DATE			
APR - - 2016			

how to st

Event P

HOME-BASED BUSINESS SERIES

how to start a home-based Event Planning Business, fourth edition

Jill S. Moran, CSEP

TAYLOR TRADE PUBLISHING
Lanham • Boulder • New York • London

This book is dedicated to my family.

Published by Taylor Trade Publishing

An imprint of Rowman & Littlefield

Distributed by NATIONAL BOOK NETWORK

British Library Cataloguing in Publication Information Available

Library of Congress Cataloging-in-Publication Data

Moran, Jill S.

How to start a home-based event planning business / Jill S. Moran, CSEP. -- Fourth edition.

pages cm. -- (Home-based business series)

Includes bibliographical references and index.

ISBN 978-1-4930-1170-4 (pbk. : alk. paper) -- ISBN 978-1-63076-106-6 (e-book) 1. Special events--Planning. 2. Special events--Management. I. Title.

GT3405.M67 2015

394.2068--dc23

2015012922

∞™ The paper used in this publication meets the minimum requirements of American National Standard for Information Sciences—Permanence of Paper for Printed Library Materials, ANSI/NISO Z39.48-1992.

Contents

Preface

Welcome to the fourth edition of *How to Start a Home-Based Event Planning Business*. It has been rewarding for me to journey down the path of putting my thoughts and experiences in event planning on paper to help others create their own business and bring to life their dreams of becoming professional event planners. Through the course of my professional growth over the past twenty-eight years, it has been both challenging and exhilarating to see the field of event planning change and grow to the industry it is today.

To complement this book, its companion book, *How to Start a Home-Based Wedding Planning Business*, and my fifteen years of lecturing to students in event planning, it has become a passion and pleasure to develop an online resource for training in special event planning called the Special Events Institute (www.specialeventsinstitute.com). This certificate program is designed for those venturing into the field of special event planning who desire a strong foundation from which to begin a career in the special events industry. My goal is to help students develop the necessary skills to enter the industry with the knowledge, confidence, and credentials to set themselves apart from the competition. I hope you enjoy this new edition and invite you to visit the Special Events Institute to take the next step in your journey to becoming a professional special events planner.

Acknowledgments

I would like to acknowledge the following:

The event professionals and student interns who helped in the research for the fourth edition, including Samantha Farrell, Marissa Welch, and Brittany Ryan.

I would also like to thank my family, clients, colleagues, and friends for their support and inspiration in writing this book.

My father, Russell Schofield, who supported me in everything I did and taught me to believe that I could be whatever I chose to be. My mother, Amelia, who planted the first creative seed in me and continues to feed it with projects, inspiration, and example. My siblings and cousins who helped create a "party" environment throughout my life!

My husband, Peter, for his willingness to walk down the road of life alongside me. My children, Kate, Kevin, and Paige, for their understanding, support, confidence, and patience with their crazy event planning mom!

My clients, who trust me with their projects and defer to me for my creative and professional advice, many of whom have become dear friends and forever left a mark on my life.

My event colleagues, who share their ideas, seek my advice, believe in my leadership, and support me with their talents and energy.

My close friends, who listen, advise, and laugh with me as I negotiate the many twists and turns of my life.

For all of these wonderful people whom I have been blessed to have in my life, I am grateful. All have added to my confidence to plan event after event and put it all down in writing for others to learn from.

01 So You Want to Get Serious about Planning Special Events?

Maybe you always knew you were meant to be a special event planner. You know who you are! You're the one who organizes your sister's wedding, the family reunions, the friends' birthday parties, and the school fund-raisers. You get the call to run the school auction, "fun day," or town road race. You decide to organize a float in the town parade just because. If any of these scenarios sounds familiar, you've identified your slot in life and can begin to take the first step in realizing a lifelong dream! Maybe you never thought making a living could be so much fun. Or you weren't willing to put the time and energy into formalizing your business. Whatever the case, the following pages will help you to identify your skill set, zero in on the gaps, offer suggestions on filling them, and set up an event planning business in your home.

Once upon a time, the planning of parties and celebrations was assigned to an exuberant family member, a creative co-worker, or an ambitious volunteer. Fund-raisers, class reunions, and wedding celebrations were planned by the person with the most energy or time on his or her hands and a passion for the event and people involved. These individuals were usually well equipped with little black books of favorite caterers, florists, or helpers to call on and the talent to get the results they wanted.

Flash forward to event planning of today. The goals for gathering people may be the same, but the methods for achieving the right results are very different. Pulling together a successful fund-raiser still requires a person with enthusiasm and creativity, but also someone equipped with a full range of skills to take the project from concept to completion and to navigate the obstacles along the way. Event planners of today are business minded, have an insatiable appetite for new ideas, and reach out to find opportunities wherever they can. The events they produce have clear goals and expectations, are executed using timelines and production schedules, and are supported by vendors and professionals who weave the fabric of the event. Risks are considered, permits secured, and contracts signed to ensure safe and successful experiences for everyone involved.

You may be that volunteer raising your hand to handle the next big event for the school, or the in-house planner who has learned the ropes by trial and error. You may feel that your experiences with events have given you a taste of what it may be like to be an event planner, but you'd like to take it to the next level. Since you have picked up this book, you also may have an entrepreneurial spirit and wonder if you could indeed make a career out of this "hobby" of yours. The question is, what do you have to do to make owning your own event planning business work, and what do you need to make it *rock*?

Whether your goal is to be better equipped to head up the school fund-raisers, to use the knowledge you have gained on the job to become an independent planner, or to launch a full-scale wedding planning business, you'll get a broad perspective on how to better prepare yourself for the fun but challenging business of planning special events.

Self-Assessment

So how do you know if event planning is right for you? Take this quick quiz:

- What would you rather do . . . sit on the sidelines or jump in and play?
- On a rainy Saturday . . . read a book or redecorate your living room?
- Do last-minute changes excite or frustrate you?
- Do you enjoy creating a menu or ordering take-out?
- Would you rather host a party or attend one?
- Do masquerade parties excite or frustrate you?
- Are your favorite shops fabric boutiques, design centers, and art supply stores?
- Can you juggle several tasks at once? Or do you like doing one project at a time?
- Do you enjoy solving problems?
- Do you love spontaneity . . . or hate it?

Your responses should give you a sense of whether you're someone who likes to jump in and get things done and could manage the dynamic nature of event planning—or if you'd be overwhelmed by the many moving parts of an event and the responsibility of taking an idea from seed to flowering tree.

If you like the excitement of taking the ordinary and turning it into the extraordinary, the good news is that you hold one of the basic traits critical to being a good event planner. The bad news, however, is that you can't operate a business on flair alone. You must add organization, good business sense, and continual professional training to the mix to build a successful event planning business.

If this makes you a bit nervous, fear not. The following pages will show you how to combine your strengths with the right support systems to realize your dream of becoming an event planner.

The Ingredients of a Successful Event Planner

So what makes a good event planner? Here are some terms you might use to describe one:

- High energy
- Organized
- Creative
- Self-motivated
- Multitasker
- Driven
- Good with people
- Extroverted
- Calm
- Can-do attitude
- Attentive to detail
- Motivator
- Entrepreneur
- Leader
- Listener
- Focused
- Cooperative
- Flexible
- Passionate
- Team player

As you can see, it takes a lot of flexibility and sometimes a "Jekyll-and-Hyde" personality to handle all the details of the event process. In the initial stages of planning an event, you have to be a salesperson—confident, persistent, knowledgeable, and persuasive—when writing your proposal and convincing the prospect to give you the job. In pulling together the elements of the event, you must be creative, thorough, and open to ideas from vendors. You must be comfortable asserting yourself but also flexible enough to take advice from the professionals you'll hire to help produce your event. As you draft, review, and present contracts, your business hat must be firmly set atop your head. You'll need to cover all the details in writing, outlining your responsibilities to vendors and to clients. When creating timelines, you must think through all the details that will take place from the moment the client says, "You're hired!" to the final "Great job!" When requesting payment and keeping track of expenses, you must be organized and detailed, keeping your client up to date on any changes or additional costs during the planning process.

Clearly, it takes a lot of different characteristics to become accomplished at owning your own business—and being successful at it. You may have some natural talent for parts of the process but cringe at the thought of other tasks. My advice is to be honest about the skills you have and what comes natural to you and get the support you need to balance what you have with what you need. Even if you don't see yourself as a master juggler, owning a business will mean that you'll need to keep all the balls in the air, but don't be afraid to ask for help from others.

More Self-Assessment: What Do You Have? What Do You Need?

You love to have flowers around but couldn't arrange them if your life depended on it . . . you know the colors you want but have no clue how to get all the blooms to stand up and look good. So what do you do? Partner with a florist who will work with you to bring your ideas to life.

The same concept holds true for the business responsibilities you'll have as an event planner—not to mention the administration, coordination, marketing, and risk management skills necessary to successfully execute each event. Use the skills you have; develop or outsource the skills you need.

On some projects, I handle the decor, props, and linens. I pull the designs together, even purchase specialty fabric and make the sheer overlays with hand-sewn tassels on each corner. But, this takes time to purchase, produce, and set up. If the budget and time frame allow me to do it, great! But realistically, it depends what other projects are going on and if it's feasible for me to handle all the internal details to complete the look of the event. On other projects I hire a linen company to ship the linens, and perhaps even to set them up for me. I enjoy the full start-to-finish side of planning, but it isn't always efficient for me to operate that way. It takes me away from selling and managing, which are equally important—if not more so—in growing and maintaining my business. This is where building a full vendor support network is critical. Even if you have the skills, it may be more cost and time effective to delegate tasks to others, so you can focus on the management piece of your business.

Professional Assessment

I Have . . .	I Need . . .	I Must . . .
A passion for events and creating memorable experiences for people	The skills to plan events professionally	Commit to training and education to start my career off on the right foot
An understanding of how to price events, but little skill at keeping track of expenses	Lessons on budgeting and using spreadsheets	Hire a part-time accountant or bookkeeper
Ideas on how to make spaces into fabulous events; the ability to create themes that are new and exciting; a sense for what my company is all about, but no skill at putting it in writing	A good writer and graphic designer	Partner with a marketing company, printer, or intern from a local college who can create brochures and work on proposals
The desire to plan event after event	A way to get business—a marketing plan	Network, join civic or professional groups, and follow up on sales leads
Lots of good ideas	Support to bring my ideas to life	Hire good vendor partners—florists, designers, and rental companies who can help me bring my ideas to life

Laying the Foundation: Skills

Take stock of your present skill set. What qualities and skills do you possess that will help you provide event planning services? Do you come from a hospitality background, for instance? Do you have experience in marketing, communications, or entertainment? You probably have skills you've developed from previous jobs, and it's time now to take a serious look at transitioning those talents into a career in event planning. Once you have assessed your strengths and made the commitment to start your business, it will still be important to continue to build your skill set to offer the level of quality services necessary for a successful full-service event planning company.

Event Skills

Talk to the pros. Contact area planners, or meet with facilities that use planners and see what they look for when they hire event planners or work with them. Become an apprentice or understudy with an event planning company. Start at the lowest level possible to fully understand what goes into the overall process. Get experience in all stages of the event life cycle and event planning from setup to sales to breakdown. If you feel you have a general understanding of the business from a prior job or position but need to fully embrace the many minute details of event planning, attend industry meetings that offer educational seminars to focus on the specifics.

Wendy Joblon, of Wendy Joblon Special Event Planner, left her position at a country club to open her own event planning business. She had worked on outings and weddings at the club for many years and had a complete knowledge of the planning process before she started out on her own. The on-the-job training she learned in her early career helped her to hit the ground running when she secured her first wedding client.

When I decided to become certified as an event planner, I signed up for a three-week course on fund-raising events to gain a better perspective from a specialist in this area and round out my understanding of these events. I met many interesting people and learned some new tricks on how to present budgets to nonprofit boards of directors. The mind-set you need to produce these events is the polar opposite of what corporate clients call for, and the course was a real eye-opener for me. This class was offered in my community through the Boston Learning Center, an adult education program that offers educational opportunities in many towns surrounding the city. It was not related to a degree program or university, but it provided excellent insight delivered by a seasoned event professional. There are educational opportunities that range from one-hour seminars on specific topics to multi-course programs that result in a certificate or degree. Check your newspaper, high school flyers, or community college calendars for sessions related to the event or meeting industry. There may be more training right in your backyard than you're aware of. Taking online courses is also a way to get exposure to training without even leaving your home! After spending many years in the industry and becoming certified, I wanted to share my knowledge and make it easier for those

Planning for Success!

Consider setting your goals on an achievement such as a Certificate in Special Events Planning. In my online education program, the Special Events Institute (www.SpecialEventsInstitute.com), graduates receive a Certificate in Special Event Planning. They can continue with Specialty Courses for a Specialty or Masters Certificate as well. Getting a certificate of training will allow you to set yourself apart from the competition and approach each event and client as a real pro. Courses cover the foundations of event planning, production, logistics, marketing, business management and entrepreneurship, and risk management. There are also courses on weddings, nonprofit events, community events, and corporate meetings and conferences. This training program allows students to experience the steps of planning successful events through presentations, videos, case studies, and discussion groups. There are also webinars that allow participants to ask questions from seasoned planners who are willing to help them get started on the right foot. Graduates can approach their careers with the confidence that they have all the right tools!

just starting out. I developed the Special Events Institute (www.SpecialEventsInstitute.com) as a way for novice planners to learn from experienced professionals in a collaborative setting through forum discussions, videos, and presentations that cover the basics of event planning. The online learning environment makes it easy for event students to study when and where they want to and engage with event enthusiasts from across the globe. I saw the need for event education and also knew that not every community had educational offerings available like mine did. I'm happy to say that we've had graduates from many countries who have gone on to start successful businesses, be promoted in their current jobs, and even win awards for events they have produced. (I'll tell you more about other educational programs for planners, as well as the certification process, in chapter 13 and the appendices.)

Besides enrolling in a certificate or degree program, signing up for continuing education, or getting on-the-job training, you could find a mentor who is willing to share his or her know-how with you. When I began to diversify my event services, a colleague who specializes in social events gave me numerous tips and vendor contacts for a wedding I was planning. The planning process was similar to that of the corporate events I'd produced, but my friend pointed out a few of the nuances that characterize a successful wedding. I had plenty of contacts for audiovisual services and trade show support, but just didn't have wedding cakes or a justice of the peace filed away in my contacts folder! As long as you won't be direct competition, most seasoned professionals are willing to share some pearls of wisdom with a fledgling planner.

Other critical components of your start-up include business skills, management skills, selling skills, and technical skills. While you can certainly hire specialists to fill such needs, when you're just starting out you may not have the willingness (or ability) to spend money in these areas. Check out some current books on time management, business planning, budgeting, and managing a staff from your local library. Many of these topics are covered in the best-seller list by authors sharing fresh ideas on the subject. Sign up as a member of an online discussion forum or visit blogs on event and business topics. If your computer skills are a bit rusty, now is the time to board the technology train. Be willing and ready to change your approach so your business can get off to the right start. Take classes at your local high school on general business topics. Read articles—either online, in newspapers, or in industry magazines to stay current on trends and techniques. Many business software programs also come with material that can help you familiarize yourself with the process of running a company. Read them and put the ideas to use in your new business.

Business Skills

Managing a business is no easy task. There are daily activities you must do to keep things running smoothly. First and foremost is keeping track of your expenses and income—the latter being one of the main reasons you're going into business. A good software program such as QuickBooks by Intuit will allow you to invoice your clients, write checks, keep track of account details, and prepare for tax time. You can order personalized business checks through Intuit, which help in presenting your company in a professional manner. The program even allows you to personalize your invoices and track multiple jobs from one client. I've found that the best way to become versed with any new software is simply to use it. Even a basic spreadsheet program such as Microsoft Excel will allow you to keep track of itemized expenses and will help you price your events properly. Start using these business programs at the beginning, and you'll soon be proficient and efficient at budgeting, forecasting, and controlling the finances of your company. You'll also want to make sure you use and understand contracts and agreements, and have a knowledge of any requirements for business licenses, permits or legal documents you will need to start and run your business. You may need to do some investigative work on the front end to make sure you approach your new venture professionally. This will help you to avoid costly mistakes that may arise by not taking the right steps in the early stages of your business.

Management Skills

Managing the people with whom you come into contact during the event planning process can also be a challenging prospect. In the event world you'll be dealing with your client, the setup crew, the chef, the servers, the photographer, the entertainer, and even the guests. You must be able to listen, assuage, persuade, consult, support, convince, and inspire—sometimes all in the same fifteen-minute period! It's a good idea to be aware of your own natural talents in this area, and to find ways to improve upon them. While it's easy to hire support on the technical side or even on the selling side, ultimately you are the one who inspires, supervises, motivates, and manages your company and those who work for you.

If you feel you are challenged in the people department, get some training. Take an honest look at how people respond to you when they're working for you. Watch how you deliver your requests. Do you show appreciation for a job well done? Can you criticize constructively? Can you fire and hire people? Can you bring your creative energies and forces out in a positive and complete way . . . getting your point across and giving the event team the information they need to make it happen? All these things are done in the course of running an event business and are skills that can make the difference between good and great!

I read business magazines such as *Inc.* and *Fortune* and check out new business books from the library for inspiration and fresh ideas. My online subscriptions range from event-specific magazines like *Best Events Magazine*, *Exhibitor*, and *Meetings News* to updates from group memberships on LinkedIn and Facebook that cover a variety of topics, including business, health, event planning, and finance. Even taking a course or a seminar can help you strengthen your skills and keep your techniques contemporary and fresh. The local chamber of commerce or professional business groups will list these in the newspaper on an ongoing basis. The best way to stay on top of your management style is to ask for feedback, listen to the responses, and take action. Be honest and critical of yourself and your events, and you'll always be working toward improving upon what you've created.

Selling Skills

As a company owner you are the best advertisement for your business. Present yourself with confidence. Exemplify the quality and style your company offers. Gather great success stories to share. Sell your company to your colleagues, friends, business associates, and potential clients. If you don't enjoy talking to people—on the phone or in person—to ask for business, you can certainly hire someone to do it for you. Be prepared to pay for the service either through a commission (the most motivating) or for a flat fee. You will need to monitor the success of your sales representative to ensure that you're getting your money's worth. While this is an area you can outsource, it's up to you to make sure you are facing off with the right messaging for your brand and company. You'll want to make sure your vision is delivered each time an email is sent or "ask" is made, so be sure to train your support staff and reinforce and realign as needed.

My greatest challenge is to be selling and producing at the same time in order to keep business in the pipeline and create a continuous flow of income. This is crucial to the financial strength and viability of your company as a full-service, full-time enterprise. It means organizing your time so you fit it all in. It's easy to do the tasks that are most pressing—such as creating production schedules, meeting with vendors and being onsite at events, but once your big event is over, you'll want to make sure another one is waiting in the wings. Consider scheduling a few hours each week to reach out to new customers or vendors or attend a networking event monthly to make sure your name stays top of mind to new clients and vendors.

Technical Skills

Can you operate your computer with relative ease? Can you create and deliver a PowerPoint presentation? Can you design a flow chart and seating chart for an event? Can you set up and manipulate a spreadsheet to create a budget and manage a budget? If not, start practicing! I've found that most of my computer knowledge has come from simply using my computer again and again. You may want to grab a *Microsoft Office for Dummies* book or take a refresher course on using a basic office computer program. Microsoft Office offers free tutorials for their office suite programs. It's worth spending time to build your skills slowly before a deadline is looming. For those Mac users, there are compatible versions for the Mac as well as those unique to the Mac, such as Pages, Numbers, and Keynote. You will need to be versed in these basic office programs or similar ones, to present and track your events in a professional way. Most of it will just take time and constant practice.

Still, while I've learned the basic programs through hours of use, when a real computer glitch hits I call the Computer Guy—an independent repair technician who comes to my home, usually the same day, to get me up and running again. He suggests updates or new products that will enhance my system and even orders and installs them for me. This is an area in which I definitely need help, and it has been invaluable having the right person to come to my rescue! Look for similar services in your area to save you time and get the results you need for creating a professional business. You should decide what is worth learning to do and what is worth delegating to a professional to make the best use of your time and money.

Finding Your Niche: Types of Event Planning Services

What do you enjoy? What are you good at? These questions can help you pinpoint the area in which you could focus on and start to build your event planning business. Then you can expand as your confidence and skills grow.

What follows are some general descriptions of the various types of planning you might focus on. (Each will be dealt with in depth in a later chapter.) What interests you or intrigues you? Could you develop the team you need and lead them in creating one or more of these events?

Social Events

If you enjoy creating events that celebrate life milestones, the social client is for you. These are weddings, birthdays, bar and bat mitzvahs, anniversary events, and the like. They are usually one-time affairs, but the possibility of follow-up business exists if you focus on creating a good relationship and ensure that the event is produced in a high-quality way. These clients can and will refer you to friends or relatives—or even call back themselves when the next family celebration takes place.

A social client can be fairly emotional. You'll see social clients joyous over their special celebrations, overwhelmed by the prospect of making choices, and shocked at the budget that is needed to create the event of their dreams. It takes patience, support, and persuasion to match their dreams with reality. At times you must be patient with a client's emotional moments while remaining grounded enough to carry on with the planning to create a flawless event that meets their expectations. At many social events, too, you'll have several contacts or layers of decision makers to deal with. Finding out who is the ultimate decision maker will be important, but always remember to be sensitive to the wishes of all parties. A bride may have her heart set on one thing for instance, only to be stifled by a mother or father who really has a much different picture of how the day will flow. Being able to balance the wishes of these two stakeholders can be challenging! The theme of the bar mitzvah will have to appeal to the younger set attending but also not create an uncomfortable or inappropriate setting for the adult attendees. These kinds of balancing acts are where the true value of a planner comes into play!

Corporate Events

The corporate market offers a very different feel from the social. While some of the same characteristics are present—a long chain of command, stakeholders with different ideas to be addressed, budget considerations—the corporate client is approached much differently. Most companies are used to hiring professionals to fulfill certain specialized roles and will often let the planner make final recommendations and suggestions. Corporate clients are less emotionally volatile than social clients, but their expectations for creativity, quality, and execution are every bit as high.

A single corporate client may have multiple programs for which you can provide services, in departments such as sales, human resources, and marketing. Creating a lasting relationship is thus critical with the corporate client—it can give you additional business beyond the first event. Networking internally will be necessary, because the sales department might not know what human resources is doing, and vice versa. From company outings to award dinners, team-building events to trade show events, depending on your interest and capabilities; a corporate client can give you a smorgasbord of event opportunities.

Downsides to the corporate market include the changing economy and changes in management. Companies have lucrative periods when money is flowing and they're comfortable spending on either marketing or internal events. Then come the times of cutbacks, and the extras like company outings and luxurious client events are eliminated. In addition, you may form a strong relationship with a top decision maker at one of your best companies—then see him or her change jobs. If another executive with his or her own favorite event planner takes over, you may lose your ongoing relationship. Still, if your original contact moves to a competing company, you could gain a new client—so stay in touch! Often in difficult economic times, internal departments can be downsized, opening up

Event Categories

- Social events
- Children's events
- Weddings
- Corporate events
- Outings
- Fairs and festivals
- Parades
- Birthday parties
- Bar and bat mitzvahs
- Religious events
- Fund-raising events
- Awards dinners
- Sales events
- Incentive events
- College events
- Event marketing
- Hospitality events
- Tours and charters
- Destination management
- Meeting planning
- Team building
- Product launches
- Ground-breaking events
- Business celebrations
- Community events
- Fun runs and walks

Event Services

- Invitations
- Entertainment
- Talent
- Decor
- Floral arrangements
- Rentals
- Linens
- Incentive gifts
- Photography
- Videography
- Inflatables
- Novelty items
- DJ
- Staffing
- Tent scenery and backdrops
- Audiovisual and sound
- Lighting production
- Catering
- Carnival and casino rentals
- Transportation
- Parking
- Security
- Ice sculptures
- Bakery and wedding cakes
- Bleachers and skyboxes
- Amusements and games
- Professional speakers
- Novelties and caricatures
- Costumes
- Decorative and specialty fabrics
- Flags and banners
- Ticketing services
- Restroom trailers
- Insurance
- Special effects
- Pyrotechnics
- Calligraphy

opportunities for independent planners to assist on a per project basis. While you may not have a large staff supporting you, often you'll have a chance to start a relationship and get your foot in the door.

Community Events

Special events take place in every town and city, every year. These gatherings are held to celebrate holidays or town anniversaries, to host sporting events, or as fund-raisers. They can involve merchants in the town, city officials or VIPs, the general public or specialty groups within the area. They also can involve large numbers of people, from volunteers to attendees to vendors. A good planner is needed to manage the process from setup to teardown. If you like to work big, these events are for you! You must have a great sense of organization, logistics, and contingency planning. Ultimate people skills are crucial here, because you often have to deal with permits, town officials, and the press. The vendor lists for fairs and festivals include tenting companies, staging companies, and lighting and power supply vendors; often they also involve artists, crafters, and the selling of stalls or booths. A good sense of the area and the attendee interests is a must if the fair is to draw both vendors and visitors. City-wide events such as walks, runs, or parades also involve many moving pieces, such as flatbed trailers, organized groups walking, and often young children who can pose unique safety issues. Crowd management and safety are focal points, as are advertising, sponsorship, and public relations.

Nonprofits

Nonprofit organizations typically have staff who organize and plan events throughout the year. These events can range from "fun walks" and golf outings to black-tie dinners and annual balls. Internal staff usually juggle multiple projects at any given time under the supervision of an executive director. The planning team generally involves an honorary board and a team of volunteers. Some nonprofits recognize the value of a professional planner and will hire one to oversee the project. Another approach is to offer your services in return for visibility to the community, the executive team, and the guests at the event. These sponsorship opportunities, while not direct moneymakers, can provide great advertising and marketing mileage.

Another way to benefit from involvement with nonprofit organizations is to use them as training grounds. If you're in the start-up stage and feel you could use some hands-on experience, volunteering at a fund-raising run or working on planning a benefit could offer some great learning opportunities. It can be especially meaningful if you're passionate about the cause!

Academic Events

Educational institutions such as universities, colleges, and technical or specialty schools host events annually for a wide range of stakeholders. There are typically events for students, alumni, benefactors, professors, and administrators that need to be produced on time and on budget while considering the unique styles of each event participant. An academic event planner will need to be savvy to protocol, safety, event preparation and flow, and vendor/supplier relations to stay within their institution's fiscal constraints and satisfy branding goals. Academic planners will be responsible for annual events, such as commencement or parent's weekend, but may also need support with special events such as an anniversary, gala, or fundraiser. It's always wise to keep a lookout for schools in your area that may be celebrating a special event and could use the support of a professional planner to lend a hand from time to time.

Specializations

Regional Events

If you want to focus on one geographic area and become the "go-to" person there, think about becoming a destination planner. A DMC—destination management company—provides hospitality services or event-related services in a specific geographic location. Activities can include meeting out-of-town guests at airports and transferring them to a hotel, group activities for visitors attending a conference, or team-building events and other general corporate or social events held in the area. Other programs associated with local conventions or conferences include themed events, recreational or "spouse" programs (activities for spouses who are attending the conference but not participating in the educational or meeting components), "step-on" tours (those that familiarize visitors with highlights of the area), museum tours, and hotel arrangements. For success in this area, familiarity with local tourist attractions, special venues, and restaurants is a must. It's also important to have great resources to support you during busy times. You'll need to establish relationships with hotels, restaurants, convention and visitor bureaus, and the chamber of commerce to get leads on groups coming into town well in advance.

Children's Events

If you enjoy children and have a tolerance for guests with high energy levels, children's events can be the niche for you! Birthdays, bar and bat mitzvahs, and annual school events can offer an opportunity to bring laughter and magic into the lives of children and take a huge burden of stress off parents who don't know where to go for the clown, singing storyteller, balloon artist, or reptile show. If you gather a wealth of resources for this market, you can provide new and exciting themes and entertainment for young folks. Advertise yourself as offering the newest and most unusual theme parties for the small set, as well as start-to-finish service—including set up and tear down. Extend your services to offer crafts, invitations, party favors, and the like. With more families having both Mom and Dad working full time, time can be a valuable commodity; pulling together special events often just doesn't fit into the schedule. Price your services right, and your referrals can keep your business going strong.

Fund-Raisers

Many fund-raising events are driven by committees of volunteers who are passionate about their cause. Events are held every week to raise money for schools, hospitals, and associations or for special causes or people in need. While the many volunteers who rally behind the cause make up the engine that drives an event's success, a good navigator behind the steering wheel is essential. As a chairperson of a fund-raising event, you'd be responsible for various committees, such as sponsorship, decorating, silent auction, and communications. Knowledge of the overall planning process and keen interpersonal skills to manage the volunteers are critical to the success of a fund-raising planner. The ability to garner support from corporate sponsors or local vendors and be a spokesperson for the cause is equally vital. While a board of influential advisers can drive attendance and large donations, an understanding of the market and community is helpful to allow the event to raise the projected funds.

Lending a Helping Hand

We have a small but wonderful art gallery located in my town. I heard through the grapevine that they could use some help with fundraising and decided to chat with the director about possible options. He was enthused by the thought of a party—something to bring the town together and create support for the gallery. We decided on a simple tented event—the Zullo Art Festival—located on the green between the gallery and library. We reached out to area restaurants to donate one item (enough for 200 people) and offered a "taste of the town" sampling. Local shops gave gift certificates and items for raffle baskets. The liquor store donated wine and craft beer. With the support of some sponsors, the rental items were covered and over the past few years, the gallery has increased their fundraising efforts, gained visibility in the community, and provided a great night out for the town. They also began renting the gallery for events and offer my name for event planning support. It feels good for me to help a gem in our town and offers a great way for me to market my services both at the event as an in-kind sponsor and after as a planning resource.

The Pitfalls of Event Planning

Starting a home-based event planning business is certainly not for the weak-hearted. Here are some of the field's top pitfalls. Have a good look; how will you avoid these?

Not Enough Time

Owning your own business means you need time to continue your education and build your skills; time to organize your office and work environment; time to focus on sales and marketing, proposal building, and vendor networking; not to mention time to plan events! And all of this is time away from what you were doing before this fabulous idea struck you—perhaps a full-time job or parenting. Whether you're switching careers or getting back into the workforce, it will take time and energy to give birth to your dream. The amount you put into your business will directly affect what you get out of it. Don't be afraid to take the time you need to successfully launch your new business and career. It will pay off in the long run!

War Stories: Faux Pas

It's a good idea to review all the pertinent information with your staff and vendors prior to each event—right down to the names. Make sure you have people's and company's names written down, as well as their pronunciations. I've heard of a venue who posted a welcome sign at an event with the planner's name instead of the host company's; a planner who announced the wrong company's name over the microphone; and a DJ who even announced the father of the bride when he'd passed away earlier that year. In some cases it's hard to be as invisible as you'd like!

Incomplete Skill Set

Before you decide to start your business, you must make sure you have the necessary skills to be an effective planner. There are many seasoned professionals already in the marketplace; developing a foothold for yourself won't be easy. Be prepared to fine-tune your skills, decide how you can set yourself apart from the competition, and be the best you can be. You can accomplish this by using skills gained in past jobs, through education and training, and with ongoing involvement in the industry. Take a good look at how you can update your skills to create a business you're proud of.

Lack of Commitment

Growing a business takes commitment to your clients and the event industry. You must be prepared to take each project from start to finish; there's no room for halfhearted attempts once you've made a presentation or signed a contract. Prioritize your "to-do" list and eliminate activities that may prevent you from reaching your goals.

Don't Be Afraid to Toot Your Own Horn!

I was nominated for Boston's Best Wedding Planner in a contest run by a local TV station. I posted the good news on social media and encouraged everyone to vote online. This included clients, friends, and family. As a result, a friend in my book group shared the good news with her sister, who was just starting to plan her wedding. She was beginning to feel overwhelmed by the details, was delighted to find someone familiar to help, and hired me as her planner!

Lack of Knowledge

If you're not completely confident in your skills as a planner, take a step back and prepare. Volunteer, become an apprentice, take a class. Consider enrolling in an online class at Special Events Institute as an affordable way to grow your skill set one course at time. Confidence can be a great asset, but evaluating your abilities honestly is even more important. Education is an ongoing process, and by gaining credentials in the field, you'll be showing your commitment to professionalism for yourself and your company.

Lack of Contacts and Connections

Tell everyone you know about your exciting new plans to start your business. Scour your e-mail contact list or social media contacts for anyone who might be able to refer business to you. Whether you are at your class reunion or mingling with friends at your exercise class, the more you publicize your plans, the more real they become. And as you share your passion and your ideas, your business will begin to take shape.

Trying to Do Too Much

If you've decided to start your own home-based business, now might not be the time to become a room parent, chair the PTA, or volunteer to run the school fair. Divide your day into the tasks that are necessary to grow your business, and give yourself the time to complete these tasks. I try to do the things I least enjoy first, or do the items that come due first. A friend also shared her own secret: When folks call soliciting her volunteer help, she now tells them she'll get back to them. Then she waits a day and thinks about whether the activity truly fits into her schedule.

Overpromising

Be willing to say no or refer business to a more experienced colleague if need be. Don't agree to a deadline if you aren't sure you can meet it. It's always more impressive to come in under budget rather than over when providing pricing estimates or event proposals.

Not Charging Enough for Your Services

There is no crystal ball to tell you what a customer will pay, or what you're worth. Setting your price is based on what the market will bear, your experience, and your complete understanding of the scope of the project. I will be honest and say there are times I have undercharged for my services and times I have underestimated the time needed to plan an event. In doing so, I have undercut the client's understanding of the event process and the value of a professional planner. It's true that the bidding process can sometimes leave you without options; it's all too easy to negotiate beyond a reasonable limit just to get the job. Your own experience and the state of the economy have huge influences on pricing as well—it's one of the most dynamic aspects of owning a business.

Remember that you're starting a business, not a hobby. Once you know you have a service that you're proud of and are ready to go, set a price that's in line with what you're offering. Don't be afraid to charge for your time. Whether you're consulting on theme and decor, creating invitations, or running an event from start to finish, time is money. And you should be compensated for it.

Top Ten Mistakes in Starting Your Home-Based Event Planning Business

10. Not separating your work and home environments.
9. Not having a plan.
8. Not charging enough for your services.
7. Not being prepared to deliver what you promise.
6. Not giving clients what they ask for.
5. Not listening to what clients want.
4. Not taking all the necessary planning steps—risk assessment, contract planning, sound budget management, and so on.
3. Not saying no to a project you can't handle. (Knowing your limits.)
2. Not saying yes to a project you can handle. (Asking for help when needed.)
1. Not setting your professional standards high enough and reaching for them!

Falling Behind on Business Responsibilities

Staying afloat requires ongoing attention to the financial and logistical details of each event. My suggestion is not to let things slip. Address difficult issues, contracts, or financial situations immediately and on a regular basis. This will keep you emotionally and fiscally sound.

Not Finding the Balance between Your Business Life and Your Personal Life

Your business becomes your life when you're an entrepreneur and business owner. It's hard to avoid! Still, balancing your passion for event planning with other interests will keep you refreshed and renewed. I belong to a monthly book club, for instance. I'm not always able to finish the assigned book, but I try my hardest to attend the meetings to catch up with my neighbors and friends. My husband and I share a love of music as well and try to stay involved in the music program at our church or catch a concert from time to time. No matter how difficult juggling our work and family schedules becomes, we always know we'll have this to enjoy together when we can fit it in!

Failing to Hire Help When You Need It

Running an event from start to finish is no easy task. The fun part is developing the theme and creating the mood for the event. The hard part is knowing when

Ten Suggestions for Success

10. Be committed for the long haul.
9. Ask for help.
8. Learn to say no to too many responsibilities, commitments, and projects.
7. Learn to say yes to something that's challenging but that you can accomplish with success.
6. Look for opportunity—for new areas to get involved with.
5. Don't be afraid to look at yourself critically; there's always room for improvement.
4. Always try to plan the next event better than the last.
3. Say thank you.
2. Stay on top of your game.
1. Have fun! Enjoy what you do.

it's time to hire help and finding the right people to make it happen. You can't do it all yourself, so be ready to bring in help when you need it—even for small events. It's never too soon to start building a quality vendor directory.

The Challenges of Event Planning

Based on what you've read so far, you can probably begin imagining the challenges of starting your own business—time, energy, knowledge, skills, marketing, growing the business, day-to-day management. . . . Take a moment now and look at some of the specifics listed below. Are you ready to do what it takes to start your own home-based business?

Dividing Your Time and Your Space

This topic is so important; I've devoted all of chapter 12 to it. It's imperative to set guidelines for family and friends—and stick to them. Write them down, deliver them in a firm and loving voice, and make sure your loved ones know how important it is for you to follow your dream of owning your own business. Set limits for yourself, too. Go to your office when you want to work, and leave it when you're ready to stop. Be fair when determining your time commitments. If you can afford to take extra time for friends and family, do it guilt-free and love it! Remember, you'll inevitably need to ask for forgiveness and flexibility in the near future, when you're racing to meet a work deadline.

Saying Yes and Saying No

If you aren't sure you should take on one more commitment, don't say yes. Think about it, consult a friend or colleague, and follow your instincts. Most people who own their own companies are doers. They're the ones who want to make things better, so they instinctively say "Sure," "Absolutely," "I would love to!" But remember the other priorities in your life and face the fact that there are only twenty-four sweet hours in every day. And you do need to sleep! When you say yes, know that doing so will allow you to maintain or improve the standard of your life or the quality of the events you produce.

Pacing Yourself

Don't feel you have to do it all now. You don't have to buy the best equipment, go to all the networking meetings, get every degree or certification, attend every conference or training program, or handle every project that comes through your door. You also don't have to be the same event planner, friend, or volunteer that you see someone else being. We all have our own mix of priorities, capabilities, commitments, and stress-tolerance levels. Listen to yourself and your loved ones. Build your company in the way and at the pace with which you are comfortable.

Building Your Toolbox

Your toolbox is the "guts" of your business. Work on it from the moment you head out on your own, and add to it as you gather new ideas and resources. Visit trade shows and conferences. Talk to your vendors about new products and services. Get your theme ideas from blogs, websites, apps, magazines, and books. Stay on top of current trends to deliver new, fresh, successful events each and every time.

Should I *Take the Leap?*

Do I have what it takes?

- Skills
- Industry knowledge
- Drive
- Business savvy and sense

Can I afford to start my own business?

- Time
- Money
- Energy
- Capital investments
- Space

Can I make the commitment?

- Passion
- Interest
- Independence
- Self-motivation

Am I willing to get what I need to make it work?

- Professional assistance
- Ongoing education
- Refinement of skills
- Support where it counts

Marketing

Marketing your business is an ongoing prospect. To keep your business dynamic, marketing has to be on your to-do list every day. One phone call. One contact. One follow-up on a lead. Just one a day will help keep the cycle going for your business. For more tips, check out chapter 5, which is devoted to marketing.

Remember . . . Rome wasn't built in a day! And you don't have to build Rome. A home-based business can be as simple or as complex as you make it. It can provide you with a part-time work experience or a full-time career. And the good news is, you are in the driver's seat. You can say yes or no to business, and stop the world and get off if you so desire!

When I came into the industry in 1990, I never dreamed I would eventually plan international events or events covered by TV networks—but I have. There are times when I can't help but get involved with the little details of an event, but I also really enjoy looking at the "big picture" of how I can impact the lives of those just starting out through my educational program or mentoring someone just starting out in the field. It's an exciting and fun career, but also takes perseverance and hard work. In the end, it's fun to step back and be proud of what you've accomplished!

Frequently Asked Questions

Should I quit my job to start my own business?

Depending on the financial support or savings you currently have, it may make sense to begin your event business on a part-time basis. Many events can be done in the evenings or on weekends. You may be able to begin working with other seasoned planners to get your experience and once you have a solid working knowledge of the process, go out on your own. To move from a part-time to full-time commitment will take a solid client base that will guarantee repeat business and repeat income. You also need to consider the cost of health care and your fixed living expenses. Make sure your event business can offset these costs and put you in a positive cash-flow position.

I am not very organized and hate the minute details of things, but I love parties . . . can I be an event planner?

There are some basic skills that will be necessary to build a successful event planning business. Creativity is one of them, but organization and attention to detail come right behind. Building a successful business will require a good reputation and delivering excellent service. If the little details drive you crazy and you can't be bothered to figure out how to "right" the "wrongs," you may be better off filling your schedule with parties to attend, not plan. If you think you have what it takes but need some honing of skills or support in a few areas of business know-how, consider teaming up with someone who complements the skills you have.

How do I build on my background in catering to launch my own event business?

It is helpful to have a background in hospitality or business if you want to focus on special events. You can take the training and experience you have and round it out with specific training in events or management from local colleges, from universities, or at industry conferences. The online program at Special Events Institute lets you study at your own pace while working or attending to other responsibilities. You also meet and network with other event enthusiasts to build your skills and confidence and are mentored by your course instructors. You'll have a lot to bring to your new business as you try out your creative event ideas and practice the planning process throughout the program.

I love all kinds of celebrations . . . what type of events should I focus on doing?

Plan to focus on the type of events with which you are most comfortable or have the most experience. If you come from a corporate background, it may be easier for you to relate to the corporate market—and vice versa with a bride or groom if you have experience in social events. You already may know the lingo and the culture. Start with something with which you are familiar and see where your successes take you. If you are chomping at the bit to make a big change, just get the training you need before taking the leap! Volunteering or offering to shadow an experienced planner can also give you a sense of what each event type is truly like before you commit to a paid client.

02 The Home Office

A Space of Your Own

The first step to starting a home-based business is having an area from which to work. Start with an office setup. Perhaps you have an unfinished basement, spare room, or library that you can take over for your home office. You won't need to worry about decor or fancy furniture, but you should have a minimum of equipment and supplies to carry out the support tasks involved with creating an event.

Your office space should allow you to make phone calls uninterrupted, have enough room for you to compile proposals or file resource materials, and even allow you to store miscellaneous event supplies. If you start with a corner of your bedroom, have plans in the works to eventually move to a separate room, where you can work behind closed doors.

My first home office was set up in the basement of our first home, in a neat and tidy corner blocked in by plywood and featuring a small window to let in a peek of the outside. I went into labor with my first child while working in that office. As we changed homes, my office conditions changed, too. In one home I had the whole family room as my workspace. My family consisted of only three of us, so it was a simple feat to take over the space in its entirety.

Only once did I have less than a room. For a short period of time, a part of my bedroom housed my desk, fax, phone, and file cabinet. I will say that faxes arriving from international clients did present a level of irritation at midnight or 4:00 a.m. . . . Still, my business did extremely well. I maintained a professional image while on the phone and while traveling and produced some wonderful events for clients worldwide. This setting was by no means optimal, but it did offer me a small space to organize my client and event files.

The best-case scenario is a separate room that can be closed off by a door. This isn't always possible, but it does allow you the privacy to work without interruption (if you set the rules and limits early on), and a quiet space for professional phone conversations. It helps that event planners don't usually have to meet with clients at their place of business; holding a meeting at a client's office, at a venue, or at a restaurant for lunch is quite acceptable.

If you may someday use office assistants to help with filing, proposal preparations, or event planning, a larger office would accommodate this. A converted garage, a finished basement, or a large room in your home should suffice. When you grow to the point of having several employees or need to store a large number of props or supplies, it's time to think of renting space. Still, for the small-scale home-office planner, a space in your home, set up with the necessary office supplies and equipment, will do just fine.

The Three Bs

When my children were small and my business was in its infancy, my rule of thumb for family interruptions while I was working was known as the three Bs. Only if something was burning, or someone was bleeding or not breathing . . . then they could interrupt at will. Although I have been through the experience of a child racing in to alert me to a neighbor's burning house and have taken a child to the hospital for stitches, these emergencies have been infrequent, and the client or vendor on the phone who was rudely cut off was always very understanding, given the circumstances. The moral of the story: don't be afraid to set parameters that will help you achieve your professional goals, but still allow you to manage the other parts of your life.

Equipment and Technology

Your business "starter kit" should include a telephone; answering service, machine, or voice mail; cell phone; computer (desktop or laptop); and a color printer/scanner. If you can only invest in one computer, a laptop will allow you to make presentations to clients as well as handle the other administrative tasks of your business. All your business functions should be automated. Get the most up-to-date technology possible when selecting your equipment. Also consider purchasing specialized programs such as QuickBooks (Intuit) for accounting, Vivien (Cast

Software) for event space design, and Photoshop (Adobe) for photo editing. If you are handy with building spreadsheets and diagrams on your own, these may not be necessary, but they are a ready-made alternative and will produce a more sophisticated end result.

Marketing materials can be created using a simple word processing program, supplemented with actual photos of your events. Accounting procedures should be handled each month, including billing and budgeting. A computer fax program will let you send and receive faxes without the cost of an additional machine. I advise keeping your start-up costs down at first by learning to do these tasks yourself, using software tools provided with a basic software suite.

Start off using equipment and supplies you may already have in your home. As you advance in your business and have the additional income to allow for the extras, then you can go for it, but in the beginning it's wise to keep your expenses low while purchasing only those items that will give you the professional image you're looking for. I once sadly watched a colleague lose her business and her self-confidence as she struggled to pay the rent on her office and administrative staff—without having the projects to support either. By starting slowly from an

Software Suggestions

Here are a few software products to consider for event planning, management, and related hospitality services.

Accounting: QuickBooks, Quicken, Microsoft Small Business Accounting, NetSuite
Catering: Caterease/Horizon Business Services, CaterPro, Caterware, Culinary Software Services
Event Design: Vivien (room and event layout), TimeSaver, Event 411, Visio
Event Management: IntelliEvent, Certain, Lanyon – RegOnline and Smart Events Cloud, Party Tack, Synergy International, EventPro, Certain Software's Event Planner Plus, PlanSoft
Marketing: Photoshop, Paintshop Pro (photo manipulation)
Office Tools: Microsoft Word (letters, proposals), Access (database management), Excel (spreadsheet design), PowerPoint (presentations), FrontPage (website design)
Office and Computer Supplies: Staples, OfficeMax, Office Depot, Circuit City

(See appendix D for contact information)

What It Costs

Software:

- Basic Microsoft Office (Word, Excel, PowerPoint, Outlook): $399
- Office Professional (additional: Access, Publisher, Outlook with Business Contact Manager): $499
- Microsoft FrontPage (website development): $199
- Event-specific software: $99–$2,000

Equipment:

- PDA/smart phone/media: $99–$600 and up
- Computer: Desktop (with accessories) $999 and up
- Laptop: $500–$3,000
- Digital camera: $99–$2,500
- Fax (thermal, inkjet, or laser): $50–$500
- Internal modem fax: $8–$80

Printers:

- All-in-one printer/scanner/copier: $80–$1,000
- Inkjet: $99–$1,000
- Photo inkjet: $89–$700
- Color laser: $140–$2,540
- Laser: $130–$1,250
- Scanner: $99–$1,500

office in your home, you won't be faced with choosing between your mortgage and your business rent.

As I noted previously, most people will never see what the "behind the scenes" really looks like, so don't bother spending money on fancy office furniture. If you're dying to put your personal stamp on a new purchase, my vote would be for that classic suit or jazzy outfit that really screams, *Hire me!*

You will need a desk or table for your computer and phone, a bookshelf for storing reference materials, and suitable file cabinets for proposals, resource literature, and supplies. An additional table or area for organizing your files and proposals, or for assembling projects, is helpful as well. My dining room table is often "stationery central" as I assemble a hand-designed invitation or announcement or put together "goodie bags" or client incentives.

As you progress and can afford it, consider buying an iPad or other tablet to show your work to new clients or manage files while onsite or perhaps a digital camera to snap those great event shots. Think about the least expensive way to get your point across to clients while still performing at the highest level possible. For most situations, you can take bulk copying or printing projects to a printer or an office center and eliminate the major purchase of a copier. Remember, you're an event planner, not a printer, decorator, florist, or caterer. Purchases in all areas should be limited to a few basics you know you'll need on an ongoing basis.

Office Supplies

Your office supplies should include the basics you need to operate in a professional way. You don't need imprinted notecards or pens unless you're planning to send an incentive gift to potential customers to announce your business opening. Try to make do with the basics to get your business off the ground with the least amount

Office Needs Checklist

Must have:

- Basic supplies.
  - pens
  - pencils
  - tape
  - file folders
  - binders
  - notepads
  - white lined paper
  - ruler
  - stapler
  - self-stick notes
  - pencil sharpener
  - paper clips
  - business cards
  - letterhead

large envelopes
blank CDs and DVDs
assorted labels
envelopes

- Basic equipment.
  telephone
  computer
  printer/scanner
  fax (or fax program)
  phone
  Internet connection

Need:

- Supplies.
  paper cutter
  hole punch
  binders
  labels
  binding machine for quick professional proposals
- Technology.
  additional phone line
  laptop computer
  iPad or other tablet
  digital camera
  DVD and CD burner
  thumb drive
  answering machine

Want:

- Copy machine
- Color laser printer

of stress to your bank account. Start off using equipment and supplies you may already have in your home.

Customized business cards, stationery, and letter-sized envelopes will allow you to follow up with prospects in a consistent and professional way and are worth the investment. Pens, notepaper, and pencils let you function in your office, draft proposals, take notes, and keep track of phone messages. Basic supplies—things like tape, glue, a stapler, and paper clips, which you may already have in your home—will need to be replaced as you use them for prospecting and projects. You'll likely need to purchase supplemental items such as binders, file folders, labels, and large envelopes to support the organization of your office and your business. Once again, purchase and store only those items you need on a regular basis to create a professional image. Rely on a printing or office supply center for specialty items such as binding proposals or preparing large-quantity printing projects.

Event Supplies

While you don't necessarily need large quantities of props or decorations to get your business off the ground, some basic supplies and equipment will allow you to start up in a professional way. I like to have an "event tool kit" to take on every job.

The Event Tool Kit

- Tape—single-sided and double-sided
- Twist-ties
- Zip-ties
- Glue gun
- Rope
- Ribbon
- Nails, screws, and tacks
- Hammer and screwdriver
- Assorted adhesives
- String
- Scissors
- Grommet maker
- Extension cords
- Smartphone or digital camera with memory card
- Batteries
- Assorted pins (pearl-topped, T-topped, straight)
- Needle and assorted thread
- Pre-moistened hand wipes

My event tool kit contains items I may need for last-minute repairs on site at an event. While a first-aid kit may seem like a good thing to have on hand, you should exercise caution when administering any first aid. It's best to plan for an EMT or nurse for larger events or put a good Emergency Response Plan in place in the event of illness or an accident at an event. Know who to call, when and what the chain of command will be, and share your plan with your staff, venue, and vendors. This will cover you legally against any malpractice suits and shows you are taking risk seriously at your events.

It's probably wise not to purchase any event equipment or decor until you secure the first project that includes a budget for it. If you're doing a wedding and need votives, for example, it may make sense to purchase a suitable quantity and charge the client a rental fee to help offset the cost. If you foresee using these for future events as well, they will quickly pay for themselves. They are small and won't pose a huge storage problem.

Be cautious when it comes to other, larger props; it may make more sense to rent these from a decor company and purchase only the items you'll definitely reuse or can store easily. Items in my storage area include basic colored fabric for draping, miscellaneous theme tabletop decor that is unusual or unique, vases, bamboo poles, and some basic black sheer table toppers, which I now have used and reused on numerous occasions.

You must determine if you can properly clean, store, and preserve any items you decide to purchase for your events. Some will go out of style, become worn, or be damaged over time. Instead, consider this an opportunity to build up your vendor relationships; add a decor company to your team, and let them worry about the transportation, setup, and storage of themed props.

Your capital equipment checklist may also include a vehicle. Obviously, transportation to and from your events is essential, but a new cargo van isn't. I occasionally rent a van when I have a lot of supplies to transport. For most events and sales calls, though, my Toyota RAV, fresh from the car wash, is just fine. If you live in the city, public transportation might provide you with all you need to get yourself going in business.

The important thing, as always, is to present yourself in a professional way; this is a point worth repeating! If you can do this with supplies you already have, rather than making a large investment in these early days, you'll be much better off financially.

Frequently Asked Questions

I am ready to launch my business! Why shouldn't I take a five-year lease out at the most prestigious office park to really get attention for my business and start out on the right foot?

Unless you have had a recent inheritance or have large sums of money buried in your backyard, it is wise to start slowly. Most clients will not need to have meetings at your office, so in the beginning it's best to spend your start-up costs on office equipment, specific event supplies, or education to get you up and running. If your start-up costs are too high before you have the income to support them, it could put you in a stressful position. Spend wisely and enjoy the feeling of having reserve funds in your bank account just in case you need them.

What software will I need to get started?

Check out appendix D and the Software Suggestions sidebar to get a good idea of the options out there. There are many programs that will help with basic office support and, more specifically, event planning and logistics. They range in cost from nothing to thousands of dollars. My advice would be to start slow. Try to get a trial version of the software and use it to see if it suits your needs. You may find that you use it too seldom to warrant its purchase. In some cases, a vendor can provide access to planning tools such as floor plan designers and offer this as a free planner resource. If you can envision yourself using it to support your sales or planning, consider charging a small administration fee on each job to help offset the cost.

Do I need a separate phone and fax line?

Absolutely! Being able to know clearly which calls are for business is essential in putting forth a professional image. If you add an additional line to your home, you will not get business support and any extras such as toll-free options, but it will be less expensive. Taking out a full business line may give you Internet access or additional features that will help your marketing efforts as well. Some fax services offer online products, eliminating the need for an additional phone line for faxes. Check with your local phone service provider for benefits and features that best suit your needs.

Where could I have an alternate meeting site for client appointments? My home office just doesn't seem professional enough!

It's a good idea to have a couple of places that are professional and accessible for client meetings. I often meet at a hotel with which I do business, and they are happy to give me a conference room to set up any centerpieces, show my portfolio, or have a light lunch or coffee with a client. Sometimes even a coffee shop that is comfortable and trendy can set the atmosphere you want to create for your new business. Some cities have community offices where, for a small monthly fee, you can utilize a central conference area and even have a company name listed on an entrance directory. In any case, opt for a professional location that allows you to put your best foot forward.

03 Developing Your Business

Your Business Structure

The next step to bringing your business to life is to formalize it. What kind of business will it be? What will you call it? Are you going it alone or joining forces with a colleague and forming a partnership? Where do you start?

First, do some research. Scour your local library or search online for information on starting a business. Government agencies such as the US Small Business Administration are also great resources. Most cities have a local SBA office; or you can visit them online at www.sba.gov. Local business groups or your chamber of commerce can provide helpful tips, too.

Take a look at business plans of friends or of other small businesses. Don't be afraid to ask advice from retired business owners. Contact your local office of SCORE, "Counselors to America's Small Business," for more information or the names of members who can offer guidance. You may find a mentor who can walk you through all the details of small-business setup and management.

The type of business structure you choose will affect how you are taxed and the type of record keeping you must do. Running the business as a sole proprietor is the simplest, most informal arrangement; incorporating, on the other hand, poses more financial record keeping but also greater asset protection. If you have a colleague who shares your dream and enthusiasm for starting a home-based business, then a formal partnership might be your best business structure option. There are pros and cons to each structure, so think it over carefully. In any case, I recommend consulting with an attorney who can help answer questions and guide you through the process.

Let's take a look at the options.

Sole Proprietorship

This is the most common form of small business ownership. One person owns all the assets and liabilities. The owner has exclusive control of the business but also total financial responsibility to the full extent of the assets of the business as well as the owner's personal assets. It's relatively simple to complete the documents necessary to set up a sole proprietorship, once a name search is done. If the name of the business is not the same as the name of the owner, a "Doing Business As" (DBA) certificate must be filed in the city or town hall where the business is conducted. You may also be able to do this online, so check your state agency for the right process.

Pros: You have exclusive control of your company, and the setup process is simple. You also receive all the income.

Cons: You're liable for all financial obligations to the extent of all your business and personal assets.

General Partnership

Starting a partnership would mean finding a kindred spirit who shares your drive and passion for the business. It also should be someone with whom you work well, who balances your business style, and who is willing to approach the business in a serious manner. You and your partner (or partners) will be sharing in the profits as well as the losses of the business, according to your respective ownership interests. Partners owe each other the duty of utmost good faith and loyalty. The relationship is governed by a written agreement if you and your partner have one, and if not, it's governed by statutory provisions. If you are doing business in the United States, DBA certificates must also be filed, and a separate tax identification number obtained from the IRS.

A limited liability partnership is the same as a general partnership, except some of the state statutes permit partners to limit any liability caused by another's negligence or breach of contract toward the investment in the partnership. In any case, a partner is still liable to the full extent of his or her personal assets for liabilities incurred.

In a limited partnership, the general partner has full liability and management of the business; limited partners have limited management. Their liability is limited to their investment in the business. A joint venture is organized for a brief time and a specific event. If the relationship or activities continue after the initial engagement, a general partnership should be formed.

Pros: Partners can divide up the work, including sales, administration, and site visits. They can cover each other during vacations and illness. They can work together to take on larger, more complicated projects. While the partnership must file a tax return, it pays no income taxes—the profits and losses flow from the partnership return to each partners' individual tax return.

Cons: Liability is still an issue. Each partner is personally liable for any obligation incurred by another partner. Thus, a partner is responsible to the full extent of that partner's personal assets for any liability incurred by another partner, through contract or negligently causing someone injury, whether or not that partner had anything to do with it or even knowledge of it. Partners may find that they do not get along, making it difficult to carry on the business. Partner's need to clearly define their roles and anticipate what will happen to the business in the event that any partner ceases to work due to disability, death, or otherwise.

Incorporation

By incorporating your business, you form a legal entity solely for the purpose of conducting business. A person or group of people forms the business entity and elects a board of directors to control the company. This board in turn can elect officers to run the business on a daily basis. Many corporations are closely held, meaning that the shareholders also serve as the board of directors and officers. The corporate entity itself becomes the business, not the individuals who run it. Ordinarily, a corporation bears a separate burden for taxes and liabilities.

Pros: The main benefit of incorporating is the avoidance of personal liability. If there should be a lawsuit, the corporation would be held responsible, not the individual. A Subchapter S election can be taken, allowing earnings to be taken as distributions and passed through your personal tax return.

Cons: Record keeping becomes more detailed, and the fees for running a corporation are higher. Articles of Organization must be filed with and approved by a state government, as must annual reports with attendant filing fees. Bylaws must be adopted and followed, along with minutes of meetings. These filing formalities must be adhered to, or a creditor could impose liabilities for the corporation against the shareholders as if there were no corporation. By filing a Subchapter S election with the IRS, you can avoid the double taxation and pass the income and losses of the company to your individual tax returns.

Limited Liability Company (LLC)

This is also a separate business entity created by the provisions of special state laws. It's similar to a corporation that has made a Subchapter S election to be taxed as if it were a sole proprietorship or partnership, except that it doesn't have some of the limitations that the Subchapter S corporations have, such as restrictions on the different classes of stock, number of owners and management and other tax arrangements. Your attorney should be able to spell out this structure thoroughly if you feel you would benefit from it.

Pros: Profits and losses are noted on individual tax returns, but the LLC is held responsible for any liability issues.

Cons: Much as with a corporation, an LLC requires more record keeping than a sole proprietor or partnership.

Once you've laid the foundation, take a look at what you'll construct on it. Put it in writing. As an event planner, you know the importance of planning, so start the planning process with your own business. What kind of event planning services will you provide? Only if you identify your goals clearly from the start will you be able to chart your successes and make the necessary changes along the way to ensure you reach your goals.

Business Planning 101: Market Research

Getting a sense for your business potential is essential. Before you take the plunge, test the water. A thorough and honest investigation of the viability of an event planning business in your geographic area or in your select specialty area will help you start off on the right foot. Your research may even uncover information that will help you focus your business strategies and save you from costly and time-consuming mistakes.

Identify the Competition

Check your local listings, social media sites, or search online for event planners in your area. Read business journals, specialty magazines, and newsletters looking for event advertisers in your area. Research online for providers and their marketing techniques. What can you offer that is different? How can you put a spin on your company to create more interest or create a niche market? Identify whom you are up against and prepare yourself to go into battle well informed.

Identify Industry Growth Potential

Read up on the role events play in today's economy. When you present your services, you must make sure you show the value you bring to the event planning process. In the 1990s events were lavish and over the top. We saw website premiers, launch parties, and client events that kept getting bigger and better. Budgets supported events that were designed to impress, and having a professional planner involved could help make that happen.

In the early twenty-first century, the focus changed as wallets tightened. Likewise, the events that were created had to reflect the prudence people were showing in their daily lives. Events were still fun, but scaled back. When clients look for ways to cut cost, they can sometimes cut the most important line item—the planner. It's up to you to show how you can take a vision and bring it to life on time and on budget and in a way that no one else can. Assess what skills you need and how you can be viewed as a top-tier planner. Put the necessary steps in place to position yourself to be ready for the business that is in the marketplace.

Identify Potential Markets

As you scan the web or read up on business opportunities, look for areas that are ripe for event services. Match this with your interests and skills. If your local business pages or event directories show a slew of wedding planners but no planners for children's events, take note. If a nearby community seems ripe to hire event planners given its changing demographics, take a closer look at focusing here. Markets could be based on geographic territories, types of services, types of customers, or even budget levels. Planning fifteen smaller events might bring as much income and satisfaction as two large events. Look for the right segment or client that has the vision but not the planning skills, time, or vendor resources and show how you can fill that need.

Event Specialties

Take a look at these unique markets for events. Consider alternate demographics, specialty segments or groups, and other potential clients that would benefit from holding special events but lack the planning know-how.

- Children's and teens' parties
- Senior citizen or retirement community events
- Sporting events or sports-related gatherings
- Religious events
- Fund-raising events: walks, runs, auctions, galas
- Specialty meetings or conferences, such as meetings for funeral directors, massage therapists, or sporting groups for instance

Identify and Quantify Market Share

You have decided you must stay in your 50-mile radius and limit yourself to social events. You know who your competitors are. Now take an honest look at what business they are getting and what would be left for you. Is there something they're missing that you could provide? Are they handling all the country club events, for instance, but none of the hotel events? Develop your checklist of potential clients and event venues and vendors, and start doing your homework. Ask them what they like most in a planner. What are they not receiving and need? Try to discover a hole you can fill. Most professionals will be happy to chat with you, especially if you can make their job easier or solve a problem for them. This will give you an indication of the opportunities available. Remember, it takes time to develop business; be consistent and persistent with your efforts.

Identify Your Strengths and Opportunities for Success

As you begin to consider your options, you'll want to see where your forte may lie. If you're coming from a corporate background, you may be comfortable dealing with professional clients. Or perhaps your background is more on the social end, and planning celebratory events would suit you better. Do you enjoy the excitement of children's or community events? If you can find an area you love and are good at, this would be the place to start. Perhaps there are some old employers or friends who would be willing to give your new business a chance and use you for an event. Make a list of all the reasons that you would be a good fit to plan someone's event and practice your "elevator speech." Remember, it starts with believing in yourself, then others will believe in you too!

Consider Your Marketing Plan

How will you get your business off the ground and running? Chapter 5 will walk you through the creation of your marketing plan in depth, but it's wise to start thinking about it now. Start a database of contacts, and keep track of your initial calls and plans for follow-up. It takes effort to develop a relationship with a client, so be prepared to pay your dues. Out of sight, out of mind is an old saying that holds some truth. Your marketing plan should include creating a brand and vision statement, developing solid marketing materials, and reaching out on an ongoing basis to get your name out there. Even a seasonal card with a few business cards can remind someone that you are ready and willing to be an event solution for them or someone they know!

Business Planning 102: Selecting a Business Identity

Now that you've done your research and thought about your plan of attack, it's time to put it in writing.

The Business Brand

Before you even begin, take a hard look at what your company will stand for. What is the style and feeling you want to portray to the world. Is it classic, casual, whimsical, or serious? Based on your style and the kind of business you want to take on, this is the message you'll want to deliver loud and clear. Start with your brand statement—who you are and why you are unique. From this, you can create your business name, marketing materials, and marketing plan. The time you spend taking a hard look at the essence of your business will pay off in the long run as you develop your supporting materials.

The Business Name

When selecting your business name, first do an online search to see if the name is currently being used. It's not necessary to trademark your name, but if you plan to do business in various geographic areas or internationally, it's not a bad idea to consult with an attorney and explore your options to best protect your company name. You'll also want to make sure your URL or web address isn't being used by anyone else so there is no confusion when people search for you online.

When I selected my company name—*J. S. Moran & Associates, event planning & management*—I wanted my identity to be tied into my company name and added the tagline to identify what type of business I was. I later updated my company name to *jsmoran special events planning & management*. My website address is www.jsmoran.com, and the subtitle allowed me to reach out to a social client looking for a celebration or a corporate client wanting planning support. This covers the need to clearly identify who I am and what I do.

There are many options for great names. The important thing is to select something you can live with for the long run and that isn't already being used by someone else. Once your attorney has done the research, you can file the appropriate papers both locally and nationally to protect your investment. You will be spending time, energy, and money to publicize your company; you don't want to find out you're being sued by someone who already registered your name!

The Business Logo

A logo can be a great way to market your identity visually. It can be created from a combination of letters in your name or be a symbol that represents the style or type of events in which you specialize. When creating a logo, you will need to work with a professional graphic designer who will create what you are looking for and work with you to complement your business cards, letterhead, or brochure material. You will incur some up-front costs for this, but once you have your logo finalized, you'll have it on file to reproduce in the future on marketing

Sample Business Names—Pros and Cons

Events by Ellen	This shows that you do events but not specifically what kind.
Parties to Go	This lets people know you provide party services with some sort of portability option.
Corporate Events, Inc.	No mistaking what this company does!
John Smith Events	Seems reasonable, but make sure there are no other John Smith event planners out there!
Fabulous Events, Inc.	Clearly an event company—catchy and creative, but not too trendy.
Designing Divas	A partnership of creative designers—but what kind?

materials such as your website, proposals, incentive items, or wearables for your planning team.

If you think about the many products and services you use and the logos associated with them, you'll understand the impact a logo can have. When you see a logo, a company and impression immediately come to mind. Consider the long-term viability of your selection and ask for the advice of your graphic designer. You will want to select something that speaks of the flavor of your business. Whether it be simple, fancy, fun, or modern . . . select an image that you feel will withstand the test of time and reflects the heart of your business.

The Business Plan

Now you're ready for the key element: Your business plan. This is a document that formalizes your dream of owning your own business. It'll also be the measurement tool by which you can evaluate your success. Although you probably won't be presenting this plan to potential investors, or even showing it to clients or colleagues, having it will give you direction and confidence. You have both goals and a way to reach them. If you ever decide to apply for funding, a bank or investor will also want to carefully review your business plan. As you navigate the inevitable changes in your business, look at your business plan from time to time to see if you're still aiming in the right direction.

What goes into a business plan? What follows is a rundown of a good plan's most important elements, along with some samples to help you get started.

Mission Statement

What is the purpose of your business? Create a short, concise statement that you can deliver and on which you can build your business. This might include your values and offer keys to success. It will also allow you to stand out from the crowd and reveal how your services differ from the competition.

Sample mission statement:

jsmoran, special event planning & management, is a full-service special event company focusing on corporate and celebratory events worldwide. We are a resource to nonprofit and corporate management teams to support growth and visibility through the flawless execution of special events, meetings, and conferences. We help groups and individuals create unique and memorable events through creative planning and professional execution.

Objectives

What are the objectives of your business? Why are you offering your services? What will you provide to your clients to improve the quality of their lives? This information can be added to your website and your marketing materials; it can also be used to measure how well you've satisfied your clients' needs.

Sample objectives:

The objectives of my business are:

To design, execute, and evaluate events or meetings that support and promote social celebrations, marketing efforts, or internal or educational programs.

To offer a worldwide presence with events/meetings presented at major trade show cities or international venues, at company locations, or at specialized venues.

To offer a valuable service to company planning teams, directors, and those responsible for creating events with professional advice and experience that will help streamline the process, save money, and create dynamic experiences.

Types of events include:

Trade show–related events
Company outings
Award dinners
Website premiere events
Commemorative events
Golf outings
Grand openings
Product launches
Client incentive events
Educational and user meetings
Social celebrations
Recruitment events

Credentials

What qualifies you to start an event planning business? The "Credentials" section of your business plan is where you must take an honest look at what you bring to your business. Just enjoying parties won't cut it. You should have a track record of event planning, have experience within the hospitality industry, or have worked in an event-related industry with an understanding of the planning process. You may need to build on what you have in order to sell yourself as a full-service planner. Decide where the gaps in your training are, and set out to fill them.

Your "Credentials" section should list all the jobs or activities that have led you to your decision to start your own business. Also describe your plans to build on and enhance the experience you already have: the courses or programs you'll enroll in, any certifications you plan to get, and the educational conferences you can commit to attending. This will show that you're motivated to be the best and will be savvy to the most current trends and event services. As an active member of the industry, you will ensure that your customers receive state-of-the-art advice by using the most up-to-date products and themes.

The biography below shows a solid balance of basic knowledge backed by an understanding of what is necessary to complete training as a self-employed event professional. This self-examination, coupled with a team of solid business professionals, could start you on your way.

Sample credentials:

Having been the event coordinator for a top five-star resort, I have covered all aspects of coordinating special events within a specific venue. I have worked with existing clients who are holding meetings within the facility and have produced special events representing a variety of creative themes.

I have interfaced with food service managers to create menus, worked with in-house audiovisual services to complement the client/vendor relationship, and hired outside production and prop companies to carry out my theme ideas. I have built a file of contacts for many event support services, including graphic designers, florists, balloon artists, and entertainment providers.

While I have been responsible for many of the planning procedures, I have not had direct selling responsibility or the opportunity to work in a variety of venues or with a variety of caterers. There are some services I am unfamiliar with, such as transportation companies and tent companies.

I plan to enhance my expertise by completing a certificate program in special events planning through the Special Events Institute. As a member of my local International Special Events Society chapter, I will seek out additional vendor support and get referrals on reliable services from my colleagues.

Organizational Chart

How will your business be managed? This will be based on its formal structure. If you are the sole proprietor, you will be the CEO or president. You can identify your support team as the group of professionals who help you reach your business goals—whether or not they're employees of your company.

In chapter 6, I offer suggestions on developing your team, including vendors and support staff. For most home-based event planning businesses, the organizational chart is fairly simple: It shows the owner and professional staff, with most services provided by trusted vendors.

Sample organizational chart:

CEO and president: *Patty Planner, PBC*
Duties: *Business management, sales, marketing*
Accounting: *Doug Detail, CPA*
Duties: *Financial management, including tax planning*
Legal: *Larry Lawyer, Esquire*
Duties: *Legal issues, including contracts*

Marketing Plan

Here you state how you'll launch your business. This is the path from your heart to your customer. Nothing happens without a sale, so this is a crucial stepping-stone to getting your business off and running. After doing your research, decide on your focus market and go for it. You may include an array of strategies including direct mailings, social media campaigns, advertising, and cold calling. Remember that this may change as economic or local business conditions evolve. Be prepared to review and update as necessary.

Sample marketing plan:

To reach out to customers, I will become an active member of the Greater Boston Convention and Visitors Bureau and become a useful resource for the business community. I will achieve prominence and recognition by attending monthly meetings and by following up on business contacts and leads promptly.

I will also join at least two professional organizations and offer to serve on a committee. This will give me recognition in the community and afford me lead opportunities as well as professional growth.

I will direct my sales efforts to specific markets and create a strong campaign that clearly defines my skills and the benefits of using my services. This marketing campaign will include developing a website, a blog to showcase my projects and ideas, active participation on social media sites, a brochure that will be sent to my target market, and a quarterly postcard with seasonal information. I will follow up all direct-mail pieces and e-mail blasts with a personal telephone contact and periodic checks to pursue opportunities.

Operations Plan

Broadly identify the many ways in which you'll facilitate an event. Begin building a directory of vendors who will support your events. This will also show your understanding of what's involved with the event process and serve to broaden your support base.

Your support team can include invitation designers, caterers, florists, rental companies, production and lighting companies, decor and prop houses, and general staffing support. By incorporating these vendors into your plan, you lay the foundation to carry out your creative ideas.

Sample operations plan:

As a full-service event planning company, I will offer strategic planning, design and execution, vendor management, and evaluation. The daily operations team will consist of a project manager who will interact directly with clients and oversee all aspects of the planning. Appropriate and unique vendors will be secured to supply all necessary components of the event; professional staff will support all levels of planning, including administrative, staffing, and professional services.

The team will be prepared to offer twenty-four-hour service when needed for weekend and evening events; members will be available via text, cell phone, and pager to address all client and vendor needs. The day-to-day operations will be driven from office headquarters with a master resource file listing pertinent vendor contact information. Timelines and production schedules will drive the execution of events and provide valuable benchmarks for monitoring success.

Financial Plan

Before you start daydreaming about cashing the first big check from your first client, consider what you need to do to get to this point. What funds will you need to start your company? How will you pay for your office supplies and marketing materials? How will you cover your operational costs? Most service-based businesses do not require a great deal of start-up funding. The items you need can usually be purchased with savings, bought on credit, or postponed until your sales allow for such expenses. Be careful not to overspend in the early start-up stages—wait until your cash flow allows for additional purchases for your business.

Sample financial plan:

In the initial start-up phase of my planning business, I will utilize existing space in my home for office and administrative activities and will invest in a new computer and printer, paid for on credit. Additional expenses in the start-up phase will include the services of a graphic artist to assist with marketing materials, including website, stationery, and logo development. These will be financed through savings, with ongoing funding of additional services paid for by event income when funds are available.

Setting Goals

The final segment of your business planning involves setting business goals, both short term and long term. What are you setting your sights on for this month, this year, in five years? Once you've mapped out your long-term goals, then you can break them down into the weekly tasks that will allow you to achieve them.

What It Costs

Professional Fees
Attorney: $150–$350 per hour
Accountant: $500–$2,000, consulting and tax returns
Bookkeeper: $25–$50 per hour
Graphic designer: $25–$125 per hour, $500–$1,500 per project
Web designer: $25–$150 per hour, $200–$2,500 per site

Short-Term Goals

Getting new business might be one short-term goal. Setting up your office might be another. Keeping your vendor list fresh, gathering new event ideas, keeping your blog up to date, or preparing an article for a newspaper could be added to the list. Once you've determined your goals, you can work backward to create a timeline allowing you to meet them.

Long-Term Goals

Your long-term goals are an extension of your short-term goals. By achieving goals on a monthly basis, you can look at what you are accomplishing over time. Long-term goals tend to be more general and broader in scope. They are less specific and task oriented and more results oriented. As I noted above, breaking down the long-term goals into smaller components will show you how to achieve the results you're looking for in a series of manageable steps.

Your long-term goals are the vision that keeps you going through the ups and downs of your business. As the entrepreneur, you will deliver this vision to your clients, vendors, and staff as you offer your services.

Here are some examples of long-term goals:

- To create a business that I can sell in ten years
- To plan events in ten major cities within a five-year period
- To become a leader in an international organization
- To become recognized as one of the top five planners in my city
- To develop a strong social event planning company creating two events per month
- To grow my business to five employees
- To become certified in five years

Short-Term Goal: Secure a Wedding Client in Three Months

Week 1:

- Contact ten associates and ask for a referral.
- Drop a note to friends and family saying hello and sharing your dream.
- Make appointments with five wedding facilities to tour the property in exchange for sharing your service presentation.
- Develop a blog on wedding resources and ideas.
- Take out an ad in a wedding guide.
- Write an article on "Ten Steps to a Stress-Free Wedding Day."
- Drop off business cards at bridal shops, caterers' offices, and florists.

Week 2:

- Write eight blog posts to add weekly.
- Follow up with sales efforts.
- Create new contact lists if no positive responses are received.
- Make appointments with brides.

- Attend bridal fairs for ideas and leads.
- Make plans to exhibit at local bridal fairs.
- Contact wedding venues to showcase at any open houses.

Week 3:

- Follow up with sales efforts.
- Make appointments with brides.
- Send and sign contracts.
- Start planning.

Week 4:

- Continue responding to inquiries from ads.
- Follow up with venues and vendors.
- Follow up with potential brides.
- Continue planning events under contract.

Weeks 5–8:

- Same as above: Call, contact, and follow up.
- Respond to all inquiries.
- Make appointments with potential clients.
- Keep the planning process going.
- Hire help as your wedding business begins to boom!

Weeks 9–12:

- Continue updating wedding blog.
- Continue to incorporate prospecting for business into weekly goals.
- Continue to manage new appointments.
- Continue the planning process with booked business.

To reach these goals, you can use your short-term timeline to break each dream into weekly steps. These may include education, volunteerism, and investing time and money. They will be achieved by the work you do on a daily basis to build your business and reputation. Be prepared to change them as your situation changes. The economy, business trends, and your lifestyle may create a dynamic environment for your business. Still, if you don't set goals, you'll never reach them.

Frequently Asked Questions

Should I team up with a friend or go it alone?

It depends on how much time you have to put into your business; if you need the help, motivation, or support of a co-worker; if you can trust and depend on your partner-to-be; if you share the same work ethic, passion, and financial motivation; and if you have a good gut feeling about going into business with this friend. It takes a special relationship built on honesty, flexibility, shared vision, and commitment to make a partnership work. But for some people, the support and camaraderie of a partner can make, not break, the success of a new business. A good rule of thumb is to be careful when partnering with family or friends; it could put your relationship on shaky grounds. Go into business in a professional way with another professional. Go into it in writing, laying out all the details of your business partnership.

Is it worth it to pay for marketing lists or to enlist a company to do market research for me?

In most cases, you will learn a great deal from digging into your market and doing the research on your own. Even though it is time-consuming, you may learn more about what areas of events really interest you and will be most financially or personally rewarding, and you may actually uncover markets that you never knew existed! Resources such as business journals that generate yearly compilations of industry-specific lists with contact numbers, names, and addresses can be extremely helpful if you are planning an e-mail campaign, postcard blast, press release, or want to include them in your social media outreach.

How do I decide on a name for my company? Do I need a logo?

Choosing a company name can be very personal. It can also be expensive if you decide to print marketing materials and then realize the look isn't working for you. Spend some time brainstorming and get input and comments from friends, family, or clients. Everyone will have their own preference on look and feel, but try to choose something that fits your style and has staying power over the long run. Try to stay away from trendy or overly specific titles that will become outdated or limit you if you decide to expand or diversify.

Do I really need to write a business plan or detail my goals?

Absolutely. Even though it seems painful and needless to write the details down, it will help you formalize your dream and create a path that will lead you to success! By detailing the step-by-step plan you will take, you can begin to check off your successes and see the holes or gaps that may arise that will keep you from achieving your goals.

04 Dollars and Sense

Let's face it. While you may be drawn to events because they are fun, exciting, allow for a creative outlet in your life, and you just enjoy bringing a vision for an event to life and have a real knack at it—an important factor behind starting your own business should be building a fiscally sound company and venture. This can take time and will require patience and planning. Determine how you can grow your business and stay financially sound from the start. Will you be leaving full-time employment or fitting in events on weekends or evenings? How will you enhance your income to offset initial expenses? Do you have the skill needed to navigate a spreadsheet, profit and loss statement, or cash flow analysis? In any case, from your very first project you should approach the process in a professional and businesslike way. This will help you during the planning stages, at billing time, and—most importantly—as you evaluate the profitability of your business.

Tracking Your Business

There are many great general business accounting programs available. I have used QuickBooks for many years. It's simple to use and complete enough for me to track projects. I complement the program with a separate spreadsheet on which every expense is logged. If I prepare a budget for a client, I follow up on it by tracking each subsequent purchase, creating addendums if needed. The program you select should allow you to invoice your clients, pay your bills, and track expenses and income. It should also give you a snapshot of the financial health of your company and assist you in your legal and tax responsibilities. Let's look at some tools that will be helpful as you grow your business.

Cash Flow Projections

	Jan	Feb	Mar	April	May	June	July	Aug	Sept	Oct	Nov	Dec	Total
INCOME													
Weddings						$5,000	$5,000	$5,000	$5,000				$20,000
Holiday parties											$5,000	$5,000	$10,000
Fund-raisers		$5,000	$5,000										$10,000
Summer outings					$5,000	$5,000	$5,000						$15,000
Total Income All Projects		$5,000	$5,000		$5,000	$10,000	$10,000	$5,000	$5,000		$5,000	$5,000	$55,000
EXPENSES													
Professional dues and publications							$800						$800
Office supplies	$50			$50			$50			$50		$50	$250
Vehicle	$600	$600	$600	$600	$600	$600	$600	$600	$600	$600	$600	$600	$7,200
Tax payments	$1,400				$1,400			$1,400			$1,400		$5,600
Insurance	$800												$800
Telephone	$120	$120	$120	$120	$120	$120	$120	$120	$120	$120	$120	$120	$1,440
Equipment	$50	$50	$50	$50	$50	$50	$50	$50	$50	$50	$50	$50	$600
Industry conferences	$800							$800					$1,600
Travel	$1,000							$1,000					$2,000
Marketing expenses	$200												$200
Printing	$200						$200						$400
Postage		$100						$100					$200
Shipping													
Entertainment	$50	$50	$50	$50	$50	$50	$50	$50	$50	$50	$50	$50	$600
Total Expenses	$5,270	$920	$820	$870	$2,220	$820	$1,870	$4,120	$820	$870	$2,220	$870	$21,690
Monthly Cash Flow	$(5,270)	$4,080	$4,180	$(870)	$2,780	$9,180	$8,130	$880	$4180	$(870)	$2,780	$4,130	$33,310
Cumulative Cash Flow	$(5,270)	$(1,190)	$2,990	$2,120	$4,900	$14,080	$22,210	$23,090	$27,270	$26,400	$29,180	$33,310	

The Cash-Flow Statement

A cash-flow statement is useful in observing how money flows in and out each month. Here's why: The event planning business can be very seasonal; you may have slow times and frantic times throughout the year. Unfortunately, expenses often occur on a routine basis—think of your costs for your telephone, vehicle, advertising, office supplies, and so on. By being aware of the flow of cash, though, you can keep a firm grasp on your finances at all times, planning ahead for times that are a bit slower.

The cash-flow statement also allows you to make observations and respond to income flow to create and manage a healthy business bank account. You can also be creative and proactive to plan for those slower times. Perhaps you target holiday events to complement summer outings. If you're a wedding planner, the winter may be a slow time, but you could enhance your services to offer holiday stationery or in-home decorating or party assistance.

The cash-flow statement model on page 53 shows the finances of an event planner working on a mix of corporate and social accounts. You should be able to generate similar statements from the accounting software program you choose.

Take an honest look at what you would spend to maintain a professional business on a yearly basis and start from there. Consider your fixed expenses like office and event equipment, dues and rent, and variable expenses such as electricity, car leases, travel, and education. You should also consider unforeseen expenses and taxes and set funds aside to cover these items when they come due. As well as your operating costs, you'll want to set your sights on financial goals that will also allow you to pay yourself as the business owner and event planner. Partner this analysis with a solid marketing plan to make your business work!

Bank Accounts

It's imperative that you keep all your business transactions separate from your personal accounts. It'll help you enormously at tax time and validate that you're running a home-based business, as well as help keep your image sharp and professional. You can do this by opening up a business checking account and using this for all business transactions. You should likewise have a business credit card to use for charging business-related expenses.

You may also want to open up a few store or vendor accounts to begin to build credit relationships with suppliers. Pay these bills using your business checking account to keep things organized and running professionally. Even when you want to withdraw funds from your business account, write a check to yourself to help you track your personal deductions from the business.

Tax and Financial Planning

The tax responsibilities and record keeping required of a home-based business are drastically different from those for an individual. A meeting with your accountant will help you set up a system that you can stick with throughout the year and make tax preparations run that much more smoothly.

As a rule of thumb, consider setting aside 40 percent of all of the income from consulting fees if you are based in the United States. Keep a fund in your savings account to make quarterly tax payments that represent an appropriate tax burden so you will not be faced with a huge bill on April 15. Your quarterly estimates will be based on the prior year's earnings, but if you're having a banner year, it will be important to prepare for a larger tax hit by tucking the money away during the year.

Business expenses will offset your tax exposure, but not all expenses will be deducted directly from your gross income. Consult your accountant for complete details on what can be deducted and how to plan accordingly for your tax exposure. He or she will best advise you on how to plan throughout the year.

Show Me the Money: Pricing Your Services

The Budget

For any given project, create a budget. This includes the client's available or allotted funds, estimated expenses based on the event details, and your fees with details on the breadth of services you will be providing. I will go over budget components in more detail later in this chapter, but I think it's helpful to open our discussion of pricing with a sample budget:

As you can see, I feel that stating your planning fees is a crucial part of a budget. When you agree to perform the planning services, you must commit to carrying the project to fruition with all the components you've presented or that the client has requested. Based on your initial consultations with your client, you should estimate the time it will take to manage this process from start to finish and bill accordingly. Whether you show this as a percentage of the elements planned, a flat fee, or an hourly rate, you are showing that there is a value and expense associated with hiring you as a professional planner.

By pricing your services properly, you will approach the project in a positive and professional manner and the client will see the value in using your services. If you underprice, you risk not giving the project your full attention, because you can't afford to. If you overprice, you risk losing customers if they realize they're being unfairly charged. In any case, careful consideration must be given to the scope of

Birthday Party Bash

Decor	$200
Production services: lighting, sound, draping, labor	$7,000
Rentals: high cocktail tables	$100
Table linens, decor, and centerpieces	$800
Balloons	$500
Flooring	$950
Invitations	$3,500
Photography	$1,500
Catered cuisine	$4,200
Subtotal	**$18,750**
Planning fees: concept, design, coordination, planning, setup, and on-site management (20% of project)	$3,750
Estimated Total	**$22,500**

the project and the time you'll put into it. As you progress through the planning, this will also help you in constructing your timeline and project overview.

Pricing by Percentage

One way to estimate the cost of your services is to figure your cost as a percentage of the total budget. I try to use 20 to 25 percent of the total as a benchmark. This is not always how the final numbers flush out, but it is a starting point. Negotiations sometimes come into play. If you're taking on a project in part to gain exposure or contacts, you might want to make more allowances in pricing. On the other hand, if you sense that a client will be needing more than the typical amount of hand-holding, then think about fee-for-services or hourly rate pricing.

Pricing by Fee for Services

If, during the proposal stages, you get the impression that the project will require additional meetings, ongoing changes, updated progress reports, or the like, you may want to clearly define what you will do for the set fee and offer the option of additional hours at an hourly rate. This rate would be based, as in many professional industries, on experience and qualifications.

When drafting your proposal, estimate how much time it will take for basic administrative duties, event coordination, marketing and promotion, and risk assessment and management. Break down each category into the components you'll be covering and the estimated time it will take to carry out the tasks. This will give you a starting point for what you might charge for a planning fee.

Let's take a look at some examples. You are given a budget of $50,000 for a 200-guest event. If you get a sense that the event will be relatively easy to manage—say, it's held at a local country club that you work with on a regular basis; the food service will be handled internally; there will be no rentals, transportation, or outside security or lighting needed; and the only additional services will be decor—then you may be able to charge a flat fee that will cover roughly thirty hours of planning time.

On the other hand, suppose the event will be held 100 miles away. It will also need tenting as well as full rentals of tables, chairs, linens, lighting, and power—and you've been asked to coordinate outside services such as entertainment, photography, video, and florals. In this case you'll want to project a much higher fee. Consider travel time, telephone and correspondence time for all vendors, and multiple updates for timelines and production schedules. In this instance your quote may include 130 or more hours for planning.

You may also figure in a range of planning expenses based on delegating some of the tasks for which you would pay a variety of fees. You may know you can pay an assistant at $15 per hour to handle clerical tasks, favor assembly, and on-site setup, while a higher fee would be assigned for creative design and event management. Figuring in the variety of fees, you will arrive on a final project cost to cover your time and labor.

War Stories: Don't Count Your Chickens . . .

An event colleague, eager to produce a fund-raising event for a local church, agreed to hire a caterer, entertainers, and rentals for a summer fête in return for a portion of the money raised from the event. Unfortunately, the weather was bad, turnout was poor, and the caterer charged an agreed-upon minimum for food services. The planner was out $10,000 as a result of her optimism. A word of caution: Be realistic and fiscally responsible with your business funds!

Pricing by the Hour

Using the same projection format, you may decide to present an hourly fee structure and tie each action item into a cost line. This gives the client a clear picture of what it takes to carry an event to fruition and allows you to be compensated for your time appropriately. You may have to negotiate your time or make alterations based on budgets. It will be up to you, the professional, to educate your clients as to the value of your services. If you're pricing your services out of their budget, think about eliminating items that could be performed by the clients or their staff and focusing on the tasks that are integral to the planning process and that you can do cost effectively and efficiently for them.

The range for hourly fees could be as low as $25 per hour or as high as $125, depending on the type of task and the consultative value you'll bring to the table. Remember, you'll be paying for your own benefits, Social Security (US Citizens), and taxes out of the hourly rate you receive, so don't underestimate your worth.

Pricing by Commissionable Rates/Add-Ons

In some instances I have seen proposals with no line item for planning fees. The planner is compensated by adding a "handling fee" or "finder's fee" to all the services that are provided at the event. If you'll be managing the rentals, florals, linens, and so forth, you may be eligible for a volume discount, which you could take as a commission. The client will not know what this amount is but should realize this is being done if there is no indication that you're being paid clearly printed on the estimate or invoice. In this case you would handle all the billing, submitting the total invoice to the client if asked to, and reducing the amount paid to the vendor by the agreed-upon percentage.

I personally try to avoid this method. I feel that it's important to show my value to clients with a line item on the invoice. I also pass discounts on to them, showing them the savings that they will realize by enlisting my services and using my power of purchase. I think this is a much stronger way to showcase the professionalism of the industry.

Negotiating with Clients

There are times when the price you think you should get just doesn't match what the market will bear. Negotiations sometimes—though not always—come into play as you move from the proposal to the contract stage. You'll want to use your professional judgment to determine whether you want to negotiate. It depends on how much you want the business, the difficulty you'll have executing the event, and what marketing value the event might bring to you. Even if you do elect to discount your price, I advise always listing the total value of the event on your contract to give clients a clear picture of a planner's worth. From that number, you may deduct a percentage or a flat amount to reach a mutually agreeable price.

My Event Company

1 Event Way

Celebrate, ON 54321

Invoice

DATE	INVOICE #
7/1/15	001

Bill To
Beth Bride and Gary Groom 123 On Our Way Blissfield, ME 98765

P.O. NO	TERMS	PROJECT
	Payable upon recipt	Beth and Gary's wedding

QUANTITY	DESCRIPTION	RATE	AMOUNT
25 hours	Initial metting, concept development, site inspections, vendor negotiations and contracting, planning services	$75	$1,875.00
		Total	$1,875.00

Negotiating with Vendors

You can negotiate with vendors for more attractive pricing. If you can foresee using a vendor for multiple events, you might be able to set up a "quantity discount." You would pass this on to each individual client to highlight the value of using a professional planner. Try to be sensitive about the suppliers' need to cover their own costs. Fixed-cost items may be easier for a vendor to discount than disposable or high-maintenance items that require repair, cleaning, or labor. Relationships with vendors often require a delicate balancing act, and it's important to always respect that they, too, need to price their services in a professional way. When the budget allows, showcase their best products and compensate them justly. Your valued vendors will understand the difficult task you have and appreciate you for using them for the variety of products or services they offer.

A Billing Hint

As a consultant you will not need to purchase a great deal of inventory or have items in stock to show to clients. Any inventory can be purchased on a per-project basis with money you will receive in advance from the client. The best advice I can give is to set up your billing to reflect deposits and final payments prior to the date of each event. This will allow you to use your clients' funds for event purchases and vendor payments, instead of your own. You'll also eliminate nonpayment issues: no money, no event.

Budgeting

When putting together a budget for an event, you should take time to carefully estimate your costs in all areas. Step one is to start with the clients' budget. You will need to fully understand the clients' expectations for decor, cuisine, and entertainment, and counsel them on what can realistically be delivered. If their budget is $50,000, and the guest list is set at 500 people, you will be hard pressed to offer filet mignon for an entrée and still get paid as a planner. Before you spend time working up a detailed outline of services, you must educate them. Offer options for a variety of food, entertainment, and decor that will fit their budget and help them achieve their goals for the event. Provide them with options and outcomes so they can make choices that will help them achieve their objectives, and stay in budget.

In the worst case you may have to let a project go because their budget and expectations do not align. Or you might opt to use your creative license and imagination to pare down costs yet still get the results the clients are looking for and be paid for your services.

When creating a budget, I often have to present various options to help clients decide on the venue and other details that are right for them. Here is where the value of using a planner comes into play. They appreciate your expert advice and the time you've taken to compile the list of choices for their event. Once the research is done and the decisions are made, it's of course up to you to keep the project within budget.

Frequently Asked Questions

What is the best way to price my services?

That is the million-dollar question! It depends on the client, the budget, the scope of services, and your experience. Pricing also can be based on the advantage of working with a certain client, if there is additional work that can be secured by getting your foot in the door, or if there is a learning curve to the type of business that would warrant flexibility in pricing. Pricing can also be varied based on your current workload and availability, the mix of events you may have and if you want to add a new "line" of services to your portfolio, the time of year that an event is requested, and if you really want the business. It is always best to look at the time you will be putting into the event and what other work you may lose if you commit to the event. Don't forget your life balance and if other areas of your life may suffer if you take an event that doesn't give you the remuneration that you need or deserve.

Should I treat nonprofit business differently? Can I make money working with this type of client?

Working with nonprofits can be advantageous in many ways. Not only can it provide repeat business (they may hold the same fund-raiser or conference each year), it can get you referrals, provide a philanthropic experience, allow you to advertise through sponsorship of events, and also provide an opportunity to use students, interns, or novice planners who will donate their time for a good cause. I typically will discount my fees for a not-for-profit client, but will show them my full fee structure, so they realize the value they are receiving. Check with your accountant to see if you can use this as a charitable deduction for your business.

		Corporate Summer Outing			
Date:				**Venue A**	
		number of guests	**pp price**		**total**
Adult menu		125	$ 34.45	pp	$ 4,306.25
Children's menu		40	$ 12.00	pp	$ 480.00
	Total				**$ 4,786.25**
	20	Soft drinks	$ 1.50	each	$ 30.00
	45	Water	$ 1.50	each	$ 67.50
	329	Bar beverages	$ 3.50		$ 1,151.50
		Bar gratuity			
					$ 6,035.25
Gratuity			n/a		
					$ 6,035.25
		Sales tax		5%	$ 301.76
Subtotal food & beverage					$ 6,337.01
Park admission fee: under 3 years old					
Electrical outlet					$ 65.00
Boat rentals	5	Paddleboat rental	$ 85.00		$ 425.00
Boat rentals	5	Canoe rental	$ 65.00		$ 325.00
Bartenders		Beer/wine/margs			$ 125.00
Waterfront					$ 300.00
Facility rental					$ 1,500.00
Total facility charges					$ 9,077.01
Entertainment & decor items					
Disc jockey & game show					$ 2,700.00
Decor: balloons, tabletops					$ 1,200.00
Novelty activities		Prizes			$ 1,000.00
Dog Tags					$ 600.00
Postcards around America					$ 750.00
Thumbprint Artist					$ 350.00
Hi Striker					$ 300.00
Dunk Tank					$ 250.00
Speed Pitch					$ 550.00
County Jail					$ 400.00
Giant Slide					$ 800.00
Obstacle Course					$ 800.00
Pizza Chef					$ 500.00
Moonwalk					$ 200.00
Cow-milking Game					$ 400.00
Uncle Sam Stiltwalking					$ 450.00
Additional items		Photos			$ 200.00
Staff supervision	8	Staff	$ 80.00		$ 640.00
Planning fees					$ 6,000.00
Flyers, notices/gift preparation					$ 500.00
Total Outing Cost					**$ 27,667.01**
T-shirts	198	Shirts	$ 5.75		$ 1,138.50
Grand total with T-shirts					**$ 28,805.51**
		Features	Venue A		
			Private facility		
			Indoor/outdoor setting: air-conditioning		
			Indoor toilets		
			Tasting available		
			Baseball/soccer field available		

Event info: Disc jockey and game show includes all props, DJ for entire event, and equipment necessary for game show.
Novelty prizes include giveaways for children's games and props for relays.
Decor includes balloons, tabletop items, props, and incidental raffle prizes for game show—pricing based on prior year's expenses.

		Venue B				**Venue C**	
	$ 28.95	pp	$ 3,618.75		$ 50.00	pp	$ 6,250.00
	$ 9.95	pp	$ 398.00		$ 12.00	pp	$ 480.00
			$ 4,016.75				**$ 6,730.00**
20	$ 1.50	each	$ 30.00		$ 2.50		$ 50.00
45	$ 2.00	each	$ 90.00		$ 2.50		$ 112.50
329	$ 3.00		$ 987.00		$ 3.50		$ 1,151.50
			$ 5,123.75				$ 8,044.00
		19%	$ 973.51			19%	$ 1,528.36
			$ 6,097.26				$ 9,572.36
		5%	$ 304.86			5%	$ 478.62
			$ 6,402.13				$ 10,050.98
	$ 30.00	3	$ 90.00				
					Signage		$ 350.00
	$ 75.00	5	$ 375.00		Mascot		$ 225.00
	$ 75.00	5	$ 375.00		Mascot		$ 225.00
	Beer/wine only		$ 75.00				$ 125.00
		n/a			n/a		
		n/a					$ 3,500.00
			$ 7,317.13				$ 14,475.98
			$ 2,700.00				$ 2,700.00
			$ 1,200.00				$ 1,200.00
			$ 1,000.00				$ 1,000.00
			$ 600.00				$ 600.00
			$ 750.00				$ 750.00
			$ 350.00				$ 350.00
			$ 300.00				$ 300.00
			$ 250.00				$ 250.00
			$ 550.00				$ 550.00
			$ 400.00				$ 400.00
			$ 800.00				$ 800.00
			$ 800.00				$ 800.00
			$ 500.00				$ 500.00
			$ 200.00				$ 200.00
			$ 400.00				$ 400.00
			$ 450.00				$ 450.00
			$ 200.00				$ 200.00
			$ 640.00				$ 640.00
			$ 6,000.00				$ 6,000.00
			$ 500.00				$ 500.00
			$ 25,907.13				**$ 33,065.98**
			$ 1,138.50				$ 1,138.50
			$ 27,045.63				**$ 34,204.48**
	Venue B				Venue C		
	Open to public				Private		
	Outdoor only/tent with no sides				Under bleachers in protected area		
	Outdoor toilets				Indoor toilets		
	No tasting offered				Tasting available		
	No ball fields				Soccer available		

Should I show my fee directly to the client, or should I bury it in the total costs of the event?

I like to present a line item for my services so the client can clearly see the value of my work. I often will create a detailed task analysis showing the hours it will take for planning, which then will give me total hours and a total fee. Sometimes a commission or fee for securing sponsorship will allow for more flexibility for the client, and can offer more of an incentive, but also is a more risky fee structure

Should I get payment in full before an event takes place?

If you can, it is an excellent way to keep your company in a positive cash-flow situation. If you are paying for event expenses on behalf of the client, it will also allow the client's check to clear your bank account before you have to issue checks to vendors. If you present your payment structure up front, when you are in the contract-signing phase, there will be no surprises for either you or the client. As long as you keep your budget up-to-date and get approval for any additions or changes, presenting the final bill to your client should be a positive experience. You will also be building good relationships with your vendors as you pay them in full and on a timely basis.

05 Marketing Your Services

To successfully start and grow an event planning business, you must have the magical mix of superior service and a strong and loyal customer base. You've already formalized your business identity and set up financial procedures; now you're ready to begin the search for a paying customer.

Specialist or Generalist? Defining Your Position

As a full-service event planner, you'll want to maintain a clear focus on what you do and be able to communicate how you execute the planning process. This will allow you to deliver concise information to potential clients. Some planners feel specialization allows them to focus their energies on one area. A specialty could be the type of planning you offer or the industry you target. Niche marketing, in the right industry or area, can position you as an expert and give you an edge by saturating one specific market. Others feel that by maintaining a broad scope of services, they are better poised to take advantage of changing business climates and industry highs and lows.

I have done both in my own career. In the 1990s my client portfolio included companies in the telecommunications industry as well as Internet companies. They were booming at the time and great sources of ongoing projects and referrals. In the early 2000s, however, these clients mysteriously disappeared from my schedule. The changing economy has forced me to redirect my energies and seek out other sources of corporate business. I've chosen to expand my services to include social and not-for-profit events, areas that I hadn't developed in the past. I've now opened up my services to wedding clients, high-end social events, and fund-raising events. While making a move to market to new types of event clients, I have stayed as close to my forte as possible, dealing with customers who are looking for a professional implementation of their event—a planner who is experienced in managing all aspects of the process, from creative development to contract management, professional execution, and the final stages of follow-up and evaluation.

Wouldn't it be nice if there were a crystal ball to tell you the future of the field of event planning! Unfortunately, so many factors can affect who chooses to hold an event and why. My advice would be to find an area you enjoy and at which you are naturally skilled. Whether that means dealing with the concerns of a bride or responding to the empty look of a CEO who has no clue what she wants for her company awards dinner, target the clients to whom you can most easily relate and go for it. Be the best you can be, build your skills in event planning and share your passion to build your business into a success.

More on Image

It goes without saying that in developing your company image, you should carry your marketing initiatives through to your presentational plan as well. Attire, portfolio, and presentational material . . . all these should reflect the company image you have chosen. Think about the clothing you wear. Would a contemporary Armani suit over a sparkly top best reflect your style—or maybe a classic blazer or suit? If you're dealing with children's events, on the other hand, taking a more casual approach won't jeopardize your reputation or the impression you make with your clients. In any case, professional, organized, knowledgeable, and prepared should be the impression you leave after meeting with potential customers. This can also be reflected in your prompt follow-up, quick delivery of promised proposals, and timeliness at meetings.

Branding Your Company

The Defining Statement

Begin crafting your marketing materials with a defining sentence that will serve to brand your company identity going forward. You will use this as your marketing statement when you introduce yourself, meet potential clients, make presentations, or pitch your services to prospective customers during sales calls. *Fun, upscale, creative, classy, whimsical* . . . these descriptors and many more can be woven into your marketing statement.

Here are a few samples of defining statements:

- Hi, my name is Claire of *A Wedding to Remember*, and I specialize in weddings. I work with couples to bring their vision to life and help make their special day stress-free and memorable. I make the details of the wedding flow smoothly and assist with the selection and management of the wedding vendors—florists, entertainment, linens, special transportation—to allow the bride and groom to create and enjoy memories of a lifetime!

- Hi, my company, *Pizzazz Party Planning*, creates events for children, including birthday parties, bar and bat mitzvahs, sweet sixteen parties, school fund-raising events, and children's fairs and festivals. We provide and manage the specialty entertainment, inflatable games, festive novelties, and theme decor that make each party truly unique for kids and families!
- Hello, I'm with *Corporate Event Strategies*. We handle the details of creating corporate events with our staff of event professionals through creative theme development, event production and execution, and ongoing attention to detail. We produce internal events, marketing events, or training events internally at a corporate headquarters or at unique venues worldwide.

Communicating with Your Clients

Once upon a time, making a personal visit and using the telephone were the only ways to connect with clients. The use of the World Wide Web to collaborate and share information has become the go-to communication tool for both social and corporate clients. In today's high-speed technology age, consider some of the following methods to market your services and connect with new clients:

Event Peeps: a live event-industry social and professional networking site
Events Network: an international event networking site similar to Facebook
Facebook: a social networking site that allows you to create a business page, add and share "friends," and post photos, messages, videos, and information about your business
LinkedIn: a relationship-building site for professional networking
Skype: free software that enables global conversations in video and audio
Google+: connect with clients and colleagues in organized circles
Instagram: photo enhancement app to showcase your work
Pinterest: boards of favorite photos and creations to show your style and interests

Sharing Information across the Web

These sites will let you post news about your events, share videos and photos, and offer tips that others may find interesting:

Flickr: an online photo management and sharing application

Instagram: a photo sharing app that followers can like and share; great for posting event photos or inspiration!

Pinterest: a place to collect your events photos and arrange them by themes or categories.

Twitter: a tool that allows you to tweet (type) information from your phone or computer for "followers" to read

YouTube: a website that allows you to post and view videos

Creating Your Marketing Materials

Marketing materials are essential tools that help a customer make the decision to hire you. They communicate what you offer, who you are, and how you can solve the needs of the client. Methods of delivery for this important information about your company and services can range from newsletters, websites, blog posts, brochures, and postcards to PowerPoint and video presentations. Online methods of communication also include a website, Facebook, Twitter, and YouTube. In designing your marketing materials, you want to be clear, succinct, colorful, and persuasive. Some clients will not be able to visualize your talents by reading a description. Photographs, sketches, or video clips can add a great deal to your marketing materials. Long-winded explanations will go unread, so short, powerful statements that show your style and value are essential.

A website is the first stop along the marketing highway. It's essential that you have a presence on the web if you are to be taken seriously as a business. Most potential clients will use online searches to find resources and to check your style and professionalism as well as your background, list of services, and client profiles and testimonials. Be sure to use high-quality photos, check for proper grammar and spelling, and make sure all the information you post is approved to share by your past clients. If you only have played a small role in an event, be accurate with your description of your involvement and do not take ownership if you haven't had a leadership role in the event. If you aren't tech-savvy, hire a professional to secure your domain name, secure a hosting company, and build your site. There are many low- or no-cost templates that will allow you to build your message and update it on a regular basis as you grow your business.

Website Basics

Make sure you create a website that is easy to navigate and captures your company style. You'll want to include these essential elements to make a good first online impression and let prospects and visitors find the information they need quickly. Choose a template that is mobile-friendly (can be viewed on all devices) and captures your style in design and color. Be sure to keep your logo, image, and branding consistent from one social networking site to another (website, Facebook fan page, Twitter feed, or Pinterest board) so visitors begin to get to know you better and to recognize your style and flair.

- Home Page—tell them what you do, why you do it, and how you can make their lives easier.
- About Page—share your story—who you and your team are and why you are passionate about events. You can divide this into sections based on the kind of events you do with dropdown menus off the main tab.
- Contact Page—make it easy for them to reach you.
- Blog—to share your good news and photos and let prospects know what you are doing; also great for search engine optimization.
- Testimonials—you can create a full page for this or add it to every page.
- Photo Gallery—this can be a separate page or be included in specific event pages.

Other elements to consider:

- Lead Capture Form—consider offering a free consultation or a "Tip Sheet" in exchange for their email information to begin to grow your user list for subsequent mailings and outreach.
- Social Media Links—share links to your other accounts such as Twitter, Facebook, Instagram, and Pinterest.

Not everyone is computer savvy, however, and some clients will want to "touch and feel" the service they will be buying. Participation in social networks such as Pinterest, Instagram, LinkedIn, Facebook, and Twitter allow you to post your credentials and inform participants of your business achievements and needs. Printed materials such as brochures, personalized folders with inserts, or even postcards can capture the basics of your business and respond to customers' needs. You may choose to develop an e-newsletter or seasonal postcard to send to a target audience, but in general mass mailings are costly and do not offer the return you will want from the investment made. An advertisement in a specialty magazine can serve as a good marketing tool. Facebook also provides the opportunity to purchase ads and "boost" posts to reach the audience you are looking for. Creating a Pinterest board, posting a news item on your blog, or "tweeting" will showcase your business to followers if managed effectively. Just remember to match the advertising vehicle with the customer base you're hoping to reach for maximum benefit. For instance, if you are trying to market to your church congregation, take an ad out in the weekly bulletin. If you are trying to reach high-end wedding clients, a booth at a high-end bridal event may be more suitable.

Dos and Don'ts of Social Networks

Don't share too much! While some social networks are business oriented (such as LinkedIn and Event Peeps), others can be both social and professional (like Facebook and Pinterest). It is wise to screen all the information you post on the Internet to make sure it presents you in a professional and appropriate way. Err on the side of caution and limit any photos or discussions that could present you in a compromising fashion. It's always wise to ask permission from your clients before posting any references to or photos of them on the Internet.

Don't brag if it's not the right forum! If you join a discussion group that shuns direct selling, make sure your comments are geared toward getting and sharing helpful information rather than just tooting your own horn. It will give you more credibility among your peers.

Do connect! Consider your past relationships when seeking networking groups. Past education (colleges or universities), social groups, vendor organizations, professional specialties . . . all have groups that welcome new members with whom to share and connect. Screen invitations, though, to maximize the right connections. Social networking can be time consuming to maintain, so choose the best connections to build your business.

Don't waste your readers' time! Consider what you say when you are tweeting or blogging. Make sure you are adding value, sharing important business information, and not just chatting for the sake of filling up the page or character count. Readers don't want to know what you had for breakfast, but will want to know if you found a great restaurant that offers new cuisine at a great price for newly engaged couples. Don't be afraid to snap a photo and pin it on Pinterest or include it on your blog or tweet. Visuals always capture a viewer's attention and can help you gain a strong and loyal following.

Once you have your defining statement mapped out, you can use it to brand your marketing materials. At first you may choose or need to develop your own. This would be the most cost-effective way to get started. If you have photos or descriptions of events that you've produced, use these as a foundation and partner it with written descriptions of your services. If you're starting from scratch and have done any volunteer work, you may want to showcase your accomplishments for these projects. If you were in charge of the decorating committee and managed a staff to develop a theme and create the event decor, this could serve as an initial building block. Photos or words of praise can be included to show the success of the event. Be careful not to take credit for a project in which you had only a small part or with which you were not directly involved. If you helped another planner with an event, it would not be appropriate to describe that event in your portfolio or marketing material. If you feel you don't have enough experience to print a marketing piece, wait until you've done a few events on your own to create personalized materials.

To get started, you might address the elements that go into planning an event in a general way (just be ready to deliver these elements with an experienced support staff!). This would show your clients that you understand the process and can help them work through the many decisions required to create an event reflecting their goals, objectives, and personal tastes.

Here are some sample marketing pieces:

Affairs with Flair

Open your doors and allow us to set the table with fine linens upon which we place exquisite florals and gourmet cuisine prepared expressly for you and your guests.

At Affairs with Flair we offer event planning services with complete coordination of catering, linen, fine china, and serviceware rental; small musical ensemble entertainment; and floral and theme decor to complete the look of your special event! When you have a dream, but not the time to make it come true . . . let Affairs with Flair come to the rescue.

◊ ◊ ◊

Party Pizzazz

Turning Forty, Getting Married, Celebrating an Anniversary . . . whatever the milestones in your life may be . . . let us help you celebrate with style! Party Pizzazz can assist with home parties or special events at restaurants, hotels, or specialty venues. We complete the planning process with unique invitations, personalized decorations, full-service catering and beverage service, and entertainment to make your party the event of a lifetime!

◊ ◊ ◊

Corporate Events Unlimited

At Corporate Events Unlimited, we specialize in the details of the event management process including strategic event planning, site selection, vendor management, and execution of your internal or sales events. Partnering with you, we provide initial consultations, ongoing communications throughout the planning process, professional event execution, and complete evaluation to ensure that each event meets your company's goals and expectations. Leave the business of special event planning to the pros at Corporate Events Unlimited.

What It Costs

Membership in a professional organization: $400 average per year, $25–$75 per monthly meeting
Ad in an industry publication: $50–$1,500
Article in an industry publication: free
Website: $150–$2,500 (includes hosting fees and site development)
Television advertising: $50 (local)–$10,000 (national)
Ad production costs: $250–$2,500
Booth at a trade show: $400–$1,200 (regional or national)

Developing a Marketing Plan

The Sales Challenge

It's not enough to formalize your event planning business . . . now you need clients. If you're lucky enough to have a few projects lined up, the pressure may be off for the time being. But one of the greatest challenges as a small-business owner is to be marketing your services while you're handling current planning tasks. You should try to set aside a certain percentage of your time to focus on securing new business. Try to answer inquiries when they come in. Turn proposals around on a timely basis in an attempt to have business in the pipeline. In a perfect world, when one project is complete, you'll have another waiting patiently to begin. Sounds good, but having the perfect balance of business is seldom a reality.

Either you're too busy to handle all the work coming your way, or you have time on your hands between projects wondering when the next event will arrive. Both situations come with solutions. If you're too busy working on projects to market on an ongoing basis, develop an automated mailer that you can send out monthly. MailChimp is a great email system that has this function built in. Commit to a weekly post on a wedding or event blog you create. Either write a newsletter or have someone do it for you. Perhaps a student intern could update your weekly blog or create a monthly flyer, which could be easily mailed to your target list of clients. Take time to get a website up and running. It will serve as an ongoing advertising vehicle. Keep it up to date with new photos, client testimonials, and event ideas. By staying in front of your existing clients and continually introducing yourself to potential customers, you keep the wheels of business turning. When an opportunity comes up, you'll be fresh in their minds.

Taking Care of Business!

Developing a solid system for categorizing leads is critical in the first stages of growing a business. Some possible lead management tools run from a basic Microsoft Office database such as Outlook, Access, or Excel; others provide a more professional management software system, such as ACT! by Symantec. There are many software tools on the market; ask at your local computer store for the latest and most popular software package, or do an Internet search to see what's new on the market. If you prefer jotting things down on paper, you might want to develop a file system using either file folders or index cards that contain key contact information and notes you make on an ongoing basis. For many years, I filed business cards in three-ring binders sorted by category. I now depend on my iPhone and love the simplicity of accessing everything from one device. Phone calls, appointments, web searches, and applications—even a camera for taking event photos—are all accessible on my iPhone. While I still carry a notebook for jotting down ideas and daily lists, the important information gets logged into my computer calendar and iPhone for quick access.

Put together your target "sales" list and mark your calendar with a plan of attack. Most sales are completed only after making many contacts. It takes persistence and a belief in your services and what you can bring to this client to make a lead turn into a sale. The sources of leads can vary from word-of-mouth referrals to lists that you purchase, leads from newspapers, and research you do on a particular market that you're targeting. However you develop your lead list, set up a system you can manage over time and set aside a portion of your planning week to take care of the business of selling!

Getting Your Name Out There

There are many ways you can connect with the right customer. Here are a few suggestions:

Website. Build and maintain a website showcasing your services.

Social Media. Facebook, Pinterest, Twitter, Instagram, and YouTube—post frequently to get and maintain a following.

Connect Online. E-newsletters, webinars, special offers on your social media sites.

Advertising. Shopping guides, newspapers, local magazines, industry magazines.

Print. Develop a print piece (like a postcard or brochure) to mail to potential customers.

Multimedia. Develop a PowerPoint presentation, a video portfolio, or a CD to show potential clients.

Networking. Start a blog, join online event-related groups, and attend industry or local meetings.

Volunteerism. Offer your services and/or advice.

Community. Participate in career days, industry functions, merchant fairs.

Trade Shows. Take out a booth in a local or national expo to reach the right customers. These could include bridal fairs, event expos, or educational conferences that have a trade show component.

Professional Involvement

Involvement in industry groups not only allows you to continue your own training and skills improvement, but also gives you an opportunity to build your vendor support as well as to form bonds with colleagues to whom you can refer business—or who could refer business back to you. A group of wedding planners in my area meets monthly for lunch to share vendor information, solutions to planning problems, and new wedding ideas or products they have discovered. They give each other "the scoop" on who's delivering the best or worst in vendor services. In a friendly way these competitors work together to stay on top of their game.

Attending monthly meetings of industry organizations can put your face and business on the map. It takes perseverance and dedication to carve an evening or two a month into your busy schedule to market yourself and your services. When my children were small, it was very difficult—if not impossible. Between the travel obligations for my clients and the family extracurricular commitments, I just wasn't able to attend a majority of these meetings. Over time, though, I made a commitment to become active in a leadership role in my local International Special

Events Society (ISES) chapter. And by doing so, I've made business contacts and professional friendships that I couldn't live without!

Industry Networking Groups Worth Joining

Consider joining allied associations and networking groups specific to the event or meeting industry. It can be time-consuming to attend meetings, but it's also a great way to get to know colleagues who could refer business to you. Below you'll find the websites of the hospitality and event industry's key organizations. Some of these sites also list other related professional organizations. Check appendix B for a complete list of hospitality-related organizations and their contact information.

People like to do business with friends, and attending networking events is a great way to get exposure. Consider joining a professional organization such as the International Special Events Society or Meeting Professionals International. It's an investment in time and money, but one well worth making. When you become a member, you have the option of joining a local chapter. Once you join, offer to serve on a committee—or better yet, begin to familiarize yourself enough with the chapter to chair a committee. In any of the related hospitality organizations, the best way to reap benefits is to become active. Everyone will know who you are. And when someone is looking for a planner, your name will be the first to come up.

- International Special Events Society (ISES): www.ises.com
- National Association of Catering Executives (NACE): www.nace.net
- Meeting Professionals International (MPI): www.mpiweb.org
- Professional Convention Management Association (PCMA): www.pcma.org

Network

Networking is a great marketing tool that allows you to sell your services in a more personalized way. You can make an instant impression on a possible client—and vice versa. While you may not walk away with a direct sale, you plant a seed for a relationship that can grow. You may even be recommended to someone else who also needs your services. Face-to-face contact with a prospect also allows you to ask for a commitment for a follow-up meeting—even to set up a day and time.

Networking can occur at professional meetings, social or civic gatherings, or within community groups. Check your local papers for lunch-hour networking groups. Inquire as to the types of companies that are currently members. Assess the value of joining before spending any money on dues. If members could potentially use your services or refer you business, it's worth at least trying out a meeting

Sources of Leads

Professional organizations. Serving on committees gives you great exposure. Networking at monthly meetings also can help develop contacts.
Chamber of commerce directories. As a member of a chamber or business association, you have access to information on incoming groups and activities.
Newspaper want ad sections. Look for event-related needs.
Online listings. Check out Meet Up, Craig's List, or LinkedIn for postings on event needs.
Newspaper or Online articles. Look for companies launching products, holding meetings, or expanding.
Newspaper social pages. Look for leads on engagements, fund-raisers, or annual events.
Specialty magazines. Business journals, meeting or incentive magazines, and bridal or corporate journals can give you advertising opportunities as well as names of vendors to contact.
Internet. Join networking sites and discussion groups; post to a blog or tweet. Being visible on the Internet will get you noticed.
Vendors. All vendors have access to event clients who may need additional services.
Past clients. Satisfied customers can provide you with referrals to other events.
Colleagues. Event associates can refer business that they cannot or do not handle.

or two. Some groups have limits as to how many meetings you can attend before committing to membership. In any case decide on how much time you have to give to this piece of your marketing strategy, and choose the groups that best meet your needs.

For me the broader industry groups like ISES and MPI as well as membership in my local convention and visitor bureau offered me a broad range of corporate and social opportunities. The local CVB gave me access to incoming groups and leads on clients that would need planning services for trade show–related events. If your target market is social business, a wedding or catering organization might provide stronger leads. If you're targeting a certain geographic area, a local business networking group might be the right fit.

The best way to approach networking is to go in with a plan. This isn't a time for free food and wine—it's a chance to gather leads, take notes, and make plans for follow-up. Check the sidebar for some pointers to get you off to the right start.

Networking Dos & Don'ts

Do . . .

- Arrive early.
- Bring plenty of business cards and a pen.
- Jot down information on a card about each person you speak to and when you'll follow up.
- Be ready—have a one- or two-sentence description of what you do.
- Gather more than you give.
- Be an attentive listener.
- Make a good impression.

Don't . . .

- Try to juggle a plate of hors d'oeuvres and a drink while you try to shake a new acquaintance's hand.
- Stick only with people you know.
- Spend more than three to five minutes with each person.
- Oversell. Instead, plan a follow-up meeting at which you can give your full sales presentation.

Places to Network

Networking opportunities can be found in industry meetings, at locally sponsored events, and even at social gatherings. All of these offer an opportunity to tell your story and gather information.

- **Hotels.** Quite often people start their event planning process with the place where they'd like to hold the event. Hotel professionals may be able to offer venue and catering services, but not extended event services such as entertainment, decor, invitations, lighting, or party favors. By coming up with a list of possible hotels that attract the type of clients you'd like to work with, you may be bringing a service to the hotel as well as its customers. Positioning yourself as a "preferred vendor" or "strategic partner," you can add value to what the hotel can offer while expanding your business at the same time.
- **Specialty venues** such as ballrooms, meeting halls, museums, aquariums, and restaurants can offer the same opportunities as hotels.

Their clients often need the support services of an event planner, and by becoming a resource to the venue you expand your opportunities.

- **Vendors** can be a major source of new business. Once you establish yourself with a group of colleagues, it's as if you've expanded your own sales force. A caterer may have a client who's looking for invitations, for instance; a tent rental company that's exclusive to a country club may be asked to recommend a planner. Vendors have become a major source of referrals for my business over the years. Treat your vendors well by thanking them for their quality work and products.
- Develop a presence **online**. Join groups, create and make consistent posts to a blog, engage in discussions either on a specialized Facebook or LinkedIn group that you create and manage. Don't be afraid to share your ideas or comment on things you see in the event industry. Showcase your success and accomplishments. Folks who are interested in events will discover you and you may find a new customer as a result!

Join the Conversation

A great way to connect with like-minded event enthusiasts is to be active in event-related discussion groups. I invite you to join me at Special Events Institute and on LinkedIn at the following chat spots!

Facebook: www.facebook.com/specialeventsinstitute and a Closed Group—Starting a Career In Events

Pinterest: www.pinterest.com/eventsinstitute/

Twitter: twitter.com/eventsinstitute

Instagram: instagram.com/eventsinstitute

LinkedIn: Jill S. Moran, CSEP and The Special Events Institute—The Premiere Group for Event Education Forum

YouTube: www.youtube.com/c/SpecialEventsInstitute

More Ways to Gain Exposure for Yourself and Your Company

- **Volunteer.** Remember, "What goes around, comes around." Donate a portion of your time. Stand out from the crowd . . . raise your hand . . . don't wait to be asked. Volunteer opportunities abound, from fund-raising events to industry or meeting committees. By giving your time, energy, and creative ideas for all to see, you create visibility and recognition for yourself.

- **Educate yourself.** Take courses on event-related subjects at local colleges or universities or online. Many schools are adding event-related courses to their continuing education programs. Most cities offer seminars or conferences for the hospitality, meeting, and event industries. These are great places to meet colleagues and pick up ideas. Whether the courses cover professional skill building, event design and trends, or business management tools, they'll add to the knowledge you need to grow and manage your business. After getting e-mails and calls from new event planners asking where to go for solid training, I decided to launch an online certificate program through the Special Events Institute (www.SpecialEventsInstitute.com). The curriculum offers the tools needed to approach event planning with confidence and skill in a convenient, affordable way. All of these educational opportunities add to your value, give you additional contacts, and let you have more to talk about when in a meeting with a client or following up with a prospect. (See chapter 13 and the appendices for a full discussion.)
- **Be a leader.** Share your expertise with those in your field or industry, in your community, or in other industries. Each year I participate in career day at our local middle school. I talk with the kids about my career and take a group of students with me for "a day in the life of an event planner." Depending on the mix of students, I try to schedule a visit to the site where an upcoming event will be held. I've taken the kids to a sports stadium that was being prepared for a company outing. In past years the field trip has included a visit to a design center for theme materials, and lunch and discussion with a chef regarding the menu for an upcoming event. I discuss theme and giveaway ideas with the students, and even do some pre-event shopping when possible. These students get not only a behind-the-scenes view of a special venue, but also a glimpse at what goes on when an event is planned. They also have parents whose employers might someday need event services—or who may need help with a particular celebration themselves.
- **Be seen.** Write articles for local and industry magazines sharing your experiences. If there are publications that address event topics, perhaps you can offer insight on a venue you've used, ideas on current

themes or decor trends, or challenges that your customers may face and how to address them. Over the years I've made contact with several event-related magazines and had articles published in them. I let my colleagues know that I like to write, and they refer me on as well. The key to getting new business this way is to get your event-related articles into magazines in other industries—say, journals in the pharmaceutical, meeting management, or trade show fields. Find out who to contact and offer to share your expertise on event topics. When these magazines hit the hands of the executives who need event services . . . you're the expert.

- **Be heard.** Offer to speak at local or national events within or outside your industry, as well as at colleges, local schools, and public or charity events. This will help you define your skills and clarify your game plan.

Everything starts with a sale. Remember, somewhere out there, someone is looking for you and needs your services. You just have to make the connection. If you've honed your skills and have an excellent service to offer, you will make it happen. Believe in yourself, and approach the task of marketing your services with determination and a positive attitude.

As you progress through the phases of getting your business up and running, be aware that you'll be constantly defining and refining your skills. Your marketing efforts should thus let customers know about the changes you're making to add value to their event experiences. Take a long hard look at your skills and what you do best, and present them in the best light possible. Be visible in your industry, among your peers and competitors, and (especially) potential clients. Take every opportunity to spread the word that you are an event planner who will make a difference.

Frequently Asked Questions

Should I specialize or generalize?

It depends on your skills and interests. I have developed a broad scope of services for my company, which has allowed me to ride through economic and seasonal changes. It also provides variety in events and clients and keeps me fresh with my ideas and concepts. The downside of variety is being diluted in your approach or confusing to clients that really want that "wedding planner" or "meeting planner." I have tried to keep my website organized and easy to search for clients that only want to see my new social events or learn more about nonprofit work I am doing. If you are passionate about weddings, be a wedding planner. If you love to work with kids, be the best children's party planner around. Don't be afraid to throw all your event eggs in one basket. But if you like variety, make sure you are up on the differences between event markets and can switch hats easily.

Do I need to take out advertisements in local papers or do a paid Facebook ad?

It's not a bad idea to advertise if you know that the ad will reach the people who will buy your services and if the cost is within your budget. There are other ways to get your name out there, including sponsorship, trade show attendance, networking, and volunteering in your community. Word of mouth goes a long way in passing your name to the right potential client. Build your reputation event by event by delivering the kind of service you are proud of. Don't underestimate nontraditional ways of advertising. All of these marketing tactics can help get your name out to those who may need your services.

Should I join a professional organization?

Joining a professional group will benefit you through networking with vendors, potential clients, and potential staff; provide education and resource information; and give you a chance to perfect your skills while serving as a leader in the industry. There are plenty of opportunities to assist with monthly meetings and industry events and try your event skills out as a volunteer. You will also develop a reputation in the industry and make contacts that can generate business. Don't expect to get a lead at every meeting or justify your expenses at a conference with direct business. Sometimes it takes months or years for your name to be recognized and for business to come your way. But in the meantime, you build your event skills and people skills by being active in the industry.

06 Developing a Team

A business begins with passion, hard work, and knowledge of the product or service to be offered. While some entrepreneurs have a broad range of skills to bring to their new business, most companies are made of a palette of support personnel. Different staff members will fulfill administrative, customer service, and project management duties. In the field of event planning, the owner of the business is typically the one with the creative and entrepreneurial spirit. Unfortunately, to run a business successfully, this often just isn't enough; you must balance the skills you do have with the ones you don't. In other words, even if you're not good at—or enjoy—financial planning, record keeping, and risk analysis tasks, they still need to be part of your daily and monthly routine. Take an honest look at your skill set, and be prepared to complement your strengths with outside support for your weaknesses.

Support, Part I: Vendors

To plan and execute your first event, you may be able to do quite a bit on your own, but you also may need some helping hands. As you grow, your support team will grow with you as well. For your first event you may want to do most of the decor yourself or enlist some volunteers to help with setup or teardown. Soon, however, you won't have time to inflate all the balloons (for instance), and you'll look for a pro who can handle this important decor element. I enlisted Christine Bernstein of Balloon City of Boston for a corporate anniversary event many years ago. While I don't use balloons in every event, Bernstein keeps me up on new techniques and decorating ideas incorporating balloons to keep me on the cutting edge. The same goes with my favorite lighting designers, caterers, or linen rental companies. There's no way I could keep up on all the latest designs and techniques in every discipline, so I look to experts to help me offer the latest and greatest to my clients.

If you pull together the right team, your events can meet or exceed your expectations time after time.

Show Me the Talent

Here's a sampling of some of the vendors you might want to utilize to bring your creative event ideas to life. These are the pros you'll call on for linens, rentals, floral arrangements, and photography; the ones who'll add that final touch of lighting and design to your event; the people who will capture the essence of your event with photography or video. This "human tool kit" will allow you to offer so much more to each and every client as you start your event planning business. You may not need every type of vendor for every event you plan, of course. Still, it's never too soon to start pulling together your list. Be sure to keep adding to it as you gather experience and references.

- Caterer
- Florist
- Invitation designer
- Photographer
- Videographer
- Rental company
- Balloon artist
- Makeup artist
- DJ
- Caricaturist
- Entertainment agency
- Casino table provider
- Fabric supply company
- Magician
- Prop company
- Tent company
- Venues: casino, hotel, ballroom, country club
- Transportation: bus, limo, etc.
- Decor provider
- Staffing company
- Lighting designer
- Electrical provider

. . . and many others

What Skills Do You Need?

Running a successful event planning business involves a sweeping range of skills:

- Administrative skills. Setting up your business. Tracking and analyzing your finances.
- Computer skills. Using financial programs, developing proposals, and using the Internet to market your business and educate yourself on ideas and competition.
- Marketing skills. Getting and keeping clients. Promoting your business.
- Sales skills. Touting yourself and skills and closing the deal.
- People skills. Balancing conflicting needs while making everyone happy.
- Creative skills. Making each event an artful, memorable experience.
- Execution skills. Flexibility, organization, negotiation, customer-service, and being detail and solution-oriented. Preparing seventeen dozen gourmet canapés, inflating fourteen dozen balloons, repairing a flickering spotlight, interviewing seven jazz bands, decorating a six-layer cake, arranging several thousand dollars' worth of flowers, finalizing what to capture with a videographer, designing invitations that are traditional—yet trendy—and setting up a half dozen portable toilets.
- Project management skills. Overseeing all of the above at the same time . . . well and doing it all with a smile on your face!

If you think you might be lacking in some of these areas—read on.

Vendor, Vendor, Wherefore Art Thou, Vendor?

How do you find good vendors? Everywhere and anywhere. Be sure to file every lead you come across in an organized way for easy retrieval when you need it. As you build your list of vendor resources, you will want to make sure they come with solid references both from clients or other planners to ensure they meet your expectations. On page 85 there is a sample form you might use to record vendor information for your files.

I receive many brochures and other pieces from suppliers and vendors, which I file away until the right project calls for a certain specialized service or product. You may not need a juggler, circus group, or magician for every event, but if the call comes in, you'll want to have a reference number on hand. Here are a few places to start:

- Industry groups (events, meetings, conferences, trade shows)
- Local business networking groups and chambers of commerce
- Online searches

- Referrals from other planners
- Referrals from venues (hotels, country clubs, event facilities)
- Referrals from industry contacts who have exposure to a variety of services
- Professional trade shows and conferences
- Trade magazines
- Colleges or universities

Vendor Information Sheet

Name: ____

Address: ____

____

____

Phone: ______________________ Fax: ________________

E-mail: ____

Years in business: ______________________________________

Current clients: ______________________________________

____

____

Types of business services: ______________________________

____

____

Types of events services: ______________________________

____

____

Specialties: ____

____

____

Pricing: ____

____

____

Payment structure (COD, credit card, purchase order, thirty-day invoice):

____

Referral letters: ______________________________________

____

Evaluating Vendors

How do you know if a particular vendor is a good match for your company? Here are some things to look for:

- Service specifics
- Professional training
- Experience
- Customer base
- Years in business
- Communication skills
- Attention to detail
- Flexibility
- Professionalism

Support, Part II: Staffing

You may go into your business as the chief cook and bottle washer, but it won't be long before you realize you can't do it all. It may be difficult to have a team readily available to help you put together invitations, dress tables with linens, or park cars, but these are the very real nuts and bolts of the event business. Where can you turn to get support in delivering the quality of which you boast?

Students

Not a week goes by that I don't receive an e-mail from a college student looking for advice and experience. Due to the nature of the business, it is often feasible to use these ambitious young enthusiasts for weekend or evening events. It may be worthwhile to meet with them, do some preliminary screening, and compile a list to use for future projects.

Some schools have work-study programs that provide paid or unpaid job experience. Contact the career placement or financial aid office at institutions in your vicinity to sign up for eligible students.

Relatives and Friends

Many start-up entrepreneurs enlist family members in the company's early stages. I was lucky enough to work side by side with my dad in his moving and storage business from the time I was in high school. It offered me great training in business and served as the foundation for my future event business. Now my daughters and son (and sometimes my husband) work with me at my events, and they often bring several of their friends to staff the kids' area at company outings or help with setup and teardown. You, too, may have relatives or friends who can offer reliable hands-on support when you need it most.

War Stories: Helper Horror

For a corporate event I hired some extra staff to assist with setup. Since these were older folks, I didn't go over event etiquette during my pre-event briefing. During the event, however, one woman proceeded to behave like a guest—helping herself to the open bar and food and circulating with the attendees. I gently guided her back to her post, but the incident was certainly a poor reflection on my company. Remember to hold your staff accountable for their behavior, and be clear about your expectations up front before the party begins.

Colleagues

Once you begin publicizing your new business, you'll begin to uncover like-minded event enthusiasts who share your passion for the events industry. Keep in contact with them. They can be excellent referral sources for business you cannot handle (and of course they might pass business on to you). You may be able to partner up with your peers on a project that's beyond your scope at a given time, or use them to supplement your resource team. There's nothing better than having a staff familiar with the event process who'll approach it in the same professional way you do.

Don't forget to repay the favor by helping out your colleagues when they need you, too!

Nonworking Professionals

Nicole Samolis of The Events Company from Syracuse, New York, uses a group of at-home moms as her team. She selects women in her community who are trustworthy, capable, and dependable to arrive for early setup and to return to the events for teardown at the end of the night. She no longer has to personally attend each event from start to finish, opening her schedule up for more important leadership duties. And her team members have a part-time job that's flexible, fun, and easy to fit into their lives.

Professional Organizations

The beauty of belonging to a professional organization like the International Special Events Society is how easily it puts you into contact with a network of event professionals. Whether your events are in your local area or produced around the world, trusted colleagues are ready and waiting for your call. Don't be afraid to perform a quick check of references to get an overview of their skills and make sure they match your needs.

Trained Staffing Agencies

Staffing agencies can provide insured, bonded professionals to provide services from wait staff and food preparers to bartending services. For many years, Betsy Duffy of House Helpers provided catering staff for an array of intimate dinner engagements and parties, including full kosher meals. Agencies such as Boston's Event Temps and Providence's the Pour People handle bar service with staff who are TIPS certified, guaranteeing their completion of a certification program that includes all bonding procedures and training, and emphasizes responsible alcoholic beverage service. Some agencies can also provide drink-related products and the latest in specialty liquors, mixers, colored sugars, and the like.

The best place to find good sources for temporary help is to ask colleagues or friends for referrals. If you aren't coming up with any leads, you can always check online under local employment agencies, staffing services, employment contractors, or temporary help. Working through agencies can provide you with insured and bonded staff but will be more costly. Refine your search to your specific need such as security, food service, catering staff, and valet services when searching the web or your local yellow pages.

Don't fall into the trap of paying a worker as a subcontractor to avoid US responsibilities such as workers' compensation and payroll taxes and the other commitments that go with hiring an employee. If you control not only what a worker does but how it is to be done, that worker is likely an employee, and you can be held liable for failing to carry workers' compensation insurance or to pay payroll taxes.

You may reach a point where it makes sense to hire someone either full or part time. Perhaps you find someone who can handle administrative duties, works well on site at events, learns quickly, works efficiently, is resourceful, and shares the same passion for events as you do. Making the commitment to hire an employee increases your financial responsibility (you will have a weekly commitment to pay your new employee), record keeping (you must take proper deductions for tax purposes and file appropriately), and legal and risk exposure (you are legally responsible for employees' actions while they are representing you and your company). Growth is a great thing, but it does have its fair share

Staffing Needs

What kinds of needs should you look to your staff to fill? Here are some functions to think about:

Event Preparation:

- Assembling invitations, gift or goodie bags, favors, name badges, briefing booklets, and programs
- Decor production, including purchasing, ordering, assembling, constructing, sewing, painting, and decorating specialized decor you select for your events
- Registration Management, including the guest list, preferences, and special requests

Catering:

Most of the time, the caterers you hire will provide the support they need, but make sure they cover all the bases:

- Food and beverage preparation, delivery, and service
- Serviceware rental and setup, including china, glassware, utensils, napkin folding
- Tray decorations for passed hors d'oeuvres
- Buffet treatments, including all serviceware and utensils
- Cleanup and refuse removal

Decor and Event Execution:

Some vendors will handle production specialties, such as tenting, lighting, and audio-visual or power service. But there are some functions that you may choose to handle through your own staffing:

- Linen placement
- Floral placement
- Tent accessories, such as light strings, vines, florals, and fabric draping
- Room decor, including buffets, walls, ceilings, dining tables, and specialty stations such as gift tables, sign-in areas, and ceremony basics (runners, aisle markers, arbors)
- Teardown and removal

Event Staffing:

You may prefer to select professionals to handle such tasks as security or parking, or you might choose to support the venue's offerings with additional staffing:

- Set up
- Registration
- Directing guests
- Instant photographers

- Gift dissemination
- Help desk
- Security
- Valet
- Coat check
- Cleanup

of complications and responsibilities. Plan for the changes you want to make by having a strong book of business in the pipeline and by carefully screening your contract staff before you hire.

Working with Your Support Staff

Partnering with Vendors

For the most part many vendors on your list can provide you with lists of their services and prices. Most will also offer a range of prices to respond to a variety of customer needs. This way, once you find a reliable rental or linen company, you simply select from its options and styles to fit your clients' budget.

Some vendors will have sample books, catalogs, or price sheets for you to examine; look for these among linen companies, tableware rental companies, and invitation designers. On the other hand, production or lighting companies whose services include extensive setup and labor charges tend to quote each project individually. Many factors can affect the price they'll quote you, including

What It Costs

Office Assistant: $0 (intern)–$30 per hour (to complete proposals, input data, or do market research)
Event Assistants: $0 (intern)–$50 per hour (depending on whether design or preparation work is required and on their experience level)
Event Manager: $25–$50 per hour. It can be difficult to get an event manager on a per-project basis, so it may be worth compensating them to ensure they will be available when events arise. If you find someone who works well and you are keeping them busy, it may be time to hire your first employee!

Subcontractor vs. Employee

Subcontractors

Pros:

You don't undertake any long-term financial responsibility.

You don't have to pay employment taxes or workers' compensation insurance.

You don't have to provide employee benefits such as health insurance, vacations, holidays, and sick days.

You can select the best candidate with the best skill set for each project.

Cons:

It may be difficult to find consistent help.

The best help may not be available when you need them.

More effort must be made in training as you use new staff for different projects.

Employees

Pros:

You can train employees to maximize their performance in your business culture.

You can delegate more tasks to your employees to allow for more effective use of your own time (management, marketing, and so on).

Cons:

You must have enough business to keep them busy.

Record keeping for payroll and employer tax returns becomes more complicated.

You have more responsibility for supervision.

You're directly liable for employees' acts or omissions.

the location of the event, the time of year or day the event is being held, setup and teardown requirements, and how their services will be used in the overall event process.

You should be able to get a range of pricing quotes—prices for everything from a la carte items to comprehensive services, and from high to low budgets. It's always wise to have a wide array of options to choose from to best fit your needs and the needs of your various clients. Vendors may also have suggestions to trim your budget or boost your event's thematic flair, based on their special focus or inventory.

Compensating Your Staff

You will want to build a reliable and motivated team to assist you during the many facets of the event process. You should pay them a fair wage while providing a stimulating and educational environment in the midst of the long hours and sometimes stressful moments of executing an event. Some of your staff might be young teens assisting with family events or working behind the scenes. Others

When to Bring in the Pros

When you realize the scope of writing your contracts or reviewing your insurance programs is beyond your ability to address prudently, it's time to bring in the pros. You work hard to convince others of the benefits of hiring an event specialist—and the same goes for the specialists who can help you in your business. If you select wisely, they are worth every cent you pay them.

Here are some of the professionals you might consult in the course of doing business:

- Accountant
- Lawyer
- Marketing specialist (web/social media)
- Computer professional
- Insurance agent
- Bookkeeper

When looking for professional support, select people who are versed in your business or at least in small home-based businesses. They should be familiar with the unique qualities of special events, the liabilities to which you are exposed, your cash-flow patterns, and the way you use technology. They should not only respond to your questions but be proactive about advising you of current changes, trends, techniques, or opportunities.

Try to engage these experts on a specified or as-needed basis. You will not need an accountant to meet with you monthly, but you may need a bookkeeper more regularly and your accountant semiannually to support your ongoing record keeping. The same holds true for your legal counsel. If you can commit to a flat fee for a specified number of calls or consulting appointments, you can be more relaxed about calling your attorney when something doesn't look right in a contract or you are concerned over a liability issue. Look for someone who appears interested in your business, is available for you in small increments of time, and doesn't mind that you're not a big-name client.

might be seasoned hospitality pros looking to brush up on their planning skills and earn some extra money on the side. Each will be treated differently. Their wages will be based on a combination of their experience and the type of work they're doing, while keeping in mind what your event budget will bear. I always figure in extra costs for staffing my events. It also helps to tip your support team based on the hours they work and their overall effort and willingness to be at your beck and call. Your main goal will be to grow a team that you can rely on and who'll be there for you when you need them, so it's best to make the job worth their while!

Job Requirements and Expectations

It's always a good idea to go over all of your expectations with each vendor and staff member in advance. This can be accomplished during an initial meeting and repeated at the pre-event walk-through. Duties can change from job to job, and client to client, so make a thorough review of your needs in writing prior to each event. The overall production schedule you create will drive most of the specific timing—arrival, setup schedule, and post-event pickup. You might want to go even further, however, spelling out such details as who will set up the tables once they're delivered, and who will set the linens out and collect them at the end of the event. All of this should be confirmed prior to signing contracts and placing final orders. Remember, time is money. If you'll be paying your staff to perform duties that relate to vendor rentals, you should be compensated for it. You may have to

Responsibility Chart

Well before your event, spell out who is responsible for each of the following:

- Rental setup, teardown, and pickup
- Permits and licenses
- Power limitations or enhancements
- Safety measures
- Security
- Food requirements for vendors and staff
- Trash removal
- Rental returns

Make sure you get it in writing or at the very least have a discussion and review of responsibilities so there is no confusion the day of the event.

include additional fees for this work, so consider these issues before you submit your final proposal to your client.

Evaluations

Just as important as thanking people for a job well done is letting them know when they haven't met your expectations. Sometimes the problem can be due to poor communication up front. Perhaps you didn't adequately stress the importance of lighting in the catering tent or failed to mention that you'd need wheelchair access for guests. Even if you perform a pre-event walk-through, don't take for granted that vendors and staff will know what you want. Write it down. Insert it into a contract. Discuss any special needs you may have well in advance of the event.

When the event is over, it's critical to hold a discussion with each vendor and staffer. Review what worked, what didn't, and what could be changed to improve the process next time. If done in a constructive way, this conversation can offer encouragement and demonstrate that you're interested enough in the relationship to work on improving it and create an even better event the next time around.

Once you've assembled the various support systems, you can begin to envision your company as an entity—an orchestra, if you will. You are the conductor of this fabulous ensemble, which sometimes performs classical music, sometimes modern, and sometimes rock! As the conductor, you're in charge of keeping the parts together and creating an end result that leaves your audience in awe. It's a sizable task but, with the right team, it's also rewarding for everyone involved.

Frequently Asked Questions

How can I make sure my vendors and contract labor will provide the kind of service I really want?

Clearly outline your expectations to all parties involved. It is a good idea to issue a vendor contract and even provide your contract labor with an agreement formalizing your expectations and payment policies. As these folks are not employees, your requirements for insurances, taxes, and payments may be different for each person and may vary from event to event. You should review your event in full: the client, the venue, the theme, and most important your production schedule and timeline. Even if a client has a short production schedule and there are last-minute decisions being made, make sure you update all parties involved. It's always a good idea to have a pre-event meeting, even if it is only hours before the event, to identify the key people and any nuances of which you want everyone to be aware. This will ensure that the event has your stamp of approval on it!

I need quite a few extra hands for an upcoming fund-raiser, but I don't have the money in the budget for staffing. How can I make things happen without working 24/7 the week before the event?

Volunteers can be a great way to staff events if you find the right people. Local colleges or universities can be an excellent source of interns, many of whom may have experience already or may be in hospitality or event-related degree programs and are motivated to do a great job and make an excellent impression. Some schools will require a minimum number of hours; others will allow students to sign up directly with you when opportunities arise. You may have a post-event evaluation to complete, but using students can be an inexpensive way to solve staffing problems and give you a chance to test potential employees before you hire them.

How can I build a list of good vendors to use?

Most of the time, you can get referrals from other event planners on whom they use for specific services. It's best to ask at industry meetings and begin forming a list before you need them. Visit their offices, check out their portfolios, and get references from satisfied clients or planners. Don't wait until you absolutely need a service to begin looking; you'll be left scrambling and may have to use someone who is not the best fit for your event.

Should I plan to take all the labor costs out of my commission or fee?

I typically will add a line item to reflect labor on events. This may include the cost of setup, teardown, table dressing and setting and chair tying, and invitation or goodie bag assembly. These are all items that also can be reflected in the cost of the service. Some linen companies will ship you the linens and you are responsible for setting them up. The same holds true with rentals of tables and chairs. You will be left with racks of chairs, bins of plates, and unfolded napkins to set up and fold yourself if you don't plan ahead. You can group the labor costs into the item, but don't forget to add these on to the material costs before inputting it as a line item for your client's budget.

07 Legal and Ethical Issues

As you'll learn very quickly in the event planning business, it's not enough to know the tricks of the trade in decor, florals, or production techniques; you must also take a hard look at the elements of each event that could open you up to liability, and learn how to minimize your risk and increase the safety of your clients and event attendees. While you should be aware of any changing regulations that affect the event industry, staying abreast of changing laws and requirements is best left for the professionals in the fields of law, management, and insurance. For this reason I suggest selecting an attorney who can guide you through the important task of creating basic contracts and updating these on a per-event basis as needed. Establishing a business relationship with an attorney is a prudent step to take for the safety and security of your business as well as the events you produce and the guests who attend them.

Liability

According to attorney James N. Decoulos of Decoulos Law in Peabody, Massachusetts, who specializes in legal and insurance issues for event professionals, you must be aware of liability throughout every phase of the event planning process. Events are often emotionally charged, and they may contain elements of surprise that could result in disaster if not planned for appropriately. As you create dynamic environments with decor, offer food prepared off site, and select artists and entertainers who bring their own set of performance issues and dangers, you may become liable for damages sustained by vendors, venues, and attendees at your events. Issues can range from an injured guest to food poisoning, falling props, and misfired pyrotechnics. While most of these unplanned occurrences aren't necessarily the fault of the event planner, it's critical that you show due diligence, taking all necessary precautions to avoid problems. These include thoroughly researching the qualifications, experience, and reputations of everyone you deal with. More potential issues that could involve liability include the consulting contract, site selection, food and beverage service, entertainment, subcontracts, security, and licensing.

Decoulos highlights the importance of liability issues by noting that failing to cope with them can lead to business failure and even personal financial ruin. Here are some of his tips for responding to the tremendously complex issues surrounding event liability:

- Learn to understand what in the course of conducting an event represents exposure to liability and how best to minimize it.
- Embrace liability as an ally. Liability is at once a sword and a shield. Use your contracts both to protect yourself and to bind clients.
- Don't overlook details about the fundamental business relationship between you and your clients, especially at the proposal phase. This is particularly so for last-minute bookings, which you may take on hoping to impress a client and gain repeat business. In the flurry of work such bookings involve, it's easy to neglect even issues as obvious as when and how you'll be paid.
- A contract is not fully formed simply with agreement upon a price. In fact, a price isn't even required for a contract to be considered in effect. What is necessary is enough detail to create a binding relationship between you and your clients. (See the "Contracts" section on page 100 for more information.)
- Be succinct and specific. There's a fine art to reducing into writing all the essential details about what you will and won't provide—and this is an art worth cultivating. Does obtaining an event license mean paying for the licensing fee or other costs such as bonding or producing a floor plan? Often a licensing authority will require special police and fire details at additional cost. When such requirements are discovered, and the additional expense becomes an adjustment of the contract price, immediate written notification must be made to (and an acknowledgment received from) the client.

Short simple letters written during the progress of work function well, even if only to document the efforts that are being made to fulfill the contract. If you fail to do so, you may well be forced to absorb additional expenses from your profit. In the case of the event licenses mentioned above, failure to discover the licensing

War Stories: Sick and Sicker

Mike Gallant of Perfect Parties was providing musical entertainment at a wedding when he received word that an elderly guest had fainted on the dance floor. Trained in CPR, Gallant knew what to do, but he quickly realized that the situation was serious. He requested immediate medical attention—and the townwide siren sounded to notify EMTs. The raid signal, in addition to the very ill woman lying prone on the dance floor, panicked everyone in the room, and they began fainting and vomiting. By the time the victim was removed by stretcher to the hospital, at least twenty more partygoers had taken ill. To avoid continued mass hysteria, Gallant requested the use of an adjacent empty ballroom to move people away from the chaos.

The moral of the story? Think through an evacuation and safety plan before you start any event, and share it with everyone involved.

requirement in the first instance may subject you and your clients to fines, cease-and-desist orders, or both. It is reasonably unlikely that all such details will be available at the contract formation stage. Therefore provisions should be made for modifying the basic contract in the course of performance.

Carefully review your client engagement letter. It should contain essential terms such as the date of contract, date of performance, contract amount, deposit, progress and final payments, time and manner of payment, and specification of all goods and services to be provided, as well as any items unique to the special event. If a guarantee is offered, it should be worded to an objective

War Stories: Crowd Control

If you deal with large public events, be prepared for misconduct and disorderly behavior. Even if liquor isn't available at a particular event, guests could arrive intoxicated. The owner of a local inflatables company shared with me his commitment to putting safety first. He and his staff must often make the call whether unruly guests should be allowed to partake in the fun. Saying no could result in a very angry patron; saying yes can be even riskier. Have enforcements ready, beyond the scope of your staff, to make sure things stay calm. If problems seem possible, don't hesitate to hire a private security firm or request a police detail.

standard. Use disclaimers to detail what isn't guaranteed—for example, the weather and a good turnout.

Contracts

The safest and most responsible way to approach any business transaction is to clearly outline what you will do and for what price. Rather than approaching contracting as something that makes the event process more cumbersome, approach it as protection for your company and your client. Formalizing your relationship will also help you avoid any misunderstandings.

You may know as an experienced planner that you'll perform certain duties during the event process, but your inexperienced clients may not have a clue. It's thus up to you to educate them so that the process is successful from start to finish. Following is a rough outline of a typical consulting agreement that I use—first an overview, then a more detailed description of its specific elements. I strongly suggest that you consult with an attorney, preferably one who is knowledgeable in event management, who can draft a contract that contains all the elements necessary to adhere to your own state and city laws.

Contract Essentials: An Overview

- Duties
- Payment
- Payment obligation and consequences
- Additional information
- Interpretation
- Cooperation
- Change orders
- Important dates
- Delays and extensions
- Inspections and approvals
- Termination
- Abandonment
- Payment of fees and permits
- Deviation from laws and regulations
- Completion of event
- Indemnity agreement
- Applicable law
- Agreement to perform
- Witness and signature line

Duties

In this paragraph you clearly identify the parties involved and the parameters of the event. Then list each specific category of items and services you'll be responsible for providing (the more detail, the better). These categories might include event preplanning and preparation, production scheduling, vendor selection and management, theme development, budgeting, promotion and marketing of the event, production of gift items, coordination of event details, on-site implementation, support and staffing, and evaluation. You can also break each of these down into sublists. For example, the vendor selection and management category might detail catering, rentals, linens, lighting, photography, decor, and transportation. The documents you'll continue to create during the planning process itself (production schedules, timelines, and so forth) will likely cover each of these entries in even further detail—but do be sure that the contract includes a thorough listing of categories.

Payment

Here you'll identify the payment agreed upon and the payment schedule. You might break this down into two or more payments based on the size and scope of the project. Also list any expenses for which you expect to be reimbursed. These might include office or travel expenses unique to the project. It would be appropriate to promise detailed lists of expenses and statement summaries to support the cost of the event as the event progresses. You should also identify your payment policy. This includes specifically when you expect advance payments and when the clients must pay based on any bills you present.

Payment Obligation and Consequences

Just as you're committing to deliver a service, you're also asking that your clients commit to compensating you for your time. In this area you would identify consequences of nonpayment, which could include termination or cancellation of contract, as well as collection agency or attorney involvement if necessary. Once again, this is not meant as a scare tactic but as recognition of how seriously you take your relationship with the clients and the obligations you're undertaking.

Additional Information

This section of your contract acts as a request for cooperation from the clients in submitting any information or materials that would be necessary or important in the planning and execution of the event. It doesn't spell out in detail all such requests, but notifies clients that requests may be made for information—and without their timely response, you cannot guarantee the event schedule.

Interpretation

This paragraph acknowledges the creative license and interpretation integral to the event process. It states that as the planner, you'll be using your creative skills to develop the event; once the theme or layout is approved by the clients, you'll proceed accordingly.

Cooperation

Further outlining the dynamics of the event process, this section notes the need for the clients' cooperation with both you and any contracted vendors. It also commits you to the same cooperation.

Change Orders

It's imp ortant to formally note that event planning is a dynamic process that may need frequent updates. Known as "change orders," such updates can be issued for signature during the course of planning without invalidating the original contract. Change orders may include additional items or expenses or revisions to the scope of the event. They will also outline any costs associated with these changes.

Important Dates

The date section will formalize the start and end dates of the project. It also validates the time you'll be putting into the planning. This section will complement

The Vendor Contract

Among the duties to specify at the outset for each contract is whether you will serve as the clients' agent and contract on their behalf or whether you will enter into vendor contracts directly. In either case you'll then secure agreements with each vendor.

Here are some of the elements you'll want to include:

- List of all parties involved
- Date
- Load-in time
- Event start time
- Event close time
- Load-out time
- Vendor services
- Event manager services
- Vendor requirements
- Breach of contract
- Independent contractor definition
- Payment to vendor
- Acceptance and signature

your production schedule and timelines and show your commitment to the planning process. You might want to insert language such as *expeditious and skillful proceedings* and *use of sufficient labor, materials, equipment, and supplies to bring the event to fruition*. You can also mention reports and schedules to further document event progress.

Delays and Extensions

Reference to delays due to clients, vendors, or causes beyond your own control can be noted here. The communication of delays or of extensions and any necessary alterations in the schedule should be provided verbally and in writing, and guaranteed here. In most situations, an event date is set and you work from the present forward to allocate planning time. It's not typical that an event would be rescheduled due to delays, but additional labor or time may be required if this is the case. This could result in additional costs, which you'd submit to the clients through a change order.

In the event of delays due to clients, you'd request an appropriate extension. This section of your contract could also include reference to any damages you incur because of delays—vendor penalties or forfeited deposits, for instance. You might also wish to note the time frame for settling any expense disputes, and when and if arbitration can be used.

Inspections and Approvals

It's a good idea to show your willingness to have the client participate in any progress inspections during the course of planning. This shows not only your faith in your work, but also your commitment to giving clients what they want. If they should decide to make alterations, it's best to do so as early as possible—before you reach the point where it would be costly or inappropriate to make changes. These inspections and approvals may be made during scheduled meetings, or more informally via spot checks of tabletop design, color or material samples, or schematic drawings. They should be documented.

Termination

This section is important for the protection of your client should they ask you to cease performing your duties. Terms for payment to you for services rendered or a refund to your client of any funds paid for work not completed should be spelled out. The client is then free to contract with another planner to complete the project, bearing in mind that you are entitled to compensation for your work, your creativity, and the opportunities you've forgone to devote yourself to this project.

Abandonment

Should the project be abandoned or canceled by the client, this part of the contract protects you up to the amount of time and expenses you've invested to date. It's an unfortunate truth that events will be canceled more often than you'd like. Make sure your contract guarantees you at least partial payment—and try to end on a good note, in the hope that future opportunities for planning arise.

Payment of Fees and Permits

As a planner you'll often find yourself taking out permits or paying fees on behalf of your client. This section acknowledges that such costs may arise. In some instances you're required by law to file for permits—for instance, for tented events, events with pyrotechnics, and events on public property where liquor is being served. It's your responsibility to know what's required for each unique situation, but it's the client's duty to pay or reimburse you for these expenses. It's always best to avoid advancing expenses in the first place, but in some cases it is necessary and makes the planning process run more efficiently. Communicating what you will do on behalf of the client is always best done in writing at the contract phase of your engagement.

Deviation from Laws and Regulations

You must notify the client in writing about any phases of the event that will deviate from laws or regulations before proceeding with the planning process.

Completion of Event

Here you commit to making sure that all appropriate items are removed at the close of the event, including equipment, rubbish, or props that were used in the production process.

Indemnity Agreement

You should request that if you incur injury, damage, or claim caused by the conduct of your clients or the attendees at their event, your clients will hold you harmless for any loss you sustain as a result.

Your clients, based on their or their counsel's interpretation and impression, may strike or modify this as well as any of the sections of your contract. If so, I recommend that you in turn consult with your legal counsel and make any necessary modifications to protect your business in the course of your relationship with the client. Depending on the reasonableness of the requested changes, you will probably work to modify the contract and move forward with the project. Many times this provision is made mutual so that each party indemnifies the other.

The indemnity provisions must be consistent with your liability insurance policy, particularly when you are asked to name your client or the venue as an additional insured.

Applicable Law

This short statement will define which state's laws will govern the contract—typically the state where your business is located or where the event takes place.

Agreement to Perform

The closing statement commits all parties to perform the covenants stated in the contract. The signature lines, titles of all parties involved, and date follow this brief statement.

A contract like this will prove to be a vital tool for your business. The days when a "gentlemen's handshake" was enough to formalize a relationship are, for better or worse, over. Today a formal written contract is the best way to protect both yourself and your clients. It also gives you and your business a professional, reliable aura that will impress your clients event after event!

Witness and Signature Line

This is where you will sign and date your agreement and have it witnessed, if needed. In most cases, having a line for both parties with the date underneath is sufficient.

Permits and Licenses

The terms *permit* and *license* are interchangeable and refer to any permissions that must be issued by governmental authorities for any aspect of an event. When you contract to provide planning services, you will be expected to know what approvals are necessary to perform the event in a safe and legal manner, and you must make it clear whether you or your client will obtain the necessary approval. Never take it for granted that a government authority will issue the approval; you may discover that your request has been denied only days before the event is scheduled to take place. It's always best to start the process early to better your chances of a positive outcome and to give yourself time to respond to any requests governing bodies and officials may make.

Such approvals are often required by local, state, or federal agencies in association with gaming activities, parades, demonstrations, tents, street closings, the use of Dumpsters, utilities, the service of food, parking and transportation issues, music use, pyrotechnics, or outdoor signage and banners. Again, it's your responsibility to know which situations warrant prior approval; to know how to secure it; and to make allowances for the time it will take to obtain it.

For example, if you're holding a tented event at which food and alcohol will be served and a fireworks display will close the celebration, you'll need an array of approvals. Begin with the clerk in the city or town hall where the event is being held for information on what boards or agencies will issue each approval. You may have to continue through to federal agencies depending on the situation. If you aren't sure, ask. Discuss each situation with your vendors, venue staff, and fellow professionals. If they provide a service such as food or liquor, they may already have the approvals in place or know where and how to apply.

In situations where music is being used or signage reflecting a copyrighted image is copied, as a planner you must know when such use is appropriate, legal, and ethical and when it isn't. Any copyrighted material may require a license prior to usage. Check with the American Society of Composers, Authors and Publishers (ASCAP), Broadcast Music, Inc. (BMI), or a performing rights organization such as Society of European Stage Authors and Composers (SESAC) for information on when a license is required and how to get one. Fines and even lawsuits could result if you are ignorant in this area. To run your business as a true professional, take the time to research the proper use of copyrighted material. Your client will respect you for your knowledge and prudence.

War Stories: No Signature, No Enlargement

When preparing graphic decor for an anniversary celebration, I proposed using enlarged and mounted photos to decorate the walls of the dining room. My investigative work led me to the prints I wanted, but when I went to enlarge them, the reproduction company told me that I needed permission from the original artist or photographer or I would be in copyright infringement. I sent letters and made calls, and ultimately I got all the necessary approvals to ensure that my creative vision would come to life, but only after much more legwork than I had planned for. A word to the wise: Cover all bases when using anything that's copyrighted, even in the proposal stages!

Insurance

Despite all your contractual and risk management precautions, your liability exposure cannot be completely eliminated. Thus, make it a point to review with your insurance specialist what business coverage you should have. Let's take a look at the array of business insurance policies available. First acknowledge that you are the key to the success of your business. Life insurance, health insurance, disability insurance, and key person insurance would all apply to you as business owner. You should consider comprehensive general liability and property insurance at the very least, with options for other specialty policies such as cancellation insurance, employment practices insurance, and/or business interruption insurance. If you have employees, most states require workers' compensation insurance, which you cannot avoid by calling someone you hire, yet control, a subcontractor. You may also choose to purchase errors and omissions insurance to cover you for claims against your business for errors you may make in the course of rendering the professional service of event planning. These are but a few of the many insurance options available.

What It Costs

Attorney Fees: $100–$500 per hour or flat fee for services provided and location
Tax Accountant Fees: $20–$55 per hour. Typical minimum of $1,200 for general tax preparation services and yearlong consulting advice
General Liability Insurance: $500–$3,000 (based on the specialty services you provide, your event experience and track record, and the area in which you are located)
Errors and Omissions Insurance: $3,000+
Lawsuit by Client or Guest: Varies widely

Locate a broker who comes well recommended with experience in plans for small businesses, home-based businesses, or event or meeting management companies. A trusted adviser can walk you through the pros and cons as well as the cost and feasibility of taking out each policy for you and your company.

Attorney James Decoulos suggests becoming aware of any new standards developing in the event industry. Failure to comply with these standards can lead to liability problems. The Accepted Practices Exchange (APEX) project of the Convention Industry Council (www.conventionindustry.org) has been reviewing and developing industry standards that could be the yardstick against which such claims are measured. Familiarize yourself with APEX and consider these issues in your risk management and insurance programs. You can find more about the APEX initiative and progress from your local industry, event, and meeting groups, or online by searching the key words "Accepted Practices Exchange."

War Stories: Oops!

A gala event nearly created more drama than expected when an oversized vase holding a massive floral arrangement burst during setup. The designer was whisked off to the hospital to receive stitches, returning in time to make finishing touches before the event began. Be very careful of containers, especially those that are in poor condition or fragile.

At another tented event the designer set tall frond-laden vases filled with fresh fruits on top of mirror bases. When the winds picked up, the vases began to topple, pouring water and fruits out onto the lovely tablecloths. Luckily, I stumbled onto the scene in time to grab some "gaffer" tape (specialty lighting tape) and tape all of the vases in place; I then concealed this precautionary measure with some scattered floral buds. It is always wise to consider all conditions, even if it means stepping down the "look" of the design just a bit!

Ask your insurance adviser about the special risks you face as both a home-based business owner and an event planner. Bring your coverage up to date to avoid legal or financial disaster.

Improving Your Risk Exposure

This overview of the legal and risk implications that you face as a planner may reveal areas in your own procedures that need review and attention. If you don't have a contract you feel is thorough enough, revisit it. Find a legal adviser who's savvy about special events and seek advice on preparing your documents so you and your client are approaching your relationship professionally.

Become more critical of the way you produce your events. Are the electrical wires or extension cords taped down so guests don't trip? Are any open flames located well away from loose fabric or decorations? Does the fabric you use meet local or state fire codes? Are all your permits and your vendors' permits in place? Are you using insured vendors? Are you named as an additional insured on their policy for the specific event date you contract with them? Do you risk fire or explosion from the materials you use or the way you present them? Is security in place for the safety of guests? Do you meet any state or federal regulations concerning the Americans with Disabilities Act or other mandated laws for public events?

Creating a Risk Assessment Plan

Work through a risk assessment plan for each event. How likely is it that an accident or injury might occur? Think about:

- Location
- Guest profile
- Decor
- Entertainment
- Transportation
- Cuisine and beverage service
- Lighting and production services
- Safety and security
- Evacuation procedures

Will your entertainment require any staging or rigging? How will you move people from one location to another? Consider your food preparation and storage. Examine how clearly fire exits are marked, and what evacuation procedures are in place.

These are just a small sampling of the questions you should ask yourself as you plan each event. Depending on the size, location, and type of event you're planning, not all issues will be weighed equally. Still, I hope I have given you a sense of the seriousness of your task as a planner and the risk you assume when you accept the responsibility of overseeing an event. If some of this seems overwhelming, I suggest taking a course or completing an education session at an industry conference or meeting that deals specifically with risk and legal issues. Regulations and requirements are changing by the minute and vary from city to city, state to state,

War Stories: Precooked and Ready to Blow!

A catering manager shares this story about a colleague who was running late for a job: "His truck was loaded, but he knew with traffic he'd be cutting it really close. In the interest of time, he decided to light the Sterno units under the chaffing dishes in the back of the truck to start the heating process. As the caterer was driving, he noticed black smoke coming from inside the cab. Yes, he did catch the truck on fire. Luckily he was able to put the fire out and still made it to the job." Moral of the story: It's better to make it to the job late than not make it at all! It's never worth taking chances.

and from country to country. The most responsible and professional position to take is to be prepared. Know what your legal and contractual obligations are for the safe and smooth production of your events.

Event Ethics

Ethical behavior in our society is continually under scrutiny. Whether you're a high-level official with the ability to touch the lives of thousands or an event planner who works with a few clients and vendors, you are responsible for your actions and how they affect others.

In 1987 a group of event professionals joined together and formed the International Special Events Society under the direction of Dr. Joe Jeff Goldblatt, CSEP. Upon becoming a member of ISES, participants in the group agreed to adhere to the ISES Principles of Professional Conduct and Ethics. Among other things this means that each member will "promote and encourage the highest level of ethics within the profession of the special events industry."

The fact that our industry is insisting its members consistently do the right thing can only enhance our reputation among the public. Still, ethics often involve moral considerations that can differ across cultures, geographic locations, circumstances, and professions. In other words, the questions and decisions you face in your business may not always be easy ones.

When you consider your own standards, take a look at the mission statement you created in your business plan. What elements can you reflect on during the event planning process? As you negotiate with vendors or clients, are you behaving in a manner that you are proud of? Are the gifts or compensation you receive necessary to your work and appropriate? Do they affect your ability to make sound, unprejudiced decisions?

We are in a highly creative field, and it's sometimes difficult to protect our unique ideas. We share them with clients and colleagues in the proposal process and during networking events. Few experiences are more disheartening than presenting a fabulous theme and ideas for execution to clients—who then fail to hire you and put on the event themselves. As frustrating as this may seem, you must realize that ideas alone are not legally protected and do not themselves make the event successful. Instead, it's all the components that transform an event from a piece of paper into reality that count. It's the risk assessment, the attention to detail, the wealth of information on sources for products and services, and the way you as a professional planner are able to carry it all out to perfection. It's the training and attention to detail that allow you be an event creator, not merely someone who follows an instruction booklet.

Ethical Quandaries

- Gift giving and accepting
- Taking credit for other people's creative ideas
- Failure to acknowledge others' contributions to your events
- Use of others' material in your promotional work
- Payment policies: commissions or kickbacks?

There are no right or wrong answers to some ethical questions. It is up to you to make the choices you're proud of and that represent professional behavior as you understand it.

Frequently Asked Questions

I have just presented a terrific event plan to a client. How can I prevent them from going ahead and implementing it without hiring me as the planner?

First, don't let too much of your idea out of the bag. Give them broad strokes of your thematic elements, and then emphasize the implementation process you will oversee. Second, consider charging for doing a proposal, especially if it involves a unique creative component or concept development process and storyboard. You may even propose that you enter into a contract at the outset that provides for a fee for the proposal, which will be credited if you are hired as the planner. It may be hard to secure any payment up front, especially if you are in a competitive bidding situation. The best plan would be to put your best foot forward and convince them that you are the one for the job!

I am halfway through planning a wedding, and the bride and groom have split. How much should I expect to get paid, and can I get reimbursed for the down payments I have made to vendors?

This is a matter of contract. You should expect to get paid for everything that you have done and get reimbursed for all your obligations to your vendors. List this out in your contract to fully protect yourself. Progress payments should be consistent with your performance, and you should be attentive that they are made in a timely fashion.

I have a client who has started going directly to my vendors for events and cutting me out of the picture! How can I avoid this?

Your contract should note that your client should not contract directly with your vendors, and likewise your vendor contract should state that they will not contract directly with your client. However, your contracts cannot obligate your client and your vendors indefinitely for future events. It is best to work with vendors who know where their bread is buttered and that you will not give them work in the future if they contract directly with your client. Ethically, it would make sense that they respect the parameters of a client/vendor relationship and support you in this. Similarly, be on the lookout for clients who are contracting behind your back. This could also create limited revenue for you if you charge on a percentage basis as they contract for higher-priced services directly and cut you out of the action.

Am I required to pay for health insurance or workers' compensation for my contract labor?

That depends upon whether your contract laborers are truly independent. Requirements for employee health benefits are subject to change, so it's best to ask a benefit or insurance professional what the current requirements are. If you control not only what they do, but also how they do it, the worker is an employee and you may be responsible for all benefits as well as payroll tax withholdings. Workers' compensation auditors often assess an audit premium for contract laborers who do not have their own workers' compensation and liability insurance. Sometimes, this can be challenged; however, if those contract laborers have employees who are not covered by their workers' compensation, you will be required to do so, even if they are only contracted by you. It is best to hire contract labor with their own insurance and keep a current copy of their certificates of insurance on file. Your contract should require them to do so.

Should I go to contract with every client, even if it is a last-minute job or a small piece of business? What about changes in their requirements?

It is best to have a written contract for every job, no matter how little the lead time is or how small the job is. This protects you during the planning process and minimizes misunderstandings about the scope of the project and payments. There's no reason in these days of e-mail capability for failing to forward your contract as an attachment and request that it be completed and e-mailed back to you—and then preferably that it be signed and faxed or mailed back. At least send an e-mail with the details of performance and payment in the body of the e-mail and request a confirmation reply that includes the legal name and address of your client and the full name of the individual stating the nature of the authority to contract for your client.

08 Planning Basics: The Event Process from Proposal to Follow-Up

You've got your crisp business card and letterhead; your office is complete with desk, phone, and fax. You've made it clear to family and friends that you're serious about your passion. You've honed your skills through job experience, volunteerism, and education. You're ready to begin planning your first event.

If you're coming from a job or position in which you're used to seeing only one part of the event process, it will be important for you to get the full snapshot of what a client will expect when you sign on to plan your first event. Even if you choose to focus on only one area of events, knowledge of the steps from concept to completion is a critical element to your success as a prepared event professional.

Whether you get your business from referrals or inquiries from your website or Internet search, most clients will expect a presentation of some sort on what the event will look like. A true professional will do this in writing with graphics, diagrams, or photographs to support the descriptions of the event elements. This first step, the proposal, can be broad or very detailed; it can also give options from which clients may select their final choices. Whether it's a simple birthday party or a lavish fund-raiser, the proposal will begin the formal process of your relationship with the client and should be treated thoughtfully.

Facts and Figures

"Proposal Elements" lists the basic information you should include in every proposal; if you feel you must add other information, such as references or samples of other events, do so. Some clients have great imaginations and can picture, from your verbal and written descriptions, how an event will look. I have found this to be the exception, however, rather than the rule. Most clients know they want a fabulous affair, but have no idea how to get there. That's why they need the help of a pro! Take the time to describe and support all the elements of your proposal, and your clients will feel more comfortable with their decision to hire you.

Proposal Elements

Purpose of event
Guest list profile
Event specifics
Event description and theme presentation
Decor elements
Entertainment suggestions
Catering and cuisine
Marketing/invitations
Cost analysis presentation
Evaluation measures and goal recap

Purpose of Event

Step one is to state the purpose of the event. Why are your clients spending the money and taking the time to create this event? This very basic step will spell out the event's goals and give you a tool to measure its success. Is it a birthday celebration, a gathering to build company spirit, an evening of recognition, or an opportunity to showcase a new facility? Take time to explore the clients' expectations and you will better match each element in the design phase. You may want to add a brief description of the style of the host or hostess, or the corporate culture as you see it. This will allow the client to comment on your accuracy and provide additional, valuable information to help with your creative development.

Guest List Profile

Who will be attending? List the number of guests, their ages, and their profiles. Will spouses and children attend? Will this be an affair open to the general public? Will you set a limit on attendees? Will you need special services based on age profiles? Will you need to please a broad spectrum of ages and tastes with the food and entertainment you select?

Clarifying these elements reveals your knowledge of the planning process. It also makes clear that the needs of the clients will drive all of an event's ingredients. Think about risk analysis, security, and wheelchair-accessibility procedures, a variety of entertainment options . . . everything you need (based on the guest profile) to create a safe and successful event. When you reach the budget and cost phase, you can show how your pricing closely reflects meeting guests' needs and supports why you may be including some elements.

Event Specifics

List the items that are set in concrete. *The client only has $10,000 to spend. The event must be held from 11:00 a.m. to 4:00 p.m. on a Saturday in June. The location will be the local art museum.* With these and any other givens in place, you can then explore the options available under these circumstances. You'll quickly eliminate venues that are previously booked, cuisine selections that are out of budget, or themes that don't make sense for the particular event. Remember, pay close attention to your clients' desires throughout the proposal phase. This will help you best match their goals to create a successful outcome.

Event Description and Theme Presentation

Here's where you pull out all stops and strut your stuff. You've clarified your clients' wishes, and you'll present to them your plan for how you'll carry out all their dreams and desires. You should select one theme as your primary one—but be prepared to shift if this isn't received well. Your event elements will support your theme through decor, entertainment, and catering.

Decor Elements

How will you bring your theme to life? Dig deep into the "whys" of the event to present a theme that is innovative and will reach the clients' goals. This is one place to insert photo images of your suggestions. It will help your clients visualize your thematic plan. Don't forget a full description of linens, florals, entry decor, bathroom appointments, and so on, to secure the image in your clients' minds.

Entertainment Suggestions

This very important element—the life of the party—will naturally flow from the event's givens and guest profile. The selections you recommend for music, dancing, or performance-based entertainment should all reflect the purpose for the event. Budget, of course, will drive many of your selections as well. Don't forget entertainers who may greet guests, circulate among them, or serve as event highlights.

Catering and Cuisine

Hot dogs or filet mignon, plated or buffet, full seated dinner or buffet-style hors d'oeuvres . . . your recommendations should fit both the budget and the concept of your clients' event. Creative food presentations and descriptions are a great way to show your flair and capabilities as a professional planner. Consult with trusted catering managers for the latest in food and serving trends.

Marketing/Invitations

From invitations to parting mementos, marketing or print materials may be featured at the event and should tie into the theme or purpose. Here's where your file cabinet or electronic "favorites" folder can be perused for just the right novelty or print piece. Relying on good vendors can also be a time-saving way to stay up on the latest and greatest in these specialty areas. An annual visit to the stationery or gift show or a Google search can uncover great local or online resources. When I need imprintables, awards or give-aways, I email or call Linda Bodker of Advantage Promotional Group (http://advantagepromotionalgroup.net/). She not only delivers quality products ahead of time and on budget, she also gives me a jump start on ideas and trends. Bonny Katzman of BK Designs (http://www.bkinvitesu.com/), a premier invitation designer, is also a "must call" for creative advice on theming each event invitation with flair. These are the pros that will save you time and money and make you look like an idea rock star! Keeping some reliable sources on hand will put you at the top when it comes time to support your event with these items.

War Stories: *The Client Is Always Right*

I was hired to produce a celebration for a sweet sixteen birthday. Although these parents could easily afford the most lavish of treatments for the party, they were concerned that they might appear ostentatious and frivolous at a time when family budgets were being tightened. I presented elements that supported their wishes, such as invitations that were traditionally shaped yet still produced in a modern and creative way, thus meeting the clients' needs but still delivering a unique and fun result.

Cost Analysis Presentation

After you've laid out the who, when, why, where, and what . . . it's time for the "how much." This should not come as a shocking surprise to your client. Many times, people will be evasive when discussing budget: "I don't know, just tell me how much it will cost." If you've firmed up all of an event's other components with them—style,

Project Estimation Sheet

Task	Est. Hours	Actual Hours	Rate
Administrative			
Proposal/contracting			
Memos/corrrespondence			
Budgeting			
Evaluation			
Billing			
Event Management			
Venue selection/visits			
Vendor evaluation/pricing			
Vendor management			
Project management			
Timelines/production schedules			
Promotion			
Print/invitations			
Promotional items			
Risk Assessment and Monitoring			
Legal documents/contracts			
Guest needs			
Vendor quality control			
Venue inspection			
Safety plans			
Safety enhancements			

purpose, guest list—but the issue of money is left dangling, use your professional skill to set a price and go for it. On rare occasions I've seen clients completely floored to learn that in order to host an outdoor event, the cost of tenting, lighting, portable lavatories, tables, and chairs had to be figured in. Most of the time, however, the clients who ask for filet mignon know what it'll cost and are prepared to pay for it.

Sometimes event decision-making is handled by a committee—and this can be very time consuming. It's best to consider your client's style and composition of stakeholders to best figure your costs and time. If you think they will need some hand-holding or education as to the event production process, figure some extra time in the pre-planning phase so you'll be compensated for the education process that you offer the board on the cost and planning procedures of a special event. If the event doesn't come to fruition, you'll be covered for your time and expenses.

The budget should include all elements of the event. The best tactic is to include all elements in broad categories, then break things down additionally on a per-person basis. In the proposal phase you can be general, but remember to figure in all your costs for labor, permitting, security, transportation, rentals, and so on, so that you don't have to come back later with revisions. You may not get an increased budget after the fact.

Evaluation Measures and Goal Recap

In the final paragraph, state how you plan to measure your success at reaching event goals. Some of these evaluation procedures can be subjective: *People had a good time, guests stayed to the closing remarks, people crowded the dance floor.* Others can be noted objectively: *Employee turnover decreased, people accepted overtime assignments, donations for the auction items were up 40 percent from the prior year.* Measures for evaluation might include questionnaires or surveys filled out on paper at the event, or a verbal survey or e-mail afterward. The shorter and more concise and specific, the better. It could be helpful to offer an incentive for responses—perhaps the respondents' names can be entered into a drawing for a grand prize. You may mention suggestions for evaluation in your proposal. This is a great way to generate ongoing business and show your commitment to helping your clients get results. If it worked out this year, they may want to do it again in the future.

Timelines

Another important part of your planning process is creating a timeline for your team and your clients. This crucial planning tool helps you keep your project on target and keep expectations clear throughout the process. Start with a month-by-month plan of activities, then shorten the time increments as the event date draws near. Outline the tasks involved and the parties responsible for them. This allows you to monitor progress and identify expectations. It will also help you budget your time and show your clients your progress month by month. This timeline will partner nicely with your production schedule, which serves as your event implementation and management tool. (I'll turn to the production schedule shortly!)

In the best-case scenario, you will have ample time to prepare and plan for each client's event. Sometimes, however—and more often than we'd like—we are called on to create an event in a short period of time. Here are two scenarios, one with a four-month lead time and another with a twelve-month planning schedule.

Sample Fund-Raiser Timeline and Services Overview: Four-Month Lead Time

Four months prior to the event:

- Discuss budget.
- Explore support (guest list compilation, key sponsor list).
- Formulate theme and complementary print pieces.
- Create detailed timeline and production schedule draft.
- Research vendors, raw materials, cost and production of invitations.
- Review database/compile guest list.

Three months prior:

- Finalize guest list.
- Develop theme for use throughout the event.
- Review venue and service providers (entertainment, props, food services, transportation, lighting, AV).
- Create invitation and complementary print structure (brochure, incentives, signage) as well as any online tools to support marketing efforts.
- Sponsor management.
- Publicity: Create press release and explore press coverage pre- and post-event.
- Raffle items: Decide on donations, purchased items, sponsored items.

Two months prior:

- Review and order placement of giveaway items.
- Continue review and updating of vendor services (contracts, deposits, orders, logistics).
- Hold management and planning meetings.
- Manage publicity including follow-up.

Six weeks prior:

- Print and mail invitations.
- Database management: monitor RSVPs, special needs, transportation, update info.
- Continue review and updating of vendor services (contracts, deposits, orders, logistics).
- Hold management and planning meetings.

Four weeks prior:

- Continue managing guest list.
- Continue vendor management (deposits, logistics, scheduling).
- Continue signage and print support.
- Work on staffing and scheduling.
- Hold management and planning meetings.

Two weeks prior:

- Finalize guest list (gifts, VIP lists, transportation, hospitality).
- Finalize timeline and production schedule.
- Review and confirm all event activities: vendors (entertainment, rentals, photography, videography, props, decor), publicity, parking, staffing, food services, sponsorship, raffles, gifts.
- Hold final meetings and walk-through.

Event date:

- Conduct on-site management of event and prepare for post-event review.

Sample Corporate Timeline: Twelve-Month Lead Time

Twelve to sixteen months out:

- Formulation of theme and complementary print or online pieces.
- Venue walk-through and initial layout discussion.
- Review of service providers:
  - Vendors
    - Entertainment
    - Rentals
    - Photography
    - Videography

Props/decor

Linens

Lighting

AV

Publicity

Gifts

Parking/transportation

Security

Staffing

Food services

Sponsorships: purveyor or other partnerships

Raffles

- Creation of detailed timeline and production schedule draft.
- Research into vendors, raw materials, cost, and production of invitations.
- Database review of guest list.
- Finalization of guest list.
- Demo room: selection and confirmation of equipment to showcase.

Ten to twelve weeks out:

- Management and planning meetings.
- Creation and proof of invitation and complementary online or print structure.
- Giveaways: Review and final selection of giveaway items.
- Demo room: Plan setup and supplies/staffing.

Eight weeks out:

- Management and planning meetings.
- Publicity: Press coverage pre- and post-event.
- Giveaways: order placement.
- Printing and mailing of invitations (envelopes).
- Raffle items: donations, purchased items, sponsored items.
- Partner management.

Seven weeks out:

- Vendor confirmations

  Contracts

  Deposits

  Orders

Six weeks out:

- Management and planning meetings.
- Decor.
- Table props.
- Signage: Entryway, demo room, event flow, raffles, history.

Five weeks out:

- Management and planning meetings.
- Food service planning.
- Continued review and updating of vendor services (contracts, deposits, orders, logistics).
- Database management: monitoring RSVP, special needs, transportation, updating info.

Four weeks out:

- Management and planning meetings.
- Signage development/schedule of events.
- Database management.

Three weeks out:

- Management and planning meetings.
- Staffing and scheduling.
- Giveaways: receipt and packaging.
- Final production schedule.
- Final event schedule.

Two weeks out:

- Final timeline and production schedule.
- Review and confirm all event activities:
    - Vendors
        - Entertainment
        - Rentals
        - Photography
        - Videography
        - Props and decor
        - Publicity
    - Parking and transportation
    - Staffing

Food services
Sponsorships
Raffles
Gifts

- Final guest list (gifts, VIP lists, transportation, hospitality, name badges).
- Name badge printing.

One week out:

- Final meetings and walk-through.
- Technical walk-throughs.

Event date:

- On-site management.

One week after:

- Post-event review.

Making It Happen

The production schedule serves to record all activities necessary to fully prepare for the event. It will help you think through all the steps in the event planning process. It should list each activity, what time it needs to take place, and who is responsible. Activities such as deliveries, setup, staging, and teardown should be noted. All parties involved should have this schedule and know when they fit in and what their responsibilities are. You can note any task you must do—think of it as the "Master To-Do" list.

For example, in order for guests to enjoy their meal, you will have tables delivered and set up; linens ordered, delivered, and laid (and packaged for pickup after the event as well); serviceware ordered, delivered, and set (then cleaned and returned after the event); centerpieces made, delivered, and positioned; food and beverages ordered and prepared; and your staff oriented and in place to serve. And these are just a few elements of your entire event; other issues may include getting licenses or permits, organizing speaker transportation and briefings, taking care of electrical wiring and fire safety, and brushing up on parking regulations. You should prepare a moment-by-moment detailed list and assign someone to make sure every item is carried out. In the beginning you may be doing it all yourself, or assigning a production manager this responsibility. Don't leave anything out of your production schedule!

Sample Social Event Production Schedule

Location ______________________________

Date ______________________________

Time	Staff	Activity
10:00 a.m.	Planner/ project manager/ venue manager	Arrive for initial setup with florals, supplies, linens, bathroom amenities
	Planner/ project manager/ venue manager	Walk-through with hostess for parking, setup, delivery
	Planner/ project manager/ venue manager	Review of teardown time and staging locations
10:00 a.m.–12:00 p.m.	Rental company	Deliver four high-top cocktail tables
12:00 p.m.	Production/ lighting company	Arrive and begin installation of production, lighting, video
2:00 p.m.	Balloon vendor	Arrive with inflated balloons and begin installation
3:00 p.m.	Caterer	Arrive and begin setup and installation of food/equipment
4:00 p.m.	Planner/ project manager	Buffets dressed
5:00 p.m.	Planner/ project manager	Tables dressed/decor in place
	Balloon vendor	Setup complete/depart
6:00 p.m.	All vendors	Pre-event walk-through
	Planner/ project manager	Staff for check-in prepped
7:00 p.m.		Guests begin to arrive
	Vendors	In place for start of event
	Planner/ project manager	Gate, coat, and shoe check-in staff in place
9:00 p.m.	Planner/ project manager	Check-in staff departs
Midnight	Vendors	Event ends/teardown begins

Sample One-Day Conference Production Schedule Overview

Time	Activity
7:00 a.m.	Breakfast
8:00 a.m.	Signage setup
	Room check: beverage, AV, tables/chairs
9:00 a.m.	Photographer, videographer meeting (content, key people, objectives)
10:00 a.m.	Security in place
	Speaker dry runs: See speaker schedule
11:00 a.m.	Voice mail to each sponsor/exhibitor re meeting at 5:00, post-show meeting, overview and etiquette, objectives (get room)
	Voice mail to each staff person re preshow meeting
12:00 p.m.	Solution room move-in
1:00 p.m.	Review special event lineup: entertainment needs (prep room, food services, special needs), decor
2:00 p.m.	Coordinate room drops
3:00 p.m.	Emcee and executive meeting: briefing
4:00 p.m.	Sponsor/exhibitor meeting
5:00 p.m.	Special event setup: decor, band, banquet/dining tables, food services
6:00 p.m.	Preshow meeting: show etiquette and conference overview and schedule
7:00 p.m.	Special event begins
8:00 p.m.	CEO gives toast, recognizes and introduces sponsor
9:00 p.m.	Sponsor speaks
10:00 p.m.	Event ends

Production schedules will differ from event to event. A tented wedding will require a longer list of vendors than a small social event hosted in your clients' home. Still, every schedule must include all preparations, a complete vendor list, delivery schedules, setup and teardown plans, and how messages will be communicated to all parties. The previous samples can be broken down even further, if you wish, depending on the number of activities, the number of vendors, and the size of the event.

The Critical Elements of Every Event

Theme and Concept Development

The theme of the event is one of the first and most important elements in the development process. Many times your effectiveness in presenting and executing your theme will be the deciding factor in getting you a planning project. The way you develop your theme shows your creativity, experience, and intellect.

You should approach theme development in an adventuresome way, but remember that not all clients may be as daring as you. Sometimes it can take a while for clients to learn to trust your suggestions, and they may need added assurance to fully embrace your creative concepts. You may need to balance your creative urges against your clients' tolerance levels, too. If you have very conservative clients, you may not want to suggest a burlesque show as the main entertainment. On the other hand, if your clients have planned several failed fund-raisers with cheese and crackers as the main course, it may be time for them to think sushi and cosmos! Thoughtful fact finding with your client during the initial stages will guide you in the right direction.

Location

Budget, convenience, size of the group, time of year, theme choice, and many other factors can drive the selection of the event location. Often clients will look to you for suggestions and advice on selecting an appropriate venue. Turn to your lists of venues you've inspected as well as recommendations from colleagues and vendors to suggest the right fit for each project.

Some locations will require additional on-site services—for example, a tented event on the water's edge. Permitting, rain date planning, toilet facilities, and lighting are just a few of the additional services needed to make a tent environment safe and enjoyable. Other venues will offer one-stop shopping, even nearby sleeping rooms, as in a hotel ballroom. Once again, the initial fact-seeking meeting should give you some clues as to what direction your clients would like to go.

Customer Service

Depending on the type of event planning you provide, you may have clients for a short time, as you would in planning a wedding, or you may be developing long-term relationships with corporate and other clients. Building these relationships may require meetings or lunches that give you a chance to get to know your clients—their tastes, their hot buttons, and how you can create events they'll be proud of. Creating a reputation in this manner takes time, but it's what determines how satisfied your clients are at the end of the day.

I typically schedule check-in meetings with my clients during the event planning process to share ideas or samples. I also set up visits to discuss change orders or last-minute requests. I check in with the client during the event itself and, most importantly, plan for a follow-up or evaluation meeting. This gives me a nice overview of the whole process and helps me make sure that all my clients get what they want.

Moreover, this frequent contact is what will give you your follow-up business, because it creates happy clients willing to use you again or refer you to others. Time spent on the client relationship may be the most important investment you can make in your business.

Guest List

Typically, your clients will compile the guest list. In some cases, such as in a fundraising event, clients may request assistance in achieving attendance goals. This enters into a very different level of responsibilities and should be treated as a separate function from the event planning and management services you will provide. I'll cover the unique features of nonprofit events in chapter 11.

The guest list will affect the cost of the event and could drive other decisions you make in the production process. As a full-service planner, you may offer to provide database management and/or mailing services. Should you decide to do this, just remember *time is money*. Estimate or keep track of the time you spend providing these extras and charge your clients accordingly. If clients prefer not to be involved with this phase of the planning process, your attention to this detail will ensure a correct headcount and help with the final planning stages.

Vendors

The cuisine you recommend for an event should come after thoughtful consideration of budget, theme, and guest profile. Having a solid list of caterers who can accommodate various needs and budgets is essential. Keep your preferred caterers'

Websites for Finding and Sharing Event Resources

Take a look at these applications and websites that will help manage your online resources:

Digg: a site to share and discover non-edited web content

Del.icio.us: a site that collects bookmarked sites (stored web addresses of interesting and informative websites)

Google Bookmarks: lets you save and organize your favorite bookmarks (web addresses) in Google and access them from any computer

Blog Play: a plug-in (application for your computer) that lets you share blog postings

Blink List: lets you find, save, and share websites quickly

Stumble Upon: helps you discover and share favorite websites with other like-minded people

Reddit: a source for what's new or hot on the web that allows members to rate sites for effectiveness

availability, pricing, and menu suggestions in mind during the proposal and contracting phase. Even though this may mean more research and time for you before the project is finalized, it will mean fewer surprises and misunderstandings in this very important part of the event.

The same is true for other event vendors such as entertainment, decor, rentals, and production services. Dig into your tool chest and peruse your collection of flyers, brochures, advertisements, and other marketing materials from vendors or competitors. If you're used to doing quick Internet searches to find products and services, don't discount the effectiveness of photographs, articles, or Pinterest boards, which can offer a more visual experience when you're digging for ideas or inspiration. Consider adding the link to your online proposal, directing the client to your suggested vendor's website. A thorough knowledge of vendors' pricing structure, availability, and capabilities will let you deliver what you promise. A quick call or e-mail to double-check such information will save you time and possibly your reputation in the long run.

Staffing

As you walk through the event, from planning through setup to teardown, don't forget the labor and staffing needs you may have. You may consider outsourcing to professional specialty staffing companies for wait staff, security

War Stories: Covering All the Bases

Even after you've held a pre-event meeting and assigned all the event tasks to the proper staff, it pays to double-check and make sure that everyone is clear about their duties and the equipment they're responsible for. At a large tented event in Newport, Rhode Island, one catering manager learned this lesson the hard way. The truck from the catering facility was all packed up, everything ready to go. The operations manager asked the driver, who was fairly new, to bring the truck around, and they'd be on their way. After driving the hour or so to the site, they opened the roll door to the truck . . . to find it completely empty. Apparently, the new driver had brought the wrong truck around—the empty one rather than the full one. Whoops!

personnel, or valet service. Or you might prefer to bring in your trusted contract pros to handle the specific jobs needed. Remember to figure these items into your price proposal. Don't forget any management and training time you may need to set aside.

As you coordinate the support staff and vendors, your role as a manager becomes even more critical. Putting your stamp on the event, and "inspecting what you expect," includes sharing your vision, training, delivering clear and concise expectations, and developing evaluation measures to let your hired help know how they performed. Taking the time to think through the process and how you will quantify success is critical in building your reputation and your company. It will also help your vendors work effectively with you for future events and build strong relationships with both vendors and clients.

Technology

Don't underestimate the role that technology will play in your events. From the preplanning resources such as programs to create budgets, floor plans, marketing and graphic materials, registration and attendee management to onsite elements such as check-in, auction and bidding, lighting, production and main stage management—these essential technology tools can allow you to work efficiently and effectively. Many of your vendors can suggest and even handle the latest in technology to make sure your program and event runs smoothly, but do your due diligence to stay up to date with what you use and offer your clients. The simple cell phone can do so much more now than it did even two years ago! It can allow you to pull up documents that you store in the Cloud such as through a service like Dropbox, and avoid carrying bulky binders. It may not be a solution for everyone, but if you can streamline your process and automate, it could make your life easier. Communication onsite through text messaging provides a discreet way to contact essential partners without the sound of a walkie-talkie or having to speak. If an auction component is part of your event, guests also can take advantage of bidding on items through apps that are downloaded prior to the event to their cell phones. You'll just have to make sure you have a Wi-Fi or Internet connection to keep the lines of communication running smoothly. Browse the Apple App store or the Internet to check out the latest apps that can make your life easier and keep you on the top of your event technology game.

Marketing Your Events

Whether by invitation only or through paid admission, every event has a marketing component. The first step of announcing the event may take shape through a save-the-date card one year before a wedding, or through advertising a fundraising event on a clients' website, in a local newspaper or through a mass e-mail. Assisting your client in planning his or her marketing campaign will include pricing, thematic development and flow, multimedia options, gifts and give-aways, and branding. Consideration should also be given to protocol and hospitality to fit your client's style and event goals. From the initial presentation of your event to the follow-up thank-you notes, the marketing of your event will help your client maximize attendance and achieve the event goals.

Risk and Safety Precautions

Whenever you open your arms and doors to guests, it is always wise to think of any special needs or provisions you might take to make their experience most pleasurable. For social events, your clients may know when special arrangements are needed for guests with disabilities or dietary restrictions. These are usually easier to identify and determined by the host or hostess. In public events, as an event planner, it is imperative to consider the legal implications of offering fair access to all participants (the Americans with Disabilities Act requires compliance in public events) and taking precautions for safe execution of all aspects of the event. Festivals and citywide events open planners up to a wide array of compliance and safety issues. It is wise to prepare fully when undertaking events of this nature to protect both the client and yourself. Legal implications of events can include proper contracting, licensing, permitting, and compliance with all local, state, and federal regulations. It also includes taking business insurance and ethics seriously and covering all bases before the event begins.

Event Evaluation

It bears repeating that the evaluation of your event is crucial both for you as a planner and for your clients. It will help you improve your services and also help substantiate your value as a planner. In all phases of the event planning process, evaluating the success of the proposal, training and staffing, marketing, execution, and attention to the details of safety and risk management will make the difference in success for your event, for you as a planner, and for your client.

Frequently Asked Questions

How much should I spend to create a proposal?

It depends on the client and the scope of the project. A PowerPoint presentation made from your laptop with photos and diagrams may be appropriate for the corporate client. Multiple bound, tabbed binders presented to the board of directors for a nonprofit might make an impressive statement. A DVD with photo slideshow from past events might "wow" a prospect. Find out who will attend the meeting and how many other companies are bidding, and ask them what they prefer before you spend the time, energy, and money on creating something that they would not appreciate or is not necessary.

Are production schedules really necessary?

From setup schedules for equipment and rentals to time for the caterer to arrive, prep food, and heat up the ovens . . . all the preparations should be clearly laid out so everyone is ready to go when the party begins. All the necessary details to execute your event should be included in your Production Schedule. If you want to make sure you don't miss the details leading up to the big day, make sure your Planning Calendar is up-to-date, thorough, and includes all the necessary details. Ordering monogrammed materials or securing permitting from local authorities for tenting needs may take more time than you realize, so make sure your calendar starts well in advance and is monitored and updated as event elements are added so no one is disappointed.

Does every event need marketing materials?

You would not necessarily think of a wedding as needing "marketing materials," but consider how you will help your client present the event to the guests. Information including a personalized website, save-the-date cards, and in-room welcome cards listing the schedule of events would be appropriate to develop for a social client. Professionally printed materials may work for corporate or nonprofit clients, while a computer-generated and copied flyer or an e-mail blast or evite (web-based invitation) would be acceptable for a school fund-raiser or community dance. Base your suggestions for marketing materials on the event, budget, and culture of the client to develop print or advertising materials that are a perfect match.

Do I need to worry about what resources my vendors need?

Absolutely! If you have a lighting company providing decor lighting, you will need to know what power they will need and make sure your venue has this available. If it is a tented event, you may need to secure a generator. Once the band, the caterer, and the lighting company all tie in, you may blow a fuse and end the party in one flip of a switch! Other needs include tables for caterers to prep on or for a DJ to set equipment on. You may need to consider listing a section in your vendor contract that asks them to detail what their needs will be including food, rentals, services, or utilities. This will help avoid any disappointments once the event begins.

09 Social Celebrations: Weddings and More

Planning social events can be one of the most exciting areas of event planning. You're helping bring people's dreams to life! Weddings, anniversaries, bar and bat mitzvahs, showers, and other celebratory events mark milestones in people's lives. For those who are completely overwhelmed by the thought of inviting six people to a dinner party, let alone organizing an event for a hundred, an event planner becomes an indispensable partner—not only by imparting a knowledge of the planning process, but by juggling the many traditions, vendors, and details as well as offering advice with the often overwhelming decisions the social client will have to make.

The Joys of Planning Social Events

One benefit to specializing in social events is that people will always have milestones in their lives that they want to celebrate: from births, through religious celebrations like baptisms, to the teenage years of bar mitzvahs and birthdays, followed by engagements, weddings, anniversaries, housewarming parties, bon voyage parties, and retirement parties! Your relationship with any given social client can be long and lucrative if cultivated properly.

Another benefit is the recession-proof nature of the social market. Although spending may be cut back in slow economic times, milestones still occur. After the tragedy of September 11, we saw a trend toward "don't wait to celebrate," and more weddings and celebrations were scheduled. While planning cycles may be shortened in tough economic times, and budgets may be shaved, the social client still wants all the pomp and circumstance to commemorate special moments. To be successful as a social planner, you should be creative with your use of and suggestions for event elements—as well as with your fee and service structure.

If managed properly, the social client can be a built-in marketing resource. Referrals from satisfied clients can be invaluable for getting future projects. Don't overlook satisfied vendor partners and facility managers. If you do your job properly and cultivate good relationships, you can set the stage for ongoing business. It makes vendors' jobs easier if they know a reliable planner is handling the details. Follow up with a card of thanks after an event to keep your name on the tips of their tongues for other social projects.

Why Plan Social Events?

- The business is recession-proof, at least to a degree: The general public will always have milestones to celebrate.
- You can get referrals from satisfied clients and vendors for other social projects.
- You can be as creative as you like.
- Once you know your way around social events, you can become a pro at all types of them: weddings, bar mitzvahs, and so on, and so on.

Creative Themes

A full palette of social clients will let you push the limit of your creative prowess. If you're planning bar and bat mitzvahs in a particular area, you can be sure the guests attending will want to see fresh themes and ideas at each event. The guest lists for these events could overlap from party to party, because many of the children may be friends and will want to share in each other's celebrations. Once you're established as a social planner with a creative flair, you'll become a valuable resource to the entertaining community.

Similar Processes

While all events share basic elements, some social events have additional unique features with which you should be familiar. Wedding traditions, for instance, include the processional, ceremony content, recessional, reception with party introductions, cutting of the cake, and special dances. Once you're comfortable with the flow, you can be a valuable resource to new brides who don't have a clue as to what they should be doing and when. Do be prepared to learn the various wedding nuances based on religion, social customs, and ethnic traditions before you commit to planning a specialized ceremony. Take a look at my book focused on the wedding client, *How to Start a Home-Based Wedding Planning Business*, for more details on specializing in this market or enroll in the online specialty course, Weddings, at the Special Events Institute. This will give you resources and tools to approach the wedding client with confidence as you hone your skills on this important social event market.

Types of Social Celebrations

- Weddings
- Anniversaries
- Bar and bat mitzvahs
- Religious ceremonies
- Baptisms
- Confirmations
- Birthdays
- Sweet Sixteen Parties
- Quinceañeras
- Engagement parties
- Bachelor and bachelorette parties
- Galas
- Bon voyage parties
- Housewarming parties
- Holiday parties
- Seasonal celebrations

Social Planning Pitfalls

Of course, it's not all smiles and sunshine as a social planner. One challenging component can be dealing with the strong emotions that arise throughout the planning process. It's a time of hope, fear, frustration, expectation, and elation. For wedding clients, couples are preparing for one of the most special moments of their lifetimes, and mothers and fathers are preparing for a major life change in their relationships with their children. Knowing this, you must handle issues delicately so as not to offend or escalate the natural volatile state of the social client.

In social events, especially in weddings, there is a tendency to have multiple managers—mother of the bride, father of the bride, bride, groom, even stepparents and bridesmaids. Some of these people will have an impact on the financial management, others on the flow of the event or the design ideas. It's important to keep things in perspective and try to pinpoint the one person who is the final decision maker. *A word of caution:* This may not be the person who initially hired you! Be prepared to be flexible and open to change during the planning process.

Wedding Checklist

Rehearsal:

- Ceremony rehearsal
- Rehearsal dinner

Getting ready:

- Hair
- Makeup
- Clothing (bridal party)
- Snacks

Ceremony:

- Justice of the peace
- Musical ensemble
- Bridal party
- Florals and decor

Printed materials:

- Program booklet
- Escort cards
- Signage
- Menu

Vendor services:

- Transportation
- Rentals
- Decor
- Lighting and production
- Power
- Restrooms
- Photographer
- Videographer

Reception:

- Decor
- Florals
- Entertainment
- Photo session
- Cocktail hour
- Party introductions
- First dance
- Family dance
- Dinner or other food
- Toasts
- Cutting of the cake
- Garter and bouquet toss
- Socializing and dancing
- Wedding party departure

Budget Constraints

One very important skill a planner must have is the ability to balance dreams with reality. This is especially true when it comes to budgeting. Every event is driven by a budget. The higher it is, the more choices you'll be able to offer your clients. But always be prepared to counsel your clients as to what's possible given their budget. Present suitable alternatives no matter how large the purse may be, and you'll be substantiating your value from the start.

Knowing the Rituals

Many social events, especially religious celebrations, feature defined rituals that must be followed. Meetings with your clients will give you a sense of what they expect and how flexible they can be. Make sure to factor in additional time or staffing that will be necessary to meet their needs on the day of the event. In the case of a high Jewish wedding, one wedding planner shared with me her frustration at being asked at the last minute to incorporate many additional traditions into the wedding ceremony. You may wish to seek advice from an expert, such as a rabbi or priest, or ask your client to map out the day's activities in detail well in advance, including everything they'll need from you and your team.

Swim Before You Sink

Before you take your first project, go through a thorough checklist of the traditions and event elements and make sure you understand what you will be called upon to execute and support. Rely on your associates to support you in your weak areas or to be that second set of hands as needed to make sure the event goes smoothly. Do a dry run and walk through all the components of the social event so you're ready to be a valuable partner when your first client walks through the door.

Tapping into the Social Planning Market

After seeing the movie *The Wedding Planner*, who wouldn't want to don a headset and be the one racing around pulling all the pieces together for the most fabulous event of someone's lifetime? Unfortunately, while it looks glamorous, the steps from engagement until the wedding couple walks down the aisle are many and filled with oodles of details.

The first important detail of being a social planner is getting customers. Chapters 3 and 5 cover the development of your business and general marketing strategies. The social market offers some unique features and avenues for success, however, so here are some tips for breaking into this market.

Take out a specialized directory listing. If you've held off on using your marketing dollars, perhaps a very specific directory ad would be more beneficial and help you hit your target market. In my area there are several wedding guides listing lots of vendors who offer specialty services to wedding clients. These directories are available at bakeries, from caterers, and at venues that focus specifically on this clientele. While you would be one of many names, it will give you credibility and a presence in the marketplace.

Become a preferred vendor for facilities. Most venues try to be as accommodating to their clients as possible. If they like you and feel you can enhance the wedding experience for their venue and their clients, they may allow you to become a preferred vendor. They will list you on their website, allow you to place brochures in their office or showroom, and suggest you to clients when asked. Some facilities may have requirements for being a preferred vendor, such as having a track record with them or producing a certain number of events using their services.

Ask for referrals. If you've enjoyed success with particular clients, they'll happily refer you to their friends and associates. Brides have sisters and friends getting married; couples have neighbors and family celebrating similar milestones. Don't be afraid to ask; you could be surprised at the leads you get.

Participate in local trade shows. Many areas host specialized trade shows for social clients. Temples, hotels, and special venues often put on expositions or trade shows specializing in the wedding or bar mitzvah market. Check with your favorite vendors for advice on which shows in your area have reaped the best results.

Offer brochures or postcards at vendor shops and meetings. Do some cold calling to your existing and potential vendors, asking if you can set out your marketing materials in their office. At professional meetings, inquire about vendor display tables and ask to showcase at a monthly meeting. Once you develop these relationships, good vendors are happy to refer a reliable planner to clients.

Be seen and heard. Once you become seasoned in your specialty area, write articles for local magazines on industry topics. Develop a blog on event or wedding planning. Offer to speak on event-related issues in panels or at training sessions. If you know one aspect of the process well—catering or linens, for instance—you can stand out by strutting your stuff.

The Challenges of Social Planning

- The events can be highly emotionally charged.
- You may have to deal with multiple managers—mother or father of the wedding couple, bride, groom, grandparents . . .
- There are almost certain to be budget constraints.
- You must have a thorough knowledge of event rituals.
- You may need to educate your client on cost, services, timelines, and options.

Social Planning Basics

The fundamental skill that any event planner brings to a client relationship is organization. Clients who hire a planner are looking for someone to pull all the details together. They need advice, organization, and attention to detail. Your main focus will be to show that you can meet your clients' needs for a successful outcome. Any social clients will look for these same skills, whether they're planning a wedding, bar or bat mitzvah, or birthday party. Your job is to use your natural skills in combination with your specialized training to make it happen!

Communication Skills

Even if you're the most organized and detail-oriented person in the world, if you can't communicate your ideas to your clients to set their minds at ease, it will be difficult to develop a solid relationship. While clients don't need to know every detail, such as the challenges you face in securing your vendors or negotiating pricing, or your frustrations in getting the necessary permits, they will need to be given spot-check updates to be sure things are moving along. Remember that the reason they hired you was so that you could handle the details. Give them the end results but not every step that got you there. This will keep them comfortable that things are moving in a positive and forward direction, without growing overwhelmed by the process.

What It Costs

Weddings, Mitzvahs, Birthday Parties: \$30–\$3,000 per person based on the guest count, location, culinary selections, decor, and entertainment
Invitations: \$1 and up based on personalization, calligrapher, and ribbon tying
Favors: \$1–\$200 based on item, engraving, materials
Entertainment: \$400–\$3,500+ (DJ), \$200+ (live musicians per performer/hour), \$1,200–\$25,000+ (band)
Linens: \$5–\$50 per table (rentals), \$100+ per table (custom overlays and cloths)
Florals: \$20–\$500+ (centerpieces), \$75–\$150+ (bouquets)
Rentals: \$5+ (tables, chairs), \$0.50+ (flatware, dishes, votives, decor)
Photographer/Videographer: \$1,200+
Lighting and Production Services: \$2,500+
Tent Rentals: \$1,500+
Limousine Services: \$350+

Sample Wedding Production Schedule

Wedding Party ______________________ Date ____________________

Contacts:

Client: ______________________ Venue: ______________________

Cell: ______________________ Contact: ______________________

Office Phone: ______________________ Office Phone: ______________________

E-mail: ______________________ E-mail: ______________________

Tent Company: ______________________ Staff on Site: ______________________

Contact: ______________________ Cell: ______________________

Office Phone: ______________________

Cell: ______________________ Staff on Site: ______________________

E-mail: ______________________ Cell: ______________________

Vendor 1: ______________________ Vendor 2: ______________________

Information: ______________________ Information: ______________________

Contact: ______________________ Contact: ______________________

Office Phone: ______________________ Office Phone: ______________________

Cell: ______________________ Cell: ______________________

E-mail: ______________________ E-mail: ______________________

Thursday, July 2, 2015

9:00 a.m.	Tent setup
	Delivery of wine, supplies
	Easel, luminaries
9:45 a.m.	Planner arrives, lighting company arrives; oversee setup
6:15 p.m.	Rehearsal
7:30 p.m.	Arrive at dinner location
8:00 p.m.	Dinner

Friday, July 3, 2015

9:00 a.m.	Rental delivery
12:00 p.m.	Setup of tables/linens/chairs
1:00 p.m.	Dress tent poles
1:15 p.m.	Set out ceremony chairs
1:30 p.m.	Set out luminaries

Sample Wedding Production Schedule (Continued)

3:00 p.m.	Caterers arrive
4:00 p.m.	Florals
4:00 p.m.	Photographer arrives
4:15 p.m.	Cake delivered
4:30 p.m.	Wedding party arrives, gets dressed, photos with bridesmaids
4:45 p.m.	Musicians arrive
5:00 p.m.	Assistant goes to the hotel
5:00 p.m.	Band arrives, starts setup
5:15 p.m.	Justice of the peace arrives
5:30 p.m.	Back upstairs
5:30 p.m.	Trolley pickup at hotel
5:45 p.m.	Trolley arrives at wedding location
6:00 p.m.	Wedding begins
	Procession starts, runner is rolled down, bride proceeds
	JP conducts ceremony, wedding couple kiss, confetti is released, party begins
6:40 p.m.	Cocktail hour/reception begins
	Wedding couple take photos together on lawn
	Guests sign book and picture, get name/table cards
7:00 p.m.	Catering captain invites guests to tent
7:30 p.m.	Guests move into tent, dinner begins, first dance
7:40 p.m.	Introductions of bride and groom into first dance
7:50 p.m.	Toast, salad served
8:15 p.m.	Entree served
	Music plays
	Band eats
8:50 p.m.	Entree done, cut the cake, parents dance
9:30 p.m.	Cake served, dessert buffet out
	Dancing continues
	Planner and staff depart
12:00 a.m.	Dancing ends

Saturday, July 4, 2015

before	Decor removed
10:00 a.m.	Rental company picks up linens
	Lighting company removes lights

Creativity and Knowledge of Trends

Every planner has a responsibility to be aware of trends in the industry. If you're focusing on the social market, think in terms of children, brides, couples, families, and seasonal celebrations. Take the knowledge you gain about trends and put them in the creative context of the events you'll plan. Take the traditional, and factor in some untraditional. Use basic themes, and add the unexpected touches that show your clients they've hired a professional. By using your own creative juices, partnered with industry knowledge, you exemplify the value of a special event planner.

Knowledge of Risk Reduction and Legal Requirements

Another responsibility of a planner, social or otherwise, is knowledge of the latest requirements for legal and risk evaluation procedures. Planners must know how to limit risk and plan for safety throughout the event process. Good contracting will reduce your level of liability or place responsibility with the appropriate party, but the goal is to make sure legal action is never called for during one of your events. Knowledge, preplanning, and precautionary measures help ensure safe and trouble-free celebrations.

Knowledge of the Planning Process

Social clients will expect you not only to come up with the jazzy ideas, but also to make them happen. It takes timing and planning with the right team players to bring your greatest ideas to life. Everyone has to be on board, to know how his or her piece of the puzzle falls into place.

Develop a production schedule and share this with all your vendors. Let clients know when you'll begin setup and be ending your breakdown. Give them confidence that you have all the details in place to build a strong and ongoing relationship with these critical partners in your business.

Social Venues

Social clients will look to you to recommend and secure unique venues for their events. Make sure you keep your eyes open for unexpected spots to hold parties and gatherings. Be well versed in the capacity of your area's hotel ballrooms, country clubs, and reception halls, but also consider the unusual spots. Aquariums, historic buildings, barns, bowling alleys, museums, or private homes could offer just the right space for hosting an event. Or what about a park or boat? Some private areas are available for rental during the off-season or rent out their facilities for public functions only at specific times of year. Take a field trip to gather the details on venue options and keep them updated. Bringing the most interesting venue choices to your client could mean the difference between getting a project or not.

Decor Basics

One of the unique features of an event is its personality. A good planner will bring out the "event personality" through the theme development and the creative use of decor. Here is just a sampling of areas where you can use your special touch to build the personality of the social event:

- Tables. Tablecloths, overlays, votives, confetti, petals, themed decorations
- Centerpieces. Florals, unusual decorations, tablescapes
- Lighting. Room corners, outside and inside a tent, pin-spotting tables, table underlighting, special treatments for the buffet and band
- Linens. Dining, cocktail, reception, buffet, gift, cake, guest registration, guest book signing, and name card tables
- Placeware. Chargers, plates (dinner, salad, dessert, bread), glasses (water, white wine, red wine, champagne), coffee cups, silverware, service or buffet platters and bowls, staging equipment
- Room decor. Props, lighting, effects (fog machine, gobos, lasers)
- Tent decor. Poles, tent entrances, sides
- Favors. Edible favors, donations, keepsakes, personalized gifts
- Restrooms. Flowers, potpourri, candles, amenity baskets, mints or other candies

By using your vendors and colleagues and staying up on the latest event trends, you'll create unique and memorable events for your social clients. Don't be afraid to think outside the box to create fresh new looks. Start with the basic style of your clients and work to stretch them to the edge—but not out—of their comfort zones.

Weddings

One of the most exciting areas of social planning is weddings. Wedding planning provides an opportunity to specialize in an area of events that offers unique and varied characteristics. There are features of wedding planning that are driven by religious customs, nationality, budget, family expectations, age and background of the couple, colleges or universities attended, and of course style and personal preferences. Weddings can be small, intimate gatherings or lavish multi-day events. They can be created as simple or sophisticated celebrations with an ample or narrow budget. For a planner, they offer a chance to build on the couple and family's ideas by creating memories of a lifetime.

War Stories: No-Shows

In the very first wedding I planned, the musical ensemble scheduled to play during the ceremony failed to arrive. The bride had confirmed some of the details, and I confirmed others. This one element fell tragically through the cracks. When I realized the predicament (only ten minutes before the ceremony was to begin), I reacted promptly by asking the bandleader—the first of the band members to arrive—if he could possibly play recorded classical CD music during the procession. I had to let the bride know what was going on! I used humor and firmness to calm her: "The bad news is, the ensemble isn't here. The good news is, Mike is, and you're going to marry him in ten minutes." I quickly shared my proposed solution and assured her that the music would be appropriate. Luckily, the pianist arrived moments later and played a wonderful solo rendition of Pachelbel's *Canon* for the processional. The guests never realized that anything had been amiss, and the wedding continued without another hitch!

Destination Weddings

Destination weddings, ceremonies held in exotic or unusual locations away from the primary residence of the bride and groom, have become more and more popular. Many contemporary couples are professionals who have moved away from home for employment, have traveled and want to share their favorite destinations with family and friends, or who see the wedding as an opportunity for guests to enjoy an extended vacation while joining them in their special day. Typically destination weddings involve multiple events, from welcome receptions to gal and guy events. The rehearsal dinner can also be as elaborate or as time consuming as the reception as you create activities for guests to enjoy throughout their stay. When budgeting your time for a destination wedding, be sure to list all the events for which you will be responsible and price your services accordingly.

LGBT Weddings

Catering to the LGBT (Lesbian, Gay, Bisexual or Transgender) client calls for an understanding of critical nuances to the traditional treatment of weddings. From how you address your bridal couple, to the photos you present on your website, to their preferences for the procession, vows, and reception—you'll want to bring

My Event Company
1 Event Way
Celebrate, ON 54321

Invoice

DATE	INVOICE #
7/1/2015	001

Bill To
Bette Bride 123 Lovebird Lane Celebration, ON 12345

P.O. NO	TERMS	PROJECT
	due upon receipt	

QUANTITY	DESCRIPTION	RATE	AMOUNT
4	Hours of consulting services. Met with bride, discussed vendors and services, set appointments to meet with florist and linen companies	75.00	300.00
100	Save-the-date cards: production and mailing services	10.00	1,000.00
Thank you for your business		Total	$1,300.00

yourself up-to-date on how to appropriately market and address this important wedding client to make them feel comfortable during the planning process. I cover this segment of the wedding client market in the Weddings specialty course at the Special Events Institute and would also recommend the book by Bernadette Smith on LGBT weddings. With more and more states recognizing the union of LGBT couples, it's a great segment of the wedding market that would benefit from the services of a professional planner to make their wedding celebration come to life.

Becoming a wedding specialist requires you to know the nuances of the ceremony, the reception, and the religious, sexual orientation or cultural beliefs that are important to your client. It will also demand you work carefully with all parties—family and friends included—to meet your client's expectations and deliver as stress-free a day as possible. I go into the nuances of wedding planning in more detail in my book, *How to Start a Home-Based Wedding Planning Business*. If this is where your love of events really lies, consider picking up a copy to enhance your know-how in the area of wedding planning. Your services also may include being a resource for attire, invitations, favors, gift baskets, and other personalized items that the couple will want to include. Your list of vendor partners to support these requests will also grow as you are asked to assist your client in the various details of the wedding process. Don't be afraid to call in the pros, such as a graphic designer or personal stylist if the couple's expectations warrant it. Just update your budget and give the couple options to select the level of service and price with which they are comfortable.

Frequently Asked Questions

I received a call from a bride-to-be to assist with her wedding. But when I met with the client and her mom, I got the clear impression that the mother of the bride would be doing most of the planning. How do I proceed with my client without getting anyone upset, especially myself?

It is often a delicate balance to satisfy both a bride who is feeling overwhelmed with the planning of her special day and is asking for professional assistance and the mother of the bride who has waited a lifetime to create a magical day for her daughter. This is when you must listen, be tactful, and put it in writing. Try to get a commitment on the scope of your relationship from the start so you aren't spinning your wheels to develop theme ideas and concepts that ultimately won't be received with open arms. Incorporate the ideas from the mom and bride with your experience in execution so you create a win-win for everyone. But don't try to sell them on something they do not want—if they want tulle, let them do tulle, but guide them toward ways to take a fresh approach.

I really love children and think I could offer great ideas for parties and favors. How do I make money at it?

For children's parties, think in terms of simplicity and numbers. You may not be doing lavish floral arrangements, but if you develop a decor package that you can personalize for different themes and is at the right price-point, you may hit the mark. For a children's party, itemize the elements that are critical—theme, table decor, favors, and games—and produce an array of these for clients to pick from to do their one-stop shopping. It will save parents time in putting together all the details, and once you have the system in place, it will take you little time to execute!

I provided my client with a list of services and charge on a percentage. Now she is going directly to vendors that offer the higher-priced elements of the event and having me do the items on which I make the least amount of money! How can I get paid for my ideas and vendor contacts?

It's hard to make an exciting pitch for an event without giving too much information away. I would suggest you talk in "wide brushstrokes" and not get into the finer details of how to execute. Don't give away your resources either. Keep your vendor list close to your chest. If a trusted vendor gets a call directly from a client, you can ask them to provide you with a finder's fee, or to direct the client back to you for contracting and production planning. Let your vendors know you are thinking of using them for an upcoming event and clear the date with them beforehand. Give the client's name, and work out how they will handle any direct contact.

What other services could I provide to enhance my social event business?

Try providing home decorating for parties—table accent items, ideas on themes for in-home parties or holidays. Stationery items such as invitations or announcements are also a good way to round out services you can offer to your social clients. You may consider offering gift items such as welcome baskets or party favors. Think of the accoutrements of the party, from favors to decorations, and try to find a niche with which you can showcase your services.

10 Corporate Events

The corporate event market offers a variety of planning opportunities. If you enjoy a more businesslike approach to special events, the corporate client is a good match for you. If you think in terms of strategic development, measurability of event goals and objectives, and accountability, you'll be on the same wavelength when meeting with a corporate client. Even if your client isn't bringing up these topics, such issues will be the heart and soul of the corporate event and should be the driving force behind your planning techniques. The corporate client is more foundation than fluff, more process than parade, more results driven than emotion driven.

The Various Corporate Events

If you're working with a marketing department, you may see product launches, sales promotion events, or trade show–related events. These tend to be held in various locations, based on the industry exhibit schedule or the company's target market. The attendees will be customers, existing or potential, with whom your clients would like an audience. They may also be employees or sales staff who are receiving special recognition or training. Special events are perfect vehicles for promoting goodwill between customer and client and allow sales and executive staff to get to know their business partners on a more casual and friendly basis.

The human resource department will be the contact for employee-related events such as award dinners, holiday outings, team-building events, training programs, summer outings, or incentive events. They can be held at or near the company headquarters or at a location chosen for its exclusivity to serve as a reward for sales or superior efforts within the company.

A CEO may drive the arrangements for a corporate anniversary celebration or retirement event for a high-level officer. You may deal directly with the executive, his or her administrative assistant, or the board of directors. As an outside planner, you can be a valuable resource to small and midsized companies in many ways. Once your foot is in the door, explore opportunities to offer your planning services to other departments.

Types of Corporate Events

- Product launches
- Conferences and meetings
- Sales events
- Customer appreciation events
- Team building
- Employee training
- Anniversary events
- Award dinners
- Incentive events
- Trade show–related events
- Retirement parties
- Holiday outings
- Summer outings
- Ground-breaking ceremonies
- Ribbon-cuttings or grand openings

Familiarize Yourself with Your Clients

Before the planning of a corporate event begins, you should familiarize yourself with the corporate culture. In chapter 8, I covered the elements of a proposal and questions to ask in order to plan an appropriate event, but there are other areas to be aware of when managing a corporate event. Knowing your audience and the goals of the event will allow you to recommend the elements that best suit your client and his or her budget.

If you'll be dealing with a mostly male crowd and spouses aren't invited, don't plan on a dance band. If you have a high percentage of attendees who prefer vegetarian meals, don't plan a filet mignon entree. Choose event elements that match the profile and expectations of the host. It may make sense, but unless you ask important questions, you may suggest event elements that are inappropriate or off-target. Thoroughly investigating the background of your group will help ensure success on the day or evening of the event!

It's critical to discuss certain event components with corporate clients very early in the planning process. These include the time span for serving alcohol, the monitoring of alcohol consumption, the handling of after-parties, and liability issues. It's important to advise your clients on the ethical and legal implications of the decisions they make in these areas. In some situations certain behavior may be more acceptable, but this could still invite disaster if implemented at a corporate-sponsored event. As a planner you are responsible for achieving the best outcome for the event, and it's important to cover all bases to protect yourself, your clients, and the attendees.

The benefits of working with corporate clients include larger budgets (pharmaceutical, healthcare, and technology sectors tend to offer the most opportunities for event professionals), the chance of repeat or additional projects, more professional planning expectations, and an understanding of the need for a professional planner to assist with their event strategies.

Get It in Writing

Be sure to add a line in your contract requesting permission to use any photographs or references to your project for your own business purposes. If you want to tweet about the event, post it on your Facebook page, or show photos from your event on your website to promote your work, make sure your corporate client is aware and approves. You wouldn't want to jeopardize any future business by sharing confidential information that the client does not want publicized.

Nuances of the Corporate Client

Unlike the social client, who tends to rule with the heart, the corporate client rules more by the wallet. Most events revolve around driving the success of their business. Sales events, award dinners, and trade show events are held for the ultimate purpose of improving the bottom line. I don't mean, by the way, to paint a picture of misdirected values—the goals of making a profit and running a successful business are valid. Indeed, chances are that you share them in your own home-based enterprise! Successful companies hire workers, drive a strong economy, and keep the wheels of commerce running strong. And events, which provide a unique opportunity for interaction within the business setting, are essential vehicles in bolstering business success.

Corporate clients will look for professional methods in the event development process. While they may not need to know all the details of the planning, they will

Challenges of Corporate Events

Changing of the guard: When decision makers leave the company, look at ways to continue the relationship. New management can often bring a new support team with them. They may have prior relationships that they feel obligated to honor or with which they are more comfortable. Through no fault of your own, then, you can be easily replaced when new executives come in and bring their favorite planner on board.

Keep connected: Do stay in touch with transferred executives, however, because you may be able to pick up event projects at their new place of business. Indeed, if you do your job well, you'll find that the relationships you've begun often extend beyond the workplace. I've made many lasting friendships as a result of working closely with clients on events. Events are very personal, and because you give so much of yourself in the process, you touch people's lives on a much deeper level than with most jobs. To me that is one of the most rewarding parts of event planning!

Create value: You may find that once you set the processes in place for an annual event, you may not be needed in subsequent years. Offer new and different twists to yearly events and provide services and discounted prices that the client may not have access to. This will keep you in the picture with your client, year after year.

Communication processes: The way information concerning the event is disseminated and managed is quite different for the corporate event planner. Social events have invitations; corporate events may have e-mails, internal news releases, or flyers, or may involve the public relations or corporate communications department. You may have nothing to do with this dissemination, or you may be asked to do it all. You might be able to offer suggestions to tie in your theme from the very beginning by offering to manage the invitation or announcement design and production.

Hear ye, hear ye: If clients want press coverage for an event, you may want to team up with someone experienced with media to write press releases, develop a press kit, and manage follow-up with press agencies. Bringing in the media involves a specific process, so you'd be wise to familiarize yourself with it or outsource it.

Gatherer of information: Small clients may ask you to develop announcements and manage the database of responses. This can easily be done with a good database management program. With fax and e-mail blasts, planned follow-up with invitees can help drive up attendance percentages. Once again, if you cannot manage this yourself, hire someone to help—another way you can add value to your client relationship.

want to be kept abreast of changes to your proposal or contract that affect the event outcome or pricing. They may let you choose the color of the flowers, but they'll want to make sure you've been thoughtful about the decor and will want to see your recommendations. The social client, on the other hand, is often more of a micromanager, wanting to choose the flowers, the vases, and the way they're placed on the table to complement the room or attire of the hostess. The corporate client is more hands-off with the details but more demanding on results. If an event does not achieve the desired objectives, its life cycle will be relatively short. Most events have natural life cycles that range from three to seven years. Companies look for fresh approaches, and if you aren't acting as their creative consultant developing new vehicles to meet their goals, you'll be out of a client in short order.

In a corporate relationship you'll typically be working with a manager, such as a human resource director for employee events, a marketing director for sales and marketing events, or perhaps a CEO for companywide events or in the case of a small business. The closer you are to the top, in terms of your relationship with the client, the better: It means fewer channels to go through for approval; less chance of confusion over goals, expectations, and budget; and less hands-on involvement by the client in the process of planning. Most executives choose a planner because they see the value of selecting an expert to do a job they themselves are not prepared to undertake.

Corporate Event Checklist

- What type of event is planned?
- What are the purpose and goals for the event?
- What is the guest profile? Age, background, ethnicity?
- What is the ratio of male to female?
- Will spouses be involved?
- What is the time of event—evening, day, during work, at a conference?
- What is the mix of management and staff?
- Are there any health or physical restrictions?
- Are there any security issues or concerns?
- How many host executives will be attending?
- Will they have any special needs, such as lodging or travel arrangements?
- What key clients will be attending?
- What host staff members will be attending?
- What evaluation methods are desired?

Working on a corporate project calls for strong written and verbal communication skills and the ability to work both independently and as a team member. Depending on the scope of the event and the size of the company, many tiers of the organization could be involved—all of which need information on the event planning process. Or you may find that once the budget is approved, clients want to do nothing more than arrive at the event and enjoy the festivities. Because you must handle all styles of leadership and corporate management, you'll need systems in place to deliver with ease. Use complete timelines and production schedules to drive the planning process, and keep your budgets up to date and accurate. (Refer back to the sample timelines and production schedules in chapter 8.) Be able to answer the treasurer's questions as well as those from the marketing director. You'll want to keep everyone who's involved comfortable and informed during the planning process.

What It Costs

Proposal Development: $25–$1,200 (laptop presentation with photos to full diagram, schematic, and model prototype)
Incentives: $15–$150 (cards, logo incentives, wearables for staff, or client gifts)
Specialized Invitations: $15–$150+ per invitation, including mailing costs
Travel: $1,000–$5,000 (for pre-event site inspections and on-site supervision; may include airfare, hotel, consulting fees, and expenses)

Events at Trade Shows

Corporate exhibitors are always interested in ways to stretch their exhibition dollars by making the most of the trade show experience. Receptions and hospitality events may be held at hotels, off-site venues, and unique locations to increase attendance. Smaller events offer more one-on-one opportunities with sales or executive staff and clients; larger events, such as international galas, allow for sales staff and executives to entertain many guests in one location rather than traveling worldwide for sales calls. This strategy covers enormous ground considering transportation cost and travel time for sales staff.

As a planner, you can assist with corporate-hosted dinner events by blocking off premier restaurants for sales staff to entertain clients. This gives a salesperson attending the show the opportunity to book a luncheon or dinner with customers either in advance or at the last minute.

Announcements or Invitations

Kick off the event's introduction with a website news post, e-mail blast, or newsletter-style print piece that covers the upcoming show, city highlights, industry news, company info, and service profiles. Send them out well in advance of the show. Follow up monthly or quarterly to keep your client's name in front of customers.

An event invitation can range from a specialty hand-designed three-dimensional boxed piece that creates a sense of mystery and excitement about the upcoming event, to a high-end item such as a customized bottle of wine for an excursion to a vineyard. For a more economical invitation, try a fax or e-mail version with clip art and the event basics. (Note, however, that many businesses are becoming averse to downloading attached files due to the possibility of contracting computer viruses. Creating PDF files or enlisting a web-based invitation service can help facilitate this process.)

Follow-up is essential, preferably by salespeople who personally know the invited guests. If the list is large and doesn't allow for this, follow-up faxes or e-mails can elicit responses and help drive strong attendance.

The Event

An off-site event at a trade show will stretch the face-to-face time your clients have with customers. If they're looking for broad coverage, try to hire name entertainers to lure in the crowd. If quality, not quantity, is what they're going for, select a site that represents the city they're visiting and theme it up. Try a theme based on their product or corporate culture, an entertainment theme (disco, Beatle Mania) or other specialty theme (southwest, space age, art, or sports). Or base the theme on the venue they select—perhaps a winery, aquarium, or museum. Go for the unusual and layer on another theme, such as Moulin Rouge, Hooray for Hollywood, the 1950s (or 1960s, or 1970s), Space Odyssey, or the like to create a fun environment.

Forgo the props and hit them with sound, lighting, and stretch fabrics for a contemporary look. Don't forget to pack in the entertainment. Offer something to everyone. A mix of stationary and moving musicians will keep the evening dynamic. A high point should always be planned for the close of the event. This will leave folks with a lasting memory and keep them eager to receive next year's invitation.

Food services should complement the theme. Complete themed menu suggestions are available through members of professional organizations such as the National Association of Catering Executives. This can help you create extraordinary and trendy selections and provide your guests with a unique dining experience.

Evaluation

Make use of the information your corporate clients have on their booth attendees and invited guests. Track their sales activities, hosted events, and exhibit experience for solid quantitative information on the benefits. Use the database for follow-up e-mails or mailings containing post-exhibit or post-event news.

Track not only direct increases in sales, but leads generated from these clients or their willingness to see the sales staff after the event date or listen to product updates. Compare sales generated following the event to sales during similar periods with no marketing event activities. Although this may not be an "apples-to-apples" comparison—market conditions, competition, and a variety of other factors can all influence the outcome—it could offer an interesting and valuable perspective.

At some level, the goodwill and strengthening of relationships that come from a successful event can provide clients with a long-term benefit not easily reduced to a percentage or number on a chart. By using both qualitative and quantitative evaluations, you can enhance your clients' understanding of the value of their events.

War Stories: Dove Soup, Anyone?

A corporate planner, trying to pull a memorable "Wow," scheduled a dramatic dove drop during a convention center ballroom luncheon event. He planned for everything, it seemed . . . except the very warm weather. When the dove nets were opened, hundreds of expired birds dropped suddenly to the beautiful tables below. Guests got more than they ordered at that event!

A word to the wise: Consider the environment in which you're working and the props you'll be using. Think through all the pros and cons and balance the risk of failure against the benefit of success.

Current Trends in Corporate Events

Corporate strategists are always looking for ways to deliver their key messages, and events can provide a powerful outlet if care is taken to understand corporate objectives and weave these into all aspects of your event delivery. Many event planners are using integrated programming—scaling back to one core concept, and integrating this into all aspects of their event. From premiums to speakers to programming, every element of the event reinforces one message to achieve a seamless implementation of the corporate objective. Your corporate clients will call on you to present their chosen theme throughout all the event elements. Be organized and creative. Don't be afraid to share your challenges with your vendors. They may be able to offer ideas on how their product or services could be incorporated to meet your clients' goals.

Get to Know Your Audience

One planner I know responds to her clients' needs by fitting the right entertainment into corporate events. It's a good strategy: Use an entertainment company that has access to top national headline entertainers to deliver hot acts that draw attendees to events. If the budget allows and you can bring a popular act into an intimate setting, it's a draw. People won't want to miss seeing Tina Turner or the Rolling Stones at a small venue . . . it's a once-in-a-lifetime opportunity to get up close to a celebrity, with the added benefit of photo ops and autograph sessions. By researching what drives your attendees—their ages and demographics—you can increase your chances for a strong turnout by showcasing the right artists.

Consider your audience's socioeconomic mix, the male–female ratio, international representation, and corporate culture. All these factors should drive your suggestions for music (an older group may not appreciate rap, or a younger crowd a classical ensemble); food (some cultures might not enjoy certain cuisine, so offer variety—and always a vegetarian option); and decor (don't make it too wild for a reserved group). Consult with the client to choose the best elements for your audience.

Tracking Your Success

Once you have created an event you're proud of, don't forget to measure the success with your end user. Consider both the client and the guests when evaluating whether the meeting or corporate event has met its goals. Information can be gathered through written on-site evaluations, with post-event surveys, or by keeping your ears and eyes open when attendees are milling about. An online registration and attendee management system like Attendee Management Inc. (www.attendeenet.com) can help with website development, registration, and tracking. If documentation of attendance is critical, I-Attend offers a product to track attendance and registration at events with i-Attend (www.i-attend.com) and Event Attendance (www.event-attendance.com). Other programs include Event Track (www.jollytech.com/products/event-track/index.phpo), Conference Tracker (www.attendance-tracking.com), or Event Pro Planner (www.eventpro-planner.com).

Pack a Punch with Technology and Imagery

The best in tech is still the way to stay on the edge of design and decor. A specialty production company can help you find ways to stay within tight budgets by pairing a state-of-the-art lighting and video entertainment package with more traditional fabric backdrops to create dynamic event environments. All the lights, music, and action can be softened with high-quality painted fabric to tie in with any themed event. Backdrop companies offer images ranging from African safaris and Moroccan villages to fantasy, western, or city skylines; these can turn an ordinary hotel ballroom from simple to spectacular in a few hours. DreamWorld Backdrops (www.dreamworldbackdrops.com) is a great resource for small and large backdrops.

Create a Well-Oiled Machine

Developing a strong network of professional vendors should become an essential part of your business plan. They will help you bring the latest and greatest with the snap of a finger to any event. At one company outing, I called on my event colleagues from the International Special Events Society to create an interactive circus experience for the participants. I pulled together members of our local New England chapter to bring their talents to the table for a day of hands-on fun for the 200 attendees.

Guests enjoyed trying their hands at juggling, plate spinning, and tightrope walking. Artists performed throughout the day, culminating in a multi-performer grand finale show under the big top. An interactive DJ laid down background music interspersed with fun games and contests. The event ran smoothly because these pros knew what was expected of them—and what to expect of each other—and worked together as a team. I have duplicated this experience with a formal gala as well. No matter what the situation, the right team will help you create a stress-free event.

Remember to continually build a strong list of vendor partners that offer the quality of service and competitive pricing that builds your value with your clients. Attending industry meetings allows you to forge rich personal relationships that you will use throughout your career. Networking events aren't only for sipping wine and noshing on hosted food—they are for growing and building your critical vendor partners and friends. While you may not have an event that you will need them for today, you may need them in the future and they may also be able to refer business to you.

Selecting the right combination of elements and services for successful corporate event planning is continually redefined, minute by minute and project

Sample Corporate Invoice

My Event Company

1 Event Way

Celebrate, ON 54321

Invoice

DATE	INVOICE #
7/1/2015	Client 02

Bill To
Mr. John Smith Corporate Client One Financial Way Profit, CT

DESCRIPTION	AMOUNT
10 hours of consulting services. Event planning and management services for Employee Awards Dinner, meetings to discuss progress, presentation of award options, update on vendors and event progress, ongoing management of vendors	$1,000.00
300 award plaques personalized	$4,500.00
Tax and Shipping	$250
Total—Thank you for your business	$5,750.00

by project. You must be aware of tightened budgets, more stringent evaluation measures, and a company's constant need to validate the expense and time spent on the event process. Think of it as a challenge—a way to stay on your event planning toes!

Frequently Asked Questions

Where can I get ideas for corporate clients to deliver events that really hit the mark?

Listening to your clients is the first step. Give them what they really want, not what is in vogue or you are dying to try out. If you have a client looking for out-of-the-box ideas for his or her events, try attending a regional or national event trade show or conference that offers exhibits and state-of-the-art showcases so you can stay up on the latest products and services available.

When coordinating an off-site event, how many planning trips should I make beforehand?

It depends on whether you are using a reputable local resource to assist you and how far away it is located. You should certainly make a preview trip to interview local vendors that you will use and to preview locations. Try to schedule any tastings or walk-throughs at venues as well. Things like demo tapes or schematics for room layouts can be sent or e-mailed as the project unfolds. If you have a reliable local company or planner, you may only need one trip. Try to arrive several days in advance of the event to work out any last-minute details.

How can I tap into business events in my small town?

Join a local chamber of commerce to get to know your business community. Consider doing grand openings or auto dealership events that need decor, balloons, or catering support. Try to assist in marketing efforts at banks. Consider a booth in a merchant fair or day. Take out an advertisement or sponsor a sports team by getting a listing in their program booklet. Eventually your company name will get around as a resource for event planning.

Where is the best place to start to get business in corporate events?

Depending on the area in which you want to specialize, you may start with human resources for company outings, the marketing department for sales incentive events or trade show–related events, or investor relations for grand openings and community outreach events. In a small company you may even work directly with an owner or his or her administrative assistant to help with special events.

11 Nonprofit and Fund-Raising Events

The nonprofit segment of the event planning field offers a wide variety of opportunities. Many professionals get their start working as volunteers on town-sponsored events, school fund-raisers, or citywide health fairs and activities. Besides the satisfaction of working on an exciting event, the altruistic elements of a fund-raising project can also be very rewarding.

Getting Your Foot in the Door

Because the goal of a fund-raiser is to raise money for a not-for-profit organization, the tendency is for these clients to be very cautious about the ratio of expenses to income. For this reason developing a relationship with nonprofits is very different from the process involved with social or corporate clients. Many large groups have paid staff in place who manage their special events. Other organizations look for volunteers to handle details and may sometimes hire a few key professionals to oversee areas with which they're unfamiliar. Small local organizations—say, school or church groups—may be used to relying totally on volunteers and may not embrace the expense of a professional planner.

One way to get started in this area of event planning is to offer your services as a sponsor. You may charge event elements such as decor, rentals, or catering at cost, or offer to pass on any volume discounts you receive directly to the group. You could donate your planning skills as an event sponsor. In exchange, you should request visibility for your company in the invitation, the program booklet, or the event's signage. Depending on the event, you could gain access to many prestigious attendees, who'll see your work and perhaps call you for more lucrative projects.

Consulting to Nonprofits

When working with a nonprofit, you should clearly define the event goals. Typically, you'll be reporting to a board of directors that makes

Nonprofit Opportunities

- Medical or health causes
- Environmental groups
- Children or family organizations
- Museums
- Religious organizations
- Schools, universities, and colleges
- Hospitals
- Human service agencies
- State or government groups

decisions for the group. In initial meetings with a board, you should determine the level of support they can offer for a special event and make sure the members embrace this as the answer to their fund-raising or capital campaign goals. (Efforts to raise the major funds that cover a group's operating expenses are often referred to as *capital campaigns*.)

A key donor who's interested in holding a celebratory event may hire you to oversee the planning. Even in this situation, the board has the ultimate decision-making power, and you should seek its support and approval. The board may ultimately decide to use the donor's funds for operating expenses and forgo the event. This has happened to me in the past. Despite all my efforts to educate the group about all the positive results an event could bring—gathering new donors into the fold, creating *esprit de corps* in the community, spreading out the donor base to include more than one major contributor—the board chose to pass up the large gala. Fortunately, I was compensated for my planning time up to that point and will hopefully have an opportunity to work with the group on future events.

As a professional planner, you can help your nonprofit clients develop a plan for incorporating special events into their fund-raising and capital campaign efforts. You can educate them as to the advantages of special events, as well as the planning process such events entail. Mary Beth Miller, a seasoned event pro, shared some ideas on educating the nonprofit client during a fund-raising basics course and developed the core elements of a planning tool that I now use. The questionnaire and project overview helps me walk my clients through the planning process, forces them to make decisions on the scope of the project, and addresses some critical issues.

Nonprofit Service Questionnaire and Project Overview

Purpose of event:

- What are the financial goals and other goals of the event?
- What is the overall theme or underlying force driving the event?
- What is the attendance goal and mix?
- What are the sponsorship goals?
- What promotional activities will be planned?

Ownership of event:

- Who are the directors, leaders, and/or committee members?
- What will the roles or chain of command be?
- What are the responsibilities of the nonprofit board and of the event planner?
- Will the planner attend every management, staff, or planning meeting? If so, how many such meetings will there be?
- Who manages accountability?
- How will recognition of achievement be handled for committee volunteers?
- What is the volunteer-to-paid-staff ratio for the nonprofit?

Expectations:

- What are the sales, sponsorship, and donor projections for the event?
- What net proceeds are expected?
- What's the budget of income and expenses? The organization's financial commitment?
- What are the contingency plans and priority lists for the event?

Management policies and provisions:

- What legal policies and provisions are in place?
- Tax policies and provisions?
- Insurance?
- Accounting?

Database management:

- Is an initial guest list available? How will it be updated?
- Is a target list of donors and attendees available?
- What will the registration process be?
- The follow-up procedure?

Event scripting:

- How will the production schedule for the actual event be coordinated?
- Are contingency plans and outcome variables available?

- Who will manage staff? Is a duty outline available?
- What are the roles and responsibilities of the volunteer staff?

Event evaluation:

- What is the measure of success from board, guests, sponsors, donors, volunteers?
- What would we change (if anything!) for next year?

Nonprofit Event Basics

The same basic elements make up a nonprofit event as any other. Theme, decor, cuisine, and so on should all partner with the goals of the organization. Whether it's a fun walk or a black-tie gala, the planning will start with the theme of the campaign and include all the elements supporting it. Announcements, public relations involvement, site selection, entertainment, and safety measures—all the familiar planning components should be factored in.

Meeting Financial Goals

Working with nonprofits has some special features, however. Unique elements of a fund-raising event include silent auctions, live auctions, and sponsorships. Engaging key donors to support ticket sales and to secure products and services for auctioning is crucial. Key event sponsors receive publicity in programs distributed at the event, on the event's signs, and so on. There also may be levels of visibility, based on sponsorship levels. When budgeting with a board, I often present scenarios comparing funds raised with combinations of ticket sales and sponsorship or auction dollars. This helps my clients set goals and focus on results.

Gaining exposure for the event may also be a key objective for the board. Reaching out into the community, getting local media coverage, or even holding a press conference to create excitement about the event can all increase the group's visibility and, ultimately, its public support. As a planner you may not want to assume responsibility for this role; it may be more appropriate to draw on the board's publicity staff and experience or on a professional public relations person.

Working with a Board

The key to putting on successful fund-raising events for nonprofits is a strong advisory board and/or sponsor. Along with a working board, or board of directors, comes the nonprofit's advisory or honorary board. Members are usually key community figures who embrace the mission of the nonprofit and have the desire and

School Fund-Raising Options

Fund-Raising Event

Opening Night Gala and Family Fun Day

Scenario One: 50 couples attend/50 families attend

Revenue	#	Cost per	Total
Gala ticket sales	50@	$1,000	$50,000
Family Fun Day ticket sales	50@	$10	$500
Raffle proceeds			$1,000
Silent auction proceeds			$20,000
Live auction proceeds			$10,000
Sponsorship donation			$33,000
Income			$114,500
Expenses			
Gala F&B—couples	100@	$200	$20,000
Fun Day F&B--families	150@	$30	$4,500
Entertainment: ensemble, soloist, magician, performance artists			$4,000
Invitations			$1,000
Decor, signage, banners			$5,000
Planning services			$10,000
Expenses			$44,500
Balance to school			$70,000

Scenario Two: 100 couples attend/100 families attend

Revenue	#	Cost per	Total
Gala ticket sales	100@	$1,000	$100,000
Family Fun Day ticket sales	100@	$10	$1,000
Raffle proceeds			$3,000
Silent auction proceeds			$30,000
Live auction proceeds			$10,000
Sponsorship donation			
Income			$144,000
Expenses			
Gala F&B—couples	200@	$200	$40,000
Fun Day F&B--families	400@	$30	$12,000
Entertainment: ensemble, soloist, magician, performance artists			$4,000
Invitations			$3,000
Decor, signage, banners			$5,000
Planning services			$10,000
Expenses			$74,000
Balance to school			$70,000

ability to drive results. Their names should be visible on any print material that identifies the event. Members of the advisory board typically don't participate in planning or working meetings but rather offer their prestige in the community to drive ticket sales and auction success. You may also choose to pull together an Event Committee comprised of influential volunteers from the community who have the time and passion to help support the strategic planning you will provide. This group can meet regularly and assist with activities such as community outreach, ticket sales, auction item solicitation, and set-up the day of the event.

What It Costs

Keynote Speaker: $2,000+
Auctioneer: 3 percent to 10 percent of sales
Auction Software: $250+
Membership Dues for the Association of Fund-Raising Professionals: $100 to $250 per year

Managing Volunteers

Nonprofit events often engage large numbers of volunteers. While this of course keeps staffing expenses low, it also calls for more training and management work on your part. Volunteers will be needed for greeting guests and managing on-site activities. You'll want to schedule training sessions to equip these volunteers with the information they need to carry out the goals and objectives of the board. Besides a passion for the nonprofit and enthusiasm for special events, they'll need clear direction and specific duties to keep things running smoothly. Expect to find a wide assortment of abilities and knowledge in the group, and start with the basics of proper event execution to put everyone on the same page. Develop a clear organizational chart, with a specific chain of command and procedures in case of emergency or if contingency plans kick in. Don't let volunteers bear the responsibility of making final decisions on important issues. Let them know who to report to in all situations.

You'll use all your basic planning tools and procedures—timelines, production schedules, vendor agreements, and contracts—with a fund-raising event. The larger the effort, the more important the attention to detail becomes. If you're working on a citywide fun run or walk, for instance, safety measures and licensing or permitting must be in place. For a carnival or children's event, consider the unique precautions necessary for safe execution, such as a medical station, help desk, and lost-and-found area. Plan for a police detail, if necessary, or on-site medical personnel. Be sure to discuss your insurance requirements with your executive director and board and make sure you or they are appropriately covered.

Celebrity Appearances

Everyone loves a celebrity—and that includes nonprofits. There may be no easier way to pump up event attendance and proceeds than to book a star appearance. Sometimes celebrities can be secured for little or no cost through personal or professional relationships. Whether you pay for a celebrity or are lucky enough to garner one pro bono, here are some suggestions to make the process run smoothly!

Checklist for Choosing a Celebrity

- What's the profile of the target donors (age, expectations, interests)?
- What's the event theme?
- What's the capital campaign theme?
- Where will the event take place?
- What's the nonprofit's message?
- What's the budget?
- Do any board members have existing relationships with suitable celebrities?
- Are there any sponsor relationships that would be advantageous?

Selecting the Appropriate Celebrity

Begin by examining your target audience. What are the ages, expectations, and interests of your group? Would a sports figure, local politician, or movie star be the most exciting draw for your event? What public figure might best complement the nonprofit's campaign theme, and your own event theme?

Depending on the location of your event, you may have access to suitable celebrities who live locally, thus eliminating or reducing your transportation and lodging expenses. Brainstorm with your board to generate a list of people passionate about the nonprofit's message. There may be a local author, war hero, politician, or educator who can offer support for the health, education, social, or environmental cause that your group embraces.

Although you will always want to work within your group's budget to select the appropriate charismatic figure for your event, board members or sponsors may

Celebrity Requirements Checklist

- Security
- Travel arrangements
- Transportation at destination
- Transportation to and from event
- Accommodations
- Hospitality arrangements—suite, incidental gift, floral and food arrangements
- Briefing booklets—details of celebrities' activities, timeline, important contact information, including cell numbers and e-mail addresses
- Special requirements—dietary, physical, additional security
- On-site coordination—staff assistance, security, press assistance

have existing relationships that allow you to secure a celebrity for little or even nothing. You'd be surprised at who knows whom, or whose relative is the next-door neighbor of such-and-such movie star or sports hero. Ask and you just may receive!

As a good planner, you'll want to be hospitable to your celebrity guests as well as make sure you're well-versed with their personal requirements. Depending on their level of renown, they may need security, limousine service, hotel accommodations, or even airfare if they're coming in from out of the area. Inform your staff of the details of the visit, including pertinent phone numbers and contact information. You might wish to include a small gift or welcoming basket or flowers as part of your greeting. Special needs such as food limitations or medical care should be addressed as well. You should plan for a complete contract or rider that lists your responsibilities and expectations and allow your guest to express his or her needs such as water, a changing room, or special requirements during the appearance.

Publicity

Good public relations can help you get maximum mileage out of your celebrity appearance. Publicity decisions will be governed by your target audience, of course, as well as by your budget and the approval and support of your board.

What kinds of publicity options are available to you? Think about doing the following:

- Develop a press kit to send to key contacts in print and broadcast media.
- Host a VIP reception allowing the nonprofit's top donors to meet the celebrity face-to-face.

- Make a general announcement in newspapers or local, national, or industry publications.
- Advertise on radio or television for the widest possible reach.

The Celebrity's Contract

Even if celebrities agree to appear at your fund-raising event for free, it's a good idea to draw up a contract or rider formalizing everyone's needs and expectations. Will you want them to sign autographs, have photos taken with key members or guests, have their names in the paper and identified with your group and the event? Don't forget, celebrities may already be working under an agency contract that limits their exposure. Ask about this from the start rather than risk disappointment on the day of the event.

You'll want to make sure all of the following are spelled out in writing in any contract with a celebrity:

- **Fees.** Spell out monetary arrangements clearly. Will a board member arrange for a complimentary appearance? Will you work through a speaker bureau or entertainment agency? Get everything in writing.
- **Celebrity requirements.** Discuss these fully, and document them for clarity.
- **Nonprofit expectations.** Think about the length of the visit, autograph signing, photos, a VIP reception, audience, and so forth. Consider amenities you'll provide such as transportation or accommodations.

How you time your information release can be a critical factor in getting the message across. You can make the initial announcement when the celebrity contract is signed and the date and event are confirmed. Plan on staggering your follow-up publicity for the most effective outcome. Again, think about your target market, the number of attendees you're looking to draw, the exclusivity of the appearance, and the price tag for attendance. If you'll be charging $500 per ticket for a VIP reception, for instance, you might want to send an elegant invitation to the nonprofit's top donors. Once again, a strong advisory board is critical to put this list of key people together.

Also consider whether the celebrity visit can be linked to such current events as book releases, movie premieres, social or cultural achievements, and so on. These may create opportunities for autograph or photo sessions, keynote messages, or event theme tie-ins. Would other activities such as visits to schools, hospitals, libraries, or civic centers be appropriate? Consider the options and outside community interest to maximize your celebrity appearance and investment.

War Stories: Preparation Is Key

Prepping a celebrity for a speaking engagement can be as important as hiring one. At one event where a young man was presenting a motivational speech to middle school students, not enough attention was paid to preparing him for his presentation in front of such a large audience. Although he had started his own foundation for children of cancer victims during his high school years, had made key appearances on national TV during college, and had been hired by a major corporation as a spokesperson, he was not prepared to deliver an eloquent and meaningful speech to the youngsters. This event might have run much more smoothly if a planner had helped him review his material, giving him suggestions on timing, delivery, and the kinds of questions he could expect from the audience.

Auction Basics

Most nonprofits include fund-raising in their special event game plan. Online, live, and silent auctions all play a big part in generating income and contributions. Soliciting gift auction items and coordinating packaging, display, and print support help to create interest, excitement, and ultimately donations for the nonprofit organization. Make sure you have a strong network of volunteer support to assist with sponsorship, auction solicitation, ticket sales, decorating and setup, registration, closeout, checkout, and cleanup. Even sending thank-you notes and asking for participation in next year's event are important duties to assign to volunteer helpers. You will want to make sure that the auction items you receive are appropriate for your event, so be sure to inspect them and vet them prior to listing them in a program or promising to offer them in your auction.

When setting up your auction items, take time to package them in an attractive way. Bundle single donations together into a "gift pack" to increase bidding prices. Take high-quality photos of items to post online. Lay the items out in an organized way in your program booklet, and arrange them on decorated tables with signage and bid sheets that will list bidders' numbers and bid prices.

Plan your charity event and auction carefully. Try not to burn out volunteers or donors by asking too much or too often. While it can be exciting to create a

Items to Include in a Silent, Live, or Online Auction

- Trips, including accommodations, airfare, and stipends, ranging from weekends to full weeks. Destinations can be a country home, exotic island, ski resort, or warm-weather bungalow.
- Beauty or spa items, including products, services, clothing, or travel packages.
- Sporting events and packages that include equipment, signed memorabilia, or event tickets.
- Artwork (can be personalized for bidder).
- Photography.
- Art, music, or theater event tickets.
- Home services, including cleaning, repair, automotive.
- Lessons—music, sporting, art, photography, language, tutoring.
- Large items such as pianos, automobiles, televisions, or video/music equipment.
- Purebred pets or pet training services.
- Priceless items, such as lunch with a principal or lesson with a pro.
- Experiences such as cooking lessons with a famous chef or visit to a television station, show, or magazine publishing company.

high-end charity event at a country club or hotel, watch the costs that go into room rentals and food minimums. Your guests may be just as happy at a local restaurant snacking on cocktails and hors d'oeuvres and mingling around the auction tables rather than dining on a plated dinner and stuck at an assigned table all night. As long as you spell out the purpose, attire, and event parameters, most guests are happy to attend to contribute to a reputable charity.

Online auctions are another way to reach supporters who cannot make it to the event but want to stay involved. You will need to familiarize yourself with the software and program to create a website, post items, and manage the process including payment and checkout. Consider Greater Giving (www.greatergiving.com, 800-276-5992) as a possible software solution for online fundraising. Other programs include Silent Auction Pro (www.silentauctionpro.com) and Rain Worx (www.rainworx.com).

Working with not-for-profit groups can be both exciting and rewarding—not to mention offer a strong business base for the special event planner. A wide variety of fund-raising organizations—schools, communities, medical and health organizations, and church, religious, and family groups—may all host events that range from galas to parades, fairs to fetes. You'll have the opportunity to expand your skills as you work with volunteers, boards of directors, and new and existing vendors; you'll also be pushed to stretch your management skills, planning abilities, and decor dollars. All these benefits, plus the chance to raise money for a wonderful cause, make nonprofit events well worth the challenges along the way!

Frequently Asked Questions

My client wants a big-name celebrity to attend her event to drive ticket sales. How can I make this happen?

Start with your advisory board to see who has connections to secure a big-name star. Many advisory members can pull in a favor or brainstorm to find out who knows whom. This is the easiest and least expensive way to approach celebrity appearances. The second approach would be to contact a speaker's bureau and contract the celebrity for a fee. Fees will include time, travel, and other expenses. And don't forget the hospitality items you will want to plan to make your celebrity guest comfortable.

I am coordinating a school fund-raiser. Do I need to get permitting or licenses to sell food or have any amusements?

Treat a fund-raising event like any other event and cover all bases. Check with your school on their policies on food preparation and sales. Follow through to local agencies concerning taxes, permits, and licenses. Don't forget tenting and rain dates if it is an outside event. Consider safety features such as a help desk, EMTs, or nurse station. Depending on the location of the event, activities, and the expected ages and attendee numbers, an on-call ambulance service may make sense as well.

Is it possible for me not to charge for my services and to take a cut of the proceeds?

Anything is possible, but the success of the event and donations will depend on the type of event, the history of donations, the current economic situation, what other events you may be competing with, and the strength of the advisory board to drive attendance and donations. Find guidelines on compensation for fund-raising professionals on the Association of Fundraising Professionals website (www.afpnet.org). The site will also guide you on ethics and standards so you can approach your project in the right way. You will also have to look at your ability to execute and "sell" the event. I would recommend doing your homework and starting slow with commitments to the nonprofit to ensure you cover your labor, time, and materials.

I have volunteered for years and want to get paid for my time in coordinating fund-raising events. How can I get started?

Find a nonprofit that is looking for someone to oversee the process. There may be internal staff that can do behind-the-scenes work, but aren't able to handle the execution to maximize the fund-raising efforts. Present your skills as professionally as possible. Make a list of the things you can do that internal staff cannot. Mention any training, credentials, or certifications specific to event planning that you may have, so the client can see the value of paying you for your services to make more in the final analysis.

12 Balancing Your Life

As you make your commitment to your business, you are also investing in yourself. I happen to love what I do, and if you're considering starting your own business you probably do, too. In fact, if you aren't passionate about it, I strongly suggest you reconsider. Owning your own business involves time, hard work, and many difficult choices.

And yet . . . as much passion as you have for your event business, it needs to be balanced with the rest of your life. Creating balance in your life is always a challenge—and if work is your hobby or passion, the lines between what you *want* to do and what you *should* do just seem to become blurrier the busier you get.

To be honest, I don't really think of my business as work. I have so much fun at it that I sometimes have to convince my family I really am working! At the same time, I am perhaps overzealous about creating a professional image for myself and for challenging my colleagues to raise the bar within the industry. I take time to consult with peers, set standards, take a leadership role, and meet and formulate long-term goals for the industry, as well as attend and speak at conferences. I spend extra time on the phone, at meetings, and traveling to accomplish these goals. I feel that I have made our industry a better one—but unfortunately, it's often at the expense of my family and friends. They are the ones I leave behind when I go on a business trip, the people I put on hold until I finish my business tasks. This is my own balancing challenge.

You no doubt face challenges of your own in trying to be an event planner, an entrepreneur, a parent, a spouse, a friend, a family member . . . and yourself. Let's take a look at some of these challenges.

Home-Office Guidelines for You, Your Family, and Your Friends

Being in business, especially your own business, requires a full and ongoing commitment. Every day you'll handle inquiry calls, create proposals, think of ways to get new business, discover ideas for new themes or decor, research vendors or contacts, and consider different ways to evaluate your events. Owning a home-based business, while giving you flexibility and freedom, means you never leave your place of work. It's up to you to close the door and create a separate environment. It also means that you work whenever you can or want to. Your level of commitment will affect the time you give to your business and how you prioritize whatever else is going on in your life. You choose how you balance business and personal life, and it's up to you to check to make sure that your spokes are all even so your wheel is rolling at a smooth pace.

Fitting It All In

When my children were young, the minute the last child was out the door in the morning, I made a mad dash to my computer. Today my home life includes walking my two rescue dogs with my husband, frequent visits to my elderly mother living nearby, and balancing multiple jobs, appointments, and projects. In any case, each day, preferably in the morning, I try to carve some quiet time to check e-mails, type proposals, send memos, plan my daily call list, and follow up on prospects and projects. On any given day the race could be interrupted by runs to the bank, to the post office, or even to answer a stray non-work-related phone call. To fit your new home-based business into your plans, you must take a long, hard look at what makes up your day and life. You must decide what you need to do, want to do, and can't live without. Then you must factor in this new exciting relationship with your home-based business.

Hours of Operation

A prime benefit of owning your own business is being the master of your own time. Running a business from your home gives you the flexibility to create your own schedule, take lunch when you want to (or eat at your desk, which often happens!), and do your errands or family activities when they need to be done.

For your own sanity and to operate at your peak, however, set limits. Mapping out your schedule allows you to plan for the time you spend on your work, for the time you devote to friends and family, and for the time you take for yourself.

Family

It can be difficult to make the transition from work time to family time when your office is in your home. Having a home office lets you slip in some work between dinner and bedtime or between after-school activities and dinner preparations. But it also means that to your family, you're always working! My youngest child occasionally puts her foot down and demands that we do something alone together. A walk with the dogs or a trip to the mall has replaced the bike ride or walk in the park, but taking time to connect will usually ground us again. Multi-tasking is a necessity for a busy person, so combining activities can give you some quality time, let you get in some exercise, and allow you to check off some weekly tasks that help keep the house running smoothly.

Although I am often faulted for having the "in the zone" look on my face when one of my children comes into my office to ask a question, I usually am available to field questions or chat about problems or concerns. I do remind them that I'm working when I am in my office, but they don't always see me as "unavailable" when I'm sitting in the next room at my computer.

Extended-Family Time

"Family time" can include parent or sibling time (or aunt, or uncle, or cousin . . .). When I'm traveling on business, I try to plan visits to relatives in the area, giving me an unexpected chance to catch up with a brother or sister-in-law or see how much a niece or nephew has grown. When my children were young, my mother and mother-in-law had a chance to spend more time with them; they often shared baby-sitting duties when trips would take me away for more than a day or so.

To address your family's need for quality time, setting a day or time that you will go over issues or sit and talk may be the best way to go. Being available at a given time and on a regular basis to give your undivided attention will keep the frustration level down on both your part and your family's. That could be having a meal together each day or driving to school together—an activity that you can give your focused energy to and leave space for connection and conversation. The unique balance you create between career and personal time will work if you communicate your needs and expectations and are willing to listen to how everything's working for others. Flexibility and compromise will allow you to "do it all"—or at least do as much as you can to feel good about who you are and what you do!

A Day in the Life of an Event Planner

Here's a look at a typical schedule when my children were young. Now that they have grown, their needs have been replaced with the needs of my elderly mother and mother-in-law, both who sometimes need to be driven to appointments or assisted occasionally each week.

5:30 a.m.	Alarm goes off. Dress and head out for a forty-five-minute walk with the dogs, husband, or friends.
6:30 a.m.	Return home, make coffee, prepare lunches for the kids, make sure everyone's up and moving. Scan the paper. Throw in the laundry.
7:15 a.m.	Wake up third child, Paige; move laundry through; tackle a few household chores.
8:15 a.m.	The house is empty of family. Check e-mails, check daily calendar, plan day accordingly.
9:00–11:00 a.m.	*Scenario One:* Plan for 1:00 p.m. appointment. Finish proposal, print map, assemble sales kit, copy CD demo. Respond to online requests for information, send out memo regarding committee work. Shower, change, get ready to leave at noon. *Scenario Two:* No appointments scheduled. Spend the morning responding to e-mails, finishing necessary memos for committee work, making follow-up phone calls to vendors regarding pricing and other details for upcoming events.
Noon–3:00 p.m.	*Scenario One:* Travel to appointment. Make presentation. *Scenario Two:* Make new-business sales calls. Log into database or file for follow-up.
3:00–5:00 p.m.	*Scenario One:* Stop at vendors for update on new linens. Return to home office, touch base with family, take child to practice/game/meet/appointment, answer messages and e-mails. *Scenario Two:* Work on final touches for upcoming event. Develop final timeline and vendor payment list. E-mail to clients. Discuss changes and make updates. Check on orders for weekend event.
5:00–7:00 p.m.	Family time: Take hockey players to practice. Bring laptop and update projects. Write follow-up thank you notes to clients. Watch part of practice.

7:30–8:30 p.m.	Dinner.
8:30–9:30 p.m.	Household chores. Family time.
9:30–bedtime	Check and answer e-mails. Put final touches on any outstanding projects.

Friends

My friends know what I do during my day. Occasionally a dear friend will timidly knock on the door to announce that she was passing by and thought she'd stop by for a quick "catch-up." While I seldom take a lunch hour, I welcome an occasional unexpected break in the day to get rejuvenated! I let friends know, though, that if I don't answer my door, it's because I'm on a call and can't be interrupted.

Many of my friends are artists and designers who give me so much inspiration. Others are nurses and caregivers who create a refreshing counterpoint to the crazed pace that I keep. All of them are important to me, and I constantly remind myself to take time to respect our friendships and give back to them what they give to me.

Colleagues

Owning your own business means you are decision maker, idea creator, and chief cook and bottle washer. It's not easy. My advice: Create a network of professionals off of whom you can bounce ideas and from whom you can get advice to build a strong business. Find other small-business owners who might share your frustrations or challenges and seek advice on what has worked for them.

Caring for Your Children While You Work

If you have or plan to have children, child care is an important consideration. You should plan to commit to a professional image in all aspects of your business, and the fact that it is in your home will not matter to your clients if you start and maintain strict guidelines.

Full Time or Part Time?

When you're just starting out, you may not need full-time care for your children. Still, if you're aggressive with your selling skills and committed to your business, understand that your clients will often demand your full attention. Thus, you must be prepared to cover the child care bases at a moment's notice. You can certainly aim to schedule appointments at convenient times; just remember that meetings often run late, and unexpected events can take you away from your family at any time. Put contingency plans into place just in case you need them. Perhaps you have a neighbor or friend with children you can call to pick your child up from school if you are running late. Consider enrolling your youngster in a program that offers flexibility or transportation from school if needed. Have some contingency plans in place before you need them to keep your business plans on track.

In-Home Child Care

If you choose in-home child care, make sure your caregivers know that you must not be interrupted when you're in your office. Here's where having a separate area for your office is essential—and preferably not right next to the nursery or playroom! Give care providers all the tools they need to care for your child from the moment they arrive straight on through lunch, nap time, and playtime. Set up your daily schedule so they can move from activity to activity without depending on you for information or approvals. And confirm a start and end time to each day so that everyone can plan their schedules accordingly.

What It Costs

Child Care: In-home, $15–$35 per hour (based on level of other assistance they provide, such as transportation, food prep, or light housekeeping when children are napping).
Off-site, $50–$350 per week (based on days and time and number of children attending).
Janitorial Services: $10–$35 per hour/per cleaner
Bookkeeping/Office Support: $15–$25 per hour
Stylist/Personal Shopper: $75–$125 per hour based on a four-hour minimum
Organizational Consultant: $50+ for telephone or in-home consultations
Spiritual Advisor: $0–$250+ per hour
Contribution at Local House of Worship: $0–$20+ per week

Nanny

A live-in nanny is a great way to handle child care if you need support outside a typical nine-to-five day. Should your event scheduling demand overnight or weekend child care, a live-in can offer the flexibility you're looking for. Au pairs can offer your family multicultural exposure as well. Be sure to specify your requirements for transportation and scheduling as you screen potential nannies, including details such as getting the children to and from activities after school or on weekends. There are many reliable sources for hiring au pairs. Check in local parenting newspapers or ask colleagues and friends for referrals.

Support from Family/Spouse

Child care support from a relative or your spouse can be a wonderful solution and opportunity for everyone. It can offer a bonding experience to both kids and caregivers, and you can concentrate on your work knowing your children are in good hands. Would your children's grandparents, aunts or uncles, or other relatives be available for such an arrangement? Consider compensating the caregivers, and be fair about the time and energy they'll invest. Remember how much energy it takes to chase after a two-year-old. Keeping expectations reasonable will create a positive experience for all parties.

Developing Guidelines

Just as you would with a vendor or client, create a daily schedule for child care professionals. Let them know what is expected of them and the children. Give them the tools to do a great job so you won't be disturbed when you're working. If you're traveling, be sure to provide your caregivers with all pertinent contact information, medical information, and contingency plans in case of emergency. Create a release form to keep on hand in case emergency services need to be provided to your child. Give caregivers a list of their responsibilities and even reward them for going

Choices, Choices

I often forgo leisure activities to finish a proposal or clean up the details of a project. These are the choices I make. On the other hand, I do allow myself to take daily walks. Yes, they're often in the wee hours of the morning, or after a glaring look from Lily, my rescue dog, or my husband, but nonetheless I make sure to fit them in. I try to stay up-to-date on current events by skimming the daily newspaper either online or print, but I don't often have time for television. I don't go to lunch with friends on a regular basis, but I do meet clients for lunch or dinner. I love to entertain, and many times invite close industry colleagues or even clients to join me for cocktail or dinner parties as well as friends and neighbors to catch up on their lives. These are choices I've learned to make to create a balance I enjoy.

above and beyond the call of duty. They may be willing to perform more than child care duties if you ask them to and pay them for it. Shopping, laundry, and cooking can be wonderful bonuses—as long as they don't interfere with the attention your children receive, of course.

Priorities

On any given day, we have commitments. They drive our decisions on how we spend our time. In the best-case scenario, we split our time and energy among several choice areas that we enjoy. More typically, there are the things we have to do, want to do, and wish we could do. Finding the right mix for these items is the test for any well-balanced individual. Throw in the prospect of starting your own business, and you already know what will happen . . . a business takes time, time, and more time. With a generous amount of passion and a large quantity of energy! You will have to make choices that will affect how your life is balanced.

Daily Schedule

What does a "typical" day look like for you? Put this down in writing. (No, there are no typical days as an event planner; you'll just have to do your best!) This is the time to simply record items on your priority list and how you spend your time. Remember to account for the basics—sleeping, eating, and caring for your basic needs. And don't forget driving time as well as routine activities like caring for your home, running errands, and grocery shopping. Make sure you consider the things most important to you and that you *actually* do.

Typically my daily list includes work (meetings, current projects, proposals, and marketing calls), self-care (a daily walk), family time (including my husband), and caring for my home (cooking, cleaning, laundry).

Now expand your scope. What items do you add to your schedule on a weekly basis? For me, these include professional meetings, larger-scale household and yard chores, visits with my aging mothers, and volunteer obligations. Add your items to your list.

Step back even further and look at your monthly schedule. My own monthly list incorporates visiting family, a book group with friends, entertaining and dining out, and catching a concert or show. You may find that all the really fun things in your life get pushed to your monthly list—it happens all too easily. Whatever *fun* means to you, remember to make time for it.

Now for the hard part: Let's take a look at how the way you actually spend your time compares to your ideal.

Commitments

Make up a list of your own priorities and personal commitments. Be honest about how much time you actually devote to each item, and how much you wish you devoted to it. Everyone's list is different, and there are no right or wrong answers here. Besides starting your home-based business, your list could include self-care, family, spouse, home, spiritual needs, friends, exercise, and any number of leisure activities, including reading, bike riding, watching television, travel, and volunteering.

Take a look at how you can organize your time to accomplish most of the goals you set—if not all of them. In any given week you may decide that your business schedule needs to include time for office work, new-business calls and appointments, current project planning and preparations, information gathering and education, and networking. Set up your calendar for each day with these activities scheduled in. Start with deadlines and work backward, adding in a time buffer to ease your stress. If you have to borrow some family time one week to meet a business deadline, pay it back the next week by spending a spontaneous hour with loved ones. They will appreciate being kept on your priority list!

Be realistic about how your business goals fit with your other personal commitments. This will determine what you will get done and when. You may ultimately decide to focus your time on meeting a proposal deadline and attending a special event course, leaving you with only a few hours a week to develop new business and network. You'll also find that your schedule rarely fits into the traditional nine-to-five parameters. That's the beauty of a home office. Don't be afraid to stretch the limits of a "typical" day to allow yourself to accomplish your goals each week.

In a perfect world you could create this list of life values and incorporate each of them into each day—maybe with a different mix of time and priority, but you'd make sure to touch base with them every day. . . In the real world, though, you'll probably want to aim at balancing it on a weekly basis.

Still, here's something to think about: By not putting up a bar, you never raise it. If your priorities and where you actually spend your time don't line up, then it may be time to make a plan for change and put it into action!

Balancing Your Wheel

Home

There's an old saying: None of us ever leaves this world wishing our house was cleaner. Everyone has a different level of tolerance when it comes to living space.

Typical Day Timeline

Time	Self	Family	Work	Volunteerism
Midnight	Sleep			
1:00 a.m.	Sleep			
2:00 a.m.	Sleep			
3:00 a.m.	Sleep			
4:00 a.m.	Sleep			
5:00 a.m.	Exercise with friend			
6:00 a.m.	Self-care			
7:00 a.m.		Organize for day and prepare meals		
8:00 a.m.	Chores	Household chores		
9:00 a.m.			Office	
10:00 a.m.			Appointments	
11:00 a.m.			Calls	
Noon	Eat (quickly!)		E-mails, calls, memos	
1:00 p.m.			Appointments	
2:00 p.m.			Proposals	
3:00 p.m.		Give rides	Calls	
4:00 p.m.		Grocery shop/ errands		
5:00 p.m.		Doctor appointments		
6:00 p.m.				Choir rehearsal
7:00 p.m.	Dinner	Dinner		
8:00 p.m.		Chores, family time		
9:00 p.m.			Office work	
10:00 p.m.			Office work	
11:00 p.m.	Bedtime			
Items	**Current %**	**Optimal %**	**Path to Success**	
Self				
Family				
Work				
Volunteerism				

How clean, furnished, and organized your home is really depends on your own style and personality.

The organizational piece of the equation is probably the most important. I find that organization is the key to keeping my stress level down. If things are a mess around me, it's hard to concentrate and comfortably go about my day. For this reason I handle a flurry of household tasks at the very beginning of the day . . . but then I step away from it. Once a week the house gets a top-to-bottom cleaning. Even though I tend to be a creative collector—adding lots of seasonal decor to my tables, walls, and doorways—I also try to be as streamlined as possible to help keep things tidy looking. My two suggestions for keeping your home and your office pleasant: Streamline and organize.

The Balancing Act

Effective scheduling requires you to weigh your priorities against your deadlines. Scan through the must-do, should-do, and want-to-do lists. What are their various time requirements? How can they be balanced reasonably? If a particular task on my own lists has to be completed by a firm deadline, it moves up in priority so I can make it happen. If I find that my lists are overcrowded or that I'm not accomplishing what I need to, I limit the time I spend on some things. Volunteerism is a big part in my life, for instance—but if I can't find time for my business or family, I need to start limiting my volunteer work.

Health

It's true what they say: If you have your health, you have everything. Stress, poor eating habits, and a lack of exercise can all slow you down and keep you from operating at your best. The hour you take from your workday to exercise will renew you and help you process your tasks more efficiently. The event industry is a creative business. Ideas and fresh thoughts flow from nature, people around us, things we experience and do. By stepping away from your desk to go for a walk or run, you participate in a mini retreat. Enjoy the world around you and mull over your challenges and problems as you take that hour or even half-hour break. You'll be refreshed and approach your "to-do" list with a new perspective.

Self-Care

Just as exercise can offer you a chance to step outside your stress zone, other self-care activities can be critical in helping you operate at an optimal level. Getting in touch with your inner self through meditation, worship, or other introspective practices can help clear your mind and wash away negative and ineffective thoughts and influences. Keep an eye on the positive around you. Look at that half-full glass—and consider the option of no glass! Taking the time to focus on what you need for your soul is as important as meeting your physical needs. The food of life comes in many forms, so treat yourself to a full menu for a strong mind and body.

Outsourcing Your Life

You've learned to outsource your event planning duties . . . now think about whether some parts of your life can be sourced out. My dad once wondered why I insisted on going to the dump each weekend. I'd encourage my husband to put it on the top of his list for Saturday and stressed over it right up until the moment I saw the car leave the driveway with our trash barrels. Of course, this was not my husband's favorite thing to do after a week of work. So my wise father asked me how much trash pickup might cost. I found out it was $10 per week. Was it worth $10 per week to cross this constant worry off two "to-do" lists? Absolutely! I also realized how much time it took me to grocery shop each week. At the time, a delivery service was available that included online ordering and weekly delivery of a full array of groceries: meats, produce, and packaged items. I used that service for several years and cried the day they discontinued it.

Support

My home-based business was born at the same time as my first child. Running a business from my home gave me flexibility and freedom, while still offering challenge and stimulation. The first year I produced one event. The second year I handled two.

Year after year, my business grew. When my children were very young, I had my family care for them when I traveled. Or I took them with me. One trip to San Francisco included my mother and seven-month-old daughter, whom I was not ready to wean at the time. It worked perfectly. I transitioned from pre-event meetings to morning feeding . . . from event setup to afternoon feeding. My mom had a great time, and my little one didn't skip a beat! It was a great memory for my mother and me, and we still look at the photos of Paige riding in the back of a limo in style at the age of seven months!

As my children grew older, they became more independent and realized that even if I might leave for a few days, I would always return. They didn't love the travel, but they loved the goodies they got when I walked back through the door. All three children have worked with me at events. They have seen what it takes to succeed in business from the beginning. I think it has helped them make choices in their lives to follow their passion and give it their all. My husband has helped me through the downtimes with encouragement and a helping hand when needed, which allowed me to travel and give each event my all. I couldn't have done it all these years without him!

Being in a supportive relationship can make or break your business. No matter how much confidence you may have, hearing about your abilities from someone you love can help you keep your chin up when the going gets tough. And honest advice when things aren't quite at their best is better received from a loved one than an angry client. If you don't have a partner, your family or friends can offer this support. Share your dreams, ask for assistance—and listen to their candid comments. But be kind and good to these important people, and take time to let them know you care for them just as much as they care for you.

Self-Support

Remind yourself from time to time of everything you've accomplished. It'll help you get through those times when you feel like you're going nowhere fast. When you assess your progress or your events, you tend to see all the things you could do better and not necessarily all the things you've done right. Make a list. Write down your achievements. Ask your clients for both a written and verbal evaluation. Take time to notice the smiles on the guests' faces when they are enjoying the fruits of your event labor. And take time to pat yourself on the back for a job well done!

Words of Wisdom

Painting an Accurate Picture

Many people think the life of an event planner is glamorous. Event planning is HARD WORK! Television and social media can make our profession sound like all we do is select flowers for brides and put finishing touches on tablescapes. They may not realize or have insight into the many hours that go into that beautiful end result. Not everyone has the patience, determination, and organizational skills to do this job, so take pride in your work and try to change people's minds about the profession. The hospitality and event planning business is a wheel that turns 24/7, 365 days a year. You work hard and put in long hours, so be proud of each event you do or take part in.

Technology Trap

Taking time to connect with friends on Facebook is important, but stepping away from technology can be just as important. In today's world, we are connected to everyone with smartphones, e-mail, and social media. While being that connected can be helpful, it is just as important to make sure you put your phone on "do not disturb" for an hour or so to relax at the end of each day. While it can be fun to stay connected with those you love on social media, it's also important to have the personal touch to relax and take care of yourself and family in person as well.

Know When to Say No

Set priorities in your life and work, and know how and when to say no. If you feel that you are overwhelmed, it's okay to reach out for a helping hand. Don't be afraid to turn down an event that you don't have the skill to produce or the time to give to it. You would rather do the best you can on one or two events and get great reviews than spread yourself too thin and produce events that you are not proud of. The same goes for other activities that take time and energy away from what you really want to be doing. Be true to yourself and learn to say no when you really need to. I have always tried to "listen to my gut" and let my inner self help me make final decisions on tough questions I face.

Frequently Asked Questions

I am having a hard time separating my work from my family responsibilities. How can I make better choices in dividing my time between the two?

Starting your own business is a total commitment, but given the other elements of your life, you will need to create a balance everyone can live with. Maybe you can walk away from the phone after 6:00 p.m., or step away from the computer from

6:00 to 9:00 p.m. and come back to it after the dishes are done and the kids are in bed. Consider how much additional money you will make from the efforts you are putting into your business and the extra time you are taking from your family or personal commitments. Evaluate your choices and prioritize. Let go of the time-consuming projects that may not reap the financial benefit but use your precious time.

Is it worth getting a sitter for my children when I am working from the home?

If you do not have a spouse who can pick up the slack or an older child to keep an eye out for the little ones, it's worth the peace of mind to get a paid professional to help with child care. Even a student who is willing to act as a mother's helper will allow you to take uninterrupted time for your business. Know your caregiver's limits and your children's needs to make sure they are in good hands and it's not an overwhelming task for the student-helper. It will also help create a more professional appearance not to be interrupted when you talk on the phone with clients.

I feel like my business could really take off if I didn't have any other responsibilities in my life. How can I make my dream come true?

Pace yourself. Make a list. Develop a plan of attack. Check off your successes and feel good about the steps you take. It's easy to look at folks who are wildly successful and say, "Why not me?" The deal is, they may have a bevy of assistants, no other responsibilities other than their business, no family, spouse, or significant other to share their lives with. So in the scheme of things, the baby steps you take can be more impressive in the big picture than you think, and each step you take will get you closer to your goal and dream of owning a successful event planning business.

My business is taking up all my time. I've given up my gym membership, quit my Bunco group, and stay in to work most evenings. Do you think I am on course for success?

It depends how you define success. Many ideas come from allowing yourself time to think, be creative, and get ideas and input from others. Walking the dog can combine exercise with pet care and—if you join a friend—with companionship. It can also give you a chance to throw out creative ideas and get feedback. Don't feel that you can live in a vacuum or that you are cutting your business time short by taking a break. Let your mind relax, and it just may be the break needed to let the next good idea take root. Joining clubs or volunteer groups can also be a good source of networking and new business. Balancing your wheel will help your business run smoothly!

13 Being the Best: Education and Training

The fact that you are interested in starting your own event planning business shows you have the desire to work in the field of special events. But do you have the necessary skills to start and grow a home-based event planning company? The event process is full of challenges, as you've seen throughout this book. With the right tools and training, though, all these challenges can be met with safe and creative solutions. You have many options for formal training to help you build your skills for a rewarding and exciting career in special events.

Formal Education

In chapter 1, I talked about the basic skills you'll need to run your business. While it may not be necessary to get an MBA, it's not a bad idea to take business courses. They will certainly help you run your business in a professional way and will save you time and money in the long run. To balance the business skills you'll gain, you'll want to focus additional training in the area of special events.

Currently many two- and four-year degree programs in areas related to special events are offered both throughout the United States and internationally at colleges and universities as part of a Hospitality, Communication or Business program. The four-year programs will give you a wide-ranging foundation of knowledge to begin your career in event planning. If you aren't in a position to study full time and want a very focused course of study in event planning, distance learning classes and part-time programs may allow you to work and study at the same time. You can enroll in courses through the Special Events Institute one at a time, giving you the flexibility to study and pay at your own pace. Other local programs may be seminar- or workshop-based and offer a one-day or weekend program to get you started without making a long-term commitment.

Even after completion of a degree program, be prepared to allow yourself time to gain the very necessary experience that school training just can't provide. You can do this through volunteering or understudying with a pro. You'll certainly understand the process of developing an event with your degree or certificate in hand, but not the unexpected curveballs that the job will throw you. Even with meticulous contingency planning, you'll find yourself challenged to solve problems at almost every event.

Being the Best

Education:

- Formal education
- Monthly professional meetings
- Semiannual or annual professional conferences

Experience:

- Networking with colleagues
- Apprenticeship with experienced planners
- Critical evaluation procedures

A combination of a good formal foundation in events and business, monthly professional meetings that offer strong educational content and the chance to network with colleagues, yearly conferences, and critical evaluation of your planning procedures will help you continue to offer the very best in planning services.

My recommendation is to balance ongoing formal education with apprenticeships and strong mentors. Formal training will at least give you exposure to the event preparation process. The danger, however, is that you won't realize everything you *don't* know. If you don't stay up to date on risk procedures, for instance, you may not realize how dangerous some event situations can be. If you don't understand permitting, a surprise visit from the fire chief might shut down your event while the guests are arriving. If you don't know the importance of involving the venue's engineering department when you're using fog machines, you may end up with the fire alarms blaring and the hotel evacuated an hour after the event begins. These are just a few of the ways that events can end in disaster. Both training and experience will help you fully prepare for a career in event planning.

Professional Designations in the Special Event and Related Industries

Special events:

- Certified Special Events Professional (CSEP): www.ises.com
- Professional Bridal Consultant (PBC): www.bridalassn.com
- Accredited Bridal Consultant (ABC): www.bridalassn.com
- Master Bridal Consultant (MBC): www.bridalassn.com

Meetings:

- Certified Meeting Professional (CMP): www.conventionindustry.org
- Certification in Meeting Management (CMM): www.mpiweb.org
- Certified Association Sales Executive (CASE): www.pcma.org
- Certified Association Executive (CAE): www.asaenet.org
- Certified Planner of Professional Meetings (CPPM), Certified Internet Meeting Professional (CIMP), Certified Global Meeting Professional (CGMP): www.cimpa.org

Destination management:

- Destination Management Certified Professional (DMCP): www.adme.org
- Accredited Destination Management Organization (DMO): www.iacvb.org

Hospitality:

- Certified Hospitality Account Executive (CHAE), Certified Hospitality Technology Professional (CHTP): www.hftp.org
- Certified Hospitality Marketing Executive (CHME), Certified Revenue Management Executive (CRME), Certified Hospitality Sales Competencies (CHSC): www.hsmai.org
- American Hotel & Lodging Education Institute certifications: www.ahlei.org

Travel:

- Certified Incentive Travel Executive (CITE): www.site-intl.org
- Certified Corporate Travel Executive (CCTE), Certified Government Travel Executive (CGTE): www.nbta.org

Exhibition:

- Certified in Exhibition Management (CEM): www.iaee.com
- Certified Manager of Exhibits (CME), Certified Manager of Exhibits/Healthcare (CMEH): www.tsea.org
- Certified Trade Show Marketer (CTSM): www.exhibitoronline.com

Venues:

- Certified Facilities Executive (CFE): www.iaam.org

Food:

- Certified Professional Catering Executive (CPCE): www.nace.net
- Foodservice Management Professional (FMP): www.nraef.org
- Certified Culinary Professional (CCP): www.iacp.com

Professional Designations and Certificates

There are many designations available in the hospitality industry, all designed to provide qualifications in various key areas.

If you are looking for the convenience and flexibility of online coursework, consider enrolling in certificate classes at the Special Events Institute (www.SpecialEventsInstitute.com). This program was developed to provide basic and advanced training and be a valuable educational resource to individuals entering into the field of special events. The course of study will provide a complete training program in special events culminating in a certificate of competency (Certificate in Special Events Planning).

Graduates would go on to work in an existing event business; work with an event-related vendor such as a caterer, venue, or rental company; work within a corporate event department; own their own event planning service; or provide planning services to communities, churches, schools, or other public places that hold events. The certificate program provides a foundation for those who wish to work in the industry and aspire to a professional designation such as a CSEP (Certified Special Events Professional) or CMP (Certified Meeting Professional).

The Certified Special Events Professional (CSEP) designation is a certification for seasoned planners (with more than five years of experience) if you want to truly stand out in the special events industry. The requirements for the CSEP title combine basic knowledge of the event planning process with experience. This is a great natural stepping-stone if you've completed online or classroom training, have worked for more than five years in the industry, and want to elevate your professional credentials.

This designation is offered by the International Special Events Society (ISES). The process involves filling out an application that includes verification of experience in the industry. Once approved, you begin preparation for a two-part exam on core competencies in event management that is offered four times a year at various testing sites. You can find more about this certification at www.ises.com/csep/home.

Achieving certification or striving for a professional designation shows your ability to combine basic knowledge with implementation. It indicates your commitment to professionalism in the industry. It also will set you apart from your competitors who aren't certified.

If you plan to focus on the wedding industry, a Professional Bridal Consultant designation would be an excellent goal. If you want to focus on partnering with the meeting and convention industry, the Certification in Meeting Management or a Certified Meeting Professional designation may be a good choice. There are many other designations within the hospitality industry focusing on disciplines such as catering, exhibit and display, and travel. See appendices A and B, pages 201–15, for an overview of issuing organizations and their websites.

More Ways to Refine Your Trade

On-the-Job Training

While formal training provides a sound start for your business, on-the-job training will complement your strategy and provide the much-needed experience to turn you into a "think-on-your-feet" professional. Rather than experience the event process on paper alone, plan to put your learning to use. You might begin by working on projects with other experienced planners or volunteering for a community event. Be critical of your skills, and you'll know when the time is right to start out on your own.

Continuing Education Programs

If you're already working in the industry and want to round out your skills, check local listings for community college, university, or high school continuing education courses. Offerings can include courses in basic business skills, events skills, nonprofit planning, catering, floral design, use of costuming or theatrical components in events, entertainment, public speaking, and marketing.

These courses can be relatively inexpensive, are usually offered at convenient times and locations, and can provide an in-face learning environment on which to build your business and event skills.

Industry Conferences and Courses

To really get an educational shot in the arm, commit to attend an event industry conference. These conferences are great ways to receive training, network with fellow event professionals, and stay on top of current trends. They allow you to gather resources and ideas on how others execute the event process.

The International Special Events Society traditionally holds a two-day conference each August called ISES Live. The days are jam-packed with sessions on an array of event topics; evenings typically showcase the host city's best venues decorated in contemporary and unique themes created by local event professionals. The ISES Esprit Award Dinner is held on the final evening, with prestigious industry awards being given to winners throughout the world. These conferences also provide ample time to network with fellow planners and chat about the event industry. Information can be found on the ISES website at www.ises.com.

The Special Event (TSE), held each January, delivers a similar experience. This conference has an additional trade show feature, with exhibitors showcasing products and services specifically used in the event industry. It's a great way to pick up new ideas and products to add to your events. Daily educational sessions, evening parties, and a closing gala celebration with an award dinner are also offered. The event is produced by Primedia Business Exhibitions; for more details, check out www.thespecialeventshow.com.

Event Solutions Expo (www.event-solutions.com) is held yearly at varying times and offers a similar conference experience combining education and a trade show. Additional conferences include the CSE LIVE, held each spring in Canada. Information on this can be found at www.canadianspecialevents.com. See appendix B for a listing of professional organizations and associated conferences and expos.

Regional Education Conferences

Other options for conference attendance that may be closer to home are the regional education conferences offered by the International Special Events Society. These are held throughout the world and are organized by regions (Northeast, Southeast, West, Midwest, Asia Pacific, and EurAfrica). These are scaled-down versions of ISES Live, with a similar combination of education, evening activities, and networking. There are sometimes award presentations and exhibitor showcases as well. These are often an accessible way to gain information, enjoy valuable educational sessions, and network with colleagues without breaking your travel budget.

Trade Shows

Trade shows can help you update your supplier lists—and can provide networking opportunities as well. Many of the industry websites offer information on shows that focus on event-related products and services. BizBash Live (see www.bizbash.com) is specifically designed for the special event industry and held in various locations across the United States throughout the year. Others, such as the National Stationery Show (www.nationalstationeryshow.com) held in New York City in May of each year, focus on a narrow aspect of the business but can provide excellent up-to-date resource information. Keep an eye on professional publications or do a thorough online search to find exhibitions or shows in your area.

Mentors

If you look through your resource directory or card file, I'm sure you'll find a list of colleagues whom you regard as professionals in the industry. They can be an excellent source of advice and training as you start and grow your business. As long as you aren't perceived as direct competition, many planners are flattered by an interest in their business practices and will welcome the opportunity to coach you. You will also see how others handle business duties such as billing, training employees, and event execution.

Another great place to find mentors is at your local professional meetings such as NACE, MPI, or ISES. Most seasoned professionals are happy to help someone avoid the pitfalls they weathered, while sharing the lessons they learned along the way. If you decide to complete coursework and have the opportunity to intern with a planner, you can often develop a connection that will stay with you and your business as you grow.

Don't discount the importance of a business-focused mentor to support your growth in running a home-based business. I have received invaluable advice from other successful home-based entrepreneurs on how to balance home and work, how to find good temporary help, and how to manage my business like a pro.

Apprenticeships

Before you begin the time-consuming and emotionally intense process of starting a business, consider serving time as an apprentice. There may be a seasoned planner out there who's looking for someone to handle day-to-day tasks and would be willing to train you and bring you up through the ranks. A retirement-age planner with no plan for passing the business to a family member might be willing to sell you his or her business when the time is right and provide you with a ready-made book of business to work with.

Above and Beyond

As you develop your business and planning skills and gather a strong portfolio of projects, you may reach a point where your home-office setting just isn't working for you. You have outgrown the two file cabinets you proudly purchased when your business was a fledgling. You walk into your home and see evidence of your business in every room and on every surface. Perhaps you cannot park your car in your garage or have run out of storage space for those unique "must-have" decorations that you've come to realize you'll use infrequently. It's time to think about the next step.

Expanding

If you truly like your home-office setup, consider staying where you are and expanding. Depending on your real estate market and your own personal situation, home expansion may allow you to create an office above a garage, or build another wing onto your home that can be later used as an in-law apartment or au pair suite. For some planners a small home-based business gives them the flexibility they want with the option for added income. It can be the perfect balance between family and work, without having to commit to climbing a corporate ladder. Only you know if your business is where you want it to be, or you're craving more.

Partnering

Perhaps joining forces with another planner may be attractive to you. Before you reach the breaking point, begin to examine the work style, ethics, and personalities of planners you may consider partnering with. They may have an office outside the home that would provide the necessary space for your blossoming business. You may find that your portfolio will complement theirs to provide an even wider array of services to clients.

With partnering comes consideration of the legal implications. Check with your attorney for issues relating to partnerships and ownership of your business. If you are both home-based and are leaving your homes to begin this new larger business, you'll be on an even playing field and have fewer issues with ownership fairness.

Adding Staff

When your business is at the point that you just can't do it all yourself—and your work is generating profit—it may be time to make the commitment to hiring employees. Depending on your home, this may necessitate a move to a larger space to provide a professional and productive environment for work. It would be wise to consider a storage area at this point as well to take back the personal space you've given up over the years with your event props and decor.

Hiring formal employees brings with it an array of legal and personnel issues. Consult with your attorney to find out the full ramifications of this move to make sure it's right for you.

What Else Is Out There?

You will reach a point in your business when you consider retirement or moving on to another venture. What kind of plan can you put into place for passing down or selling your business? If you've managed your finances well and show strong profits, you may have created an entity that is viable and attractive for purchase. Perhaps you've nurtured a strong assistant who has proven him- or herself and is interested in taking over the business. At the start of your business, these issues seem inconsequential, but as time goes on they become real decisions for you to ponder.

As you've worked through the exciting and challenging aspects of building your special event planning business, you may have discovered other areas that interest you. You may be intrigued to expand your offerings as you uncover skills and interests you didn't realize you had. You may see a niche market or unique aspect of the business that you want to explore. Don't be afraid to follow your heart, your talents, and current trends and market conditions to enable yourself to continue making money and enjoying what you do. There are no top secrets to running a successful business; it's simply a matter of passion for what you do, the ability to look at yourself critically, and the urge to be the best you can be. Take it one step at a time, and be proud that you create such pleasure for others by your excellence in planning special events!

Appendix A: School and Degree Programs

The following organizations and links offer online resources to locate educational opportunities relating to event and meeting management, travel and tourism, hospitality, culinary sciences, and trade show management:

American Hotel & Lodging Educational Institute: www.ahlei.org/

Convention Industry Council: www.conventionindustry.org/ or hospitality-1st.com/PressNews/Schools.html

Degree Directory: degreedirectory.org/articles/which_schools_offer_online_degrees_in_event_planning.html

Grad Schools: www.gradschools.com (www.gradschools.com/all-levels/hospitality-management)

International Special Events Society (professional development and education): www.ises.com

Meeting Professionals International: www.mpiweb.org/Professional Development

Special Events Institute (online certificate program): www.specialeventsinstitute.com

Appendix B: Professional Industry Organizations

AMC Institute
700 N. Fairfax Street, Suite 510
Alexandria, VA 22314
Phone: (571) 527-3108
Fax: (571) 527-3105
www.amcinstitute.org
AMC Institute is an international nonprofit trade association comprised of companies that provide association management and professional services to volunteer-governed organizations and for-profit companies. AMC Institute includes member companies that are demonstrated leaders in the association industry, committed to high quality and value-added association management and professional services.

American Hotel & Lodging Association (AH&LA)
1201 New York Avenue Northwest
Suite 600
Washington, DC 20005
Phone: (202) 289-3100
Fax: (202) 289-3199
www.ahla.com
The American Hotel & Lodging Association (AH&LA), founded in 1910 with over 11,000 hotel members, represents the interests of the US lodging industry at the national level on federal legislative and regulatory affairs, the national media, the educational community, research groups, and the general public.

American Society for Training and Development
1640 King Street, Box 1443
Alexandria, VA 22313-1443

Phone: (703) 683-8100
Fax: (703) 683-8103
www.astd.org
The American Society for Training and Development (ASTD) is the world's largest association dedicated to workplace learning and performance professionals. ASTD's members come from more than one hundred countries and connect locally in 130 US chapters and thirty global networks. Members work in thousands of organizations of all sizes, in government, as independent consultants, and as suppliers. ASTD started in 1944 when the organization held its first annual conference. ASTD has widened the profession's focus to link learning and performance to individual and organizational results and is a sought-after voice on critical public policy issues.

American Society of Association Executives (ASAE) & The Center for Association Leadership
1575 I Street Northwest
Washington, DC 20005
Phone: (202) 371-0940
Fax: (202) 371-8315
www.asaenet.org
The American Society of Association Executives (ASAE), founded in 1920 with 24,940 members, is dedicated to enhancing the professionalism and competency of association executives, promoting excellence in association management, and increasing the effectiveness of associations to better serve their clients.

Association for Convention Operations Management (ACOM)
191 Clarksville Road
Princeton Junction, NJ 08550
Phone: (609) 799-3712
Fax: (609) 799-7032
www.acomonline.org
The Association for Convention Operations Management (ACOM), founded in 1988 with 400 members, is an international organization for convention professionals. The association is dedicated to providing needs-directed continuing education, enhancing professional values and standards, and advancing and promoting quality customer services, to encourage growth and recognition of the convention services profession.

Association of Collegiate Conference and Events Directors–International (ACCED-I)
Colorado State University
2900 S. College Avenue, Suite 3B
Fort Collins, CO 80521
www.acced-i.org
Founded in 1980, the Association of Collegiate Conference and Events Directors–International (ACCED-I) is a nonprofit organization committed solely to the collegiate conference and events profession. Its mission is to improve, promote, and recognize excellence in the collegiate conference and events industry. Celebrating more than thirty years of service, ACCED-I is the premier resource for collegiate-based conference and event planners. Currently, ACCED-I has a membership of more than 1,400 professionals representing approximately 640 educational institutions and forty-one corporations in the United States, Canada, and the United Kingdom.

Association of Destination Management Executives (ADME)
PO Box 2307
Dayton, OH 45401-2307
Phone: (937) 586-3727
Fax: (937) 586-3699
www.adme.org
The mission of ADME is to increase the professionalism and effectiveness of destination management through education, promotion of ethical practices, and availability of information to the meeting, convention, and incentive travel industry and the general public.

Association of Fundraising Professionals (AFP)
4300 Wilson Boulevard., Suite 300
Arlington, VA 22203-4168
Phone: (800) 666-3863
www.afpnet.org
The Association of Fundraising Professionals (AFP) represents more than 30,000 members in 207 chapters throughout the world, working to advance philanthropy through advocacy, research, education, and certification programs.

Center for Exhibition Industry Research (CEIR)
12700 Park Central Drive, Suite 308
Dallas, TX 75251

Phone: (972) 687-9242
Fax: (972) 692-6020
www.ceir.org
CEIR is a nonprofit organization with the mission of advancing the growth, awareness, and value of exhibitions and other face-to-face marketing events by producing and delivering research-based knowledge tools. For more than thirty years, CEIR has been highlighting the importance of exhibitions in today's business environment.

Club Managers Association of America (CMAA)
1733 King Street
Alexandria, VA 22314
Phone: (703) 739-9500
Fax: (703) 739-0124
www.cmma.org
The Club Managers Association of America (CMAA) is the professional association for managers of membership clubs. With close to 7,000 members across all classifications, members run more than 3,000 country, golf, city, athletic, faculty, yacht, town, and military clubs. The objectives of the association are to promote and advance friendly relations among persons connected with the management of clubs and other associations of similar character; to encourage the education and advancement of its members; and to assist club officers and members, through their managers, to secure the utmost in efficient and successful operations.

Connected International Meeting Professionals Association (CIMPA)
info@cimpa.org
www.cimpa.org
Founded in 1982, CIMPA is an online association of buyers and sellers of meeting and travel products and services with a mission. The mission of CIMPA is to connect people of different cultures through meetings, travel, and the Internet for the purpose of promoting understanding, tolerance, and friendships. By being connected to each other and to resources on the Internet, members of this community will more easily share tools, information, and ideas to plan cost-effective and successful meetings, travel, and incentives. With more than 3,000 members in thirty-two countries on five continents, CIMPA's members collectively plan more than 100,000 meetings annually. Its annual International Technology, Meetings and Incentives Conference is held in different locations all over the world.

Convention Industry Council (CIC)
700 N. Fairfax Street, Suite 510
Alexandria, VA 22314
Phone: (571) 527-3116
Fax: (571) 527-3105
www.conventionindustry.org
The Convention Industry Council's thirty-two member organizations represent more than 103,500 individuals, as well as 19,500 firms and properties involved in the meetings, conventions, and exhibitions industries. Formed in 1949 to provide a forum for member organizations seeking to enhance the industry, the CIC facilitates the exchange of information, develops programs to promote professionalism within the industry, and educates the public on its profound economic impact. In addition to the CMP Program, CIC is also responsible for the Hall of Leaders Program as well as the Accepted Practices Exchange (APEX).

Destination Marketing Association International (DMAI)
US Office
2025 M Street Northwest, Suite 500
Washington, DC 20036
Phone: (202) 296-7888
Fax: (202) 296-7889

DMAI European Office
Avenue de Tervueren 300
Brussels, B-1150
Belgium
Phone: + 32 (0)2.789.23.44
Fax: + 32 (0)2.743.15.50
www.destinationmarketing.org
Destination Marketing Association International represents 1,350-plus professional members from more than 600 destination marketing organizations throughout thirty countries. Called the International Association of Convention & Visitor Bureaus until August 2005, the association has worked to enhance the professionalism, effectiveness, and image of CVBs and tourism boards since 1914.

Exhibit and Event Marketers Association (E2MA)
(formerly Trade Show Exhibitors Association [TSEA])
2214 NW 5th Street

Bend, OR 97701
Phone: (541) 317-8768
Fax: (541)317-8749
www.e2ma.org
E2MA is the premier content development organization for corporate marketers and their suppliers, who employ exhibit and event marketing. Driven to benchmark and promote the business value of trade shows and events, the mission of the E2MA is to optimize exhibit and event marketing programs by identifying, evaluating, and advancing new tools, new technologies, and best practices for the face-to-face marketing medium.

Exhibit Designers & Producers Association (EDPA)
10 Norden Place
Norwalk, CT 06855
Phone: (203) 852-5698
Fax: (203) 854-6735
www.edpa.com
Exhibit Designers & Producers Association (EDPA) members include exhibit designers; producers; systems manufacturers; distributors and marketers of custom, portable, and modular exhibits; show services contractors; exhibit transportation companies; event marketers; and organizations that provide related products or services to the exhibit industry. EDPA provides members with industry-specific education, advocacy, research, and marketing networking opportunities.

Exhibition Services & Contractors Association (ESCA)
2340 E. Trinity Mills Road, Suite 100
Carrollton, TX 75006
Phone: (877) 792-ESCA (3722) or (469) 574-0698
Fax: (469) 574-0697
www.esca.org
Exhibition Services & Contractors Association (ESCA) is the professional organization of firms engaged in the provision of material and/or services for trade shows, conventions, exhibitions, and sales meetings. ESCA is the voice of the exhibition service industry, and its purpose is to be a source of facts and answers to special problems that confront the convention service industry.

Financial and Insurance Conference Planners (FICP)
303 N. Wabash Avenue, Suite 2000
Chicago, IL 60611
Phone: (312) 245–1023
www.ficpnet.com
Financial and Insurance Conference Planners (FICP) is an association whose membership is comprised of meeting, convention, and conference planning professionals who work for or are under contract to insurance or financial services companies. Members exchange meeting management techniques and ideas that enhance the value of conferences and promote the professional stature and career growth of planners.

Healthcare Convention & Exhibitors Association (HCEA)
1100 Johnson Ferry Road, Suite 300
Atlanta, GA 30342
Phone: (678) 298-1183
Fax: (404) 836-5595
www.hcea.org
The Healthcare Convention & Exhibitors Association (HCEA) is a trade association of more than 670 organizations united by their common desire to increase the effectiveness and efficiency of health care conventions and exhibitions as an educational and marketing medium. HCEA promotes the value of exhibits as an integral part of health care meetings. HCEA offers its members a continuing opportunity to become more knowledgeable in their profession through meaningful communication, the exchange of ideas with other members, and the many services provided exclusively to HCEA members.

Hospitality Financial and Technology Professionals (HFTP)
11709 Boulder Lane, Suite 110
Austin, TX 78726-1832
Phone: (512) 249-5333; (800) 646-4387
Fax: (512) 249-1533
www.hftp.org
HFTP is an international professional association serving over 4,800 members working in hospitality. Since 1952, HFTP has been dedicated to providing members with extraordinary networking opportunities, industry-leading certification programs and events, and essential resources for professional growth.

Hospitality Sales & Marketing Association International (HSMAI)

US Office

1760 Old Meadow Road, Suite 500
McLean, VA 22102
Phone: (703) 506-3280
Fax: (703) 506-3266

European Region Office

Solli Plass Postbox 2418
0256 Oslo, Norway
Phone: +47 913 98 344
www.hsmai.org

The Hospitality Sales & Marketing Association International (HSMAI) represents travel sales and marketing professionals. Founded in 1927, HSMAI is an international individual membership organization comprising more than 5,000 members representing seventy-nine chapters in thirty-five countries, dedicated to enhancing sales and marketing management skills in the travel and hospitality industry through education and networking opportunities with peers and customers.

International Association for Exhibition & Events (IAEE) (formerly IAEM)

IAEE Headquarters

12700 Park Central Drive, Suite 308
Dallas, TX 75251
Phone: (972) 458-8002
Fax: (972) 458-8119

IAEE European Office

Brussels Expo
Place de Belgique
B-1020 Brussels
Belgium
Phone: +32 (0)2 474 85 37
Fax: +32 (0)2 474 84 88

IAEE Asia Pacific Office

1 Maritime Square, #09-43 HarbourFront Centre
Singapore 099253
Phone: (65) 6 278 8666
Fax: (65) 6 278 4077

IAEE China Office
Phone: +86-1084476820
Fax: +86-1084476822
www.iaee.com
The International Association for Exhibition & Events (IAEE) is the professional association for more than 3,200 individuals located in forty-one nations, and it is involved in the management and support of the global exhibition industry. IAEE's mission is to promote the exhibition industry throughout the world and to provide for the education and professional growth of its members.

International Association of Conference Centres (IACC)
35 E. Wacker Drive, Suite 850
Chicago, IL 60601-2106
Phone: (312) 224-2580
Fax: (312) 644-8557
www.iacconline.org
The International Association of Conference Centres (IACC) is the only global professional association that represents small to medium-sized venues focused on meetings, training courses, and conferences. All members conform to a comprehensive global set of criteria and standards. IACC serves its members as the global leader in the meetings industry and currently has 400 members in twenty-one countries in the Americas, Europe, and Australasia.

International Association of Culinary Professionals (IACP)
1100 Johnson Ferry Road, Suite 300
Atlanta, GA 30342
Phone: (404) 252-3663
Fax: (404) 252-0774
www.iacp.com
IACP is a not-for-profit professional association that provides continuing education and development for its members, who are engaged in the areas of culinary education, communication, or in the preparation of food and drink. The worldwide membership of nearly 4,000 encompasses more than thirty-five countries. This diversity not only offers unique insight into the world's cuisines but provides excellent networking opportunities. IACP's vision is to be an international forum for the development and exchange of information, knowledge, and inspiration within the professional food community worldwide.

International Association of Speakers Bureaus (IASB)
4015 S. McClintock Drive, Suite 110
Tempe, AZ 85282
Phone: (480) 839-1423
Fax: (480) 603-4141
www.iasbweb.org
IASB member bureaus subscribe to a code of professional conduct and accepted practices. Being in direct contact with an IASB member bureau assures the meeting professional of securing the right speaker and/or trainer for their event. In many cases, IASB speakers' bureaus hold the key to a successful event.

International Congress and Convention Association (ICCA)
Toren A, De Entree 57, 1101 BH
Amsterdam
The Netherlands
Phone: 31-20-398-1919
Fax: 31-20-699-0781
www.iccaworld.com
With more than 600 member organizations and companies in eighty countries, ICCA provides a worldwide network of meeting professionals, experts in all aspects of hosting and organizing congresses and conventions. ICCA offers its members unique opportunities to access comprehensive meetings data, exchange business leads, and meet potential clients. ICCA represents all the various professional meeting suppliers, such as congress travel and destination management companies; airlines; professional congress, convention, and/or exhibition organizers; tourist and convention bureaus; meeting information and technical specialists; ICCA meeting hotels; and convention and exhibition centers.

International Special Events Society (ISES)
330 N. Wabash Avenue
Chicago, IL 60611
Phone: (312) 321-6853
Fax: (312) 673-6953
www.ises.com
The mission of ISES is to educate, advance, and promote the special events industry and its network of professionals along with related industries. To that end, it strives to uphold the integrity of the special events profession, acquire and disseminate useful business information, foster a spirit of cooperation among its

members and other special events professionals, and cultivate high standards of business practices.

Meeting Professionals International (MPI)
3030 LBJ Freeway, Suite 1700
Dallas, TX 75234
Phone: (972) 702-3000
Fax: (972) 702-3070

Canadian Office
6700 Century Avenue, Suite 100
Mississauga, Ontario L5N 6A4 Canada
Phone: +1 905-286-4807
Fax: +1 905-567-7191
www.mpiweb.org
Established in 1972, MPI is the largest association for the meeting profession, with more than 24,000 members in sixty-eight chapters and clubs across the United States, Canada, Europe, and other countries. As the global authority and resource for the $122.3 billion dollar meetings and events industry, MPI empowers meeting professionals to increase their strategic value through education, clearly defined career pathways, and business growth opportunities. MPI launched Pathways to Excellence in 2003, which has taken meetings to the next level of inclusion in the business world.

National Association of Casino Party Operators
PO Box 5626
San Francisco, CA 94083
Phone: (888) 922-0777
www.nacpo.com
The professional members of NACPO are committed to providing the best possible products, services, and assistance to achieve the objectives of its members' customers. They strive for excellence in all aspects of the profession, and maintain the highest standards of personal and professional conduct to bring credit to the association. In all industry practices, they use only the highest legal, ethical, and safety standards.

National Association of Catering Executives (NACE)
9881 Broken Land Parkway, Suite 101
Columbia, MD 21046
Phone: (410) 290-5410
Fax: (410) 290-5460
www.nace.net
The National Association of Catering Executives (NACE), founded in 1958, is the oldest and largest professional association for caterers in all disciplines and their affiliate vendors. With more than 3,000 members in forty-six chapters, NACE serves hotels, off-premise, club, military, and on-premise caterers, providing top-quality educational and networking opportunities and affiliate vendor interaction.

National Business Travel Association (NBTA)
123 N. Pitt Street
Alexandria, VA 22314
Phone: (703) 684-0836
Fax: (703) 342-4324
www.nbta.org
The National Business Travel Association (NBTA) is the source for critical information on the business travel industry. For more than thirty-five years, NBTA has dedicated itself to the professional development of its members through advocacy, education and training, and networking opportunities. NBTA represents more than 4,000 corporate travel managers and travel service providers, who collectively manage and direct more than $200 billion of expenditures within the business travel industry.

National Coalition of Black Meeting Planners (NCBMP)
700 N. Fairfax Street, Suite 510
Alexandra, VA 22314
Phone: (571) 527-3110
www.ncbmp.com
The National Coalition of Black Meeting Planners (NCBMP), founded in 1983, is a nonprofit organization dedicated primarily to the training needs of African American meeting planners. It is the purpose of NCBMP to be the preeminent organization in education of the African-American meeting planner in all aspects of the meeting planning profession.

National Speakers Association (NSA)
1500 S. Priest Drive
Tempe, AZ 85281
Phone: (480) 968-2552
Fax: (480) 968-0911
www.nsaspeaker.org
The National Speakers Association (NSA) is an international association of more than 3,800 members dedicated to advancing the art and value of experts who speak professionally. For more than twenty-five years, NSA has provided resources and education designed to enhance the business acumen and platform performance of professional speakers.

Professional Convention Management Association (PCMA)
35 E. Wacker Drive, Suite 500
Chicago, IL 60601
Phone: (312) 423-7262
Fax: (312) 423-7222
www.pcma.org
The mission of the Professional Convention Management Association (PCMA) is to serve the association community by enhancing the effectiveness of meetings, conventions, and exhibitions through member and industry education and to promote the value of the meetings industry to the general public.

Religious Conference Management Association (RCMA)
7702 Woodland Drive, Suite 120
Indianapolis, IN 46278
Phone: (317) 632-1888
Fax: (317) 632-7909
www.rcmaweb.org
The Religious Conference Management Association (RCMA) is a professional nonprofit interfaith organization of men and women who have responsibility for planning and/or managing meetings, conferences, conventions, or assemblies for religious organizations. Founded in 1972, RCMA is dedicated to enhancing the professionalism of its members and to improving the experience of religious meeting attendees throughout the world.

Society of American Florists (SAF)
1601 Duke Street
Alexandria, VA 22314
Phone: (703) 836-8700
Fax: (703) 836-8705
www.safnow.org
SAF is the only national trade association that represents all segments of the US floral industry. Its 15,000 members are the industry's top retailers, growers, wholesalers, importers, manufacturers, suppliers, educators, students, and allied organizations. SAF is the face and voice of a strong, unified floral industry.

Society of Government Meeting Professionals (SGMP)
908 King Street, Lower Level
Alexandria, VA 22314
Phone: (703) 549-0892
Fax: (703) 549-0708
www.sgmp.org
The Society of Government Meeting Professionals (SGMP) is dedicated to improving the knowledge and expertise of individuals in planning and execution of government meetings through education, training, and industry relationships. The society has twenty-eight chapters with more than 3,500 members.

Society of Incentive & Travel Executives (SITE)
330 N. Wasbash
Chicago, IL 60611
Phone: (312) 321-5148
www.siteglobal.com
The Society of Incentive & Travel Executives (SITE) is a worldwide organization of business professionals dedicated to the increased recognition and use of incentives as a motivator and reward in programs designed to achieve defined objectives. Founded in 1973, SITE is comprised of thirty-five chapters with 2,100 individual members representing more than eighty-seven countries.

Appendix C: Recommended Reading

Business Books

Applegate, Jane. *201 Great Ideas for Your Small Business*. Princeton: Bloomberg Press, 1998.

Jones, Laurie Beth. *Jesus, CEO*. New York: Hyperion, 1995. Third Edition, Bloomberg Press, 2011.

Kantor, Rosabeth Moss. *World Class: Thriving Locally in the Global Economy*. New York: Touchstone, 1995.

Parinello, Anthony. *Selling to Vito*. Holbrook, Mass.: Adams Media Corporation, 1999.

Pine, B. Joseph II, and James H. Gilmore. *The Experience Economy*. Boston: Harvard Business School Press, 1999.

Williams, Terrie. *The Personal Touch*. New York: Warner Books, 1994.

Creativity Boosters

Magazines: *Architectural Digest, Elle Decor, Garden Design, House Beautiful, House & Garden, Martha Stewart Living, Metropolitan Home, Real Simple, Town & Country, Veranda, BizBash Special Events Magazine, Wedding Planner Mag, Meetings Net, Meeting and Conventions www.slideshare.net/BrooksSpeakersBureau/top-magazines-and-publications-for-event-planners (this has a list of popular magazines for event planning)*

Event Basics

Goldblatt, Joe, CSEP. *Special Events: Creating and Sustaining a New World for Celebration*. Seventh Edition. New York: John Wiley & Sons, 2013.

Goldblatt, Joe, CSEP, and Kathleen S. Nelson, CSEP. *The International Dictionary of Event Management*. Second Edition. New York: John Wiley & Sons, 2001.

Hemela, Deborah Ann. *The Sourcebook: Props, Set Dressing & Wardrobe*. Altadena, Calif.: Debbies Book, 2002–2003.

Nonprofit Risk Management Center. *Managing Special Event Risks*. Washington, D.C.: Nonprofit's Insurance Alliance of California, 1997.

Professional Convention Management Association. *Professional Meeting Management*. Birmingham: Professional Convention Management Association, 1996.

Tutera, David, and Laura Morton. *A Passion for Parties*. New York: Simon & Schuster, 2001.

Silvers, Julia Rutherfor, *Professional Event Coordination*. Second Edition. New York: John Wiley & Sons, 2012.

Wiersma, Elizabeth A., CSEP, and Kari E. Strolberg. *Exceptional Events: Concept to Completion*. Weimar, Tex.: Chips Books, 2003.

Home Office

Morgenstern, Julie. *Organizing from the Inside Out*. New York: Henry Holt & Company, 1998.

———. *Time Management from the Inside Out*. New York: Henry Holt & Company, 2000.

Life Balance

Ford, Debbie. *The Dark Side of the Light*. New York: Riverhead Books, 1998.

McGraw, Philip. *Self Matters: Creating Your Life from the Inside Out*. New York: Free Press, 2001.

Richardson, Cheryl. *Life Makeovers*. New York: Broadway Books, 2000.

———. *Stand Up for Your Life*. New York: Free Press, 2002.

———. *Take Time for Your Life*. New York: Broadway Books, 1998.

Networking

Carnegie, Dale. *How to Win Friends and Influence People*. New York: Simon & Schuster, 1982.

Darling, Diane. *The Networking Survival Guide*. New York: McGraw-Hill, 2003.

Appendix D: Internet Resources

Bar and Bat Mitzvahs

www.myjewishlearning.com/life/Life_Events/BarBat_Mitzvah/Practical_Aspects/Planning_Guide.shtml

www.mitzvahorganizer.com

www.bnaimitzvahguide.com

www.barbatmitzvahguide.com

Budgeting/Financial Planning

Microsoft
smallbusiness.support.microsoft.com/en-us/gp/expert=tips

Career
www.eventmanagerblog.com/top-5-qualities
smallbusiness.chron.com/top-10-customer-service-skills-events-coordinator-13268.html

Resources
www.emcvenues.com/education-connections/education-resources#mtgplannerresource

Home Business Magazine
www.homebusinessmag.com

About
financialplan.about.com/msubbudg.htm

Intuit—makers of QuickBooks, Quicken
www.quicken.com

Expense Watch
www.expensewatch.com

US Small Business Association
www.sba.gov

Business Week Online
www.businessweek.com/small-business

American Express
www.americanexpress.com

Business Planning

US Small Business Administration
www.sba.gov

Score
www.score.org

American Express Small Business
www.openforum.com

PricewaterhouseCoopers
www.pwc.com

Small Business Info Canada
sbinfocanada.about.com/od/businessplans

SoYouWanna.Com
www.soyouwanna.com/site/syws/bizplan/bizplan.html

Entrepreneur Magazine Online
www.entrepreneur.com/businessplan/index.html

Microsoft Small Business Center
http://smallbusiness.support.microsoft.com/en-us

Small Business/About
sbinformation.about.com/od/businessplans

Event Planning Tools

The Great Event
www.thegreatevent.com

Meetings Industry Megasite: Tools, resources, articles, and news
www.mimegasite.com/mimegasite/index.jsp

Catering Resources

Caterease/Horizon Business Services
(800) 863-1616
www.caterease.com

CaterPro
(916) 645-8484
www.caterprosoftware.com

Caterware
(877) 513-2263
www.caterware.com

Culinary Software Services
(303) 447-3334
www.culinarysoftware.com

Synergy International
(800) 522-6210
www.synergy-intl.com

Event Business Management Resources

NetSuite
(800) NETSUITE
www.netsuite.com

Event Management Software

ReServe Interactive/Efficient Frontiers
www.efficient-frontiers.com

TimeSaver Software
(512) 943-9110
www.timesaversoftware.com

Vivien Layout Software/Cast Software
www.viviendesign.com

Rental Resources

Party Track/Event Rental Systems
(520) 777-0712
www.partytrack.com

General Special Events Resources

thestir.cafemom.com/food_party
www.evite.com
www.orientaltrading.com
www.paperlesspost.com
www.partyspot.co.za
www.party411.com
www.party.lifetips.com
www.shindigz.com
specialevents.com
www.thepartyspotonline.com
www.windycitynovelties.com

Fund-Raising/Nonprofit

www.usa.gov/Business/Nonprofit.shtml
npconnect.org
www.not-for-profit.org
www.fundraising.co.uk
www.fundraisingnetwork.org
www.fundraisingdirectory.com

Legal/Ethical Issues

ASCAP
www.ascap.com

BMI
www.bmi.com

Performing rights organization for songwriters and publishers:
www.SESAC.com

Convention Industry Council
www.conventionindustry.org
www.conventionindustry.org/Blog.aspx

APEX
www.conventionindustry.org/StandardsPractices/APEX.aspx

Marketing

Entrepreneur magazine
www.entrepreneur.com/topic/marketing

U.S. Small Business Association
www.sba.gov/category/navigation-structure/starting-managing-business/managing-business/running-business/marketing

More Business
www.morebusiness.com

Small Business UK
www.smallbusiness.co.uk

About.com
marketing.about.com/od/marketingbasics/a/smmktgbasics.htm

Microsoft
www.microsoft.com/enterprise/business-leaders/reimagine-marketing/default.aspx#fbid=7PLSPoFfwM8

Small Business Canada
sbinfocanada.about.com

Business Link
www.gov.uk/browse/business

Meeting/Conference Planning

Star Cite
(800) 430-8027
www.starcite.com

Eventbrite
www.eventbrite.com

Certain Software
(888) 237-8246
www.certain.com

Successful Meetings
www.mimegasite.com

Decor

Dream World Backdrops: www.dreamworldbackdrops.com

Registration Systems

www.cvent.com
www.regonline.com
www.ersvp.com
www.certain.com

Liability and legal issues

www.corbinball.com/articles_legal/index.cfm?fuseaction=cor_ArticleView&artid=498&sectionCode=art_legal

Contracts and insurance

www.northeastern.edu/events/planning_resources/legal_issues.html

Skills and customer service

smallbusiness.chron.com/top-10-customer-service-skills-events-coordinator-13268.html

Products/Vendors

BBJ Linen
www.bbjlinen.com

Cloth Connection
www.clothconnection.com

The Candle Shop
www.candleshop.com

NJ Candle Company
www.njcandle.com

Rentals Unlimited
www.rentals-unlimited.net

Sensia Candles
www.sensia.com

GBS Linens
www.gbslinens.com

Table Toppers
www.tabletoppersinc.com

Wedding Resources

www.weddingsolutions.com
www.brides.com
www.knotforlife.com
www.theknot.com
www.yourwedding101.com

Work/Life Balance

management.about.com/od/lifeworkbalance

www.business.com/directory/human_resources/work_and_life

www.worklifebalance.com/work-life-balance-defined.html

www.humanresources.about.com/od/glossaryw/g/balance.htm

Organization

www.homeofficelife.com/ask_expert.html

www.queensofclutter.com

www.organizingresources.com/1index2.htm

Stress Management

www.stressbusting.co.uk

www.helpguide.org/articles/stress/stress-management.htm

Time Management Tips

www.timemanagementgoals.com

www.ineedmoretime.com/time_tips.htm

Other websites that could be helpful:

www.entrepreneur.com/article/37892

eventplannersassociation.com/education-resource-event-professional-event-toolbox-newsletter-archives/

Index

About the Author

Jill S. Moran, CSEP began her career in special event planning in 1990 by planning a client reception for five hundred guests attending an international trade show. Drawing on her background in the arts, exhibit and display experience, and instinct for creativity and planning she expanded her event business to include nonprofit events, weddings, and social celebrations.

She has grown her award-winning event planning and management company, jsmoran special events, by providing creative advice and full-scale implementation and production services for special events ranging from multi-day destination weddings, corporate outings, sales and marketing events to conferences, trade shows, galas, and exclusive parties. She has hosted events and weddings in cities across the country and internationally in locations ranging from museums and yachts to convention centers and wineries. Her events have been televised on Entertainment Tonight and E!. She has been showcased on Boston's Channel 7 WHDH-TV sharing design and party decorating ideas.

She has served on several international committees for the International Special Events Society and has been president for the New England chapter. She was one of the first designated Certified Special

Events Professionals in the New England area. She has won five prestigious ESPRIT awards including Best Industry Contribution for *How to Start a Home-Based Event Planning Business, How to Start a Home-Based Wedding Planning Business,* and the Special Events Institute. She has lectured at the Canadian Special Events & Meeting Expo, Eventworld, The Special Event and ISES Regional Education Conferences, has participated on panel discussions for industry conferences throughout the United States and in Canada, and is an adjunct professor at Newbury College, located outside of Boston, Massachusetts. She is passionate about education and special events and is proud to have developed the Special Events Institute, an online certificate program providing valuable training for event planners.

Her varied background includes a degree in Education, MBA coursework, and continued involvement in the arts and education. She lives in Massachusetts with her family and continues to enjoy creating the life of the party!

The University of Padua

Eight Centuries of History

Edited by Piero Del Negro

Signumpadova
EDITRICE

Editorial Direction
Paolo Scapolo

Technical editor
Italo Novelli

ACKNOWLEDGEMENTS
The editors and publishers are grateful to the following bodies for permission to reproduce photographic material.
The Musei Civici of Padua for the photographs on pages:
23, 32, 69b, 83, 87, 93, 95, 96, 97, 103, 104, 114, 146a, 147, 149c, 154, 183a, 191a, 193, 198, 205b, 212a, 212b, 213a, 217a, 224a, 224b, 232b, 247a, 252b, 262, 265, 271;

The University Library of Padua for the photographs on pages:
18, 27b, 74, 148a, 150, 168b, 210b, 210c, 214

The Messaggero di Sant'Antonio for the photographs on pages:
22, 27a, 223

The valuable advice of the Centre for the History of the University of Padua is gratefully acknowledged.

The photographs on the cover and pages 29, 42- 43, 46, 47, 56-7, 66, 76, 85, 90, 131, 133, 134, 194, 228, 233, 249, 250, 258, 272, 274 and 283 are by Francesco and Matteo Danesin.

ISBN 88-8475-008-3

Photolithography and printed by:
Offset Invicta Padova s.r.l. – Limena (Pd)

Original title: L'Università di Padova. Otto secoli di storia
Translation from the Italian:
Hilary Siddons, Helen Deborah Walberg

Via Adria, 27 - 35142 Padova
Tel. + 39 049 8827622 - Fax + 39 049 8826740
signumeditrice@interfree.it

Index

Gymnasii Patauini Rector.

Pro-Rector & Syndicus.

I believe that history is an irrefutable dimension of life, that ignorance of the past renders us blind when confronting the challenges of the present. This is even more true when the life in question is that of a centuries-old institution like the University of Padua, after Bologna the oldest Studium generale in Italy, and one of the most ancient in Europe. It is therefore with the greatest satisfaction that I present The University of Padua. Eight Centuries of History, *a volume whose rich illustrations do not mask, as can occasionally happen, a paucity of content, but on the contrary offer the reader a brilliant synthesis of the complex politico-institutional history of our University and its principal contributions in the scientific and cultural sphere, the work of some of the major specialists in these areas.*

The need for a publication of this type, of a historical synthesis that unites scientific validity with a popular format, has been profoundly felt for a long time – one could say since 1922, when Antonio Favaro published a clear historical-institutional profile as part of the University's celebration of its seventh centennial. These eighty years have not been lacking in attempts to promote a collection of studies which would allow the history of the University to be retraced in its broad outlines, and which could have made use of the patrimony of monographic studies and editions of sources which have been accumulating since the late nineteenth century, thanks in particular to Andrea Gloria, Favaro himself, Biagio Brugi, Paolo Sambin, Lucia Rossetti and Loris Premuda. But the target was unfulfilled by the Magnificent Rector Carlo Anti, the promoter, on the eve of the Second World War and in view of the Exposition of 1942, of a collection of studies destined for the most part to remain unpublished, and by the Magnificent Rector Mario Bonsembiante, when he relaunched a similar initiative a decade ago.

I am therefore most grateful to the Centre for the History of the University of Padua and, in particular, to its director Piero Del Negro for having stressed, on the occasion of the inauguration of the timely Project Bo 2022, *the necessity of producing as soon as possible– and besides* The University of Padua through the centuries, *a great collection of documents of political-institutional history, whose first volume is soon to be published - the volume which I present here. I would also like to extend my thanks to Del Negro for having edited this volume; to the authors of the studies collected here, who for the first time have allowed a complete picture to be drawn of an institution which has played a prominent part both in cultural and civic history; to the publisher Paolo Scapolo, who has believed in and devoted much time and energy to the initiative; to Italo Novelli, who has expended enthusiastic care on the visual aspect of the book; and to the* Fondazione Cassa di Risparmio di Padova e Rovigo, *which has offered its backing for its publication.*

GIOVANNI MARCHESINI

Rector of the University of Padua

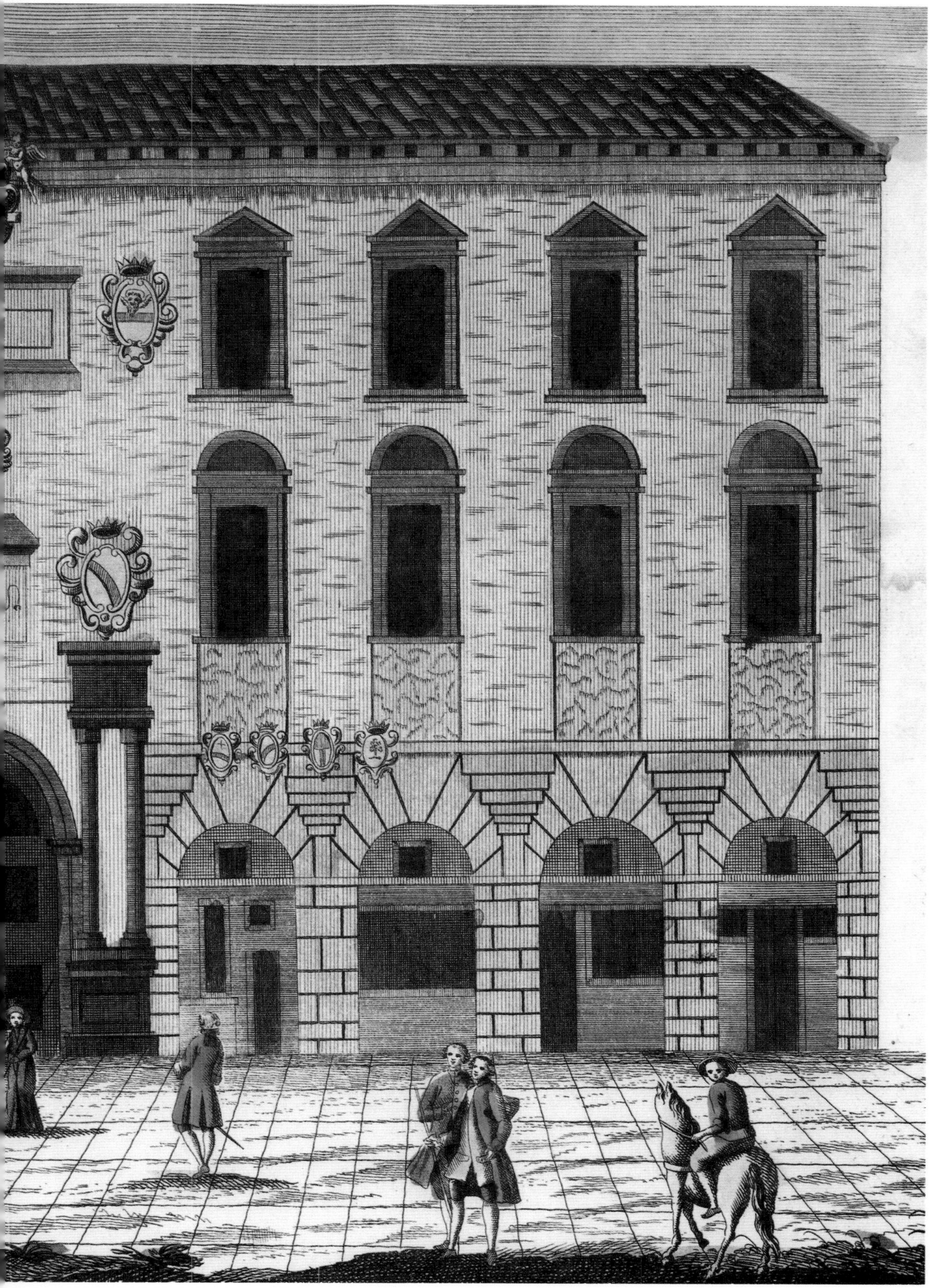

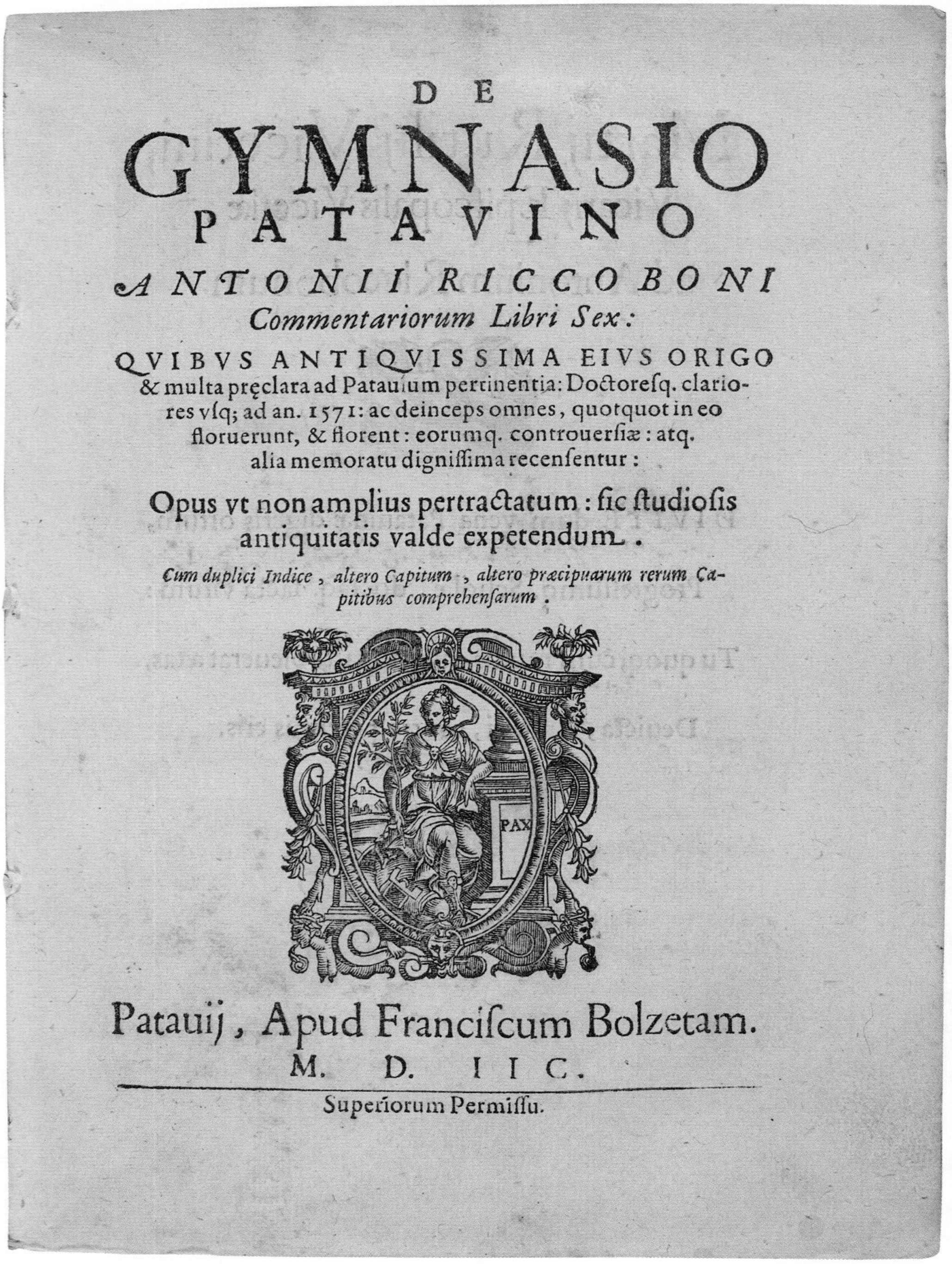

DE

GYMNASIO PATAVINO

ANTONII RICCOBONI

Commentariorum Libri Sex:

QVIBVS ANTIQVISSIMA EIVS ORIGO & multa pręclara ad Patauium pertinentia: Doctoresq. clariores vsq; ad an. 1571: ac deinceps omnes, quotquot in eo floruerunt, & florent: eorumq. controuersiæ: atq. alia memoratu dignissima recensentur:

Opus vt non amplius pertractatum: sic studiosis antiquitatis valde expetendum.

Cum duplici Indice, altero Capitum, altero præcipuarum rerum Capitibus comprehensarum.

PAX

Patauij, Apud Franciscum Bolzetam.

M. D. IIC.

Superiorum Permissu.

PIERO DEL NEGRO

Introduction

The University of Padua boasts an important tradition of studies on its extremely long history (it is enough to remember that from 1739 to 1806 its staff included a professor of the History of the University of Padua, certainly the first academic formalization of this disciplinary field in Italy, and probably in the world), yet it has remained up till now without a historical synthesis able to satisfy the needs of the general public and at the same time reach the standards demanded of a scientific publication. Perhaps it was the very richness of the sources, both published and inedited, and the overabundance of monographic studies on various aspects of the history of the University which have long discouraged any attempts in this direction. What is certain is that *The University of Padua. Eight Centuries of History* is intended to fulfil the function of intermediary between specialized research and the wider public, but also act as a stimulus for further research, since it tackles historical periods and themes that have remained until now in the margins of historical debate.

The volume presented here is organized around two major themes: the institutional and political history, and the history of science and culture. From the chronological point of view, the most important division is that between medieval and early modern history on the one hand, and modern history on the other. The date for the watershed is 1806, the year in which the Veneto region became part of the Napoleonic Kingdom of Italy and the University of Padua lost the institutional autonomy it had enjoyed under the previous political regimes, from the Padua of the Commune (1222-1318), and the signoria (1318-1405), to the Padua of the long Venetian domination (1406-1797) and the very brief first Habsburg rule (1798-1805). After 1806 it was rendered uniform to the other two Universities of the Kingdom, Pavia and Bologna, which had already received a single organizational structure a few years earlier. In the course of the second and third periods of Austrian rule (1813-48 and 1848-66: two phases separated by the revolutionary blaze of the spring of 1848, one of the first manifestations of which was the riot of students and citizens in Padua on February the 8th), the institutions which the University referred to were those of Vienna, Prague, and Pavia, while, after the annexation of the Veneto to Italy in 1866, it was inserted - not without resistance - into the

Antonio Riccoboni, De Gymnasio Patavino

University system of the Kingdom of Savoy and was run on the basis of the Casati Law of 1859.

1806 was also an important date for the history of science and culture in so far as it marked the disappearance of the traditional bipartite division of the Studium into a 'university' of jurists and a 'university' of artists (that is to say, physicians, 'philosophers' and theologians), and the beginning of a system based on faculties. With the passing of the decades, this new system was to take ever-increasing account of the professional needs of society, and was therefore to add to the centuries-old tradition of lawyers, physicians, and theologians, those more or less recent figures the engineers, pharmacists, veterinary surgeons, agronomists, mathematicians, physicists, biologists, diplomats and experts in politics in general, statisticians, teachers of literary subjects, psychologists, and economists, to name a few.

A place of teaching, but also of research, the University of Padua has had among its masters and students figures of great international renown in the most disparate fields, from medicine to law, from theology to philosophy, from literature to engineering, from astronomy to physics, from politics to religion. Among these, to quote but a few from the medieval and early modern period, centuries which saw Padua attract teachers and students from all of Europe, were figures such as Pietro d'Abano, Albertus Magnus, Baldo degli Ubaldi, Marsilio of Padua, Nicolaus Cusanus, Vittorino da Feltre, Pico della Mirandola, Nicholas Copernicus, Erasmus of Rotterdam, Francesco Guicciardini, Girolamo Fracastoro, Pietro Pomponazzi, Andreas Vesalius, Francis of Sales, Torquato Tasso, Stefan Báthory, Francis Walsingham, Gabriele Falloppia, Girolamo Fabrici D'Acquapendente, Tommaso Campanella, Cesare Cremonini, Galileo Galilei, William Harvey, Saint Gregorio Barbarigo, Elena Lucrezia Cornaro Piscopia (the first woman in the world to graduate), Geminiano Montanari, Bernardino Ramazzini, Giovanni Poleni, Antonio Vallisneri, Giambattista Morgagni, Carlo Goldoni, Giacomo Casanova, Melchiorre Cesarotti, and Giovanni Capodistria.

An immense cultural and civic heritage, a role at the very forefront of the education of scientific, political, and professional *élites*: it is to the rediscovery of the past of a University which Erasmus exalted as "a highly-equipped and most famous emporium of the best disciplines", of a past in which the present has embedded its roots and rediscovers its own identity, that this volume is dedicated.

Political and istitutional history

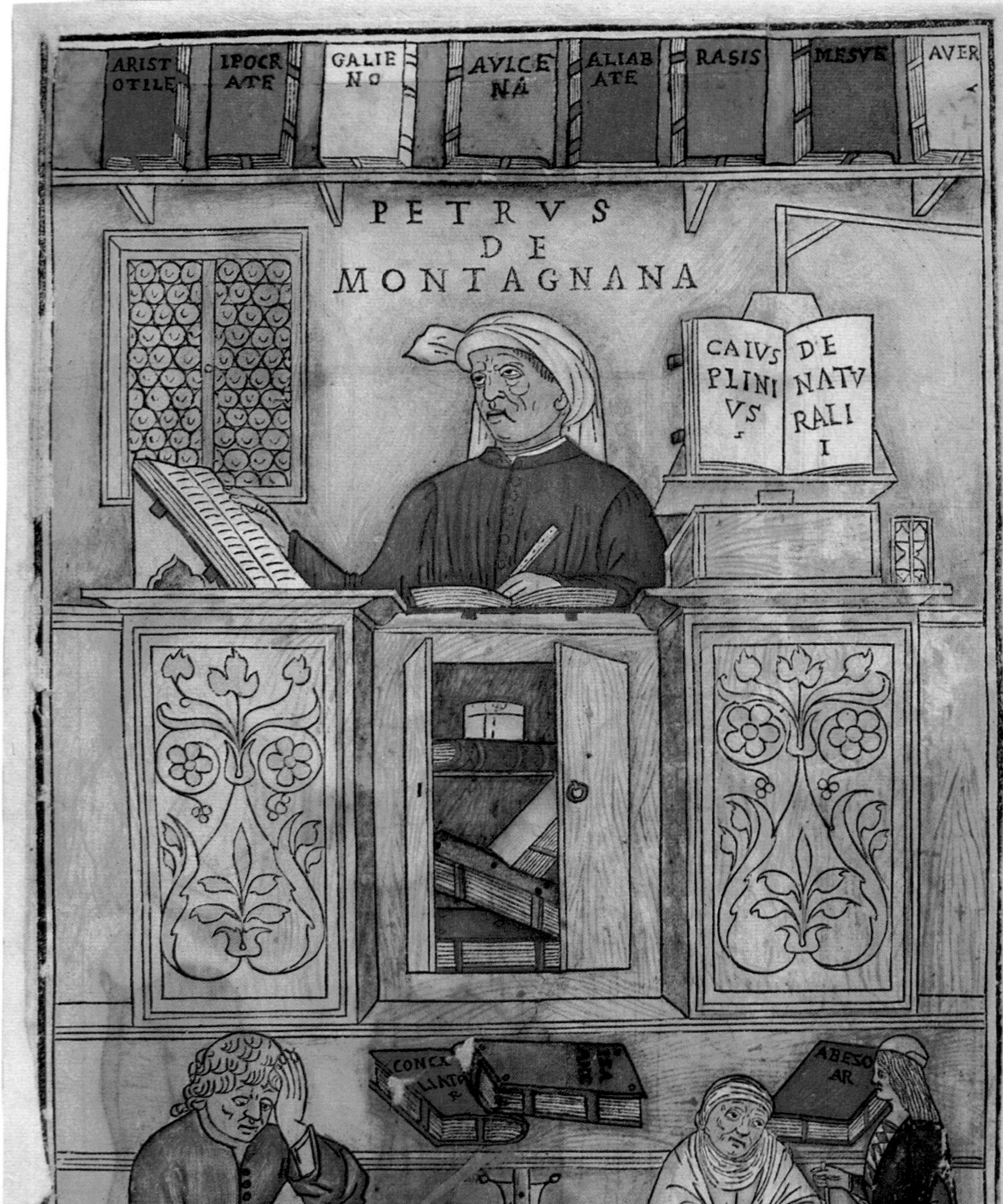
ARIST OTILE
IPOCR ATE
GALIE NO
AVICE NA
ALIAB ATE
RASIS
MESVE
AVER
PETRVS DE MONTAGNANA
CAIVS PLINI VS
DE NATV RALI
ABESO AR

DONATO GALLO

The Medieval Period

Origins and the Age of the Commune

"1222. Messer Giovanni Rusca of Como, podestà *of Padua. In this period the Studium of Bologna was transferred to Padua, and on Christmas Day after mass there was a great earthquake".*

This piece of information, included in the ancient compilations of the thirteenth-century *Annals* of Padua, attests the foundation date traditionally accepted for the origin of the University of Padua. The concept of 'foundation' is ambiguous and substantially inexact, however, in the case of medieval University institutions, with few and circumscribed exceptions. Andrea Gloria, the nineteenth-century Paduan historian who employed his gifts as paleographer and archivist to reconstructing the first two centuries of the University, established that the beginning of lessons for the academic year of 1222 would have been either the 29th of September or the 1st of October: a likely-enough date, even if the final months of 1222 were not particularly propitious due to the violent earthquake known as "of Brescia". But of course we must not take the transferral of the Studium of Bologna literally since it could not have been total, and we must not imagine a framework already completely structured in forms and rituals that were substantially of a later date.

The University of Padua however represents one of the paradigmatic cases of a medieval University born from the migration of a group of students from a pre-existing University seat. In the first decades of the thirteenth-century students flocked from every part of the western world to the schools made famous by the jurists teaching in Bologna; but in order to escape the increasing controls imposed by the Commune on the student corporations against the traditional "scholastic freedom" guaranteed by the Emperor Frederick I, on several occasions they swarmed to other cities which had shown themselves hospitable to their studies or which were able to attract the learned with the prospect of better living conditions.

Unlike the experiences of ephemeral Studia, the transplant of the University schools to Padua had a successful outcome, analogous to what had happened a few years earlier in another context for Cambridge with respect to Oxford. Above all, the functioning of the University was undoubtedly continuous, documentable for about twenty years, from the

Table of the Fasciculo de medicina, *Venice 1494*

mid-1220's to the beginning of the 1240's. This fact clearly distinguishes the Bolognese migration to Padua from the slightly earlier one to Vicenza (1205-1209), which was not able to take root completely.

Regarding the origins of the Studium it must be stressed, however, as the latest historical research has shown, that beneath the 'spontaneous' origins of the University of Padua there existed a network of favourable conditions, both internal and on a wider level, of connections with other cities. There existed in the environment of Padua itself a growing request for a cultural formation at a high level (already detected in the second half of the twelfth century, when some Paduans studied at the Studium at Bologna), both in the context of the Commune and in that of the local ecclesiastical institutions, and this, together finally with its connection with the powerful dynasty of the Marquis of Este, meant that in the first decades of the thirteenth century Padua represented the ideal soil on which to build a school of University level. There is significant documentary evidence of teachers and pupils, even if they are numerically limited. Nevertheless, following the fundamental observations made by Girolamo Arnaldi, there are many clues to indicate the consolidated existence of schools of jurists over a reasonable period of time, and it is possible to attest to the existence of the associative organization assumed by the 'university' of the students and masters, thanks, for example, to their receiving the official collections of papal decretals in the 1230's. Moreover, as Grado Merlo has recently pointed out, the arrival in the city from 1226 of the Dominican friars, with their initiative of proselytism among the schoolmen, allows us to place Padua on a level not that far from the other major University seats of the time, Paris and Bologna, or the more recent Toulouse and Vercelli.

In Padua between 1224 and 1241 we find students and doctors from various European countries, above all from the German-speaking areas, but there were also Frenchmen, Provençals, Englishmen, Spaniards, Poles, Czechs, and Hungarians, besides the students of Italian extraction. In 1228 a migratory movement of cisalpine and transalpine students (but, from what we know, not the Germanic group) left Padua in the direction of the Studium which the city of Vercelli, in the west of the Po valley, wanted to open; but the Paduan schools continued to function for more than another decade. After Padua succumbed to the power of Ezzelino III da Romano in 1237, the schools of jurists survived for a few years, only to disappear after 1241 without leaving a trace. In the following years, however - gathering clues from very little documentation - presences were limited to the sector of the liberal arts, the presence of notaries, and certainly medicine: in 1250-52 Bruno of Longoburgo, author of an important treatise on surgery, was active in Padua. It was precisely the field of the philosophical and medical sciences that was in the forefront of the University revival of the post-Ezzelino period: in 1262, in fact, in the cloister of Sant'Urbano (one of the various seats of teaching, since the University schools, which did not acquire a centralized seat until the end of the fifteenth century, were scattered mainly throughout the district of San Biagio), Rolandino of Padua presented his vast chronicle, which summed up the preceding turbulent decades in a passionate but also reticent portrait, and presented it for approval to his colleagues, the masters of 'arts' and of medicine, now reunited into a corporation.

Regarding the structure of the medieval University, Giorgio Cencetti has spoken rightly of a "conceptual unity" that "is not translated into an organic unity", writing "that the concept of university as a complex of courses, masters, and students [...] is totally modern. The Middle Ages, though not refuting the idea of a conceptual unity of the *Studium*, preferred to attribute legal status and corporate regulation to the single entities which added together constituted it".

One can easily recognize three distinct components in the Padua Studium too. Indeed the Padua Studium was structured in a way completely analogous to that of Bologna in its mature (thirteenth-century) model, and was tightly linked to it because of an evident influence which was often a conscious imitation of its organizational model: the corporations of students or 'universities' in the strict sense; the colleges of doctors, with the function of administering examinations, including doctors who were effectively teachers, and also non-teaching doctors; and the chancellor.

The structure of the student corporations, after the initial decades characterized by the many-nation 'rettorie' attested to in 1228 and in 1241, are clearly defined in the statutes of the student jurists, which were completely revised in 1331. These statutes open with a sort of historical preface, which retraces not without obscurity the activity begun in 1260 by some enterprising personalities who had held the office of rector, and who had distinguished themselves for having contributed to the formation of the statutes of the student body. These people are a sample collection of students from all over Europe, from Spain to Poland, standing out among whom is the Spaniard Gosaldo da Cuenca (who Domenico Maffei has identified as Gonzalo, an important figure and future archbishop of Toledo).

The students were divided into two large groups, the *Ultramontani* (or Transalpines) and the *Citramontani* (or Cisalpines), divided into national groups (*nationes*). In the fourteenth century there were nine national groups of *Ultramontani* (but the *natio Teutonica* had two votes, being numerically in the majority) and ten *Citramontani*. These two groups converged in fact into two closely related but distinct associations which had as their heads two rectors, or, on several occasions, only one, according to a recurrent feature of the Studium of Padua that seems to have become the norm in the course of the fifteenth century, when a single rector from the *Transalpini* and one from the *Cisalpini* normally alternated.

The Padua Studium, precisely because it was born as an offshoot from a typically student reality - that of the Bolognese 'university' of jurists - undoubtedly enjoyed from the beginning the support of the local church,

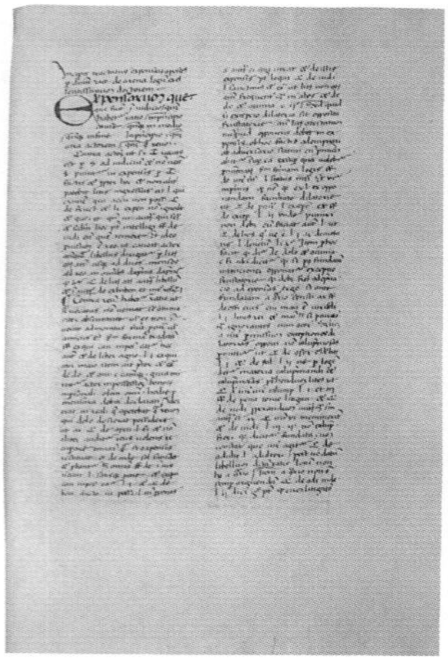

Giacomo Dall'Arena, Tractatus expensarum

thanks also to the active interest of Giordano of Modena, the bishop in 1222, who knew the Studium of Bologna well. When it was definitively consolidated in the second half of the thirteenth century, the Padua Studium drew its own legitimization from its antiquity, according to a theory attested very early, for example, in the opinions of the famous jurist Giacomo Dall'Arena of Piacenza, who was in Padua in 1260-1264 and later in 1287-88. Thus born without any previous authorization from the highest medieval powers (the Empire and the Pope), as happened to the few Universities with pre-ordained foundations, Padua assumed the prerogative of a *de facto* 'Studium generale'. And yet even Padua ran the risk of being deprived of its Studium on at least two occasions (not unlike what happened in Bologna): when it was hit by the threat of Papal interdict in 1289-90, in a moment of acute tension due to the initiatives of the Commune (even though according to tradition it was normally Guelph) against the fiscal privileges of the clergy; and then in 1312 when Emperor Henry VII of Luxemburg wanted to punish the city, guilty for having adhered to the league headed by Florence. That the threats were taken into serious consideration, including the disastrous consequences that they would have had on the prestige and the economy of the city, is demonstrated by the fact that in 1319 the Commune obtained from Frederick of Austria, elected king of Germany and of the Romans in competition with Ludwig of Bavaria, remission of the preceding imperial condemnation with the explicit confirmation of the lawfulness of the Studium in all the disciplines.

In the Italian Studia born from the thirteenth to the fifteenth century the office of chancellor was in general held by the bishop. The most remarkable exception, apart from the royal University of Naples, is represented precisely by Bologna, in which another ecclesiastic dignitary, the archdeacon of the cathedral, acted as chancellor from 1219. For Padua there was a first papal confirmation in 1264 of the procedure relative to the completion of the course of study and the conferral of the "licentia docendi", which was attributed to the bishop after the examinations were completed by the masters, in the form in which it had been introduced – perhaps in 1261 – in the statutes of the autonomous 'university' of the law students. The prerogatives of the bishop-chancellor, confirmed by two important papal privileges of 1346 and 1439, did not go much beyond the exercise of the chairmanship, either personally or delegated to vicars, in the administration of the final exams (in the more common terminology, analogous to that of other medieval Universities, the "licentia" or "examen privatum" and the "publica examinatio" or "examen publicum" or "publica doctoratus"). The chancellor guaranteed the regularity of the procedure of the exams, accepting the binding advice of the commission formed by members of the distinct doctoral corporations (the jurists, the artists and the physicians, and from 1363 also from the College of theologians), while the redaction of the documents relative to the academic degrees was the duty of one or more public notaries in the service of the bishop. The procedure of conferral of the licence and the doctorate is shown by a few but important examples of original documents that have re-emerged, dating from the second half of the thirteenth century (1281,1295), and by an abundant documentation which dates sporadically back to the beginning of the fourteenth century and becomes very rich from the middle of that same century. This documentation, with the series of the acts of the academic degrees of the fifteenth and sixteenth centuries, is a collection – despite the inevitable lacunae – impressive for its abundance and quality that finds no comparison in any other University in Italy or perhaps in Europe.

The mature Paduan communal rule (the so-called "Second Commune"), beginning from its resumption after the end of the twenty-year dominion of Ezzelino III da Romano (1236-1256), developed a constant vigilance to ensure the presence of the Studium in the city through legislative statutes, the financing of the fundamental chairs, the safeguarding of the juridical state of the students (the "libertas scholastica"), and the internal autonomy proper to the 'university', thanks to precise obligations based on pact and through the reception of these into the civic statutes in 1262. In this way the Commune guaranteed certain essential conditions to increase the student presence: the availability of lodgings, loans at a modest rate of interest, and copyists for the book production necessary for the transmission of the disciplines taught, which were based on a definite body of obligatory texts.

In addition there existed a civic magistracy functioning as a link between the Commune and the University: the *trattatori* of the Studium. These appear in the Paduan statutes of the second half of the thirteenth century, where there is a normative description that sets out their competence, together with the rectors of the student corporations, essentially in matters of engaging teachers with the system of 'condotte' (contracts), while autonomously, on behalf of the Commune, they established the amount of the professors' salaries. Any decision relative not only to the condition of the contracts, but also to the disbursement of the teachers' pay, had to be authorized with proper deliberation by the civic Council. This is shown, among the generalized loss of documents, by a surviving measure taken in 1303 to pay the salaries owed to two teachers, Tommaso Lamandini of Bologna and Pietro da Dozza, who had substituted, respectively, Pietro da Ferrara on the 'ordinary' chair of "decreti" (canon law), and Pietro of Suzzara on the 'extraordinary' chair of civil law (on 'ordinary' and 'extraordinary' cf. below Zordan). Likewise we also have the model for a letter of invitation to a teacher dating to 1310, designated by election by the 'university' of students and confirmed by the communal Council. This example called Iacopino Ruffini of Parma, doctor of law and knight, to the teaching of civil law for the subsequent triennium, to begin on 29 September, with a honorarium of 400 *lire di piccoli* a year.

At the service of the Commune, the doctor jurists of the University (among whom we can recall the names of Riccardo Malombra of Cremona and Oldrado of Lodi) were highly sought after as consultants regarding relations with other cities - such as Venice, the economic metropolis of the area in which Padua was situated - with Italian and foreign leaders, and with the Papacy. These doctors thus represented a group of the highest social prestige. The College of doctors, including teachers of civil and also canon law (the latter no less important in the University environment), included both the "dottori leggenti" (lecturers) of foreign provenance, for the period of their teaching at Padua, and citizens with an academic qualification in law, forming a corporation very distinct from that of the palace judges, which was already powerful in the communal assemblage. Among these latter, the graduates were only a small percentage until the late fourteenth century, even if all were obliged to attend at least five years of law studies.

Between the year 1300 and approximately 1310 Padua, last surviving city in the Veneto with an autonomous communal regime, reached perhaps the most splendid phase of its independent history before the magnificence of its subsequent period under the signoria. A later chronicler, Guglielmo Cortusi, described it as "full of the splendor which was given to it by learned men and doctors of every liberal art", a beacon and "refuge of safety" for foreigners from diverse regions. Among the foreigners, the social group of the students in the field of law and in the ever more representative sector of the arts and medicine constituted a true international élite, highly mobile, and in any case recognizable.

In 1318, at the culmination of the factional conflicts and the crisis of the communal regime which led to the conferral of the 'capitaniato' on Giacomo il Vecchio da Carrara, the judges and Paduan doctors who carried out the transfer of power from the Commune to the *signore* were clearly concerned about the Studium. Indeed the explanatory articles of the statute with which the civic Council transferred full power to Giacomo contain an explicit reference to the University, inserted in the paternal provisions of the signoria among a range of incumbencies aiming at ensuring the peaceful and prosperous state of the city. In the twenty years after 1318 – years of political vicissitudes in which, in order to defend itself against the expansionism of Verona, Padua had given itself first to Frederick of Habsburg, king of the Romans, and then to his vicar Heinrich, Duke of Carinthia (1320-1328) - but above all in the period when the city was directly included in the well-organized rule of the Scaligeri (1328-1337), the functioning of the framework of the Studium seems to have been ensured by a deep-rooted symbiosis between University environments and communal magistracies, even in the succession of different external regimes.

The University of Padua derived more than a few advantages from repeated episodes of student diaspora from the nearby Studium of Bologna in the thirteenth and fourteenth centuries (above all in 1306 and 1321), while it did not appear to suffer particular disadvantages from the rise of other Universities in the same geographical area (which however represented only a limited part of a much larger catchment area), universities which were sometimes precarious or existing on paper only, in Treviso, Verona, and Cividale del Friuli. The competition was to become fiercer, however, in the late fourteenth and fifteenth centuries, when the University panorama was enriched by new Studia founded by various signorie, such as those of Pavia and Ferrara.

Certainly the new migration of the Bolognese law students in 1321 took place in the context of a well-established communal University policy. Having first sought refuge in Imola, they later swarmed in part to Siena, in part to Padua, where a group arrived after having negotiated highly advantageous pacts with the emissaries of the Commune, among whom was the historian, notary, and poet Albertino Mussato. The event of 1321 was rightly assumed by Girolamo Arnaldi to be the final moment of the Paduan Studium's first century of life. The civic Commune, there is no doubt, had clearly sensed the favourable circumstances and had established four 'trattatori generali', true plenipotentiaries who were charged with confirming previous pacts and establishing others, in order to return the local Studium to a high level. This was done through the adoption of the norms which had been accorded to the students at Bologna but above all through the guarantee that the University would be governed according to the customs, statutes, and regulations of the University of Bologna, thus ensuring the transplant of the internal law that the corporation of the students of the 'Alma Mater' had created for themselves over the previous seventy years.

Altichiero, Francesco il Vecchio and Francesco il Giovane da Carrara

The Epoch of the da Carrara signoria

In the period of the second definitive signoria of the da Carrara family (1338-1388, 1390-1405) the Padua Studium was at the centre of a complex movement which involved the ruling powers and which nevertheless continued and updated a model of intervention which was already present in the preceding period.

In its preoccupation for the healthy state of the University, the mature da Carrara signoria inherited and followed certain attitudes that dated back to the communal epoch. At the time of their succession to the signoria, the da Carrara did not have a plan for a coherent 'University policy', but from the 1340's they were able to work at various levels to make the University flourish, especially during the very long government of Francesco il Vecchio (1355-1388) and that of his son Francesco il Giovane (1390-1405). Certainly these men found the cultural environment of the city already distinctly characterized by the presence of the Studium; but the interchange between the signoria, the higher urban classes, and the University culture was only one of the peculiar aspects of the physiognomy assumed by the court of the da Carrara, an aspect also perhaps dictated by

Tomb of Ranieri Arsendi of Forlì

their intuition of the propaganda and image value that could be drawn from the culture and the presence of the Studium, which enjoyed notable international prestige. With regard to the University, in fact, there was clearly a tendency to take practical measures, such as calling famous professors, in order to qualify the level of the teaching on offer, principally to attract foreign students. Various clues point to a direct involvement of the signoria (or rather, of the apparatus of the seignorial government) with acts that, although they do not constitute a true University policy, can be considered at least as a "policy of chairs".

Very early on, even as the signoria was still taking root and developing, we find the first (and only, as far as we know) statement by Paduan chronicles to refer explicitly to a very well-known person being called to the Studium as a teacher. In September 1344 Ubertino da Carrara called as a teacher of civil law, with a salary of a full 600 florins, the famous jurist Ranieri Arsendi of Forlì, who had already held positions in Bologna and Pisa and who played an important role as counsellor to the court of the da Carrara until his death in Padua in 1358. We know that already a few years earlier, perhaps in 1338, a request had come from Padua to Taddeo Pepoli, *signore* of Bologna, asking for permission to be given for certain Bolognese professors to be employed by the Padua Studium, a request that was not granted, however.

Another relevant aspect of the action carried out by the same Ubertino da Carrara does not directly concern the Studium, but testifies to a primary interest in the cultural qualifications of the city, which ever since the late thirteenth century had been distinguished by a series of relations with the Paris Studium in the field of philosophico-medical studies. Twelve young Paduans were sent to Paris, at Ubertino's expense, to study the liberal arts, according to the relationship which existed in that period between the philosophical disciplines and medicine: it was an action of re-qualification with results useful both for the citizen class of physicians and artists and for University teaching. In the mid-fourteenth century, indeed, the University boasted people such as Giovanni Dondi (c. 1330-1388), a singular figure: an encyclopedic intellectual, astronomer, and physician to the court of the da Carrara and then the Visconti; and members of the Santasofia family, a dynasty of physicians active in the major University centres in Italy and abroad (Bologna, Padua, Pavia, Perugia, and Vienna).

It was as far as we know above all Francesco il Vecchio da Carrara, in parallel with a true transformation of the signoria into an autocracy, who rendered the interference of the prince in the choice of teachers ever more real, through a dense network of patronage and an articulated ministerial machinery. Francesco also exercised his influence in support of the request that the Studium be accorded the College of Theology, which was granted by Pope Urban V in 1363, a fact that crowned the University, according to the medieval hierarchy of knowledge, and rendered Padua (in the words of some contemporary chronicles) "ornamented with the flower of all the sciences". In 1375, in response to a letter recommending Andreasio

Cavalcabò of Viadana, doctor of law, for a teaching post at Padua, Francesco wrote to Ludovico Gonzaga, lord of Mantua, stating that he was for the time being "well provided with doctors" for the University.

A notable example of the praxis also followed at Padua in the teaching contracts is represented in 1384 by the arrangements agreed for the engagement of a figure well-known in medieval philosophical thought, Biagio Pelacani of Parma, to public lectureship (i.e. to the course or the chair) of philosophy and astrology, in which Antonio Cecchi of Moncalieri acted as Francesco da Carrara's vicar general. In the field of law we can recall the engagement of the great Baldo degli Ubaldi (1376-1379) and the Florentine canonist Lapo of Castiglionchio (1379), a choice which involved the participation, if not directly of Francesco, then certainly of members of his court entourage. A few years later (1384-1386) Angelo degli Ubaldi, younger brother of Baldo, was also in Padua, again at the request of Francesco.

Baldo degli Ubaldi

The search for and the engagement of teachers from outside Padua had to be carried out by special agents who enjoyed the absolute trust of the prince - it is not clear whether in competition with or as an alternative to the actions of the 'trattatori' (as is documented in 1398 at least). Otherwise other professors were used, as for example, when Giovanni Ubaldini, professor of canon law, acted as agent of the da Carrara in 1399 to make contact in Bologna with Pietro d'Ancarano, who had already taught at Padua in the past, in order to stipulate a new contract. But it is rather curious to note that in the following year four 'trattatori', elected by the civic Council, reappear to elect and hire professors (both in law and arts, medicine and surgery). On 15 October 1400 they reached an agreement with the Bolognese Bartolomeo da Saliceto, contracted to teach civil law for three years, with an annual salary of 600 ducats. Even in the age of the signoria, although relegated to the function of an administrative body, the Commune preserved in principle its direct commitment to the University arena through the 'trattatori' of the Studium, whose jurisdiction was defined in the age of the signoria with a civic statute of 1339. The later fifteenth-century transformation of the 'trattatori' into 'Riformatori dello Studio' under the Venetian domination increases our doubts as to the effective role played by this communal magistracy.

The signoria played roles which were apparently contingent, but which were nevertheless destined to have a profound impact on the juridical structure of the University organization, when it was entrusted with the function of mediating the conflicts which arose among the members of the Studium who during the course of the fourteenth century were still in the process of defining their respective spheres of autonomy. In this action, in the long run the signoria was to substitute the function traditionally covered by the bishop-chancellor, without taking on any specific role but with a real and very concrete influence. The interventions of the signoria took the form of arbitration between the parties in conflict, as a form of justice external to the institutional University environment: a choice that in some aspects was almost inevitable, given the powers invested in the prince (de facto but also de iure: it should not be forgotten that the da Carrara, from Giacomo II on, were also bestowed with the Imperial vicariate over Padua). The signoria, therefore, seems to have gradually acquired a stabilizing function which amounted to a form of control over the Studium.

The first act of mediation carried out by a member of the da Carrara family happened during the conflict which in 1346-47 set the bishop-chancellor Ildebrandino Conti in opposition against the rectors of the universities of students. The student corporations demanded to be allowed to participate with the right to vote and interrogate in the exams for the license and the graduate degree, which was denied by the chancellor. The arbitrators' decision regarding the parties was pronounced by Giacomo II da Carrara on 26 November 1347, and he recognized the participation in exams by the rectors of the two distinct universities of jurists, the Transalpine and Cisalpine, but without any possibility of suffrage in the voting. The official sanction, which accorded the rectors the right to be present at the exams, was the confirmation of a residual function of the student body, a formality necessary in the licensing and the conferral of doctorates, destined to remain through the obligatory presence of the rectors or the pro-rectors at the proceedings of the conferral of the academic degrees.

The most significant episode of this assumption of a stabilizing role between the different bodies of the Studium took place at the very end of the fourteenth century, when the question of the relations of subordination between the associative organization of the students of arts and medicine with respect to those of law flamed up again. In 1360 the corporate bond that linked the students of arts and medicine had already achieved an initial partial autonomy from the jurists, thanks to the intervention of the bishop Pileo da Prata. Nearly forty years later, the self awareness of the philosophico-medical corporation had reached the point of demanding complete organizational independence - within a general growth in prestige of the discipline professed by the 'artists' with respect to the jurists, with reference also to the contemporary "dispute of the arts", regarding the primacy of the various disciplines - and this independence was expressed by the election of the first autonomous rector, the student Benedetto Greco of Salerno.

The events took place in the year 1399 and involved Francesco Novello da Carrara, lord of Padua, who was called to resolve the controversy between the artists - supported by the College of physicians - and the universities or corporations of the law students, to which the College of doctors of civil and canon law gave their support. The quarrel was submitted by the united wills of the opposite parties to an arbitral commission, which was headed by Francesco III da Carrara, acting as a commissioner for his father, together with six doctors from the two disciplinary areas, three jurists (Francesco Zabarella, Antonio of Sant'Angelo and Pietro Alvarotti) and three physicians (Baldassarre of Padua, Bartolomeo of Mantua and

Giacometto, called "dal Santo"). In the end it was decided that, similarly to what had happened in other Studia, the artists could elect a rector with full jurisdiction in the civil controversies among their subjects, with the abolition of every form of oath of observance to the statutes of the jurists. As redress for the revenues which the latter would no longer receive from the graduation of the artists after the definitive division of the corporation of the arts and medicine from that of the jurists, Francesco donated, in the same year 1399, a house in the Piazza Sant'Antonio to the two rectors (the Transalpine Francesco Mella of Cataluña and the Cisalpine Giovanni Suffuda of Reggio Calabria); the building still exists today.

We find an interesting consequence of the mediation of the signoria several months later, on 16 September 1400, when Francesco il Giovane provided a letter of introduction for two representatives of the students of arts and medicine of Padua, Dino del Garbo of Florence and Lorenzo Sassoli of Prato, who were going to Bologna to make copies of the statutes of the local 'university' of arts students, statutes which were probably entirely accepted in Padua as an already well-established body of norms. Initially and for several decades of the fifteenth century the 'university' of the artists, like the contemporary structure at Bologna, had only four nations called the Tuscans, the *Ultramontani* (Transalpines), the Lombards, and the Romans; later, in the revised statutes of 1460-65, which were re-elaborated in 1496, the nations of the 'Oltremarini' (Oltremars), the March of Treviso, and finally the March of Ancona were added.

It is interesting to note how, in the short period (1388-1390) in which Padua became part of the vaster Visconti dominion, the Studium was directly controlled by the court of Gian Galeazzo Visconti, and in the academic year of 1389-90 at least, there was direct intervention by Gian Galeazzo. Indeed the rolls (or lists of teachers destined for various courses) of the University of Pavia – founded shortly before as an expression of the power of the Visconti lordship over a broad State of multi-regional dimensions – also include the names of a small group of professors sent expressly to Padua. The Visconti model certainly represented a stimulus for the da Carrara towards ever greated intervention in the University world, though the privileges that the students and teachers traditionally enjoyed were left in place.

The First Venetian Century

The Studium of Padua was the only University centre in the regional State of the Venetian dominion from the fifteenth century until the fall of the Republic in 1797 which obeyed what Piero Del Negro has termed the "logic of the signoria", characteristic of the relationship between government and University structures at the end of the medieval and the beginning of the early modern period. From the moment Padua fell under Venetian domination, the position of its Studium was also felt to be essential to the external, international prestige of Venetian rule. The influence exercised by Venice on the University in fact demonstrates the tendency of traditional components to be absorbed into vaster contexts of territorial sovereignty.

After its armed conquest (22 November 1405) and the destruction of the da Carrara dynasty, the submission of Padua to Venetian dominion was formally completed on 3 January 1406, when the representatives of the ruling classes (noble knights, doctors, nobles not decorated with knighthood, and merchants) handed over to the doge the symbols of their lordship over Padua. Venice responded to the requests the Paduans had made with their act of submission with a solemn document, the *Bolla d'oro*, the "Golden Bull", which was to constitute the fundamental framework of the relations between dominant city and dominated Commune. The Paduans asked to maintain the privileges enjoyed by the corporations, both the commercial guilds and the University. This latter lay within the city but was in a position of substantial autonomy from the urban context, and also represented an important pole from an economic point of view. Venice carried out every initiative regarding the University's advancement.

On a practical level Venetian intervention was mediated by the rectors (the *podestà* and the captain) sent by Venice to the conquered city and endowed with extensive powers of control, intervention, and initiative. These men were vigilant and attentive in safeguarding and ensuring the growth of the Studium; standing out among them are the figures of Zaccaria Trevisan and Fantino Dandolo (who were among the few Venetian nobles to have obtained prestigious doctoral degrees from the Studia of Bologna and Padua at the end of the fourteenth and in the first years of the fifteenth century). The civic Council, last residue of the Commune, on the other hand, became the typical place in which a sort of Paduan patriciate came to define itself over the course of the fifteenth century, not without internal contrasts, and the families which had had an active role within the University represented an essential component both in terms of prestige and in their public activity.

From 1406 – not unlike what happened in the Visconti State with regard to Pavia - Venice imposed substantial scholastic protectionism in favour of the Paduan Studium. In the following year all Venetians and the subjects of the territories under Venetian rule were forbidden to pursue academic degrees at Universities "al di qua delle Alpi" (on this side of the Alps, that is to say in Italy), forcing them to attend the University of Padua alone. This imposition was not rigorously observed initially, since for some time both Venetians and citizens of other subject cities (above all Verona and Vicenza) were found outside the Paduan Studium, and indeed the prohibition was repeated subsequently, in a more vigorous form, in 1444. Thus, within the territorial range of the Venetian Republic a substantial monopoly on University instruction was created, concentrated on the Padua Studium. At the same time the surviving requests for a local University which cities like Treviso, Vicenza, and Verona could still cultivate, by appealing to papal and imperial privileges or to deep-rooted cultural traditions, lost all their effectiveness.

Venice aimed first at defining the financing of the University, through a policy which very soon arrogated both the finding of financing and, as a consequence, the control over expenses, to the state authority. A budget was allocated for this purpose which was initially derived from the income from taxation that the Republic collected in Padua and in the surrounding district, to the sum of 3,000 ducats, raised to 4,000 on 12 September 1407. The Paduan Commune was excluded from the management of the budget, even though it initially contributed half the funds.

This was, in practice, the removal of the civic Council of Padua from all direct interference in control of the choice of the teaching body too. In the fifteenth century there was in practice a tri-polar system - teachers were designated by the student 'university', checked by the Venetian rectors, and confirmed by the Venetian government - from which any intervention by the communal Council was eliminated almost immediately. Recalled back into existence in 1415 and then inserted into the revised form of the Padua statutes of 1420, even the 'trattatori' were deprived of any autonomous room for manoeuvre and were reduced to diligent solicitors with the Venetian podestà and captain, who chose them in full autonomy.

The concrete act of governing was carefully exercised in the policy of professorial chairs, pursued with the conviction that "famous professors draw many students". Hence the University's financial budget had to be used to pay famous professors attractive salaries. This line, also repeatedly expressed in official Venetian documents, constituted a solid defence against the risk of the University of Padua's becoming provincialized for the entire fifteenth century, while in the same period many other Italian Studia were subject to closures and limitations of a localistic nature.

The Venetian government itself could directly call foreign professors, as happened for example in the case of Raffaele Fulgosio, a highly famous jurist, who in September of 1407 was to be employed in the teaching body of the Padua Studium: for his arrival even diplomatic channels were used, and finally in October of 1408 he was welcomed into the College of jurists. Shortly after came the call to the similarly-named Raffaele Raimondi of Como, and so (to demonstrate the saying, well-known in Venice, that "the students follow the great masters"), "from the whole world they rushed to Padua to the two Raffaeli", up until the death of the two professors in the course of 1427, a year of grave pestilence.

One very important aspect of the traditional corporate liberties was represented by the designation of the chosen teachers for the lectures (the courses) which, taken as an ordered whole, constituted the 'rotulo' (the roll, or official list), as stipulated in the statutes. The norms however often faced restrictions and expansions, and were very limited from 1444-45, when riots broke out within the 'university' of jurists.

Even the Venetian podestà and captain sometimes acted to call some

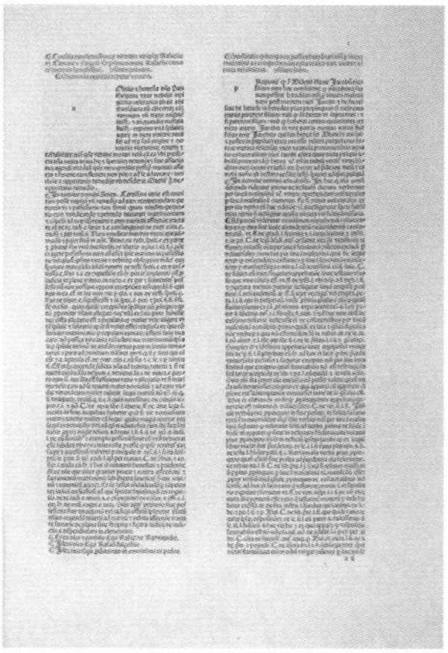

Tomb of Raffaele Fulgosio

Raffaele Raimondi, Consilia

famous teacher. If the testimonies are not numerous, they are nevertheless enough to show that recourse to private enterprise in contracting the professors was generalized. In 1414, for example, the Venetian podestà created two agents, one to recruit a professor of canon law at Bologna, the other with the specific task of making contact with another celebrated representative of legal science of the time, Giovanni Nicoletti of Imola, in anticipation of the academic year of 1414-1415. The responsibilities which the Venetian rectors of the city exercised in choosing the professors can be clearly seen in a document, a 'rotulo' showing the distribution of the courses both in the legal and the medical field, for a total of ten teachers of law courses and eight professors of medicine and the arts. The 'rotulo' is conserved precisely within the deliberations of the Venetian Senate, dated 22 September 1430, which also record traces of the discussions regarding the confirmation and the hiring of teachers. It was prepared in Padua in the context of the student corporations, sent by the Venetian rectors to the government of the Republic, and was finally subject to the approval of a vast deliberative organ, the Consiglio dei Pregadi (the Senate); then it returned to Padua as a "manifesto of studies" just in time for the beginning of lectures.

At the beginning of 1439, on the suggestion of Paolo Dotti, a professor of law in the Studium and a high-profile exponent of the city's ruling class, the civic Council requested that in order to meet the rising financial demands, the Venetian government should recommend that several ecclesiastical benefices be destined as a grant for six public 'lettori' (lecturers), to be chosen from among the many young and able-bodied Paduan doctors: a system that had no known precedent in the Padua Studium. Certainly the request was not put into effect then, because of the turbulent situation that year, due in part to a failed anti-Venetian plot. These minor chairs became the so-called 'third ranks', defended to the bitter end by the communal Council more than once in the course of the century, as the last resort for doctors native to the city who wanted to take up teaching.

The presence of professors of great renown brought obvious repercussions: the catchment area of the University of Padua was particularly varied and extensive in the fifteenth century and beyond, a longer period than for other Universities. The extremely rich documentation provided by the academic acts, that is the conferral of degrees, remains as a confirmation of the truly international character of the University throughout the course of the century, and shows the extraordinary range in provenance of the doctoral candidates and students from all over Western Europe, with a prevalence, among the non-Italians, of the *natio Teutonica*; it also provides significant testimony of relations with central-eastern Europe and with Venice's Mediterranean possessions.

In the first Venetian century the privileges of the student 'universities' in the field of jurisdictional autonomy and exemption from taxation were certainly not touched; indeed Venice defended the corporative structure into which the student world was organized according to long-standing tradition, while it did not hesitate to intervene very rapidly in the Colleges of doctors and even regarding the prerogatives of the bishop-chancellor. In the course of the fifteenth century the 'university' of law students subsequently took it upon itself to systemize its own body of norms: unfortunately only the statutes of 1445-1463 have survived in a form that does not allow us to see the chronological stratification of the additions and corrections with respect to the fourteenth-century statutes. The single rector of the jurists, to whom both the Ultramontane and Cisalpine students were subject, appears regularly from 1417-18. But by now 'student power' had acquired a very different weight with respect to that not only of the thirteenth, but also of the fourteenth century. Certainly the 'student universities' were still very attentive to the privileged status of their own members, especially if those students were also clerics. It is in this context that we can understand the final papal intervention in favour of the Studium of Padua, the solemn bull issued by the Venetian Eugenius IV on the first of December 1439, which confirmed the previous papal concessions and extended to doctors, masters, and students living in Padua all the indults and privileges, of whatever nature and denomination, that had already been granted by popes or emperors to the Studia of the Roman Curia, Paris, Oxford, Bologna, and Salamanca.

The Collegio Pratense

In the middle of the fifteenth century the signs of a decline in the splendour of the Studium became more and more evident. For a long time historians have spoken of a "mid-fifteenth-century crisis" (Vittorio Lazzarini): a crisis of attendance and of prestige (the absenteeism of the official teachers was to lead Venice to accuse them of being the reason for the Studium's lack of appeal to the students); competition from other Universities, which were seen as more attractive above all for the more advantageous conditions they offered in gaining academic degrees; and the corporative closure of the Colleges, defenders of their social prestige and of the revenues due to the 'promotori' (the members of the Colleges presenting the students) at graduation.

In this crisis, the numbers speak for themselves, besides the fact that they represent some of the very few quantitative data available for the entire medieval period regarding the student presence in Padua. Whatever figures have been calculated regarding the quantity of students - a numerically élite group - for the previous period (thirteenth and fourteenth centuries), they have no firm foundation. In 1457, in fact – as the Venetian Senate lamented – there were more or less 300 students, while in the past the number had usually reached 800. Times in any case had greatly changed with respect to the two preceding centuries: even the 'libertas scholastica', the condition of guaranteed circulation and safe permanence for the students, a substantially mobile and restless group, was by now subjected to politics and relations between States. As had already happened in 1413, in 1451 students from Florence and the cities under Florentine rule - having been expelled or having prudently gone of their own accord - left Padua as a result of the crisis that had threatened relations between Florence and Venice.

But it was precisely in the years of the crisis, however, that Venice attempted to reorganize the financing of the University through various, not always effective, means, among which the attempt at least (in 1461, 1463, 1475, 1480) to divert sums from the tax revenues of other cities of the Terraferma under Venetian rule (Bergamo, Treviso, Verona), thus overcoming the civic and municipal character that was the normal way of providing the Studium's income, moving decidedly towards a State approach that was absolutely new to the Italian Universities of the period.

Substantial groups of students, above all among the Italians, had been diverted from Padua by competition with other old and new Universities, a highly diversified offering, the initiatives attempted by many Universities to re-qualify themselves, and by the tendency of various ruling powers to force their subjects to study in centres directly under their control. In Tuscany, for example, the University of Pisa, re-founded by Lorenzo the Magnificent as the centralized University of the Florentine dominion, represented an attractive choice. In Northern Italy the Studium of Ferrara, practically revived in 1442 and financed by the court of the Este to the detriment of Bologna, Padua, and Pavia, attracted bands of students from the south of Italy and even from outside Italy, who at the end of a complicated academic pilgrimage found highly advantageous conditions there for attaining an academic degree. This happened in the well-known case of Nicholas Copernicus, who had passed through Bologna and Padua, but who actually obtained a doctorate in canon law from Ferrara.

Venice also faced growing difficulties finding and employing truly famous professors: while it removed the designation and the reconfirmation of the contracts from the hands of student groups, putting them directly under government control, and exempted the most illustrious and esteemed professors from reconfirmation, it suffered more and more from the prohibitions which the cities of great cultural tradition - such as Bologna, Siena or Pavia, natural reservoirs of doctors - placed on their teachers preventing them from taking on courses in external universities.

And yet the last quarter of the fifteenth century represented in many respects the true "golden age" for the Padua Studium, as François Dupuigrenet-Desroussilles has pointed out, and as is attested by those precious sources, the academic degrees, which have now finally been published. Nevertheless, it was also the epoch of a strict surveillance by the signoria over the students, who became riotous on more than one occasion; and it was the age in which the Padua civic Council reassumed its grievous laments in order to save some academic posts for doctors from among its own citizens, whose numbers had multiplied excessively.

Indeed as from 1467 the Paduans had been allotted merely the minor chairs known as 'third rank' chairs, with an extremely modest salary, though Paduan professors of a certain prominence certainly still found honourable contracts. The crisis of the mid-fifteenth century involved various levels of the classes of Paduan doctors, jurists and physician-artists, who with their respective Colleges found themselves involved in the transformation of Paduan society in the direction of an oligarchy. Not by chance, in the decade prior to the mid-century, there arose problems of precedence in the civic processions between the two corporations of doctors, problems that mirrored more profound contrasts than the needs of public self-representation. The conflict for places in the processions, in fact, was not only ceremonial but, demonstrating yet again the greater social weight and the greater self-consciousness of the corporation of jurists, brought to light a conflict with the College of arts and medicine that alarmed the Venetian authorities. In 1447 the podestà intervened not only to keep the peace between the two bodies but also to defend the "honour of the Dominant city". In 1451 a further Venetian measure stated that in the Paduan processions the four distinct corporations of the Studium (doctors and 'university' of the jurists on the one hand, doctors of arts and medicine and the 'university' of arts students on the other) should march separately in future.

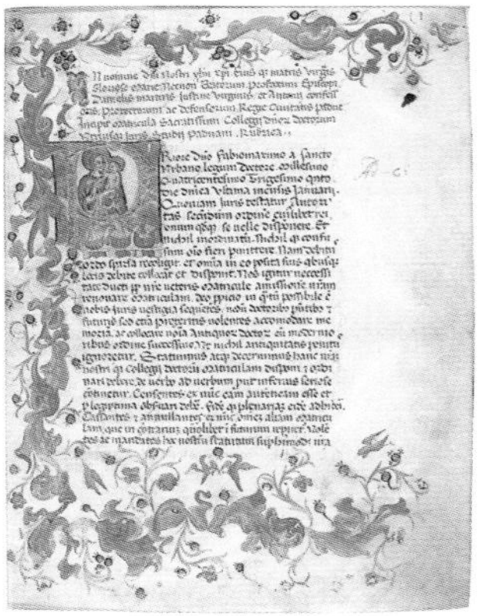

Matricula of the College of law

The College of jurists already existed at Padua in the second half of the thirteenth century, uniting both the city's professors in effective service, and the doctors of civil and canon law native to the city or naturalized as Paduans, even if they were not teachers. The internal structure of the Padua College is documented in detail by a normative source which was added to in time by several deliberations and reforms, that is to say the statutes of 1382, which collect and organize in three books norms dating from 1349 onwards, when the College was probably re-organized after the calamitous years of the Black Death. A fixed number of twelve members was then established, increased gradually to twenty, then to twenty-five and thirty; finally, in 1382 it was decreed that as many members could be appointed as pleased the doctors already in the College, thus making the open number depend solely on the decision of the effective members. Around 1437 the members of the College already amounted to about fifty, and the number grew subsequently thanks to the formation of family dynasties of Paduan lawyers.

We can follow the extremely important task of administering degree examinations which the College of jurists carried out - as did the College of medicine and arts in its own field - in its external relations, through the documents of the academic degrees. It is nevertheless difficult to obtain a sufficiently detailed picture of the internal activity of the College in this field because the acts of the curia of the bishop-chancellor still prevailed. The normative statutes of the College are very meticulous both for the procedure of the exams, and for the high fees which the candidates had to pay those who presented them (the aforementioned 'promotori') and the other members of the commission: incomes that could become the subject of contestation, as is shown by fragments of decrees of the College of jurists in 1419-1422. Linking the rates of the payment of the examiner's fee and other exactions to the value of the most valuable Venetian currency, the gold ducat, it was possible to tie the University rights to the rate of

Doctors of the Capodilista family

inflation, as Jacques Le Goff has demonstrated.

The Paduan graduates in arts and medicine entered the College of physicians and artists, but not necessarily the doctors who lectured. An additional corporation was open to physicians who had not graduated, surgeons who had a diploma, and practitioners, which controlled medical practice, not unlike what happened in other local situations; but it was distinct from the College of doctors. The origins of the College of arts and medicine, which in the fourteenth century was to adorn itself with the title of "sacred", are undoubtedly connected to the original link between philosophy and medicine characteristic of the medieval Studia. The College of artists must have already had a well-defined structure at the beginning of the fourteenth century, with a "preposto" or prior at its head. In 1330 a new organic collection of statutes was perhaps compiled, of which a few fragments remain, while later, in 1376, new statutes were prepared by a commission elected for that purpose within the College and submitted for approval to the chancellor of the Studium. The stratifying of additions and modifications made further revisions of the statutes necessary, and they assumed a new systematic form in 1433, the year of the surviving fifteenth-century redaction.

In the same century one element decisively characterized the structure of the College of arts and medicine with respect to the parallel corporation of the jurists: its fixed number of members. Initially limited to twelve, then raised to sixteen members, reduced again in the second half of the fourteenth century, the number of members of the College was raised to twenty thanks to the intervention of the government of the Republic of Venice in 1407, and revised in 1422. This allowed the entry of Venetian doctors of arts and medicine, a fact which gave the College a somewhat different nature, through the juxtaposition of two distinct components based on citizenship and not on academic qualification. In addition, through the definition of a complex procedure for the choice of new members, a double system was created, which, without disgruntling the doctors of Paduan citizenship, opened the way for privileged access to the Venetian graduates who were in possession of the necessary qualifications.

The College of artists and physicians was therefore placed under strict control by the Venetian republic and was in no way exempt from the pressures exercised by the government. Emblematic of this situation is the fact that the statutes refer to Venetian intervention and incorporate it almost literally, prescribing the registration of all the Ducal letters relative to the College itself. The fifteenth-century statutes of the College of arts and medicine document, therefore, a transition towards the direct intervention and control by Venice over this as over other components of the Padua Studium. The fixed number of members of the College of arts and medicine, which Venice had wanted to maintain, became the reason for repeated clashes within the corporation. Faced with the repeated requests from the ever growing number of Paduan and Venetian graduates who asked to be admitted, the medical College first rejected new appointments,but in other cases it accepted the intervention of Venetian authority for admitting certain "public professors" who would have been excluded as foreigners, as happened in 1469, for instance, for the philosopher Nicoletto Vernia of Chieti.

Between 1445 and 1449, with the eye of an external and detached observer, the Sienese Enea Silvio Piccolomini outlined an essential picture of the Studium of Padua, which took the form of a dry list of the most representative teachers of a recent but practically finished past. This was a different perspective, but ultimately also convergent with that of the Paduan physician Michele Savonarola who – writing within a culture connoted by a strong sense of municipal and class membership – dedicated himself in the same span of years to illustrating the "magnificent ornaments of the royal city of Padua": among these were the great doctors of law, philosophy, and medicine, who brought such lustre to the city. The testimony of Piccolomini clearly shows what must have been perceived as the salient characteristic of the Padua Studium towards the middle of the fifteenth century: the presence of highly-renowned teachers, of both local and non-local extraction, often enjoying fame of European proportions; but above all its nature as the University of Venetians. To Piccolomini, the future Pope Pius II, the inseparable bond between Padua and the nearby Venice was clearly apparent.

His brief characterization somewahat anticipates the famous, justified, but also abused definition of Padua as the "Latin Quarter" of Venice, which dates back to Ernest Renan. The Padua Studium is understood, that is, in its complete transformation into the University of the Venetian Dominion, the University which in the following century was to be precisely the Studium of Saint Mark.

An example of the centralization and the State control over the University exercised by Venice is to be had in the infrastructures destined to house the teaching. In 1493, in fact, to make a central seat available for the law schools, the rector Bernardo Gil of Valencia and the counsellors of the law 'university' obtained in emphyteutical concession the buildings of the old inn under the sign of the ox, the origin of the Palazzo del Bo, which in 1522 also became the place for lectures in the arts and medicine, and which was rebuilt as from 1539.

PIERO DEL NEGRO

The Early Modern Period

1. *The Early Sixteenth Century: from the University of Students and Paduans to the Studium of Saint Mark*

In a study on *L'Università di Padova dal 1405 al Concilio di Trento* François Dupuigrenet Desroussilles entitled the paragraph dedicated to the years 1475-1509 as "the age of gold". Without doubt those who lived through the tormented period after the outbreak of the War of Cambrai understandably tended to mythicize the previous years and celebrate them as the "good period of the Studium of Padua" (Marin Sanudo), for in the span of only a few years Padua had changed masters twice, had been twice besieged, and had changed from being a city of studies to one of arms as a result of its fundamental strategic and logistic role in the defence and reconquest of the Terraferma by the Venetians. The war had placed the very existence of the University at risk and it had forced it to suspend most of its activities for nearly a decade. But at the same time, however, precisely because of the extreme situation that it had created, the war had stressed the contradictions and conflicts of power that characterized the life of the Studium at the dawn of the early modern period.

At the turn of the sixteenth century Padua's University policy was like a battlefield where different centres of power met and clashed without establishing a clear hierarchy. For example, both the University (which, as we know, identified itself from the institutional point of view as student corporations: the 'universities' of the jurists and the artists, and the thirty-odd 'nations' that were their fundamental components), and the Paduan civic authorities (in particular the Council of nobles) could intervene in the key question of the recruiting of professors, to the same extend as could the Venetian government. It was up to the students to approve the teachers at the University from year to year, while the Council of nobles demanded, among other things the right to designate the "*sollecitatori* and *riformatori* of the Studium", who then had to cooperate with the Venetian representatives in Padua in the choice of "good doctors". The Venetian government influenced the designations, both reserving for itself the authority to approve the 'rotulo' (the list of courses), and directly opening negotiations with the foreign professors it wished to bring to lecture in Padua, and submitting their nomination or their confirmation to the Senate (they were almost always fixed-term agreements: as a rule the contracts and their renewals did not exceed six years).

A Professor of the University of Padua

Even if collaboration between the three principal poles of University politics might appear to be something taken for granted, given that the "expansion of the Studium" guaranteed by Venice when it annexed Padua to the Republic of Saint Mark was in everybody's interests - Venetians and Paduans, students and professors - it rested in fact on an equilibrium made unstable by the interests and the divergent perspectives of the institutions concerned. The student corporations intended to safeguard their autonomy in a situation of objective weakness. Among other things the choice of professors by the students had been fully justified as long as the latter had financially supported the former with their collections, but once the weight of financing the Studium fell exclusively on the shoulders of the Serenissima (it is also true, however, that the University budget was supplied almost exclusively by certain taxes paid by so-called 'territorials', the inhabitants of the province), it became difficult for the students to oppose what was decided in Venice regarding the contracts.

As for the Paduan ruling class, everything points to the conclusion that precisely the loss of sovereignty induced it to accentuate the parochial characteristics of the Studium. In that respect too, Padua looked to the Bolognese model, the model of a University that preferred professors from the local nobility. In the second half of the fifteenth century the Council of nobles had obtained the establishment of six (then eight) chairs reserved for citizens of Padua and the inhabitants of the walled cities of the territory (the so-called 'third ranks'). The chairs were assigned, respecting the policy of collaboration between the three principal poles of the University system, by a commission which was made up of both the Venetian authorities resident in Padua (the *podestà*, the captain, and the *camerlenghi*, the treasurers), the student leaders (the rector of the 'university' in question), and the communal leaders (a deputy *ad utilia*, that is to say one of the members of the Council at the head of the civic administration). On the other hand Venice had refused Padua's request for a chair to be set aside for them in each of the disciplines taught at the University. Moving entirely in the opposite direction, the Senate had instead established that two Paduans could never read courses 'in concorrenza', that is to say be placed on chairs destined to teach the same canonical text at the same time.

The Serenissima undoubtedly believed that the chairs reserved for the Paduans and, more in general, the monopoly on University teaching granted to the Padua Studium - a monopoly that implied not only that the Paduan Studium was the only University of the Republic, but also that the subjects of Saint Mark were obliged to take degrees there if they aspired to public employment – were part of the pact made with the city at the moment of its 'submission' to Venice. The Studium had to be considered a sort of reward that the Paduan nobles had received as an indemnity for the loss of sovereignty after the surrender of the city, and it was therefore taken for granted that the University would continue to remain from every point of view, symbolic and economic, a municipal resource. It was with this conviction that the Serenissima had prohibited Venetian patricians from teaching at Padua. Nevertheless Venice also realized that a completely 'Paduanized' University would not have been able to remain in the top ranks of the international panorama for long, hence the need to put an end to the Paduans' requests which not only risked compromising the balance between foreign and local professors (these latter had their institutional bastions in the three sacred colleges of law, arts and medicine, and theology), but also risked destroying student autonomy.

It is not surprising then that the Paduans and the Venetians were forbidden to hold the office of the rector of the 'universities'. It was clear that Venice wanted to prevent a transformation of the student corporations into a Trojan horse of Paduan interests. These interventions by the Serenissima in defence of the autonomy of the student corporations with respect to Padua (and Venice) could, in light of the typology of the relationships between the State and the University set out by Willem Frijhoff, lead one to place the relationship between the Serenissima and the Paduan Studium in the category of "distance" ("the political powers trust the University, which lives almost autonomously, like a private corporation").

In effect the relative detachment of the Republic with respect to the University in the fifteenth and early sixteenth centuries appears to be the result of the convergence of a series of factors more contingent than structural. There was above all the need to move with caution in a context such as that of the University, which found the Venetian State entirely unprepared. It must be considered that, despite its overly complex structure, the Republic did not have a magistracy or a Council available with competences specifically concerning education or more generally culture, and consequently, depending on the problem, the University had to call on the Council of Ten (for public order), the Senate (for financial and in a broad sense political questions) or the *Collegio* (the intermediary between the Venetian government and the 'outside' world, including cities subject to Venice). In Padua the Serenissima was represented by a *podestà* (who held judicial and political authority) and a captain (whose duties concerned the financial and military sectors). Even in the local context the Venetian authorities had to tackle problems which as a rule were alien to their experiences in governing and often to their training. It should in fact be remembered that the Venetian patricians who studied in Padua in the fifteenth to sixteenth centuries were relatively few (a minority, nevertheless, that was very qualified and influential), while in the seventeenth to eighteenth centuries, if one excludes the young men destined for ecclesiastical careers, they constituted an absolutely marginal phenomenon.

We should perhaps remember that typical Venetian government was a mixture of conservatism and pragmatism. The politics of the Serenissima always respected tradition in the conviction that continuity through time was in and of itself a guarantee of success. In Padua tradition was identified with a student autonomy founded on papal bulls, and thus it is no surprise that Padua University remained the last Italian University to per-

Pietro Bembo

mit the students to choose professors, nor that the modifications introduced into the statutes of the 'universities' after the inclusion of Padua under Venetian rule, were sanctioned by the pope. It must not be forgotten either that the student vote guaranteed that the courses conformed, both in their teachers and the contents of their teaching, to the changeable expectations of young men, and at the same time favoured the recruitment of professors from among the ranks of the new doctors and the students themselves. It was logical to expect that this participation attracted many students to Padua, thus satisfying the objective which was most important to Venice.

The gradual abandonment by the Serenissima of the strategy of "distance" in favour of the opposite "guardianship" (in the definition of Frijhoff, "the State places no faith in the University [...] and assumes control of all aspects of University life both internal and external") was justified by taking into account - besides the transformation of the Republic of Saint Mark from a Commune of Venetians into the dominant power of a 'regional' State - the specific problems of the University institution. Venice had to reckon with a market of University teachers that extended, despite the tendentially protectionist politics practised by certain princes, over most of the Italian academic world (for example, between 1518 and 1528 the teaching body at Padua was joined by professors from the Universities of Bologna, Pavia, Ferrara, Rome, Perugia and Salerno), and included also, in exceptional cases, certain Studia outside the peninsula.

The Serenissima did not only mobilize its ambassadors and its representatives in the subject cities to single out, often in collaboration with the rectors of the 'universities' and with other students, the most valid candidates for the leading Paduan chairs (in particular the so-called 'first ranks'), but it also entered into negotiations with the most highly esteemed professors in order to convince them to come or to remain in Padua, offering them higher remunerations and benefits than those guaranteed by its competitors (throughout the entire early modern period Padua enjoyed the fame as the Italian University which paid its professors the highest). For this reason it was logical that the Venetian government could not accept that the students' vote should risk tearing apart the fabric of agreements it had woven.

It is not surprising then, that from the second half of the fifteenth century onwards the Republic intervened more and more often to remove from the rite of the student vote the most famous teachers, who for their part were content to avoid such bitter trials, and at the same time it claimed the right to sanction with the authority of the Senate the new statutes drawn up by the two 'universities', sanctions which, it must be remembered, incorporated what had been decided in Venice concerning the Studium. In addition Venice intervened more often to modify the roles of the professors elected by the students. In 1503 the Senate established that it was not necessary to subject to the student vote those lecturers, the *lettori*, who had a salary of at least sixty florins and who had occupied their chair for at least five years. In the ranks of the prominent Venetian patriciate the belief was by now confirmed that the "growth of the Studium" was not guaranteed so much by respect for the student autonomy as by the choice of "good doctors", and indeed that the residual power of the students would be an obstacle on the road to the optimal management of the Studium.

Certain episodes occurring on the eve of the War of Cambrai testify that, while the strategic line of "guardianship" had already planted firm roots in the Venetian ruling class, on their part the students were by no means resigned to being placed in the sidelines of the new University equilibrium. In 1507, when the captain of Padua threatened to punish the students who, wishing to anticipate the carnival festivities, demanded that the professors suspend classes, "the indignant students broke all the benches of the schools, and the chairs of the professors, and they could not give lessons". Nevertheless, when the Venetian rector beat a retreat and allowed the vacation to begin, the students changed their mind too, and wanted the professors to continue lessons: a total reversal of the two sides, a fact which the Venetian chronicler Marin Sanudo attributed to the fact that the "students in this did not want to be subject to our rectors". Perhaps, beyond the almost complete disappearance of the transalpine students, the slump in the number of graduates (from more than fifty to around fifteen) can be attributed to this unrest in the years immediately before the war.

Nevertheless, when, in May 1509, the Venetian army suffered its defeat at Agnadello and the rule of the Serenissima on the Terraferma collapsed, the majority of Paduan nobles - among whom more than a few professors were in the front line - demonstrated with weapons in their hands that they did not want "to be subject to our rectors". Padua remained for too short a period under the government of emperor Maximilian I to allow the local oligarchy to carry out a reform of the Studium. What is evident is that the Paduan nobles attributed a particular importance to their refound hegemony on the University scene, and it is not by chance that on their return the Venetians were concerned to break the bonds between the pro-imperial nobility and the doctor and professorial class, the bonds which had fed the revolt. Among those condemned to death was even the jurist and deputy *ad utilia* Bertuccio Bagarotto, called by Sanudo the "best professor in Padua".

After the second half of 1509, when University life had been suspended, the Studium returned to work on a smaller scale (between 1513 and 1518 less than ten students a year graduated, among whom not even one foreigner) until 1517, when a truce in the war between Venice and the Empire induced the Paduans to protest and the Venetians to concede reopening the University or, more exactly, to attempt to "bring the Studium back to that flourishing state it was normally in". The most significant innovation was the hard-won launching of a Venetian magistracy (in fact initially a commission with a fixed-term mandate and limited jurisdiction) made up of three senators, the "deputadi a redur lo studio" or rather - as they were called from the following year - the "Riformatori sopra el Studio de Padoa" (Reformers of the Studium). The mandate of the *Riformatori* was initially limited to "bringing those professors and lecturers to the Studium of Padua, with their stipend, or salaries, and those conditions which they will judge to be convenient"; subsequently and gradually, however, it was extended not only to the entire management of the University and the financing and control of other Paduan cultural institutions in the state sphere, but also to Venetian institutions of cultural relevance, from the press to schools of every order and level.

The *Riformatori* of the Studium of Padua not only came, as we know, to occupy a pigeonhole in the Venetian organization that had remained empty, but were also the expression of the oligarchic tendency prevalent in sixteenth century Venice up until the turning point of 1582-3. In any case, it was only in 1528 that the *Riformatori* gained a fixed place in the crowded organizational framework of the Serenissima, while their recognition as exclusive coordinator of Venetian University policy dates to 1536. If on the one hand the crisis the Studium faced after the war due in part also to the difficulty of bringing the University budget back to the pre-war levels – favoured an attempt by the Venetian oligarchy to provide itself with a tool – the *Riformatori* – indispensable for the policy of "guardianship" of the University, on the other it again questioned the organization of the University which had been set out at the beginning of the sixteenth century. The Paduan nobility's 'betrayal' had evidently weakened its position in the short term: not by chance only five of the nineteen chairs assigned in 1510 and four of the twenty-four awarded in 1517-18 were given to Paduans, while the Council of nobles had to wait until 1538 before returning to the Senate with a request for the establishment of six chairs of Roman Law reserved for Paduans, a request which was to be rejected. At the same time, the need to make students return to Padua in consistent numbers induced the Republic to be lavish with its concessions to the 'universities'.

It is not surprising then that the proposal advanced initially by the *Riformatori* and then by the *podestà* of Padua to remove the right to vote on the list of courses from the students was rejected by the majority of senators, and that in 1523 the Senate indeed decided that "all the doctors reading in the said Studium, both principal and substitutes", excepting ten primary professors, "had to be balloted" by the students. It is no marvel either that a serious event in 1519 – an attempt by the students to attack the houses of the Jews was blocked by the captain of Padua, who was wounded in the arm by a lance during the fight – ended in naught: the *avogador de comun*, the magistrate sent from Venice to draw up the trial decided in fact that there was no case to proceed with, since it was to be considered as a scuffle. Three years later the Senate refused with an eloquent "move more leniently" the proposal of another captain to banish twenty student hoodlums.

Until the beginning of the 1530s there remained few students, even though it must be noted that from 1517 the University rapidly refound its cosmopolitan clientele. It is not by chance that in that period a prestigious lawyer such as Andrea Alciato and a very famous philosopher and man of letters, Erasmus of Rotterdam, agreed in judging Padua to be the best of the Italian Universities, and indeed the latter was to celebrate it as "a most furnished emporium and renowned for the best disciplines". But, when the Studium went back to being generally considered, as one captain of Padua wrote in 1532, "most beautiful", when, that is, the ranks of professors were newly increased, thanks in part to the expansion of the University budget (in 1527, after a slow increase, it regained its pre-war level and in 1538 it reached 50,000 *lire*, a figure which could finance sixty chairs), and when the student presence started to climb again (in 1542 the Venetian rectors at Padua estimated that there were a good 1,300 students at the University, the highest known number from an official source regarding attendance at the Studium in the sixteenth century), then the Republic was forced to consider the intemperance of the student body with a much less benevolent eye, and it again embraced a University policy that aimed to consolidate the relationship of "guardianship" of the Studium, making use of the *Riformatori* and the, at the time, omnipotent Council of Ten.

Zamoyski coat of arms

As from 1531 an attempt was made to make the students respect the ban – destined in fact to be eluded until the late eighteenth century – on carrying arms without the permission of the Venetian authorities, while the banishment of the most unruly students multiplied and the Council of Ten took to intervening more and more often in University matters which were in one way or another in the interest of public order. In the years around 1530, both because of the rise in the number of students and as a consequence of the attempt to discipline a 'structurally' turbulent environment like the University, less permissive regulations were passed and more generous financial concessions were made to some of the most important colleges for the students. In general the sixteenth century was a very favourable century for the multiplication of the *commissarie*, the student grants, and the colleges for the students: there were in fact nine new foundations, more than double the four listed in the course of the fifteenth century.

The principal phases in the drastic decline in student power at Padua around the middle of the sixteenth century followed on from one another in the years 1544-45, 1550, 1560, and 1562. In 1544 for the first time the revision of the statutes of the 'university' of jurists was entrusted to a commission which, besides the students chosen by the corporation, was also made up of certain lecturers appointed by the Venetian rectors in Padua. In the following year the Senate authorized the *Riformatori* to buy the entire Palazzo del Bo, where a little while earlier the schools of the arts, once located at San Biagio, had been joined together with those of the jurists, who had been located at the Palazzo del Bo since the late fifteenth century, and to promote the necessary building work, which was be conti-

On the two following pages: the ancient Courtyard of the Palazzo del Bo

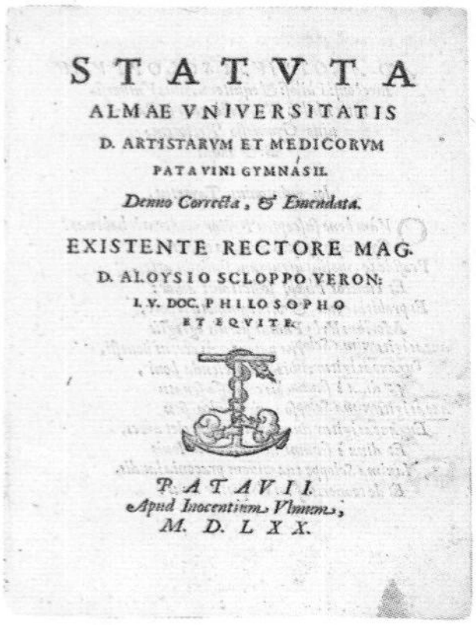

Statutes of the 'university' of arts

nued until 1552 "with dignity and ornament of our Studium and the schools and pre-existing locality that must be completely public".

"Situated opposite the new palace of the *podestà*, with its façade adorned with the lion of St. Mark" and decorated with the coats-of-arms of the Venetian representatives, the "completely public" Palazzo del Bo was not only, as Dupuigrenet Desroussilles has stressed, "the immediately noticeable sign of the undisputed dominion of the Signoria over the Studium, and an instrument of prestige to foreigners, an example quickly imitated at Pavia and Bologna"; but it also annulled the bond that had until then united the schools to the 'universities' who had been the proprietors or tenants of the rooms used for didactic purposes. Moreover, the concentration of the courses at the Bo foreshadowed, in a certain sense, the supersedence of the binary system based on the two 'universities', in favour of a single 'public' Studium, of a State University which would considered its main axis to be in the hierarchy of *Riformatori* – professors – students.

In 1550 the first printed edition of the statutes of the jurists was promoted by the rector of the jurists, but the editing was entrusted by the *Riformatori* to a professor. Among the innovations introduced in the statutes, two are worthy of being singled out for their symbolic value: one which stipulated that the inaugural mass celebrated by the 'university' was no longer to be dedicated to the Holy Spirit, but to the patron saint of Venice, Saint Mark, and the statute stipulating that a delegation of the corporation should go to Venice to pay homage to the doge on the occasion of his election. The crucial turning point came in 1560, when since riots had broken out during the election of the lawyers' rector, with dozens of wounded, some of whom quite seriously, the Senate, at the request of the Venetian rectors and many professors at Padua, decided to remove from the students what remained of their medieval right to elect teachers.

In this way the slender thread that still testified to the ancient bond of dependence of the professors on the students was cut once and for all, while relations between the *Riformatori* and the teachers were further consolidated, and the teachers were confirmed in their role as interlocutors and the principal tools of the Venetian government within the Studium. It is not surprising, then, that in 1562 another revision of the statutes of the jurists was entrusted to a commission made up only of professors. The shift in the balance of power in the direction of the professors was also favoured by the gradual increase in the percentage of Paduans in the ranks of the lecturers: a sixth, as we know, in 1517-18, but around half of the total in the last decades of the century. Perhaps the increase in the clashes between the students and Paduans after 1560 and in particular in the 1580s could be attributed to the fact that, once the right to nominate professors was taken from the former, the latter became much less tolerant with regard to student misbehaviour.

As we have seen, the major weight of the offensive against the power of the students lay on the shoulders of the law 'university'. This depended not only on the fact that the law 'university' occupied the principal place in the corporate organization of the Studium, and therefore what was decided with regard to it could be automatically extended to the 'university' of arts too; but it probably also depended on a phenomenon characteristic of the central decades of the sixteenth century, the upset of the quantitative relations between the student jurists and those of the arts. As the outgoing captain of Padua Mattio Dandolo brought to light in 1547 in a report presented to the Senate, "it is an unheard of thing in that Studium that there are not more than 300 law students and there are more than 700 students in the arts, something that always used to be to the contrary, since the law students always used to be twice as many as the artists".

Filippo Mainardi

To what factors, other than the "quality of the lecturers that [were] many and excellent in the arts", according to Dandolo, can one attribute the "unheard of thing", it is not possible to determine in the absence of specific research into the question of graduates in particular. What is certain is that in 1553 the artists of the German 'nation', the most important among the transalpines, felt themselves to be sufficiently strong after the increase in their number that they decided to separate from the jurists. It does not therefore seem to be totally wide of the mark to hold that the 'offensive' by the Venetian government against the 'university' of the jurists also sought to profit from the state of uneasiness in which the law students found themselves in those decades.

The crisis of the power of the students ran its course without significant reactions on the part of the students, both because of its gradual nature and because the Venetian authorities knew how to sugar-coat the bitter pill with certain concessions. It must in fact be recalled that the *Riformatori* and the Senate were always ready to give due consideration to the requests of the students which aimed at a greater qualification of their studies. As Dupuigrenet Desroussilles has underlined, in the mid-sixteenth century there appears an obvious convergence between the Venetian government and the students in favour of an education focused on "practical knowledge", both in the legal field (this is demonstrated, for instance, by the appointment to a professorship in criminal law – a discipline requested by the students – of an ex-functionary of the Venetian administration, and by the importance given to feudal and Roman law at the expense of canon law), and in the medical field (a tendency that found its apogee in 1545 in the decision to found a botanical garden, the first scientific 'laboratory', together with the Hospital of San Francesco, in a Studium that up to then, as was the rule in the medieval University, had had an exclusively didactic character).

2. *The Sixteenth and Seventeenth Centuries: The Counter Reformation and the "Patavina libertas"*

Venice had yet another – and perhaps even more important – card up its sleeve in the game of relations with the students (but also, as in the pre-

Botanical Garden: general view, greenhouse, dried sample collection

vious case, in its dealings with the professors): their protection from the repressive politics of the Counter Reformation. At least in principle, the Serenissima was forced to align itself with papal positions and therefore to admit into its territories the main instruments of the control of Rome over the soul, from the Inquisition to the Index of prohibited books. Nevertheless, that did not prevent it from recognizing, indeed with some justified deviation (as happened in the period of the War of Cyprus), the need for having the pope as a friend in the fight against the Ottomans, in a policy so attentive to the defence of the State with respect to the Church as to induce the pope in 1606 to excommunicate the Senate and to prohibit the celebration of the holy rites throughout the dominion of the Republic.

In the sixteenth and seventeenth centuries the Republic's University policy was developed along the lines of substantial continuity and coherence, notwithstanding the fact that at the summit of Venetian government, and in particular among the *Riformatori* – who quickly imposed themselves as one of the most prestigious magistracies in the Republic – there alternated representatives of very different ideological orientations. This was due to a political system based on the role of notables, which attributed much importance to the offices already held, and which tended therefore to reconfirm high-ranking people even when the political equilibrium had been modified to their disadvantage.

The fundamental directive remained that of the "guardianship" of the Studium by the *Riformatori* (the Senate gradually lost importance and its role in University issues was reduced to the ratification of the decisions made by the magistracy). Nevertheless the Venetian authorities no longer applied this line, as they had done mainly in the middle decades of the sixteenth century, solely in the view to subordinating the different components of the Studium to Venice; but, rather, they concentrated on the defence of those professors suspected of heresy or misbelief and, above all, of the students, who were persecuted - be they Lutheran or Calvinist, Orthodox or Jew - by the Counter Reformation. The University of Padua had to remain, notwithstanding the religious tensions, a universal source of knowledge, precisely that "universa universis Patavina libertas" which is still today the motto of the University.

This 'liberal' attitude of the Serenissima with regard to the University has been justified, or rather, exalted by the majority of historians on the basis of very different considerations. They have insisted at times on the foreign policy of the Serenissima (at the end of the sixteenth and in the first decades of the seventeenth century Venice fought, allying itself with France and making pacts with Protestant powers, from England to Holland, against the axis between Rome, Madrid, and Vienna; against, that is, the Counter Reformation union between the Pope and the Habsburgs); at times on the particular character of its political form (in a Europe dominated by absolute States Venice continued to hold high the banner of republican liberty); at times on its tolerance towards religious and ethnic minorities, typical of a city-state devoted to trade (hence a "Patavina libertas" as a University variant and derivative of the "Veneta libertas"); or at other times on the presence, in the ranks of its ruling group, of people of libertine inclination, who did not believe in anything "dai copi in su" (above the roof tiles).

Except for the last, these are all arguments of weight, but they must slip into second place with respect to the question of the peculiar nature of the relationship between Venice and the Studium. As Frijhoff reminds us, "in the Renaissance period the feudal State was transformed into the early modern State" and this latter has "need of a measure (an ideology) and of qualified and devoted controllers (counsellors, judges, and high functionaries)": the early modern State found both, ideology and controllers, "in the Universities, whose autonomy of management, thought, and teaching was from then on placed under the guardianship of the *raison d'état*". As with the majority of the other Italian States, even though it kept the characteristics of the city-State, the Venetian Republic had greatly changed through time, even playing on the mercantile character of its leading class, into a territorial State having in part surprisingly modern features. Also, as we have seen, the Studium of Padua had acquired before other universities the characteristics typical of a State University.

The "guardianship" of the Republic over the Studium coexisted however with the "Patavina libertas" and indeed to a certain extent was its most solid guarantee. How does one explain this paradox? One must consider that Venice, as an aristocratic Republic, could not identify itself in the 'strong' version of the Renaissance State depicted by Frijhoff (just as, in the eighteenth century, it could not really conform to the model of the absolute State proposed by enlightened princes). Since the Venetian patriciate was a political class by right of birth, it could do without a preparation and cultural legitimization in the classrooms of the Palazzo del Bo, as Francesco Gritti caustically observed in verse in Venetian dialect after the fall of the Republic. Gritti, a enlightened member of the old aristocratic body, made fun of a typical representative of his order, who considered himself by "inborn right" "equipped [...] to govern the populace": as a patrician, therefore he did not have, nor feel, the need to take a degree.

On the other hand, even the high-level Venetian bureaucracy, the secretaries and chancellors belonging to the élite of the 'cittadini originari' (native citizens) were not concerned, as a rule, to acquire an academic education. Certainly, the Sacred College of Law produced vicars, assessors and other personnel of Venetian administration, but their position was rigorously subaltern. This was also true for the teaching body of the University, which, after the 'submission' of Padua to Venice, had ceased to constitute a component of a political and bureaucratic class and had been closed – with few exceptions which, however, did not concern its Paduan component – in a sphere of local influence. In short, the State of St. Mark did not ask the University of Padua to be an ideological instrument at its service (among other things, Venetian law claimed its extraneousness with

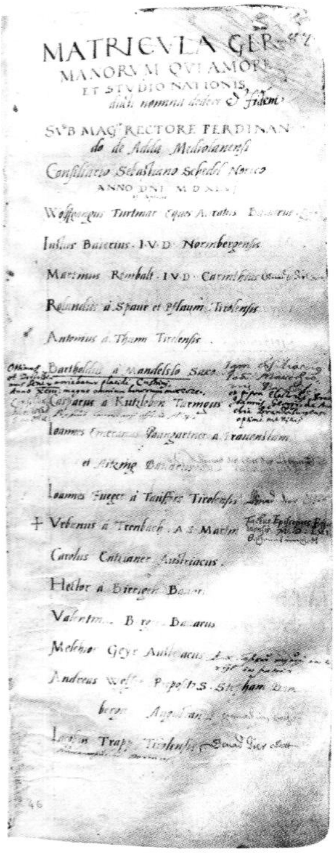

Matricula Nationis germanicae

regard to the Roman law taught in the Studium), nor a reservoir for the recruitment of its political class. As a consequence, the pressure exerted by Venice was minor, at the expense not so much of the "autonomy of management" as of the "autonomy of thought and teaching". Indeed the "autonomy of management" remained only symbolic after the state control of University finance, the complete transformation of teachers into 'public professors', and the drastic reorganization of student power.

The "autonomy of thought and teaching" benefited, to a certain extent, from the peculiar mixture of 'weakness' and 'strength' that distinguished the policy of the Venetian republic, not only in the University field. As State University the Studium of Padua was by and large protected from clerical influence and interference (despite being the chancellor of the University, the bishop normally had to remain in the margins of University life: even the control over what could be defined as his natural preserve, the Sacred College of Theology, was to be taken away from him by the *Riformatori*); and it was not excessively conditioned by the local political powers – if the Paduan case is compared to those of Bologna, Siena, etc. However, the *Riformatori* and the Senate knew to keep the harness tight on the neck of the student organizations, the teachers, and the Paduan professional corporations within the University archipelago (see, for example, the tighter control that was exercised between the fifteenth and seventeenth centuries on the consultations that the Sacred College of Law issued at the request of rulers and cities).

On the other hand, the limits of the Venetian State – we must add to the structural ones the rising fear that radical innovations might irrevocably ruin a political order which, it was believed, no longer was able to tackle the most demanding international challenges – impeded the completion of the transformation of the medieval Studium into a modern 'national' institution. It should not therefore appear strange that the principal tool of Venice's policy of "guardianship" of the University was a "distant" magistracy, the *Riformatori*, who met in the Venice, "far from the eyes of the lecturers and students", as Ingolfo Conti was to emphasize at the beginning of the seventeenth century. A magistracy which in the course of the sixteenth and seventeenth centuries was to visit the Studium from which it took its name only twice, in 1675 and 1771 respectively.

In the Venetian strategy the University was certainly a political tool, but above all to the extent to which it could be presented to the outside world as the prestigious cultural showcase of the regime. The attendance of students and the fame of the masters had to celebrate Venice, besides Padua. Consequently it is not surprising that, for example, Erasmus of Rotterdam mentioned Padua University using metaphors ("emporium", "quiet port") taken from the context of the ruling city. The Venetian authorities conceived of the Studium as a basically cosmopolitan institution, open to cultural exchanges, in the same way that Venice was for the exchange of merchandise, merchants, and travellers. From this there arose the conviction that it was necessary to guarantee the arrival of students from every part of the world, removing those religious or political barriers that could in one way or another impede them.

The attack brought by the Counter Reformation on the University of Padua was twofold: on the one hand it aimed at purging the Studium of the various elements considered heterodox; on the other it established parallel institutions against Padua University, which were destined to recruit from a catchment area partially coinciding with that of the University, but which were based on radically different educational designs. If Venice succeeded in coping reasonably well with the first of the two offensives, and even managed to counterattack with great efficiency, carrying out a reform of the University structure which was to paradoxically accentuate its national (and, if you like, lay) character, the outcome of the second challenge appears controversial. Without doubt the most direct and dangerous threat was warded off, the establishment of a Jesuit Studium in Padua. But it is also true that the competition of the colleges of the Company of Jesus and the other religious orders committed to secondary education (a task carried out in the territories of the Serenissima above all by the Somaschi and Barnabites) was one of the causes of the crisis which hit Padua University between the end of the sixteenth and the beginning of the eighteenth century.

As from 1520, when even the University of Padua was first affected and then more and more concerned – not only because of the presence of the German students – by the spread of the Protestant Reformation, "Venice left to the jurisdiction of the University tribunal all accusations of heresy and blasphemy launched against matriculated youths, thus showing it assimilated heresy easily and simply into the contravention of the civil laws", which the jurisdiction of the tribunal within the corporation was limited to, "instead of considering it a crime" (Sandro De Bernardin). The establishment in 1542 of the congregation of the Inquisition and, twenty years later, the solemn condemnation of Protestantism by the Council of Trent forced the Republic to make use of all its diplomatic resources to manoeuvre among the opposing requirements of catholic orthodoxy and the protection of those students (and teachers) who were heterodox in varying ways. The major stumbling block facing Venice's University policy was the papal bull *In Sacrosancta* of 1564, which prescribed that whosoever wished to be admitted to take the graduation examination had to make a profession of faith, which confirmed the tenets of the Tridentine decrees and with which one swore to give "true obedience to the Roman pontiff".

Venice attempted to obtain from Rome for the profession of faith - a "thing", as one *podestà* of Padua wrote, that was comprehensively "abhorred by the German, English, Greek and other nations" – not be imposed on foreign students, but the pope would not accept any compromise, and the Paduan ecclesiastical authorities profited by the papal inflexibility to re-launch its campaign against students suspected of heresy. The Serenissima was forced to put on a brave face: as from March of 1565 the

Palazzo Capodilista

profession of faith was required from those who intended to take the degree in the sacred Colleges. Nevertheless Venice's 'surrender' in the face of Roman pressure was far from being total. Although with some tactical withdrawals, and always limited to single cases, the Republic sought to guarantee an effective safety net for the Germans in particular to whom a document was granted in 1587 that protected them from investigations "for reasons of religion".

As for the question of the profession of faith, a way round the obstacle was found which exploited the fact that the baccalaureate diploma could also be granted by the counts Palatine, besides the sacred colleges. Appointed by imperial authority, the Palatine counts were not obliged to conform to what the papal bull prescribed, in contrast to the 'parallel' order of the counts of the Lateran, an order recently instituted by the Pope and granted the same rights of public jus as the Palatines, such as the right to create doctors and notaries, and to legitimize bastards. In addition the counts Palatine could also meet the needs of the less well-to-do students, who encountered growing difficulties in graduating in the sacred Colleges due to the increase in the cost of the degree and the restrictions on the number of free degrees.

Nevertheless, in 1612, when the Republic decided to expropriate for itself the powers of the counts Palatine and Lateran, powers which it believed were exclusively of state competence, the problem of the non-catholic students' degrees returned to front stage. In 1616 the Senate decided, on the request of the German 'nation' of the arts and on the proposal of the *Riformatori*, to give the "task for three years to one of the Colleges of arts, with the title of president, to confer, according to the usual style and assistance, the degree of doctor auctoritate Veneta gratis" "in the arts, to poor students and others". In 1635 an analogous measure was approved, again upon the demand of the German students, in favour of the jurists. In appearance these were blocking-measures to the benefit of the poor students (only in 1636 were the mysterious "others" identified by the Senate as "ultramontanes and Greeks", that is to say, translating the 'national' component into religious terms, Protestants and Orthodox), which were limited to substitute the counts Palatine and Lateran with members of the sacred Colleges chosen by the *Riformatori*. In any case, it was this version that Venice - which always alluded to the scabrous question of the religion of the laureates by simply adopting, in the Senatorial decrees, enigmatic formulas like the "public observances well known to the prudence of this Council" - sought to have credited by the justly suspicious Roman authorities.

In fact the resolutions adopted in 1616 and in 1635 have to be considered, also in light of the successive decrees of 1636 and 1640 which were supposed to interpret and integrate them, as the pillars of a high profile reform, without a doubt the most important of those adopted in the University sphere in the seventeenth century. The even more significant point is that hidden behind the Latin formula "auctoritate Veneta". As far as we know, it was the first time that a State had explicitly questioned the umbilical cord that united the general Studia and, beyond these, knowledge in its highest manifestations, to the universal powers of medieval Europe, that is, the pope and the emperor.

Just as the Republic arrogated the right to "confer [...] the degree of doctor" by means of teachers designated by itself, the University of Padua, though preserving its own identity which can be defined as papal-communal and which was guaranteed in particular by the sacred Colleges, made a further, fundamental step towards its transformation into a State University. At the same time higher science was preparing to undergo, for better or worse, a 'national' modification, which sooner or later was to be reflected on the didactic level, and which was to lead, among other things, to the difficult and gradual substitution of the universal language of the medieval and renaissance Studia, Latin, with - in the case of Padua – Italian. What is paradoxical is that this fundamental pressure in favour of the State University originated in Padua in the desire to preserve the Studium's cosmopolitan character. Furthermore, the road to the 'laicization' of the University was trod with the purpose of preventing the religious standardization required by the Counter Reformation (De Bernardin has summarized the rebuttals of the Senate to the protests of Rome, pointing out that the Studium "was only concerned with certifying the scientific preparation of the student and the fact that a heretic was a good physician did not at all prejudice the true faith").

The instrument of this turning point was initially identified, as we know, in a member of the "College of arts", on whom the "title of president" was conferred by the *Riformatori*. Between 1636 and 1640, however, the birth of two august Venetian Colleges, made up of the eight principal chairs of the two 'universities', was formalized. In this way not only was the bond between the universities and the degrees "in the name of the Venetian Republic" destroyed – objectively embarrassing, if not counterproductive, given the sacred character of the Colleges of Paduan doctors – but the organization of the Studium was also radically modified, juxtaposing and, as we will see later, in practice opposing two of the three preexistent doctoral Colleges, which were, as we know, expressions of local interests, with the Venetian Colleges. Given the tendency of the Republic to assign the 'first ranks' to foreigners, these Venetian colleges contained above all University professors born as a rule outside Padua, who therefore have to be considered the spokesmen of the interests of a 'category'. In other words, through the Venetian Colleges the non-Paduan teachers of the University received for the first time an institutional recognition, which in the subsequent decades would allow them to present reports and projects to the *Riformatori*. As a consequence, the axis between the *Riformatori* and the professors (above all the foreigners) was made stronger than ever, an axis which as from the 1530s had assumed a central position in the Padua University context.

The other important challenge which the Counter Reformation set the

University was that of the colleges for the education of the ruling classes, primarily the nobility. In Padua, as in the rest of the Catholic world, the most insidious threat to the University were the Jesuits, who in 1542 opened a college in Padua initially destined for the training of the members of the Society, and then gradually transformed into a para-University institute (in 1590 it was decorated with the title of *Gymnasium Patavinum Societatis Jesu*). Even worse: as the philosopher Cesare Cremonini was to complain, it was transformed into a proper anti-Studium (it must not be forgotten that the most usual Latin name for Padua University was *Gymnasium Patavinum*), both because subjects were taught, from the humanities to philosophy and theology, which also appeared in the 'rotulo' of the University, and because it was frequented by just under five hundred students (among whom about sixty Venetian patricians and Paduan noblemen), half of whom pursued studies at a University level.

At the beginning of the 1590s, based on the few figures available - almost all relating to the law 'university' - the number of students at Padua had not only dropped to a notable extent with respect to the exceedingly high levels reached in the 1540s, but it had fallen below the rather low average recorded in the early 1560s (just over five hundred students enrolled). This was perhaps due to the continued conflict between the students and the Paduan nobility, but was certainly a result of competition with the Jesuit college. It is not surprising, therefore, that the Senate considered the "new form of the Studium, with the sounding of the bell and printed course lists, at the same times, with open doors and public schools" introduced by the Jesuits at Padua "almost in competition and with manifest prejudice against that of our Signoria". As a consequence a decree was approved in 1591 which ordered that the reverend Fathers "could not lecture except among themselves, to the benefit of their own, and no others, without infringing in any manner on the Statutes and privileges of our Studium in Padua". In other words, the Jesuit college had to return to its origins as a Seminary for the members of the Society.

Nevertheless it must be stressed that the decree "destructive" – as the Jesuits defined it – of the *Gymnasium Patavinum Societatis Jesu* was passed by a narrow majority of Venetian senators, and that the noble Council of Padua, both before and after 1591, always continued to side with the Jesuits. In effect the pedagogical project of the Society had gained the approval of the richest and most conservative members of the two ruling classes directly involved in the problem. As a memo by the noble Council of Padua pointed out in favour of the Jesuits in 1594, the opposition between the "tumultuous schools" of the Palazzo del Bo and the "virtuous schools" of the Society, the students who carried "weapons" and the "boys [...] who lived with discipline", could only be resolved in favour of the educational programme of the reverend Fathers.

The Counter Reformation model, founded on the premise that, as one Jesuit wrote, "it is a universal custom in all parts of the world to employ in this" - that is to say in the pedagogical field - "for the most part priests and religious persons, since it is not very safe to entrust the instruction and education of children to secular persons of loose life and customs", not only de-legitimized all the lay lecturers of the Palazzo del Bo, but it did not even accept the "loose life" of the students, and therefore clearly seemed to lead in the mid term to the suffocation of that "Patavina libertas" which on an institutional level continued to exist in the form of the student corporations. It is not surprising therefore that not only the teachers directly involved in the Jesuit "competition", such as Cremonini, but also both the 'universities' of the students, incited by the German 'nations' and the professors of arts, ended up by backing recourse to Venice against the Anti-Studium of the Society.

Cesare Cremonini

Even after the "evident danger of evil consequences and destruction" of the Studium as a result of the unjust Jesuit "competition" was warded off, the Venetian authorities and various elements of the Padua Studium came to consolidate the identity and the specificity of the University by means of a series of initiatives conducted on many fronts. On the didactic level the custom of dictating the texts, typical of most Italian Universities and Jesuit colleges, was prohibited: a teacher at Padua had to demonstrate his mastery of the discipline (and academic Latin) by holding his lesson without using any 'paper'. In this way, as Francesco Grimani Calergi, one of the many eighteenth-century critics of this practice, pointed out, "the lessons were reduced to a truly vain and unfounded pomp of memory with manifest damage to the student and displeasure to the master, who was obliged to waste much time memorizing his lectures".

If, as will become clearer further on, the attempt to emphasise the particularity of the teaching at Padua had become exceedingly counterproductive, another innovation in the final years of the century, on the other hand, seems to have had entirely positive repercussions: the construction of an anatomical theatre within the Palazzo del Bo, a recognition of the excellence acquired by the Paduan school of medicine and the importance attributed to it by Venice (which also profited by shedding light indirectly on the limits of the Jesuit "competition", which certainly could not vie with the public University in the education of physicians and lawyers). In turn the anatomical theatre was to promote further important scientific developments, as confirmed by William Harvey and Johann Georg Wirsung among others. Finally it must pointed out that in 1598 the first history of the Studium, *De Gymnasio Patavino* was sent to the press, compiled by one of the most decisive adversary of the Jesuits, the professor of Greek and Latin humanities, Antonio Riccoboni. Although it was dedicated by the editor to the counsellors of the German 'nation', the work reflected above all the author's interest in the "literary controversies" of the University teachers, and was a confirmation of the central role that the professors had acquired in the life – and therefore in the history – of the Studium.

On the two following pages: the Anatomical Theatre

3. *The Seventeenth and Eighteenth Centuries: from Baroque Stagnation to the Reforms of the Enlightenment*

In the course of the seventeenth and the first part of the eighteenth century the University of Padua, like most other Europe universities, underwent a critical phase in which the shadows clearly outnumbered the rays of light. The Republic, and in particular the *Riformatori*, were not only unable to oppose the degradation of the teaching system with the energy and shrewdness they had shown in the defence of the "Patavina libertas" against Counter Reformation pressures, but they even contributed to the establishment of a vicious downward spiral. Without a doubt their objective remained – as Conti stressed in 1614 – the "preservation and growth of that Studium which has for centuries and centuries been deemed the finest in Europe"; they also wanted, as one *podestà* of Padua insisted in the same period, "to maintain the Studium in its greatness", in such a way that the University would continue to be the cultural flower in the buttonhole of the Venetian republic, and therefore contribute to elevating its prestige world-wide.

But the conception, typical of the Baroque age, that Venice had of "greatness" itself tended to privilege form with respect to substance, rites and traditions rather than the content and the effectiveness of teaching methods. Among other things, the lectures given at the Palazzo del Bo after the reform approved by the Senate in 1591 testify to this. In 1711 the Kingdom of Savoy's ambassador to Venice, Francesco Filippo Picono, observed that these lectures were held in a "haranguing" manner, "somewhat like someone who preaches or recites a discourse *ad pompam* than a lecture or explanation by a man who teaches". Picono was willing to recognize that these were lectures that were "most erudite and always with great decorum"; nevertheless the students derived very little "utility" from them, since they were "compositions, accompanied by figures, and animated with gestures [...] that make them very delightful to hear, but for he who wishes to accumulate a doctrinal capital they are most displeasing for the speed with which they are pronounced and the multitude of the doctrines that are presented".

In those same years Francesco Grimani Calergi, an influential Venetian patrician to whom Scipione Maffei was to dedicate his celebrated '*Ricordo*' [memorandum] 'for the Reform of the Studium of Padua' in 1715, declared himself convinced that "the need for the *puntisti* [see below] is born from having removed the dictation, because the students, not able to learn the doctrines needed to graduate by simply listening to them in the Bo, have to look for specific private masters to instruct them"; vice versa, "the students being sufficiently educated by these *puntisti* to take a degree do not go to the public lectures", unless forced to by the need to show the proof of attendance required when taking the doctorate. In other words, following the late sixteenth-century turning point in the teaching at the Studium of Padua, two or rather three parallel teaching circuits co-existed, or rather opposed each other: a) the official circuit, the "haranguing" lectures held at the Palazzo del Bo, which could only benefit the particularly well-prepared or talented students; b) the circuit of the *puntisti*, the "private lecturers", who illegally imparted the fundamental notions in the juridical field (a task carried out in particular by the *istitutisti*, that is, those who taught the institutions of civil law) or the medical field to the student 'mass', training the students above all in the *punti*, the "points", that is to say, to answer questions which were chosen by lot from a pre-established list at the degree exams; c) the circuit of private lessons imparted, almost always for payment, by the official professors in their houses to students who often used to rent rooms from them too.

Francesco Bertelli,
Gymnasii Patavini pars exterior
and Gymnasii Patavini
pars interior

This last circuit, which although in some periods acquired notable importance thanks to particularly prestigious teachers (we can think, for example, of the importance of the private schools of Galileo Galilei and Giambattista Morgagni), nevertheless involved a more or less reduced minority of students (also because it is known that many professors did not want to teach privately the discipline which they were officially charged with teaching, but preferred to become illegal *istitutisti* or *puntisti*), at least until the reforms of the second half of the eighteenth century which were to integrate them into the circuit of the lectures at the Palazzo del Bo. It can be affirmed therefore that in the seventeenth and at the beginning of the eighteenth century what distinguished academic teaching was the competition between the public Studium and those who Conti defined, not by chance using a term adopted by Cremonini regarding the aborted Jesuit University, as the "private anti-Studia". Padua was "full" of these "anti-Studia" from the beginning of the seventeenth century onwards, and in the following decades they were also to proliferate in the principal cities of the mainland and in Venice, thus diverting hundreds of potential students from the University classrooms.

In 1614 a decree by the Senate noted that "a wretched corruption in our Studium of Padua had recently been introduced, that the lecturers do not lecture [in private] to the students on the texts by authors of those professions in which they intend to make progress, but only on the *punti* that serve to gain the title of doctor", and hence allowed the official professors to "drill [their students] in these *punti*" only fifteen days before the degree. The punishment was to lose their chair and receive a heavy fine, while the law inflicted the same fine and two years of banishment on "doctors not reading public lectures", who dared to work as *puntisti*. These repressive norms remained, in fact, a dead letter. Not by chance, at the end of the seventeenth century the Senate returned, in vain, to legislate with "the object of severing this scandalous abuse" and extirpating a "profession so detested and abhorred". Even throughout the first half of the eighteenth century the denunciations of the "quantity of private lecturers" and the "incredible number of *puntisti*" continued, always without results.

The proliferation of the *puntisti* was also favoured, besides by the substantial didactic inefficiency of the lectures held at the Palazzo del Bo, by the scheming which went on at the degree examinations. As a decree of the Senate recorded in 1655, degree candidates did not find difficulty in "acquiring the *punti*" (the questions) - which the statutes stated were to be chosen by lot twenty-four hours before the examination - "on which they were to be examined". This happened "by means of persons who are enemies of virtue, disturbers of good order". The *Riformatori* sought in vain to fight the phenomenon, raising excessively the number of *punti* and electing, in 1664, some official *puntisti* (two per 'university' beginning in 1665), who had to assist the students in their preparation during the last year of their studies (from 1665 only in the two months preceding the degree). The attempt to combat the "private anti-Studia" by legalizing, de facto, the "most detested and abhorred practice" of the *puntisti*, was a complete failure, as is attested by a report presented in 1738 to the *Riformatori* by Giovan Francesco Pivati, a functionary of the magistracy entrusted with watching over the Studium.

At Padua – Pivati wrote, among other things – the students continued to graduate with "vile methods" and "shameful easiness". "Instead of choosing the *punti* by lot, many times they are given months, even years ahead of time"; "instead of making a young man study, he is made to study nothing of law or medicine besides those two given *punti* and nothing else, then pretending to draw them by lot, the *puntisti* turn their heads the other way"; "the subjects that must be taken at the degree, are sent home ahead of time, to the dishonour of the oath that every doctor in the College takes"; "the *arguenti*" (that is to say those members of the College who had to participate in the debate), "who must be chosen by lot, are those very ones who have sent the subjects home to the student" and, finally, "in the recapitulation of these arguments the student is prompted word-for-word by a nearby professor". It is not surprising that in this way "every incredible ignoramus" could be graduated by the doctoral Colleges of Padua, and that the anonymous author of a contemporary *Regolazione sopra i proffessori dello Studio di Padova* [Regulation relating to the professors of Padua University], affirmed that it had become a "proverb" that "anyone, no matter how ignorant, can get a degree from the University of Padua".

Pivati attributed all this to the corruption or at least the connivance of most of the members of the doctoral Colleges. But one must also bear in mind a 'structural' cause for a practice so indulgent with the student degree candidates: the real competition between the Sacred Colleges and the Venetian Colleges, a competition which induced the rivals to be more or less permissive with their degree candidates to keep them from turning to the 'enemy'. Based on the decrees of the Senate, the boundary between the students who could have access to the Venetian Colleges and those destined to take degrees in the Sacred Colleges was very clear: among the former were only the Greeks, the ultramontanes, and the poor. Nevertheless the paternalistic laxity of the *Riformatori* was to add to these three categories not only all those who were not subjects of the Republic, but also those subjects whose families could prove a foreign origin (thus in 1731 Carlo Goldoni, who was born in Venice of a father born in the city, but who could vaunt a grandfather born in Modena, was able to graduate from the Venetian College of law).

Carlo Goldoni

In the last decades of the seventeenth and the first eighty years of the eighteenth century, while there were no significant variations in the number of students belonging to the 'nations' who were allowed to take their degrees in the Venetian Colleges, these latter were hit by a succession of anomalous waves of 'popularity'. While, for example, in the relatively rigorous 1720s the Venetian Colleges granted degrees to 27% of the graduates, that percentage reached 45% in the first years of the 1740s and even exceeded 75% (in the case of the artists) in the exceedingly permissive 1770's. These waves favourable to the Venetian Colleges were weakened or interrupted by the intervention by the Senate or the *Riformatori* (as happened in 1711, in 1760, and in 1780), at the request of the sacred Colleges and the noble Council of Padua, which demanded the substantial respect of their "privileges" within the context of the University.

The protests by the Paduan notables were not surprising, given that the students' preference for the Venetian Colleges greatly damaged them on the financial level. What was at stake was in fact the "deposit" which the candidates had to pay before presenting themselves for the exam, an expense which with the continuous and often arbitrary increases had in fact reached such heights that the degree cost as much as a year of room and board at Padua (until 1777, as Pivati recalled, besides the "published public tariff" there was also a "hand-written addition, that was given secretly to the candidate at the time of his degree"). It was a preoccupation of the same type that pushed the students literally to forge their papers to be able to graduate from the Venetian Colleges. These latter took in fact more adroit measures (less serious procedures, as the sacred Colleges maintained, an accusation that the Venetian Colleges not only denied disdainfully, but turned back against their competitors), but above all they required a considerably lower 'deposit' (a third less in the case of the artists) than that requested by the sacred Colleges. It is not by chance that in 1780 the question of the competition between the Venetian Colleges and the sacred Colleges was resolved once and for all by a reform which established that the character of the College no longer affected the amount of the 'deposit', nor the *sportula* (that is to say the remuneration) given to the professors who formed the Venetian Colleges. Once the convergent interests of the candidates and the professors, respectively, in choosing and recommending the Venetian Colleges had disappeared, the quota of graduates in these latter was to quickly drop below the threshold of a fifth of the total.

Around the middle of the 1730s a Venetian patrician who desired to restore the University to its "original splendour and prosperity", and in particular to "procure and facilitate the increase in the number" of students, advised the *Riformatori* to "consent frequently to the wishes" of the students. In reality, as the concessions regarding the *puntisti* and the Venetian Colleges demonstrated, the *Riformatori*, although they had sought to take into account the need to safeguard the function of the lectures at the Palazzo del Bo and the "privileges" demanded by the Paduans, had not simply been awaiting this suggestion to carry out a policy which respected the "wishes" of the students and their relatives. After the turning point of 1560, the crisis of the 'universities' had deepened. Even most of the foreign 'nations' navigated through rough waters, with the important exception of the Germans, who were to preserve a notable importance throughout the seventeenth century (in particular, the annual average number of students enrolled in the German 'nation' of the arts was twenty-one between 1553 and 1599, thirty between 1600 and 1649, twenty-eight between 1650 and 1699 and eighteen between 1700 and 1721), the 'Ultramarines' (the Greeks) and the Poles.

In 1608 an English traveller declared himself convinced that "there are at Padua more students of foreign origin and from remote nations than in any other University in the Christian world", but in fact in those years the Studium was very much less cosmopolitan than it had been in the recent past. If in 1591 nearly half the students came from abroad, twenty years later the Ultramontanes slightly exceeded a quarter of the total. It is still not clear what structural causes most influenced this phenomenon: most obvious and taken for granted is the impact of circumstances adverse to the influx of the students: wars and the great plague epidemics. One must undoubtedly note, following Maffei and Grimani Calergi, "the immense number of Jesuit and Somaschi colleges, in which a large part of the young nobility is educated, whereas once everyone went to the public Studia"; but important as well were the establishment of new Universities in states which had remained without one up until then, and, above all, the related protectionist practices of sovereigns to prevent their subjects from studying outside their own country. Perhaps the continued decrease in influence of the students on academic events also had some weight. What is certain is that from the beginning of the seventeenth century the over costly office of rector no longer had any candidates. The second rank below the rectors, the pro-rectors and 'sindaci' (auditors), were placed at the head of the corporations, but in the absence of candidates their place was sometimes taken by counsellors from the German 'nation'.

The loss of prestige of the student representatives was accompanied by an evident decline in their interest in an improvement in their studies. In the seventeenth and eighteenth centuries the students no longer demanded, as they had done in the sixteenth century, the institution of new chairs, nor did they contribute, even unofficially, to the appointment of professors. The "wishes" of the students no longer went beyond the elementary, one could say instinctive, need to graduate as soon as possible and at the lowest possible cost. The *Riformatori* consequently attempted to lower the cost for the degree examination (the institutions of official *puntisti* ran basically on the same lines) fixing, among other things, a limit to the number of promoters. But it appears clear that in the short run they were not capable, as we have seen, of moderating the demands of the doctoral colleges.

On the other hand the Venetian magistracy did not encounter obstacles in its path when it decided to satisfy the "wishes" of its student subjects (an exception was made for the Oltremars who, like the Ultramontanes and the foreigners in general, were exempted from obligatory attendance) concerning the reduction of their stay at Padua. This was done by both reducing drastically the length of the course of studies (in 1636 the six or seven years set by the statutes of the two 'universities' was brought down to five, and in 1700 to four; in the course of the early eighteenth century a reduction of the courses to three years was also considered), and by permitting the academic year to be shortened more and more. In 1771 the consultants of the *Riformatori* Natale Dalle Laste, Gasparo Gozzi, and Giambattista Bilesimo, calculated that in fact the year had reached the point of including only three months of lectures.

It is true that at the same time the *Riformatori* managed to render the – residual – presence of the students even more effective, by imposing on them certifications that at first sight were ever more difficult to obtain. Thus in 1638 the burden of certifying the presence of the students at the lectures at the Palazzo del Bo was placed on the shoulders of the teachers, and in 1665 tertiaries were instituted, that is to say that the students were obliged to be issued, every third part of the academic year, with a certificate of attendance first by eight, then by four "primary" first-rank professors. But – as the *Regolazione sopra i proffessori* complained – it was quite a widespread practice for the students to limit themselves "to showing up a few times at the school of one of the less scrupulous professors to swindle the sworn oath of the tertiary".

In the same way the aims of a decree by the Senate in 1655 were not achieved. The decree prescribed that "the period of the [...] residence [of the student] at the same [Studium] is not intended to begin except from the day that he presents himself to the fiscal chamber, where he has to give his name, surname, father's name, and country, and his address is to be noted alphabetically in a book kept for this purpose", and it also stated "that no one can enjoy the exemption of the matricula if he is not inscribed in the said book, and the same *matricula* must in future be numbered and dispensed according to numerical order". As Pivati was to complain in 1738, even after the decree there continued to be a "theft of *matriculae*" so very "vituperous" as to make one look very suspiciously at the official data concerning enrolment, which in any case had a very uneven course: indeed at the beginning of the eighteenth century a *podestà* of Padua calculated that, despite his efforts to contain the phenomenon, the "effective and legitimate" students were less than half of those present in the "alphabetical book".

While at the close of the sixteenth century the number of matriculations was under the five hundred mark, in 1610 it reached a thousand. The

Thirty Years War caused the enrolment trend to take another downward turn. In 1640 the lowest point of the seventeenth century was perhaps reached with barely 379 students enrolled; a peak in enrolment was reached in 1682, one of the years of peace that separated the end of the War of Crete from the beginning of the War of Morea, when 1362 students figured in the "alphabetical book". As had happened in the course of the sixteenth century, even in the seventeenth the quantitative relationships between the law students and the students in the arts varied in a way that was difficult to decipher: if in 1592 there were four matriculating students of the former to one of the latter, in 1673 there were double the number of artists than law students. One of the protagonists of the period of reform, the then professor of medicine Simone Stratico, pointed out in 1760 that in those decades of the seventeenth century "matriculation reduced to the indirect profit of the *sindaci* made the number of students appear notable, with a pleasant deception, something that was not true". It may be possible therefore that these strong variations were also caused by the greater or lesser 'generosity' of those who were at the top of the two 'universities'.

In any case, critically evaluating the information which can be derived from the matriculation registers is a precaution suggested by a comparison with the still partial data we have regarding the degrees. While, for example, the statistics concerning the number of students enrolled show a drop in the number of Ultramontanes beginning in the years around 1680 (26% in 1611, but 10% in 1677 and 5% in 1681), we know that at the beginning of the eighteenth century (more precisely in the years from 1719 to 1747) more than a fifth of the graduates at Padua still came from the area of the Holy Roman Empire. The difference between the serial data of the matriculations and the degrees conferred is justified if one takes into account above all the fact that while at that time Venetian subjects - except the Greeks – were required to attend the University for four years, the average stay for the Ultramontanes and the Oltremars was less than two years.

As from the last decades of the seventeenth century, while it suffered an evident tarnishing of its cosmopolitan lustre, the Studium was also neglected by that part of the civic society which had contributed to its success in the past, alleviating the students from the burden of their stay. In the first two thirds of the seventeenth century two new colleges had been founded for the students (both to favour the Greeks, a 'nation' which not by chance was to undergo a phase of expansion in the course of the century, in contrast to its foreign sisters), and seven *commissarie* had been established. After 1664, however, no new benefits for the students were created, and the network of aid which favoured their stay in Padua accelerated its breakdown so rapidly that a century later Stratico asserted that only ten colleges continued to remain open, while nine others had "vanished" or had been converted to some other use.

The *Riformatori* needed no convincing that one of the principal reasons that induced parents to keep their sons away from the Studium was the "bad impression that is spread about the students' excessive liberty"

(1. Conti) - an "impression" though that was merely confirmed by the riots in which the students were often protagonists (there were very few visitors to Padua in those decades who did not complain of the dangers that one encountered there after dark because of the forays of groups of armed students). Despite this, however, the same *Riformatori* and, before them, the Venetian rectors of Padua, failed in their repeated but often ritual attempts to discipline the rowdy student body. This defeat must be attributed above all to the lack of an official teaching circuit, which kept the students far from the lecture halls, but also to the tendency of the Venetian government to turn a blind eye to the "excessive liberty of the students", on the assumption that an indulgent policy would attract a greater number of them to Padua.

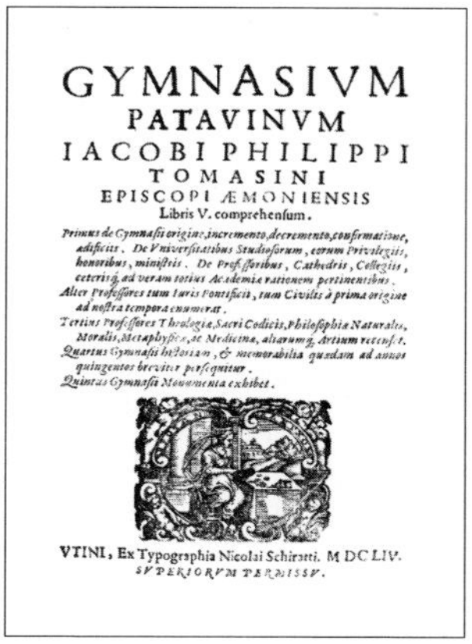
GYMNASIVM
PATAVINVM
IACOBI PHILIPPI
TOMASINI
EPISCOPI ÆMONIENSIS
Libris V. comprehensum.
Primus de Gymnasii origine, incremento, decremento, confirmatione, ædificiis. De Vniversitatibus Studiosorum, eorum Privilegiis, honoribus, ministris. De Professoribus, Cathedris, Collegiis, ceterisq; ad veram totius Academiæ rationem pertinentibus.
Alter Professores tum Iuris Pontificii, tum Civilis à prima origine ad nostra tempora enumerat.
Tertius Professores Theologiæ, Sacri Codicis, Philosophiæ Naturalis, Moralis, Metaphysicæ, ac Medicinæ, aliarumq; Artium recenset.
Quartus Gymnasii historiam, & memorabilia quædam ad annos quingentos breviter persequitur.
Quintus Gymnasii Monumenta exhibet.
VTINI, Ex Typographia Nicolai Schiratti. M DC LIV.
SVPERIORVM PERMISSV.

Gymnasium Patavinum
by Giacomo Filippo Tomasini

Neither did the *Riformatori* seriously counter the pressures brought to bear by the Paduans to preserve that municipal character of the Studium celebrated in the mid seventeenth century by the local man of letters Giacomo Filippo Tomasini in a new history of the University entitled *Gymnasium Patavinum*, which was dedicated, respecting an almost worn-out corporative tradition, to the Germanic 'nation'. Throughout the seventeenth and the first half of the eighteenth century the number of Paduan teachers, mostly patricians, remained around 50% of the total number of professors reached in the late sixteenth century. Nevertheless one must also remember that Venice, although it was lavish in its concessions to the Paduans (in 1657 it formally removed the prohibition that kept them from occupying the 'first ranks'), also sought, as a French traveller wrote in a hyperbolic vein at the end of the seventeenth century, to fill "the chairs with the most knowledgeable men in the world, that they [the Venetians] attract with high salaries" (in 1700 the professors who were not subjects of the Republic amounted to nearly a third of the entire teaching body).

In the seventeenth century the Studium's budget fluctuated between fifteen and thirty thousand ducats, that is to say an amount decidedly higher not only than that invested in the sixteenth century, but also, once inflation is taken into account, than that destined for the University in the age of reform. And yet, despite the financial power (which among other things allowed the establishment in 1629 of the *pubblica libreria*, the first Italian University library), and despite the fact that the "most knowledgeable men in the world" were called on to occupy its chairs, the University of Padua - although it continued to be exalted in foreign guidebooks as "the most beautiful and celebrated in Italy" - did not avoid the crisis which in that century and later struck the Studia of Europe with few exceptions. The serious limitations in its teaching and its fidelity to a framework of studies that did not take into account the new directions of modern science, together with the rumours that circulated regarding the behaviour of its "malicious and impious students" (as Johann Caspar Goethe, the father of the more celebrated Johann Wolfgang, defined them), contributed to lowering the prestige of a University which ever since the end of the seventeenth century had been increasingly judged to be in "decline". And its

Monument to Elena Corner Piscopia in the Palazzo del Bo

fame could certainly not be re-launched by episodes pointing to the future, but sterile at the time, such as the first female graduate in the world, that is to say the only – and not only for this reason typically baroque – degree in philosophy conferred in 1678 on the Venetian patrician Elena Corner Piscopia.

In the eighteenth century, the history of the Padua Studium can be divided into two main periods separated by a watershed, the reform of 1761. In the first period the running of the University by the *Riformatori* and the Senate was characterized, as it had been in the previous century, by the defence of traditional norms and arrangements. The most important innovation was the reduction of the University budget, which did not even keep pace with inflation. Between 1700 and 1750 the number of teachers fell from fifty-one to thirty-nine. Hunting for "the most knowledgeable men in the world" became a rare event: more and more the chairs given to young men who had graduated from the University of Padua itself and who, unlike foreign celebrities, were content with low salaries. Not by chance the percentage of teachers who were not subjects of the Republic fell in this period from 29% to 13%, while that of the Paduans rose from 43% to 54%. This was accompanied by an increase in the clerical component of the teaching body (from 23 to 38%), which was due in part to the fact that the churchmen were willing to accept lower salaries than the laity since they were housed in convents or enjoyed benefices. At the same time there was a reduction in the percentage of nobles: two tendencies destined to become consolidated in the second half of the century.

The need for a "correction and reform" of the "matters of the Studium" which would ensure the presence in Padua of a "good number of students", but which above all would give them a solid cultural and professional training "so that once their course of studies has finished they will return to their countries true doctors", was noted early enough, as is testified by a document of 1712 by the presidents of the Venetian Colleges. But this precise denunciation, like the most advanced and detailed proposals made a few years later by Maffei and Grimani Calergi - which instead pointed above all to the need for a radical reform of the traditional teaching curriculum - fell substantially on deaf ears. Priority was given to propagandistic works such as the *Historia Gymnasii Patavini*, published in 1726 by a professor of law, Nicolò Comneno Papadopoli. Papadopoli's work can be considered the first 'political' history of the University, insofar as it was not only promoted by – and dedicated to – the *Riformatori*, but above all because it made the "splendour and the majesty reached" by a University exalted without reservation depend on Venetian rule: "no other Studium in Italy has had greater and more famous professors in every type of discipline or has educated more learned and illustrious students".

In the first decades of the century the chronicles of a University unable to abandon the organizational, disciplinary, and didactic "old school" were fuelled above all by the "mournful events" which in 1715, 1723, 1735 and 1737 saw the students come to blows either with the Paduan nobles, the police, or the artisans of the urban militia. These episodes following one after the other, and the evident crisis of the student corporations induced the Venetian government in 1738 to dissolve the 'universities' and entrust the offices of pro-rector and *sindaco* to the professors and the distribution of the *matriculae* to the Venetian rectors of Padua. This latter decision, even though it certainly did not put an end to the traditional "rubbamento" (theft) of this document, reduced in any case to a significant extent the category of the "alleged" students. After the suppression of the student organizations the number of those enrolled, which in the course of the preceding decades had oscillated between the annual average of eight hundred at the beginning of the century, and that of a little over six hundred in the 1710s, dropped by almost a third, confirming the worst suspicions; it remained however above the five hundred mark until the reforms of the 1760s.

The *coup de grâce* to student autonomy had been recommended as well as by the *podestà* of Padua then in office, also by Pivati, the functionary placed by the *Riformatori* in charge the "literary matters" of the University. That year Pivati had presented the magistracy with some *Riflessioni sopra lo stato presente dello Studio di Padova* (Considerations on the present state of the Padua Studium), which among other things suggested adopting the "new scientific method" with "new chairs and new subjects", as well as inaugurating a new reform of the "disappointing" teaching at the Palazzo del Bo and a degree exam that no longer gave any guarantees of competence. But the *Riformatori* preferred not to embark on a general reform of the University, and limited themselves to the establishment of a new chair in experimental physics. The physics laboratory, together with the acquisition of the museum of natural history belonging to Antonio Vallisneri Sr. and the institution of a chair in navigation and naval architecture, represented in any case an important move towards a University based on scientific "establishments"; a University, therefore, not only ready to adopt the "new experimental method", but also to consolidate the mathematico-scientific field that had long remained stifled by the disciplines of professional worth, like law and medicine.

In 1752 Jacopo Facciolati, the first holder of a chair in the History of the University (instituted in 1739) also insisted on the "structures necessary for the practice of physics" in his *De Gymnasio Patavino syntagmata XII*, to a certain extent an anticipation of the more demanding *Fasti Gymnasii Patavini* (published in 1757). Nevertheless, Facciolati, unlike Pivati, accepted the "new method" only in homeopathic doses (the *Plan for the reform of a University of study* compiled in the same period, in which Facciolati proposed to rationalizing the existing arrangement with few innovative improvements, also testifies to this), and he preferred to take refuge, when the arguments permitted it, in an exaltation of the good old days.

The reform of 1761 was promoted by a trio of relatively 'young' *Riformatori* (their average age was just over fifty, while that of the previous three had been barely under eighty) open to European culture: Angelo Contarini, Bernardo Nani, and Francesco II Lorenzo Morosini, the latter of whom was the protagonist of the University reforms of the Venetian Age of Enlightenment. It is true that at first the policy of the magistracy did not stray from the beaten track which limited the action of the *Riformatori* to "reviving", from time to time, the "execution" of more or less remote and neglected "public laws". But the project for reform which Stratico had presented at the end of 1760 to a collaborator of the Riformatori with the aim of rendering "the University of Padua illustrious, profitable and well connected", and of restoring it "with splendour and usefulness", induced the *Riformatori* to aim higher.

Even if they rejected some of Stratico's proposals which were most innovative and anticipatory of the future developments of the University - and not only of the Paduan institution - (the suppression of the medieval bipartition of lawyers and artists, the introduction of degrees in "philosophy" and "mathematics", that is to say science and engineering; the adoption of textbooks; the transformation of the University into an academy...), in 1761 they passed an important reform of the teaching. They decided, among other things, on the transferral of private lectures to the Bo (in which Italian was to be used, *al tavolino*, that is to say sitting round a table, in the style of a seminary), the inauguration of proper curricula, and the introduction of the teaching of "useful" disciplines both in the juridical (public law) and in the medical-scientific field (medical and surgical clinics, a chair in gynaecology, paediatrics, and industrial medicine and agrarian science).

But in 1762 the traditionalists returned to power in Venice and, as a consequence, the Senate decided to re-establish the "ancient method" regarding teaching. However this counter-reform did not stop the gradual institution of new chairs established in 1761, and more generally, it was not able to compromise the substitution of the traditional 'vertical' 'rotulo' with a 'horizontal' 'rotulo'. At the beginning of the eighteenth century two-thirds of the chairs were dedicated to the elucidation of five disciplines: practical medicine, theoretical medicine, philosophy, canon law, and Roman law, whereas the 'horizontal' roll, after having recognized that the area of recruitment of the students by this time largely coincided with the territories of the Serenissima, aimed at enlarging the range of the University subjects by taking into account the needs of the State, the economy, and Venetian society.

In particular a chair in public law was activated, a decisive recognition of the existence of a third area of legal studies besides those of civil and canon law; it was decided to construct an astronomical observatory, the most costly and striking intervention - together with the rental of a little land for the experiments of the chair in agriculture - in an age of University reforms which endowed the Studium with a dense network of scientific 'establishments'. Those which stand out, like the clinics already mentioned, are the reforms which contributed to push medicine in an

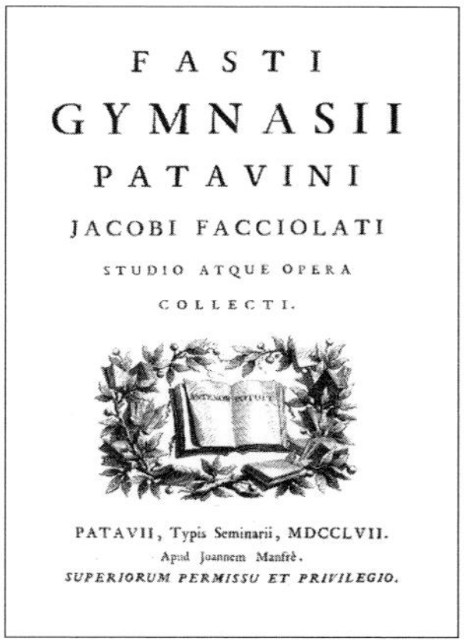
FASTI
GYMNASII
PATAVINI
JACOBI FACCIOLATI
STUDIO ATQUE OPERA
COLLECTI.

PATAVII, Typis Seminarii, MDCCLVII.
Apud Joannem Manfrè.
SUPERIORUM PERMISSU ET PRIVILEGIO.

Iacopo Facciolati, Fasti Gymnasii patavini

Francesco II Lorenzo Morosini

experimental direction, and those which were more attentive to the needs of society. The investment in these research "establishments" caused the University budget to soar, and in 1770 it reached a peak of 46,000 ducats, almost double with respect to the levels of the early eighteenth century; in addition, while before the reforms 80-90% of the expenses were represented by salaries of the professors, in the years of the development of the network of laboratories, etc., this percentage fell to 60%.

The most important year for a new University course, this time irreversible, was 1768. After having collected the suggestions of two trusted teachers, the jurist Bilesimo and the physician Leopoldo Marc'Antonio Caldani, Morosini, one of the authors of the reform of 1761, had the *Riformatori* approve much more detailed and rational teaching plans than those adopted in 1761, and he established a course in ecclesiastic public law, a discipline destined to bolster the offensive of the State against the Church which characterized the political battle of that period. In 1771, for the first and only time that century, the *Riformatori* visited the University: it resulted in the decision to endow the Studium with a largely new teaching structure, not so much because of the modifications caused to the curricula of 1768, but rather because of a drastic reduction in the number of holidays, the adoption of textbooks, the introduction of a preparatory course in Latin (which in any case after the teaching reform had fallen to second place with respect to Italian), and a session of exams at the end of every year of courses.

The crisis of the student colleges found a partial solution in 1772 with the institution of the college of Saint Mark - where, after seven colleges had been closed, more than fifty "fellowship holders" were concentrated - and with the re-organization of the three remaining colleges. In this way an attempt was made to discipline a body of students which continued to cause problems to public order, even if to a more limited extent than in the past. The number of matriculations, which in the 1760s were just under three hundred, regained height in the last decades of Venetian rule, nearly reaching the five hundred mark (for different reasons: as a result of the fact that as from 1771 even the Paduans were obliged to enroll; as a consequence of the reforms, and finally as a result of the attempts to make the physicians and men of law who were subjects obey the obligation to take their degrees at Padua). In addition the reforms – in particular the introduction of annual exams, textbooks, and Italian as the primary language of teaching – ensured that University studies achieved a formative value never reached in the past except in the immediate circle of some great masters. At the same time they updated the profile of a cultural apprenticeship which had until then had an almost exclusively bookish connotation excessively dependent on medieval models.

In 1773, an important reform concerned the University library, which Stratico tried to transform into a functional tool of research. In 1779, one of the proposals made by Stratico in 1760 was carried out: indeed an Academy of sciences, letters, and arts was established in Padua on

Morosini's initiative, based on a plan by the aforementioned Stratico. The Academy was destined to stand alongside the University as a stimulus for research by teachers, as a sounding board – thanks to the publication of the Acts – of their activities, as a centre of consultation for the Venetian government, and as an opportunity for many professors to integrate their salaries significantly. On the eve of the fall of the Republic of Venice the Studium of Padua, even though it still had a confused and debatable politico-administrative organization, presented itself in other respects as radically renewed with respect to what it had been at the beginning of the eighteenth century. If it had almost completely lost its international character (95% of the teachers and students were subjects of the Republic), it had however acquired a more valid didactic profile and had laid the groundwork for its scientific modernization.

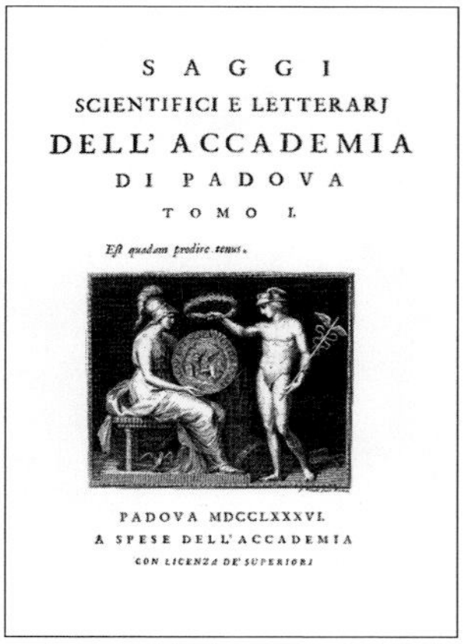

Scientific and literary essays from the Academy of Padua, *1786*

MARIA CECILIA GHETTI

From 1797 to 1866

At the end of April 1797 the French forces had already set up camp in the Venetian ex-dominions, including Padua. The University body hesitated to express itself regarding the new turn of events: more than a few of its members (Simone Stratico, Marco Carburi, Pietro Sografi, not to mention others) had for some time cultivated 'revolutionary' sentiments which now seemed to find the concrete possibility for their realization in the new Jacobin climate.

The ancient Studium was placed among the "objects" of the third section of the first department of the new Central Government of the "Padovano, Polesine di Rovigo e di Adria": even if the academic year ended for obvious practical reasons by respecting Venetian traditions, the democratic regime demonstrated from the beginning its desire to dedicate time and energy to the planning of a new University organization inspired by the revolutionary and enlightenment principles which were simultaneously redrawing the pedagogical and didactic map in France.

The task of "putting studies in order" was thus entrusted to a specific body, the Committee for Public Education of the Municipality of Padua, to which, among others, the professors Melchiorre Cesarotti, Giuseppe Toaldo, and Stefano Gallini, were appointed with the aim of elaborating a general plan for the reform of the ancient University that "through regularity, extension, and plenitude", was to constitute the framework of a cultural and didactic restructuring that was subsequently to receive the approval of the "immortal Bonaparte".

However, the ambitious revolutionary theory had to reckon with a budget reduced to a minimum (as with, more in general, the economy of the entire region): the Committee was forced therefore to limit itself to adopting measures of a very reduced significance, measures however that allowed the academic year of 1797-98 to open without problems.

The pro-rectors and *sindaci* were substituted by "adjuncts" to the first department, while the president of the central government at the University exercised the function of controlling the discipline of the students, who were also the object of the watchful surveillance of the police authorities.

With the single exception of certain measures (among which, the adoption of Italian as the official language of research and teaching turned out to be politically meaningful), the University organization of the democratic period remained substantially faithful to the Venetian model: the pressu-

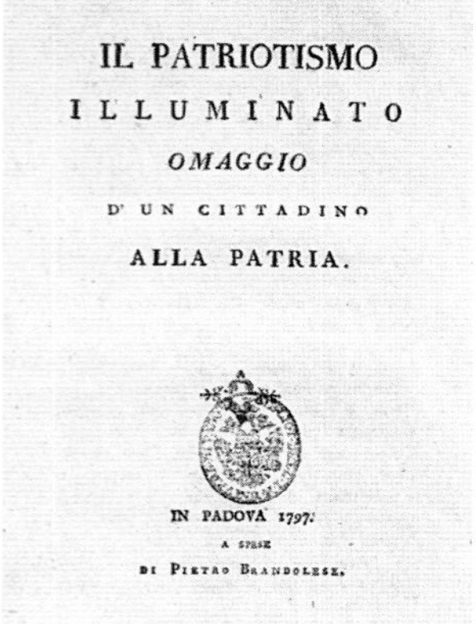
IL PATRIOTISMO
ILLUMINATO
OMAGGIO
D' UN CITTADINO
ALLA PATRIA.
IN PADOVA 1797.

Melchiorre Cesarotti, Il patriotismo illuminato *(Enlightened Patriotism)*

res, both economic and political, deriving from the continuous state of war in which the region found itself, were too many to allow the new government to carry out those radical changes that would break any continuity with the *ancien régime* that the municipal proclamations emphatically declared they wanted to repudiate.

Thus the revolutionary commitment ended up by translating itself above all into measures of a formal nature: the professors, who were forced to wear a tricolour sash (red, white, and green) fixed at the end by a gold medallion with engraved republican mottoes, figured as simple "citizens" even in the catalogues which, printed in Italian, replaced the Venetian 'rotuli'.

Various chairs were suppressed, both for economic reasons (and this is the case for those known as "of the city", the *lecturae civitatis*), and for ideological motives, as information regarding the chairs of public ecclesiastical law and feudal law demonstrates. In the same way, some teachers were replaced: even in this case, the only political connotation involved the chair in Greek and Latin Humanities, which having remained vacant after the death of Clemente Sibiliato, was 'passed back and forth' between Pier Luigi Mabil – who turned it down to occupy himself full-time in municipal government – and one of the 'glories' of the University at the end of the eighteenth century, the celebrated Cesarotti.

As we have already seen, the events of war and politics which, over a brief period of time assailed and devastated the region, did not leave much room for a specific and constructive didactic experimentation: with rare exceptions, far from dedicating time and energy to the realization of a truly new University, the professors had to confront daily the economic hardship which derived from the irregular payment of their salaries, payment obtained sometimes only at the price of repeated and humiliating supplications to the central administration. The students were no better, continually requesting the academic authorities to be admitted to the degree exams without the established compulsory proof of four years of attendance: the difficulties linked to moving around the streets, the 'tolls' paid by the families in the form of requisitions or expropriations by the French occupants, are the reasons most frequently given in support of these petitions. The democratic authority sought in vain to stop the requests, decreeing on 7 Nivoise/27 December 1797, that these would be accepted only in cases of proven seriousness, so that "the State itself should not be depopulated by such disturbance of the public order, and every scholastic discipline be subverted".

Notwithstanding the many difficulties, some results were obtained however: among the most significant is the unification of the two Venetian Colleges, arts and law, into one national seat, where it was possible to obtain the final degree without any preventive profession of faith. Events however came to a head, and every further academic transformation had to be postponed. The classrooms of the Palazzo del Bo were used to organize the military draft for the students, while the Treaty of Campoformido consigned the Veneto and its University to the Habsburg court.

In January 1798, Padua University thus passed under the control of what by now had become the "Noble Provisionary Central Government of the Padovano, Polesine di Rovigo e di Adria", in its turn subordinate, through the central government seat in Venice, to the supreme will of Vienna. The pro-rectors and *sindaci*, promptly 'dug up' from the now obsolete Venetian 'choreography' (such was the desire for 'normality' after the revolutionary shock, that the offices were reassigned to the same teachers who had held them in the last year of Venetian rule), once again represented the two distinct 'universities' of arts and law. Then they awaited, with the rest of the public functionaries, to find out the consequences of the "act of restoration" that General Wallis issued on 6 February 1798, after his troops had taken full control of the region.

While the citizens of Padua seemed to welcome the new occupants, hoping that they would be less demanding in fiscal terms than the French, academic life proceeded following the indications set out in the democratic catalogues (but the lecture schedule was promptly reprinted in Latin, which started again "ab auspicatissima die XX ianuarii", coinciding with the arrival in Padua of the Habsburg troops).

Perhaps by effective political choice, or perhaps because they were forced by the conditions of a region already at the end of its resources thanks to the events of war and politics, the Austrian authorities oriented themselves from the beginning in favour of a cautious return to the Venetian model, which became the basis for the activities of the new "caesareo-regia Academia Patavina".

The professors who had been 'involved' on a politico-ideological level with the French government were removed from teaching, but not even on this occasion were particularly rigid or punitive measures adopted: the authorities simply suspended the chairs of ecclesiastical history and sacred scripture, once assigned to Giuseppe Maria Pujati and Placido Maria Tadini; that of obstetrics, once belonging to Pietro Sografi; the teaching of mathematics, nautical theory, and experimental physics, up until then in the hands of Simone Stratico; theoretical and experimental chemistry, once belonging to Marco Carburi; and the lectures in civic architecture, assigned to Giacomo Albertolli, but they did not however question the tenure of the courses, and put off to more tranquil times any definitive decision. These defections of a political nature were supplemented by vacancies in other chairs, due however to the normal generational succession of the occupants of the various disciplines.

The imbalance between the number of courses set out in the restored 'rotuli' and the number of courses effectively taught remained constant throughout all the so-called "first Austrian domination". However the recovery, in many respects obligatory, of the Venetian didactico-organizational structure did not mean that Vienna did not contemplate the prospect, although not in the short term, of bringing the ancient Studium into line with the criteria in force in the other University centres of the Empire, in such a way as to follow the practice of subordinating scholastic and cul-

Façade and cloister of the Giustiniani Hospital

tural policy to the more general interests of the State, which in the Habsburg territories constituted perhaps the most vibrant and vital inheritance of the recent past of Maria Theresa and Joseph II. It is in this context that we can understand, for example, the suppression of the teaching of experimental agriculture ("considering that a similar chair does not exist in any other University in the hereditary States"), and the institution, in Venice, of a course in jurisprudence destined to spread the principles of Austrian law throughout the new Venetian provinces.

These were, however, innovations of little importance, and the impact of other measures with which Vienna sought to loosen the forced but at the same time cumbersome bonds with Venetian tradition (for example, the abrogation of the degrees *more nobilium*, the special degrees reserved for the nobles) was also limited: its anti-Napoleonic effort forced Austria to concentrate means and resources on the military front, postponing *sine die* that "general ordering" of the Venetian University which the documents of the time announced and re-announced with monotonous regularity.

Order and tranquillity became then the watchwords of the new rulers, and the University representatives also adapted themselves to them with apparent facility, pursuing any effort aimed at "serving public tranquillity and public security". The definitive measures taken against those professors who had openly sided with the democratic regime remained mild, inspired by an attitude of pacification rather than by what had now become an ideologically sterile confrontation: Tadini, Albertolli, Gallini the professor of medicine, and the librarian Giuseppe Greatti were dismissed (leaving "the entirety of their credits" intact) and the same measure was also applied to Pujati and Giuseppe Dubravcich a little later (in 1805 Sografi and Carburi were "most clemently" authorized to "apply for the vacant chairs in their sphere in the University", thus putting an end to the exile which they had endued for several years).

The Austrian government did not soften their appeals to severity and discipline with regard to the students, involved in student-like 'acts of bravado' more than in demonstrations of political dissent. Such appeals were particularly insistent at the beginning of the new century, when the echo of French deeds in neighbouring Lombardy seemed to revive the up till then fairly tepid political passions of the Paduan students: these were episodes of little importance, however (altercations, swearing, the spread of "bad and dangerous books"), which the Austrian authorities sought to transform into moments of force, anticipating that rigor that was to render them notorious and disliked some years later, after the end of the new occupation by the French, who in the meantime, as from the autumn of 1805, had retaken possession of the region.

The University, which was visited in December 1805 by Eugène Beauharnais, fully reflected the difficult conditions in which the region found itself-exhausted from years of war, requisitions, ever higher and more greedy taxation. Formally represented by the pro-rectors Bonato and Cromer, who had been appointed by the Austrians, the University once again awaited instructions from the new occupants who, mindful of the brief democratic past of '97, immediately decided to reintegrate some of the professors whom the Habsburg government had removed as "revolutionaries" back into their academic roles. (It should however be remembered that even during the first months of 1801, when the French had briefly retaken possession of the territory around Padua, the "evicted and suspended" professors were promptly reintegrated into their proper academic functions, if only for a brief period).

On 25 July 1806 the decree of Saint Cloud was issued, which in art. I stated: "The University of Padua is preserved. Within the next year it will be placed on the same level as the other Universities of the Kingdom".

The proverbial autonomy which the ancient University had enjoyed over the many centuries of its glorious existence, through different dominations and governments, was now negated in the name of a new University, submitted to a central power which expressed a cultural and institutional project aimed at the construction of a general model *super partes*, more than at local needs and particularities, a model able to translate in a homogeneous manner throughout the various lands of the Empire the supernational dimension which inspired Napoleonic policy.

On the basis of French legislation, which became operative immediately, public education was placed under the authority of the Minister of the Interior, who in turn entrusted it to the care of a general director. The equalization to the Universities of Bologna and Pavia, where the new directives entered into force slightly earlier than in Padua, signalled the end of the Venetian academic structure which, willing or not, both the preceding 'Jacobin' and Austrian governments had - with obvious adaptations - preserved.

The traditional division into 'universities' of arts and law disappeared definitively, giving way to a more agile structure guided by a single regent or rector and subdivided into three distinct classes (mathematical sciences and physics, moral and political sciences, literature) and into as many faculties (physico-mathematics, medicine, and law). Theological studies were relegated to the Seminary, thus decreeing the definitive secularization of University life: the Colleges, both Venetian and Sacred, were also suppressed (thus acknowledging the absolute power of the State in the conferral of academic degrees), and the *nationes* were also abolished, having by now become the occasional survivors of a past that had long lost the cosmopolitan dimension of its most splendid periods.

The Napoleonic University thus acquired a modern physiognomy: the rector, elected directly by the Viceroy, represented the principal intermediary between the organization and the central government. A dean was appointed at the head of each faculty, who was also placed in direct contact with the Milanese authorities. Rectors and deans constituted the anchors in a profoundly hierarchic structure, of which the professors, appointed by the government, constituted the base.

With the last echoes of the Venetian past thus abolished, the members

Napoleonic Proclamation of 1811

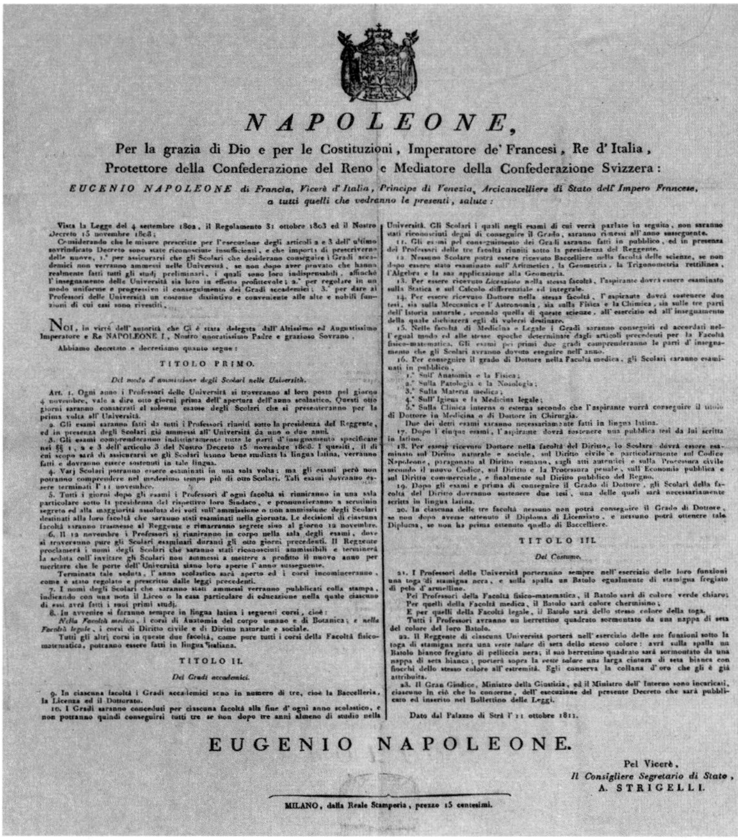

NAPOLEONE,

Per la grazia di Dio e per le Costituzioni, Imperatore de' Francesi, Re d'Italia, Protettore della Confederazione del Reno e Mediatore della Confederazione Svizzera:

EUGENIO NAPOLEONE di Francia, Vicerè d'Italia, Principe di Venezia, Arcicancelliere di Stato dell'Impero Francese, a tutti quelli che vedranno le presenti, salute:

Vista la Legge del 4 settembre 1802, il Regolamento 31 ottobre 1803 ed il Nostro Decreto 15 novembre 1808;

Considerando che le misure prescritte per l'esecuzione degli articoli 2 e 3 dell'ultimo sovrindicato Decreto sono state riconosciute insufficienti, e che importi di prescriverne delle nuove, 1.° per assicurarsi che gli Scolari che desiderano conseguire i Gradi accademici non verranno ammessi nelle Università, se non dopo aver provato che hanno realmente fatti tutti gli studj preliminari, i quali sono loro indispensabili, affinchè l'insegnamento delle Università sia loro in effetto profittevole; 2.° per regolare in un modo uniforme e progressivo il conseguimento dei Gradi accademici; 3.° per dare ai Professori delle Università un costume distintivo e conveniente alle alte e nobili funzioni di cui essi sono rivestiti,

NOI, in virtù dell'autorità che Ci è stata delegata dall'Altissimo ed Augustissimo Imperatore e Re NAPOLEONE I, Nostro onoratissimo Padre e grazioso Sovrano,

Abbiamo decretato e decretiamo quanto segue:

TITOLO PRIMO.

Del modo d'ammissione degli Scolari nelle Università.

Art. 1. Ogni anno i Professori delle Università si troveranno al loro posto pel giorno 4 novembre, vale a dire otto giorni prima dell'apertura dell'anno scolastico. Questi otto giorni saranno consacrati al solenne esame degli Scolari che si presenteranno per la prima volta all'Università.

2. Gli esami saranno fatti da tutti i Professori riuniti sotto la presidenza del Reggente, ed in presenza degli Scolari già ammessi all'Università da uno o due anni.

3. Gli esami comprenderanno indistintamente tutte le parti d'insegnamento specificate nei §§ 1, 2 e 3 dell'articolo 3 del Nostro Decreto 15 novembre 1808. I quesiti, il di cui scopo sarà di assicurarsi se gli Scolari hanno bene studiata la lingua latina, verranno fatti e dovranno essere sostenuti in tale lingua.

4. Varj Scolari potranno essere esaminati in una sola volta: ma gli esami però non potranno comprendere nel medesimo tempo più di otto Scolari. Tali esami dovranno essere terminati l'11 novembre.

5. Tutti i giorni dopo gli esami i Professori d'ogni facoltà si riuniranno in una sala particolare sotto la presidenza del rispettivo loro Sindaco, e pronunzieranno a scrutinio segreto ed alla maggiorità assoluta dei voti sull'ammissione o non ammissione degli Scolari destinati alla loro facoltà che saranno stati esaminati nella giornata. Le decisioni di ciascuna facoltà saranno trasmesse al Reggente e rimarranno segrete sino al giorno 12 novembre.

6. Il 12 novembre i Professori si riuniranno in corpo nella sala degli esami, dove si troveranno pure gli Scolari esaminati durante gli otto giorni precedenti. Il Reggente proclamerà i nomi degli Scolari che saranno stati riconosciuti ammissibili e terminerà la seduta coll'invitare gli Scolari non ammessi a mettere a profitto il nuovo anno per meritare che le porte dell'Università siano loro aperte l'anno susseguente.

Terminata tale seduta, l'anno scolastico sarà aperto ed i corsi incominceranno, come è stato regolato e prescritto dalle leggi precedenti.

7. I nomi degli Scolari che saranno stati ammessi verranno pubblicati colla stampa, indicando con una nota il Liceo o la casa particolare di educazione nella quale ciascuno di essi avrà fatti i suoi primi studj.

8. In avvenire si faranno sempre in lingua latina i seguenti corsi, cioè:

Nella Facoltà medica, i corsi di Anatomia del corpo umano e di Botanica; *e nella Facoltà legale*, i corsi di Diritto civile e di Diritto naturale e sociale.

Tutti gli altri corsi in queste due facoltà, come pure tutti i corsi della Facoltà fisico-matematica, potranno essere fatti in lingua italiana.

TITOLO II.

Dei Gradi accademici.

9. In ciascuna facoltà i Gradi accademici sono in numero di tre, cioè la Baccelleria, la Licenza ed il Dottorato.

10. I Gradi saranno conceduti per ciascuna facoltà alla fine d'ogni anno scolastico, e non potranno quindi conseguirsi tutti tre se non dopo tre anni almeno di studio nella Università. Gli Scolari i quali negli esami di cui verrà parlato in seguito, non saranno stati riconosciuti degni di conseguire il Grado, saranno rimessi all'anno susseguente.

11. Gli esami pel conseguimento dei Gradi saranno fatti in pubblico, ed in presenza dei Professori delle tre facoltà riuniti sotto la presidenza del Reggente.

12. Nessuno Scolare potrà essere ricevuto Baccelliere nella facoltà delle scienze, se non dopo essere stato esaminato sull'Aritmetica, la Geometria, la Trigonometria rettilinea, l'Algebra e la sua applicazione alla Geometria.

13. Per essere ricevuto *Licenziato* nella stessa facoltà, l'aspirante dovrà essere esaminato sulla Statica e sul Calcolo differenziale ed integrale.

14. Per essere ricevuto Dottore nella stessa facoltà, l'aspirante dovrà sostenere due tesi, sia sulla Meccanica e l'Astronomia, sia sulla Fisica e la Chimica, sia sulle tre parti dell'Istoria naturale, secondo quella di queste scienze, all'esercizio ed all'insegnamento della quale dichiarerà egli di volersi destinare.

15. Nelle facoltà di Medicina e Legale i Gradi saranno conseguiti ed accordati nell'egual modo ed alle stesse epoche determinate dagli articoli precedenti per la Facoltà fisico-matematica. Gli esami pei primi due gradi comprenderanno le parti d'insegnamento che gli Scolari avranno dovuto eseguire nell'anno.

16. Per conseguire il grado di Dottore nella Facoltà medica, gli Scolari saranno esaminati in pubblico,

1.° Sull'Anatomia e la Fisica;
2.° Sulla Patologia e la Nosologia;
3.° Sulla Materia medica;
4.° Sull'Igiena e la Medicina legale;
5.° Sulla Clinica interna o esterna secondo che l'aspirante vorrà conseguire il titolo di Dottore in Medicina o di Dottore in Chirurgia.

Due dei detti esami saranno necessariamente fatti in lingua latina.

17. Dopo i cinque esami, l'aspirante dovrà sostenere una pubblica tesi da lui scritta in latino.

18. Per essere ricevuto Dottore nella facoltà del Diritto, lo Scolare dovrà essere esaminato sul Diritto naturale e sociale, sul Diritto civile e particolarmente sul Codice Napoleone, paragonato al Diritto romano, sugli atti autentici e sulla Processura civile secondo il nuovo Codice, sul Diritto e la Processura penale, sull'Economia pubblica e sul Diritto commerciale, e finalmente sul Diritto pubblico del Regno.

19. Dopo gli esami e prima di conseguire il Grado di Dottore, gli Scolari della facoltà del Diritto dovranno sostenere due tesi, una delle quali sarà necessariamente scritta in lingua latina.

20. In ciascuna delle tre facoltà nessuno non potrà conseguire il Grado di Dottore, se non dopo avere ottenuto il Diploma di Licenziato, e nessuno potrà ottenere tale Diploma, se non ha prima ottenuto quello di Baccelliere.

TITOLO III.

Del Costume.

21. I Professori delle Università porteranno sempre nell'esercizio delle loro funzioni una toga di stamigna nera, e sulla spalla un Batolo egualmente di stamigna fregiato di pelo d'armellino.

Pei Professori della Facoltà fisico-matematica, il Batolo sarà di colore verde chiaro;
Per quelli della Facoltà medica, il Batolo sarà colore chermisino;
E per quelli della Facoltà legale, il Batolo sarà dello stesso colore della toga.

Tutti i Professori avranno un berrettino quadrato sormontato da una nappa di seta del colore del loro Batolo.

22. Il Reggente di ciascuna Università porterà nell'esercizio delle sue funzioni sotto la toga di stamigna nera una *veste talare* di seta dello stesso colore: avrà sulla spalla un Batolo bianco fregiato di pelliccia nera; il suo berrettino quadrato sarà sormontato da una nappa di seta bianca; porterà sopra la *veste talare* una larga cintura di seta bianca con fiocchi dello stesso colore all'estremità. Egli conserva la collana d'oro che gli è già attribuita.

23. Il Gran Giudice, Ministro della Giustizia, ed il Ministro dell'Interno sono incaricati, ciascuno in ciò che lo concerne, dell'esecuzione del presente Decreto che sarà pubblicato ed inserito nel Bollettino delle Leggi.

Dato dal Palazzo di Strà l'11 ottobre 1811.

EUGENIO NAPOLEONE.

Pel Vicerè,
Il Consigliere Segretario di Stato,
A. STRIGELLI.

MILANO, dalla Reale Stamperia, prezzo 15 centesimi.

of the University body became simple functionaries, entirely absorbed in teaching (which was conducted primarily in Italian) and subordinated to a collection of behavioural regulations so rigid as to induce the French historian Henri Taine several years later to compare the University to the "vestibule of a barracks" (Napoleon himself, on the other hand, compared the professors to a body of lay "Jesuits", completely devoted to the good of the institution).

There was no echo of the revolutionary fervour which, with the inevitable naivety of every movement in its "new-born phase", had shaken the quiet and decadent order of the Venetian Studium a few years earlier: the revolution had by now given way to a rigidly organized national reality, capable of controlling and directing every aspect of public life, fruit of that successful equilibrium between political *grandeur* and police rigor that characterized the imperial parabola.

Once a pupil had completed the 'ginnasio' (the first five years of secondary school) and, where they had been instituted, the 'liceo' (the final three years of secondary education), he entered University courses, regularly marked by trimesters: the procedure ended with the final degree examination, which could be taken only by students capable of proving that they had completed the entire cycle of studies in one of the three national Universities. The academic year, from November to June inclusive, concluded with the rite of the exams, conducted in Italian: having passed the tests which admitted them to the bachelor and licence degrees, the candidates received their final qualifications (a degree for the lawyers, physicians and surgeons; a simple academic qualification for the architects, engineers, pharmacists, the surveyors, that is for those who had received a more technical training).

The variations in the curricula were numerous, significant above all in the legal field where Roman law, which Venice had always considered as a privileged subject, was substituted by the French codification. New disciplines, like history or the study of languages, completed the preparation for the future lawyers, who also acquired the rudiments of economics, thus giving rise to professional figures who were more agile, ductile, and concrete with respect to those of the past.

Even in the field of more specifically scientific studies there were numerous changes, such as, among others, the new courses in sublime calculus, geodesy, military architecture, design, and mathematics. This attention to scientific and technical development, an area in which France boasted a consolidated scholastic tradition, represented a constant in Napoleonic reformism: here arose, in the wake of the French *écoles d'application*, the new school of waters and streets, the school of legal eloquence, opened in 1809 in Milan, the military Schools in Modena and Pavia, the Academy of fine arts in Venice, reorganized on the basis of the analogous centres in Milan and Bologna.

The new bourgeois world, which included all the categories involved in those productive activities that the aristocratic classes had, save rare exceptions, always disdained, required different dynamic, active, professional figures. The Napoleonic government was fully aware of this, and aimed its scholastic reforms at the creation of an intellectual ruling class capable of acting as a protagonist in the scenario which was rapidly being created.

The University thus became a sort of 'consensus factory', churning out the *homines novi* who represented the driving force in the bourgeois Napoleonic empire, which had one of its strong points precisely in its monopolistic control over the field of education. All didactic and cultural activity was subordinated to the supreme interests of the civic power and its wishes, which were often translated into successfully modern measures: the development of the scientific and economic disciplines, the new organization of legal studies, the 'rediscovery' of history and literature (of which the regime took skilful advantage in nationalistic terms), were phases in a progressive modernization which involved, and sometimes even overwhelmed, the ancient Studium.

The students, who initially adhered with enthusiasm to the wave of reforms, were however very soon to see their expectations crushed by the rigor and the centralism of the French regime. Organized in veritable *battaglioni* (rigorously equipped paramilitary structures) the students of the University – who during the centuries of Venetian control were known for their proverbial and indeed too ostentatious anarchy – were subjected with evident discomfort to the choreographic display of police control by the French regime.

Even more difficult was the position of the teaching body, deprived of the privileges which it had traditionally enjoyed in the Venetian epoch, and forced to adhere to the *ukasy* of the Napoleonic regime, which preserved nothing of the brief enthusiasm associated with the 'Jacobin' 1797. Thrown back and forth between old and new "masters" (in 1809 the Austrians retook possession of the region for a brief period, and more than a few of the teachers presented petitions of submission to the Habsburg representatives, consequently incurring not long after the predictable anger of the French, who had in the meantime retaken control of the territory), professors and students of Padua University appeared to look on the Napoleonic adventure with indifference, besides their required formal homage: in November of 1813, the beginning of the second period of Austrian rule did not seem to be accompanied by particular laments for the recently fallen regime (from 1798 to 1815 Austrian rule had been interrupted by a brief French interlude).

Once the inevitable uncertainties of the initial period were over (in which, from the end of 1813 to 1816, the Napoleonic academic organization was maintained almost intact) and once the Habsburg rule over the region had become stable, on 12 September 1815 a notification of the imperial-royal Venetian government regarding the "renovation of the University of Padua and the fixing of the course of its studies" confirmed Austria's will to bring the Venetian University into line with the norms in force in other analogous seats in the Empire, with particular reference to Vienna and Prague. The contacts between the University and the supreme authority of the capital were guaranteed by the 'mediation' of the government in Venice (in this particular case, the presidentship of the lieutenancy set up in Venice), which received and transmitted every, even the smallest, petition.

Among the initial consequences of the new regulations was the reopening of the theology faculty, which the French had confined to the Seminary: those who enrolled, after finishing the three-year course of study and the final degree exam, acquired the title of "doctor in sacred theology". New on the other hand was the philosophico-mathematical faculty, which conferred the degree in philosophy and in mathematics (this latter coincided in practice with the specialization in engineering and architecture): the first two years, which could also be followed in the "licei" which existed in various cities of the region, was conceived as preparatory to subsequent more specific courses of a theoretical (legal, medical, theological) or professional (surveying and engineer-architects) nature.

The medico-surgical faculty maintained its traditional courses, acquiring in addition a two-year course for pharmacists and a three-year course aimed at the training of surgical personnel destined, following a practice already in force in the other Habsburg States, for service in rural and mountainous zones. The politico-legal faculty preserved in its principal aspects the organization it had received under the French administration, limiting itself to substituting the courses connected to the principles of Napoleonic law with courses inspired instead by the Austrian legal tradition.

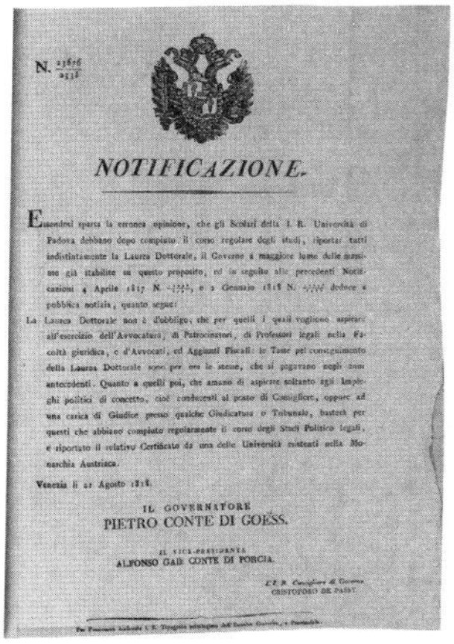
NOTIFICAZIONE.

Essendosi sparsa la erronea opinione, che gli Scolari della I. R. Università di Padova debbano dopo compiuto il corso regolare degli studj, riportar tutti indistintamente la Laurea Dottorale, il Governo a maggiore lume delle massime già stabilite su questo proposito, ed in seguito alle precedenti Notificazioni 4 Aprile 1817 N. [illegible], e 2 Gennaio 1818 N. [illegible] deduce a pubblica notizia, quanto segue:

La Laurea Dottorale non è d'obbligo, che per quelli i quali vogliono aspirare all'esercizio dell'Avvocatura, di Patrocinatori, di Professori legali nella Facoltà giuridica, e d'Avvocati, ed Aggiunti Fiscali: le Tasse pel conseguimento della Laurea Dottorale sono per ora le stesse, che si pagavano negli anni antecedenti. Quanto a quelli poi, che amano di aspirare soltanto agli Impieghi politici di concetto, cioè conducenti al posto di Consigliere, oppure ad una carica di Giudice presso qualche Giudicatura o Tribunale, basterà per questi che abbiano compiuto regolarmente il corso degli Studi Politico legali, e riportato il relativo Certificato da una delle Università esistenti nella Monarchia Austriaca.

Venezia li 21 Agosto 1818.

IL GOVERNATORE
PIETRO CONTE DI GOËSS.

IL VICE-PRESIDENTE
ALFONSO GAB. CONTE DI PORCIA.

I. R. Consigliere di Governo

Austrian Proclamation of 1818

Even if the regulations described up to now were of an avowedly temporary nature, they nevertheless reveal something of the guidelines which inspired the Austrian rulers in matters of education, conceived as a political "object" and, as such, finalized to support the most general interests of the State. Such a formulation found further confirmation in the supreme resolution of 7 December 1816, which officially defined the didactic and administrative organization of the "restored" University, on the basis of which the faculties just mentioned remained in force, according to a scheme common to the other Universities of the Empire as well.

Still, there were some modifications to the curricula of studies, which were enriched with new or 'revised' disciplines like pedagogy, agrarian science, statistics, history, aesthetics, mercantile law and, obviously, Austrian civil law. In the medical field, semeiotics, toxicology, dietetics, hygiene, and legal medicine, all entered the plans of study, confirming a pragmatic and professional approach also testified to by the courses set up for pharmacists, midwives, and veterinary surgeons. Unchanged on the other hand were the programmes for engineers, architects, and surveyors (partially restructured afterwards in 1839). Latin reacquired a position of hegemony, above all in the scientific sphere: finally, for all the students, except Jews and Protestants, an obligatory course in religious institutions was established.

Even the administrative life of the University was subjected to a series of changes: at the head of the structure figured the *rettore magnifico*, who could also be elected from outside the teaching body and who exercised his functions with the help of the academic senate, in turn made up of directors, deans, and the seniors (or elder members) of the different faculties. Among the functionaries just mentioned, the figure of the director merits particular attention, as a newly-established figure who had the tasks of surveillance not only over the correct functioning of the teaching activity, but also over the moral and political conduct of all the personnel of the University (professors, students, and administrative staff).

Indeed the rigid Habsburg apparatus required, as a *condicio sine qua non*, obligatory respect for the "virtues" of discipline, morality, and good conduct: obliged to comply in the course of their lectures to a written text approved beforehand by the censors, not even the teachers could escape the control exercised by the directors and his zealous 'spies'. The private courses were thus progressively suppressed, to be revived, in exceptional circumstances, only in the two years 1849-50, when the Universities of Padua and Pavia, involved in the revolutionary uprising of '48, were temporarily closed. Finally, the teaching class received mediocre treatment from Vienna from the economic point of view, following a trend already in force during the Napoleonic regime, and it suffered a sharp slump in its image and social prestige with respect to the far-off Venetian "extravagance".

The *Regolamento generale per le Università del Lombardo-Veneto*, promulgated in Vienna on 8 April 1825 responded to the need to give order and stability to the complex University machine. Backing up, in its general outline, the layout that had already emerged from the norms of 1816-17 (with the already-mentioned subdivision of the disciplines into four distinct faculties: theological, politico-legal, medico-surgical, and philosophico-mathematical), the new regulation constituted the framework around which Paduan academic life was based in its various aspects for the fifty years of Austrian domination.

The theological faculty – which in 1822 returned, though maintaining University status, within the walls of the Seminary – underwent a partial reform at the end of the 1850's, a somewhat natural and 'physiological' consequence of the adoption of the Concordat of 1855: Vienna did not withhold resources and attention from this area of study in its effort to train a clergy prepared both for the indispensable cure of souls, and the realization, as loyal and faithful subjects, of the superior interest of the State (superior even to that of the Church).

The field of legal studies was also affected by various modifications, above all during the three years 1855-58: these were mainly variations in the area of the taught disciplines, with particular attention to those most linked to the German tradition, such as Austrian history and statistics (however, the institution of the first chair of history of Italian law, which dates back to 1857, must also be mentioned).

More limited, however, was the destiny of the faculty of philosophy, which was practically suppressed in 1852, when the reform of secondary school studies, going from six to eight years of obligatory attendance, rendered superfluous the presence of the two-year preparatory course, which exactly coincided, as we have seen, with the philosophical course. To compensate, from the academic year of 1846-7 the mathematical faculty was activated, which presented a 'practical' slant (as shown by the teaching of the science of machine construction or technology, among others), targeted for the preparation of graduates ready to enter their respective professions immediately. (In this respect it is interesting to point out how, already at the beginning of the 1820's, the problem of the relationship between graduates and the world of work imposed itself, with significant repercussions above all in the legal sector which produced too many graduates for the actual needs of the market). There was little or no change, finally, in the medical field, except from the partial restructuring of pharmaceutical studies in 1859.

The few measures taken in the administrative field (from 1853, for

The customers of the Caffè Pedrocchi

example, the nomination of the rector passed to the Minister of Rites and Public Education) also suffered from the climate of "waiting" which permeated the entire period of Habsburg rule over the Veneto, a period of uncertainty hanging between the forced maintenance of an unsatisfactory status quo and the promise of a hoped-for organizational restructuring, which was always deferred and never even completely planned.

The omnipresent and vigil eye of the Austrian authorities controlled every aspect of the life of the students, whose presence at the University of Padua rose from 620 enrolled in 1816-17 to 1265 (plus 90 seminarians) in 1830, finally to reach the figure of 1889 in 1842-43, and to then decrease (apart from the exceptional point of 1742 present in 1851-52) to 862 in 1859-60 and 619 in 1860-61 (there was a considerable rise in 1865-66, with 1379 students enrolled, but we are by now dealing with the final throes of a situation that was soon to end).

The students of the University came mostly from the Veneto region, with a small percentage (about 10%) from nearby Lombardy (above all Brescia, Bergamo and Mantua), and small groups from Friuli, Istria, and Dalmatia: an explanation of this 'Italian' presence can be found in the decision of the Austrian authorities not to include the study of German among the required courses, and German also remained optional in the secondary schools, at least until the reform of 1852. Contrary to this, however, was the much less liberal provision that prohibited Italian scholars from frequenting foreign Universities, with the sole exception of those situated in territories of the Habsburg Empire.

In the case of the teaching class we also see the constant decline of a professional figure which was by now comparable to the other categories of State employees, subjected to an extremely rigorous disciplinary control, to a no less oppressive intellectual censure, and *dulcis in fundo*, to an extremely unrewarding economic situation (the professors' salaries varied in the fifty years of Habsburg domination between 800 and 2,000 florins a year). Almost all the professors in service in Padua, generally hired in competitions held contemporaneously in Padua, Pavia and Vienna, were of Italian origin, with the few significant exceptions of some Austrians and Hungarians (which Italian patriotic tradition has long accused of opportunism, and sometime of veritable espionage, in favour of the Viennese 'enemy').

The difficult cultural and ideological conditions which created the backdrop to the teaching at the University of Padua in the first half of the nineteenth century did not mean, however, that high-profile names could not be found among the ranks of the teaching class, of figures distinguished for scientific merit, and in several cases, also for their civic and political commitment (among others, the astronomer Giovanni Santini, the mathematician Giusto Bellavitis, the hydraulic engineers Gustavo Bucchia and Domenico Turazza, and the Latinist Pietro Canal). In 1842, on the occasion of the fourth congress of Italian scientists held in Padua, the scientific isolation of the University world of the Veneto was temporarily suspended, allowing for new and profitable contacts with Italian and foreign colleagues.

There were important names also among the students: Antonio Rosmini, Niccolò Tommaseo, Giovanni Prati, Arnaldo Fusinato, and Ippolito Nievo were students at Padua, together with Alberto Errera, Giuseppe Lorenzoni, Antonio Favaro, Enrico Nestore Legnazzi and others, who also remained later with the University in a teaching capacity.

The bureaucratic drabness of the life of the University of Padua during the first half of the nineteenth century was interrupted however by moments of ideological and political tension, of which the mythical events of 1848 represented the most intense and significant point.

As we have already had pointed out, the young men who frequented Padua University in the first half of the nineteenth century were not distinguished by any particular cultural or political merit: the students seemed mainly committed to honouring their most notorious reputation, that of the violent and rowdy troublemaker, inclined to alcoholic excess and protagonists of repeated fights with the citizenry, with whom they were always unpopular (despite the fact that they represented an irreplaceable source of income for various categories of merchants, innkeepers, and landlords *in primis*). During the period of the Restoration (which by extension can be made to reach the eve of 1848), the conflict between students, the citizenry, and law enforcement was revived with regularity. This was fuelled by

Palazzo del Bo, the Aula Magna today

violent and criminal undergraduate activities which until the 1840s maintained an essentially apolitical connotation, evidence rather of an "environmental unease" which was a constant leitmotiv in Paduan student life.

The Austrian authorities thus found themselves confronted, on one hand, with an increase in the University population that they themselves sought in various ways to nourish (until the creation of that already mentioned 'exuberance' of qualified personnel); on the other, with the problem of public order inevitably connected to a student presence on the rise. Notwithstanding this, it can be stated that until the eve of 1848 the conduct of the Paduan student body did not present a particular threat to the governing authorities, and that the various clashes between 'cops' and students rarely assumed characteristics serious enough to really worry Vienna (it should also be added that more than once exponents of the Austrian government, Metternich in particular, did not hesitate in exaggerating that potential threat of student disorders, transforming them into an instrument of pressure to obtain further restrictions in the control over discipline and behaviour).

With the exception of a couple of episodes of real importance (two students returning from Bologna in 1831, which had risen up against the papal government, were found with tricolour cockades and radical publications; and the arrest of the student Virgilio Brocchi, accused of high treason, held under arrest for two years and finally, in the absence of certain proof, expelled from the University), the students of Paduan seem to be merely protagonists of completely innocent acts of bravado, very far from the political commitment that in the same period Pellico or Mazzini tried in vain to invoke in them. Maddened by the fumes of alcohol, more than once in the 1830's and 1840's the students of the University provoked brawls and gave rise to altercations with the populace: the excessive propensity to drink shown by a percentage of the students (detected to a greater extent among those of non-Paduan origin, forced by the chronic lack of lodgings to stay in taverns and inns), together with the inadequate presence of law enforcement capable of controlling the phenomenon, was translated almost inevitably into 'brawls' with soldiers of the Austrian garrison, fights which however only rarely presented that political connotation which a certain rhetoric of the Italian *Risorgimento* sought to imbue it with later.

At the beginning of the 1840's the situation seemed to change and give way to a new solidarity, in an anti-Austrian sense, between the students and citizens (these latter belonged predominantly to what the documents of the period defined as the "lower class"). These were sporadic episodes which in any case prefigured that unforeseeable moment of 'communion' between different social forces which was the wave of revolutionary activity that, in February and March of 1848, seemed to sweep away regimes, governments, princes, and emperors in various parts of Europe. The events of the 8th of February in Padua can be clearly seen from this revolutionary viewpoint: they took the form of a veritable organized movement with clear pre-insurrectional characteristics, to which Padua University adhered with force and conviction.

Beginning in the autumn of 1847, students and citizens became protagonists in a series of episodes aimed at hitting, in a deliberately political way, the most widespread sources of Austrian revenues, that is to say the lottery and, with the celebrated boycott of cigars, the State monopoly on tobacco. The echo of the serious disorders occurring in Milan and Pavia (in this latter city two students were killed), contributed to exacerbating the tension in Padua too, where part of the student body gave rise to demonstrations of provocative protest, immediately suppressed by a series of arrests (others, in the meantime, began to support the armed battle, gradually constituting an ever vaster and more determined movement).

The 'pretext' that burst the revolutionary tension which had 'incubated' for so long was provided by a sad but absolutely casual event: the death, by illness, of a student, one Giuseppe Placco. At his funeral, which took place on 7th February, over 5000 people from all the social classes participated: among those who followed the bier, covered with flowers in the

Austrian Proclamation, 5 January 1848

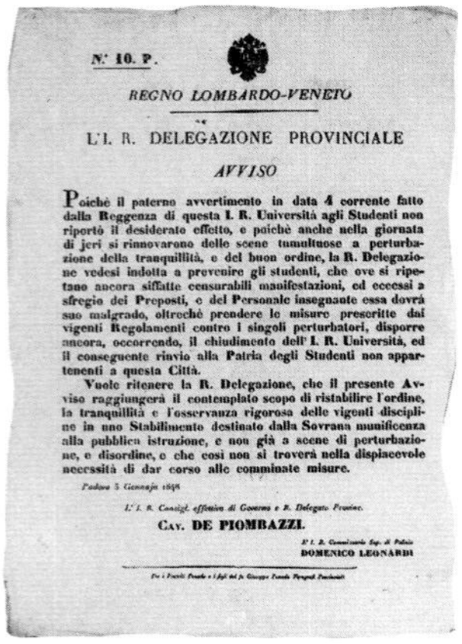

N.° 10. P.

REGNO LOMBARDO-VENETO

L'I. R. DELEGAZIONE PROVINCIALE

AVVISO

Poichè il paterno avvertimento in data 4 corrente fatto dalla Reggenza di questa I. R. Università agli Studenti non riportò il desiderato effetto, e poichè anche nella giornata di jeri si rinnovarono delle scene tumultuose a perturbazione della tranquillità, e del buon ordine, la R. Delegazione vedesi indotta a prevenire gli studenti, che ove si ripetano ancora siffatte censurabili manifestazioni, ed eccessi a sfregio dei Preposti, e del Personale insegnante essa dovrà suo malgrado, oltrechè prendere le misure prescritte dai vigenti Regolamenti contro i singoli perturbatori, disporre ancora, occorrendo, il chiudimento dell' I. R. Università, ed il conseguente rinvio alla Patria degli Studenti non appartenenti a questa Città.

Vuole ritenere la R. Delegazione, che il presente Avviso raggiungerà il contemplato scopo di ristabilire l'ordine, la tranquillità e l'osservanza rigorosa delle vigenti discipline in uno Stabilimento destinato dalla Sovrana munificenza alla pubblica istruzione, e non già a scene di perturbazione, e disordine, e che così non si troverà nella dispiacevole necessità di dar corso alle comminate misure.

Padova 5 Gennajo 1848

CAV. DE PIOMBAZZI.

DOMENICO LEONARDI

Stamp of the Committee of the students of Padua, 1848

shape of a large tricolour flag, several hundred students stood out, dressed in the Italian fashion (at the time forbidden) and the liveries of domestics, sent by all the noble families as a clear challenge to Vienna.

The tension grew: on the morning of the next day (were are now at the mythical 8th of February) a delegation of notables, citizens, and students placed before the Austrian command a series of requests, which were rejected. A physical confrontation was by now inevitable: the students sought refuge within the University and the walls of the Caffè Pedrocchi. Many of the soldiers were wounded (the number of dead was not determined) as were the civic population: two students were killed. On the following day the inevitable wave of arrests began: seventy-three students were expelled from the University and four professors were stripped of their appointments. Viewed independently from the any Risorgimento tendency to turn the episode into a myth, the events of the 8th of February, sustained by the joint participation of students and citizens, nevertheless testify to a new political maturity which fully involved the academic world of the Veneto region, and signalled, as has recently been observed, the beginning of a civic commitment that from then on represented an inalienable feature in the history of Padua University.

The University was reopened 11 November 1850: the revolutionary events did not seem to have been able to soften the rigid approach. Maintenance of formal order was accompanied by an exacerbation of the measures of control, which became even harsher and more obstinate and which set "exemplary" repressive sanctions in the case of their being broken. In his celebrated Secret chronicles of my times, Carlo Leoni pointed out how the students were "melancholy and frightened", very far, at least in appearance, from the revolutionary euphoria to which they had abandoned themselves two years before.

In reality, under the appearance of apathy and conformism, there persi-

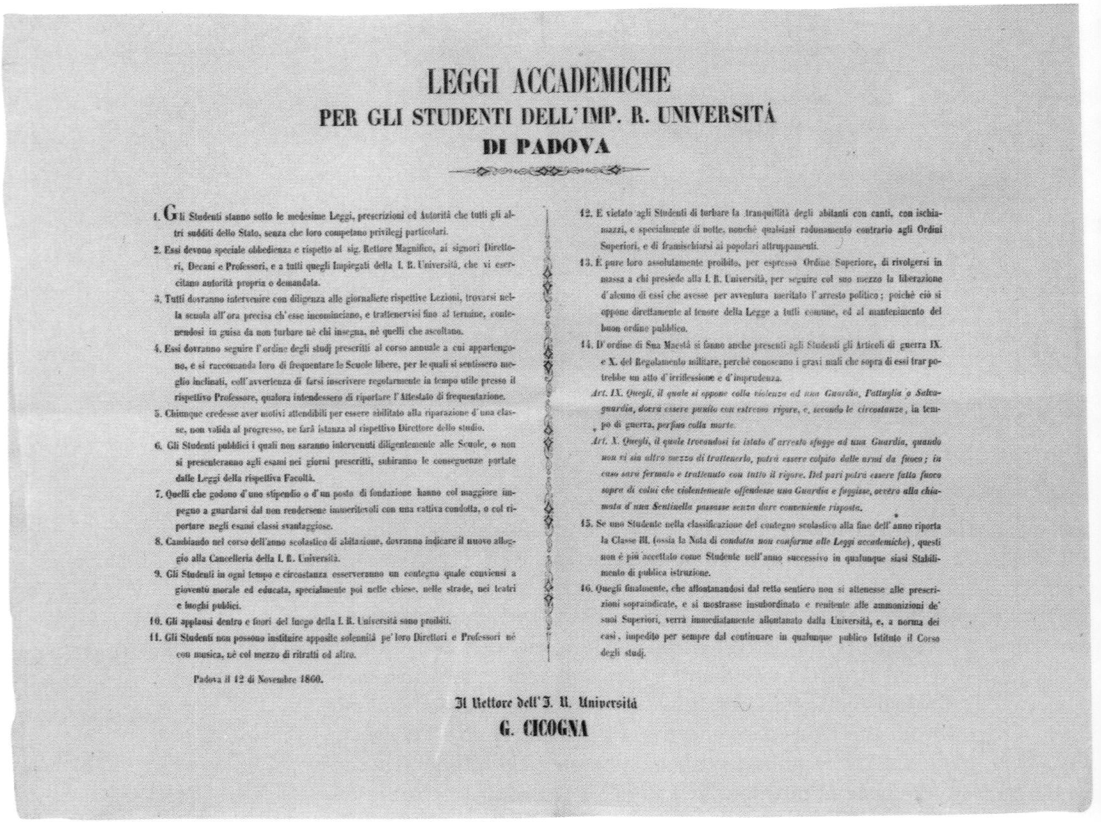

LEGGI ACCADEMICHE
PER GLI STUDENTI DELL'IMP. R. UNIVERSITÀ
DI PADOVA

1. Gli Studenti stanno sotto le medesime Leggi, prescrizioni ed Autorità che tutti gli altri sudditi dello Stato, senza che loro competano privilegj particolari.
2. Essi devono speciale obbedienza e rispetto al sig. Rettore Magnifico, ai signori Direttori, Decani e Professori, e a tutti quegli Impiegati della I. R. Università, che vi esercitano autorità propria o demandata.
3. Tutti dovranno intervenire con diligenza alle giornaliere rispettive Lezioni, trovarsi nella scuola all'ora precisa ch'esse incominciano, e trattenervisi fino al termine, contenendosi in guisa da non turbare nè chi insegna, nè quelli che ascoltano.
4. Essi dovranno seguire l'ordine degli studj prescritti al corso annuale a cui appartengono, e si raccomanda loro di frequentare le Scuole libere, per le quali si sentissero meglio inclinati, coll'avvertenza di farsi inscrivere regolarmente in tempo utile presso il rispettivo Professore, qualora intendessero di riportare l'Attestato di frequentazione.
5. Chiunque credesse aver motivi attendibili per essere abilitato alla riparazione d'una classe, non valida al progresso, ne farà istanza al rispettivo Direttore dello studio.
6. Gli Studenti pubblici i quali non saranno intervenuti diligentemente alle Scuole, o non si presenteranno agli esami nei giorni prescritti, subiranno le conseguenze portate dalle Leggi della rispettiva Facoltà.
7. Quelli che godono d'uno stipendio o d'un posto di fondazione hanno col maggiore impegno a guardarsi dal non rendersene immeritevoli con una cattiva condotta, o col riportare negli esami classi svantaggiose.
8. Cambiando nel corso dell'anno scolastico di abitazione, dovranno indicare il nuovo alloggio alla Cancelleria della I. R. Università.
9. Gli Studenti in ogni tempo e circostanza osserveranno un contegno quale conviensi a gioventù morale ed educata, specialmente poi nelle chiese, nelle strade, nei teatri e luoghi pubblici.
10. Gli applausi dentro e fuori del luogo della I. R. Università sono proibiti.
11. Gli Studenti non possono instituire apposite solennità pe' loro Direttori e Professori nè con musica, nè col mezzo di ritratti od altro.
12. È vietato agli Studenti di turbare la tranquillità degli abitanti con canti, con ischiamazzi, e specialmente di notte, nonchè qualsiasi radunamento contrario agli Ordini Superiori, e di framischiarsi ai popolari attruppamenti.
13. È pure loro assolutamente proibito, per espresso Ordine Superiore, di rivolgersi in massa a chi presiede alla I. R. Università, per seguire col suo mezzo la liberazione d'alcuno di essi che avesse per avventura meritato l'arresto politico; poichè ciò si oppone direttamente al tenore della Legge a tutti comune, ed al mantenimento del buon ordine pubblico.
14. D'ordine di Sua Maestà si fanno anche presenti agli Studenti gli Articoli di guerra IX. e X. del Regolamento militare, perchè conoscano i gravi mali che sopra di essi trar potrebbe un atto d'irriflessione e d'imprudenza.

Art. IX. Quegli, il quale si oppone colla violenza ad una Guardia, Pattuglia o Salvaguardia, dovrà essere punito con estremo rigore, e, secondo le circostanze, in tempo di guerra, perfino colla morte.

Art. X. Quegli, il quale trovandosi in istato d'arresto sfugge ad una Guardia, quando non vi sia altro mezzo di trattenerlo, potrà essere colpito dalle armi da fuoco; in caso sarà fermato e trattenuto con tutto il rigore. Del pari potrà essere fatto fuoco sopra di colui che violentemente offendesse una Guardia e fuggisse, ovvero alla chiamata d'una Sentinella passasse senza dare conveniente risposta.

15. Se uno Studente nella classificazione del contegno scolastico alla fine dell'anno riporta la Classe III. (ossia la Nota di *condotta non conforme alle Leggi accademiche*), questi non è più accettato come Studente nell'anno successivo in qualunque siasi Stabilimento di pubblica istruzione.
16. Quegli finalmente, che allontanandosi dal retto sentiero non si attenesse alle prescrizioni sopraindicate, e si mostrasse insubordinato e renitente alle ammonizioni de' suoi Superiori, verrà immediatamente allontanato dalla Università, e, a norma dei casi, impedito per sempre dal continuare in qualunque pubblico Istituto il Corso degli studj.

Padova il 12 di Novembre 1860.

Il Rettore dell'I. R. Università
G. CICOGNA

Academic laws for the students, 12 November 1860

sted profoundly anti-Austrian sentiments, which chose various ways of revealing themselves, more subdued with respect to the insurrectional surge, but equally important and significant. The "cigar boycott", which saw the students smoking a pipe as an alternative; the Italian fashion of hats, worn with provocative ostentation; the mural graffiti singing hymns to an *italianità* that ever broader sectors of the population now felt possible, and hoped for: all these elements confirm that the explosion of '48 had not passed in vain, but had deeply marked a transformed political reality.

The 1850's were punctuated by repeated demonstrations of a patriotic nature, of which the students of the University were convinced and symphatizing protagonists: in March of 1858 about 600 students crowded into St. Antony's basilica for the requiem mass in memory of Felice Orsini; the following year, in 1859, more than 1,000 accompanied the coffin of the physics professor Bernardo Zambra, whose last name, shouted over and over, became a patriotic acronym ("zitto, Austria muoia, bella risorge Ausonia" –"be silent, Austria is to die, the fine Ausonia is reborn"), which so inflamed the young participants that it gave rise to fights and scuffles after which the University remained closed for over a month.

At the end of the decade, the patriotic commitment of the Paduan students translated itself into a veritable political emigration: a number of young men left the city of the Veneto to fight beside the Piedmontese troops during the Second War of Independence, while others (about sixty) abandoned the classrooms to embark with Garibaldi's men on the celebrated Expedition of the "Mille" ("One thousand").

With the beginning of the 1860's (the University remained closed from May 1859 to October 1860) the episodes of insubordination which saw the students of the University as protagonists were further intensified. The students were then repeatedly involved in anti-Austrian demonstrations which regularly ended in arrests and expulsions, and culminated (we are already in March 1865) with a massive demonstration of several hundred students in the ancient courtyard of the Palazzo del Bo, where copies of the *Syllabus* of Pius IX were burned.

The time was by now ripe for decisive political change, which was shortly to see Padua and its ancient University pass under the young Italian government and begin, once again, a new cultural and ideological season.

PIERO DEL NEGRO

From 1866 to 2000

1. *In Liberal Italy*

In 1866 the transition from the last period of Austrian rule to the Italy of Vittorio Emanuele II was a traumatic event for the University of Padua. It is true that the institutional and didactic organization of the University was substantially preserved exactly as it had been, except for the inevitable adjustments in a liberal-national vein (for example, regarding the teaching, the substitution of Austrian history with Italian history, or the introduction of constitutional law) until 1873, until, that is, the law which rendered the University equal to the others in the kingdom came into effect. But the teaching body suffered the negative consequences of the change in regime in the immediate future. This is testified to by, among others, the few notes that the Paduan patriot Carlo Leoni dedicated in these months to "our University" in his diary. On 26 June he recounted how a few days earlier, after his arrival in Padua, the royal commissioner Gioacchino Pepoli "gave back their former posts to the professors [Enrico Nestore] Legnazzi, [Jacopo] Silvestri, [Stefano] Agostini, [Antonio] Valsecchi, who had been removed by Austria, and suspended many professors [eighteen in all, including the adjunct calculator astronomer] among whom were [Francesco] Panella, [Tito] Vanzetti, [Alessandro] De Giorgi, [Lino] Rizzotto, etc.".

A year later, on 8 November 1867, Leoni, taking up the subject of the sudden changes in the University teaching body again, pointed out that "the new professors are truly talented and our University in a few months can be said to have regenerated; besides the Paduans [Ferdinando] Coletti and [Francesco] Marzolo [who in effect was not so new, since he had already taught surgery at Padua in 1847-8, losing his job that year because of his participation in the revolution], people like [Eugenio] Ferrai, [Luigi] Luzzatti, [Filippo] Lussana, [Lodovico] Brunetti [...] are enough to illustrate it". The purges, the re-integrations, and admissions which had affected over half the professors had obeyed a fundamentally political logic, which had penalized the *Austriacanti* (supporters of Austria) and rewarded the patriots, with a final result in every case of raising the average quality of the Paduan professors.

The academic substitutions had take into account, in particular, the wishes and idiosyncrasies of that handful of Paduans of a moderate tendency – first among whom were Coletti and Legnazzi – who, after having

Arturo Martini, Palinuro, *the partisan Masaccio, Palazzo del Bo*

often played prominent roles in the events of 1848-49, committed themselves in the years preceding 1866 to an intense conspiratorial activity in the heart of secret committees. There were few University professors – and among these must be mentioned the mathematician Giusto Bellavitis, who not by chance was to be the first 'Italian' rector of the University in 1866-67 – who had collaborated, mostly in the background, with the initiatives of Coletti and the other organizers of the fight against the Austrians; this is also explained by taking into account the fact that the government in Vienna had taken steps to distance from the classrooms of the Palazzo del Bo those professors who had shown patriotic convictions.

The heavy conformist mantle which the Austrian regime had imposed on the entire academic body had favoured the spread of a behaviour which was considered by the intransigent wing of the *Risorgimento* movement to be a veritable defection. It is not surprising then that the purges of 1866 touched or in any case aroused unjustified fears in many of the professors, including those who, like the statistician and economist Angelo Messedaglia and the engineer and mathematician Domenico Turazza, were subsequently to be appointed senators of the Kingdom of Italy. It is known that from 1797 onwards politics had a direct impact on Paduan academic life, though not at the levels of 1866. What in any case distinguished the turning point of this latter year from those preceding it, was that it transformed the "professor-functionaries of knowledge" beloved of the Napoleonic and Habsburg regimes into "professor-citizens" who were placed, in some cases despite their wishes, in a politico-cultural setting which, in so far as it identified itself in the formula of "national science" and assigned the University a fundamental role in the construction of the State, threw open the doors of the ruling class to the professors, and at the same time identified the Universities as the places for the education of that class.

1866 in Padua saw a renewal of that student radicalism that had been the protagonist of the glorious 1848, and which in 1859-60 had contributed to the political migration and the expedition of the "Mille" to free the South of Italy. A University Association was established that was openly liberal, whose honorary president not by chance became Giuseppe Garibaldi, and which in 1867 published a periodical, the *Avvenire*, for a few months, which was subtitled "University journal". On the evening of 8 February 1867 several hundred "students in movement" celebrated, for the first time publicly, the "anniversary of the deeds of Padua of 1848". The student agitations unleashed by the defeat of Garibaldi at Mentana forced the postponement of the opening of the University until 9 December. In January of 1868 "a swarm of student *garibaldini* [supporters of Garibaldi]" (C. Leoni) was at the forefront of a series of anticlerical demonstrations culminating in the invasion of the Cathedral and the Seminary. In the following year the funeral of a student was the pretext for another similar episode, which aroused the anger of the bishop and the prefect.

Francesco Marzolo

But neither the "movement" of the student *garibaldini*, nor the intransigent patriotism - it too of anticlerical tendency - of Coletti and the other instigators of the "regeneration" of the teaching body in 1866-67 had a decisive influence on the way the University of Padua was introduced into liberal Italy. Without doubt the general ideological climate can help to explain the progressive marginalization of the Theology studium, a process that in any case Padua shared with the other Universities of the Kingdom, and that had to be put to an end by the Italian parliament in 1873, when it was decided to suppress the studium. Greatly hit by the purges of 1866, the professors of theology were reduced from ten to five; deprived of funds, the theological studium wearily dragged on to a closure largely anticipated by the catastrophic drop in the number of students, which decreased from 120 in 1865-66 to two in 1869-70. It is no wonder then that not even one of the eight rectors, who between 1866 and 1873 succeeded each other with a year-long mandate (as established by Austrian legislation) to the head of the University, came from Theology, while the last three rectors of the Austrian University of Padua had come from this studium.

In the years subsequent to the Unification the rectors were an expression, on an equal basis, of the remaining four studia of the University of Padua. The alternation between the studia engaged the 'mathematicians' Bellavitis and Turazza respectively in 1866-67 and, once the legitimate needs for representation by the other components had been satisfied, in 1870-71. There then followed the 'philosophers' Giuseppe De Leva and Giacomo Zanella in 1867-8 and 1871-71, the physicians Marzolo and Coletti in 1868-69 and 1872-3, and finally the jurist Giampaolo Tolomei in 1869-70 and 1873-9 (in the meantime Padua had been brought in line with the other Universities of the Kingdom and the rector's mandate had not only received a *de facto* long-term extension, but also, as a result of the regulation of 1876, had acquired greater importance to the detriment of the competence of the academic Council, called the senate from 1923). The office of rector was not infrequently a sign of esteem accorded to the most important man in the studium (from 1873 faculty), who was granted the right to represent the University - and it was a characteristic that was often to be confirmed in the subsequent decades: this was in particular the case of De Leva, the director of the philosophical studium and then, after the 'equalization' of the University of Padua with the other Italian universities, dean of the Faculty of Philosophy from 1866 to 1873 (and then from 1892 to 1895). It was also the case of Tolomei, director of the legal studium from 1866 to 1873 (and dean of the Faculty of Jurisprudence from 1881 to 1893). Turazza and Marzolo had however also occupied the office of director or dean, respectively, of the Faculty of Mathematical, Physical and Natural Sciences (from 1872-76: from 1876 to 1891 Turazza had directed the School of Applied Engineering); and of the Faculty of Medicine and Surgery (from 1875 to 1879).

In 1866 Tolomei attempted, in this particular circumstance without success, to be elected as a member of parliament. Such an objective was attained however in the first electoral round after the annexation of the Veneto to Italy by his colleague in the studium Messedaglia and by the 'mathematician' Gustavo Bucchia. While this latter was linked to the circle of Coletti and Marzolo, which was represented in particular, as we have seen, in scientific studies and was above all close to the self-employed middle classes, Tolomei and Messedaglia were not only close to the aristocratic élites and the upper-middle class who supported the historical right wing, but they could also be considered the spokesmen of "national science": they were, that is, expressions of the attempt to form a strong link between the technical expertise of a juridico-economic type and the political class and high bureaucracy, and they constituted a sort of interface between the University and the State. This was also true of their friends and pupils Luzzatti and Emilio Morpurgo, whose two careers followed a different order - Luzzatti was to debut as a professor and Morpurgo as a member of parliament – but who were united by their high profile bureaucratic office, that of Secretary General of the Ministry of Agriculture, Industry and Commerce.

Messedaglia and Tolomei, the former in Rome, the latter in Padua, were the protagonists of an attempt to reverse the terms of the problem that the University faced just after Unification. Convinced, to a large extent correctly, of the basic superiority of Austrian organization with respect to Italian, they sought not only to avoid Padua being simply brought into line with the national University system, but also to make Padua a point of reference for the university reform that was being discussed in Rome, and in any case they took up a position against the centralist approach of the Italian University policy. Although they obtained some undoubted successes on a tactical level (the reform of the curricula of the legal faculty in 1875 took into account certain key proposals by Messedaglia), from the strategic point of view the 'political' wing of Jurisprudence lost the match: Padua was to renounce its own tradition. Moreover it must be pointed out, on another level, that the transformation of the Paduan professors into Italian politicians (or into very high-level functionaries), if it guaranteed Padua a certain visibility on a national level in the short term, it also favoured the academic transferral of those teachers to the capital (this was, for example, to be the fate of Messedaglia and, twenty years later, Luzzati), and therefore constituted an impoverishment of the Paduan teaching body.

On the internal front, that of university policy in its own house, the action of Tolomei was not particularly decisive. This is the impression we get at least from the interpellation which Giovanni Canestrini, professor of zoology, anatomy and comparative physiology from 1869 and the greatest proponent of Darwinism in Italy, presented to the mayor of Padua on 29 March 1882, as a councillor for the Progressive Constitutional Association. Tolomei "assembled the various faculties, and asked each one what needs they had, and these, wanting to reach an ideal in order to place themselves in the mainstream of science, made a list of needs, which in order to obtain satisfaction would have required the availability and the commitment of enormous sums of money". In this way the project ran aground, as did the attempt by Marzolo (newly made rector in 1879-80, a mandate cut short after a few months by his death), following the particularistic logic of the faculty to which he belonged, to transfer the obstetrics clinic to a building in its own right.

Antonio Tolomei

Marzolo's successor, Morpurgo, rector from 1880 to 1882, took up Tolomei's wide-ranging policy. He failed, however, following what had already happened in many other Italian University seats (eight, among which a great University such as Turin), when he tried to establish a consortium between the University and the local agencies with the support of the State. Canestrini's intervention was not limited to a tirade against the University policies of the Commune and the Province of Padua - accused of having made the University many declarations of "sympathy and esteem", but "never any material assistance" - and to a denunciation of the failures of the rectors. Indeed the interpellation stressed the problem of the "decline" of the Padua Studium, or more exactly, that of the possibility of its successfully "competing with the other Universities of the Kingdom". In any case, the fact that the University was passing through a critical phase was shown by the trend of student enrolment.

Before 1859 – before, that is, the separation of Lombardy, which became Italian, from the Veneto, which remained Austrian – the number of students fluctuated around 1,500. The formation of the Kingdom of Italy had reduced Padua University's catchment area and removed streams of students: in 1860-61 a low point of just over 600 students had been reached. In the last years of Austrian rule the curve had swung upwards again, reaching nearly 1,400 enrolled students in 1865-66, a tendency that was increased following the annexation of the Veneto region to Italy. In 1867-68 it reached a peak of 1,660, but in the subsequent years the spectre of decline materialized: the lowest point of the curve was to be touched in 1882-83, with fewer than 900 students.

Regarding the "battle", indeed the "war" against the other Universities, Canestrini pointed out the limits of the approach of the moderate Paduans who controlled the Commune (the mayor, whom he addressed, was Antonio Tolomei, a son of Giampaolo) and the University. Perhaps because their mainstay was a humanistic faculty, Canestrini's adversaries were convinced that "the fame and importance of the University will always be in relation to the scientific and moral quality of the men who teach there". But, the zoologist answered, "the effect of the teachers, if it could once be considered as 99% useful, is today greatly diminished because they need laboratories and instruments to render their teaching profitable". "Ample spaces" and "well-equipped laboratories" required new buildings and hence a policy of building expansion. This was the path that the scientific faculties had already taken: during his rectorship Coletti had transferred the pre-clinical teaching of medicine from the hospital to the buildings

Palazzo del Bo, end of the nineteenth century

obtained by the restoration of the convent of San Mattia. In 1874 a School of Pharmacy and in 1876 a School of Applied Engineering were founded, the latter autonomous from the Faculty of Sciences. But new institutional structures were still waiting, in 1882, to be given the necessary classrooms and laboratories: in particular the "Institute of Applied Engineering has no buildings, has no schools, and lessons take place in the classrooms of our Faculties".

The second rectorship of De Leva (1882-85) is to be remembered above all for the great student agitation of March-April 1885, which caused the University to close. Even though the episode that roused the students was the arrest of a professor of medicine who was involved in a row with the rector and his faculty, the occupation of the Palazzo del Bo with the bell sounding the tocsin, an event that had not taken place since 1848, can be situated within a cycle of student protests in some of the greatest Italian Universities, provoked by an increase in student fees decided by the government, but also fuelled, above all in Padua, by "irredentism", that is, by an aversion to the alignment of Italy with the Vienna-Berlin axis. Perhaps another important factor in the crisis of the mid-1880's was the increase in the student population (gradual, but continual in the case of Padua: in 1884-85 it again surpassed a thousand and in 1890-91 it reached a peak of 1,300). The increase must be attributed, as the rector Carlo Francesco Ferraris pointed out in 1891, "not only to a greater need for culture [or, if one prefers, an increase in the job market], but also to the fact that the poor economic conditions of the country have diverted many from other occupations to turn them to the acquisition of academic qualifications as a safer defence against the vicissitudes of life". The University reverted to being, as it had been above all in the years around 1840, contemporaneously and contradictorily a temporary refuge from intellectual unemployment and a driving force of this phenomenon.

Succeeding De Leva was the anatomist Giampaolo Vlacovich (1885-91), dean of Medicine from 1879 to 1885, who was committed, without much success, to overcoming what the same Vlacovich defined as the "humiliating shabbiness of the present". "Certain improvements were made to our too humble University classrooms"; some laboratories were built in the ex-convent of San Mattia; the transfer of the School of Applied Engineering to the ex-Palazzo Cavalli was planned; "the Institute of General Physics and that of Geology were given a larger and more convenient seat in the building next to the University"; "the University acquired drinking water"; the Institute of Obstetrics was finally transferred to the ex-Palazzo Negrelli donated by the Commune. But the project which was dearest to the University, the institution of an inter-provincial consortium in the Veneto in which the Commune of Padua and the State would participate, did not get off the ground because of the Paduan moderates' lack of sensitivity towards higher education.

Even the last two rectors of the nineteenth century – the 'jurist' (he taught statistics) Ferraris (1891-96) and the great clinician Achille De Giovanni (1896-1900) – failed in their attempts to form what Ferraris was to call "the ever desired and ever lacking University consortium". Already division head of the Ministry of Agriculture, promoter of the science of administration in Italy, member of parliament from 1886 (in 1905 he would also become Minister of Public Works), Ferraris, who was very close to Morpurgo, was elected as head of the University without ever having held the office of dean. Scholar of the University's problems besides those of administration in general (after his rectorship he was to teach administrative law), Ferraris can be considered the first rector-manager of the University of Padua. It is not by chance that in his reports the "worthy officials of the secretarial staff" appeared for the first time, in addition to those "colleagues" who had been the exclusive recipients of Vlacovich's interventions.

Ferraris showed he possessed a by no means conventional view of his duties. In his addresses inaugurating the academic year he spoke directly to the students – this is a novelty worth being pointed out – whom he defined as the "pars magna" of the University, "our pride and our hope", "the paramount element in the life of our institution". The rector did not limit himself to urging them, as his predecessors had done and – needless to say – all his successors would do, to "the rigorous observance of University discipline": in 1894 he even invited them, in violation of the ministerial regulations of 1885 which prohibited student associations, to assemble in "a sodality, where without distinction of studies, opinion, parties [they would find themselves] all united as University students". Certainly, Ferraris expected that "a delegation of students [...] in continual relationship with the academic authorities" would mean the avoidance of the "dissentions and misunderstandings" which derived from the student custom of nominating "temporary committees, improvised sometimes riotously", every time a "wish or need" appeared on the horizon. And his attempt to overcome the divisions into "parties" that had characterized University life until then (in the preceding decades clerical, moderate, democratic, and radically-leaning circles were born and often soon died), responded to the understandable desire to keep politics out of the University.

But the rector would also have liked the University association, which in effect he was able to create in 1895 and which was to guarantee a "dignified calm" "in moments of great agitation in other Universities", to provide "aid to young students who find themselves in temporary hardship", to function, that is to say, as a sort of society of mutual assistance based on the "co-operative spirit", in a period in which the number of students continued to increase (during the rectorship of Ferraris the number of students enrolled rose from over 1,300 to over 1,600), bringing the less wealthy middle class into the University too. Perhaps the 'official' student association was also conceived by the rector to 'fence in' the typical riotous student behaviour (*goliardia*) triggered by the celebrations that occurred in 1888 for the eighth centennial of the University of Bologna. It is not surprising that right after the Bolognese festivities, in which students from

Padua also took part, and after inaction lasting a third of a century, publication began again by and for the students, with *Lo Studente di Padova* (The Student of Padua), which even though it did not exclude 'serious' articles, nevertheless privileged the 'goliard' aspect.

Although Ferraris was convinced, as we know, that "the strenuous competition of young men for higher studies in order to move into already excessively crowded liberal professions cannot always be considered a social good", he also realized that as long as the number of students enrolled was considered an indicator of the "force of attraction" and the "didactic fame" of a University, statistical data was a weapon to be used in the "race with the other institutions of higher education", which Canestrini had also insisted on. It was therefore logical that the rector attributed particular importance to the fourth place which Padua won in 1894-95 in the national University classification behind Naples, Turin, and Rome, and he was anxious that this position should also be preserved in subsequent years.

The great building enterprise carried out by Ferraris was the adaptation of the ex-Palazzo Cavalli as a seat for the School of Applied Engineering, a project made possible thanks to the involvement of the "Cassa di risparmio" bank, which anticipated the necessary 180,000 lire, the government, which accepted the task of paying in instalments nearly three-quarters of the sum, and the Commune, which was saddled with the rest of the cost of renovation. The rector expected that this would be the first in "a series of single, practical and effective measures", which, once added together, would obtain the same result that the 'great' consortium was to have reached. But things were to happen differently.

And thus in 1892 Ferraris had declared, when the approval of the convention in favour of the new seat of the School of Applied Engineering was in sight, that this put an end to "the ugly legend that the citizens of Padua [...] did not possess a full awareness that the University is the institution which reunites the greatest interests of the City, just as it is the centuries-old glory, the supreme intellectual centre"; yet in the final months of his term he wrote a bitter act of accusation against the communal administration that was in no way inferior to that of Canestrini. In Italy a good thirteen of the seventeen State Universities had managed to establish a consortium; as far as Padua was concerned, in almost thirty years the Commune had spent 130,000 lire for its University, that is to say not even 5,000 lire a year when, for example, Catania guaranteed 70,000 lire per year, Messina 60,000, Bologna 50,000, etc.

Carlo Francesco Ferraris

Even though Ferraris sought to provide for other pressing needs of the University (for example, in 1892 he drew up a contract with the administration of the civic hospital, which "resolved all the controversies which had lasted over a half a century" by the clinics handing over rooms to the administration itself), it might be thought that his commitment in favour of the engineers also responded to his convictions regarding the needs of a country that had still not experienced an industrial revolution. If there were too many physicians and lawyers, there were too few engineers and technicians in general and it was therefore necessary to invest in them. As the governing council of the School of Applied Engineering pointed out a few years later, "the awareness [...] that the greatest hopes for the future must be nourished in the progress of technical applications, and that the people expect an increase in their riches and an improvement in their conditions of life above all from the engineers" was by now widespread.

Antonio Favaro

Ferraris' rectorship deserves to be remembered above all for the "cult of the most glorious [...] historical past" of the University, for his firm desire to rescue the University's past in order to "maintain and increase the prestige of the city and the University". The grand celebrations in honour of Galileo which took place in December 1892 under the direction of Antonio Favaro, the great Galileo scholar, like those three years later in memory of Tasso, were not a ritual event, but an occasion to rekindle the splendours of the University before the national and international scientific community, and also to exalt "the rights of the University and lay science against the usurpation of the Jesuits". In 1892 Ferraris had placed the controversial memorial plaque commemorating the 8th of April 1848 in the Palazzo del Bo, which had been requested ten years earlier by the students, but had not been inaugurated in 1885 because it condemned the "Austrian hordes", a expression judged too strong by a government that had just allied itself with Vienna. It is true that the plaque was set in the wall only after "Austrian hordes" had become the more imprecise "foreign troops", but it should be noted that in his report the rector referred to the "foreign hordes", thus suggesting a mix halfway between the two versions.

Among other things Ferraris had the archives of the University reorganized and inventoried by expert functionaries: the historical archive was transferred to the University library to facilitate consultation; the rector also sought to obtain the documents relative to the University which had been deposited in the episcopal curia, but he had to be satisfied with their reorganization. Ferraris also initiated the restoration of the "incomparable museum" of the coats-of-arms of the Palazzo del Bo ("the first heraldic monument in Italy" according to the president of the Heraldic College Antonio Manno), and he also had a topographical list drawn up of it. In addition he re-established the historic seal of the University and had the degree diplomas decorated with a frieze created on the occasion of the Galileo celebrations. The anatomical theatre was transformed from a lecture hall into a monument. As his decision to send the University yearbook as a gift to 222 Universities and higher institutions abroad indicates, Ferraris contributed enormously to restoring an identity and an international appeal to the Padua Studium.

Compared to that of Ferraris the rectorship of De Giovanni was very insignificant. De Giovanni, who had fought with Garibaldi in 1859 and 1866 and afterwards militated in the progressive camp, had been dean of Medicine from 1885 to 1896. His election could be interpreted as the consecration of "lay science", of a positivism whose greatest interpreter was

Achille De Giovanni

the philosopher and pedagogue Roberto Ardigò, dean of Philosophy and Letters in 1895-96, who was to be solemnly honoured precisely during De Giovanni's rectorship. But that election was also an indication of the shifting of the academic body to politically more advanced positions. Canestrini had been dean of Sciences from 1885 to 1891; head of Pharmacy from 1900 to 1903 was to be the professor of mineralogy Ruggero Panebianco, a former *garibaldino*, who became the leader of the socialist party in Padua (having become member of parliament, he was forced to flee to Switzerland in order to avoid a condemnation that he had received as a subversive). Even in the Faculty of Jurisprudence, which had always been a bastion of moderatism, one can witness an opening to the Left: in 1893 Achille Loria, a Marxist Positivist of great notoriety who had adhered to the Socialist league of Panebianco, was named to the chair of Political Economy, while in 1896 Giulio Alessio, a professor of the Science of Finance who was to be minister many times between the end of the Great War and the arrival of Fascism, initiated his long career as a member of parliament with the radical party.

De Giovanni had sought to forge closer links with the city, inviting to the inauguration of the academic year "the honourable representatives of the civic and military Authorities", and establishing a group of 'Friends of the University' "belonging to all the parties": but the plan for University building reform, which the rector presented in 1898 to the Commune and the government and which put forward the creation of an adequate seat for the Institutes of Mineralogy and General Chemistry and the transferral the University library to the Palazzo Bo, made little progress because of the convulsive end-of-century crisis. The failure of the attempt to show that the University "was not only a royal institution, but also one of local patriotism" was made even more bitter by the fact that throughout the De Giovanni rectorship, and even in the first years of that of his successor Raffaele Nasini, the student population declined year after year, falling under the 1,600 mark in 1897-98 and reaching the lowest point on the curve in 1902-03 with fewer that 1,300 students.

The reduction in the number of students, which hit Sciences, Medicine, and the School of Applied Engineering above all, was justified by De Giovanni and Nasini sometimes citing specific causes (the crisis of enrolment in Engineering was, for example, attributed to the absence of a course in Industrial Engineering); other times by consoling themselves with the observation that – as was stated by Nasini in 1901 – "the fatal decline" was shared by all the Italian Universities and that in any case, given the excessive number of graduates in circulation, the fall in enrolment should be considered beneficial; yet again by contesting – as De Giovanni did in 1897 – the criterion of "determining the level of importance of a University centre by the number of people attending it" (he proposed as an alternative "the statistics of the lessons held during the academic year"). Perhaps the basic cause of the phenomenon was once again to be identified in the negative effects of an economic cycle that was positive this time: it is probable that in the short run the launch of commerce and industry kept young men with a broad scientific vocation away from the University in so far as there were greater employment opportunities at the end of secondary school.

The chemist Nasini, rector from 1900 to 1905, had also been first the dean of a faculty, in this case Sciences (1897-1900). Unlike De Giovanni, Nasini, who was inspired above all by Ferraris' example and went, among other things, to Glasgow to participate in the celebrations for the fifth centennial of the local University (the first visit abroad by a rector recorded in the reports), Nasini was able to benefit from a fairly favourable political climate created by the victory in Padua of a "popular block" dominated by the radicals of Alessio, and in Rome by the liberal-progressive component headed by Zanardelli and Giolitti. The greater stability of the administration at the centre and in the periphery and above all their greater willingness to invest in teaching were exploited with great ability by the new rector, who tried, with the full support of the dean of Jurisprudence Vittorio Polacco (*de facto* rector of the University during the long months when Nasini was in Rome) to forge close links with the Minister of Public Education, Nunzio Nasi, who even came to visit the University, remaining impressed – as he announced to the Chamber of Deputies – by the "spectacle of the very sad conditions of those scientific laboratories", and with the "popular" mayor Vittorio Moschini, "who with so much affectionate intelligence watch[ed] over the improvement and the well-being of the city".

Raffaele Nasini

Nasini did not limit himself to putting forward De Giovanni's plan again, a plan which he held to be wrong in part (he did not share the idea of transferring the library to the Palazzo del Bo), and whose narrow vision he criticized above all; but he outlined, in a memorandum he presented in October 1901 to the government, the Commune, and the Province of Padua, a very ambitious plan of both building expansion and restoration of the University, which was to cost 2,200,000 lire (at the end nearly two million were granted), more than a third of which to be paid by the local organizations. The law instituting the consortium between the University, government, Commune, and Province was approved in December 1903, after the relative conventions had been signed. At the same time the indefatigable Nasini also managed to create an inter-provincial consortium, to which the principal cities of the Veneto belonged, and which integrated, although by a modest amount, the ministerial funds for the acquisition of books and equipment for the University.

When the funds granted were translated into works, one saw "rising from the *Macello* (slaughterhouse), surrounded by gardens, a new, tranquil and elegant quarter of the city dedicated to the Sciences; in the quiet street of San Biagio rose the pretty and graceful Library" (inaugurated in 1912, it was the first Italian University library to be housed in a building constructed *ex novo*); the Palazzo del Bo was restored and enlarged in the direction of the canal, as were the rooms in San Mattia and the other buildings in

Enlargement of the University: demolition of a building against the medieval wall along the Riviera dei Ponti Romani

the hospital quarter and the ex-Palazzo Cavalli. In the area near the *Macello* "more land than that necessary for the moment" was fortunately acquired, "taking into account other Institutes" – besides those originally planned, General Chemistry and Zoology – "which necessarily must be built there, and the enlargement of those that will be built immediately".

On the ideological level Nasini justified his grand plan of development for the University in two ways. First he dealt with the local interlocutors, in particular with the count and liberal-progressive member of parliament Paolo Camerini, president of the "Cassa di risparmio" bank (which not only loaned the sums necessary for carrying out the plan, but also contributed directly to the development of the University with substantial donations, such as that which allowed the creation in 1901 of a electro-technical laboratory), and "star of first magnitude in the ownership and the capitalism of the Veneto" (A. Ventura). With them Nasini insisted, in the light of economic and social progress, on Padua as a "future centre of strong and practical studies", and, in particular, on the necessity of developing Engineering and the clinics. But at the same time the rector presented "the cause of our University" as an "Italian cause": Padua was the "vanguard facing the Rhaetian and Julian Alps, against the once feared and still feared dangers of the Germans and the Croatians to the language and the sentiment of peoples who have Italian blood". In his reports Nasini never forgot the "brothers of Trieste and Trent", expressing, among other things, a desire in favour of the establishment of the Italian University of Trieste. Irredentism and paternalism characterized Nasini's relations with the students, whose "exuberant student joy" he willingly "excused" when it took the form of a "fierce protest [...] against those who with their native tongue would tear the Italian soul from he who is born Italian".

From 1905 to the advent of Fascism four rectors succeeded each other as head of the University in accordance with the criterion of rotation among the various faculties, including the School of Applied Engineering: the civil lawyer Polacco (1905-10), already dean of Jurisprudence from 1896 to 1905; the Italianist Vittorio Rossi (1910-13), the electrical engineer Ferdinando Lori (1913-19), already director of the School of Applied Engineering from 1908 to 1912 (he was to receive a second term as director from 1921 to 1925) and the teacher of medical chemistry Luigi Lucatello (1919-1926), dean of Medicine from 1916 to 1919. They all largely followed the tracks laid down by Nasini. On the one hand, therefore, the continuation and the completion of the building activity initiated by the first consortium (or the second, according to the rector Emanuele Soler, who in 1929 was to name Ferrari's initiative of 1893 as the first consortium); on the other fidelity to the idea that the University of Padua was the "vanguard of Italian civilization" (as Polacco said in 1908; three years later Rossi was to specify that it was a "vanguard of high Italian culture towards the eastern border").

As a consequence, the University of Padua's job was not to compete – as Canestrini, Ferraris, and De Giovanni had believed – with other Italian

The bell tower of the Palazzo del Bo

Universities for quantities of students and excellence in research, but to struggle against the Germans and Slavs at least in the defence – if not with a view to liberation – of the Italians remaining under Austrian domination. The irredentist choice was not only an updated version of that *Risorgimento* ideology which after 8 February 1848, or better, after 1866 had become a part of the DNA of the University; and it did not merely grant the "vanguard" a particular identity in addition to that guaranteed by the "lay science" of the Galilean tradition: it was also a prerogative to be asserted in the University's relations, including those financial, with Rome (Padua was presented as a 'special' University because it was a frontier University, a University which more than any other incarnated militant patriotism); and, from another point of view, it was an ideal investment which, as was to happen after the victorious war of 1915-18, was destined to increase the University's catchment area on the basis of another historic inheritance, that of the Republic of Venice.

It is not surprising that in 1919 "the last act" of the Lori rectorship was "the invitation to the sculptor Sanavio to model the lion of San Marco" – an "emblem" that was "the pure symbol of the reunited Venezie" – "to be placed above the main entrance of the University building, as it had been in the past". And it is not surprising either that Lucatello was to celebrate the Italian victory by adding "the longed-for border regions of a liberated fatherland" to the "scientific jurisdiction" of Padua University, that coherently transformed itself into the "University of the Tre Venezie [the Trentino, Veneto, and Friuli Venezia Giulia regions]". Nor should it surprise us that on the same occasion Lori made it clear, remembering the Dalmatians, "Oh! Unfortunately still to be liberated", that the victory was "mutilated" even for Padua.

Such irredentism was to legitimate, if not to fuel, ideological and political interventions that were more or less clearly factional, according to the needs of the moment and the developments in Italian politics. Thus in 1906 Polacco expressed the desire that young people were "open to the enthusiasms and the humanitarian ideals that the new social problems opened up", but that this did not make them "ready to renounce the fatherland, by diluting its sacred image into a utopist cosmopolitism", that is to say into socialism. Four years later the same Polacco – and it was the first time that sport was taken into consideration in the reports of a rector – addressed "words of encouragement and good wishes" to "the sports teams, where together with the muscles the character is fortified and the spirit of discipline is strengthened and patriotism is kindled". In 1911 Rossi exalted Italy's colonial mission in words similar to those of D'Annunzio: "the Nation, reawakened to the consciousness of itself, to the faith in its destiny, beats boldly at the door of the future, and a new sense of vigour, youth, and pride pervades every soul not indifferent to the greatness of the Fatherland, while a new piece of African land opens up to the civilization and the life of the third Italy through Italian wisdom and valour".

In 1914, when the First World War broke out, Lori did not take up a position in the struggle that was taking shape between the neutralistic and the interventionist wings of Italian public opinion, but limited himself to offering vows for a peace that would respect the "most natural of rights", the "right of nationality", and that would take into account in particular the "mighty [...] voice of the mother of every right, the voice of Rome". Nevertheless he also granted the University the role of "first institute for the civil preparation of the people", a "preparation" that in effect was equivalent to a general mobilization, as confirmed a few months later by the constitution of a "Council for Civil Preparation", in which even the rector was to take part. In the following year however Lori claimed his commitment in favour of intervention in honour of the University. Proof of this was the dispatching to Quarto of the "*garibaldino* senator De Giovanni [...] together with our students", to represent the University and to applaud "the voice of a poet", D'Annunzio, who, commemorating the expedition of the *Mille*, had preached the need for Italy to enter into war and the participation of "professors and students" - who had now become "a single soul with the citizens" - in the "Week of Political Passion, 10-17 May", a week which had persuaded a parliament with a neutralistic majority to approve an Italian act of intervention in the war, a course of action that had already been decided by the king and the government.

In the course of the conflict, in his reports Lori took up the themes of the most obvious cultural and political polemic against Germany and Austria, the "fortresses of militaristic and tyrannical imperialism". He presented among other things a caricatured image of the German University ("an army organized by professors and by teachers that sought with premeditated intent to sack in exclusive favour of Germany every smaller branch of the most concealed paths of knowledge which had been revealed for the most part by the Latin Genius"), ignoring the debt the University of Padua owed to it. In January 1918, inaugurating the academic year of 1917-18 in a Padua that was the capital of the frontline and in the presence of the Minister of Public Education (whose speech introduced an innovation that remained for long without a sequel, in a rite which until then had only consisted of the 'administrative' report of the outgoing rector and the scientific inaugural lecture of a high ranking professor), Lori also attacked "certain demonstrations within our Country, coming from factions without a fatherland, that [...] fashion to their evil will the appearance of more extensive ideals, without understanding that socially one cannot progress in leaps and bounds': in other words, the demonstrations he attributed to the socialists.

Lucatello also aligned himself, as we have seen, with the irredentist tradition, and, as Lori had done in 1918, strictly linked "the greater success of the Studium" to the "greater success of the arms and the valour of Italy" (in 1919, for example, he celebrated the "new ranks of young men" who came "to us yearning to draw on the purest sources of Latin culture"; and two years later he remembered the young men of Trieste "jubilant around our banner, symbol of what they felt to be their natural University"). Nevertheless, he was in favour of a rapid re-conversion of the wartime University into a University of peace. The long-awaited celebrations of 1922 for the seventh centennial of the birth of the Studium – Rossi had begun the preparations back in 1913 – were presented as a sort of academics' Versailles: in Padua "the scientists of the entire world, even those which our dutiful patriotism has distanced from our hearts and minds" were to unite, with the aim of reconstructing and sealing "forever the international fraternity of knowledge".

When the "brilliant hour of our national life" struck, that is, when in October 1922 Mussolini took power, Lucatello, though remembering that "the school of higher learning is not a political gymnasium", also specified that the University of Padua had "never isolated itself, by the fate of events, in the closed circuit of pure scientific speculation", and that, among other things, it had to continue its function as "banner and beacon of *Italianità* against the East". From this came his evident approval of a "new Authority of Government", which presented a "fatal programme of national redemption" and which had arisen from "a prodigious movement of Italian youth". It was not by chance that - in that part of his report addressed to the "excellent youths", the students, the protagonists of the "prodigious movement" - the rector claimed the University to be, once more, the "purest reflection of the moral and intellectual life of the country". If it was true that in the University there "reverberated the tremor of the ideals that touch the country", it is also true that one of the furnaces of those ideals had been, from Nasini onwards, the University of irredentist preaching.

Regarding the other inheritance from the Nasini period, the project of building expansion, Polacco was above all an executor of what his predecessor had planned (his original contribution was the placing in the ex-Villa Pisani at Stra an Institute of Hydrographics which had been created from within the School of Applied Engineering with the aim of diversifying the teaching on offer and of profiting from the recreation, thanks to Ferraris, of the Magistracy for Waters). Rossi, however, expended great energy in re-launching an initiative which did not advance with the hoped-for speed (after ten years only half a million lire of the two million allocated in 1903 had been spent). In 1913 a second consortium was established, which obtained financing for nearly three million lire and which thanks to the "broad administrative autonomy" which had been granted on the basis of a agreement arranged by the future Fascist minister Alfredo Rocco, managed to bring to a completion the construction and/or the furnishing of several institutes before the Italian entry into war. The transfer of the library from the Sala dei Giganti to its new seat in via San Biagio allowed the first step to be taken towards what was to become the Liviano building. Between 1919 and 1920 the State made six and a half million lire available to the University, which allowed for the re-opening of the building sites at the Palazzo del Bo, at the new School for Engineers near the

Piovego canal, and in the hospital quarter. Given wartime inflation, however, the sum certainly did not allow for the completion of the 1913 programme.

As from 1904-5 the number of students enrolled began what Polacco defined first as an "encouraging rise", and then exalted as a "most important increase". In effect there was a long and gradual increase: the 1,400 mark was surpassed in 1905-06, as was that of 1,600 in 1911-12, and that of 1,700 (a level not reached since the annexation of the Veneto region to Italy) in 1913-14. In the last year of peace a new record was set: 1878 students enrolled, that is to say - taking into account that the faculty was made up of 73 full and 'junior' professors, 92 deputies and assistant lecturers, and 14 temporary lecturers - a ratio of eleven students per professor. The rush of students to the University classrooms also included female students, admitted from 1874 into the University graduate programme: in 1915-15 they accounted for almost a fifth of the total, even though one must bear in mind that, once the 162 potential obstetricians were subtracted from the total of 351 – the courses in Padua and Venice had been established 140 years earlier by the Republic of Venice - and the 102 diploma students from the secondary schools who attended the special training course were taken into account (a first step towards the Faculty of Education), the female presence in the 'traditional' University was reduced to a few dozen in all, nearly all of them enrolled in Philosophy and Humanities or in Sciences. More in general, the rush of students favoured the establishment of "numerous student associations", above all on the eve of the war. The paediatrician Vitale Tedeschi also promoted a University dining hall. Together with the numbers of students the number of episodes of protest also grew: the rite of ringing the bell of the Palazzo del Bo completely lost its exceptional character. The students aligned themselves ever more in right wing positions: in 1911 they were the heart of a demonstration against the "popular" Commune, and in 1914 they were in the front line in the "Week of Political Passion" during the so-called "Glorious May".

As Lori summarized on the day after the Armistice of Villa Giusti, which put an end to the Great War, "nearly all the students, many assistant lecturers, and several professors were engaged in military duties", and "certain courses for a lack of students were not completely held, but in many the number of lectures was normal" (based on the number declared by the same Lori two years earlier, one can calculate that more than 83% of the male students enrolled in 1914-15 were drafted). "Only the classrooms of the Faculty of Medicine [were] particularly and exceptionally crowded" because, following a decree at the end of 1916, 2,189 soldiers who were in the last four years of medical study from all over Italy were made to converge on the University of Padua and on the sector dependent on it at San Giorgio di Nogaro. 524 of these graduated after an accelerated course of study. Nearly 200 students from Padua University died in the war, that is to say more than 12% of those enrolled in the last year of

Postcard for the seventh centennial of the University

peace, a percentage among the highest registered in the Italian Universities. Victims of the war were above all students from the humanistic faculties (in their case the percentage hovered around 17%), because unlike those in the scientific faculties - who were sent more often to the rear as medical officers or artillerymen or engineers - they were admitted into the ranks of the infantry, the service which was to endure by far the greatest losses.

The war consolidated an esprit de corps, also on a post-University level: in 1918 a University Alumni Association was established. In the first year after the war the enrolled students were "a good 2,475: of which 302 were from the liberated lands", which jumped to 3,609 in 1919-20 (including nevertheless 1,114 *fuori corso*, those who had failed to get their degree within the prescribed time), and it stayed above the 3,200 mark in the last years of liberal Italy, notwithstanding a reduction of the *fuori corso* (these latter dropped to 622 by 1920-21, a drop apparently in line with Lucatello's desire that the category would "naturally vanish from the University statistics": but the desire was to be proven wrong throughout the entire subsequent history of the University). The expansion of the "scientific jurisdiction" of Padua University to the "liberated lands" undoubtedly played a part in the increase in enrolment (the ex-irredentists grew from the pre-war hundred or so to just under five hundred in the early 1920's). The decisive factor, however, was probably the social remix provoked by the war through the selection of more than 200,000 reserve officers, many of whom came from social strata not yet touched by the idea of aspiring to a degree. This phenomenon had in turn led to the establishment of "courses of integration" to benefit the ex-officers, courses whose preservation was to head the list of noisy requests by the students in 1919.

The "Great Festivities of May" 1922 for the University's seventh centennial "with its wide echo throughout the world [...] formed the apotheosis of a great past and a present not unworthy of its traditions". It was on that occasion that an Institute was founded (afterwards a Centre) for the History of the University of Padua, specifically designed to cultivate those traditions. "The 25 delegates from foreign Governments and the 500 delegations from scientific institutes and academies, here convened, were the solemn and universal recognition of homage to one of the most venerable homes of thought and at the same time a recognition of homage to Italy, which with its Universities, in the darkness of barbarism, was able to pick up the torch of civilization to illuminate the world". A claim for the supremacy of the Italians, but also a celebration of "a renewed solidarity of scientific labour and human progress with the common resolution, aside from and above all differences in language and race, to return to the works of peace": it was with this "new and fertile movement towards ideal goals worthy of ancient glories" that, with all its hopes and its contradictions, the liberal age of Padua University ended.

2. *The University during the Period of Fascism and the Resistance*

Giovanni Tamassia

The adherence of the University of Padua to Fascism, visible in the report with which Lucatello inaugurated the academic year of 1922-23, should not be considered as the point of arrival of an ideological process which the University had embarked on with Nasini's rectorship. Certainly the irredentism, the interventism, the belligerence, and the fight against subversives (the "reds", obviously) were some of the ingredients of the Fascist mix. But the resulting Fascism of the line summarized in the University slogan, "vanguard of Italian civilization", was not always inevitable. This is testified to, among others, by the attitude of the great historian of Italian law Giovanni Tamassia, Dean of Jurisprudence from 1910 to 1919, who was one of the most reliable mouthpieces of irredentism and interventionism, but also a defender both of the liberal State against the liberticidal laws of Mussolini - whose fundamental choices he however approved - and of the liberal University against the authoritarian reform of Giovanni Gentile.

The alignment of the last rector of the liberal University with the positions of the Mussolini government obeyed an institutional logic in the first place (the University was pro-government by vocation), and was not backed by the convinced support of a large majority of the teaching body – this is proven, for example, by the fact that ten years later, in 1932, nearly a third of the professors at the University had not yet become members of the national Fascist party. Without a doubt there were some professors who had been among the first Fascists, like the geographer Luigi De Marchi, dean of Sciences from 1909 to 1915 (and then from 1929 to 1932), and in 1919 president of the Fascist Combat Party; nor should we minimize the importance of the group of teachers, from the jurist Rocco to the romance philologist Vincenzo Crescini and the historian of philosophy Emilio Bodrero, who shifted from nationalism to Fascism. But it is known that these and other professors ready to identify themselves with the regime can be set against those of more than a few others, who continued to cultivate anti-Fascist tendencies in the course of the twenty years, and that the Faculty of Letters in particular, but not only, prevented the realization of the cultural conformity demanded by Fascism.

The student situation was very different. Early Paduan Fascism had its strong point in the more than one thousand ex-reserve officers enrolled at the University, and its fortunes were directly in proportion to the consistency of that group. Even before the University Fascist Group (GUF) had been established in Padua in 1921 - one of the first to be created in Italy - the ex-combat students distinguished themselves by their capacity to influence academic life, imposing integration courses and special sessions of exams. In the first years of the 1920's the GUF, which was led by students for the most part enrolled in Engineering and Medicine and with a lower middle class social background, had a fairly tormented history, torn by internal battles due to the different currents of Fascism. However, even before the conquest of power by Mussolini and the transformation of the student organization into one wheel of the totalitarian machine, it asserted itself as the only 'mass' association of Paduan students (around 600 members at the end of 1921; in 1925 Lucatello indicated that the "most flourishing" Fascist student organization was "around 1,400 members strong" – but other sources show a figure of around 800 University students – while the Italian Catholic University Federation numbered seventy). One should nevertheless also bear in mind the fact that in the 'most Fascist' years of the 1930s, although it emerged as a stronger force than Padua's rowdy student traditions, the GUF never organized more than half the enrolled students.

It is not by chance, then, that in 1923 Lucatello commemorated those who had fallen in the Great War as "the divine ferment of a re-flowering youth which kindles new approaches in every branch of the State function". Combatants – Fascists – youths – students: it was on the basis of this series of so-called synonyms that the rector interpreted the turning point of 1922, and it was therefore logical that he considered the students as an interlocutor which had been greatly changed thanks to the political role they had conquered during the war and the post-war period, from the "dear youths" of the Giolitti era (youths who could still receive the paternal admonitions of Polacco, for example). Nevertheless the fascistization of the University was not to come from below, from the "re-flowering youth", but from above, from Rome, through the Gentile reform and the subsequent adjustments by the ministers who succeeded him at the head of the Ministry of Public Education (later of National Education).

The characteristic points of the University reform of 1923 - "the most Fascist of the reforms" according to Mussolini – can be identified in the following phenomena: de-professionalization (it was up to the University first of all to "promote the progress of science", a science conceived in an idealistic prospective; the introduction of a State exam for access to the professions, like the transformation of the School of Applied Engineering into autonomous higher institutes separate from the University, indicated that the "exercise of offices and professions", above all if of a technico-scientific nature, ceased to be the priority objective of the institution); authoritarianism (rectors, deans, and professors were appointed, in the first or last instance, by the government); administrative and didactic autonomy (the University could give itself its own statute – Padua's was approved by a royal decree on 14 October 1926 – but the rigidly standardizing reforms of the 1930s would notably restrict Gentile's more open policy: the administrative council, of which two professors elected by their colleagues were part – a 'democratic' survival cancelled in 1933 – guaranteed a managerial autonomy far greater than that enjoyed previously); and a welfarism aimed at tempering the class-oriented choice at the basis of the reform (the establishment of the University Aid Organization and the Scholastic Fund, set up in Padua towards the end of the 1920s).

Lucatello sought to tune the University of Padua to the new wavelength from Rome, transforming "our problem of [building] renovation" into an "urgent national issue, that cannot be put off", and also beginning works, like the student dormitory and the University dining hall, for the benefit of young people. Although his attention to the liberated 'brothers' did not disappear, as from 1923 the rector insisted rather on "the contribution that our University brings to the humanistic and cultural influence of the Fatherland on foreign Countries, especially those of the nearby East". The growing presence of foreign students – 150 in 1923, but 400 in 1925 – testifies that the "high scientific and patriotic mission" of the "cultural centre of the *Tre Venezie*" was crowned with success. Strengthened by these results Lucatello managed in 1924 to get Mussolini - who "wished", as Soler was to affirm a few years later, "that before the arriving foreigners this ancient Studium should maintain high the fame that for centuries has made it a beacon facing Eastern Europe" - to approve the convention which created the third University consortium for a total of sixteen million lire (Lucatello had requested 50% more), three quarters of which fell to the government to pay. In the following year the provincial consortium was brought back to life, annexing in this case too the provinces liberated to the Veneto.

Padua University also profited from the "broader horizons" that the Gentile reform "opened up to the Studium", establishing one of the first schools of Political and Social Sciences opened in Italy, and setting up various post-graduate courses, among which a historico-philological one on the *Venezie*. But despite the new courses, despite the carrying out of works aimed at completing the University buildings planned before the war, the student population began to fall after reaching a new record in 1923-24, with 3,400 enrolled. The causes of the phenomenon were multiple, one purely statistical due to the subtraction of the engineering students: the gradual depletion of the ex-combatant students and the economic crisis were certainly of importance, but the most relevant factor was probably Gentile's reform, which had made secondary school more selective and restricted access to university. In the course of the rectorships of Soler and his successor Giannino Ferrari Dalle Spade (1929-32) – a professor of institutions and history of Roman law who had been secretary of the Association of Fascist University Professors – the number of students fell by nearly a third with respect to the peak reached before the Gentile reform had been put into action.

In September 1926, on the eve of the end of the seventh year of his rectorship, Lucatello died. His post was taken, on the designation of the minister Pietro Fedele, by Bodrero, a much decorated commander of the arditi (special shock troops) in the Great War, federal Fascist secretary of Padua in 1923-24, and member of parliament from 1924. But the nomination of Bodrero as under-secretary for Public Education sent him to Rome. He was substituted first as pro-rector, and in the academic years of 1927-28 and 1928-29 as rector, by Soler, a professor of geodesy who had been dean of Sciences from 1925. Thanks also to "the reliable good offices of

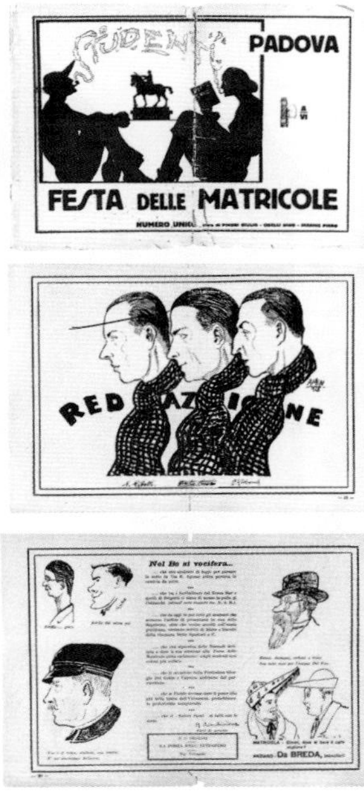

"Festa delle matricole", only issue, 1928, cover, pp. 13 and 20

The Palazzo del Bo, nineteenth-century façade and the Great Hall before the interventions of Gio Ponti

our most dear colleague Emilio Bodrero", who had become an influential Fascist party leader, Soler rapidly proceeded with the programme of "new building, destined to give our University the framework of a great modern Studium". Among other things the new wing of the Palazzo del Bo along the internal canal was completed (where Jurisprudence and Mathematics were situated); the Institute of Anatomy and Pathology was finished ("certainly it can be considered one of the largest, if not the largest in Italy"); and the furnishing of the Institutes of Engineering along the Piovego canal continued.

Although Soler was in a certain sense a product of the 'old' University (his appointment as an elderly ex-dean had been recognition of an institutional logic still along internal lines), the fascistization of the University did not cease because of this during the years of his rectorship. As from 1926 the GUF appropriated the celebrations of the 8 February for itself; that year a memorial plaque was also dedicated "to the Fascist students fallen for the liberation of the Fatherland and the defence of Victory" (four members of a Fascist action squad, three of whom were killed in the course of punitive expeditions in the province of Padua): those students were given, as had been the case for those who had died in the Great War, degrees *honoris causa*; in 1928 the "casa del Goliardo" was inaugurated. While special courses in military culture began (ballistics, sighting, and shooting), "sporting games" acquired a particular prominence. In 1926 the new Surgical Clinic was inaugurated, with a plaque unveiled in honour of Mussolini. Two years later Corporate Law was introduced.

The Fascist Ferrari – already Fascist before Mussolini took power – sought to accentuate a process that, from a medieval-corporative point of view, he believed was founded on the "ever living corporation of Doctors and Scholars". The rector insisted on the need not to neglect "besides the Library, [and] the Laboratory [...] the great air of the gymnasium and the Militia, to mould the new Italian with a proud virile soul, inflamed by a living and industrious love of the Fatherland". From this came the importance attributed to the courses for student officers of the University Militia inaugurated in November of 1929, and to those in military culture (in 1930 'technical' courses were added to the 'humanistic' ones: the first was in the history of aeronautics). As far as the teachers were concerned, the rector was convinced that they were all on the side of the "strong State" – "who could deny their fervid adhesion to a Regime that aims only at the greatness of the Fatherland and the valuing of high culture?" – and that it was important to obtain a greater scientific qualification for them. Even if he could not avoid remembering that in 1848, under the bad government of Austria, the University had been attended by around 2,000 students, a "number only a few hundred lower than that of today", Ferrari in any case found a cause for consolation in Padua's being in third place, behind Rome and Naples, as the University with most students.

He maintained nevertheless that the "great regional University", the "University of the people of the Veneto" was threatened by vaguely-defi-

Mass in the Ancient Courtyard, 8 February 1933

ned "hasty improvisations" (an allusion to what boiled in the cauldron in Venice and Trieste in favour, respectively, of a consolidation and the birth of a new University?), which he judged to be condemned to "a wretched and difficult life". It appeared to him to be more reasonable to stress the strategic choice of a "single University for all the *Tre Venezie*", and the "single University" could be none other than Padua. But the objective of Padua as "great regional University" needed "a more powerful consortium" than the one launched by Lucatello. In fact, the funds granted six years earlier were running out. In 1930 Ferrari presented a memorandum to the government with a request for fourteen million lire, which would allow the satisfaction of what he considered to be "the most impelling need for Padua", the new institute of Physics in via Marzolo (the land had been acquired in 1930), the building of an access stairway to the Sala dei Giganti, the restoration of the University buildings in via Giotto, and the initiation of the ambitious project of a modern general hospital like those already existing in Genoa, Pavia, Turin, and Bologna.

Despite the support of an ex-student of Padua University, the Fascist party leader Giovanni Giurati, the rector was only able to obtain from Mussolini a telegram, which restated that the University of Padua "should in the future be what it was in the past, a singular centre of study and experiences and pride of the land and the people of the Veneto". The plan for a "more powerful consortium" ended up on the shelf, from where it was retrieved by Ferrari's successor Carlo Anti. The Ferrari rectorship, the first after the accord between the Fascist regime and the Catholic Church consecrated by the Lateran Pacts of 1929, accelerated "the process of reconciliation between University institution and ecclesiastical institution" (M. Isnenghi), a process initiated in 1926 with the participation of the academic body in a *Te Deum* at St. Antony's Basilica as a thanksgiving for the failure of an attempt on the life of Mussolini. Among other things in 1930 the anniversary of 8 February was celebrated by the GUF with an open-air mass and the rector exalted the philosopher Francesco Bonatelli - who had been an adversary of the positivist Ardigò and "lay science" - as "a typical representative of Catholic spiritualism, and consequently, of *Italianità*". The definitive consecration of the agreement between the Church and the Palazzo del Bo took place in 1939, when Anti was able to announce that "after a secular interruption" a "pious custom, the religious inauguration of the academic year [had been] revived".

The archaeologist Anti, a convinced Fascist who came, like his friend and mentor Bodrero, from a nationalist position, had been dean of Letters from 1929 to 1932. The "changing of the guard" with "our comrade Ferrari" was marked in many respects by continuity. The ideological reference points remained traditional, even if Anti managed to define them precisely with an almost maniacal care. The role of the University was confirmed both with respect to the Great Veneto of the heirs of the Republic of Venice ("the vast land of the people of the Veneto" stretched from the "reconquered Brenner Pass to the unredeemed Ragusa"), and to an international context: the rector stressed "the vanguard position of our Italian culture before the Germans of the North and the Slavs of the East, our historical but still living influence on the whole of the Venetian Levant"; the three hundred foreigners enrolled, for the most part in Medicine, constituted "a true supremacy" for the Italy of the University and was "one of the great services that our University renders the country for the spread of Italian culture"; Padua however had to be made capable of "defending the honour of Italian culture in the immediate comparison that aliens and foreigners might make with the neighbouring Universities of Innsbruck, Graz and Lubyana".

Anti not only made Mussolini's motto of "book and musket" his own (the students had to be the "first in the *littoriali* [Fascist competitions] of sports and first in the *littoriali* of culture", a goal which in fact remained more or less distant for the Padua GUF), but he was also convinced that, more in general, the University of Padua and Mussolini's regime were following the same path: it was not merely a coincidence that "from the celebrations of the secular festivals in 1922" the University "counted its academic years back beyond the seven-hundredth, hand in hand with those of the Fascist regime". Rigging the numbers somewhat – as was often the case in his reports – the new rector outlined an exultant balance sheet for the first decade of the Fascist era: the students had increased from 2,347 to 3,093 (in reality in 1921-22 and 1931-2 they had decreased by a couple

Carlo Anti

of hundred, despite the new schools of Political Sciences and Statistics, the graduate courses and those of culture); the number of foreigners had grown from the sixties to three hundred (he forgot to state that the peak of four hundred was reached in 1924-5); and eighteen and a half million lire had been invested in building projects.

But this was no reason for resting on one's laurels. The number of students enrolled "could and must pass 4,000". The building problem - the completion of the work on the Palazzo del Bo and the Liviano, the construction of the Institute of Physics, the "modern general hospital adequate for the importance of Padua, University, and city, etc. - required an "integral solution, worthy of our times", highly unlike the fairly timid solution advanced, without success, by Ferrari. Anti knew how to play his cards with great determination with Mussolini. The fourth Consortium was not only instituted in a very short time, on a par with the regime's decision-making process, (the rector met with Mussolini on 29 April 1933, on 26 June the Council of Ministries approved the project, on 20 July the relative papers were signed, and on 6 August two hundred labourers began work), but Anti also obtained from the government nearly twenty-five million lire (another twelve were to be granted in 1938, when expenditure had reached thirty million lire), and another ten million from the local corporations and the "Cassa di risparmio" bank: that is to say more than three times the sum requested by Ferrari.

Regarding the realization of Anti's building work based on the 1932 plan, and more in general on his activity as rector, one can refer to a broad and valuable bibliography, without exception the most significant dedicated to a protagonist of Paduan academic life in the modern period (M. Isnenghi, G. Dal Piaz, A. Ventura), a collection of studies that makes it unnecessary for us to enter into details here, as certainly the great status of the character of Anti would merit. I believe that it is sufficient here to recall some of the basic features of Anti's programmes and activities, mainly taking up significant points in the extremely lucid "General report from the outgoing rector Prof. Carlo Anti to the incoming rector Prof. Concetto Marchesi", dated 7 September 1943.

Building activity: the Palazzo del Bo and the Liviano were transformed into buildings functional to their assigned tasks, a seat of representation of the rector and the academic body, offices and humanistic faculties or, anyway, of scientific institutes that have no need of laboratories (in his last report Anti was to present the Palazzo del Bo as a "vast monumental academic apartment", a "unity that without fear of exaggeration one could say is unique to the world"). The Palazzo del Bo and the Liviano were also decorated by "works of art that can acquire a significance in the history of Italian art". Lower, if we like, was the ideal investment in the new scientific institutes - the most important was that of Physics, while the "modern general hospital" remained on the drawing board. The ideal was nevertheless manifested in the attempt to secure "some supremacy" for those institutes: "for example the high tension plant of the Institute of Physics, the

The 'Littorio' Courtyard

telescope at Asiago, etc."

Relations between University and the city: a fixed point of Anti's vision was that "the University of studies in Padua is not a *local body*, but a great cultural organ with an international range and function that has its seat by chance in Padua, and that it gives the city which hosts it, morally and materially, exorbitantly more than it receives". "A great organism like this University in a relatively small environment like Padua", he had stated in 1941, "it obviously becomes in a certain sense overwhelming, positively overwhelming". It was necessary to "reverse any relationship of value between the city and the University", and therefore to ensure the latter with a physiognomy not flattened on a provincial dimension. The "monumental" building programme, the scientific "supremacy" also responded to this need.

Relations between the University of Padua and its "neighbouring" counterparts: Anti considered "possible competitors [...] in descending order of importance: Venice, Trieste, Ferrara". Naturally Venice and Trieste broke the monopoly claimed by Padua in the area of the *Tre Venezie* (and beyond: Istria, Dalmatia...). Venice was developing along complementary lines to Padua (Economics, Architecture, Languages), and therefore it was also to block the development which Anti believed opportune to institute in Padua the faculties which both Universities lacked (the rector's plans included Education, Statistics, Agriculture, and Veterinary Medicine, and

FISICA

The Liviano and the Institute of Physics

a multiplication of the degrees in Engineering). Furthermore, the foundation in 1938 of a parallel University in Trieste put Anti in serious difficulty. In the report he presented in this last year Anti would attempt to avert the fact in a patriotic vein (in Trieste there "is born a brotherly emulator, a wrestling partner"; "it is another sign of the progressive enlargement of Italy"), but it was however evident that one of the main pillars of Padua's mission, as a pan-Veneto institution, was entering irremediably into crisis.

Relations between the University of Padua and the Veneto: again with the aim of consolidating the University's grip on the region, it was necessary for Padua to reach out to "all the provinces of the *Tre Venezie*". The Astrophysics Observatory at Asiago inaugurated in 1942 and the Marine Biology station at Chioggia were joined, under Anti, with the pre-existent network of schools of obstetrics; but the rector had other plans on the drawing board aimed above all at penetrating into the Trentino-Alto Adige region.

Administration: Anti was perfectly aware that a leap in quality was necessary, that is to say the transformation of the secretariats "from a regime of familiar simplicity to a bureaucratically complex organization as required by a great modern body"; this was an objective that the small number of staff made it difficult to reach (twenty-eight jobs in all, a number that makes one smile today if set in relation to a "bureaucratically complex organization").

Issue of the professors: in his final report Anti dealt, as he had done several times in the past, with the miserable conditions of the deputies and assistant lecturers. Their number had increased excessively in the last decades, together with that of the temporary professors, to allow for an expansion in research and teaching that the seventy or so tenured professors certainly could not cope with – their number had grown by about two dozen with respect to the moment of the annexation of the Veneto region to Italy, but had remained on the level reached in the Giolitti era, when the University had benefited from the discovery that the law of equalization did not give Padua the numerical constraints that burdened the other universities of the Kingdom. The professors were ignored by Anti in his final report, but Ventura's research shows that his policy of recruitment was always inspired by the criterion of privileging the "scientific requisites of the candidates" with respect to their "political ideas". This explains the appointment of declaredly anti-Fascist teachers, and sometimes their protection and the preservation of their chair.

This deontological code rested on the conviction that the University, high culture selected with rigour from an élite corporation, was in itself "national", despite the political convictions of its single members. It was nevertheless brutally suspended when the race laws were passed, which in 1938 affected, besides more than two hundred Jewish students, also 9% of the teaching staff, including prominent figures like the economist Marco Fanno, the physicist Bruno Rossi, and the anatomist and histologist Tullio Terni. In his report that year Anti dryly presented the "Jewish problem" as "a rigid but logical and necessary clarification of positions and responsibilities", adding nevertheless a chilling coda: "as a result of the legislative measures of this period, in this and in the next year we should expect a notable movement of professors".

The students: Anti was also convinced that there was power in numbers, and therefore he committed himself throughout the 1930's to increasing the student presence, achieving a certain degree of success in tandem with the general trend of the Italian University population. The prophetic figure of 4,000 students enrolled was reached in 1934-5 (but with the decisive statistical contribution of Engineering, which in October of 1935 had returned to being a University faculty in all respects; the other institutional innovations of this year, that is the transformation of the schools of Political and Social Sciences and that of Pharmacy into faculties, was without consequence from this point of view). Two years later the threshold of 5,000 was almost reached. This last barrier was breached in 1940-41, when the 6,000 mark was surpassed; further supremacy was established in the two subsequent years: more than 7,000 in 1941-2 and nearly 9,000 in 1942-3. Anti was fairly critical with regard to this quantitative explosion, from which the Humanities benefited in a particular way as the most frequented faculty in this period, partly due to an increase in the presence of women, who found few outlets in other faculties.

Certainly the rector would have been pleased if the causes had simply been the "most healthy" results of "the natural increase of the new classes and the industrial and social development of the Nation", and if that development has translated itself into a healthy multiplication of the "technical professions". But the reasons for such an excessive leap in student numbers could only have been the suspension of the high school graduation exams (the *prove di maturità*), which were a "highly healthy restraint and filter", the widespread exemptions from university fees, and the "widespread availability of money" to the "young men at arms, who thus willingly assumed the burden of university fees to ensure themselves an honest reason for periods of leave". The result: "young men completely unsuitable for University studies due to their mental preparation and intellectual capacity enrolled, attracted only by the 'good degree market'". In particular the increase in the number of students in the humanistic faculty prepared avalanches of misfits. Anti's diagnosis is largely correct, but it does not give sufficient consideration to the fact that the "contingent causes" had a structural cause behind them: the great increase in the number of secondary school students in the 1930s, which in its turn had been favoured by the social rise of the lower middle class.

Anti's accusations against the 'mass' University might also sound like the confession of a paradoxical failure through excessive success of the policy of assistance for students, which he had pursued with great commitment and broadness of vision from his debut as rector. The University dining hall (12,000 meals in 1930-31, but 53,000 in 1931-32, and more than 80,000 ten years later: the amounts indicate that, despite the increases, only a small minority of students benefited from the dining hall); the free health clinic; the *Principe del Piemonte* dormitory ("our darling" was inaugurated in 1935, with about a hundred rooms available); the Office for Information for Financial Aid: all these interventions were without a doubt the fruit of a conviction – which came from a comparison with the Anglo-Saxon world – that the Italian Universities were "very backward [...] regarding the organization of student life", but they also took into account the students' social roots.

In 1932 the rector attempted to "reduce to a minimum" the cost of studies – through free meals, exemption from fees, etc. – in the conviction that "for the middle class, which is and always will be the supplier of aspirants to the liberal professions", that cost was a "very serious burden". However, in 1937 Anti was also to proclaim, acknowledging a recent slogan of the regime, that "even in the University field we should move towards the people": among the objectives of the Fascist revolution was to be that of "conforming the University organism to the needs and the possibilities of the Italian people, independently of the financial means of the individual". This was a theme which he took up again four years later, this time in an autocratic vein: the University spent much on aid to the student, but in a disorganized way; the conclusion was that "the aid that is offered is [not] sufficient to ensure that any poor person with intelligence could take on University studies with tranquillity". The Anti rectorship closed with a series of great contradictions: at the precise moment in which the increase in student numbers might make one think that the "University organism" had conformed to the "needs and the possibilities of the Italian people", it became clear on one hand that the "poor person with intelligence" was still penalized, and on the other that "it was not an increase that was healthy and beneficial to the national economy".

The academic year of 1934-35 was the first also to be opened, besides by the usual report of the rector, by a speech by the secretary of the GUF, which was symbolically intended to place "students and teachers" on the same plane. In reality the relationship between the academic authorities and the Fascist students was not to change, despite the fact that the most radical secretaries of the GUF challenged Anti, accused of protecting anti-Fascists. On the contrary, as testified by examples like the transformation of the "Casa del Goliardo" into a dormitory and the absorption of the GUF dining hall into the University one, the University 'confiscated' a part of that charitable activity which had previously been a strongpoint of the activity of the Fascist students. The task assigned to the GUF was one of militarizing – and normalizing, as the abolition of the festivities of matriculation shows – the traditional riotous student behaviour that was extremely lively in the 1920s and 1930s.

The University was to be, according to Anti, "first in line in this mobilization of the Nation", and the presence of the students in uniform at the inauguration was an indication of the "triumphant penetration of military life within the University walls". In fact the success of the GUF in this

Eugenio Curiel

sphere was fairly limited: the University "8th of February" battalion was made up of just under 600 students, that is to say one sixth of the enrolled males. It is true that more than a hundred student volunteers left for the Abyssinian War (nine fell "for the conquest of the Empire", and another student fell "for the triumph of the Fascist idea in the land of Spain"), and that when, in 1940, the University cohort opened subscription for 137 volunteers, it received 460 requests. But it should not be forgotten that in the final moments of the Second World War, in 1943-45, the Paduan students – the same to whose "heroic memory" Anti had dedicated the Littorio Courtyard (now the New Courtyard) of the Palazzo del Bo – mostly chose, when it decided to do so, to take part in the Resistance. With regard to the politicization of the students too the final verdict on the GUF cannot be considered as among the most positive, as is shown by the bi-weekly *Il Bo*, born in 1935, which became, thanks in particular to Eugenio Curiel (an assistant lecturer in rational mechanics and a clandestine militant in the Communist Party), "a lively tribune of leftist cooperativism, from which a wind of protest blew against the regime" (A. Ventura).

During the Second World War the University lost far fewer students than it had done in 1915-18, at least until the fall of the regime in 1943. In the thirty-eight months following June 1943, 86 students died, that is to say less than half those who died in the course of the forty-two months of the Great War, when the number of students had been only a quarter of those who took part in World War Two. Naturally this is due to the different characteristics of the two conflicts, and above all to the fact that despite its bellicose mask on the military front, the Fascist regime claimed much less than what had been required by liberal "little Italy" from the Italians and, in particular, from the University students. The "principle" was adopted that "the Universities function fully, and also technically, to help the war in progress"; this implied a limited mobilization of personnel, and, at the same time, placed "the activity of research in strict dependence on the needs of war". The teaching activity was "relatively regular" until the summer of 1943.

On the day after the fall of the Fascist regime Anti resigned: four days earlier, on 25 July 1943, Mussolini's arrest by order of the king had led to a demonstration of popular joy in Padua, during which the tricolour had been unfurled at the University and some students rang the bell of the Palazzo del Bo. On September 1st, the government of Marshall Badoglio appointed as rector the Latinist Marchesi, who had for over a year been the protagonist of an intense conspiratorial activity on the part of the Communist Party. In turn, Marchesi chose as pro-rector the Pharmacologist Egidio Meneghetti, one of the heads of the "Party for Action" in the Veneto, and he appointed as deans of faculties professors known in part for their anti-Fascism (for example, in the Humanities the Hellenist Manara Valgimigli, who was a Socialist sympathiser; and in Sciences the mathematician Ernesto Laura, who in 1925 had, along with Valgimigli, signed the manifesto of anti-Fascist intellectuals). When, on 10

September, the Germans occupied Padua, Marchesi submitted his resignation, which was nevertheless rejected by the minister of the newly-proclaimed *Repubblica sociale*, the new Fascist State in the north of Italy.

An extremely particular situation was created. Marchesi maintained that his re-confirmation by the neo-Fascists could signify, in light of the political character that his appointment had had and the fame which surrounded him, a "guarantee that the University would be immune from contacts and troublesome contagions to academic life", a hope nurtured in the awareness that the "proud tradition of liberty and autonomy of Padua University" conferred on it an "immense moral authority, it inspired in the academic and student body a dignified pride in the solid defence of their own prerogatives, and surrounded the institution with a reverential respect that even the authority of Salò hesitated to challenge" (A. Ventura). At the same time Marchesi and Meneghetti decided to establish the Council of National Regional Liberation of the Veneto, headed by Meneghetti, and to make the University the central driving force in the battle against Nazi Fascism.

On 9 November the inauguration of the academic year took place in a climate of extreme tension, in a great hall thronging with students and professors. The authorities were not invited, respecting the University line as "undisturbed asylum of industrious free conscience" (C. Marchesi): the Minister of National Education was present, but in an informal capacity. Accompanied by the applause of those present, the militant neo-Fascists who had occupied the podium were chased off, and Marchesi gave an address which – as the then-assistant lecturer in history of political doctrine and future rector Enrico Opocher was to remember – was received "like a declaration of war by the University of Padua on the oppressors of Italy". Among other things, Marchesi's peroration reaffirmed the University as a place of the civilization of work against the barbarians in uniform ("here within the civic custody of the University of Padua is confirmed"; the University "is the high impregnable fortress where every nation and every people gather their splendid and fertile energies, so that humanity is supported and lit on its way; this is the fortress which dominates and fuels the whole world of work"). The peroration concluded with an appeal to the young people to put their trust in the nation of Italy, "that cannot fall into servitude without obscuring the civilization of the people". The academic year was opened "in the name of this Italy of the workers, the artists, and the scientists".

A few weeks later Marchesi, threatened with arrest, fled to Switzerland after having given his resignation as rector - "I do not intend to appear a collaborator with a government from which I am distanced by a capital and unhealthy discord" - and invited the students to add "to the standard of your University the glory of a new, greater decoration in this supreme battle for justice and for peace in the world". Under the guidance of Meneghetti the University, and in particular the Institute of Pharmacology, did not cease to play a fundamental role in the Resistance in the Veneto.

The expulsion of the militant Fascists from the Great Hall and the inaugural address of Concetto Marchesi for the academic year of 1943-44

Concetto Marchesi and Egidio Meneghetti

"One could say that the entire University, with rare exceptions, from the professors to the porters, from the administrative personnel to the great majority of the students, was involved in conspiratorial activity in various forms, supporting it with its consensus or with a solid wall of accessory silence" (A. Ventura). Those of the University who fell in the fight for liberation numbered 116, among whom 106 students; the largest contribution was that made by Engineering (33 dead, that is to say nearly 3% of those enrolled in the course of 1942-43, against a general average of 1.7%), the faculty that twenty years earlier had supplied most of the leaders of University Fascism.

After the resignation of Marchesi a new academic senate was established, "and for the first time after twenty years the designation of the faculty deans was restored to the Faculty Councils"; in its turn the senate elected as rector the botanist Giuseppe Gola, already dean of Sciences from 1932 to 1941 and from 1940 to 1943 Anti's pro-rector. Even if the new academic heads were not politically characterized like the previous ones, and some of them – such as the rector himself - were a sign of a continuity with the Anti period, the University identified itself in the line traced by Marchesi. As the same, Gola affirmed, the University sought to "represent in neo-Fascist Italy a closed corporation, almost a State within the State", it sought "to be a united block, whose behaviour was immediately interpreted in its true patriotic significance" (in 1945 Valgimigli was to recognize that "Gola knew, with ability and extraordinary sagacity, how to defend and protect both the persons and the dignity of his colleagues and students". It must be mentioned, however, that at the inauguration of the academic year of 1944-45 a clandestine manifesto addressed to the students of the University had accused the rector of collaboration).

On 31 July 1945, restored "to the splendour of the *Patavina Libertas*" (G. Gola), the University of Padua reopened its doors, "having been through a torpid twenty-year mist, having victoriously overcome the liberating storm, having elected according to ancient democratic custom the Rector and the Deans of the Faculties". In the incoming rector's address Meneghetti traced the future of the "University of the People of the Veneto" in the context of the Italy of autonomies and liberty, in which the Resistance placed its hopes. The two central columns of Meneghetti's vision were the renewal in a democratic sense of the postulates of the University policy which had been affirmed in the Giolitti era, and which Anti had declined in accordance with purely Fascist models.

The rector vindicated on the one hand the "regional as well as national function of our University": "in a vast region, autonomous also from a fiscal point of view, a University, which like ours is alone, can find abundant means"; it was absurd that "our University, in a region where agriculture flourishes, does not yet have a Faculty of Agrarian Studies". On the other hand he assigned the "University of the Veneto" the task of "recalling foreign students" from regions "on the northern and eastern borders", "thus to fuse once more the wretched dissentions of race and nationalism in the crucible of culture and in the exalted harmony of the spirit"; the University was to be, "at the same time, the ultimate temple of liberty and a spiritual bastion against whomsoever, in the North or the East, wishes to extinguish the light of Latin thought by rejecting the beneficial coexistence of cultures and peoples".

The first academic year of peace was opened on 12 November 1945, in the presence of the head of government Ferruccio Parri, who decorated the standard of the University with a gold medal (one of the three granted to the Universities of Europe for the role they played in the Resistance). "Secular refuge of science and peace" said the explanation: "the University of Padua in the last appalling conflict knew, before anyone, how to transform itself into a centre of conspiracy and war [...] Padua had in its University a temple of civic faith and a principle of heroic resistance; and from Padua the University partisan youth offered Italy the greatest and longest tribute of its blood".

3. *After 1945*

Until the Second World War the studies and sources available, and above all the process of the critical sedimentation of the past have allowed for a relatively articulated reconstruction of the politico-institutional history of Padua University. For the decades after 1945, however, we must limit ourselves here to an account merely outlining in very broad strokes the vicissitudes of the University, based, as in the previous paragraphs, on the succession of rectors. The half-century and more, which divides us from the conclusion of the last World War, can be divided into two broad periods. The first coincides with the rectorships of Meneghetti (1945-47), Aldo Ferrabino (1947-49), Guido Ferro (1949-68) and Opocher (1968-72); the second - 'contemporary' to us in the full and original sense of the term - leads us towards the present, through the rectorships of Luciano Merigliano (1972-84), Marcello Cresti (1984-87), Mario Bonsembiante (1987-93), Gilberto Muraro (1993-96) and Giovanni Marchesini (1996-2002). In the first phase the crisis of the University as it came out of the Second World, in a version still in many respects élitist, is overcome, and it emerges, with all its contradictions – but also with its indubitable successes – as a mass University destined to grow, for good and bad, and to consolidate itself in the second phase through further, not only quantitative, developments.

As a third of a century later Opocher, another rector who had taken part in the Resistance, was to do, Meneghetti set himself the task of "the reconstruction of the buildings and [...] of the scientific heritage" destroyed by the war, but also the re-establishment of scholastic discipline" (Padua rejected a request, which was accepted elsewhere however, for the so-called "military" 18/30, a grade assigned without an exam, and a forerunner of the "political" 27 or 30/30 claimed by the demonstrating students of the 1970s). He also dedicated himself to overcoming "the tra-

Guido Ferro

ditional form of the Italian, or better the Latin, University, characterized by the lack of relations between teachers and students". The rector, who was ahead of his time in the inauguration of the 1946-47 academic year "in the name of the Italian nation and the Veneto region", aimed, on the one hand, at the "development of free student initiatives" (it is worth remembering at least the University theatre, the Arts Centre, and the "Voice of the University", a radio station that created a relationship not only between the University and the thousands of students – that year there were more than 11,000 – that the problems of the post-war period kept far from Padua, but also with a broader society, eager for culture). On the other, Meneghetti promoted "a rich organization of "houses for students" like perhaps no other Italian University had" (the pre-existing student dormitory, named after Arnaldo Fusinato, was supplemented by another named after the garibaldino Ippolito Nievo, and it was even decided to open a female dormitory as well). This organization was in turn to offer "a solid basis for the creation of true University halls of residence". Another of Meneghetti's important initiatives, already announced in 1945, was the launching of a Faculty of Agrarian Studies under the leadership of the ex-rector Gola: it was formalized to all effect in 1951.

The next rector, the historian of Antiquity Ferrabino, who had been dean of Humanities from 1932 to 1941 and in 1946-47, made an effort to establish a relationship with "the greatest economic representatives" of the Veneto region with the aim of supplementing state funding with further "financial forces". The state had already "taken on the burden of university studies almost entirely", but did not have the means to ensure the University's adequate development (only a third of the enrolled students could be accommodated in Padua's classrooms and laboratories). Ferrabino also made a firm denunciation – in many respects still valid today – of the "gloomy centralizing bureaucratic conformism, which creates daily impediments to our freedom of work and organization", despite the fact that "the Constitution establishes autonomous regulations for the Universities", and therefore one would expect it to guarantee "scientific autonomy, first of all, then teaching autonomy, and then autonomy of election and selection, and a radical administrative and financial autonomy".

Ferro, professor of maritime construction, already pro-rector with Gola and dean of Engineering in 1947-49, achieved a whole series of records: seven elections to the rectorship, which enabled him to govern the University for twenty years. He was the rector who relaunched the University after the post-war reconstruction, the rector who with far-sightedness and alacrity laid the main bases for the expansion of the University with the Italian economic boom. He was the rector, finally, who had to confront the explosive contradictions which emerged in the 1960s. It can be stated that Ferro took the most significant points out of Anti's box of plans and book of dreams, from the "modern general hospital" to the increase in the number of Faculties on offer, with a view which was both antagonistic and complementary to Venice (a view which, more in general, was founded on the axiom – still alive in 1963 – that the "spiritual dominion" of Padua "extended over the entire region"). He then ensured the execution of these points with an admirable tenacity, thanks also to his sympathy - except in the last years of his rectorship - with the politico-ideological centrism of the Christian Democracy party, which, as it had done for Anti, guaranteed, both on a national and a local level, a relative stability to his progress, and ensured him interlocutors who were very willing to listen.

During the Ferro rectorship there were clearly two completely opposing phases if we consider the evolution in the statistics of student enrolment: from 1949 to 1959, in line with the national phenomenon, there was a gradual and limited reduction in the numbers of students, which reached a low point of a few more than 9,000 against the 11,000 registered at the beginning of the cycle (from the statistical point of view the principal cause of the phenomenon was the reduction in the number of fuori corso students, which dropped in the course of the decade from over 4,000 to just over 2,000). Between 1959 and 1968, on the other hand, the numbers multiplied threefold, always in parallel with what was happening in other Italian Universities, surpassing the 27,000 mark in 1967-68. In the phase of the – relative – decline in enrolment, Ferro directed his efforts above all on building expansion and a broadening of the cultural offering. In this respect 1952 was a particularly important year: the fourth University consortium was refinanced with 1.7 billion lire (in the space of eight years it allowed for the construction of the clinics of Obstetrics, Paediatrics, and Neuropsychiatry, and the block of the general hospital); the Faculty of Education established two years earlier was recognized by law thanks to a convention with the local associations (the 'founding father' and first dean was Umberto Antonio Padovani, professor of moral philosophy); and - still true to a tradition that saw Padua as "that central driving force of high culture in a vast region" - summer courses were opened at Bressanone (as from 1954 housed in a University youth house built expressly for the purpose).

More than once Ferro proposed an 'English' vision of Padua as a "University of colleges" – a vision dear to Meneghetti. In effect, however, perhaps because he was conforted by the progressive reduction in the numbers of students, perhaps also so as to not enter into competition with the religious colleges authoritatively present in the city (at the end of the 1960s they had at their disposal about a thousand beds, in contrast to less that 700 'public' beds), in the first part of his rectorship, Ferro only increased the overall capacity of the dormitories to a limited extent (one should nevertheless remember the transfer of the women's dormitory to via S. Eufemia and the renovation work done to the Fusinato); nor did he greatly favour that "development of free student initiative" that had been dear to the first rector of the Republican University. Another evident limit and critical issue - this too destined, like the previous one, to come to a crucial point in the second phase of the Ferro rectorship - was the issue of

Bressanone, student dormitory

teaching, which was strongly penalized, beyond the possibility of any intervention by the rector, by the obtuse faithfulness of the Ministry of Public Education and its environs in favour of an élitist choice (the increase in the tenured professors was conceded grudgingly, so that for example in 1953 there were only 75, that is to say more or less the same as fifteen years earlier, while in the meantime the number of students had doubled). The phenomenon led necessarily to an exponential increase in various forms of pro-tempore teachers ('external' temporary professors and volunteer assistant lecturers), and to a crowding in the ranks of the regular assistants (an underpaid category, even considering that half its members also benefited from a teaching assignment). The strongly hierarchical, funnel-shaped organization that had already emerged in the 1930s was further consolidated, a form of organization that was totally unable to manage the sudden structural acceleration of the 1960s.

When the tide of students began to rise and at the same time the paternalistic student aid was transformed into a democratic right to study, Ferro was one of the first to note the impressiveness of the phenomenon and to try to seek a solution, again putting forward the project of Padua as a "University of colleges" with the foundation of the Morgagni and Ederle colleges, and the opening of a second University dining hall. At the same time he bravely launched himself into a policy of acquisition of land suitable for building and of large historical buildings, enough to make Anti's most ambitious plans pale by comparison. A building in piazza Capitaniato was obtained from the Commune to house Education, the Liviano was expanded towards via Accademia, the University area of via Marzolo and its environs was notably enlarged, annexing both the ex-Paolotti jail and beyond the Piovego canal. Moreover, the via del Santo was 'invaded' to locate the seats of the faculties of Political Science and Statistics (born from an offshoot of Jurisprudence in 1968) and the Institute of Geography, while Palazzo Oselladore in via S. Francesco was bought to locate a foyer destined for the students (it was later to become the seat of the Calculus Centre). Finally, seventy hectares were obtained at Legnaro to establish a "satellite University centre" destined in the first place for Agrarian Science, but also for other scientific institutes that could not be accommodated in Padua.

Even granting the building problem "a character of absolute priority over every other instance, especially in view of the notable increase in enrolment", Ferro spared no efforts to obtain a substantial reinforcement to the teaching body. Although the tortoise of teachers and non-teachers as a whole was not able to keep pace with the hare's pace of the student mass, and the quantitative relationship between students and teachers continued to deteriorate, one must nevertheless recognize the profound transformation, not only in numbers, which took place in the period in the ranks of the personnel. Between the mid-1950s and the mid-1960s the number of tenured professors more than doubled. At the end of the 1960s the University of Padua had become an important industry with 1,100 professors and assistant lecturers (the tenured professors had in the meantime surpassed the 200 mark), and around a thousand non-teachers, i.e. the administrative, technical, and auxiliary staff.

Ferro was convinced that "the enlarged and ever enlarging scholastic population" would inevitably lead "either to the creation of new Universities, or to a truly plethoric student mass in the existing Universities", two outcomes considered ruinous to the same extent. He therefore pronounced himself in favour of a decentralization of the Padua faculties in other cities of the Veneto, faculties (and satellite courses) that would however remain "within the didactic and administrative structure [...] an integral part of ancient Universities like ours". The first experiment in this direction began in 1963 with the government approval of a convention stipulated the previous year between the University of Padua and the Consortium for the establishment and development of University studies in Verona, for the financing of a Faculty of Economics and Commerce (in fact active since 1959-60). The experiment was consolidated in the following years with the establishment, again in Verona, of courses (later Faculties) in Medicine and Education.

In 1968 Ferro, who was a firm critic of the process of rendering University bodies more democratic, was succeeded by the professor of the philosophy of law Opocher, already dean of Jurisprudence from 1955 to 1959 and pro-rector in the first years of the 1960s. Opocher considered that one of the myths destroyed by the "progress, social, technical, and cultural, of our times [...was] that of a University intended and organized like a fortress inaccessible to the forces of history, the bulwark of a supposed neutrality of culture, that ends up by becoming sterile impotence". Opocher proposed in the first place to accelerate the "difficult expansion of structures still inadequate for the realization of the transition from an élite University to a mass University". This was a labour of Sisyphus, in that precisely during his rectorship "the pressure of the student masses" manifested itself with its greatest vehemence: between 1967-68 and 1971-72 the number of students enrolled grew from 27,527 to 42,200, especially following the liberalization of access to University approved by parliament at the end of 1969. The University of Padua reached the rank of fourth Italian University in the number of students enrolled, behind Rome, Naples, and Bari: a result that, unlike what had happened in the past, raised little enthusiasm.

Opocher was forced by the emergency situation to abandon the project of Padua as a "University of colleges" and to seek to satisfy the growing student demand for beds with the acquisition or the renting of apartments. His commitment was such that it was possible to more than double the number of beds available in the span of his rectorship. Moreover the number of scholarships awarded passed from 1,325 to 10,402, while exemptions from the University fees and meal vouchers increased by a very remarkable extent as well. Special courses were designed for working students, who constituted a considerable percentage in some of the humanistic Faculties. The rector set up an advisory Commission to the Council of Administration made up of representatives from the various parts of the University, an anticipation of the process of democratization of the academic bodies that was to take effect after the approval of the "Urgent measures regarding the University" of 1973. The attempt to open the "fortress [...] to the forces of history" even met with violence: on 15 April 1969 a bomb devastated the rector's office. The tensions, which affected much of the University world and with which even Ferro had to contend in the second half of his rectorship, manifested themselves in a particularly acute form in these years, even if largely still in a participatory and non-subversive form: the strikes by the assistant lecturers and the non-teaching personnel were compounded by student agitation, which in 1969 forced the University to shut down for a week.

For an analysis of what has happened in the course of the last thirty years it is possible to refer - besides the annual publications of the University - to two works of a different type, but both important for a reconstruction from the point of view of the protagonists of two fundamental rectorships in the University's recent history. I refer to *Eventi e risultati più significativi del mio Rettorato* (The more important events and results of my rectorship) (1972-1984) by Merigliano and to the *Scritti accademici* (Academic writings) 1993-1996 by Muraro. More than a few of the Merigliano years were brutally afflicted by subversion and terrorist violence; those of Muraro were the years of the difficult launching of the autonomous statute of the University, in a context greatly affected by the financial crisis. But compared with other rectorships of the recent past and the present, those were also years of important production and transformation, even though they were often, too often, caught between the hammer of erratic government and parliamentary decisions and the anvil of local conditioning and limitations. I will not even attempt to reconstruct the phases of this intense journey here, but limit myself to recalling some features through the examination of a number of facts.

The students continued to pour in in ever growing numbers due to a combination of the civic and economic growth of the region and the corresponding rise in the level of education (the strong increase in the percentage of those who chose to enrol at the University at the end of their secondary school studies was fundamental); this took place until the end of the 1970s, when the record of nearly 62,000 students enrolled was reached, 10,000 of those attending the seat at Verona. In 1982 the University of Verona obtained its independence from Padua and the number of students fell to under the 50,000 mark: enrolment oscillated around this last figure until the end of the 1980s, when the curve began to rise again, reaching a new peak in the mid-1990s with 66,000 enrolled, thanks in part to the multiplication of the degree programmes. In the last few years even Padua had seen a moderate drop in enrolment like nearly all other Italian Universities, preserving in any case a number of students in excess of 60,000. To a large extent the trend in the number of degrees conferred

The Legnaro complex: aerial view and interior of a laboratory

parallels this: nearly 5,000 in the 1970s, just over 3,000 in the period of decline.

With respect to the Italian University average, Padua distinguishes itself in its relatively high percentage of foreign students (2.1%, compared to the national 1.2%), and in its better ratio between the number of students enrolled and the number of beds available in the university dormitories and apartments (over 3%, nearly twice the national average). In both cases however these are percentages quite inferior to those of the foreigners in the early 1960s (over 3%: but the internationalization of the student body was at its greatest during the early 1930s, with a rate of 12%) and, regarding the beds available, those at the end of the 1950s and at the end of the Opocher rectorship. In any case it is unlikely that these factors greatly influence and have influenced the University's capacity to attract students, and more generally the importance of Padua in a regional and national context.

Despite the proliferation of Universities in the Triveneto (in the course of the last thirty years Trieste and Venice have grown remarkably stronger, while Universities of major or minor prominence have taken root in Verona, Udine, Trent, Feltre, Gorizia...), the University of Padua has preserved a manifest centrality in the region that until not many decades ago it could have us believe was still integrally subjected, as in the times of the Republic of Saint Mark, to its own "spiritual dominion". This must be attributed above all both - extremely pronounced in the rectorships of Bonsembiante, Muraro and Marchesini - to its ability to carry out capillary decentralization (already regarding a dozen centres in the provinces of Belluno, Bolzano, Padua, Rovigo, Treviso, Venice, and Vicenza), and to the quality and the growing development of its teaching and research, which have known how to renew themselves and to face ever new challenges. It is enough to remember that in the last few years three new Faculties have been established (Veterinary Medicine, Psychology, and Economics), while a fourth, Education, has become – a transformation not only in name – Educational Sciences. Furthermore, the recent University reform has allowed for the establishment of nearly a hundred three-year degrees, eight of which are inter-faculty and one inter-University. The creation of Agripolis at Legnaro, the multi-department Biology complex in the area of the Piovego canal, and new seats for Psychology should also be mentioned, while the further acquisition of buildings in the centre of Padua has been reserved for the humanistic faculties.

The University of Padua is no longer "the vanguard of Italian civilization" on the eastern border to defend against the Germans and the Slavs, nor the cultural expression of the Great Veneto from the Alps to the Adriatic of a nationalist and then a Fascist nature. With a teaching and non-teaching body that in its entirety exceeds the 4,000 mark, it is "the largest business corporation in the Venezie" (M. Bonsembiante), but also the incarnation of a tradition of liberty and universality summed up in the

The Departments of Psychology beyond the Piovego, and an operating theatre in Cardiosurgery

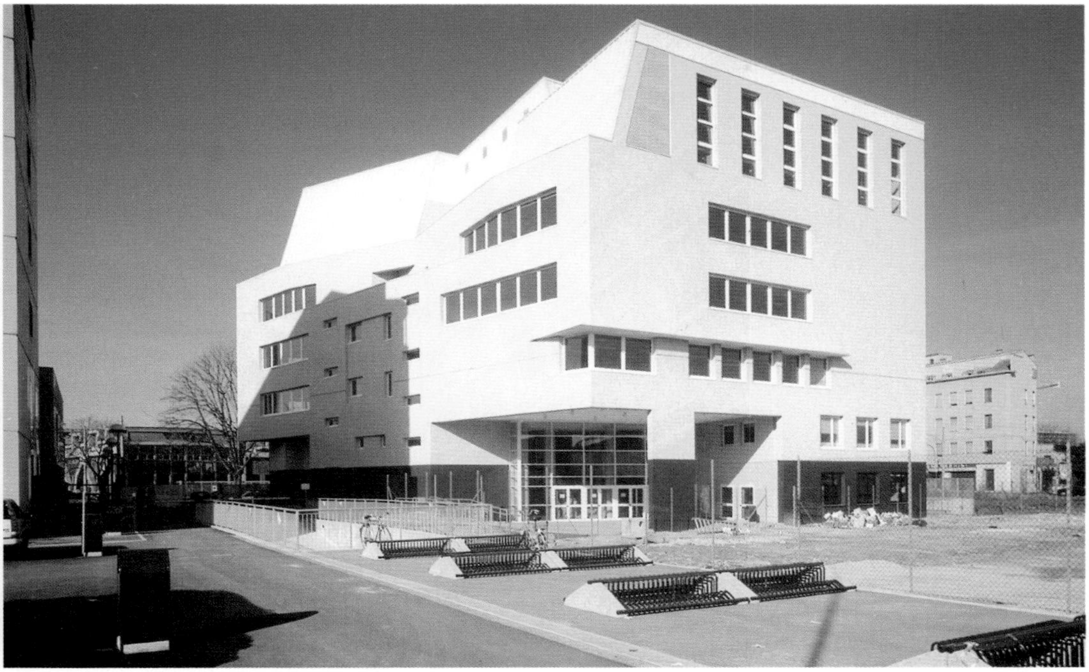

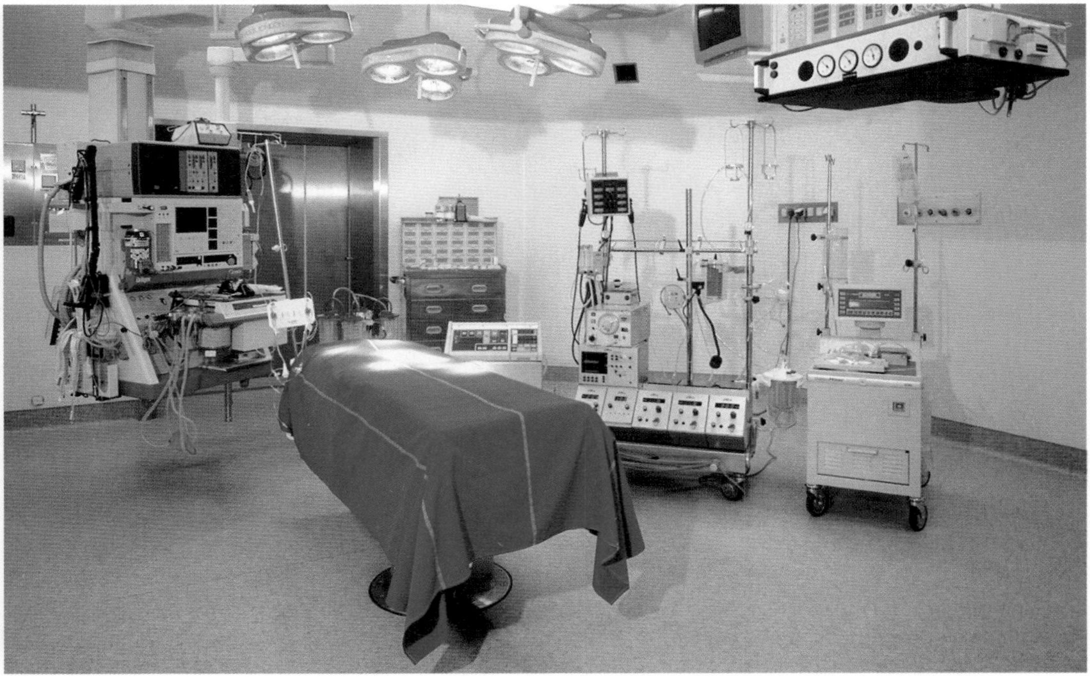

Beyond the Piovego, multi-department complex of Biology, Engineering

motto "Universa Universis Patavina Libertas". For Anti the University was not *of* Padua, but *in* Padua; a quarter of a century later Opocher would confirm, this time with respect to the Veneto, that the function of Padua University could not "be circumscribed within a particular territorial range, because the function of a University is always, as the name says, free of such limits".

I believe that this may be the key to understanding what from another point of view might appear, in light of the long history of the Italian University system, to be the Paduan anomaly or, if you like, the Paduan peculiarity: the fact, that is, that a University which flourished thanks to the "division of labour" between a political capital and a cultural capital typical of the great regional States of late-medieval and Renaissance Italy (we can also think, besides the dual concept of Venice-Padua, of Milan-Pavia and Florence-Pisa), has also preserved a great prominence in the context of Italy in the last hundred years, a context which was apt to make the importance of a University depend directly and strictly on the dimensions of the host city. If the University of Padua has been able to rescue itself from the fate to which it appeared condemned by the relatively modest demographic weight of its referent city, this has depended - besides the socio-economic characteristics of the Veneto and the particular initiative of the city of Padua - on its ability to preserve itself as a *Universitas* in the original sense of the term, on its continuous effort to revive itself as a teaching and research community, on the basis of a unique web of scientific and civic values, and on a universalistic perspective

Scientific and Cultural History:
The Medieval and Early Modern University

BALDVS PERVSINVS

GIORGIO ZORDAN

Jurisprudence

First of all, a few brief explanatory remarks on terminology, in common or conventional use, for the benefit of those non-experts in the field. The term jurisprudence derives from *iuris prudentia*, which in Latin means knowledge of law. Of more recent origin, in our particular case, is the word 'faculty' understood as a discipline, a branch of human knowledge, etc. Nowadays, in fact, we say that every University is divided into a number of faculties: as many faculties as there are branches of knowledge that the University intends to provide a teaching and a knowledge in, and we speak, even in an official language, of a 'University of Studies', an expression that for many people – rightly or wrongly – evokes, besides the educational institution, the totality of the sciences which are imparted there. Hence today, the Faculty of Jurisprudence is that part of the University organization whose purpose is the study and the teaching of law. In the past, that is to say throughout the long course of the centuries (13th-18th) that this brief historical profile will deal with, if we wish to adhere to concepts then in use, and therefore with greater linguistic accuracy, we should say in a general sense a 'university', or an association, of students (at times, and in any case outside Italy, of masters) and in this specific case a 'university' of jurists. Now, if, as an authority in the field maintains, "one should not reduce the history of the University to that of legal culture" (Dolcini), one cannot doubt either that the origin of the University of Padua coincided and, better still, was identified with the initial establishment of a corporate organization whose purpose was the acquisition of a 'sapiential' knowledge of law, higher, that is, than that already possessed by the multiform body of those practising law (judges, pettifoggers, notaries, etc.).

Far from wishing to retread the obscure paths of the pre-history of the Studium *translatum* (transferred) from Bologna to Padua in the year 1222, given that this period is little and poorly documented – the only source to refer to this are the city *Annals*, reliable nevertheless – it is enough for our present purposes to stress how this event seems to have been the most successful and enduring result of one of the recurrent migrations undertaken at the beginning of the thirteenth Century by members of the University of Bologna as a reaction against the crime, as they saw it, of the Bolognese authorities of threatening the most jealously coveted scholastic freedoms. It was not a question, then, of the movement of single individuals, but of traumatic moments of secession, of veritable torrents which carried away whole groups to other places, groups which were in their own way cohesi-

Baldo degli Ubaldi

ve and organized, made up both of students and their masters.

If, therefore, conflicts arose from time to time in Bologna within the 'university' of students, which had achieved full self-governing status in the last decades of the twelfth Century, since this was a society only of students of law, those members of the 'university' who migrated from there to Padua with their own structure and their own leaders must have been law students. And this is the point: nobody will deny that, besides law students, those who arrived in Padua were also students of other disciplines, known overall, and rather reductively as arts students (according to an ancient tradition used to include all the knowledge of the seven liberal arts). These latter, however, were not members of the 'university', in the sense that in Bologna they had not yet constituted their own corporation. Foreign to student associations, directly defending their own interests, and devoid of any external visibility (in Bologna the 'university' of arts students was to obtain formal recognition only in 1316, and in Padua not until 1399), the arts students were obliged to the law students for their means of representation and indeed had to depend on them in many respects, while for just as long the teaching they offered was accepted as merely preparatory to the study of law.

From its very first days, moreover, the University of Padua began to take on the organizational structure, teaching method, and scientific orientation of Bologna. Exactly one century after its primitive establishment, the convention of 1321 between the Commune of Padua and a numerous group of members of the University of Bologna, who had then migrated to Imola, systematizing a practice which was by now a century old, confirmed that the Padua Studium should be ruled and run according to the customs, statutes, and ordinances of the Bologna Studium. Although such sworn pacts did not produce the automatic extension of the juridical status of the University of Bologna to that of Padua, but rather somewhat mitigated norms completed by local customs, this bond of filiation remain insoluble. The first part of this book deals with the institutional development of the University, which took root in the soil of the Veneto region. It is necessary, therefore, to say something here about those aspects which specifically concern the study and the teaching of law, beginning with a consideration which was not of marginal importance. The crises which from time to time shook the University of Bologna to such an extent as to provoke a considerable and painful brain drain can all be explained – as the generally-held opinion maintains – by contingent reasons or reasons determined by the sometimes violent clashes with the public authorities: they were not, that is, internal crises of ideas or methods, nor excesses which resulted from a dissatisfaction regarding the quality of the legal teaching imparted there.

In the first few decades of the thirteenth Century, the Bologna Studium was still basking in the glow of a centuries-old juridical and academic activity. But this activity, presenting the science with the ripest fruits of an intense literary production, was about to reach the final stage of a glorious parabola which had begun its upward course when Irnerius († c. 1130), an obscure master of the liberal arts, started to study on his own (that is to say, without teachers) the 'legal books', and then to share with others what he had learnt with such difficulty, giving rise to a school which was to earn him everlasting fame. His descendants indeed were to remember him as the first man able to enlighten the new period of legal studies. And a school, it is worth perhaps pointing out, does not simply mean a teacher who explains and students who listen and conserve his teaching: a school is a current of thought, a lifestyle, an innovative scientific method; creating a school means in particular – in the past, just as it does today – training pupils and followers who will perpetuate the doctrine of their promoter, guaranteeing, that is, its cultural and spiritual descent.

All of this can be applied very well to the school founded by Irnerius: with it was taking shape that capital phenomenon of a European dimension that we call the legal renaissance, in which we can identify the origin not only of Western legal science, but also of modern continental jurisprudence itself. The object of study and teaching of such a school were the leges – laws par excellence – that is to say, the juridical norms contained precisely in the 'legal books'. Thus it became the tradition to quote the texts of the emperor Justinian (the Digest, Codex, Institutes, Novels), completely rescued from oblivion and restored to their possible completeness by the founder, and considered by his pupils as a unitary and coherent normative system: a *corpus*, or rather the *Corpus* (*iuris civilis*). The principal merit of entire generations of pupils and followers of Irnerius, known as Glossators (from glossa, the explanatory note written in the text which the teacher was reading, analyzing it exegetically) was that of having set themselves up as intermediaries between the complex legislation of Justinian and the modern forms of communal living: in other words, of having rendered ancient Roman law - thanks to its own highly original doctrinal contribution - a set of norms for the present, capable of concrete application and use in legal practice up until the nineteenth century, the Century of codification.

Cloat of arms of the 'university' of jurists

Ideally, beside *dominus* Irnerius in the prestigious empyrean reserved for the fore-runners of modern legal science, we would place the only slightly younger *magister* Gratian († c. 1160), a Camaldolese monk, teacher – again at Bologna – of practical theology. If the former is the founder of civil law as a science, then the latter – through an activity at once titanic and utopian, aimed at establishing a concordance between the thousand contradictions in the infinite normative texts produced by the Church in the first thousand years of its history, and hence often in fact opposed to one other – showed the world the spiritual face of a universal law (just as the Church was universal) and took on the task of separating logically and definitively the juridical norms from the ethical norms, law from theology from moral philosophy, in such a way as to merit the epithet of father of canon law as a science.

Gratian's work was a milestone of that which only later, and in imitation of civil law, was to be called the *Corpus iuris canonici* (canons are those norms whose source are the legislative assemblies of the Church, that is the Councils, and are flanked by other norms, the decretals, promulgated by the Popes in their guise as monocratic legislators); known concisely as the *Decretum Gratiani*, it was soon to be accepted by the legal science and its school. Its author saw to that himself when he created around his own compilation a teaching destined, in the Bologna of the law students, to triumph rapidly, before moving on to achieve success at a European level. Indeed, those who placed the Benedictine master's compendium at the centre of the study and teaching of law were known as Decretists.

At the beginning of the thirteenth Century, when pope Innocent III inaugurated the practice of conferring on collections of decretals an official status, and the papal ambition of diffusing such recently written collections among the men of learning by 'publishing' them in the Universities then active took root, the object of the teaching of canon law grew exponentially. Take, for example, the case of Honorius III, who in 1226 addressed a collection of his own papal constitutions to both the Bolognese and the Paduans; or, when in 1234, those of Gregory IX were to be made public (the c.d., *Liber extra*), as well as the exemplars sent to the masters and students of Bologna, at least one extra copy was made available for those who were in Padua. Decretalists was then the name given to the cultivators of this new law of the Church, which was studied with the same methods and using the same literary genres which the civil lawyers had made their own, above all the gloss.

To support what has been hinted at above: the exodus from Bologna was not caused by a scientific asphyxiation or aphasia, and we can recall how the years of the first 'Paduan' migration saw Azzone dei Porci († 1230) complete his infinite series of summae (systematic expositions of a more or less complete Justinian corpus), among which by far the most impressive, successful, and widely-diffused was the *summa* of the Codex, which for centuries remained the text in which students and practitioners found the most profound synthesis of civil law. Accursius († c. 1260) developed, if not completed, the *Magna glossa* or *Glossa ordinaria*, which even today stands as a monumental network of glosses (chosen with great shrewdness from among the best of the doctrinal production of his predecessors), serving as a systematic apparatus to the four parts of Justinian's compilation and its gigantic perpetual commentary. A brief word is also due to Odofredo Denari († 1265) not so much for his improbable presence in Padua as a master, as for the abundance of his writings which nevertheless clearly reveal the ineluctable exhaustion of scientific creativity in the school of the gloss. A contemporary and an emulator of Accursius, though not equal to him in the acumen of his legal thought, Odofredo was equally famous among his contemporaries and descendants: it is enough to observe how his lengthy lectures on the various parts of the *Corpus iuris civilis* were to appear, let us say, among the text books of numerous Italian

Universities even in the mid fourteenth Century. This is specifically documented for Padua by the statutes of the 'university' of law students dating to 1331, the oldest academic ones to have reached us.

At this point we would like to know more about the life and the functioning of the Padua law 'university' as well as the dimensions of this decisive cultural phenomenon in its lengthy teething period. But such curiosity must remain for the most part unsatisfied.We know that its beginning was uncertain and put at risk by external events, above all by the turbulent period of Ezzelino da Romano (1237-1256), to such an extent that some deny a continuity between the Studium established in 1222 and that revived (or reformed) in 1260 by means of statutes encompassing in all probability the nuclei of earlier norms. This was the work of a Spaniard named Gosaldo, archdeacon of Cuenca, and rector of both 'universities' (that is to say, of the Italian law students and the foreign law students). He is a much quoted character, but one little known until recent studies illustrated his later brilliant ecclesiastical career, becoming the archbishop of Toledo (1280).

If the "numerous group" of students present in Padua from the beginning can be estimated with some probability to have consisted of a few hundred (including, naturally, law and arts students), it is much more difficult to estimate the number of those who taught law at the same time. It is of little help to turn to the generic statutory norm by which the Commune guaranteed the payment of the salaries of the *domini legum* and the *magistri decretorum et decretalium* "from before 1236" (Arnaldi), a period, that is, when the title of *dominus* was the jealously-guarded prerogative of the civil lawyers, while the canonists were still known in contemporary parlance by the title of *magister*, usual but felt to be of lesser importance.

It would be hazardous to reason by analogy with what was happening in other more or less contemporary academic situations. It is enough here to recall, merely indicatively, that in the contract stipulated in April 1228 between the envoys of the Commune of Vercelli and the representatives of the members of the University of Padua regarding the transfer of the Studium to Vercelli (another migration, therefore! this one of limited duration, however), the Commune showed itself to be extremely generous – perhaps too generous – in its promises: it would allocate five hundred lodgings for its new guests, and of the fourteen chairs which it undertook to finance, three were of civil, and four of canon law.

Neither do we obtain a clearer picture if we recall this or that teacher of the earliest Paduan Studium by going through the most disparate documents which in general do no more than mention them. Without doubt the various Marquardo Teutonico, Simone Vicentino, Guglielmo Guasco, Rufino, Giacomo da Piacenza, Omobono Morisio, or some offspring (Urgerio, Falcone, Sabione...) of the proliferous 'lawyer' family of the Buzzacarini are names partly known to the specialist. But these names say little (or nothing) to the non-specialist, and simply create the distinct impression that in its first decades, though of a lesser weight or of lesser

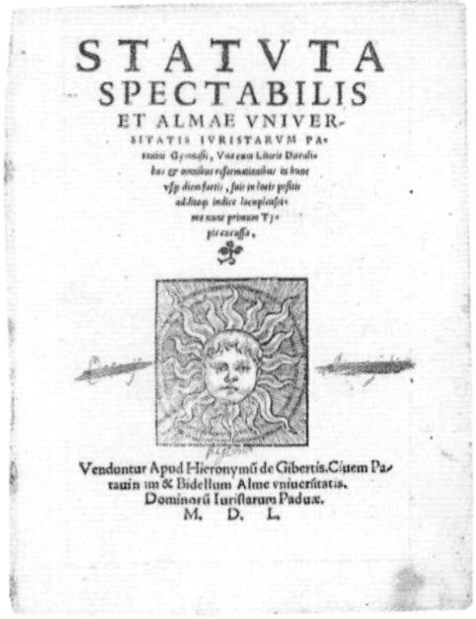
STATVTA
SPECTABILIS
ET ALMAE VNIVER-
SITATIS IVRISTARVM PA-
tauini Gymnasii, Vna cum Literis Ducali-
bus & omnibus reformationibus in hunc
vsq; diem factis, suis in locis positis
additoq; indice locupletissi-
mo nunc primum Ty-
pis excussa.

Venduntur Apud Hieronymū de Gibertis. Ciuem Pa-
tauin um & Bidellum Alme vniuersitatis.
Dominorū Iuristarum Paduæ.
M. D. L.

Statute of the 'university' of jurists

prestige than their colleagues in Bologna, the teachers of the Padua Studium were, like their Bolognese counterparts, all members of the school of the gloss.

May we be excused for the insistence with which we remind the reader of the principal point in question: it was in the specifically didactic field that the initial fidelity to the Bolognese model was realized in a complete fashion, and paid off. What enabled Padua to establish itself over the centuries as a privileged seat of legal culture at a European level, and an international magnet for those who aspired to attain a specialist knowledge, what enabled it to emulate and even – at times – contest the primacy from Bologna was indeed its immediate and decisive adherence to those models of legal learning which were irradiating from the mother University over the entire continent, so as to establish a single and universal form of legal education up to and beyond the threshold of the modern age.

Imparted according to the scholastic method (proposition of the thesis, argument *pro et contra*, solution), the *lecturae* (lessons) aimed initially at getting the students fully able to understand and perfectly to master the normative text before them, by means of the tenacious effort of interpreting in depth all the books containing the 'legal knowledge': the final objective of a hard and lengthy training. The teaching was in fact based solely on the *Corpus iuris civilis* and the *Corpus iuris canonici* and excluded any particular norm (city, corporate statutes, general and/or local customs, etc.). Everything, in other words, was civil and canon law, the reason why in time the chairs were to vary more in number than in the variety of teaching subjects, as emerges from the list or roll which was compiled and published over the centuries, together with the calendar, at the beginning of every academic year.

There existed, rather, a bipartition between 'ordinary' lessons (held in the morning and revolving as a rule around the first part of the Digest and the Codex for civil, and Gratian's Decretum and the Decretals of Gregory IX for canon law) and 'extraordinary' lessons (given in general in the afternoon on the remaining parts of the two *Corpora*). For either the one or the other type of lesson there could be 'ordinary' and 'extraordinary' masters, lecturers and their competitors or antagonists, as well as - for each discipline – one, two, or three *loci* or chairs set up or suppressed in time, suspended or conflated with others, re-established or held vacant, depending on the possibility of finding people judged suitable to fill them or on the ... financial resources available to remunerate them adequately.

This is without taking into consideration the private lessons with the aim of integration (to which the masters were held by statute to the same extent as for the public lessons) or that sort of chair of a lower rank, the *lecturae civitatis*, which also animated the panorama of law studies in various ways. It would be too lengthy to compile a chronological list of all the disciplines officially imparted or merely those qualified as compulsory: it is enough to see that from an initial body which can be imagined to be very small (towards the end of the thirteenth century we are speaking of one decretist, two decretalists, and two civil lawyers), we move on to ten fundamental chairs towards the middle of the fourteenth century, fifteen during the first decades of Venetian domination, over twenty in the year 1500, and then come down again to fifteen at the beginning of the eighteenth century and eleven in the last years of the Venetian Republic.

Not even the course of studies had a constant length, varying from the six years required by the most ancient statutes, to the five of the middle period, and the four from the eighteenth century onwards. In this period of time, students had to assiduously attend lessons and take part in the other didactic activities organized with generous frequency. Not to go to too fine a detail, we will merely recall here the *repetitiones*, lessons held outside the normal teaching timetable and devoted to a more detailed exegesis (interpretation) of the laws or of paragraphs of special importance, and the *quaestiones*: discussions on normative discordant texts with the aim of harmonizing them (*quaestiones legitimae*), or debates animated by the contrasting of arguments around some concrete example, made up by the master, which presented problems regarding a normative discipline and which stressed the content (*quaestiones de facto*), or veritable practical exercises in the form of a head-on dispute between individuals or groups of students around a case liable to different juridical approaches and solutions, which – still under the guidance of the teacher - stimulated reflection on the practical consequences of the norms (*quaestiones disputatae*).

The teaching method of the daily lessons, questions, disputes, and so on, made it easy for the masters to check the students' aptitudes and progress without recourse to periodical examinations. The only official tests took place at the end of the scholastic career: then, a special commission assigned the candidate a thesis (*punctum*) to defend in a dissertation which for the doctorate in civil law revolved around the Digest and the Codex, and for canon law around the Decretum and the Decretals. If the student should aspire to the doctorate *in utroque* (in both branches of law) there would be two *puncta*, one for each branch. With the aid of his supervisors (*promotores*) the student would first sit a private examination in which he would expound on the set topics before the commission and dispute with his counter-supervisors (*punctatores*), and then a public examination, less technical but more solemn and costly, which usually took place in a cathedral in the presence of the highest academic, civil, and religious authorities of the city. At the end of this latter, the *licentia docendi* was granted.

A *doctor* is he who teaches (*docet*), or he who in any case has the right to do so: he who has graduated, that is, and with the academic laurel has obtained permission (*licentia*) to teach pupils in turn. That a degree in jurisprudence (to use current terms) has always qualified one for the practice of the legal professions is an opinion as widely held as it is easy to refute if we simply consider that, in the Venetian Republic at least, the requirement of a University qualification was only introduced in 1668 for those who intended to practice as lawyers on the Terraferma and in 1724 for those practising in Venice. It is worth insisting, therefore, to debunk a

Riccardo Malombra
Francesco Zabarella

veritable commonplace: the purpose of the legal education imparted in the Universities was uniquely that of training masters of law; the degree, that is, was and remains, we should say ontologically, a qualification for the teaching profession, even though, understandably, the *legum doctores* (the law teachers) were not slow to find other professional outlets, above all in public administration.

In the academic environment the strong spirit of association which characterized the doctors was not of secondary importance. It was with an eye again to Bologna that the composition and prerogatives of the Padua Collegium of the doctors of law were fixed by law, doctors who were perhaps present in the city even before 1222. Constituted by indigenous teaching and non-teaching doctors and by foreign doctors teaching in the Studium, the Collegium of doctors initially had a limited number of places (twelve, twenty, thirty...) and then an unlimited number. Though institutionally separate from the University, it succeeded in establishing itself on one hand as a powerful organ which integrated and evaluated scholastic activities (it supplied the members of the degree commissions, for example) and on the other as a privileged interlocutor with the political power to whom it offered its own *consilia* (consultations) to resolve complex legal cases and to settle important judicial controversies, obtaining in exchange prestige and lavish honours.

To move on now to later scientific achievements, it must be said that the strong resurgence of the Padua 'university' of law after the defeat of Ezzelino da Romano coincided by chance with the exhaustion of that vital force which, with a grandiose civil and cultural operation, had pushed the school of Bologna to a position of fame throughout Europe. Bologna was by now on the road to losing its monopoly of the legal science and its progress. It was by now clear – in the second half of the thirteenth century – that the remarkable work of Accursius marked the decisive end of an era and that it was impossible to go any further with the method of the gloss. Through a new literary genre destined for success over the following centuries, the *tractatus* (a monograph written to contemplate in a specialized, systematic, and exhaustive fashion a certain area of law or a single juridical institution), and by developing or finalizing in various ways *quaestiones*, *repetitiones*, and *consilia* (tools, as we have said, already used by the Glossators), those labelled as the 'post Accursian' law teachers began to operate with a greater sensitivity to the daily problems of legal practice.

The revival of the University of Padua was immediately determined by the presence of law teachers of notable standing: in 1264 Guido da Suzzara († c. 1295) arrived, and after him Iacopo d'Arena († 1302), whose school produced Oldrado da Ponte († 1335) who succeeded his master, Riccardo Malombra († 1334), illustrious *consultore* (official adviser) of the Venetian Republic, and Alberico da Rosciate († c. 1360), a very prolific writer and a prominent representative of a juridical doctrine which was no longer strictly academic and, at the same time, of a literary tendency in harmony with some of the glimmers of pre-humanism which had begun to light up certain sectors of the University world of Padua.

But fourteenth-century legal science was already speaking the language of the commentary: the second school of law which came to take the place of the gloss, imposing a different way of 'reading' and expounding the legal books, also came to be known as the *mos docendi italicus* (the Italian way of teaching) and was to characterize jurisprudence – and not only Italian – up to the threshold of the modern era. A different method (the commentary) and new teaching aims came into force. What now made the study of law in Padua an appetizing prospect was the teaching, for longer or shorter periods, of eminent jurists such as Giovanni d'Andrea († 1348), pupil of Riccardo Malombra, Ranieri Arsendi († 1358), the great Baldo degli Ubaldi († 1400), Bartolomeo da Saliceto († 1411), preceded by other offspring of his family (Riccardo and Roberto), the future cardinal Francesco Zabarella († 1411), and so on. These are characters very different from one another, but all have in common the fact that they put the new techniques of critical penetration of the legal text into practice in their University *lecturae*. Such techniques aimed both to give the text a general logical presentation and to unify it, thanks to the use of an original dialectico-syllogistic procedure which bent the law to Aristotelian logic, producing juridical dogmatics with decidedly new systematic and creative results.

It goes without saying that such a sophisticated methodical tool, if used ingeniously, could lead to quite remarkable results, "but it could in turn dominate the jurist of modest ability, rendering him the slave to a clumsy and sterile mechanization" (Cavanna), and severely test the capacity for concentration of the students who had to undergo this not always enthralling experience. With the assertion of the Venetian domination of the *Terraferma* (the beginning of the fifteenth century), we reach the period of Padua Studium's greatest splendour, and, at the same time, of its ineluctable transformation into an institution 'of the prince'. Once it had reached the peak of its economic and political power, the Serenissima did not spare the means to ensure for its own University the most illustrious teachers then in circulation. A beneficiary of this, in the first place, was the 'university' of law, which was illuminated throughout the fifteenth century by masters of the greatest worth such as Raffaele Fulgosio († 1427), Raffaele Raimondi († 1427), Giovanni Nicoletti da Imola († 1436), Paolo di Castro († 1441), Bartolomeo Cipolla († 1475), Alessandro Tartagni († 1477), Angelo degli Ubaldi († 1490), Bartolomeo Sozzini († 1507), Giovanni Campeggi († 1511), and Giasone del Maino († 1519), to name some of them: in other words the *Gotha* of the *mos italicus*. They were the best exponents of that school of commentary that, if by the second half of the fifteenth century had started to show its first signs of stagnation and involution elsewhere, in Padua it was at the height of its creative tension. In this period it produced a literature which was ever more conspicuously linked to the needs of legal practice, and therefore largely alternative to University literature, even though the huge collections of consilia and the

Paolo di Castro
Giasone del Maino

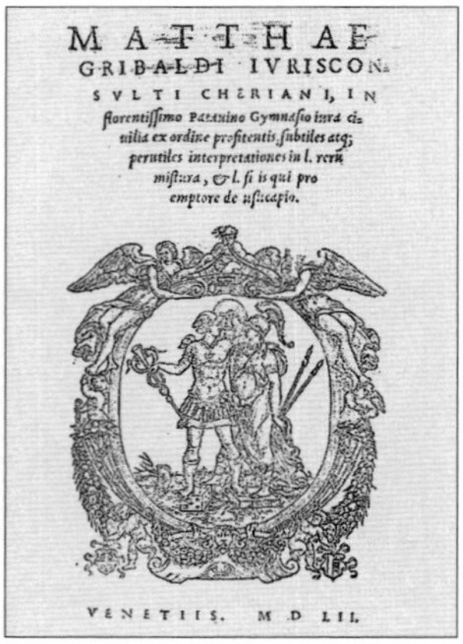

Frontispiece of the Interpretatio *by Matteo Grimaldi Mofa and the portrait of Marco Mantova Benavides*

most up-to-date *tractatus* certainly ended up by circulating in the classrooms too.

In 1493, almost as a physical crowning of such flourishing, the 'university' of law abandoned the private housing spread through the various quarters of the city (s. Biagio, s. Caterina, etc.) in which it had been forced to function up to then, to congregate in the *Hospitium bovis*, a large building already used as an inn under the sign of the ox. From this building, which underwent successive enlargements and refurbishments, the law masters and students were no longer to depart: it is, in fact, in the Palazzo del Bo that the faculty of Jurisprudence is still housed and has its official seat today.

After the enforced standstill of all academic activity (1508 - c.1515) as a consequence of the war which set Venice against the armies of the league of Cambrai, the 'university' of law showed some signs of innovation with regard to its teaching, which had been practically petrified for the last three hundred years or so. Worthy of note, in fact, is a greater complexity in the curriculum of studies. In 1540 the *lectura criminalium* (criminal law) was inaugurated; in 1544 the teaching of feudal law began; in 1578 the chair of pandects was established (devoted to the study of the sources of Justinian law with the aid of the historical and philological knowledge able to explain them) and set as a complement to the two lessons on the *instituta* (institutions) which had been in existence for around a century. Although still in a humble form, a phenomenon of continental importance was taking shape in Padua: "the beginning of the emancipation of the various disciplines of legal science from the *corpus iuris*" (Coing). The appearance of those distinct teaching subjects, however, did not reach the point of challenging the criteria of unity and exclusivity of the study matter, nor did it signify (or yet signify) an effective erosion of the area reserved for the traditional disciplines: canon law and, above all, Roman law (now officially entitled Caesarian). This latter preserved intact its characteristics of comprehensive use and validity: what was taught by those 'new' chairs was still an interpretation of certain sections of the 'old' Justinian corpus.

Though without totally precluding the most recent theoretical and didactic methods which were spreading through various parts of Europe and, in particular, the cult of jurisprudence which was producing excellent results in France (*mos docendi gallicus*), the law 'university' of Padua remained solidly entrenched in the commentary, showing – as we have hinted – a more conspicuous tendency towards practical knowledge. But this should not lead us to consider Paduan legal studies of the sixteenth century as inferior, even though – on the other hand – we cannot share the opinion of those who with excessive optimism consider it "the golden century ... corresponding to the splendour of the Venetian Republic" (Brugi). In this period the chairs of Padua were held, some for their whole life, by civil lawyers of the calibre of Matteo Gribaldi Mofa († 1562), Mariano Sozzini jr († 1565), Giovanni Cefali († 1580), Marco Mantova Benavides (†

1582), Tiberio Deciani († 1582), Guido Panziroli († 1599), Jacopo Menochio († 1607), Francesco Mantica († 1614), and by no less illustrious canon lawyers than Antonio da Burgos († 1525), Antonio Francesco Dottori († 1528), Pietro Paolo Parisio († 1554), to name some of them. These law teachers at least were able admirably to dominate the plethora of tools which the mos italicus was unable to separate itself from.

Then that prolonged and fertile noon too reached its sunset. The crisis did not arrive suddenly, simply a little later with respect to many other 'universities' of law in Italy, equally ineluctable and unstoppable. The causes of the progressive decline were numerous and complex. Among the internal ones we can indicate, extremely briefly, the process of obsolescence of the teaching method, set to exhaust itself in tired and repetitive manneristic acrobatics, and the inadequacy of the curriculum of studies, useful only in perpetuating the scleroticization of medieval legal science in the name of a conservatism at once obtuse and complacent. The external causes can be substantially reduced to the strong competition with foreign Universities, accentuated when the Padua Studium was no longer able even within Italy to act as a magnet for dynamic and innovative doctrines.

To make matters worse, a clearly perceptible climate of spiritual narrow-mindedness and cultural atrophy reigned, save meagre exceptions, above all over the teaching body ever more marked by a diffused provincialism, analogous to that which at the same time characterized the student world. The disaffection of foreign masters for the Padua Studium led to a progressive increase in the number of teachers who were subjects of the Serenissima and, among these, Paduans became the most numerous, thus accentuating the tendency towards a jurisprudence which was merely self-sufficient. It was a decline that the no longer florid Venetian economy could hardly contrast.

An ancient historiographical tradition, still today awaiting critical confirmation, perpetuates – still for the seventeenth century – the memory of several names: Giulio Pace, Marc'Antonio Ottelio, Bartolomeo Vecchi, Ottavio Livelli among the civil lawyers, Marc'Antonio Pellegrini and Lelio Mancini among the canonists, the criminal lawyer Giovanni Galvani, and so on. Then the most leaden of silences falls.

Things, moreover, were not destined to improve in the first half of the eighteenth century. We can consider the fact that the decline of the University of Padua, provoked by the scarcity of its students, hardly attracted by the archaic nature of its curriculum, became in this period almost a stereotype, both in the accounts of foreigners who visited the Palazzo del Bo during their "journey to Italy", and in the lucid and sometimes pitiless diagnoses contained in the many proposals for reform, in the numerous schemes for the reorganization of the University written by men of ability, progressive, and enlightened, on their own behalf or on a more or less official basis. By listening finally to such accounts, in 1761 the Venetian Republic established, and after a brief period of brusque reversal, in 1768 relaunched and perfected a complex restructuring of the tea-

The portraits of Tiberio Deciani, Francesco Mantica, and Giovanni Galvani

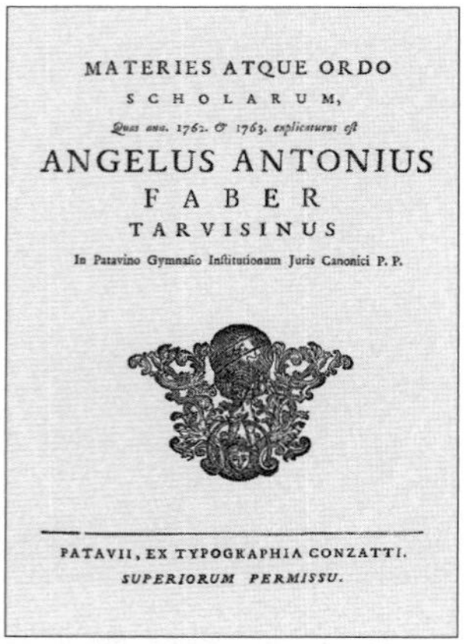
MATERIES ATQUE ORDO
SCHOLARUM,
Quas ann. 1762. & 1763. explicaturus est
ANGELUS ANTONIUS
FABER
TARVISINUS
In Patavino Gymnasio Institutionum Juris Canonici P. P.

PATAVII, EX TYPOGRAPHIA CONZATTI.
SUPERIORUM PERMISSU.

Angelo Fabbro, Materies atque ordo scholarum

ching, aiming to modernize the academic disciplines. The 'university' of law should have received particular benefit from this, too discredited as it was by an ever more vacuous and abstract legal science, by a stagnant knowledge, by an irrevocable conservatism, in such a way as not to merit the stinging judgement of authentic "petrifaction of medieval thought" (Brugi).

In 1761 the teaching of the Institutions of Canon Law was established and in 1764 that of Natural Law; then in 1768 – once seven chairs held to be of little use had been suppressed, among which that of Criminal Law (!) – some subjects were introduced from scratch as optional, or as we would say today, as an enforced choice: the chair of Public Ecclesiastical Law was established, that of Feudal Law changed to Feudal, Nautical, and Commercial Law, while Natural Law took on the wider title of Natural, Public, and Peoples' Law. To complete the curriculum were the traditional chairs of Roman Law (which was again officially known as Civil, or rather Caesarian) and Canon Law, the teaching of Civil Institutions including that of the notarial art, the teaching of Canonical Institutions, and four *lecturae civitatis*. It was also stipulated that the teachers of civil law should devote part of their time to illustrating the foundations of Venetian law and the municipal laws (city statutes).

It remains to be said, nevertheless, that the entire reform, which remained in force until the end of the Venetian Republic (1797), revealed itself to be better on paper than in practice, settled as a principle and inspired by the new ideological and cultural orientations rather than actually followed in practice and carried out by the governing organs of the University. Indeed despite having produced, this time in concrete terms, the freeing of the new disciplines listed above from the normative bodies in which legal science had for centuries been included and compressed, the reform was not able to make the logico-structural (if not strictly quantitative) weakening of Roman and canon law which it had provoked coincide with the concrete innovation in the methods and the contents of legal teaching. In other words, although thus reformed, the Padua 'university' of law could do nothing but perpetuate itself in its anodyne and sterile survival.

The convulsive and turbulent months of the arrival of democracy – from April 1797 to January 1798 – did not have an appreciable effect either on the structure or the functioning of the University. Subversive fury and utopias of a total regeneration characteristic of the Jacobin ideology very soon contrasted with the climate of political insecurity and economic precariousness, of improvisation and anxiety, typical of the experiences of independent municipal government. Thus, once the perfecting of ambitious projects for reform had been put off to better times, it did not seem possible to delay the introduction of a limited series of sectorial measures, aimed at the abolition of what was judged to be in most strident contrast with the revolutionary creed and out of harmony with French pedagogical experiences. The abandonment of Latin, substituted by

Italian as the official academic language was, all things considered, the most significant and enduring novelty of the entire libertarian period.

On the 6th of February, 1798, a proclamation issued precisely in Padua intended to overcome the status quo maintained in the first weeks after the coming into force of the treatise of Campoformido, took steps to regulate the local administration of the Venetian Terraferma according to the dictates of the new occupying force: the imperial-royal Habsburg government. Once the democratic regulations had been suppressed, the periferic organization and structures were totally restored just as they had been before the collapse of the Venetian Republic. Indeed, better to show a distance from the damage produced during the revolutionary period, there was an explicit reference to the 1st January, 1796: all institutions were to be brought back to this date, including the ancient Studium which thus returned intact to the old Venetian model. With regard to the 'university' of law, this meant the reappearance of chairs previously abolished: that of Public Ecclesiastic Law, Feudal, Nautical, and Commercial Law, as well as the four *lecturae civitatis*. It must be added, however, that the entire reassertion of the teaching order, just as it had been put together in the final throes of the Venetian government, in no way contributed to enlivening the field of legal studies, partly because many official subjects remained without teachers and were therefore not activated during the entire period of the first Austrian domination (January 1798-December 1805). "Temporarily forced to re-propose with an accentuated immobility a University model foreign to its own traditions, the court of Vienna did not for this reason rule out the prospect, though put off in time, of an 'Austrianization' of the Veneto studium" (Ghetti) which, therefore, awaiting more favourable circumstances, struggled to continue, rendered even more wretched by the rigid and repressive government control over its professors and students.

All of this could only be remedied, not much later, by the imperious will of Napoleon Bonaparte. By dismembering the centuries-old edifice, he was to supply the Padua Studium with the requisites for a modern State University and the legal disciplines – taught in the faculty of law – with characteristics completely antithetical to those abstract and evanescent ones found there up to then, thus offering a drastic remedy for the gulf between the type of education imparted up to then in the classrooms of the Palazzo del Bo and the real needs of legal practitioners who could be immediately received into the world of bureaucracy and legal trials.

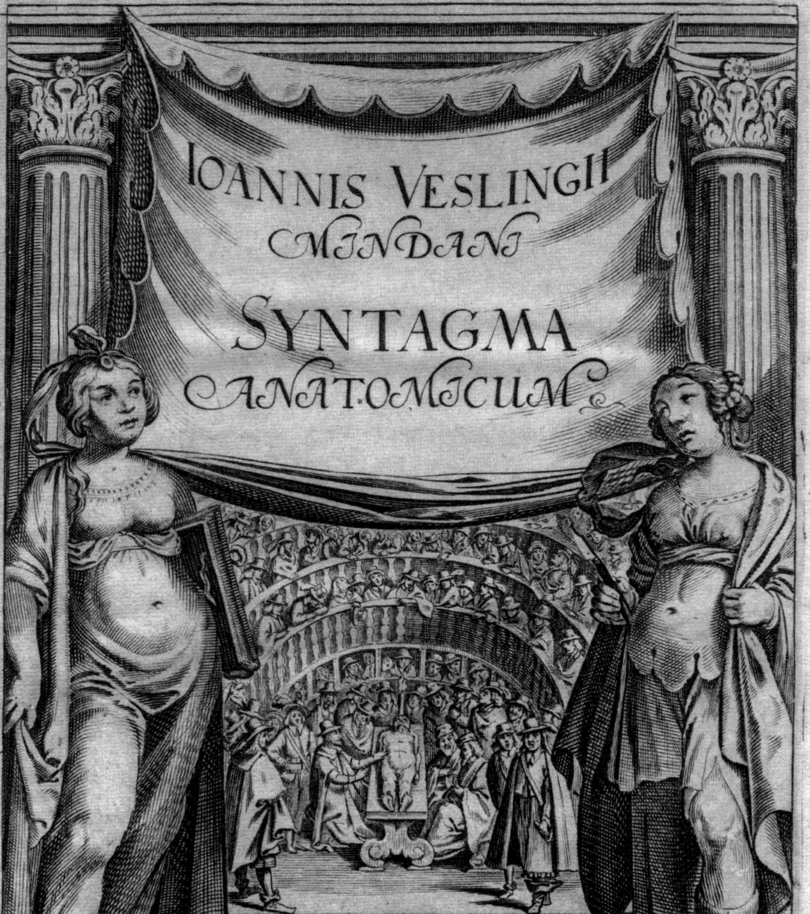
IOANNIS VESLINGII
MINDANI
SYNTAGMA
ANATOMICUM
PATAVII, CIↃIↃCXXXXVII.
Typis Pauli Frambotti Bibliopolæ Sup. permissu.
Jo. Georgius sculp.

GIUSEPPE ONGARO

Medicine

The existence of schools of medicine in Padua before the establishment of the Studium is demonstrated by the numerous names of doctors, which figure in ancient Paduan documents. But in the Studium the teaching of medicine began around 1250, with the establishment of the Collegium of medical and arts doctors. It is only around the middle of the thirteenth century that we find evidence of the presence in Padua of Bruno di Longobucco of Calabria (c. 1200-c. 1286), who was trained at the school of Salerno and was the author of a *Chirurgia magna* completed in Padua in January 1253 and dedicated to a certain Andrea di Vicenza, long used in the Universities as the official text book for the teaching of surgery. The work, which also came out in printed editions from 1498, is based above all on Abulkasim, but it is enriched by the author's numerous personal observations. After 1253, at the request of a certain Lazzaro of Padua, Bruno wrote a summary entitled *Chirurgia parva*. In this period, therefore, through Bruno, Padua felt the influence of the school of Salerno, the most ancient and illustrious medieval institution of the western world for the practice and the teaching of medicine.

Among the first masters of medicine in the Padua Studium there also figure the names of three teachers "profound and expert in physics and natural science", Agno, Giovanni, and Zambonino da Gaza of Cremona, who had completed their studies in Paris; other renowned teachers of medicine were Albertino degli Anselmi da Palazzolo, Avezzuto da Roncaglia, and the Paduan Matteo da Roncajette.

But at the beginning of the fourteenth century standing out above them all is the physician and philosopher Pietro d'Abano (c. 1250-c. 1315), one of the most characteristic and important figures of medieval medicine, who in 1306 was called to Padua from Paris as a teacher of medicine, philosophy, and judicial astrology. He had travelled widely and had been to Constantinople to study Greek and be able directly to consult the works of the ancient physicians and philosophers, then to translate into Latin some of Galen's works; in Paris, where he had written a treatise on physiognomy, he had taught medicine with great renown. With him eclectic and naturalistic Aristotelianism, not without its heterodox implications, gained a foothold in Padua, where it was to remain strong throughout the entire sixteenth century, taking on characteristics of Averroism. With his teaching and the scientific authority he enjoyed, the fame of the Studium spread rapidly throughout Italy. An extremely expert and sought-after

Johann Wesling, Syntagma anatomicum (*Padua 1647*[2]). *Frontispiece*

CONCILIATOR
CONTROVERSIARVM, QVÆ INTER PHILOSOPHOS ET MEDICOS VERSANTVR,
PETRO ABANO PATAVINO, PHILOSOPHO AC MEDICO CLARISSIMO, AVCTORE.
Quibus nunc in margine per numerum adiunximus rationes, quæ ad partes confirmandas, confutandas, atque conciliandas pertinent.
Libellus de Venenis, Eodem auctore.
Petri Carrarij Quæstio de Venenis ad terminum.
Symphoriani Champerij Lugdunensis in Conciliatorem cribrationes.
Index tum rerum, tum verborum copiosissimus, nuper additus.
VENETIIS APVD IVNTAS
M D LXV.

Frontispiece of a sixteenth-century edition of Pietro d'Abano's Conciliator

physician, he was consulted among others by pope Honorius IV and by the marquis Azzo d'Este. He was moreover among the first to teach astronomy and mathematics; a profound scholar of Aristotle, he was the author of an *Expositio problematum Aristotelis.* In 1306 in Padua, at the same time as Pietro d'Abano, we find Dante and Giotto: the intellectual relations which might have existed between them have been much discussed, and attempts have been made to find traces of Pietro's medico-philosophical influence in the works of Dante and the frescoes of Giotto.

In his most famous work, the *Conciliator controversiarum quae inter philosophos et medicos versantur* (Mantua 1472), which enjoyed an enormous diffusion, Pietro attempted to reconcile speculative philosophy with medicine, showing himself also to be an expert clinician, for whom "the art of medicine must only consider those things that can be seen or felt". His therapeutic advice is always simple and clear and shows that he is alien to charlatanism. His Averroism, however, took him into a minefield from the point of view of orthodoxy, as did his astrological research, which led him to maintain a marked determinism with regard to human events. His theoretical work imparted such a vigorous impulse to the Studium's scientific and medical orientation that its effect was to last into the following centuries.

In his *Conciliator* Pietro d'Abano shows a particular interest in anatomy. He can be credited with the first autopsy we have records for in Padua, albeit undertaken for reasons of a forensic nature. His treatise *De venenis*, in fact, tells of the dissection of the corpse of a pharmacist who had accidentally poisoned himself with mercury. Forensic activity appears very early on in Padua, even though it is not possible to find precise and trustworthy documentation for forensic studies of the corpse for the thirteenth and the first half of the fourteenth century. It is very likely, however, that the requirements set by the communal statutes for forensic doctors included the examination of a corpse, not only external but also in the form of an autopsy. Obviously an autopsy could be prescribed above all in cases of sudden death, on the suspicion of poisoning, or for a suspected epidemical or contagious illness. Finally it is worth noting that a typically Paduan tradition based itself on the dissection of the corpse: the miracle of the heart of the avaricious man found in a casket which had been indicated by Saint Anthony while preaching at the man's funeral. It is likely that this anatomical detail was added to the legend in the second half of the fourteenth century, confirming the interest provoked by the dissection of the corpse in large sections of society. We cannot doubt, therefore, that there already existed in Padua a pretty well established practice of dissection around the end of the thirteenth and the beginning of the fourteenth centuries.

A great admirer of Pietro d'Abano was the famous Gentile da Foligno (c. 1275-1348), a former pupil of Taddeo Alderotti, who was in Padua between 1338 and 1345 as the personal physician to Ubertino III da Carrara. Legend has it that on his arrival in Padua he asked to see the room where Pietro had taught, and kneeling on the threshold, removing his hat, and raising his hand, he cried "Ave templum sanctum!". Even though he did not teach in Padua, Gentile da Foligno exercised a notable influence on the Studium, suggesting that Ubertino da Carrara send to Paris twelve young Paduans to complete their medical studies: a plan which was translated into practice in part at least, given that the names of various students from Padua are registered at the Parisian Studium in that period. At least two of them, Antonio Lio and Iacopo da Arquà, subsequently taught medicine in Padua.

A colleague of Pietro d'Abano in the teaching of medicine was Mondino da Cividale († 1340), present together with Pietro in 1307 at the graduation of 'Aymericus de Polonia', whose principal work is a re-elaboration of the *Synonyma medicinae* (or *Clavis sanationis*), a dictionary of materia medica written by Simone di Genova. In 1311-1312 Dino del Garbo, the most famous pupil of Taddeo Alderotti, as well as a relative of his, also taught medicine briefly at Padua.

The first successor to Pietro d'Abano was Nicolò Santa Sofia, who had been his pupil and who occupied the chair until 1350. He was the founder of an illustrious family of physicians, who for many generations occupied a place in the forefront of both professional and academic medicine. His sons Giovanni († 1389) and Marsilio († c. 1403) were physicians and professors of great renown. Giovanni was the author of a *Commentarium universum* on the works of Hippocrates, Galen, and Avicenna, printed in Venice in 1531, and a *Consilium ad pestilentiam* for the city of Udine, published by Sudhoff in 1913. Marsilio taught first logic and then medicine in Padua from 1367 to 1381, then moving to Pavia and then to Bologna, where he died in 1403 and where he is buried; he wrote a *Tractatus de febribus*, published in the sixteenth century.

Another pupil of Pietro d'Abano to acquire great professional fame, and who in 1342 obtained the chair of medicine, was Giacomo Dondi (1293-1359), physician, astronomer, and mathematician. In 1344 he built in Padua for Ubertino da Carrara one of the first mechanical clocks, hence the nickname given to his family ('dall'Orologio'). His most important medical work is the *Aggregator medicamentorum seu de medicinis simplicibus*, a dictionary of medicinal simples, natural substances used in medicine; also worthy of note is his *Tractatus de causa salsedinis aquarum et modo conficiendi salis ex eis*, inserted into the collection *De balneis* published by Giunta (1553), in which he recommends the extraction of salts from mineral waters for medicinal purposes. His son Giovanni Dondi dall'Orologio (1318-1389) also taught at the Padua Studium: a man of enormous culture, an astronomer, mathematician, and man of letters, as well as a physician, he shared a close friendship with Petrarch. He dealt more than his father had done with the thermal waters of the area around Padua in his *De fontibus calidis agri Patavini*, written after 1372 and inserted into the collection *De balneis*, published by Giunta (1553). He also wrote, probably before 1371, a little treatise, *De modo vivendi tempore pestilentiali*, published by Sudhoff in 1911.

Pietro da Tossignano († c. 1407) studied medicine and surgery in Padua, figuring as professor of medicine in Bologna in 1364. Towards 1390, invited by Francesco da Carrara, he came to teach medicine in Padua; in 1396 he returned to Bologna, however, where he died. He wrote various medical treatises, the most well-known of which is that on the plague of 1397, entitled *Consilium pro peste evitanda*, written in 1398 and inserted into the *Fasciculus medicinae*, the famous collection of medical texts published in Venice in 1491. Also very widely diffused were his compendium of hygienic and dietary rules for staying healthy, the *De regimine sanitatis*, and the handbook of therapy and materia medica, *Receptae super nonum Almansoris*.

The titles of some of the works mentioned so far indicate how in the fourteenth century the plague strongly attracted the attention of physicians, who attempted to characterize it clinically and distinguish its various forms, and to study the presumed causes and adopt suitable preventative and therapeutic measures. In the exemplary sanitary legislation with which the Venetian Republic codified the measures to be adopted against the plague, culminating in the prohibition to enter port for ships coming from infected places, many masters of the Padua Studium played a role as authoritative advisers.

THE FIFTEENTH CENTURY

In the fifteenth century, the Padua Studium, like others, had only three fundamental chairs of medicine, that is, in order of importance, Theoretical Medicine, Practical Medicine, and Surgery. Within a three-year span, alternating between 'ordinary' and 'extraordinary' lecturers, the teaching of theoretical medicine dealt with the book I of Avicenna's *Canon*, Hippocrates' *Aphorisms* with the commentary by Galen, Hippocrates' *Prognostics*, and Galen's *Articella*. Topics of a practical nature, on the other hand, alternated from the chairs of practical medicine, such as *de febribus*, *de morbis particularibus a capite usque ad cor*, and *de morbis particularibus a corde infra*, albeit in the form of a reading and a commentary on *fen* IV of Avicenna's *Canon* and book IX of Rhazes' *ad Almansorem*. In practice, the theoretical lessons consisted of the study of aetiology, symptomatology, and the therapy of disease, while those of practical medicine involved the commentary of clinical cases already illustrated and selected from among those included in the texts by Avicenna and Rhazes. As far as surgery was concerned, the lessons also spanned a three-year period; the curriculum was analogous to that in Bologna, where the texts prescribed for study were the *cirurgia Bruni*, Galen and Avicenna's surgical works, and book VII of Rhazes' *ad Almansorem*. In the following century the curriculum of books read for surgery included the study of tumours in the first year, wounds and ulcers in the second year, and luxations and fractures in the third. The surgery teacher was also initially expected to act as incisor in the anatomical demonstrations, and only in

The physician visits a victim of the plague, from the Fasciculo de medicina (*Venice 1494*)

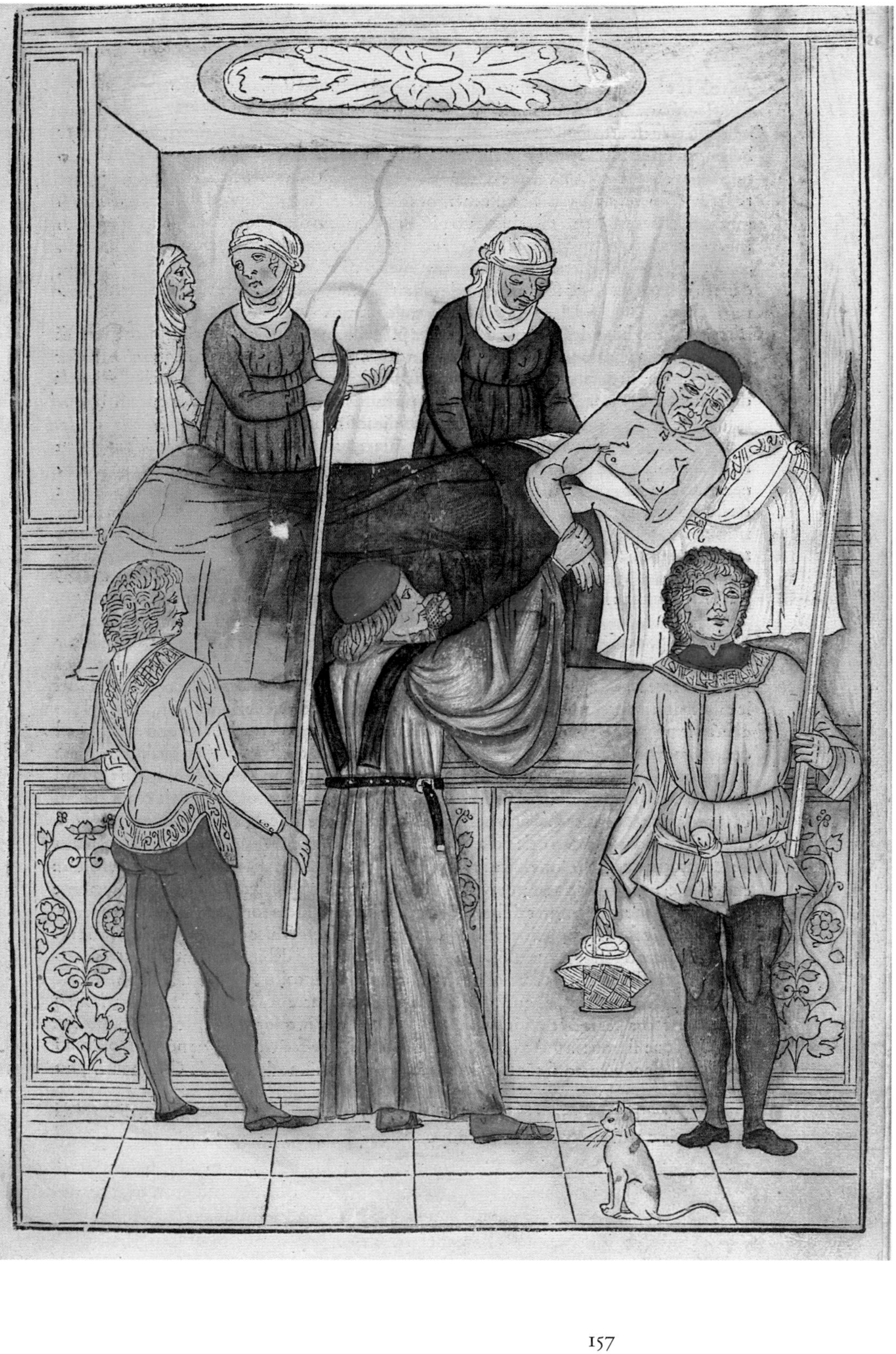

the late sixteenth century was he formally charged with the teaching of anatomy too.

The medical renaissance began with the recovery and the rediscovery of ancient medical and biological texts, which made it possible to read the original texts of the classical authors and not the Arabic translations. Towards the end of the century studies were also greatly enhanced by the spread of printing, which, in the nearby Venice, took on quite a considerable importance.

Among the masters of medicine who taught in the Padua Studium in the first half of the fifteenth century, the first name of some importance is that of Giacomo Della Torre of Forlì (c. 1360/1362–1414), who taught medicine in Padua from 1399 to 1402 and then from 1407 up until his death, whose commentary on Galen's *Articella* was prescribed by the statutes of the 'university' of arts students as the text book for theoretical medicine up to the mid sixteenth century. Antonio Cermisone († 1441), of a family from Parma though he himself was born in Padua, whose library has been reconstructed, taught theoretical medicine from 1413 up until his death; an extremely famous practitioner, he was often called to Venice and elsewhere to practice his profession. He was the author of a collection of *Consilia*, the second of such collections to be printed (1476), four months after the analogous collection by Bartolomeo Montagnana. Cermisone's *Consilia* are the expression of a lengthy and refined practical activity and include numerous personal observations. Among the numerous physicians of the Paduan family of the Santa Sofia, particularly worthy of being remembered is Galeazzo († 1427), son of Giovanni, who, after having taught medicine in Vienna from 1398 to 1405, was lecturer in theoretical medicine in Padua from 1407 up to his death, and his brother Bartolomeo († 1450), who taught practical medicine from 1392 to 1437. During his stay in Vienna (1398-1406), in Lent 1404, Galeazzo Santa Sofia undertook the first solemn public dissection, a practice which he had obviously first seen and carried out in Padua. "If we think", observes Moritz Roth, the great Vesalius scholar, "that the first dissection undertaken in Vienna was carried out by a professor from Padua, we have the impression that in the fifteenth century Padua at least reached the level of Bologna, if not actually overtaking it". Ugo Benzi (1376-1439), the renowned physician from Siena, also taught 'ordinary' theoretical medicine between 1429 and 1431: he is also a typical early fifteenth-century physician, whose medical doctrine principally took the form of a commentary on the works of the ancient masters; he is nevertheless the author of numerous *Consilia saluberrima ad omnes aegritudines a capite ad calcem*, which also contain original observations, and a treatise on personal hygiene, one of the first – if not the first – to be printed in the vernacular (1481).

Besides the Santa Sofias, the Montagnana family also provided numerous masters for the Padua Studium in the fifteenth and sixteenth centuries, the most famous of whom was Bartolomeo († before 1452), professor of practical medicine for many years. His most important work is a collection of *Consilia* written around 1444, the first of such collections to be printed, which subsequently came out in many editions, the last one of which in 1664. Preceded by an anatomical description of the parts affected, Montagnana's *Consilia* are much more advanced and methodical that those of other contemporary writers, to such an extent that in some of them it is possible to identify the elements to form a retrospective diagnosis; the personal observations are numerous and valuable, especially those relating to surgery. Montagnana also practised surgery, as is confirmed by his interest in anatomical dissections: in his *Consilia* he recounts how he always found the jejunum empty in fourteen human corpses, which he had dissected. Bartolomeo Montagnana is moreover the author of a treatise, *De balneis patavinis*, in which, besides indicating the correct way to use the baths of Monte Ortone for therapy, he also considers the accidents, which may occur during their use.

Cristoforo Barzizza of Bergamo († 1445), who taught 'ordinary' practical medicine from 1434 to 1444, is the author of works of a practical nature, the most important of which is the *Introductorium sive ianua ad opus practicum medicine* (1440). From 1426 to 1465 the chair of theoretical medicine was held by Sigismondo Polcastro of Vicenza (1384-1473), who was lecturer in philosophy from 1419, and who was author of a commentary on Hippocrates' *Aphorisms* and a number of *Quaestiones*, several of which concern medical subjects.

The most important figure in the field of fifteenth-century practical medicine was the Paduan Michele Savonarola (c. 1385-1466), whose works "mark the beginning of a healthy reaction against medical scholasticism" (Sarton). A pupil of Giacomo Della Torre, Galeazzo Santa Sofia and then Cermisone, Savonarola devoted himself for twenty years to an intensive and esteemed practical activity; he began to teach in the Studium late, as a lecturer "ad tertium Avicennae" in 1433, and in the following year as lecturer in 'extraordinary' practical medicine. In the summer of 1440 he left Padua for Ferrara, called there by the marquis Niccolò III d'Este: thus, while his brother Francesco continued the Paduan branch of the family, Michele became the founder of a new Ferrarese branch, which was to produce the famous dominican fra Girolamo, born in Ferrara on 21st September, 1452, the son of Niccolò di Michele and Elena de' Bonacossi.

A highly prolific writer, among Michele's medical works the first in order of chronology and importance is the *Practica maior* (*Practica de egritudinibus a capite usque ad pedes*), written in his Paduan period and dedicated to Sigismondo Polcastro, a younger colleague at the Studium and also a relative of his. The *Practica* includes the entire range of medical knowledge of the period and is rich in personal observations deriving from his own professional practice. The pre-eminence given to the description of clinical cases, Sarton believes, is a clear sign of the re-awakening of a clinical spirit and of an experimental rather than a speculative medicine: in effect, with his *Practica*, Savonarola joins the Paduan tradition of eminently practical medical studies inspired by a naturalistic concept of science alien to speculative interests. A humanist physician firmly rooted in the Paduan intellectual tradition, he carried forward the naturalistic work of Pietro d'Abano. Savonarola's principal work was blessed with a success, which it deserved, to such an extent that despite its size it was printed in numerous editions both in the fifteenth and the sixteenth centuries. Savonarola is considered to be the fifteenth century medical writer who more than any other dealt with obstetrics and gynaecology, and he is credited with having been the first to have spoken of the stenosis of the pelvis as a cause of difficulty during childbirth. Savonarola's interest in questions regarding conception and pregnancy is also clear in a work belonging to his Ferrarese period, the little gynaecologico-paediatric treatise in the vernacular entitled *De regimine pregnantium et noviter natorum usque ad septennium*, printed by Belloni (1952), the third part of which constitutes a veritable treatise of puericulture and paediatrics up to the age of seven, with a pedagogical appendix on children's moral education. The work thus occupies a chronological and historical place of the first order, given that its author died six years before Bagellardo produced his *Libellus de egritudinibus et remediis infantium* (1472). Paolo Bagellardo Dal Fiume († 1492/1494) was first lecturer in philosophy (1441), then from 1444 lecturer in 'extraordinary' theoretical medicine, from 1458 lecturer in 'extraordinary' practical medicine, and finally from 1472 lecturer in 'ordinary' theoretical medicine. His little work, published in Padua in 1472, has a unique historical value, because besides being unanimously considered the first Western treatise on paediatrics, according to Sudhoff it constitutes the first book on medicine which passed directly from the author's desk to that of the printer. The *Libellus* is fundamentally a compilation of information on paediatrics taken above all from Rhazes' *Practica puerorum* and from the chapters on paediatrics in Avicenna's *Canon*, integrated, however, with elements which derive from the author's own practical experience. Bagellardo's work, which he conceived of for the use of practising physicians, was very successful and was reprinted many times over the course of the fifteenth and sixteenth centuries, undergoing in some of these editions changes and additions, and it was translated into the vernacular (1486) and into French (1538).

Two other of Savonarola's works belong to his period in Padua: the *Tractatus de vermibus*, which can be considered the first treatise on parasitology in its own right to exist in medical literature, inspired by Avicenna's helminthological treatise and of an eminently practical nature; and a notable treatise on fevers, the *Practica canonica de febribus*. Finally, written mostly in Padua is his *De balneis*, published between 1441 and 1450, whose importance to the history of medico-hydrological literature is partly demonstrated by the fact that it figures as the initial treatise in the famous collection, *De balneis*, published by Giunta (1553). With it Savonarola joined the Paduan tradition of studies on medical hydrology and hydrotherapy which, beginning with Pietro d'Abano and carried forward by the Dondi, was in the fifteenth century also to see the contribution by Bartolomeo Montagnana with his *Tractatus de balneis patavinis* (1440) and which was to be enriched in the sixteenth century by Gabriele Falloppia's *De thermalibus aquis*.

Giovanni Arcolani of Verona († 1458) taught 'ordinary' practical medicine from 1427; he then moved to Ferrara (1433), where he remained until his death. Besides several consultations, he left behind him a *Practica, seu expositio in nonum librum Almansoris*, which, among other things, contains a satisfactory description of the symptoms of *delirium tremens* and an *Expositio in primam fen quarti Canonis Avicenne*. Above all, Arcolani's works are rich in original surgical observations: he considered surgery to be the principal aid of medicine, thus going beyond the distinction which still existed at the time between the work of the surgeon and that of the physician, a further confirmation of the fact that such a separation never existed in an exasperated form in Padua, as it did in other places, however. His *Practica* contains precise references to autopsies.

The name of Leonardo Buffi from Bertipaglia († after 1448) stands out among the teachers of surgery. He was not only lecturer in the Studium from 1421 to 1429, but also practised his art with great renown in Venice and in other cities. His treatise on surgery (*Recollectae habitae super quarto Canonis Avicennae*) is rich in personal observations and contains references to dissections; moreover, in his treatise *De antidotis*, added to the *Recollectae* in the printed editions, we find reference to two dissections carried out in Padua on 8th February, 1430 (1429 according to the Venetian calendar) and 4th April, 1430, the first of which was performed by Ugo Benzi in Buffi's presence, in a house near the church of s. Luca.

By the first half of the fifteenth century, therefore, the practice of dissections was well-established. Towards the close of the fifteenth century anatomical dissections became more frequent, preparing the way for the renaissance in anatomy in which Padua was to play such an important role. The teaching of anatomy was imparted on the basis of a text which had by then become a classic: Mondino de' Liuzzi's *Anatomia*, which dates to 1316. Once Mondino's *manualis operatio* had been abandoned, however, anatomical teaching was to have three protagonists: an 'extraordinary' professor who read Mondino's text, another teacher of theoretical medicine or of 'ordinary' practical medicine who explained the text, demonstrating it and checking it with a corpse, while the lecturer in surgery incised and dissected the corpse. This is the scene illustrated in the well-known xylography depicting the anatomy lesson, which precedes the text of Mondino's *Anatomia* in the Italian edition of the *Fasciculus medicinae* (1494).

Among the lecturers in medicine of the second half of the fifteenth century, worthy of being remembered, if for no other reason than for the fame which they enjoyed during their lifetime, are the names of Pietro Trapolin (1451-1509), philosopher and physician, who taught practical medicine from 1494 and theoretical medicine from 1495 to 1509, and was the author of a treatise *De morbo gallico*; the Venetian Pietro Roccabonella

The anatomy lesson, from the Fasciculo de medicina *(Venice 1494)*

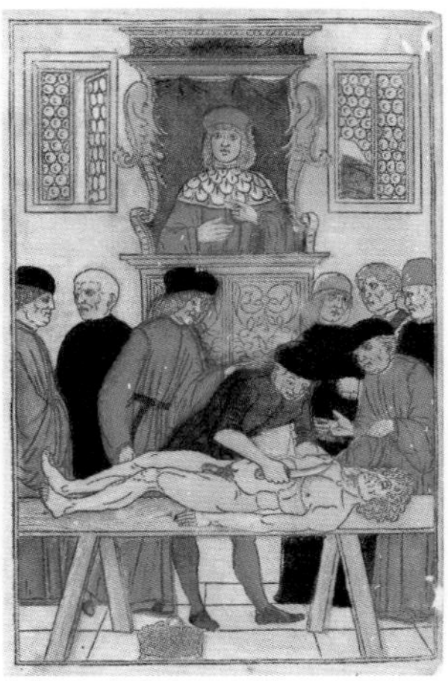

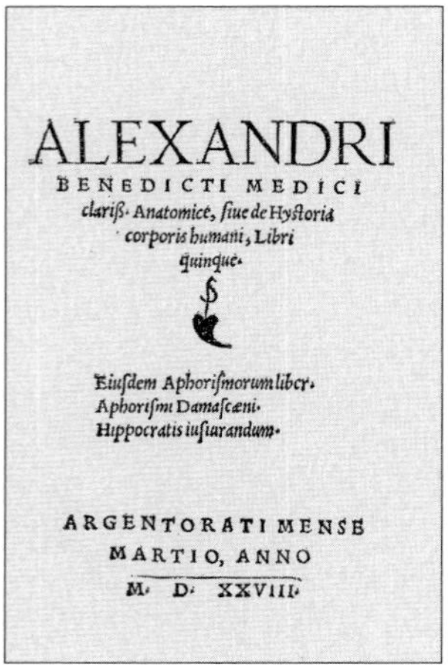

ALEXANDRI
BENEDICTI MEDICI
clariss. Anatomice, siue de Hystoria
corporis humani, Libri
quinque.

Eiusdem Aphorismorum liber.
Aphorismi Damasceni.
Hippocratis iusiurandum.

ARGENTORATI MENSE
MARTIO, ANNO
M. D. XXVIII.

Alessandro Benedetti, Anatomice, sive de historia corporis humani libri quinque (*Strasbourg 1528*). *Frontispiece*

Gabriele Zerbi, Liber anathomiae corporis humani (*Venice 1502*). *Incipit*

(†1491), who taught theoretical medicine from 1459; and Giovanni dell'Aquila from Abruzzo († 1507), lecturer first in 'extraordinary' practical medicine (1463-72), then in theoretical medicine (1487-93), and finally in practical medicine (1493-1506), who contributed to the handing down of a satisfactory redaction of Pietro d'Abano's *Conciliator*.

In the fifteenth and sixteenth centuries the names of Alessandro Benedetti and Gabriele Zerbi stand out. Alessandro Benedetti (c. 1450-1513), from Legnago, left for Greece immediately after obtaining his degree in medicine from Padua (1478), where for twelve years he practised medicine above all on the island of Crete, a Venetian possession. In 1490 he was called to the Padua Studium as professor of 'ordinary' practical medicine, but in 1495 he was appointed chief surgeon to the Italian army against Charles VIII, and he took part in the battle of Fornovo (6th July, 1495), leaving behind a written account of the military campaign, the *Diaria de bello Carolino* (1496). A typical humanist physician, Benedetti produced an edition of Pliny's *Naturalis historia* (1507), dedicated to Giorgio Merula; he was a convinced supporter of the need for naturalistic observation as the basis for any form of progress in medical knowledge. Benedetti left behind him a posthumously published work (1533), a veritable practical encyclopaedia of the medical knowledge of his age, containing numerous personal medical and surgical observations, frequently confirmed by precise anatomo-pathological findings. A careful epidemiologist, in his *De observatione in pestilentia* (1493), he maintained the possibility of the spread of the morbid principle of the plague, and therefore recommended the isolation of the patient and the disinfection of his clothing, especially woollen garments. Benedetti occupies an extremely distinguished position among writers on syphilis, as one of the first to have observed the disease in several soldiers during the battle of Fornovo. He is also the author of a collection of medico-deontological aphorisms, *Collectiones medicinae*, published for the first time in 1493. Interest in the practice of the profession produced a flowering of deontological works; already in Cristoforo Barzizza's *Introductorium*, ample space is set aside for the treatment of medical deontology, and Gabriele Zerbi published a work specifically on the subject in 1495, the *De cautelis medicorum*. In the field of anatomy, Benedetti is the author of a work, the *Anatomice sive historia corporis humani* (1502), which had a great influence on anatomical terminology. This was the first work after that by Mondino to be dedicated exclusively to anatomy, but unlike the latter's however, it is a compendium of descriptive anatomy, not a manual of dissection. Its anatomical content is not based on dissection, which Benedetti did practice, but derives from Greek sources, and therefore from Galen's authentic anatomy and not from the pseudo-Galenic medieval anatomy. In his anatomical terminology, although he used Giorgio Valla's posthumous work, *De humani corporis partibus* (1501), and Giulio Polluce's *Onomasticon* (c. 134-192), Benedetti drew fruit above all from the good knowledge of Greek which he acquired during the lengthy period he spent in Greek-speaking countries, thus introducing new terms. Benedetti's book had a notable diffusion and was reprinted many times: it was the only Italian anatomical treatise to have been reprinted in Paris (1514), hence allowing the diffusion of its morphological terminology throughout northern Europe, and giving rise to a renewal of anatomical vocabulary by humanist physicians. Benedetti's work established the norms for the construction and the organization of a temporary ("temporarium") anatomical theatre: thus anatomy also becomes a performance, as Benedetti himself realized, as the good humanist that he was, sensitive to the aesthetic aspect of dissection.

Greater contributions to anatomical knowledge were made by Gabriele Zerbi from Verona (1435-1505), whose *Liber anathomiae corporis humani* (1502) is a vast unillustrated work written in a prolix and still medieval fashion, but which contains however several original observations obtained through dissection, above all concerning the abdominal organs. Zerbi taught 'ordinary' philosophy in Padua from 1467 to 1475; he then moved to Bologna and to Rome, from where he returned to Padua in 1494 as professor of 'ordinary' theoretical medicine. A renowned practitioner, he died a violent death together with his son on his return journey from Turkey, where he had been taken by his fame as a physician. Besides his *Liber anathomiae corporis humani* and his *De cautelis medicorum*, Zerbi published the *Quaestiones metaphysicae* (1482) and a little treatise on geriatrics entitled *Gerontocomia* (1489). As well as a physician, anatomist, and philosopher, Zerbi was also a good humanist and he is attributed with the discovery and the preservation of several manuscripts of medieval scientific works.

Among anatomists active in Padua before Vesalius, we are duty-bound to recall the Bolognese Alessandro Achillini (1463-1512), much better known as a philosopher and a physician, who taught in Padua in the years 1506-1508. His *Anatomicae annotationes*, published posthumously in 1520, is a collection of notes from his anatomical lessons: although dictated according to the traditional method, there is no doubt that he personally carried out dissections, at least in the years 1502, 1503, and 1506, and therefore the *Anatomicae annotationes* might have been compiled during his period in Padua. The terminology is still medieval, as are his sources, among which Mondino in particular; nevertheless, Achillini gives a clear and concise description of structures which he had had a direct experience of, showing a more direct approach to anatomy, even if this does not yet have the status of a discipline in its own right. An important place among pre-Vesalius anatomists is also held by the Venetian Niccolò Massa (1485-1569), trained in Padua, whose *Liber introductorius anatomiae* (1536) is the best manual of anatomy to have been published until Realdo Colombo's *De re anatomica* (1559).

THE SIXTEENTH CENTURY

1. *The Rebirth of Anatomy*

The fundamental feature of sixteenth-century medicine is the definitive revival of interest in anatomical studies, based on findings obtained from direct observation, and therefore on dissection. In the second half of the fifteenth century anatomical dissections had become more frequent, thus contributing to an awakening of the medical environment to the study of anatomy, even though these dissections had not yet become a systematic part of the curriculum of studies or research but were carried out in general to verify and confirm traditional anatomy, to train surgeons, or for forensic reasons. The methodological disputes, fertile and substantial in the Padua Studium more than elsewhere, led to greater importance being given to experience, and they contributed to tilting the medical environment towards a logico-empirical approach in naturalistic research. Another intrinsic element which favoured anatomical studies was the tendency in vogue in Padua to interpret Aristotle according to Alexander of Aphrodisia, a tendency which stressed anatomical research as a means of obtaining knowledge of those essential constitutive elements of human nature which must all be present in order for man to be endowed with material intellect, that is to say the capacity to understand. Now the anatomy lesson is different from the one represented in the xylograph of the Italian edition of the *Fasciculus medicinae*: leaving the text of Galeno-Arabic medicine behind him on the book rest, Vesalius gets up from his chair, picks up the knife, and starts to dissect with his own hands in the middle of a circle of students. Corresponding to this change of scene is a radical change in mentality: anatomical reality is now no longer deduced from the text traditionally handed down, but from the direct observation of the human corpse.

1543, the year of the publication of the *De humani corporis fabrica* by Andreas Vesalius from Brussels (1514-1564), is like a watershed that separates two epochs of medicine: medieval and modern. It is the same year that saw the publication of the *De revolutionibus orbium coelestium* by Nicholas Copernicus (1473-1543), a former student in Padua. Again in the same year and still in Padua, the demonstrative method was also inaugurated in pharmacognosis and in botany, while three years later we see the publication of Girolamo Fracastoro's *De contagione et contagiosis morbis*, which established the bases of modern epidemiology and pathology.

Andreas Vesalius arrived in Padua in 1537, attracted by the freedom of research and the availability of corpses for anatomical research, which the city guaranteed. On 5th December, 1537, he obtained his doctorate in medicine from the Padua Studium and immediately afterwards, at the age of 23, was appointed professor of the first *locus* (rank) of surgery, with the express condition that he teaches anatomy. We know that he also gave lessons in surgery, but very soon anatomy was to absorb him completely. In

Below:
Andreas Vesalius. Padua, Palazzo del Bo, hall of the Faculty of Medicine and Surgery

Opposite:
Andreas Vesalius, De humani corporis fabrica libri septem (*Basle 1543*). *Frontispiece and the meditating skeleton.*

Male and female nudes, from Andreas Vesalius, Suorum de humani corporis fabrica librorum epitome (*Basle 1543*)

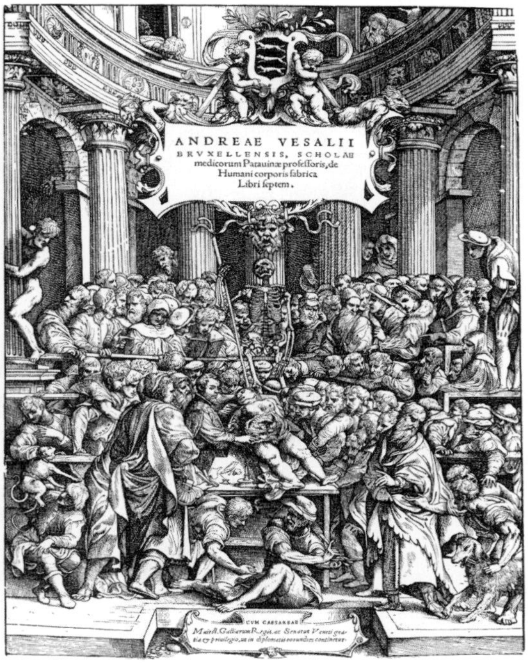
ANDREAE VESALII
BRVXELLENSIS, SCHOLAE
medicorum Patauinæ professoris, de
Humani corporis fabrica
Libri septem.
CVM CAESAREAE

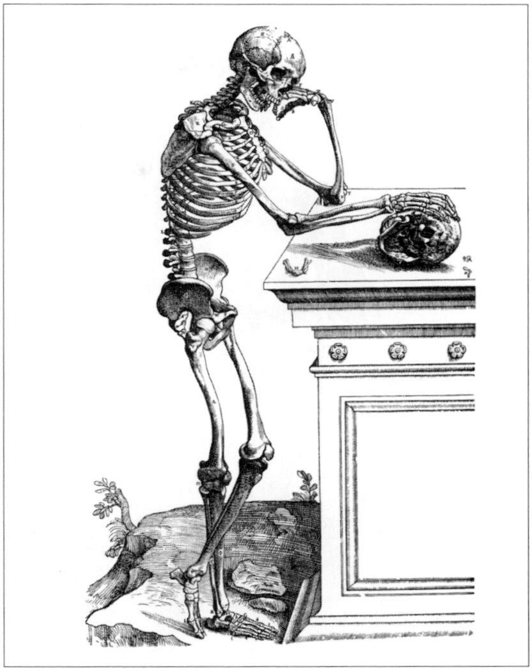

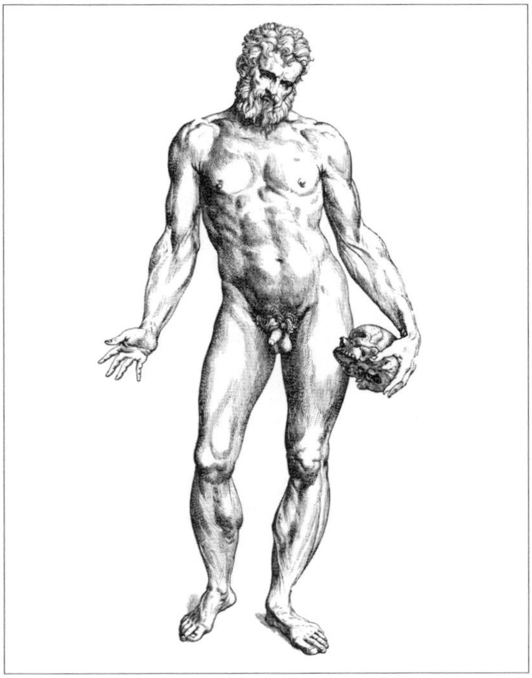

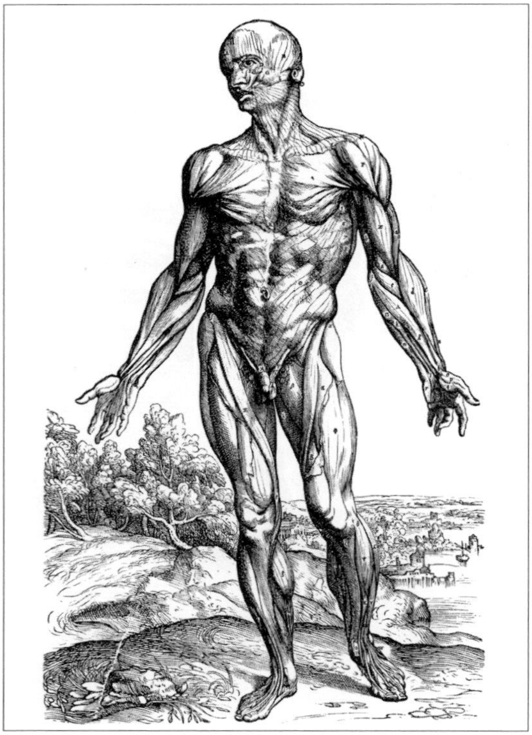

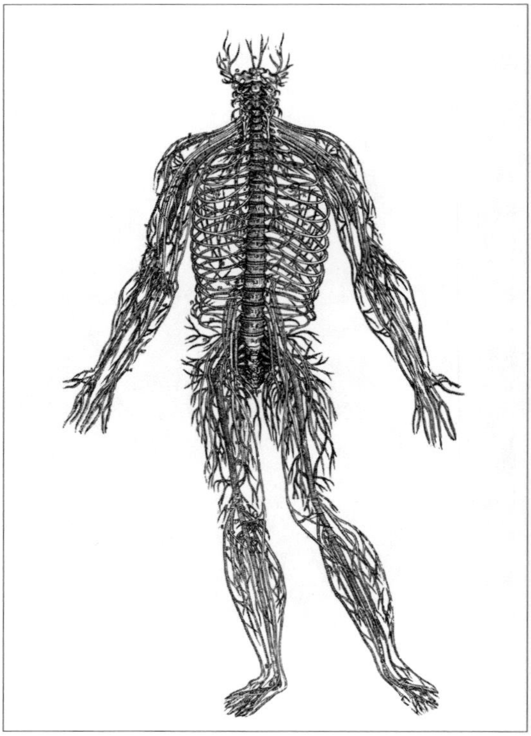

Table showing muscles and table showing nerves from the De humani corporis fabrica *by Vesalius*

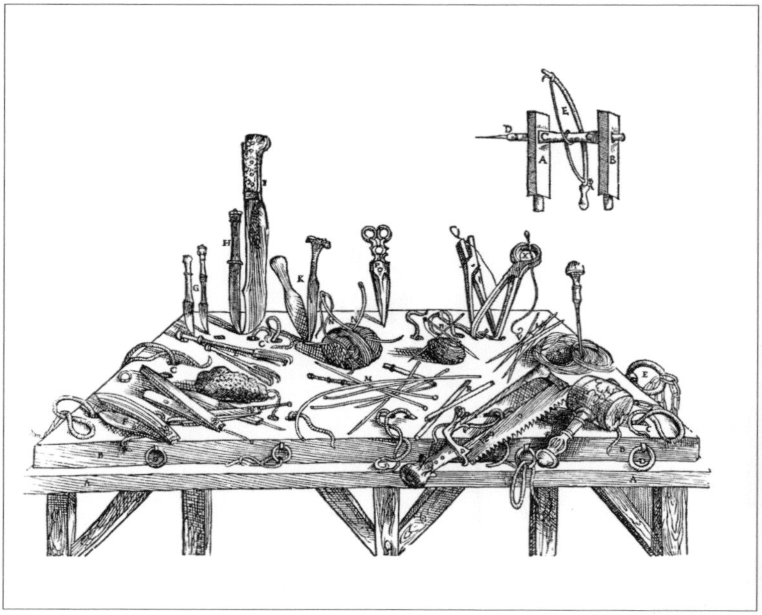

The instruments for dissection from the De humani corporis fabrica *by Vesalius*

Padua, from 1537 to 1543, Vesalius spent six years of intense activity devoted to teaching and research, having at his disposal a sizeable number of corpses, thanks to the Venetian Republic's enlightened attitude of openness. In his demonstrations he also used an entire skeleton and individual bones, often making use of drawings to illustrate the course of the vessels and the nerves. These didactic diagrams, in part prepared in advance and in part sketched during the lessons themselves, were probably the source of the *Tabulae anatomicae sex* (1538), made up of three figures of the skeleton drawn by the painter and Vesalius' compatriot Jan Stephan van Calcar (c. 1500-1546), a pupil of Titian and an extremely acute observer and excellent artist, and three diagrams depicting the vascular apparatus and splanchnology, drawn by Vesalius himself. In some places the six xylographs repeat the errors of Galenic anatomy: a five-lobed liver, a sternum divided into seven parts, a *rete mirabile* at the base of the cranium, are certainly not the result of objective observation of the human corpse, despite the fact that the drawings contain some new findings, such as the ending of the azygos vein, the structure of the jawbone, and the absence of the inter-maxillary suture, in open contrast to Galen's anatomy.

But very soon his accurate anatomical research on the corpse, together with a careful study of Galen's anatomical text, which he himself edited, brought Vesalius to the conclusion that Galen's anatomy, held to be human, was in reality fundamentally based on the dissection of animals and above all of monkeys. In January 1540, invited to Bologna, Vesalius carried out some anatomical demonstrations, during which he openly declared that human anatomy could only be learnt by means of the dissection and observation of the human body and, to prove the fact that Galen's anatomy was based on animals, he prepared the skeletons of an anthropoid monkey and a man, thus demonstrating that Galen's osteology agreed with the first skeleton, but not with the second, human, one.

In 1538 Vesalius began to write his principal work, securing the collaboration of artists from the school of Titian, and above all that of van Calcar, whose active and productive participation in the work's pictorial realization is beyond discussion. On the 1st August, 1542, the manuscript of the *De humani corporis fabrica* was complete, and two weeks later so was that of the *Epitome*. Vesalius sent them to Basle, along with the woodcuts, to the printer Iohannes Herbst (*Oporinus*, 1507-1568). In August, 1543 the printing of the *Fabrica* was complete; the *Epitome* came out almost at the same time in Latin and in German.

The reasons, set out in the preface, which induced Vesalius to compose and to publish the *Fabrica* were various. He wanted to convince the medical world, with the example of his teaching and above all with the descriptions and the illustrations of the *Fabrica*, of the fundamental and pre-eminent importance of anatomy in the study of medicine; secondly, he intended to demonstrate that it was only by applying his principles and his research methods that one could attain a true knowledge of anatomy, in contrast with the traditional and acritical acceptance of Galen's morpholo-

Realdo Colombo. Padua, Palazzo del Bo, hall of the Faculty of Medicine and Surgery

Realdo Colombo, De re anatomica libri XV *(Venice 1559). Frontispiece*

gy. Human anatomy, he maintained, can only be learnt by dissecting and studying the human body, the only authentic source of knowledge. It was however advisable that human dissections were accompanied by parallel dissections of animal bodies, in order to distinguish Galenic animal anatomy from human anatomy. Thanks to Vesalius, Padua became the first great centre for the study of human and comparative anatomy, a double field of research continued by his successors, such as Falloppia, Fabricius, and Casseri.

According to Vesalius' method, the medical student had to study directly and dissect the human corpse; similarly, the master was to get down from his chair, take the place of the surgeon who formerly undertook the dissections, and carry them out himself. The reader of the *Fabrica* must not simply be satisfied with Vesalius' descriptions, but must verify them personally: for this reason, the descriptive chapters of the *Fabrica* are often integrated by detailed instructions on dissectorial technique and anatomical preparations. The *Fabrica* is therefore the basis for a new study of human anatomy and for a new method of anatomical research, which entirely reflects the teaching method imparted by Vesalius in Padua from the end of 1539 to 1543.

The over three hundred illustrations constitute an essential part of the *Fabrica*, strictly integrated with the text, together with which they must be considered. Their anatomical details and the accompanying notes, which explain them exhaustively with numerical and alphabetical references, show that the pictures were produced under the supervision of Vesalius and always with the specific aim of explaining a certain part of the text. The value of Vesalius' work, considered from a general point of view, does not lie so much in the anatomical discoveries contained in the *Fabrica* as in the scientific principle it enunciates, which is that the only true source of anatomical knowledge is the dissection of the human body.

Vesalius' message was received by his successors. He was succeeded to the chair of surgery "with the requirement of autopsy" in 1544 by Realdo Colombo of Cremona (1516-1559), previously lecturer in logic and put forward in vain in 1541 for the second rank. Extremely interested in the vivisectional method, Colombo was the author a compendium in fifteen books, *De re anatomica* (Venetiis 1559), published posthumously and devoid of illustrations, but much used as a textbook in its numerous editions. Colombo's fame is linked above all to his assertion of the impermeability of the interventricular septum and the description of the flow of the blood from the right to the left heart through the pulmonary vessels. Colombo added to his description the experimental demonstration, through vivisection, of the fact that the "venous artery", that is to say the pulmonary vein, contains blood and not air or "soot". No one before him, he stated, had observed or described the passage of the blood through the lungs.

Colombo was succeeded in 1551 by Gabriele Falloppia of Modena (1523-1562), who was officially charged with lecturing on both surgery and anatomy, as well as on simples, posts which he held until his death. An active dissector, Falloppia was the sixteenth-century anatomist who more than any other contributed, together with Vesalius, to the anatomical renaissance. The results of his research are collected in the *Observationes anatomicae* (Venetiis 1561), which consist essentially of completions and corrections to Vesalius' *Fabrica*. Falloppia's research was more precise than that of Vesalius, and his discoveries more numerous: "Fallope avait le génie de l'invention; Vésale, le génie de la méthode" (Daremberg). Among the numerous contributions, which Falloppia made to anatomical knowledge, the best known is the accurate description of the uterine tubes, which still bear his name. With his important observations on the primary and secondary centres of ossification and on the development of teeth, Falloppia can be considered as the initiator of the study of embryology. He was the first of the modern age to treat of the "partes similares", which correspond to our "tissues", with which he attempted to go beyond the purely morphological description of organs in order to gain a knowledge of intimate composition based on several elementary formations similar to each other, though found in different parts of the body.

A paradigmatic figure of the transitional phase of anatomy from that of the renaissance to that of the seventeenth century is Fabricius ab Acquapendente (Girolamo Fabrici d'Acquapendente, 1533-1619), a pupil and the successor to Falloppia, who held the chair of surgery and anatomy in the Padua Studium for fifty years. His biological works were not published until 1600 onwards, despite the fact that the relative observations date to several years earlier. Fabricius was the first anatomist to recognize the importance and the representational effectiveness of the systematic anatomical illustration, leaving behind him a great anatomical atlas in colour, of which 167 tables remain, now preserved in the Biblioteca Marciana of Venice. His name is linked to the first permanent anatomical theatre (1594), still preserved in the palazzo del Bo, an emblematic instrument of the demonstrative method in anatomy, which constituted the model for the anatomical theatres built in the seventeenth century in the main Universities of Europe, all based on the Paduan archetype.

In his anatomical research, Fabricius applied the anatomo-comparative method with great effectiveness. With his two treatises, *De formato foetu* (1600) and *De formatione ovi et pulli* (1621), he was the initiator of scientific embryology. It appears that he did not use any means of enlargement in his research. The *De formato foetu* is a magnificent comparative study, which describes the maturest phases of development in numerous animal species; the treatise also contains marvellous drawings of the pregnant human uterus, embryonic adnexa, and the placenta. The *De formatione ovi et pulli* illustrates the various phases of development of the chick from the sixth day onwards, with numerous and excellent illustrations which remained unsurpassed until those by Marcello Malpighi (1628-1694). It also describes and illustrates for the first time the lymphatic organ of birds which goes by the name of 'bursa of Fabricius', credited in the last few decades as being the central lymphoid organ of immunity.

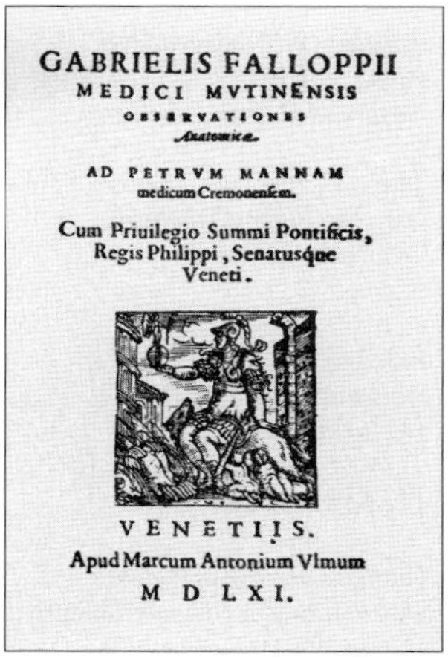
GABRIELIS FALLOPPII
MEDICI MVTINENSIS
OBSERVATIONES
Anatomicae.
AD PETRVM MANNAM
medicum Cremonensem.
Cum Priuilegio Summi Pontificis, Regis Philippi, Senatusque Veneti.
VENETIIS.
Apud Marcum Antonium Vlmum
M D LXI.

Gabriele Falloppia. Padua, Palazzo del Bo, hall of the Faculty of Medicine and Surgery

Gabriele Falloppia, Observationes anatomicae (*Venice 1561*). *Frontispiece*

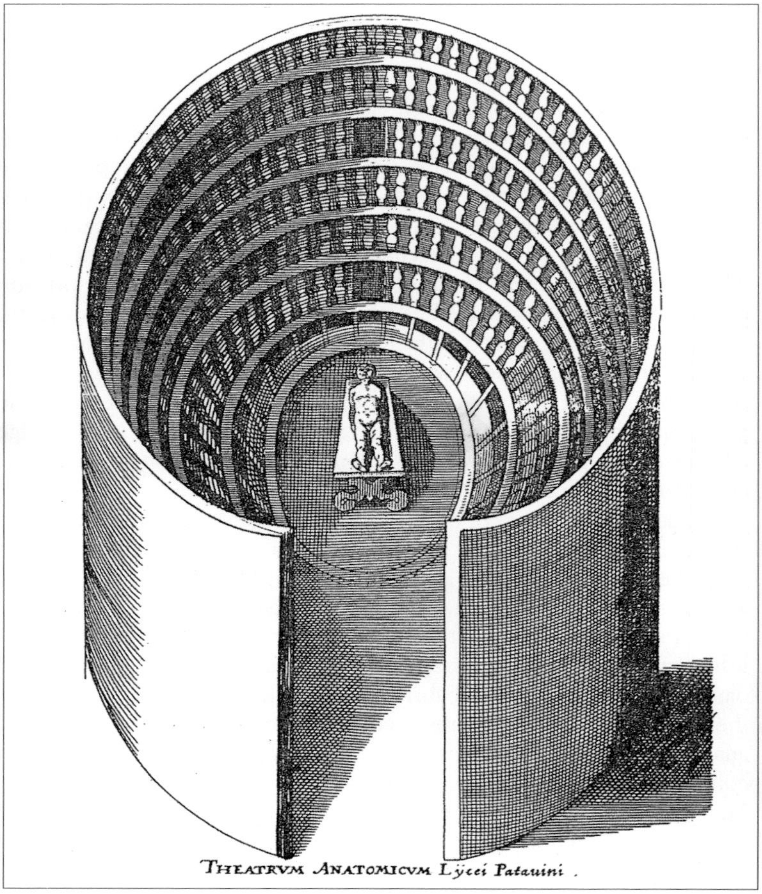

Fabricius ab Acquapendente. Padua, Palazzo del Bo, hall of the Faculty of Medicine and Surgery

The anatomical theatre, from Giacomo Filippo Tomasini, Gymnasium Patavinum (*Udine 1644*)

Fabricius ab Acquapendente, De formatione ovi, et pulli (*Padua 1621*). *Frontispiece*

The bursa of Fabricius

Fabricius ab Acquapendente, De locutione et eius instrumentis (*Venice 1601*). *Frontispiece*

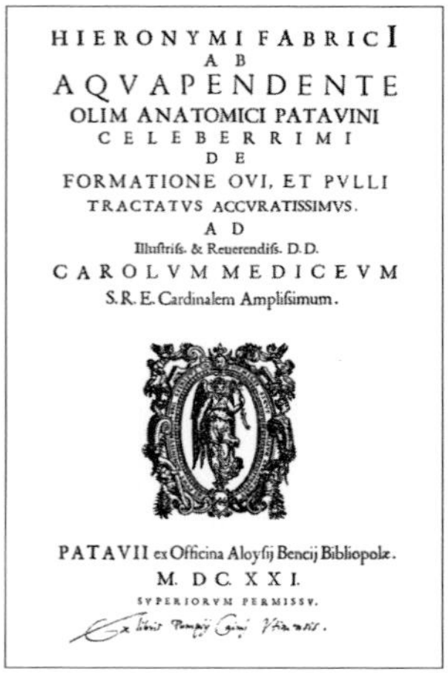

HIERONYMI FABRICI
AB
AQVAPENDENTE
OLIM ANATOMICI PATAVINI
CELEBERRIMI
DE
FORMATIONE OVI, ET PVLLI
TRACTATVS ACCVRATISSIMVS.
AD
Illuſtriſs. & Reuerendiſs. D.D.
CAROLVM MEDICEVM
S.R.E. Cardinalem Ampliſsimum.

PATAVII ex Officina Aloyſij Bencij Bibliopolæ.
M. DC. XXI.
SVPERIORVM PERMISSV.

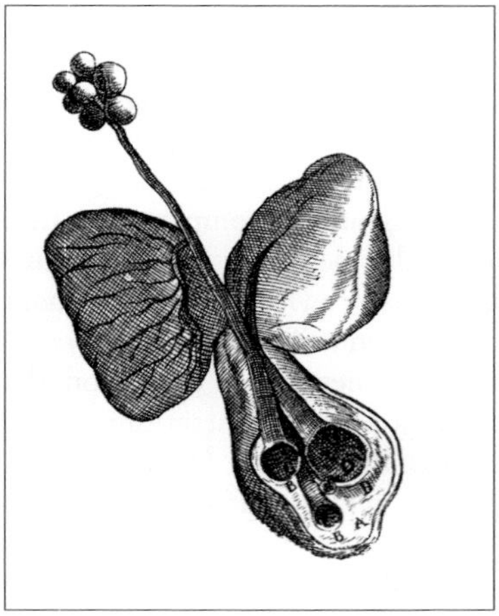

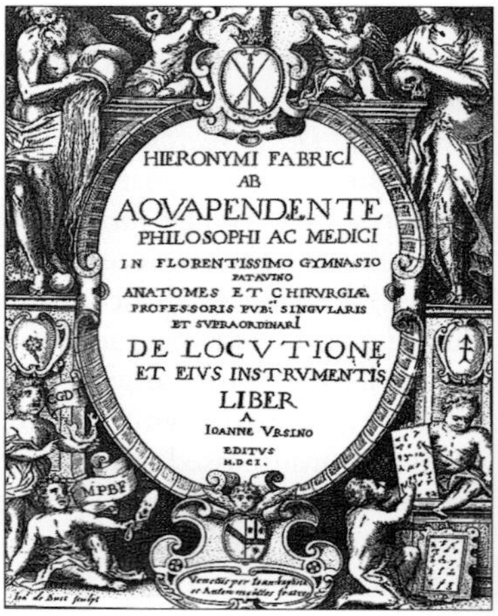

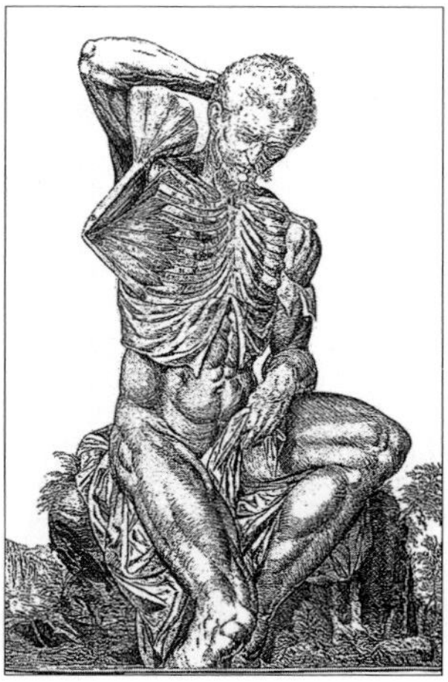

Anatomical table, from Giulio Casseri, Tabulae anatomicae (*Venice 1627*)

Fabricius also marks the transition from descriptive to functional anatomy with his works on the sense organs and the organs of phonation and respiration, the treatises *De visione voce auditu* (1600), *De locutione et eius instrumentis* (1601), *De brutorum loquela* (1603), and *De respiratione et eius instrumentis* (1615). Extremely interested in the problem of animal movement, he also left behind him a little treatise, *De motu locali animalium secundum totum* (1618), which gathers together a series of lessons he gave from the chair. But the best known of Fabricius' works is the *De venarum ostiolis* (1603), in which he systematically studied the valves of the veins, the first to illustrate them with excellent drawings. The work had a decisive influence on Harvey, who used some of its figures, basing many of his arguments in favour of the circulation of the blood on the action of the valves of the veins. The presence of valvular strips within the veins had already been observed in the sixteenth century, but it was Fabricius, Harvey's master, who introduced a valvular apparatus into anatomical science as a systematic attribute of the veins, also observing that the valvular sinuses always point towards the heart. Despite the potentially revolutionary significance of these anatomical findings, Fabricius did not understand the true function of the valves, which he attributed with the task of slowing the flow of the blood towards the periphery and hence of preventing the blood from collecting in the extremities.

The organs of sense and phonation were also the objects of the anatomo-comparative research of Giulio Casseri of Piacenza (1552-1616), who in 1609 succeeded Fabricius to the chair of surgery. He was the author of the treatises *De vocis auditusque organis* (1600-01) and *Pentaestheseion* (1609); on his death he also left behind him a series of extremely valuable *Tabulae de formato foetu* and *Tabulae anatomicae*, published posthumously in 1626 and 1627, which represent the final exalted expression of the sixteenth-century Paduan school of anatomy.

2. *Demonstrative Teaching of Simples and the Botanical Garden*

At the beginning of the sixteenth century the teaching on drugs was not imparted from special chairs, but the lecturers on practical medicine, when dealing with the care of individual illnesses, now and then when the opportunity presented itself, also considered the medicines appropriate for them. In 1533 the chair *ad Lecturam simplicium* was established in the Padua Studium, the first of its kind in Italy, and it was entrusted to Francesco Bonafede of Padua (1474-1558), who already taught 'ordinary' practical medicine in the second rank. The new teaching was clearly of an applied nature, consisting of a reading and a commentary on Dioscorides' *De materia medica* and Galen's *De simplicium medicamentorum temperamentis et facultatibus*, and therefore included the study of the therapeutic properties of natural, mineral, vegetable, and animal products: it was, in

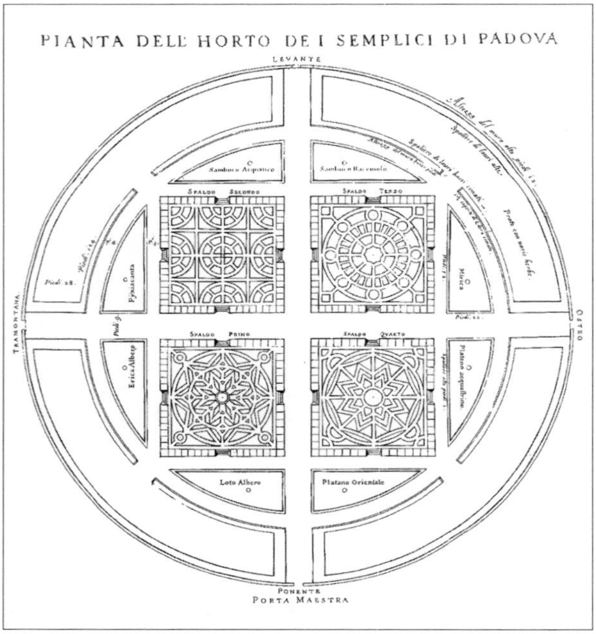
PIANTA DELL' HORTO DE I SEMPLICI DI PADOVA
LEVANTE
TRAMONTANA
OSTRO
SPALDO SECONDO
SPALDO TERZO
SPALDO PRIMO
SPALDO QUARTO
Loto Albero
Platano Orientale
PONENTE
PORTA MAESTRA

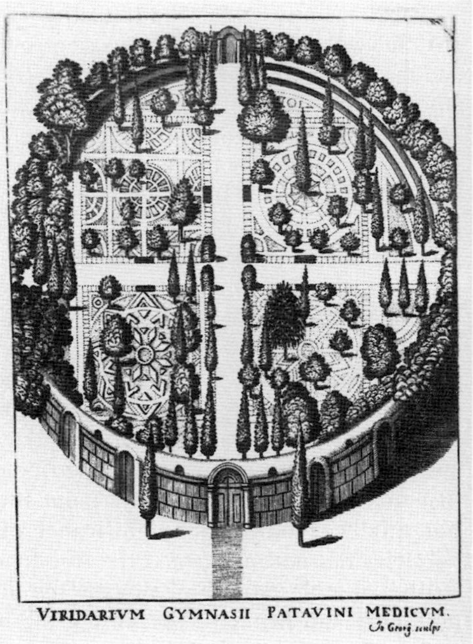
VIRIDARIVM GYMNASII PATAVINI MEDICVM.

other words, pharmacology in the strict sense of the word. It was not long, however, before the need was realized for practical demonstrations of the subject taught. In 1543, realizing the difficulty of providing a profitable and effective teaching without physically showing the simples in question, with the support of some of the other teachers of medicine, especially Da Monte, and encouraged by his own pupils who appreciated his practical approach, Bonafede made known to the *Riformatori* of the Studium the need to found a public garden where medicinal plants could be grown, especially those plants found in the area under Venetian domination. He also proposed that the garden should have annexed to it a model pharmacy, which by means of practical comparisons would ensure an exact knowledge and an authentication of the medicinal products. On 29th June, 1545 it was decided to make a piece of land available and to build the public Garden of simples. The organization of the new garden was so rapid that in 1546 it could already be visited with interest, and a few years later Conrad Gessner was able to say that he had never seen a garden so rich in plants and so orderly. This is the Botanical Garden of Padua, which has reached us in its original guise and in its original place, a precious document of the demonstrative method. The trade links with the East, flourishing in Venice, allowed exotic plants to be brought which would otherwise have been inaccessible, either alive or as seed, which were thus made available to scholars. When the work was complete, in 1546, the running of the garden was entrusted to Luigi Squalermo, known as Anguillara (c. 1512-1570). After Bonafede, the chair *ad Lectura simplicium* was given to Falloppia, who held it from 1551 to 1563. From the establishment of the garden up until 1564 its prefect was always merely its director and guardian: in 1564 Melchiorre Guilandino (Wieland, c. 1520-1589), prefect of the garden, was charged with "lecturing, explaining, and showing in the same garden the simples": thus there arose the chair *ad Ostensionem simplicium*, true teaching of botany and pharmacognosis, while the lecturer on simples continued to deal with medical botany. The foundation of the Botanical Garden of Padua was an event of extraordinary importance in the history of modern science for the introduction of the demonstrative method into pharmacognosis and botany too.

The original plan of the Botanical Garden, Padua, da L'Horto dei semplici di Padova (*Venice 1591*)

The Botanical Garden of Padua, from Tomasini's Gymnasium Patavinum

The entrance to the Botanical Garden of Padua, from Tomasini's Gymnasium Patavinum

3. *The Doctrine of Contagion.*

Among the glories of the Padua Studium we must also number Girolamo Fracastoro of Verona (1478-1553), who was a student there, a friend, and fellow student of Nicholas Copernicus, with whom he also shared a passion for astronomy. He was the pupil of masters such as the anatomist, physician, and philosopher Alessandro Achillini, Alessandro Benedetti, Pietro Pomponazzi, Pietro Trapolin, and Girolamo Della Torre († 1506), with whose son, Marcantonio (1481-1511), believed to be the master of Leonardo, he shared a great friendship. In the Padua Studium

Girolamo Fracastoro

Girolamo Fracastoro, Syphilis sive morbus gallicus (*Verona 1530*). *Frontispiece*

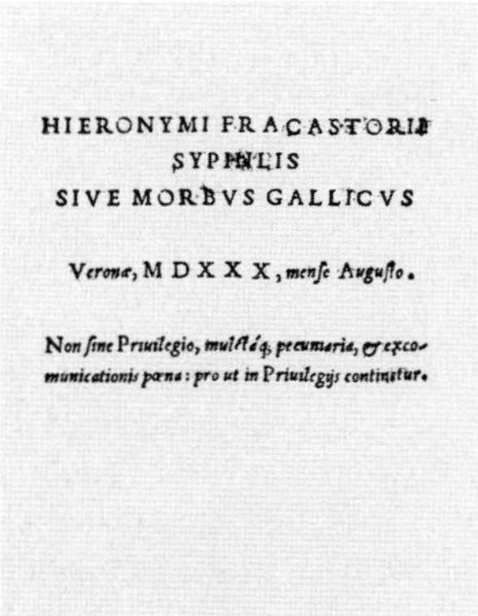
HIERONYMI FRACASTORII
SYPHILIS
SIVE MORBVS GALLICVS

Veronæ, M D X X X, mense Augusto.

Non sine Priuilegio, mulctáq; pecuniaria, et excommunicationis pœna: pro ut in Priuilegijs continetur.

Fracastoro was also lecturer in logic for a short period of time (1502), and then "conciliarius anatomicus". An encyclopaedic scientist, he was above all a physician, and it is in medicine that he left conspicuous footprints. It was his poem in hexameters, *Syphilis sive morbus gallicus* (Verona 1530), defined as the most beautiful Latin poem of the Renaissance, which earned him wide popularity. The term 'syphilis' derives from the name of the shepherd Syphilus, the hero of Fracastoro's poem, a term subsequently adopted universally to indicate the luetic infection, to which Fracastoro made an important nosological contribution. But *De morbo gallico* contains, in embryonic form, and sometimes even clearly developed, many of the theories, which were to lead Fracastoro to the formulation of his doctrine of contagions. In his three books, *De contagione et contagiosis morbis et curatione* (1546), he deals with the problem of the origin of epidemic illnesses, the essence, and the mechanism of contagion, establishing the bases of modern epidemiology and pathology. For Fracastoro contagion is "a specific infection which passes from one subject to another" and the principles of contagion are the "seminaria", that is to say something alive and viable which can multiply itself and penetrate into the body through definite gateways and in different ways. Within the complex nosology of contagious fevers, Fracastoro differentiated the true plague from other pestilential fevers, describing moreover for the first time exanthematous typhus, up until then confused with the plague and typhoid fever, also describing in detail the characteristics and the importance of its exanthema. No less clear is Fracastoro's opinion on the contagion of some illnesses, such as tuberculosis.

4. *Medicine and Surgery*

In the field of medicine we can recall a number of extremely renowned masters who contributed to spread the fame of the Padua Studium throughout Europe. In the first half of the sixteenth century, standing out above them all is Giovan Battista Da Monte of Verona (*Montanus*, 1489-1551), a lively mind, skilled not only in medicine, but also in philosophy, literature, botany, chemistry, and archaeology, who in 1539 was officially entrusted with the first chair of 'ordinary' practical medicine *in paritate loci* with Francesco Frigimelica (1490-1558); in 1543 he moved from there to the chair of 'ordinary' theoretical medicine, which he held until his death. Humanist physician and philologist, Da Monte was an extremely effective teacher, but he published very few works, among which a Latin translation of part of Aetius of Amida's medical oeuvre (1534). The numerous other works which bear his name are in reality lessons and consultations collected, not always faithfully, and re-elaborated, by his pupils. Prudent in his therapy, Da Monte felt the need for a more rational therapeutics and for this reason we have already seen him directly involved in manifesting his support to the *Riformatori* of the Studium for the establishment of a public garden.

A pupil of Da Monte, Bassiano Landi of Piacenza († 1562) taught theoretical medicine from 1545 until 1562, the year in which he was assassinated. A radical Alexandrist, Landi was the author of various medical works, among which the anatomical compendium *De humana historia*, published in Basle in 1542 by Oporino, which is a significant example of the convergence of interests at once philological, practical, and speculative, characteristic of pre-Vesalian anatomists. The Venetian Vittore Trincavelli (1496-1563) was also a radical Alexandrist; he was a practitioner of great renown, succeeding Da Monte to the chair of 'ordinary' practical medicine in 1551, and he produced the Venetian edition of the Greek text of Alexander of Aphrodisia's *De anima* (1534).

In the second half of the sixteenth century, the figure of greatest importance was Girolamo Mercuriale of Forlì (1530-1606). He obtained his degree in Padua in 1555, and held the first chair of 'ordinary' practical medicine from 1569 to 1587, subsequently moving first to Bologna and then to Pisa. A humanist physician and philologist with a profound knowledge of Latin and Greek and ancient medical literature, he published the Greek text of the works of Hippocrates with a Latin translation, collated against the manuscripts (1588), studied the authenticity of Hippocrates' writings (1583), and also published a critical interpretation of numerous obscure or controversial passages in the Greek and Latin medical writers (1570). His six books, *De arte gymnastica* (1569), the fruit of almost seven years of research in the museums and libraries of Rome, is his most famous and original work, through which he brought ancient gymnastics back to life: true precursor of modern physical therapy, he showed the usefulness of gymnastics as a means of therapy, in particular in the rehabilitation of the paralysed. Particularly worthy of appreciation is his effort to organize in an organic form the whole of medical knowledge according to the apparatus or system affected, both for didactic and practical purposes, which therefore makes him the precursor of modern medical specialization. When he was still a student he published the little work *Nomothelasmus, seu ratio lactandi infantes* (1552), the oldest treatise on breastfeeding we possess; this work and the treatise in three books, *De morbis puerorum* (1583), rich in precise and acute observations, are the starting point of modern paediatrics.

That the fervour for the demonstrative method, characteristic of the Padua Studium in the sixteenth century, included an awareness of the need to teach at the patient's bed is demonstrated by the fact that in the years 1577-78 Marco Oddi (1526-1591), chief physician of the Hospital of San Francesco and then teacher of 'extraordinary' medicine, and Albertino Bottoni († 1596), who held the first chair of 'extraordinary' practical medicine, took their students to the hospital to visit the sick, one to the male and the other to the female, reading to the students on the illnesses they observed, even authorized that "when it was necessary to show the place where these originated, that they should open the corpses". These practical exercises, highly appreciated by the students, were held,

Girolamo Mercuriale

A table from the De arte gymnastica *(Venezia 1569) by Girolamo Mercuriale*

Prospero Alpini. Portrait by Leandro da Ponte, known as 'il Bassano'*, 1586 (Stuttgart, Staatsgalerie)*

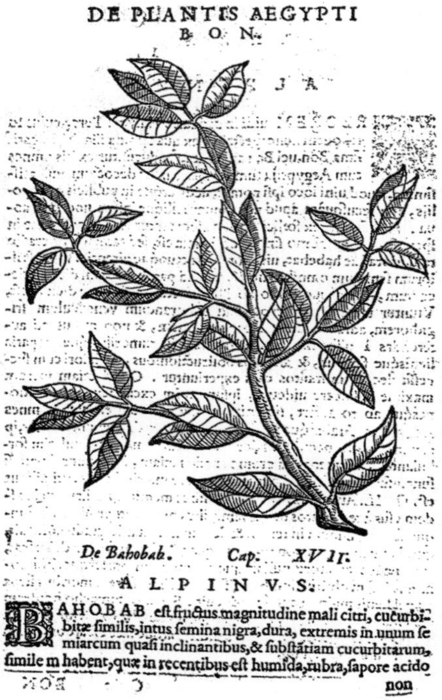

DE PLANTIS AEGYPTI
BON.

De Bahobab. Cap. XVII.
ALPINVS.

BAHOBAB est fructus magnitudine mali citri, cucurbitæ similis, intus semina nigra, dura, extremis in unum se miarcum quasi inclinantibus, & substātiam cucurbitarum, simile m habent, quæ in recentibus est humida, rubra, sapore acido non

The coffee plant, from Prospero Alpini, De plantis Aegypti *(Venice 1592)*

albeit not on a regular basis, at least as long as Oddi and Bottoni were alive. In 1601 a new chair was established, *ad secundam fen primi Canonis Avicennae*, entrusted to Antonio Negri († 1626), later called *de pulsibus et urinis*, which could be defined as semeiotic: the teaching was only theoretical, however, and only in 1619 did Negri offer to carry out practical exercises on the pulses and the urine in the hospital. With an uneven fortune, the chair survived until 1748, the year in which it was suppressed.

After a long vacancy, in 1594 the lectureship on simples was entrusted to Prospero Alpini of Marostica (1553-1616), who in 1603 also took on the charges of prefect of the Garden and the showing of the simples, following the death of Giacomo Antonio Cortuso. Under the influence of Guilandino and the naturalistic exploration which the latter had undertaken in far-off lands, Alpini travelled in Egypt from 1580 to 1584: his observations are contained in numerous works, some of them posthumous, *De medicina Aegyptiorum* (1591), *De plantis Aegypti* (1592), *De plantis exoticis* (1629), and *Rerum Aegyptiarum libri IV* (1735). In *De plantis Aegypti* he described and drew for the first time the coffee plant (*Coffea arabica* L.), stressing the therapeutic uses of the drink obtained from the toasted seeds. Alpini was also a physician of great worth and in 1601 he published a work on prognosis entitled *De praesagienda vita et morte aegrotantium libri septem*, destined for great success. The *De praesagienda* is a clinical, semeiological work, based on ancient Hippocratic thought, enriched and verified by his own personal observations. The treatise *De medicina methodica* (1611), on the other hand, is an acute attempt to reawaken the interest of physicians in the doctrine of ancient Greek 'Methodists' and therefore in solidist thought. Under his direction, the Padua Botanical Garden became an important centre of study and research, above all concerning the diffusion and cultivation of many exotic species. Alpini was in correspondence with many Italian and foreign scholars, with whom he swapped plants and seeds. A scholar of Italian and exotic flora, in particular that of Egypt and Crete, his research was always aimed at attaining a knowledge of the pharmacological properties of plants, and hence with the purpose of possible therapeutical uses. A careful observer of natural phenomena, he was a precursor of the idea of the sexual reproduction of plants with his observations (1592) on the fertilization of female palms and dates by a "powder" of male inflorescence. His name is remembered even today in the *Alpinia* genus.

The renaissance of anatomical studies and the improved knowledge of the human body, which resulted from it, were reflected in the first place in surgery, favouring its progress. Many of the anatomists of the sixteenth and seventeenth centuries eminently practised and taught surgery. Benedetti was an excellent surgeon, one of the firsts to deal with battle surgery, a forerunner in lithotripsy and rhinoplasty (1502). Vesalius, Colombo, and Falloppia were also all excellent surgeons, as well as anatomists, even though their surgical work was overshadowed by their anatomical activity. Fabricius also had vast surgical experience, and his surgical works had a notable diffusion.

THE SEVENTEENTH CENTURY

The anatomical research of the sixteenth century had demonstrated the insufficiency of Galen's anatomy, previously taken as dogma, and substituted the ancient knowledge with newly acquired, much more precise, information on the structure of the human body. In the seventeenth century, on the other hand, we see an assertion of experimental anatomical research, aimed above all at understanding the function of the organs, thus leading to a radical revision of Galen's physiology too. The attention that Fabricius and Casseri had paid to the organs of sense and phonation highlights the new approach which was asserting itself in the seventeenth century, also influenced by the dynamism which was characteristic of the Baroque period. Like the artist, the Baroque physician no longer considered man's eye, but rather his gaze, that is to say, he no longer limited himself to examining the parts of the body statically, but turned his attention to its movement and its functioning. He is now no longer content to know how the organs of the human body are constituted, but wants to know how they work: from descriptive anatomy we thus move on to "animated"

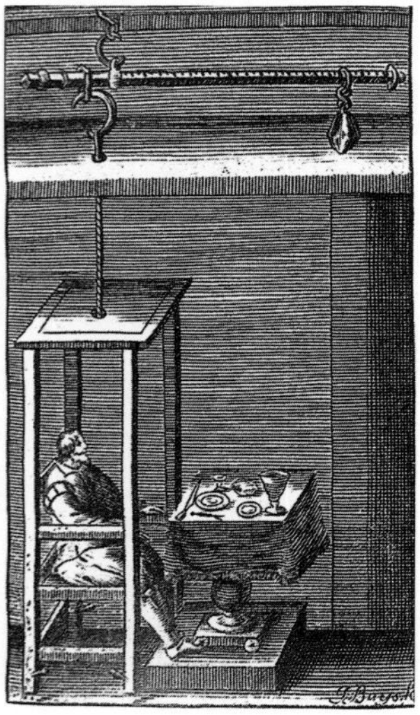

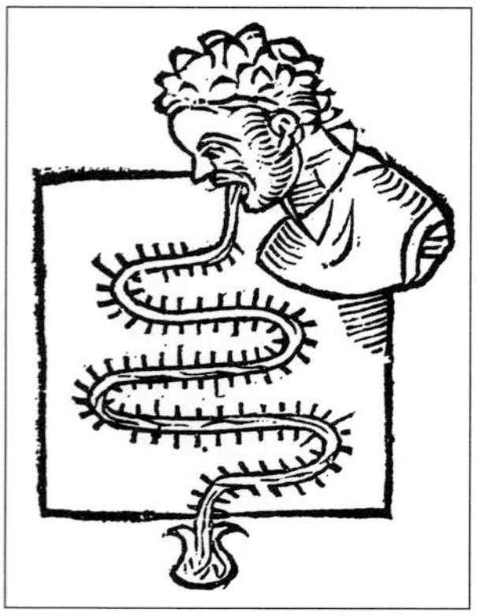

or functional anatomy, that is to say physiology. Up until the seventeenth century, however, biological experimentation had had an exclusively qualitative character, and hence the introduction of the criterion of quantity is of fundamental importance.

1. *Experimental Medicine*

Galileo Galilei (1564-1642), professor of mathematics at the Padua Studium from 1592 to 1610 can be credited for having introduced the modern conception of science, not so much for his particular scientific discoveries, which are in themselves also expressions of a new methodological approach, as for having proposed and practised a new scientific method, which set the science of nature on a course so as to render it possible to advance little by little in collaboration, obtaining results which were still partial and still temporary, but verifiable, able to be corrected and added to one another according to a reliable procedure. The fundamental procedure of scientific research for Galileo was measurement. For him, mathematics was a discipline indissolubily linked to the study of natural phenomena, which must be a quantitative study obtained by means of measuring them as precisely as possible. Any theoretical consideration regarding nature was fruitless for Galileo, who gave up the study of the metaphysical essence of things. Nature, he wrote in a famous passage from the *Assayer* (1623), is like an "enormous book which is continually open in front of our eyes [...] but it cannot be understood if we do not first learn to understand its language, and to recognize the characters in which it is written. It is written in mathematical language and its characters are triangles, circles, and other geometrical shapes, without which means it is impossible for humans to understand its speech; without these were are simply wandering in vain through an obscure labyrinth". In other words, what are objectively inherent in nature are mathematical ratios by which natural phenomena are regulated. The concept of quantity, expressed by figures and elaborated by means of mathematical procedures, has an essential importance in all of the experiments carried out by Galileo, who applied this notion to biology, albeit marginally, studying the mechanism of the movements of animals, or considering the influence that the size of animals and their limbs and organs had on their functioning and on their anatomical structure.

Galileo's influence on the development of biological inquiry and therefore on medicine on an experimental basis was decisive. The first to apply principles of measurement to biology was Santorio Santorio of Capodistria (1561-1636), who held the first rank of 'ordinary' theoretical medicine in the Padua Studium from 1611 to 1624. By using in reverse Galileo's stratagem of measuring small intervals of time by means of his own pulse, as he did in his experiments on the falling of weights and in his observations on the isochronism of small oscillations of the pendulum, Santorio thought out and built (1602) the *pulsilogio*, an instrument for observing "with mathematical certainty" the frequency and the variations in the rhythm of the pulse. In this period the study of the pulse consisted of the most minute recording of its "quality", but did not include the measurement of its frequency. The *pulsilogio* consisted of a weight suspended on a wire and oscillating like a pendulum next to a graduated scale: the length of the wire could be altered so that the frequency of the oscillations exactly coincided with that of the pulse, thus reading the length of the wire on the scale. Of greater renown were his quantitative experiments on metabolism and his measurements of body temperature. With a special balance he systematically observed the daily variations in his own body weight, thus demonstrating the existence of imperceptible transpiration (*perspiratio insensibilis*), that is to say that much of the body's excretion takes place invisibly through the skin and the lungs. In order to evaluate quantitatively the factors, which influence imperceptible transpiration, Santorio introduced a series of instruments of measurement: the thermometer, the hygrometer, and the anemometer, necessary to determine the relationship between imperceptible transpiration and humidity or temperature. The thermometer which Santorio built had its own scale, and thus represented a certain progress with respect to Galileo's thermoscope (in relation to which Santorio conducted independent research); with it Santorio systematically measured body temperature in health and in sickness. His hygrometer consisted of a lute string or a thick piece of hemp attached at both ends to two nails with a lead weight in the centre, able to slide in correspondence to a graduated scale. The fact that the works in which the thermometer and the hygrometer are described are commentaries on Galen's *Art of Medicine* (1612) and Avicenna's *Canon* (1625) demonstrates well the transitional nature of the science of the period. With his experiments, therefore, Santorio initiated the modern study of metabolism. His research on the thermometer and the *pulsilogio* were conducted independently from Galileo: they are, rather, an expression of the "fullness" of the times, even though it is difficult to consider as a mere historical coincidence the fact that he was a contemporary of Galileo and knew him personally.

It was the same desire to consider the quantitative aspects of vital phenomena which made William Harvey (1578-1657) re-examine Galen's opinion on the movement of the blood, thus substituting the concept of flux and reflux with that of circulation. It was in Padua, where he stayed from the autumn of 1599 to 1602 and where he obtained his degree on 25th April, 1602, that Harvey acquired the doctrinal and experimental instruments which allowed him to demonstrate the circulation of the blood, by far the most important event in the entire history of physiology.

Harvey drew inspiration from the concepts of Aristotle, of whom he considered himself a faithful disciple and whom he quotes around thirty times in his *De motu cordis*, regarding the themes of cardiocentrism and circular movement. For Aristotle the heart is the principle of movement and sensation, source of innate heat, origin of the veins, and point of confluence of all the blood. More than an improbable, though tempting, pres-

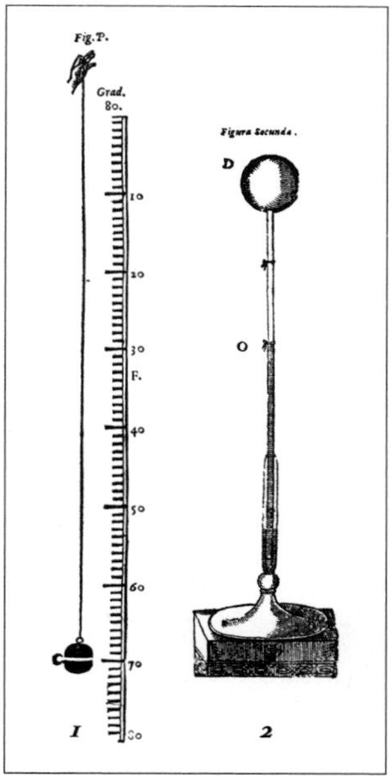

Santorio's 'pulsilogio' (1) and thermometer (2)

Opposite:

Santorio Santorio

The chair-balance designed by Santorio for his experiments on 'perspiratio insensibilis' (Santorio Santorio, De statica medicina, *Venice 1614)*

One of Santorio's clinical thermometers

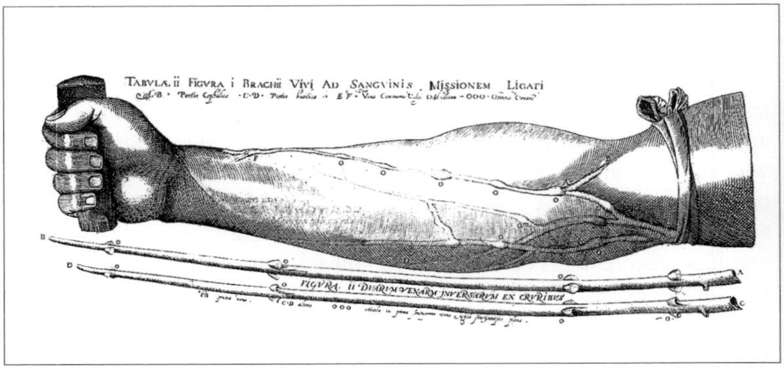

From table II of the De venarum ostiolis *(Padua 1603) by Fabricius ab Acquapendente.*
In the arm ready to be bled, the valves (o o o) appear as isolated swellings along the lines of the turgid veins. Below, two veins of the legs have been isolated and turned inside out better to emphasize the valvular hollows (those of the vein above have also been filled with wads of cotton)

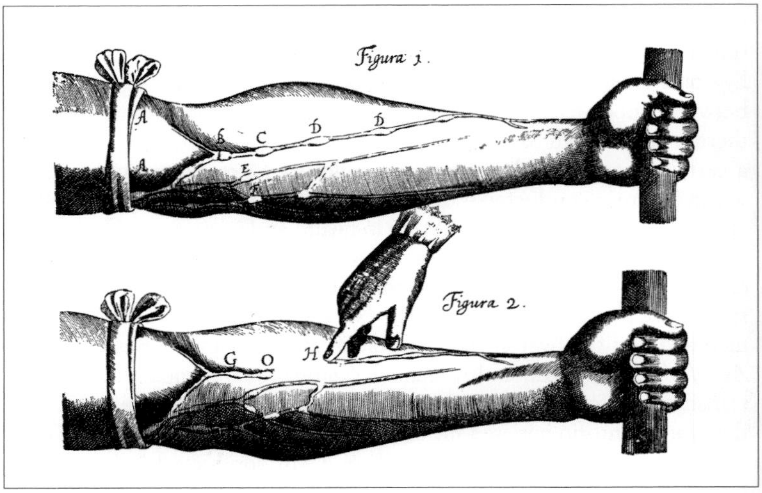

Figures 1 and 2 of the De motu cordis *(Frankfurt am M. 1628) by William Harvey. Like the other two figures which represent the entirety of the work's illustration, these are taken from the first figure of table II of Fabricius'* De venarum ostiolis, *reproduced in an inverted form for the convenience of the engraver. Harvey's four figures represent the experiments squeezing and digitally pressing the veins which he presented in favour of the centripetal flow of venous blood*

ence of Harvey at Galileo's public or private lessons, it is obvious to think of the influence which the Paduan environment might have had on him, so saturated as it was in Aristotelianism, and in particular the Aristotelian curriculum of the chairs of 'ordinary' and 'extraordinary' philosophy, such as the course *De principatu cordis ex Aristotelis sententia contra Galenum*, held by Cesare Cremonimi (1550-1631). Neither can we exclude, moreover, the productive resonance in Harvey of other Paduan lessons, such as those given by Fabricius on local movement, or those by Eustachio Rudio († 1611) who at the time dealt with the structure and the functions of the heart and the arteries from his position on the first chair of 'ordinary' practical medicine. Fabricius's *De venarum ostiolis* (1603) had a decisive effect on Harvey, who used some of its figures, basing many of his arguments in favour of the circulation of the blood on the action of the valves of the veins. We have said that Fabricius did not understand the true function of the valves of the veins, which he interpreted functionally in a way

Opposite:

William Harvey. Portrait by Cornelius Janssen (London, Royal College of Physicians)

William Harvey, Exercitatio anatomica de motu cordis et sanguinis in animalibus. *Frontispiece*

The coat of arms of Harvey in the ancient Courtyard of the University of Padua (Padua, Palazzo del Bo)

that integrated them into the Galenic system. Harvey, on the other hand, drew an important proof for the centripetal flow of venous blood from his experiments squeezing and digitally pressing the veins of the forearm.

The decisive point of Harvey's work, however, is another. He arrived at the discovery of the circulation of the blood by tackling the problem of haemodynamics in rigorously quantitative terms. The essential part of his demonstration lies precisely in his application of Galileo's principle of measurement: the mass of blood which passes through the heart or a large vessel in a unit of time is so great that there must be the periodical return of the same substance. In chapter IX of the renowned *Exercitatio anatomica de motu cordis et sanguinis in animalibus* (1628), he calculated that the quantity of blood driven by the heart into the aorta in half an hour is much greater than the total quantity of blood found in the organism: it is thus necessary to admit that it is the same blood which, with a circular movement, returns to the aorta. The "vasa per capillamenta resoluta", the capillaries, that is, hypothesized by Andrea Cesalpino (c. 1524-1602), are necessarily admitted by Harvey even though he did not have a microscope, because the trials he carried out were conducted with mathematical criteria and their existence was thus guaranteed. The existence of capillaries was later to be demonstrated in frog lungs by Malpighi in 1661.

EXERCITATIO
ANATOMICA DE
MOTV CORDIS ET SANGVINIS IN ANIMALIBVS,
GVILIELMI HARVEI ANGLI,
Medici Regii, & Professoris Anatomiæ in Collegio Medicorum Londinensi.
FRANCOFVRTI,
Sumptibus GVILIELMI FITZERI.
ANNO M. DC. XXVIII.

2. *Iatro-mechanics*

Galileo's message and the demonstrations by Santorio and Harvey imparted a great impulse to the attempt to explain the functions of the animal body on exclusively mechanical bases. Thus *iatro-mechanics* was initiated, also called *iatro-mathematics* or *iatro-physics*, whose supporters attempted to explain all vital phenomena with a series of external or internal movements of the organism, subject to the laws of mechanics. The father of iatro-mechanics was the mathematician and physicist Giovanni Alfonso Borelli (1608-1679), pupil of Benedetto Castelli (1577-1643), in turn a direct pupil of Galileo, who in his *De motu animalium*, published posthumously in 1680-81, applied the laws of mechanics to the functions of the living organism.

Also contributing greatly to the assertion of iatro-mechanics was the introduction of the microscope in biological research. Optical enlargement had its first applications in the microscopic field thanks – yet again – to Galileo, thus opening up the scope of sensible experience. Indeed, already in Padua in 1610, Galileo had applied the *occhiale*, adapted to enlargement at close range, to microscopic observation, thus inaugurating microscopic biology. Microscopic examination of the minute structures of the animal body, as well as contributing to completing in detail the diagram of the animal machine, demonstrated an unexpected extreme complexity of living matter as it appeared under the microscope, thus contributing greatly to the seventeenth-century revival of atomism. The discovery in the animal organism of previously unknown machines was a fundamental element in the construction of a new system of rational, in the place of Hipporatic-Galenic, medicine. According to the programme of iatro-mechanics, it was by now a question of studying in greater depth the structure and the functioning of organic machines and then of evaluating their anatomical and functional alterations in order to arrive at a pathogenic interpretation, leaving to clinical research the task of recognizing these alterations in the patient and of finding the means suitable for repairing them. It was a programme then too advanced with respect to the relatively few acquisitions made on the experimental level: this explains how the systems of iatro-mechanics, still too aprioristic, were destined for failure from the point of view of practical medicine, thus promoting the rebirth of empirical medicine.

No wonder that the Padua Studium, which had been one of the first to have received the message of the new experimental philosophy, reserved a particularly warm welcome for iatro-mechanics, also promoted by the vision of René Descartes (1596-1650), who, in his posthumous work *De homine* (1662) maintained that the organism is none other than an ingeniously built machine. Cartesianism had been introduced to the Padua Studium by Michelangelo Fardella (1650-1718), a former pupil of Borelli, teacher in the first rank of 'ordinary' philosophy, who played an important role in opening up the Padua Studium to modern European currents of thought. A vigorous iatro-mechanic was Francesco Spoleti († 1712), professor of 'ordinary' practical medicine from 1693, after having been professor of philosophy from 1689, who had to abandon his chair in 1707 for reasons of health. Particularly close to Leibniz, in 1686 he had published a dissertation *De secretione bilis in hepate*, in which he defended the mechanical interpretation of secretion.

But the founder of the iatro-mechanical approach of the Padua Studium was Domenico Guglielmini (1655-1710), a former pupil of Malpighi and an authoritative representative of the new science and of rational medicine in particular. In 1698 the Venetian Republic to the Padua chair of mathematics had called him, but in 1702 he was transferred to the first rank of 'ordinary' theoretical medicine. The fame of this Bolognese scientist in the field of fluvial hydraulics had undoubtedly been the decisive factor which led the *Riformatori* of the Studium to elect him, a fame which was obviously not unconnected to the scientific intelligence which he was attributed with in the *République des Lettres* throughout the whole of Europe. Nevertheless, Guglielmini considered his treatise *Della natura de' fiumi* (1697) to be his conclusive work in the field of hydraulics, and he had long planned to devote himself to "mechanical medicine", taking advantage of the knowledge he had acquired on the movement of fluids. In 1701 in the meantime he published the "exercitatio physico-medica" *De sanguinis natura et constitutione*, where some of the principal laws governing the movement of water are applied to the movement of blood. In the following year he inaugurated his new teaching with an expressively

Frontispiece of the inaugural lecture held by Guglielmini in 1702

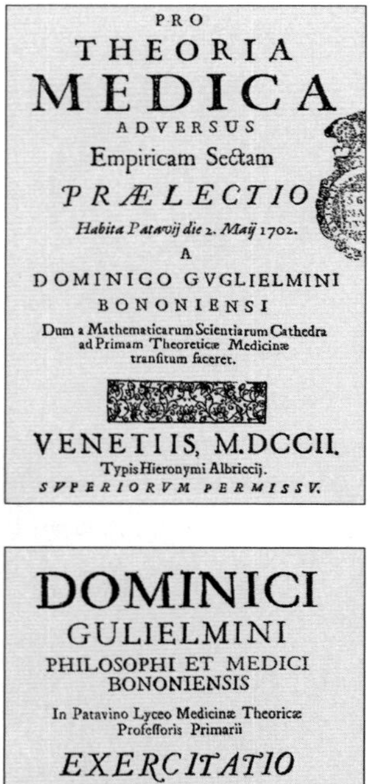
PRO
THEORIA
MEDICA
ADVERSUS
Empiricam Sectam
PRÆLECTIO
Habita Patavij die 2. Maij 1702.
A
DOMINICO GVGLIELMINI
BONONIENSI
Dum a Mathematicarum Scientiarum Cathedra ad Primam Theoreticæ Medicinæ transitum faceret.
VENETIIS, M.DCCII.
Typis Hieronymi Albriccij.
SVPERIORVM PERMISSV.

Domenico Guglielmini, Exercitatio de idearum vitiis correctione et usu (*Padua 1707*). *Frontispiece*

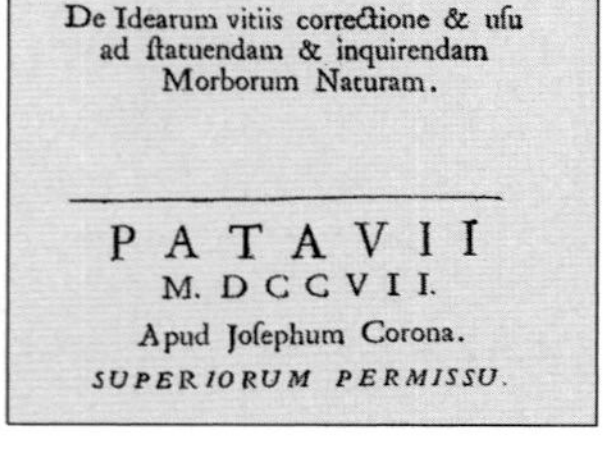
DOMINICI
GULIELMINI
PHILOSOPHI ET MEDICI
BONONIENSIS
In Patavino Lyceo Medicinæ Theoricæ Professoris Primarii
EXERCITATIO
De Idearum vitiis correctione & usu ad statuendam & inquirendam Morborum Naturam.
PATAVII
M. DCCVII.
Apud Josephum Corona.
SUPERIORUM PERMISSU.

entitled lecture, *Pro theoria medica adversus empiricam sectam*, a manifesto of rational medicine and at the same time an impassioned profession of faith in Malpighi. In his subsequent physico-chemical and medical works, however, Guglielmini maintained it necessary, as did Malpighi, to have recourse to chemistry too in setting out the bases of rational medicine. To establish a rational foundation for medicine – he maintains in his "physico-medico-mechanical" dissertation *De salibus* (1705) – it is necessary to investigate the elementary constituents of the body, of medicines, and in general of everything that composes or alters solid and fluid parts. Greatly interested in anatomy, in his *Exercitatio de idearum vitiis correctione et usu ad statuendam et inquirendam morborum naturam* (1707), he pauses at length over the importance of the dissection of corpses in the search for the causes of illness, a programme which was to be carried out in Morgagni's *De sedibus*. Guglielmini was linked to Morgagni in his final years by a great friendship, despite their difference in age: to him he "confided his ingenious physico-mathematical meditations", and a significant testimony of this bond is the precise and affectionate biography that Morgagni dedicated to him and the edition he prepared of Guglielmini's *Opera omnia* (1719).

Domenico Guglielmini

The last teacher of the Padua Studium to align himself decisively in favour of radical iatro-mechanical positions was to be Giambattista Mazini of Brescia (1677-1743), the author of numerous works, among which a *Mechanices morborum* (1723-25) which in 1726 earned him the second rank of 'ordinary' practical medicine, which he occupied until his death.

3. *Anatomy and Medicine*

Paduan anatomy of the seventeenth century did not follow the path of comparative anatomical research, but devoted itself to descriptive human anatomy, refining dissectorial investigation and consequently perfecting the descriptive results to the undoubted benefit of surgical practice. The name of Adriaan van den Spieghel of Brussels (*Spigelius*, 1578-1625), Casseri's successor to the chair of surgery and then Fabricius' to the chair of anatomy (1619), is linked to the caudate lobe of the liver, or *Spigelian lobe*, and to the *Spigelian semilunar line* of the transversal muscle of the abdomen. Johann Wesling of Minden (1598-1649) was officially entrusted with the Padua chair of anatomy in 1632, and he also held the lectureship and the showing of the simples; he was the author of a famous manual *Syntagma anatomicum* (1641) which came out in numerous editions and translations, in the second edition of which (1647) we find depicted for the first time the chyliferous vessels in man. The technique of dry anatomical preparations then in use in Padua dates back to the preparatory phase of the illustrations for the second edition of the work. Such preparations were obtained by isolating the anatomical structures from the surrounding organs and tissues and fixing them with pins to a table of fir-wood until

Adriaan van den Spieghel, Opera quae extant omnia *(Amsterdam 1645). Frontispiece*

Johann Wesling. Padua, Palazzo del Bo, hall of the Faculty of Medicine and Surgery

they became completely dry; once dry, they were covered by a coat of copal-gum. This type of preparation was not only used for practical anatomical demonstrations to students, but also to provide the material for the artists who prepared the illustrations for the treatises on anatomy. Two contemporary series of dry anatomical preparations from the school of Wesling are preserved at the Royal College of Surgeons and the Royal College of Physicians in London. Close to the chair of anatomy, though not officially employed, as we would now say, we find Johann Georg Wirsung of Augsburg (1589-1643), expert physician and anatomist who established himself in Padua after his degree and who in March, 1642 in Padua carried out the memorable discovery of the pancreatic duct, the starting point of the radical renewal which the doctrine of secretions was to undergo in the space of a few years. Wirsung's adventurous life ended tragically in Padua; besides his mortal remains, Padua still holds the *unicum* constituted by the original bronze table on which he presented his discovery, which after various vicissitudes has reached us and which is now preserved in the Palazzo del Bo.

In the second half of the seventeenth century, Paduan anatomy underwent a progressive decline, even though a number of valid scholars were not lacking. After the death of Wesling, the chair of anatomy was filled by the Venetian Antonio Molinetti († 1675), author of esteemed studies on the sense organs. He was succeed by Giacomo Pighi of Verona (1647-1682), a highly promising young anatomist who died prematurely, known and esteemed by Malpighi. In 1683 the first rank of anatomy was entrusted to Domenico Marchetti (1626-1688), known for having used intravascular injections with success in anatomical research. Leale Leali of Verona († 1726) was the author of valued research on the anatomy of the male

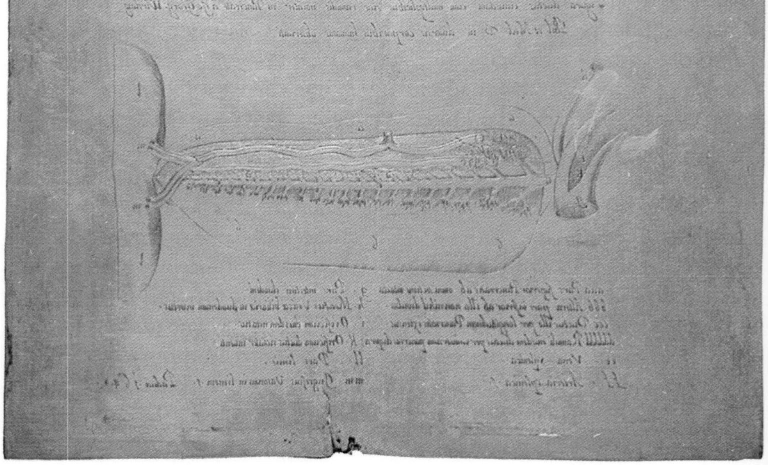

Original copper from the table depicting the pancreas with Wirsung's duct (1642). Padua, Palazzo del Bo

genital organs (1686), and he later occupied the second rank of 'extraordinary' practical medicine. On the death of Marchetti, Michelangelo Molinetti (1651-1714), the son of Antonio, rose to the first rank of anatomy: living on the fame of his father's work, he has left no trace of himself in the history of anatomy. There is no doubt that after Antonio Molinetti anatomy in Padua went into a period of eclipse, in which "anatome Patavina adeo celebris, pene sopita periit, quoad a Morgagno suscitata revixit", as Haller wrote, shrewdly analysing the causes of such a decline, soon to be arrested with the appointment of Morgagni to the first rank of anatomy.

A colleague and friend of Galileo, with whom he was also involved in several controversies, such as the famous case of the whiteness of the moon, was Fortunio Liceti of Rapallo (1577-1657). It was to Liceti that Galileo, in the final years of his life and by now blind, dictated, on 23rd June, 1640, the letter which contains the famous phrase: "Not without envy do I hear of your return to Padua, where I spent the best eighteen years of my entire life. Enjoy that freedom, and the many friendships which you have made there and in the noble city of Venice". Initially a teacher of philosophy in Padua and Bologna, in 1645 Liceti returned to the Padua Studium to the first rank of 'ordinary' theoretical medicine. A multi-faceted, versatile spirit, tireless polygraph, he has long had to bear the label of intransigent and stubborn champion of peripateticism. In the strictly medical field, Liceti was the author of a famous treatise *De monstrorum causis, natura et differentiis*, which came out for the first time in Padua in 1616, and which makes an important contribution to scientific teratology, classifying monstrosities for the first time according to morphological and not causal criteria, as had been the case in previous classifications.

The controversy between empirical and rational medicine was alive in Padua too, even though it never reached the levels of bitterness experienced in Bologna. Among Paduan teachers there also militated traditionalist physicians and hardened supporters of empirical medicine, such as Francesco Alfonso Donnoli (1636-1724), who held the first rank of 'extraordinary' theoretical medicine, and who in 1705 had entered the fray between empiricists and 'rationals' with his *De bello civili medico*, to which Guglielmini had replied with a little pseudonymous work. Alessandro Knips Macoppe (1662-1744) was a traditionalist physician who in 1716 succeeded Morgagni to the second rank of 'ordinary' theoretical medicine, inaugurated his teaching with a lecture entitled *Pro empirica secta adversus theoriam medicam*, which was in deliberate opposition to that which Guglielmini had held in 1702. In 1693 Knips Macoppe had created a notable sensation when he clinically diagnosed the fatal illness of Charles Patin (1633-1693), professor of 'extraordinary' practical medicine in the first rank, as a "polyp of the aorta", a diagnosis confirmed by autopsy: he rushed to publish the letter Patin had sent him while still alive together with the post mortem report, which depicts the "polyp" which had

Fortunio Liceti

formed inside an aneurysm of the aortic arch. Patin, a numismatist and an erudite as well as a physician, who had taught in Padua from 1676 to 1693, was the son of Guy Patin (1601-1672), who considered the circulation of the blood "paradoxale, impossible, absurde et dangereuse" and who in 1685 had dedicated his inaugural lecture to the attempt to demonstrate *Circulationem sanguinis a veteribus cognitam fuisse.* Finally, well known as one of the last to oppose the circulation of the blood was Omobono Pisoni of Cremona (1664-1748), teacher of 'extraordinary' practical medicine from 1698 until his death.

THE EIGHTEENTH CENTURY

In the early eighteenth century the official curricula of the most important medical subjects were still those established by the ancient statutes of the 'university' of arts students. In reality, the effective content of the teaching was greatly conditioned by the scientific personality of the teacher, who could limit himself to a slavish explanation of the "auctoritates", but who was also free to take them as the starting point for a modern and unprejudiced treatment, as is demonstrated by the teaching of Vallisneri for practical and Morgagni for theoretical medicine.

The teaching of medicine was radically reformed in the second half of the eighteenth century. New chairs were established which reflected not only the latest scientific approaches, such as that of natural history, physics, and chemistry, but also the emerging clinical needs, such as the chairs of obstetrics, paediatrics, oculistics, and industrial medicine. The new curriculum of theoretical medicine consisted of the alternating annual

The thermal baths of Abano, from Domenico Vandelli, Tractatus de thermis agri patavini *(Padua 1761)*

treatment of physiology and pathology and that of 'extraordinary' theoretical medicine also covered hygiene. In 1765 two new chairs of practical medicine and practical surgery were established in the hospital; in 1760 the chair of experimental chemistry was initiated, entrusted to Marco Carburi (1731-1808), while in 1786 the lecturing on simples was substituted by medical botany which was entrusted to Angelo Dalla Decima (1752-1825). In 1773 the Venetian Republic instituted a school of veterinary medicine in Padua, which was endowed with its own anatomical theatre, entrusted to Giuseppe Orus of Parma (1751-1792), pupil of Claude Bourgelat (1712-1779). In 1779 the veterinary school became part of the Studium and in 1787 Orus was officially appointed professor. The interest, which the Studium had always shown for the spas of the Euganean Hills, led in 1768 to the establishment of the teaching *ad thermas Aponenses*, which survived until 1806.

Bernardino Ramazzini (1633-1714), the initiator of the systematic study of industrial illnesses, was brought to Padua in 1700 as professor of 'ordinary' practical medicine, first in the second and then in the first rank, immediately after the publication of his classic work *De morbis artificum diatriba* (1700). In the same year one of the most important direct pupils of Malpighi, Antonio Vallisneri (1661-1730), arrived in Padua, called to occupy the first rank of 'extraordinary' practical medicine, from which he was transferred in 1709 to that of 'ordinary' theoretical medicine, first in the second and then, after the death of Guglielmini, in the first rank. Champion of rational medicine, Vallisneri effectively contributed to the confutation of spontaneous generation by showing (1700) that the larvae of insects on the galls of plants, whose presence had been demonstrated by Malpighi, were born from eggs laid by insects on the plants. In his *Istoria della generazione dell'uomo e degli animali* (1721) he showed his convinced adherence to egg preformism, following Malpighi who had observed under the microscope the first phases of embryonic development, interpreting them as the development of preformed germs. A skilled naturalist, he carried out research on the most varied of topics, on the anatomy of the ostrich (1712), on that of the chameleon (1715), on "insects" – a term which was then used to denote minute animals *en bloc* – (1713), on the generation of intestinal worms (1710), on fossils, whose organic origin he recognized, and on the origin of sources, which he showed to derive from atmospheric precipitation. The extremely rich museum he left was donated to the Studium by his son Antonio Vallisneri junior (1708-1777), who was then appointed professor of natural history. In the nineteenth century Vallisneri's museum was taken apart, on more than one occasion, and the material preserved in it – added to by Vallisneri junior – was divided between numerous institutes. At that time the doctrine of "live contagion", which derived the spread of a contagious disease from the transmission of a living being from the sick to the healthy, was confirmed in the *Nuova idea del male contagioso de' buoi* (1714) with which Carlo Francesco Cogrossi (1682-1769), later professor of 'extraordi-

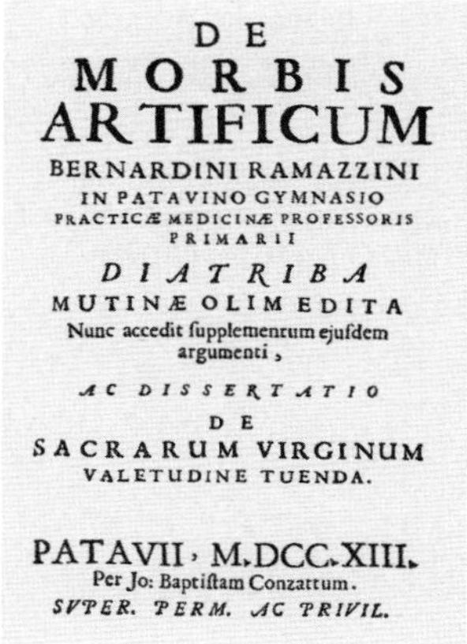
DE
MORBIS
ARTIFICUM
BERNARDINI RAMAZZINI
IN PATAVINO GYMNASIO
PRACTICÆ MEDICINÆ PROFESSORIS
PRIMARII
DIATRIBA
MUTINÆ OLIM EDITA
Nunc accedit ſupplementum ejuſdem argumenti,
AC DISSERTATIO
DE
SACRARUM VIRGINUM
VALETUDINE TUENDA.
PATAVII, M.DCC.XIII.
Per Jo: Baptiſtam Conzattum.
SUPER. PERM. AC PRIVIL.

Bernardino Ramazzini. Padua, Palazzo del Bo, the hall of the Faculty of Medicine and Surgery

Bernardino Ramazzini, De morbis artificum *(Padua 1713). Frontispiece. The definitive version of the work*

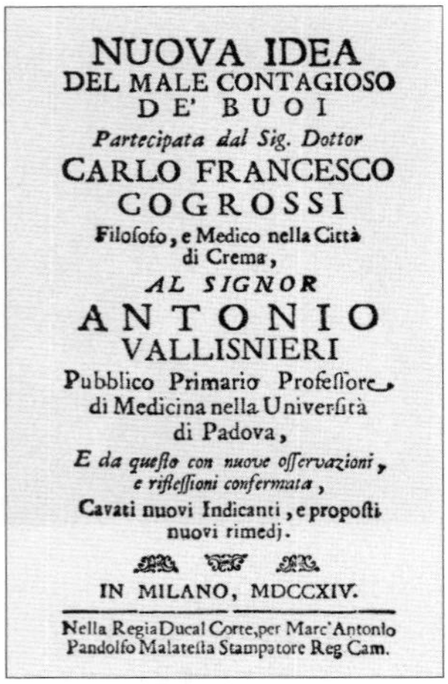
NUOVA IDEA
DEL MALE CONTAGIOSO
DE' BUOI
Partecipata dal Sig. Dottor
CARLO FRANCESCO
COGROSSI
Filosofo, e Medico nella Città
di Crema,
AL SIGNOR
ANTONIO
VALLISNIERI
Pubblico Primario Professore
di Medicina nella Università
di Padova,
E da questo con nuove osservazioni, e riflessioni confermata,
Cavati nuovi Indicanti, e proposti
nuovi rimedj.
IN MILANO, MDCCXIV.
Nella Regia Ducal Corte, per Marc'Antonio
Pandolfo Malatesta Stampatore Reg. Cam.

Carlo Francesco Cogrossi, Nuova idea del male contagioso de' buoi (*Milano 1714*). *Frontispiece*

nary' practical medicine in Padua from 1720 to 1733, entered the lively debate caused by a famous and very serious epidemic of foot and mouth disease which raged from 1711 and 1714, maintaining – with Vallisneri's authoritative endorsement – the living nature of contagion.

1. *The Pathology of the Organ*

In the eighteenth century anatomical thought made a decisive move into pathology and clinics thanks to the work of Giambattista Morgagni of Forlì (1682-1711). Called to Padua in 1711 to the second rank of 'ordinary' theoretical medicine, which fell vacant after Vallisneri's transfer to the first rank after the death of Guglielmini, Morgagni began his teaching on 17th March, 1712 with the inaugural lecture *Nova institutionum medicarum idea*, in which he presented new requirements of a didactic nature, with an up to date and complete plan for medical studies. After the death of Michelangelo Molinetti, in 1715 he was transferred to the first rank of anatomy, which he occupied until his death, always maintaining intact his exceptional mental lucidity. In Bologna he had been linked above all to Anton Maria Valsalva (1666-1723), one of Malpighi's former pupils, actively joining the Galilean and Malpighian tradition. His Bolognese period ended with the publication of the *Adversaria anatomica prima* (1706), a series of minute anatomical research conducted according to the Malpighian tradition, with which he made many new contributions to the mechanical structuring of the organism, as he did with the research contained in his five successive *Adversaria anatomica* (1717-19), his *Epistolae anatomicae duae* published in Leiden by Herman Boerhaave in 1728, and his *Epistolae anatomicae duodeviginti* on the writings of Valsalva (1740). Dating to his Paduan period are also numerous writings of a historico-medical, historical, and erudite nature, collected together with others in the *Opuscula miscellanea* (1763), among which the *Epistolae Aemilianae* in which he illustrated his own native land.

But Morgagni's most important work is his *De sedibus et causis morborum per anatomen indagatis* (1761), a title, which condenses the anatomo-clinical method, linked to his name. Fruit of sixty years of daily work, the *De sedibus* contains sixty "anatomo-medical letters" ordered topographically into five books, each one of which considers a morbid or syndromic entity (*de capitis dolor*, etc.), with the presentation of a certain number of complete cases of the post mortem report and a critical commentary on it. In all, around seven hundred cases are presented, most of which belong to his personal practice, while others derive from the experience of Valsalva and that of Giandomenico Santorini (1681-1737), whom he met during his stay in Venice; finally, some cases taken from literature are by authors he considered reliable. In each "anatomo-medical letter", Morgagni carries out an almost complete revision of the previous literature, which he systematically compares with his own observations. His synthesis is thus the

Giambattista Morgagni. Padua, Palazzo del Bo, the hall of the Faculty of Medicine and Surgery

fruit of continual comparative examinations, first separately between anatomical findings and clinical symptoms and then by establishing links between the two orders of phenomena. An expression of this work of coordination and synthesis are the four indices which take up a full seventy-eight pages, with exhaustive cross referencing above all between illnesses, symptoms, and lesions observed on the corpses, which thus renders the work of great practical use.

The parallelism between anatomical lesion and clinical symptom characterizes the anatomo-medical stories of *De sedibus*, which is organized according to a clinical and not an anatomical point of view. To a large extent, Morgagni used the new acquisitions on the structure and the function of a mechanically-conceived organism to establish a parallel between anatomical lesion and clinical phenomena. A fault in one point of the complex mechanism of the organism, investigated by means of anatomy, is the

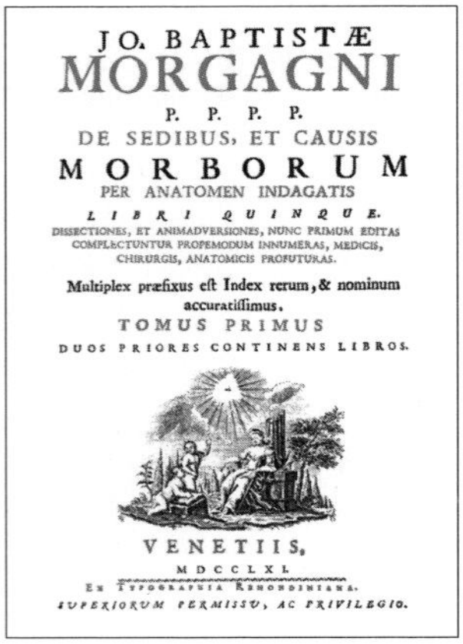
JO. BAPTISTÆ
MORGAGNI
P. P. P. P.
DE SEDIBUS, ET CAUSIS
MORBORUM
PER ANATOMEN INDAGATIS
LIBRI QUINQUE.
DISSECTIONES, ET ANIMADVERSIONES, NUNC PRIMUM EDITAS
COMPLECTUNTUR PROPEMODUM INNUMERAS, MEDICIS,
CHIRURGIS, ANATOMICIS PROFUTURAS.
Multiplex præfixus eſt Index rerum, & nominum
accuratiſſimus.
TOMUS PRIMUS
DUOS PRIORES CONTINENS LIBROS.
VENETIIS,
MDCCLXI.
EX TYPOGRAPHIA REMONDINIANA.
SUPERIORUM PERMISSU, AC PRIVILEGIO.

Giambattista Morgagni, De sedibus et causis morborum per anatomen indagatis *(Venice 1761). Frontispiece*

seat and the cause of the illness, or rather, of its clinical phenomena, which are conceivable as functional alterations derived from the fault itself. Besides this iatro-mechanical approach, with its structurist implications, Morgagni also absorbed the medical chemical one, which teaches the deduction of a local lesion from an altered chemism and the mechanical tracing back from this to the functional alteration, that is to say to the clinical phenomenology. The lesion of the organ is therefore the cause which determines the clinical physionomy of the illnesses. Aetiology, according to its current meaning, however, for Morgagni included causes he called "external", that is to say the traditional environmental factors, including lifestyle and the type of work, thus showing a debt also to Ramazzini's work.

The *De sedibus* is a veritable mine of original observations, both clinical and anatomo-pathological: we find described for the first time the syndrome characterized by a permanent rare pulse with epileptiform fits, redescribed in 1827 by Robert Adams (1791-1875) and in 1846 by William Stokes (1804-1878) and today called Morgagni-Adams-Stokes syndrome; the cirrhosis of the liver, described at greater length in 1819 by Laennec; frontal internal hyperostosis and its association with obesity and virilism in elderly women, called "Morgagni's syndrome" by Folke Henschen (1936), etc. Other masterly descriptions concern various types of aneurysms, the gastric ulcer, lobar pneumonia with the description of hepatization, the acute yellow atrophy of the liver, renal tuberculosis, the contro-lateral localization of cerebral lesion in hemiplegia ("Valsalva's rule"), the frequent otitic origin of intra-cranial suppurations, and so on, thus identifying the anatomical aspect of various important illnesses. But more than in his individual contributions, the significance of Morgagni's work lies in its having created an "epistemological rupture", since after him we no longer think and write in the same way as we thought and wrote before. His great work of synthesis led to the recognition of pathological anatomy as an integral part of medicine and was a premise for its further development. Morgagni is today unanimously defined as the founder of "organ pathology": organ pathology is precisely that aspect of Morgagni's work, which has substantially influenced the successive development of medicine. With Rudolf Virchow (1821-1902) the significance and the importance of Morgagni's work was definitively recognized (1894): for the founder of cell pathology the *De sedibus* is a great methodological work, representing the moment of the successful introduction of the concept of localism.

Leopoldo Marc'Antonio Caldani

2. *Towards a New Medicine*

Frontispiece of the first edition of Caldani's Institutiones physiologicae *(Padua 1773)*

Frontispiece of the third edition of Caldani's Institutiones pathologicae *(Venezia 1786)*

Morgagni was succeeded to the chair of anatomy by the Bolognese Leopoldo Marc'Antonio Caldani (1725-1813). Caldani initially held the chair *De morbis mulierum, puerorum et artificum* (1764); in the following year (1765) he was appointed professor of theoretical medicine in the first rank and in 1773, after the death of Morgagni, he was also assigned the teaching of anatomy, holding both chairs until 1805. He is a prominent figure in the late eighteenth-century history of anatomy and physiology above all for having assimilated, confirmed, and spread the new approach in physiology and the new research methods, introducing them into University teaching and systematizing the new acquisitions. We must recall first of all his work on the verification and the detailed experimental investigation of Haller's doctrine of irritability and the contribution he made to neurophysiology. We should also stress the influence exerted by his *Institutiones* of physiology, pathology, and anatomy not only in Italy, but also throughout the whole of Europe. Conceived of as text books for students, his *Institutiones*, particularly the *physiologicae*, had the characteristic of a manual in their being agile and clear and at the same time modern and up to date, ensuring them a vast diffusion: there were numerous editions and translations and they were the official textbooks of many Italian and foreign Universities even into the first decades of the nineteenth century. In the field of anatomy, finally, particularly worthy of being remembered is the monumental collection of anatomical tables, the *Icones anatomicae*, produced with the collaboration of his nephew Floriano Caldani (1772-1836), in part drawn from original preparations, and in part taken from those of other anatomists of the time. A lively participant in the scientific movement of the eighteenth century, Caldani maintained intense epistolary relations with the principal European scientists of his age.

The Bolognese Luigi Calza (1737-1783) succeeded Caldani to the chair of *De morbis mulierum, puerorum et artificum* in 1765. Thanks to Calza, a school of obstetrics was established in 1769 for midwives, and a museum was set up under his direction, which contained wax models of the various states of the uterus and the phases of childbirth, conserved at least in part still today. He is to be credited with the distinction, still valid today, of the uterus into three regions, the body, the isthmus, and the neck.

In 1777 the chair of surgery was entrusted to Camillo Bonioli of Lonigo (1729-1791), who acquired widespread renown as its holder. In 1794 he was succeeded by Vincenzo Malacarne of Saluzzo (1744-1816), who devoted himself above all to surgery, with particular concern for surgical and topographical anatomy, of which he can be considered the founder. His *Ricordi d'anatomia traumatica* (1794) constitutes the first treatise on traumatology. Malacarne is remembered above all for his valuable research into human neuroanatomy. He is to be credited for having produced the first detailed description of the cerebellum, distinguishing it into various parts which he attributed with names long linked to his own in anatomical language. He also studied in detail monstrosities and malformations, putting forward a new classification and introducing a new nomenclature, many terms of which are still used today.

In 1782 the chair of practical medicine in the first rank was entrusted to Andrea Comparetti of Friuli (1745-1801), who in 1780 had published a

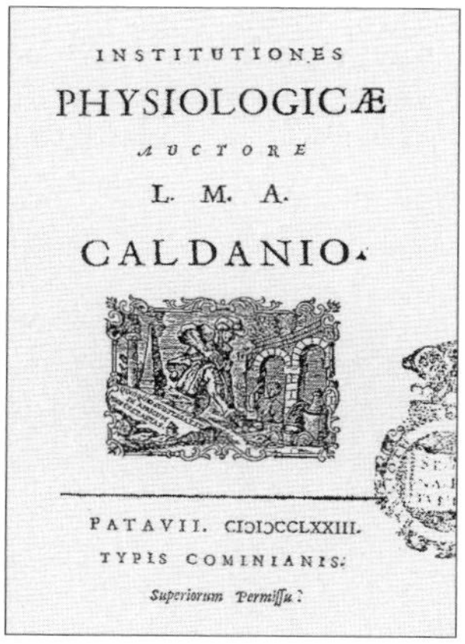
INSTITUTIONES
PHYSIOLOGICÆ
AUCTORE
L. M. A.
CALDANIO.
PATAVII. CIƆIƆCCLXXIII.
TYPIS COMINIANIS.
Superiorum Permissu.

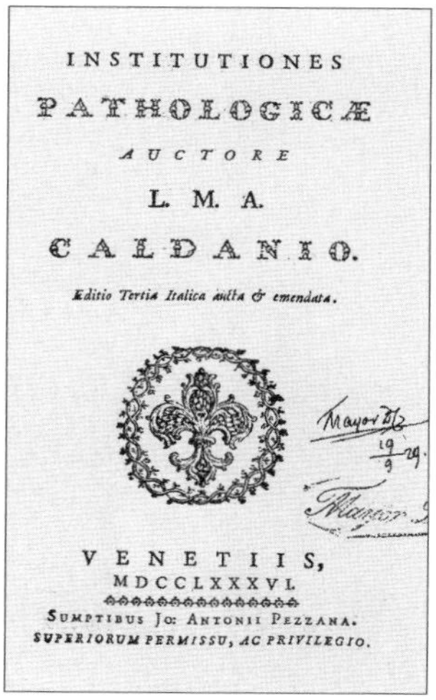
INSTITUTIONES
PATHOLOGICÆ
AUCTORE
L. M. A.
CALDANIO.
Editio Tertia Italica aucta & emendata.
VENETIIS,
MDCCLXXXVI.
Sumptibus Jo: Antonii Pezzana.
Superiorum permissu, ac privilegio.

work which had received acclaim in Italy and abroad, entitled *Occursus medici de vaga aegritudine infirmitatis nervorum*, containing extremely detailed and original observations on the structure of the sympathetic ganglions, their functional significance, visceral sympathetic innervation, and on the origin of the orthosympathetic system. In 1787 he was also charged with the teaching of practical medicine in the hospital; or rather, since in 1778 building work was being carried out on the new hospital, he was charged with preparing a plan for the reform of clinical teaching and the entire order of the hospital. The plan put forward by Comparetti – later published with the title *Saggio della scuola clinica nello Spedale di Padova* (1793) – was accepted, and he himself was entrusted with its implementation. Nevertheless, despite the scrupulous attitude, which Comparetti brought to the medical profession, and the amount of time he devoted to it, his true vocation was research. Involved in the European development of experimental physics, ever since he was young he had set out for himself a broad programme of research into physical and physiological optics; this research, which should have led to a systematic work on optics which remained unpublished, was partially issued in a series of writings published between 1784 and 1798. His double teaching assignment did not prevent him from completing other important research such as the *Observationes anatomicae de aure interna comparata* (1789), considered a mine of important observations on the anatomy, the comparative anatomy, and the pathological anatomy of the ear. His research on vegetable physiology led him to publish a *Prodromo di fisica vegetabile*, which appeared in two parts (1791-1799) as an anticipation of a complete treatise, which was never realized. In his *Riscontri fisico-botanici ad uso clinico* (1793) he outlined an adventurous plan of fine vegetable anatomy as an interpretative conduit between the external characteristics of plants and their clinically important properties. His final work was the *Dinamica animale degli insetti* (1800), an original attempt to extend to insects what Borelli had attempted for higher animals.

Andrea Comparetti.

Unlike other centres of research and teaching, Padua long remained a bastion of solidism and organicism, the fruit certainly of Morgagni's extremely long teaching, then that of Caldani. Padua remained substantially faithful to its localistic and organicistic conception even when, at the turn of the nineteenth century, the vitalist doctrines of John Brown (1735-1788) and Giovanni Rasori (1766-1837) came to the fore. Just before Brown's ideas began to have an impact in Italy, the Venetian Stefano Gallini (1756-1836), a former pupil of Caldani and from 1786 professor of theoretical medicine in the second rank, had published his *Saggio d'osservazioni concernenti li nuovi progressi della fisica del corpo umano* (1792), in which, among other things, he showed himself to be the forerunner of Marie-François-Xavier Bichat (1771-1802), anticipating the new approach for a rational division of the functions of the organism on the basis of differentiated tissues. But above all he maintained the necessity of turning to chemistry in order to understand vital phenomena, a conception which he was to develop and investigate further in other subsequent works. Gallini was thus a precursor of Maurizio Bufalini (1787-1875), the main exponent of the reaction against vitalistic doctrines, considered the founder in Italy of the modern clinical method and the forerunner of the new approach taken by Italian medicine from the second half of the nineteenth century onwards, albeit under the influence of the French and German schools. With the new organization of the faculty of medicine, from 1806 Gallini was entrusted with the chair of physiology and comparative anatomy, a chair, which he held, with various vicissitudes, until 1833.

Stefano Gallini.

GREGORIO PIAIA

Philosophy

When Shakespeare, in the opening scene of *The Taming of the Shrew*, refers to the University of Padua as the "nursery of arts", by 'arts' he intends here not painting or sculpture, but rather the seven liberal arts: the 'trivium', whose object is the world of language (grammar, rhetoric, dialectic), and the 'quadrivium', regarding the physical world or 'nature' in its widest sense (arithmetic, geometry, music, astronomy). Ever since late antiquity, basic culture had been divided into these 'arts', later enlarged with the rise of the first Universities to include the various sections of the rediscovered Aristotelian encyclopaedia: logic, first of all, and then physics and metaphysics, psychology and biology, ethics and politics, poetry and rhetoric. The teachers (*magistri*) charged with providing such a training were precisely the artists, who in Padua also imparted the teaching of medicine: initially placed under the jurisdiction of the 'university' of law students, from 1399 onwards they constituted a distinct 'university' of arts students, or rather a faculty of the arts.

Little is known about the very first beginnings of the culture of the arts in the Padua Studium and its relations with the cathedral schools. The birth of the Studium (1222) is bound up in any case with the composition of the *Quadriga* or *Ars epistolaris dictaminis* by the notary and *magister* Arsegino (1217), with the journey to Toledo (1218) by the Paduan canon and *magister* Salione, who translated several scientific texts there from Arabic and Hebrew, and with the writing of the sermons of Saint Anthony († 1231), which contain frequent references to Aristotle's *De animalibus*. In effect it is above all Aristotle the naturalist who aroused the interest of the learned circles of the city, and it is significant that in the same period studying the liberal arts in Padua was the young Albertus Magnus, who was to mention in his works several natural phenomena which he had the opportunity of observing during his stay in Padua (such as the earthquake of 1222 or the case of the Paduan woman who managed to fast for 40 days). This interest in the philosophy of nature finds a confirmation, for example, in the figure of the Pole Witelo, who – true to the custom of the *peregrinatio academica* – came from Paris to Padua in the years 1262-1268 in order to study canon law there and to teach some disciplines of the arts. In Padua Witelo wrote a treatise on the nature of demons, in which he tends to give a naturalistic explanation for several seemingly prodigious phenomena, already hinting at that attitude of "double truth" which was later to characterize the "School of Padua": dealing with the fall of the

Portrait of Galileo Galilei, Aula Magna, Palazzo del Bo

Pietro d'Abano, Palazzo della Ragione

angels (judged impossible from the point of view of the natural order of the universe), he explicitly declares that, "since I have been set a question in natural terms (*naturaliter*), I will reply to the same in natural terms", with the proviso that it comply, as far as faith is concerned, with what has been established by the Fathers and the Councils. It is an attitude which, for the first part at least, corresponds to that of Albertus Magnus (summarized in the famous motto *de naturalibus naturaliter*) and which was to find a full confirmation in the principal exponent of Paduan philosophical and scientific culture at the turn of the fourteenth century: *Petrus de Apono*, or Pietro d'Abano.

It is no mere chance that Pietro d'Abano (c. 1250-1315/1316) figures among the series of ancient and modern "illustrious men" painted by Justus of Ghent for the study of Federico da Montefeltro in the Palazzo Ducale of Urbino. The figure of Pietro evidently still occupied an important place in the cultural imagination of the late fifteenth century, so much more because his fame as a man of science was accompanied by legends which made him out to be a magician, a raiser of demons, and the author of spells. It was said, for example, that he had learnt the seven liberal arts from as many spirits which he kept shut up in a crystal ampulla, and that he was able to make the money he had already spent return to his purse. This magic halo was strengthened by the story of the three trials (one in Paris and two in Padua) which had been brought against him on the charge of heresy.

But who was Pietro d'Abano in reality? The tales of his extraordinary feats naturally belong to legend, but this does not alter the fact that Pietro was interested in magical arts and openly declared in his *Lucidator* that he had successfully practised pyromancy, the prediction of the future, that is, based on an examination of the movements of a fire and the noises and the smoke it emits. "Physician, astrologer, philosopher": these three epithets, which usually accompany the figure of Pietro, are indicative of the richness and the complexity of his field of research, which find expression in his greatest and most famous work, the *Conciliator differentiarum philosophorum et praecipue medicorum*. For Pietro the physician, and for the relations between medicine and astrology the reader must turn to the previous chapter. Here we would like to pause for a moment to consider the figure of the "philosopher-scientist", which can be taken as a symbol of an intellectual attitude recurrent in the history of the Padua Studium.

The first aspect to be borne in mind is of a biographical nature and consists in the eminently 'European' nature of Pietro's cultural formation. His teaching in Padua (which can only be reliably dated from 1307 onwards and which ended with his death) was in fact preceded by a period of study in Constantinople and then in Paris, that is in the capital of the Eastern Empire, which kept alive the direct tradition of Ancient Greek philosophy and science, and in the greatest centre of Aristotelian study of the Latin West. The impulse to go to Constantinople to study Greek and to find a copy of the *Problemata* (a collection of questions mostly on natural philosophy, attributed at that time to Aristotle himself) perhaps came to Pietro from his Paduan master, the physician Paolo Tosetto of Ravenna, who knew Greek. We thus see that welding of research and textual analysis (philology) on the one hand, and natural philosophy on the other, which was at the origin of the long process culminating in the birth of modern science. As far as Paris is concerned, Pietro's fruitful stay in the final decade of the thirteenth century, during which he wrote the *Physiognomia* and began work on his commentary on the *Problemata* and on the *Conciliator* itself, placed Pietro in contact with an extremely stimulating University environment.

We have a significant reflection of these inter-University contacts in John of Jandun, who in 1312 declared that he had been the first Paris teacher of philosophy to have received – via the "most beloved" Marsilio of Padua – a copy of Pietro's commentary on the Latin translation of the *Problemata*. John was a prominent exponent of Averroism, that is to say the current which interpreted Aristotle according to the commentary by Averroes and which raised strong opposition because of its heterodox results (in particular for the doctrine of the single and separate intellect, which excluded, on a philosophical level at least, the individual survival of the soul after the death of the body). According to some scholars, Pietro d'Abano also adhered to this current of thought and was indeed the initiator of that Averroistic tendency which was so alive at the University of Padua in the fifteenth and sixteenth centuries. It is a theory which has enjoyed notable favour and which also inspired the modern fresco of the "School of Padua" by Guido Saetti, which dominates the Hall of the Faculty of Letters and Philosophy in the Palazzo del Bo: in it Pietro is depicted on the left, seated among papers, books, and instruments, and under the aegis of Averroes, while in the centre of the fresco, as his ideal continuer, is Pomponazzi who is discussing the nature of the soul together with his pupil Gasparo Contarini in the presence of Nifo and Achillini. Certainly, the theory of "Averroism" allows one fully to justify the trials brought against Pietro and would provide a precise philosophical basis for his medico-naturalistic approach; but in reality, the *Conciliator* and his other works contain no Averroistic doctrines. Pietro's intent – and in this he can be distinguished from the "pure" Aristotelians – was to put forward a 'science' of natural things which, basing itself on experience and on reasoning, aimed at grasping the "second causes" which our intellect can know in a much easier way than the first cause or God. From this there arises a transfer of interest from metaphysics and theology (which for the most faithful followers of Aristotle constituted the speculative sciences *par excellence*) to the philosophy of nature in its various subdivisions, which go from theoretical medicine to astrology and natural or white magic. From this point of view the study of the influences of the heavenly bodies, in their play of action and reaction, aims at clarifying the tangle of individual second causes in the sublunary world, whose "entities" are not immobile and perfect, but in continual movement. Astrology as a "science",

Gasparino Barzizza

therefore, as distinct from the superstitions of the common people but also from the semi-serious interest which many people today show for the signs of the Zodiac and horoscopes. And the fact that astrology was profoundly felt in fourteenth-century Padua, even at the level of the 'general public', is testified to by the series of astrologico-religious frescoes which decorate the great hall of the Palazzo della Ragione, painted at the time of Giotto, perhaps at the suggestion of Pietro d'Abano himself, and then largely redone in the early fifteenth century.

Above we mentioned, in passing, Marsilio of Padua, the famous author of the *Defensor pacis* (1324), the work which, long before Machiavelli's *Prince*, marks the transition to a 'modern' vision of politics. Such a vision is based on the full independence of the civil power – in so far as it is founded on the will of the "whole of the citizens", or rather of the "more valid part" of them – from the ecclesiastical power, which indeed must be subject to the civil for all those acts which have some external or social relevance. Written in Paris in support of the emperor Ludwig of Bavaria, then in conflict with pope John XXII, the *Defensor pacis* presents in its first part, however, numerous echoes of communal life and medical studies in Padua which, in all likelihood, the young Marsilio experienced at the University of Padua (perhaps under the guidance of Pietro d'Abano himself) before leaving for the Paris Studium. Albertino Mussato, the greatest Paduan man of letters of the early fourteenth century, speaks in one of his letters in verse of how the young Marsilio could not decide whether to study law or medicine, finally opting for the latter. Indeed Marsilio's approach to the political problem shows medico-naturalistic tones on more than one occasion, and his interest in the immediate "efficient cause" of the organ of government (which leaves the divine will in the background like a "remote cause") is in line with Pietro d'Abano.

To go back over the most significant aspects of the evolution of the disciplines (medicine apart) which belonged to the arts, we must begin by noting the contribution made by the Padua Studium to the beginnings of humanism, thanks to teachers like Giovanni Conversini of Ravenna and above all Gasparino Barzizza of Bergamo, whose period in Padua (1407-1421) was particularly fruitful. Employed by the Venetian Senate with the double teaching assignment of rhetoric and moral philosophy, Barzizza, like other distinguished teachers, also kept a sort of private boarding school, with paying students lodging in his house whom he guided in their studies. Here we must remember that in Padua too, as in the other Universities, the teaching of grammar and rhetoric – although part of the curriculum of the faculty of arts – was often imparted by private teachers. Barzizza was a passionate admirer of Cicero – it was he who initiated the "Ciceronianism" which Erasmus of Rotterdam was later to rail against – and he had numerous pupils in Padua, among whom Francesco Filelfo, Guarino Veronese, and Vittorino da Feltre, who also followed the mathematics lessons imparted by Biagio Pelacani. In 1421 Vittorino, who had already obtained the title of *magister artium*, accepted the post as successor to Barzizza (who had moved to Milan) to the chair of rhetoric, but he resigned after only one year, returning to private teaching in Venice; not long afterwards he was called to Mantua, where he founded the "Giocosa", the most famous educational institution of the humanist period.

If several of Barzizza's students, like Guarino and Filelfo, went to Constantinople to study Greek, there were also numerous learned Byzantines who came to Italy in the fifteenth century to teach the language of Plato and Aristotle. Demetrio Calcondila of Athens, for example, was professor of Greek in the Padua Studium from 1463 to 1475, then moving to Florence and later to Milan, and he had among his students Niccolò Leonino Tomeo (1456-1531), whose father was Albanian, and who was apparently the first in Padua to read Aristotle's natural philosophy in Greek. Other Greek humanists who taught in Padua in this period were Giovanni Lascaris senior, Michele Marullo, and Marco Musuro, whose lessons were attended by Erasmus during his stay in Padua in the winter of 1508-1509.

Tomb of Paolo Veneto

What is outlined above is the "humanistic face" of the Padua Studium, which on the strictly philosophical plane, however, took on quite a different aspect and approach in the early fifteenth century, thanks to the influence of Ockham's physics from Paris and the logical and mathematical studies which had developed over the course of the fourteenth century in Oxford. Here, at Merton College in particular, there taught a group of masters known as the *calculatores* because they adopted an alphabetical symbolism in the logical calculation of propositions, then applying this method to various fields of experience. Biagio Pelacani, mentioned above, (who taught in Padua from 1384-1388 and then in 1407 and 1408-1411, dealing in particular with optics) was extremely interested in the problems of the school of Buridan, a Parisian follower of Ockhamism and the Oxford "physicists". But the most remarkable figure of early fifteenth-century philosophy in Padua was without doubt the Augustinian friar Paolo Nicoletti (known as Paolo Veneto, 1372-c.1429), who stayed in Oxford from 1390 and perhaps also in Paris, and began his first teaching in Padua around 1395. He became famous in the University environment to the point of earning himself the epithet of *monarcha philosophorum*, and was also Master General of his Order, undertaking diplomatic missions on the behalf of the Venetian Republic, until he fell into disgrace and was exiled and had to wander from University to University throughout Italy. His fame, which lasted for a long time, was due above all to his University text books: besides the *Summa naturalium* (which includes Aristotle's natural philosophy and metaphysics), he wrote a *Logica parva* and a *Logica magna*, in which he carried out a broad-ranging and organic systematization of late-scholastic logic, aiming – in the footsteps of English writers such as Rudolph Strode and William Heytesbury – to construct a more "formal" discipline, based that is on an analysis of the syntactic element of discourse. This subordination of logical inquiry to semiotic analysis, to create a sort of metalanguage, is the ripest fruit of the *logica modernorum* (that is to say the terministic and nominalistic developments of Aristotelian logic), and for the rigorous rules which accompany it, it has been interpreted by some scholars as an anticipation of modern formal logic. It must be said that this logico-speculative rigour, to such an extent as to make him neglect empirical observation, also led Paolo to formulate extravagant theories, such as in the *De compositione mundi*, where he deduces the presence of permanent water in the plains and the mountains not from precipitation in the form of rain and snow, but rather from the pressure exercised by the sea on the coasts and the consequent absorption of sea water by the land like a sponge.

The dialectic ability he had acquired in Oxford supported Paolo Veneto in his lively controversy against that group of humanists, led ideally by Petrarch, who had denounced the uselessness of the subtle and quibbling analyses carried out by the *moderni loyci*, and contrasted the new humanistic culture with the philosophy of the "British barbarians", judged unworthy of imitation. Against those who criticized the study of logic, dedicating themselves rather to the "lucrative sciences" (such as law and medicine) or involving themselves "ridiculously" in the study of the past, Paolo thus asserted the validity of his discipline, which teaches us to "dispute both in a probable and a demonstrative way", and which reveals itself to be useful to the philosophy of nature. In reality this controversy was born of two different conceptions of philosophy, understood by the professors of 'humanity' (that is to say grammar and rhetoric) as an essentially moral reflection, dealing with problems which we would now term existential, while the professors of logic, 'physics', and metaphysics conceived of it as a technical and specialized discipline, capable of offering rigorous models of rationality.

There is another aspect of Paolo Veneto's thought which must be borne in mind, and that is his fondness for some of the theories of Averroism, which already in the fourteenth century had spread from Paris to the University of Bologna. In his commentary on the famous and highly controversial passage from book III of the *De anima* in which Aristotle defines the "active" intellect as "separate" from the body and from the other faculties of the soul, Paolo seems to side with the opinion put forward by Sigeri of Brabant (the initiator of "Latin Averroism" in the second half of the thirteenth century), distinguishing between a sensible individual soul, which inheres totally to matter and is the form of the body, and the Intellect, which is not individuated by matter and is therefore unique for all individuals, simple, unalterable, and existing in its own right. The individual unites himself to this Intellect (which also includes the "passive" as well as the "active" intellect) in the cognitive act by means of "fantasy" (in which intelligibles are "in potency"), without however being "informed" by it, as Thomas Aquinas on the other hand maintained. It is with Paolo Veneto, then, that Averroism truly enters the Padua Studium, where it was variously professed by many teachers starting with one of

Paolo's own pupils, Gaetano from Thiene, who taught logic from 1422 to 1430 and then natural philosophy until his death (1465), and who was in turn master of Nicoletto Vernia (1420-1499), his successor to the teaching of the philosophy of nature.

With Vernia we arrive at a turning point in philosophical orientation, since Vernia took the field against the Parisian and Oxford masters of the previous century in the name of a return to the genuine Aristotelian text and the 'classical' commentators (Hellenists, such as Themistius and Alexander of Aphrodisia, but also medievals like Averroes and Albertus Magnus). This change of direction depended perhaps on his clear adherence to Averroism, but we cannot exclude that this hostility to the most recent interpretations of Aristotelian logic was born from the disgust – mentioned above – with which many exponents of humanism viewed French and British philosophy. It is in this period (1483) in any case that the Latin translation of the Aristotelian *corpus* was published in Venice, containing the commentary by Averroes, which was then followed, in the years 1495-1498, by the first printed edition of Aristotle in Greek. It was a great editorial and philological event, which also had repercussions on the approach to Aristotle's text: indeed with respect to Paolo Veneto, the new generation of masters placed emphasis on the methodological and "instrumental" aspect of logic, setting formalistic and semiotic analyses to one side, and extending their interest from the structure of the demonstration to the procedures of rhetoric and dialectic, which found an application in the field of practical philosophy. Though it still existed, the gulf between the two cultural perspectives, the rhetorico-moral and the logico-scientific, was narrowed; it was a gulf which was indeed to animate throughout the entire sixteenth century the fervent debates which took place between the various University environments of Padua, the School of Rialto, and the intellectual patriciate of Venice, whose members (it is enough to quote the two Contarini, Gasparo and the future doge Niccolò) had more or less regularly studied Aristotle in the University classrooms, but also used to meditate on and discuss the Platonic dialogues and their ethical and civic relevance.

But let us return to Vernia, famous in his time as the leader of the Averroists. In his teaching he stressed the superiority of "physics" (as the study of bodies in movement) with respect to metaphysics, and of medicine with respect to law which only allows one to attain a reduced happiness (relative, that is, to the relations of social intercourse), while the true and perfect happiness is intellectual and is guaranteed by "natural science". In this way, he joined the long-standing "dispute on the arts" (understood naturally as the liberal arts), initiated by Coluccio Salutati with his *De nobilitate legum et medicinae* (1399) and rekindled by the theologian Giovanni da Imola, who had claimed the primacy for law. Vernia moreover adhered to the theory of the eternity of matter, as well as that of the single intellect. The spread of such ideas led the Bishop of Padua,

Pietro Barozzi, to issue a decree in 1489 against those who upheld the unity of the intellect, in as far as the negation of the survival of the individual soul had pernicious consequences for Christian life. In fact, "thus removing the rewards for the virtues and the punishments for the vices, [they] believe they can commit with greater freedom any sin". The problem was certainly not new: back in 1277 the bishop of Paris, the great University centre, had condemned a broad series of texts judged dangerous for the Christian faith; and later the fifth Lateral Council – in session VIII, on 19th December, 1513 – had taken an official position against the theory of the mortality of the soul and the unity of the intellect, as well as that of the eternity of the world, intimating to all the *magistri* of philosophy that they should follow their presentation of such doctrines by the appropriate confutations. To tell the truth not all the Council fathers were in agreement with this condemnation. The Bishop of Bergamo, Pietro Lippomano, for example, considered it an undue intrusion of the theologians into the field of philosophy, which only dealt with Aristotle. In truth, as in Paris in 1277, the doctrinal and disciplinary relevance of these ecclesiastical condemnations, officially justified by the danger of heresy and scandal, must not lead us to neglect other possible and more earthly motivations, based on the competition between the corporation of philosophers and that of theologians, and between different philosophical schools.

And Vernia? He initially seemed to favour a transfer to the University of Pisa, but his contacts with Lorenzo il Magnifico, set in motion through Poliziano, came to nothing. He then wrote a suitable dissertation aimed at confuting the "perverse opinion of Averroes on the unity of the intellect and on the happiness of the soul", reaching the point of affirming a basic agreement – as far as the immortality of the soul was concerned – not only between Plato and Aristotle, but also among some of the great Aristotelian commentators, such as Simplicius, Themistius, and Aquinas. With this he brought himself close to the concordism of Giovanni Pico della Mirandola, who had spent two extremely intense years in Padua (1480-1482) as part of his youthful studies, following the lessons given by Vernia himself and having as his master the famous Jew from Crete Elia Del Medigo, he too an Averroist, who taught in the school of the Israelite community and was connected to the University environment. In effect at the end of the fifteenth century the cultural climate in Padua – partly due to the custom of contrasting every holder of a teaching position with an opposing or antagonistic teacher – was extremely lively and stimulating, and it was not by chance that, besides Pico, the other major Italian philosopher of the period, Pietro Pomponazzi, also studied (and then taught) in Padua. Here the discussions on Averroism were bound up with the disputes between Thomists and Scotists, in an environment open to the philological approach of humanism – we can think, for example, of the relations between Vernia and Ermolao Barbaro and Girolamo Donà, translators respectively of Themistius and Alexander of Aphrodisia.

Pietro Pomponazzi

Pomponazzi, to tell the truth, seems far removed from humanistic elegance: his Latin is of the scholastic kind, somewhat rough but enlivened – as it transpires from the numerous *reportationes* or collections of notes taken by his pupils – by salacious digressions and expressions in Italian or the dialect of Mantua. Famous were his irreverent, almost student-like, jokes against friars and theologians with which he won the favour of the students; but this mocking spirit was accompanied by a strong and aristocratic consciousness (very Aristotelian, or rather Averroistic) of the difficulties which the philosopher had to face in his solitary search for truth. Thus, in a lovely passage from *De fato*, he expresses the condition of the philosopher, inspired by the mythical Prometheus, chained by Zeus to a rock of the Caucasus and condemned to have his liver ceaselessly devoured by a vulture for having stolen a spark of fire from Olympus in order to give it to man: "Prometheus is the philosopher who, in his effort to discover the divine secrets, is continually gnawed by painful thoughts, has no thirst, no hunger, does not eat, does not sleep, does not excrete, mocked by all, held to be foolish and sacrilegious, persecuted by the inquisitors, object of spectacle for the common people. This is what philosophers earn, this their reward". Such an ascetic and almost dramatic vision of the job of the philosopher did not prevent Pomponazzi, however, from taking a wife (he married three times) and from producing two daughters, to whom he left a modest inheritance.

"Little Peter" ("Peretto") – as Pomponazzi was jokingly called because of his shortness – was born in Mantua in 1462 and in Padua he had followed the courses held by the Averroist Vernia, the Thomist Francesco da Nardò, and Pietro Trapolin, a moderate Averroist. In Padua he taught natural philosophy on two occasions: in the years 1488-1496, having as his "competitors" first the Averroist Alessandro Achillini and then Agostino Nifo, and then in the decade 1499-1509, as the successor to Vernia. He left Padua because of the closure of the Studium during the disastrous war of the League of Cambrai, and in 1511 moved to the nearby University of Bologna, where he taught natural philosophy, and sometimes also metaphysics and ethics. According to the testimony of one of his pupils he let himself die stoically of starvation, on 18th May, 1525, so as no longer to have to bear the illnesses which tormented him.

His Bolognese period was Pomponazzi's most fruitful, and it is in this period that he wrote his most famous works: the treatise on the immortality of the soul (1516), the *De fato, de libero arbitrio et de praedestinatione* (1520), and the *De incantationibus* (also 1520); but the genesis of his thought is completely "Paduan", even though the history of the two Universities of Bologna and Padua is characterized in this period by frequent exchanges of teachers. On the problem of the nature of the soul, *pièce de résistance* of all the philosophers of the time, Pomponazzi goes from an initial adherence to the theory of the Averroist Sigeri to a progressive interest in the positions of Alexander of Aphrodisia (2nd-3rd C. AD), to the point of making these latter coincide with the most faithful and correct interpretation of the thought of Aristotle. In his *De immortalitate animae* – quoting arguments used by Aquinas - he contests Averroes' radical anthropological dualism, which makes a clear distinction between the intellective soul, which is unique for all men and is immortal, and the sensible soul, which belongs to each individual and is mortal. In maintaining the unity of man as a fully knowing subject, Pomponazzi does not accept, however, the interpretation of Aquinas, who, he believes, goes beyond natural limits and seeks recourse to Christian revelation: reasoning in strictly philosophical, that is to say Aristotelian, terms, the sensible faculty becomes united to the intellective faculty, understood as a "possible or material" intellect, while the "active" Intellect is separated and transcendent, and is identified with God. It follows, again on a philosophical plane, that the human soul is to be considered mortal, albeit placed at the summit of the world of matter, and bordering on the immaterial. The immortality of the soul, just like the creation of the world, can only be admitted as an article of faith.

The appearance of the *De immortalitate animae* gave rise to notable reactions within the Paduan philosophical environment too. Gasparo Contarini, an old pupil of Pomponazzi's and future cardinal, wrote two little treatises on the subject, setting himself the task of demonstrating that the soul is indeed the form of the body, but a form subsisting in its own right and thus destined to survive on the death of the body. This is the line taken by another pupil of Vernia's, Agostino Nifo (1473-1546), mentioned above, who, after having taught in Padua in the final decade of the fifteenth century, moved to Pisa and then to Salerno, acquiring notable renown not only for his philosophical talent but also for his amorous excesses which enlivened his old age. Pomponazzi replied to these and other criticisms by accentuating his rigorously philosophical approach and he extended his reflection to other topics: in the *De incantationibus* he aimed to explain miracles and prodigious events as purely natural phenomena, making use, as Pietro d'Abano had done, of a natural causality in which the influences of the heavenly bodies play a role; in the *De fato* he tackles, without however coming up with a convincing solution, the antinomy between determinism and freedom, appealing finally to the Christian faith. Theory of the double truth or unreconcilable disagreement between reason and faith? Crypto-materialism and "impiety" (as the epithets that circled after his death would have us believe, and as the "libertines" of seventeenth-century France were to think) or agnosticism of a Kantian kind, which opens up a space beyond science for practical reason and faith? A rigorous "scientific" system which anticipates positivism, as Ardigò maintained in his time, or substantial eclecticism, which would justify the variety of solutions put forward? The contrasting plurality of interpretations is an indication of the incisive and problematic thought of this Paduan-Bolognese *magister*, who, though he did not go beyond the Aristotelian conception of nature, knew how to investigate its methods and implications in depth.

We need not go through the long list of Aristotelian professors who contrasted or succeeded each other to the chairs of the Studium throughout the entire sixteenth century and beyond. It is more profitable on the other hand to stress that the traditional distinction between Averroists and "Alexandrists" (followers, that is, of the interpretation of Alexander of Aphrodisia) did not represent the only internal positions of the "School of Padua", in which there were frequent cases of eclectic contamination; and we even find an "Aristotelian" like Francesco Piccolomini (1520-1604) who does not hide his sympathies for Plato but far from attempting to find an agreement between the two great Greek philosophers declares that they represent two distinct paths to philosophy which must remain as such. Piccolomini was the antagonist (indeed the relentless adversary) of Iacopo Zabarella on the chair of natural philosophy and succeeded him on his death (1589). Born in 1533 into an illustrious Padua family – among his ancestors was the canonist and cardinal Francesco Zabarella – Iacopo had been a pupil of Bernardino Tomitano and Marcantonio Genua, and after having taught logic for four years, in 1568 he moved to natural philosophy. His works enjoyed a large diffusion in the German Universities thanks to the coherence and the organic unity with which he succeeded in dealing with the central themes of Paduan Aristotelianism.

Francesco Piccolomini and Iacopo Zabarella

On the question of the soul, Zabarella lucidly took up the criticism of Averroism and re-proposed the Alexandrian theory, appealing to the principle of double truth. But his fame today is linked above all to his reflections on logic, whose instrumental character he stresses, instrumental that is in distinguishing what is true from what is false. Logic is not a science, but is at the service of the sciences; while the sciences deal with notions or concepts based on physical reality, logic in fact refers to "second notions", terms, which are our invention and which can be and not be. They are not necessary, but contingent, things, and therefore cannot constitute a science because science – in line with the Aristotelian tradition – is only of necessary things. The plurality of the sciences and their fields of research are made to correspond to a diversification in the methods proper to each science or "art", and in this Zabarella clearly distances himself from the position of the French Petrus Ramus and his followers (the "Ramists"), who in the same period championed the elaboration of a single universally valid method. In effect the debate on the "method", preparatory to the rise of the new science and the new philosophy and which was to have its most well-known expression in Descartes' *Discourse on the Method* (1637), was particularly lively in the second half of the sixteenth century and received a notable impulse thanks to the work of Zabarella and other Paduan teachers. In particular Zabarella distinguishes the concept of "order" (which regards the way of ordering the things to be treated in the context of a discipline and has a purely didactic function) from that of "method", which on the other hand allows the transition from known to unknown in a sort of "hunt" for new concepts, which syllogistic logic supplies with the adequate instruments. And since every syllogism proceeds from causes to effect or from effect to causes, its method has two essential moments: the "resolutive" moment, which leads us from the sensible effect to the discovery of its cause, then undertaking a return or "regress" which allows - and this is the other moment – the "compositive" process, by means of which the effect is deduced from the cause. Zabarella devoted particular attention to the *resolutio* and the *regressus*, distinguishing between common observation, which can easily deceive us, and truly scientific experience, formulated as a *demonstratio quia* or rather "demonstrative induction". This latter works on contents which present themselves as being strictly concatenated to each other, in such a way that from even a few particular cases one can arrive at a universal proposition which can then be applied to individual empirical events.

But the "resolutive" method is also clearly present in Galileo, who deals with it on more than one occasion in writings which go from 1615 to 1638; Galileo shows in any case that he has a clear grasp, and indeed agrees with, the Aristotelian theory of demonstration, which he had studied in works by the Jesuit professors of the Collegio Romano, inspired by the doctrines of Zabarella. This is the origin of the theory that the great Galileo was in reality indebted to the Paduan Aristotelians for his methodological principles: it is a theory as appealing as it is provocative, first put forward by Ernst Cassirer and then by John H. Randall jr., which has been supported more recently with new argumentation by William A. Wallace, while contributions opposing the idea of a continuity between Renaissance Aristotelianism and modern science have not been lacking. It is a game played mostly at home, so to speak, since even Galileo is – although not exclusively – a glory of Padua... Leaving aside the ideological components which have led to the exaggeration of one or the other side, it must be recognized that in its entirety Galileo's procedure faithfully follows the Aristotelian procedure, since it begins with experience (known to us) to retrace the principles (unknown to us) and then return to the empirical plane. But the meaning of the terms used by Zabarella and Galileo is different however, as they derive respectively from a substantialistic and metaphysical vision for the former, and an empirical and phenomenalistic one for the latter. Different above all is the nature of Galileo's procedure, because both the initial observation and the conclusive experiment are conceived mathematically. Thus, while the "resolutive" method of the Aristotelians moves from the empirical observation of the "qualities" to arrive at the "essence" of the phenomenon, and then from this to deduce its properties, Galileo begins from the experience of the "quantities" (which as such are measurable) to discover and formulate a mathematical law, from which he deduces further properties, always of a quantitative nature. But it is precisely this mathematical stamp which marks the difference between modern and Aristotelian science.

One final digression before we move on. The double demonstrative method (composition/resolution) theorized by Zabarella only holds for the speculative sciences such as the philosophy of nature, while for the practical sciences, in which one cannot arrive at perfect knowledge, one must rely on rhetorical and dialectic procedures, which refer respectively to the "civil discipline" (politics) and the moral disciplines. Touching on these themes, Zabarella entered the rich debate which was inspired in the course of the sixteenth century by Aristotle's *Poetics* and *Rhetoric* and which found particularly fertile ground in Padua. On rhetoric, for example, wrote Sperone Speroni (1500-1588), a former pupil of Pomponazzi in Bologna, who taught logic in Padua for several years and directed the "Accademia degl'Infiammati". The Padua chair of Greek and Latin Letters was entrusted in 1552 to Francesco Robortello of Udine (1516-1567), author of the first commentary on the *Poetics* (1548). Kind and generous to his students, Robortello was however polemical and irascible with his colleagues: he was involved in a memorable dispute with the historian and Latinist Carlo Sigonio of Modena (his colleague in Padua in 1560, where he lectured on the *Poetics*) which was only ended after the intervention of the Venetian Senate itself. Sigonio soon moved to Bologna, followed by one of his students, the young Torquato Tasso, who had come to Padua on two occasions, first to study law and then eloquence and philosophy. But, besides this hardly edifying event, we must recall the reply which Robortello – like other Paduan teachers, among whom the same Zabarella – made to the question of the relationship between poetry and logic: he considered poetry a rational discipline, thus linked to philosophy, because the poet has the task of expounding the true; Tomitano in turn held "philosophy to be necessary to the acquisition of Rhetoric and Poetry", while other Paduan teachers, such as Jason de Nores, attributed poetry with an ethico-pedagogical and political purpose, as a "teaching for civil life".

Carlo Rinaldini

It was on the 7th December, 1592, that Galileo Galilei, then twenty-eight years old, held his inaugural lecture for the course of "mathematics" in the Palazzo del Bo, with great public success. In February of the following year, he wrote to the physician Girolamo Mercuriale, who had moved to the Pisa Studium, saying that he was highly satisfied with his new position; in his reply (3rd March, 1593), Mercuriale recalled having already drawn his friend's attention to the fact "that the Padua Studium was the proper home for his genius". It was not a rhetorical phrase: the University of Padua continued to enjoy great fame, despite the growth in the number of Studia, and it was a sort of crossroads of intellectual Europe. It was not by chance that in the same few years there had arrived in Padua, for a short period of time and in truth with no great success, two restless and talented thinkers: Giordano Bruno, who then moved to Venice to the house of the same Giovanni Mocenigo who was strongly to denounce him to the Inquisition, and Tommaso Campanella, who precisely in Padua was arrested on two occasions on the accusation of heresy and was then transferred to the Inquisition in Rome. It is true however that the horizon under which the young Galileo moved from a teaching post in Pisa (which

Nicolaus Copernicus

had begun at the end of 1589) to one in Padua was dominated by more contingent and concrete reasons. In Pisa his modest annual fee of sixty *scudi* was wholly insufficient to meet his family requirements, above all after the death of his father Vincenzo (1591), and moreover the relations with his philosopher colleagues, with the exception of Jacopo Mazzoni, were not good. It was with the support of the marquis Guidobaldo Del Monte, his friend and protector, former student at Padua, that Galileo managed to have himself called there. The annual salary of 180 florins initially granted to him by the Venetian Senate was only twenty-five per cent higher than the meagre Pisan fee, but there was the well-founded hope of a future rise and furthermore the increased number of students would have made it more remunerative to give private lessons, as Galileo had been used to doing in Pisa.

Thus the long vacancy of the Paduan chair of "mathematics", which had lasted since the death of Giuseppe Molinetti (January, 1588) was over. It was a teaching position which had an illustrious history, initially joined with astrology, understood both as judicial astrology or divination and as the study of the celestial system (astronomy). A reference to Pietro d'Abano here is obligatory, in particular to his *Lucidator dubitabilium astronomiae*, where, drawing on Arab writers such as al-Bitrugi, he declares his intention of clarifying the doubts born of the different solutions to the astronomical problems given by Aristotle and Ptolemy's Almagestus. In the mid fourteenth century teaching astrology at Padua was Giovanni Dondi, who in his *Astrarium* described the complex mechanism of the great astronomical clock which still today dominates the Piazza dei Signori and which, besides the time and the day of the month, also indicates the path of the sun and the zodiac, the phases of the moon, and the movement of the planets. From the end of the fourteenth century we find among the professors of astrology, astronomy, and mathematics, Biagio Pelacani, mentioned above, and then Prosdocimo de' Beldomandi, who left behind him many works on the arts of the quadrivium. The most notable is a commentary on the *Tractatus de sphaera* by John de Sacrobosco, which was in turn a compendium of Ptolemy's *Almagest*, used at that time as a basic text book for the teaching of astronomy (even Galileo used it in his Padua lessons). Beldomandi taught astrology from 1422 to his death (1428) and it is not unlikely that his lessons were attended by the young Nicolaus Cusanus, who studied canon law in Padua from 1417 to 1423 and who always nurtured a strong interest in mathematics and astronomy as well as in theology and philosophy. The same Cusanus was later to have relations with two other celebrated professors of "mathematics" at the Padua Studium, the Germans Georg Puerbach and Johannes Müller from Königsberg (known in Latin fashion as Regiomontanus).

Nicolaus Copernicus' stay in Padua around the turn of the sixteenth century to study medicine and law should not be emphatized too strongly, given the lack of evidence for his interest in astronomy at that time. It is in any case possible that he followed the astronomy lessons given by

Benedetto Triaca, a pupil of Pomponazzi; and we should not forget that at the time the discussion of astronomical topics such as the length of the year and the reform of the calendar, homocentric spheres, the "eccentric", the "deferent", and "epicycles" also involved the philosophers. These latter had at their disposal a cosmology fully integrated into the Aristotelian system, which produced descriptive models of the physical constitution of the universe; astrologers and mathematicians, on the other hand, who based their studies on Ptolemy's mathematized astronomy, aimed at the calculation and the forecasting of celestial movements. This is the context in which we can view another two famous pupils of the Studium: Girolamo Fracastoro of Verona (1478-1553), who in his composite oeuvre also dealt with the homocentric spheres, as well as the mortality of the soul and medical questions, and Girolamo Cardano of Pavia (1501/1506-1576), a mathematician as well as a physician, who is to be credited with a formulation of the theory of cubic equations. Neither should we forget, among the illustrious pupils of the Studium, the figure of Bernardino Telesio from Calabria (1509-1587), who after having studied philosophy and mathematics in Padua elaborated a philosophy of nature alternative to the Aristotelian one.

Girolamo Cardano

It was only inevitable that in Padua, bastion of Aristotelian logic, there should be conflict – and conflict there was - between the mathematicians and the scholars of logic. This is what happened in the mid sixteenth century, when Alessandro Piccolomini published a work which questioned the thesis – held by Averroes in particular – whereby mathematical demonstrations were the most reliable form of demonstration because they start from definitions, axioms, and postulates, that is from principles which, as they are by nature known the best, act like apodictic causes of the properties of mathematical entities. A reply was made to this attack on the scientific nature of mathematics from Aristotelian positions, by the young Francesco Barozzi in 1560, who asserted the "certainty" of mathematics with reference to the neoplatonic Proclus, a translation of whose commentary on the first book of Euclid he was later to publish. For his part Pietro Catena (who from 1547 to 1576 occupied the chair which was later to be Galileo's) attempted to free Euclidean demonstration from its subordination to the canons of Aristotelian demonstration by collecting and analyzing the references to mathematics scattered in Aristotle's logical works. It is with this background, characterized by a relentless contrast between Aristotelianism and Platonism, that we must situate Galileo's teaching in Padua, during which he developed the idea of mathematics as a rigorous instrument of knowledge, able – unlike Aristotelian logic - to capture and formulate the 'laws' which constitute the structure of physical reality.

Galileo taught and lived in Padua for eighteen years, and they were, as he himself was later to recognize, "the best eighteen years of my whole life". Years of teaching and study, but also of intense friendship with Paduan and Venetian intellectuals, as well as of persistent financial diffi-

DIFESA
DI GALILEO GALILEI
NOBILE FIORENTINO,
Lettore delle Matematiche nello Studio di Padoua,
Contro alle Calunnie & imposture
DI BALDESSAR CAPRA
MILANESE,
Vsategli sì nella Considerazione Astronomica sopra la nuoua Stella del M DC IIII. come (& assai più) nel publicare nuouamente come sua inuenzione la fabrica, & gli vsi del Compasso Geometrico, & Militare, sotto il titolo di
Vsus & fabrica Circini cuiusdam proportionis, &c.
CVM PRIVILEGIO.
IN VENETIA, M DC VII.
Presso Tomaso Baglioni.

SIDEREVS
NVNCIVS
MAGNA, LONGEQVE ADMIRABILIA
Spectacula pandens, suspiciendaque proponens
vnicuique, præsertim verò
PHILOSOPHIS, atq; ASTRONOMIS, quæ à
GALILEO GALILEO
PATRITIO FLORENTINO
Patauini Gymnasij Publico Mathematico
PERSPICILLI
QVATVOR PLANETIS
MEDICEA SIDERA
NVNCVPANDOS DECREVIT.
VENETIIS, Apud Thomam Baglionum. M DC X.

Bust of Galileo Galilei, frontispiece of the Difesa contro alle calunnie et imposture... *and frontispiece of the* Sidereus Nuncius

culties, given that he had to provide not only for his family of origin, but also for the three children he had from a relationship with the Venetian Marina Gamba. Symbol of his public lessons at the Palazzo del Bo is the famous chair – now kept in the Sala dei Quaranta – which according to tradition was set up for him so that his lessons could by followed by the numerous students, both of philosophy and medicine. Moreover, as was the custom, Galileo took steps to increase his income by taking in numerous student lodgers in his large house in via dei Vignali (the present-day via Galilei, near the Basilica of Saint Anthony), and giving them private lessons. It should be pointed out that the content of these lessons, both public and private, was wholly traditional, in conformity with the curriculum in force, and that this was despite Galileo's personal adherence to Copernicanism is clear from the letters he sent in 1597 to Iacopo Mazzoni and to Kepler: a caution probably dictated by the negative reception many had given to Copernicus' theory. In any case, in Galileo's house the students had the possibility of becoming acquainted with and of acquiring the scientific instruments which he himself had one of his mechanics build from 1599 onwards. These are the years of his studies on military fortifications, the geometrico-military compass, the thermometer, and the magnet.

The appearance of a new star in the sign of Sagittarius, on 10th October, 1604, attracted the attention of Galileo, who in that same academic year of 1604-1605 was dealing with the "theories of the planets". He held three, packed, 'extraordinary' lessons in the Studium on this event, in which he took up a position against the Aristotelian doctrine of the incorruptibility of the heavens, thus provoking the anger of his Aristotelian colleagues and above all that of Cesare Cremonini who was also his friend. But the opportunity for coming decisively out into the open and leaving behind his "silent Copernicanism", was provided by the celestial observations that Galileo was able to carry out in the autumn of 1609 thanks to the telescope built in the previous months in his laboratory: the surface of the moon, the Milky Way, the nebulae, then the four moons of Jupiter, named the "Medicean stars" in honour of Cosimo II Granduke of Tuscany (with whom Galileo had been negotiating a return to his "patria" for several months, even though in August 1609 the Venetian Senate had confirmed his teaching post at the Padua Studium for life with an annual salary of 1000 florins). On 12th March, 1610, his *Sidereus nuncius*, the "announcement on the stars" was published in Venice, which gave news of the discoveries he had made thanks to the *perspicillum* (the telescope). There was an exceptional European interest in such discoveries, which threw the entire Aristotelian and Ptolemaic cosmology into crisis and seemed to confirm the Copernican system, and consequently the reactions from the Aristotelian camp were strong. But by now Galileo, attracted by the idea of being able to return to Florence and dedicate himself entirely to study under the protection of the Granduke, had on 15th June, given up his teaching in Padua. He continued his astronomical observations, however, discovering sunspots and perhaps the phases of Venus in the summer months. On 7th September, 1610, after one last morning observation of the "Medicean stars", he left Padua, having promised his friends he would return. It was a promise that Galileo was unable to keep. "Oh what good it would have done Mr. Galileo too [...] not to have left the freedom of Padua!": thus his old colleague and friend, as well as adversary, Cesare Cremonini, was reported to have commented afterwards, Cremonini the relentless Peripatetic in odour of impiety, whom the Venetian Senate, despite the accusations of the Inquisition, always guaranteed with the freedom to teach, protracted for forty years, up until his death (1631).

Geminiano Montanari

Once Galileo had left, no positive trace of his teaching remained with the Paduan Peripatetics, who were obstinately impervious to cosmological and philosophical novelties. There is a well-known anecdote regarding Cremonini, who had refused to look into the telescope pointed towards the sky, because "looking through those glasses startled his head". It symbolizes the radical difference in mentality, even before any theoretical contents, between a highly rigorous and unbiased approach to reality, bordering on heresy for the theologians, but still mediated by the books (and hence by the doctrinal framework) of Aristotle, and an approach centred on observation, measurement, hypothesis, and experiment: an approach, that is, which declines to investigate first principles and therefore refuses a dimension which, although physicistic as it was in the Paduan Aristotelian tradition, still remained 'essentialistic' and metaphysical.

The path to the assertion of the new "experimental philosophy" in the Padua Studium was not short and was accompanied by the progressive detachment of new disciplines from the trunk of natural philosophy or 'physics' or from the great river-bed of 'mixed mathematics', into which up until 1506 the teaching of mathematics and astrology had flowed. An effective turning point can be identified only from the 1560s onwards, thanks to the Venetian mathematician, Stefano Degli Angeli (1623-1697, a pupil of Bonaventura Cavalieri in Bologna and a teacher in Padua from 1662), and the philosopher and mathematician Carlo Rinaldini of Ancona (1615-1698, collaborator of the "Accademia del Cimento", called in 1667 from the Pisa Studium to the chair of philosophy), both heirs of the Galilean method. It was Rinaldini who, visiting the extremely well stocked library of Giovan Battista Cornaro Piscopia in Venice, made the acquaintance of his daughter Elena Lucrezia, and was astonished by her knowledge in the field of geometry. A true child prodigy, Elena had acquired European fame for her exceptional culture: Rinaldini guided her in her philosophical studies and was the supervisor for her degree in philosophy, which she obtained at the age of 32 from the Padua Studium on 25th June, 1678, the first woman graduate in the world. Degli Angeli in turn had as a pupil Iacopo Riccati, student of law at Padua but passionately interested in mathematics, who was to become famous for the differential equation, which bears his name.

Other protagonists of this "revival of Galileanism" were Geminiano

Statue of Giovanni Poleni and portrait of Simone Stratico

Montanari (1633-1687) and Domenico Guglielmini (1655-1710), both of whom came from the University of Bologna. With Montanari the new chair of astronomy, as separate from that of mathematics, took off in 1678. A spirit open to all the philosophical currents of his time, firmly convinced that the sciences should be at the service of "public happiness", he denounced the falsity of judicial astrology and fervently committed himself to applied mathematics, in particular hydraulic engineering. In 1698 Guglielmini also arrived in Padua, teacher first of mathematics and then medicine, a great expert in fluvial hydraulics. And several years earlier, in 1694, the Sicilian Michelangelo Fardella had been called to the chair of philosophy (where he remained until 1709, then moving to Barcellona), who after having frequented Cartesian circles in Paris had taken on the task of diffusing Descartes' mathematism, united with a profound Augustinian inspiration filtered through the thought of Malebranche. Contributing to this opening towards more recent European thought was, for several years, albeit behind the scenes, the great Leibniz, who had not omitted to visit Padua during his journey to Italy. Leibniz planned to make the Padua Studium a sort of outpost in Italy for the diffusion of differential calculus, in competition with Newton and his followers, and to this end he actively supported the appointment to the chair of mathematics of the Swiss Jacob Hermann (who held it from 1707 to 1713) and then Nicolaus Bernoulli, who was called to Padua in the same year in which his patron died (1716), but who remained there only three years.

The modernization of philosophico-scientific culture pursued by several teachers did not make an impact, however, on the traditional didactic organization of the Studium, which in the early eighteenth century underwent a deep crisis, denounced with polemical vigour in the report made out by Scipione Maffei of Verona (1715): "What idea can someone today conceive of a public University if, having taken in his hand the roll of the lectures [that is the list of the teaching subjects and their relative curricula], [...] he sees all the lecturers in all types of philosophy confined by the rules to the books of Aristotle, and Aristotle imposed even on he who has to lecture on Astronomy?". The desired reform of the Studium was carried out in 1739 and had among its major protagonists the Venetian Giovanni Poleni (1683-1761), who in 1710 had been called to the chair of "Astronomy and meteors" then moving in 1715 to that of philosophy (that is physics) in the second rank and in 1720 to that of mathematics. In 1739 he was entrusted with the newly established chair of "experimental philosophy", which in 1755 was added to by the teaching of nautical science and shipbuilding, substituting Gian Rinaldo Carli. Philosopher, scientist, and engineer, member of the principal European scientific academies (London, Berlin, Bologna, Saint Petersburg, Paris), a careful observer (in 1725 he began the first meteorological surveys in Italy, then continued by Toaldo) but also a scholar of archaeology and an expert classical philologist, he personifies an ideal of a decisively modern culture but one at the same time far removed from that conflict between the "two cultures" (the humanistic and the technico-scientific) which seems to characterize present-day learning. Poleni, who had already built a physics laboratory in his own house, promoted the construction in 1740 of the great "Theatre of experimental philosophy", a laboratory of almost 400 pieces which have partially survived the vicissitudes of time: around a hundred pieces of apparatus are today preserved in the "Galileo Galilei" department of Physics, while three great model ships have found a place in the academic halls of the Palazzo del Bo.

On his death, Poleni was succeeded by Simone Stratico of Zadar (1733-1824), who in 1801 was to be called to the chair of "navigation" at the University of Pavia, later becoming senator of the Napoleonic Kingdom of Italy and president of the National Institute. Among the novelties of the reform of 1739 was the establishment of an autonomous chair of geography, the teaching of which had been joined to that of astronomy up until then, while the first chair of experimental chemistry, which was entrusted to Marco Carburi, dates back to 1759. As far as the long hoped-for construction of an astronomical observatory was concerned, this was carried out by the abbé Giuseppe Toaldo of Vicenza (1719-1797), who had been appointed professor of astronomy in 1762 and was to reach European fame in the field of meteorological studies. Toaldo had studied and then begun his teaching career in the episcopal Seminary of Padua, which reached University level in the eighteenth century thanks to the initiatives of the bishop Gregorio Barbarigo. It was in this same institute that the most 'European' of the late eighteenth-century men of letters of the Veneto region, the abbé Melchiorre Cesarotti, had completed his studies and then taught rhetoric. Cesarotti was famous for his Italian translation of the *Songs of Ossian*, admired even by Napoleon. In 1768 he was called to the University chair of Greek and Hebrew and there devoted himself to the translation of Demosthenes and the *Iliad* and took part in the debate on the Homeric problem. An extremely lively spirit, he also tackled the problems of literary criticism (proposing new aesthetic canons with respect to the dominant rationalism) and those of the Italian language, maintaining the necessity of a linguistic renewal against the immobilism of the purists. Significant, in such a rich cultural context, is the interest which he showed for the theories of Giambattista Vico: an interest shared, albeit in different ways, by other of his University colleagues, such as Iacopo Stellini, teacher of moral philosophy from 1739, and the Greek and Latinist Clemente Sibiliato, as well as the Studium's historiographer, Francesco Maria Colle. On one hand the meteorological surveys of the abbé Toaldo, with their applications to agriculture; on the other the interest of the abbé Cesarotti in Greek and "Celtic" literature, but also in the French followers of the Enlightenment and in Vico: it is with this double cultural profile that the centuries-old teaching of the arts in the ancient and glorious Paduan Studium ends emblematically.

Giuseppe Toaldo and Melchiorre Cesarotti

Eximij theologie Professoris. M. Antonij Trombete Patauini ordis Minoꝝ Proui. Sci Antonij Mistri i pclaro Patauino studio Methaphysicã pu. legentis ad Augustinũ Barbadico Illustrissimuz Venetiaꝝ Ducem Questio de Diuina prescientia futuroꝝ contingentium sequitur.

q

Queritur vtrũ deus precognoscat futura contingentia. Et arguit̃ ꝙ nõ. Si deus scit me lecturũ cras: ergo istud futurũ necessario eueniet: ꝯsequẽs ẽ falsum q: sicut de isto: ita de quolibet alio futuro ꝯtingenti. ⁊ ita oĩa ex necessitate euenirẽt. quo dato: seqtur ꝙ nõ oporteret negociari/aut cõsiliari circa agenda a nobis. ꝯsequentia ꝓbatur. Illud necessario euenit: cui⁹ oppositũ est ipossibile aduenire. Sed oppositũ huius futuri ꝯtingentis ẽ huiusmodi. Qḋ ꝓbatur. q: vel ẽ possibile aduenire/vel nõ. si non: habeo ꝓpositum. si sic: ponat̃ in esse. ⁊ tũc deus decipiet̃ in sua cognitione quũ deus cognosceret ab eterno oppositũ. Ad oppositum est Hieronymus sup Hieremiã. Futuroꝝ scia soli deo competit. ẞ si de⁹ posset falli circa ista: nõ esset scia ipsoꝝ. q: scia est cognitio certa ⁊ euidens ex ꝑino posterioꝝ ⁊. vij. metaphysice tex. commẽ. iiij. Quoniam inquisitio de diuina prescia futuroꝝ presupponit notitiam quõ futurum ꝯtingens se hꝫ ad esse. q: sicut se hꝫ ad esse: sic ad cognosci ex. ij. metaphy. tex. cõmen. iiij. ideo pro determinatione qõnis quatuor pricipaliter facimus. Primo videndũ est quõ capit̃ a phĩs contingens. Secundo an futurũ ꝯtingens sit ad alteraꝫ ptem ꝯtradictionis determinatũ. Tertio an ꝯtingentia hẽant aliquã cãm sui esse. Quarto de quesito videbitur. Quantũ ad primum articulum sunt tres distinctiones. Prima distinctio est ista. Contingens vno mõ accipit̃ vt distinguit̃ ꝯtra necessarium. Alio modo vt distinguitur ꝯtra ens vt in pluribus. Primo mõ est illud in cuius nã ẽ possibilitas ad deficiẽdum. vt est de mẽte Auer. ij. phisicoꝝ. cõmen. xlviij. ꝯtra Auic. ⁊ tale ꝯtingens est illud qḋ est possibile esse vel nõ esse. de quo loquitur Arist. ix. metaphi. tex. commen. xvij. vbi habet hoc. Est aũt potentia nihil sempiternũ/omnis namqꝫ potentia: contradictiõis est. possibile oẽ contingit nõ actu esse. Ex qbus verbis ꝯcludit Arist. ꝙ oĩs potentia passiua/ẽ ꝯtradictõis ⁊ ita (quum possibile qḋ distinguit̃ ꝯtra necessariũ sit in potẽtia passiua ad esse post nõ esse q: est terminus potentie actiue q̃ agiꝑ motuꝫ) seqtur ꝙ tale ꝯtingens hꝫ possibilitateꝫ ad deficiendũ. ⁊ ita nullo modo ẽ necessariuꝫ. Et ex hoc hꝫ euidentiã snĩa Auic. ponentis drĩam inter ꝯtingens vt in pluribus ⁊ necessarium. Naꝫ ꝯtingens vt in pluribus ẜm ipsum habet impedimentũ. necessariũ vero nullum habet impedimentũ. Vñ primo sue phisice ca. xiij. dicit ꝙ hec ẽ differẽtia inter semꝑ ⁊ sepe. q: ei qḋ est semꝑ: non aduersat̃ ꝯtrarium impediens. ẞ bene ei qḋ est sepe. nã si ab eo qḋ est sepe: remouean̄t contraria impediẽtia: tale ꝯtingẽs erit necessariũ. Neqꝫ ẞ snĩa Auic. ꝯtradicit snĩe Auer. q: lꝫ Auic. põat possibilitatẽ ad deficiendũ extrinsecam sciꝫ ex pte ipedientis extrinseci: nõ tñ negauit intrinsecaꝫ. ẞ vna p̃supposita videlꝫ intrinseca: alterã explicuit. Quare rõ Auer. quam adducit in p̃allegato cõmẽto ꝯtra Auic. nulla est. Alio modo capit̃ ꝯtingens vt distinguit̃ ꝯtra ens vt in pluribus. ⁊ tale est ens cõtingens equaliter/aut in minori pte qḋ est ens casuale ⁊ fortuitũ. ⁊ hoc sequendo viaꝫ Auic. tenentis dari casum tam in possibilibus eq̃liter q̃ in minori pte. Nec rões Auer. aut Themistij multũ ꝯtra hãc viam vt postea declarabit̃. Secũda distinctio cõtingẽs equaliter. Quoddã ẽ ex pte effectus tm̃. Quoddaꝫ ex pte cause agentis. Ex parte effectus illud est cõtingens equaliter qḋ ab aliqua potentia actiua sic prouenit qḋ de nã sua nõ natum ẽ ab huiusmodi potentia actiua magis ꝓuenire q̃ nõ ꝓuenire. sed idifferent̃ se hꝫ ad vtrũlibet. Sed ꝯtingens ex pte cause agentis est agens qḋ ex natura sua deducto impedimento est indifferens ad agendũ ⁊ non agendũ. Tertia distinctio ꝙ duplex est cõtingentia. Quedã ꝑ se. Quedã ꝑ accidens. Cõtingentia ꝑ se est ẜm quam aliqd est possibile aliter se hẽre non ex impedimento alicui⁹ cause: sed solũ ex plenitudine ptãtis ⁊ potentie potentis ponere in esse ipm effectũ vel oppositũ ipsius. Et hec ꝯtingẽtia attribuit̃ volũtati. Propter quaꝫ ei attribuit dñiũ ⁊ pricipatũ. Phy. viij. poli. c. v. dicẽs. Aie potẽtia qua eligim⁹ ꝑ̃ncipans est. ⁊ qḋ liberꝝ ab hac potentia existit: ab oĩbus ẽ inuincibile. Et. x. ethi. Felicitas ẽ opatio optima/⁊ optimi: siue intellectus: siue alicuius alterius qḋ ẜm nãm vĩ principari ⁊ dñari. Et nono metaphy. textu. cõmen. x. distiguit potẽtias rõnales ab irrationalibus. volens ꝙ rõnalis valꝫ ad opposita. irrõnalis est tantũmodo vnius oppositoꝝ. Et vlterius vult ꝙ potẽtie rõnales sicut sunt scie ⁊ artes (quũ equaliter respiciant opposita ⁊ non magis sint vnius q̃ alterius) si sint determinate vnius: hoc est ex appetitu ⁊ pro heresi determinante. Et cõmentator prosequitur dĩ ꝙ appetitus determinãs est voluntas. q̃ lꝫ (vt iquit ipse) sit ab intellectu .s. vt oñdente ⁊ ꝯsiltante: intellectus tñ ⁊ alie potẽtie rationales sunt a volũtate impante ⁊ regulante alias potẽtias ꝑ modũ impij lꝫ ipsa regulet̃ ab intellectu ꝑ moduꝫ ꝯsilij. Neqꝫ sic regulari arguit maiorẽ dignitatẽ in intellectu. Certũ ẽ. n. ꝙ Iuriscõsultus regulat Regẽ ꝑ modũ ꝯsilij. Iste tñ Iuriscõsult⁹ nõ ẽ dignior Rege. q: Rex ipꝫ Iuriscõsultuꝫ ⁊ alios regulat ꝑ modũ impij qḋ regulare arguit ꝑ̃ncipalitatem ⁊ nobilitatẽ. Qḋ si tu diceres ꝙ intellect⁹ ⁊ scia non cõnumerant̃ iter potentias rõnales: Hoc est ꝯtra tex. p̃allegatũ ⁊ ẽt ꝯtra tex. cõmẽ. iii. vbi enumerat artẽ medicatiuã iter potẽtias rõnales que potentia inquit ipse est infirmitatis ⁊ sanitatis. Contingentia ꝑ accidẽs est illa ẜm quã aliqd est possibile aliter se hẽre ex impedimẽto alicui⁹ cause siue efficientis siue materialis siue finalis. Et hec ꝯtingentia ẽ q: cause nõ pñt agere vel pati. vñ effectus ẽ ꝯtingens seu ꝯtingent̃ euenit ex ordine ad causas accñtales comitantes causas ꝑ se ⁊ impedientes ipsas. Et ista contingentia est ipsoꝝ nãlium generabiliũ ⁊ corruptibiliũ. Huiusmodi. n. effectus cãruꝫ nãlium q̃tum ẽ ex causis ꝑ se ipsoꝝ: necessario ꝓueniunt. ꝙ aũt ꝯtingenter eueniãt: hoc est ex causis ꝑ accidẽs ꝯcomitantibus causas ꝑ se ⁊ ipsas ipedientes. Cause. n. nãles ꝑ se disposite remoto ipedimento nõ pñt non agere. quare necessario agũt. Et hoc ẽ quod dicit Aristo. nono metaphy. tex. cõmẽ. allegati. Necesse ẽ inquit qñ vt pñt actiuũ ⁊ passiuũ appropinquant: hoc qdem facere: illud vero pati. Ex hijs que dicta sunt seqtur ꝙ ꝯtingentia effectus causaꝝ nãlium hꝫ quatuor ꝯditiones. Prima ꝯditio est ꝙ est ꝯtingẽtia ꝑ accñs. nõ ꝑ se. Est eñ huiusmodi ꝯtingentia ex pte idispõnis mãe aut alterius cause accidentalis aut ꝑ accñs. nõ aũt ex ordine effectuũ ad cãs ꝑ se. Secunda ꝯditio ẽ ꝙ talis contingentia ẽ contingentia ẜm qd nõ simplr. q: est i ordine ad aliquã vnã cãm vt impedibilẽ ꝑ aliã. nõ est aũt in ordine ad totũ ordinẽ cãrum ꝯcurrentiũ ad effectum. Tertia ꝯditio est ꝙ ẽ ꝯtingentia ꝑ̃uatiua. non positiua. Prouenit eñꝫ ꝯtingentia huiusmodi ex ꝑ̃uatiõe seu ex defectu alicuius dispõnis causaꝝ. Cause. n. vltima dispõne priuate: non agunt. Quarta ꝯditio ẽ ꝙ est ꝯtingentia extrinseca

ANTONINO POPPI

Theology

Scholars have for some time now been stressing the purely lay character of the oldest Italian medieval Universities such as Bologna, Padua, and Naples, which were dominated by the study of law, medicine, and natural sciences, unlike the Universities of northern Europe such as Paris, Oxford, Cologne, etc., where the 'faculty' of theology exercised a sort of hegemony, setting itself up as the supreme summit of knowledge, unifying all of the others.

It is only in the second half of the fourteenth century that the teaching of theology began to work its way into the official structures of the Italian Universities too as a new 'faculty' *sui generis* side by side with the *universitates iuristarum* and *artistarum*. After the pioneering cases of Pisa and Florence with a bull by Clement VI (1343 and 1349), the Avignon popes also authorized the institution of a 'faculty' of theology in the Studia of Bologna (1360), Padua (1363), Perugia (1371), Pavia (1388), Ferrara (1391), and in other minor Universities. As has been pointed out, these innovations signalled the end of the predominance of Parisian theology which up until then had been the splendour of Christianity and the central column of papal teaching in the arduous problems of the faith and Christian praxis; this policy of theological decentralization responded to the papacy's need for new alliances with the forces of the Italian cities and its attempt to escape the interminable disquisitions, sometimes verging on the heretical, of the Parisian nominalist theologians. It is our intention here to outline the institutional structure of Paduan theology in its essence and then to present some of the results of the scientifico-cultural activity of its theologians.

1.The bull instituting the 'faculty' of theology in the Padua Studium, Urban V's *Sane dum fructus*, is dated from Avignon 15th April, 1363. Ardently desired by city bishops of great intellectual and diplomatic standing such as Ildebrandino Conti and Pileo da Prata, the new 'faculty' was also in accordance with the quest for prestige of the signoria of the Carrara family (Francesco il Vecchio and his brother Ubertino, canon of the cathedral), as well as with the need of the arts students to forge new academic alliances against the law students, from whom they were separating themselves. Just as the Padua Studium was famous everywhere for its teaching of canon and civil law as well as for that of the liberal arts, so the pope expected that from now on it would also shine for the study of divine science; thus receiving the supplications of the students, with his apostolic

Antonio Trombetta, Questio de divina prescientia futurorum contingenium

authority he established and ordered that in this city from now on (*deinceps*) there should be a "studium generale in eadem theologiae facultate" with all the privileges enjoyed by the teachers and students of the other faculties, recommending however that there be called to the teaching and the running of this 'faculty' masters and bachelors who had graduated from Paris or from some other famous theological Studium.

Obviously, theology was not unknown in Padua; the papal foundation marks the recognition of a more ancient and robust tradition of theological studies already documented at the end of the twelfth century in the cathedral schools which then intensified over the course of the thirteenth century with the establishment in the city of the great Mendicant orders, who almost immediately opened their own *Studia generalia* with masters and students from all over Europe, with flourishing libraries of hand-written and illuminated manuscripts of the Bible, the Fathers, the most important theologians of the respective schools, liturgy, and piety, as well as substantial collections of the Latin classics. Around 1230, in the Dominican convent of Sant'Agostino and among the Franciscans of the little church of Santa Maria Mater Domini we find two masters of biblical and theological studies of the calibre of Saint Albertus Magnus and Saint Anthony of Padua; later the Augustinian friars, the Carmelites, and finally the Servites arrived, bringing with them theologians and philosophers who had graduated from Paris or Oxford, who brought Paduan culture into the network of the higher Studia and in contact with the novelties emerging in Europe.

With the bull of 1363, we have an elevation of these private schools of theology to the public academic level, and therefore their aggregation to the older University of arts and law. The *universitas theologorum* comprised first of all the regent masters, or headmasters of the various city convents, all the 'lectores', that is to say the professors of these convents who already had a doctorate in theology, and it also incorporated the graduate students, or bachelors, who were beginning their academic career under the guidance of a regent master, explaining for two years some of the books of the Bible in a 'cursory' or introductory fashion to the young students of theology of the various schools, and for another two years those of Peter Lombard's *Sentences*. Such a composition immediately evinces the peculiarity of this corporation; indeed, we find ourselves looking at a 'university of masters' or scholars, more than a 'university of students', as were the other two faculties, given that the bachelors were young thirty-year-old professors, who had already obtained a doctorate in the arts, had studied theology in the convent schools for six years, and had been admitted to the 'faculty' on the basis of a "disputatio temptatoria" with an experienced master of theology whose task it was to ascertain and guarantee that they were suitable and sufficiently prepared for the courses leading to a doctorate in theology.

2. Right from the beginning, according to the statutes, the governing body of the new 'faculty' was constituted by the Collegium of theologians,

made up of the regent masters of the city schools and then gradually opened up to the masters who joined by means of a rigorous examination and a certain donation of money; even if they were not teachers, all of its members, however, had obtained a doctorate in theology and were exclusively men of the church (they had at least to have been tonsured, or to have received one of the minor orders): women were not even admitted to the degree in theology, as is demonstrated by cardinal Barbarigo's refusal to admit to the doctorate the noblewoman Elena Lucrezia Cornaro Piscopia, who had already been put forward by the conventual Franciscan dean Felice Rotondi in 1677. The Collegium immediately became the central legislative and executive institution of the entire *universitas theologorum*, to such an extent as to be almost identified with it (in the documents of the college we find recurring almost like a hendiadys: *Collegium et alma universitas sacrorum theologorum antiquissimi Studii patavini*), promoting and defending the 'faculty' throughout the entire course of its history, up to its suppression by Napoleon in 1806.

While the theologians were initially almost all members of religious orders and those of the diocesan clergy could be counted on the fingers of one hand, after the Council of Trent we find a great resurgence of the secular clergy, canons and rectors, or priests of urban and suburban churches, who with a view to higher ecclesiastical positions enrolled in theology courses in the 'university' of arts, crowning their studies with teaching and their aggregation to the Collegium: in Padua they initially constituted half and then two-thirds of the Collegium, carrying out a notable role in its governing (we can think of influential figures like Girolamo Zacco, Camillo Borromeo, or Mario Mazzoleni), even though later they were excluded from promotion to degrees, employed by the Venetian Senate solely as public teachers of theology, metaphysics, and Holy Scripture in the 'university' of the arts (1632).

The Collegium was presided over by a dean, chosen annually from among the regent masters of the major religious orders according to a cyclical rotation; with the statutes of 1424 the length of office was reduced to six months and from 1498 to four months by means of drawing lots among the theologians who were members. By affinity with the priors of the other two Collegia (law and medicine), in 1592 the dean was aided by a 'sindaco' and several years later (1613) by three councillors as well: all five formed the so-called 'banca', a type of council which under the vigilance of the chancellor (the bishop of Padua) or his vicar general, dealt, as they arose, with disputes between masters, checked the regular functioning of the exams for the doctorate, the faithful observance of the statutes and any need for their reformulation in the case of changed circumstances, established the fees for the various academic degrees and the incorporation of masters who had graduated elsewhere, saw to decorum and the official participation of its members in public ceremonies, defended its own autonomy and the rights it had acquired from the attempts by other Universities to incorporate it, and was responsible for the treasury and the

Saint Gregorio Barbarigo and Felice Rotondi

preservation of the documents and the other official acts of the 'faculty'. To be able to fulfil any one of these duties the College member had to be resident in the city of Padua, not in the surrounding countryside, to have been a member for at least three years, and to be at least forty years old for the councillors.

The decisional power of the 'banca', however, was particularly restricted because any decision had to be approved by the entire College of masters and finally be endorsed by the supreme authority of the bishop rector, considered the *caput universitatis theologorum*, the ultimate authority of the 'faculty', to whom each individual theologian and the whole Collegium together owed particular reverence and obedience, signified publicly in an official reception in the cathedral shortly after the arrival of a new bishop to the diocese.

The statutes formed over the centuries of its existence the 'faculty''s *magna charta*; it was with continual reference to these that deans and masters of the Collegium undertook their duties, defended their rights, and resolved internal and external conflicts. Thanks to a lucky find in the archives, father Antonio Sartori has documented the precise circumstance in which the general statutes of Urban VI for the recently-established Italian theology faculties were officially presented in Padua to bishop Raimondo on 21st February, 1385, in the presence of four regent masters of the religious orders representing the entire College. These brief norms were soon enlarged with the first of the Padua College's own statutes in 1406, immediately after Padua passed under Venetian domination, drawn up by the Franciscan dean Englesco Engleschi, and approved by the bishop Albano Michiel. They were completely reorganized and distributed into three parts in 1424 by another Franciscan dean, Giovanni di San Marino, and promulgated by the bishop Pietro Marcello: this redaction remained the basis for all the successive additions and partial reforms over the course of the years, and of the new complete reformulation with the "Statuta reformata" of 1573 and then 1612.

3. From what has been said above, it appears therefore that the 'faculty' of theologians had its own characteristics, which distinguished it from the other two faculties. In the first place, the students, who were not united in a specific corporation and different *nationes* like the law and arts students, did not have their own rector nor could they choose and pay their own teachers, the religious of the conventual schools who were not paid with public money but were dependent for everything on the Collegium of theologians and the city's bishop. This particular feature of the studies and the governing bodies, however, in no way authorizes the conclusion reached by some scholars like Francesco Maria Colle, who in his *Storia scientifico-letteraria dello Studio di Padova* (1825) simply denied the existence of an autonomous theology 'faculty' and its Collegium before the establishment of the two new chairs of Thomist and Scotist theology in the arts at the end of the fifteenth century; in this way, rather than a 'faculty' in its

own right, theology would resemble more a sort of 'degree course' for the arts students. Equally reductive is the position of the great Renaissance scholar, Paul Oskar Kristeller, recently deceased (1999), who held that in the Italian Universities, geared around the study of law and medicine, there had never been a true theology 'faculty' on the level of the Universities of northern Europe: a few courses on metaphysics, theology, and later on the Bible and ecclesiastical history set up in the 'university' of arts students were not able to correspond to a doctorate in theology and were officially part of the arts 'university', not of an inexistent theological 'faculty'.

This opinion, still highly credited among historians of the Universities, had already been provided with a reply by Andrea Gloria in his *Monumenti dell'Università di Padova (1318-1405)*, published in 1888, who wrote that those who affirm that the theological 'faculty' did not form part of the University teaching as from 15th April, 1363, "deny the most obvious truth" as it emerges from the discovery and analysis of the juridical language of a notable number of documents, where the theological masters are all held to be equal to the other teachers. A more careful linguistic examination of the establishing bull and the statutes, not to mention the self-awareness of the theologians directly involved, leads to the same historical date of the existence of a third 'faculty' beside the other two of the Padua Studium.

4. After its first century of flourishing life, in the second half of the fifteenth century the theology 'faculty' went through a period of deadly crisis, with a great reduction in the number of its students and the closure of numerous schools opened for the practice of the bachelors in view to their doctorate. The laborious *iter* of lessons and academic exercises with the rigorous final examination before the entire College of theologians was of a vastness and a complexity to discourage the less committed; moreover, and above all, the exorbitance of the fees for the final degree examination constituted an often insurmountable obstacle for the members of the religious orders, generally from the more modest social classes, forcing them to abandon this crowning of their studies, or to turn to a 'minor' degree with the Palatine counts. In the documents of the time we sense a full awareness of the gravity of the situation both by the deans and the bishops and by the arts students; thus it was that Venice decided to intervene by opening two competing chairs of metaphysics and then theology *in via Thomae* and *in via Scoti*, that is, according to the thought of Thomas Aquinas and that of John Duns Scotus, entrusting them for centuries to the Dominican and Franciscan teachers respectively. In 1551, moreover, it established the official teaching of the Bible, later supported by the introduction of Oriental Languages, and in 1718 by the chair of the History of the Church.

With the establishment of these new chairs, Venetian policy aimed implicitly at removing the theological 'faculty' more and more from its dependence on the bishop and the College of theologians, given that the public teachers were called and directly paid by the Senate of the Republic, and they had to obey scrupulously the instructions of the *Riformatori* of the Studium in all those matters which concerned the organization of studies, exams, fees, and so on.

As early as the end of the fifteenth century, therefore, a profound transformation was imperceptibly under way, even though it had not yet been felt, of the medieval theology 'faculty', which was independent from political authority, into a new institutional figure enclosed within the general organization of the Padua Studium, entirely dependent on central Venetian policy, although still distinct and autonomous from the other two faculties and their respective Colleges. It was, however, a natural and obvious transition, given that, as we have already hinted, the students and those taking degrees in theology hardly ever came from the old convents any more, but rather from the public schools of theology existing in the arts 'university', and, consequently, the public teachers became the first and the direct providers of teaching and of the academic vitality of the 'faculty' and its College. We thus move from the theology of the convents to the theology of the arts, and hence necessarily from an original obedience to the bishop to a full submission to the decrees of the *Riformatori* of the Serenissima.

The public theologians, whose influence in the Collegium became more and more decisive, felt themselves to be better protected by the civil magistracies than by the ecclesiastical authorities. As we can read in the reports of the Collegium of 1677/78 (cf. Archivio Storico dell'Università, ms. 435, fols 43v-116r), a tense stand-off was reached between those comprising the 'banca' of the theologians and cardinal Barbarigo's vicar general, Alessandro Mantovani, who insisted on interfering in the extraction of the 'puncta' for the final exam of those taking their degree, checking the proof of their studies and the dimissory letters from their respective superiors, demanded the presence of the diocesan chancellor for the "acts" in the place of the notary of the Collegium, and moreover stipulated the advance deposit of the graduating fees with the episcopal curia, and not with the notary of the theologians. The dispute dragged on for a long time and was resolved in Venice by the *Riformatori* in the theologians' favour, in the light of the statutes and the "praticato", that is to say the customary praxis according to which the bishop's presence in the "pronontia del dottorato" was simply ceremonial.

As a body by now fully integrated and recognized by the Padua Studium, throughout the entire eighteenth century the theology 'faculty' too felt the profound upheaval of the various attempts at reform with which the Venetian Republic attempted to renew the antiquated didactic organization of the two 'universities', bringing it up to date with other European Universities in the field of mathematical, medical, biological, chemical, and agrarian research, and so on, by establishing new teaching subjects, opening scientific laboratories, suppressing obsolete chairs, and substituting the fossilized Latin language with the live spoken language in its courses. Thus in 1739 the chairs of Thomist and Scotist Metaphysics were suppressed and unified into a single subject (still officially called Logic and Metaphysics in the roll) of a philosophy freed from the weight of the old schools and open to the new ideas of modern thought put forward by Cartesianism, Leibnizianism, empiricism, and the wind of the Enlightenment which was blowing across Europe; the same happened in 1771 for the two chairs of Theology, reduced to one and entrusted to the Thomist teacher Antonino Valsecchi, who reorganized the entire dogmatic around a more modern framework of interpreting the truths of the faith, leaving behind the centuries-old textbook of Peter Lombard's *Sentences*. Thus we arrive at a first temporary contraction of theology by the French Jacobins in 1797/98, then to its definitive fall with the Napoleonic decree of Saint Cloud dated 25th July, 1806.

5. The curriculum of the theology student, which for the bachelors initially stretched over a four-year period, was subsequently reduced to three years and, finally, with a decree by the *Riformatori* in 1760 and 1761, 'graciously' reduced to two, with the requirement of annual exams in theology, metaphysics, Holy Scripture, moral philosophy, and oriental languages. The ritual for the final public exam (the *vesperie*) and the conferring of the doctoral insignia (the *aulatio*), shaped in 1546 by the Servite theologian Domenico Dotti according to the indications of the statutes and the praxis (cf. ms. 423, fols 55v-60v), was substituted by a new formula specifically adapted by the *Riformatori* for the theologians and imposed on the Collegium with letters to the rectors of Padua on 10th May, 1688 (cf. ms. 438, fols 75v-76v).

At the present state of research, it is not possible to carry out a precise count of the number of theologians who passed through the Padua theology 'faculty' from 1363 to 1806, due to the irreparable loss of the relative matriculation records for almost the entire sixteenth century, and gaps for part of the seventeenth century. We can form an approximate idea by remembering that from its origins to the first years of the sixteenth century the sources document around 445 theologians; the commission for the reform of the statutes set up in 1569 declared with a hint of pride that the theologians who up until then had become masters in the 'faculty' were more than a thousand, and that among these stood out the famous names of popes, bishops, abbots, masters general of religious orders, professors and orators famous throughout all Christendom: Padua, therefore, was not to be held inferior to the other famous Italian or foreign theology 'faculties'.

As far as their scientific activity is concerned, generally speaking we must remember that the fourteenth and fifteenth centuries mark a period of weariness in theological thought, threatened on the theoretical level by nominalism and by a progressive detachment from the positive sources of the Christian faith: the Bible and the Fathers, while on the practical level,

Christendom found itself torn apart into a plurality of obediences due to the Schism and conciliarist theories. Paduan theology, although it was by nature more conservative than innovative, made its presence felt with valid and prepared men both at Constance (1414-18) and Basle, then playing an even greater role in the follow-on Council at Ferrara-Florence (1438-39) on the problem of the union with the Greek Church and the overcoming of the dogmatic obstacles involved: let us remember cardinal Francesco Zabarella, the Dominican Andrea da Pera, and the Franciscan Ludovico da Pirano.

The Paduan theologians were particularly involved in the criticism of conciliarist theories, in support of the superior authority of the pope over the Council; no less famous and at times almost violent were the discussions between the Thomist and the Scotist schools on the dogma of the immaculate conception of the Mother of God and on the cult of the adoration of the blood of Christ shed during the passion, which saw the victory of Francesco Della Rovere, the Franciscan regent master of Saint Anthony's, who was later to become pope Sixtus IV.

A first-hand contribution to the Fifth Lateran Council (1512-17) was made by two theologians of the convent of Saint Anthony, public professors of the arts created bishops by pope Julius II, Maurice O'Fihely (Hibernicus) and Antonio Trombetta; under discussion were the errors of Averroist Aristotelianism which denied the creation of the world, the personal immortality of the human soul, and the freedom of our acts. In Padua, indeed, they had endeavoured to denounce and critically confute such theories with lessons and scorching publications, theories which were passed off in the classrooms of the arts 'university' as the only rationally founded truth and the most correct interpretation of the genuine thought of Aristotle. As it is known, the pious bishop Pietro Barozzi had been forced to issue a decree of excommunication on 4th May, 1489, for those teachers who spoke on these questions even with the people in the street causing grave scandal among the simple. But the largest presence of the best Paduan theological minds was had, however, in the various sessions of the Council of Trent (1545-1563), whose inaugural oration was held by one of our own theologians, the Conventual Franciscan monsignor Cornelio Musso; various teachers, both Thomists and Franciscans, Augustinians, and so on, had already discussed the major themes of the Lutheran Reformation on justification, the Bible, the Church, the sacraments, and the other truths denied by the various currents of Protestantism, both in their lessons and in printed publications.

The Collegium took up positions and made pronouncements regarding the lawfulness of money lending with low interest at the pawn brokers, the so-called "monti di pietà", instituted in Padua in aid of the poor against the scourge of usury. In April-May, 1618, the Collegium spontaneously mobilized itself for a 'censure' of the heretical doctrines contained in the book *La repubblica cristiana* by the bishop of Split, Marco Antonio de Dominis, who had obtained his doctorate in theology from Padua and had become a member of the Collegium on 20th July, 1600 (ms. 424, fols 122v-123r); under the guidance of the Scotist arts professor, Filippo Fabri of Faenza, with the approval of the cardinal prefect of the Roman Inquisition himself, Giovanni Garzia Millini, which was sent to the Paduan inquisitor, and the approbation of the Venetian doge and Senate, an extremely strong text was drawn up and published which condemned as "haereticas, temerias, falsas et seditiosas ac scismaticas" the propositions contained in the incriminated work (ms. 426, fols 211r-214v).

On more than one occasion the support and the opinion of the Paduan theologians was sought to promote the recognition of the sanctity of Elena Enselmini (ms. 441, fols 27v-30r: with a petition to pope Innocent XII in 1693), and in particular that of cardinal Gregorio Barbarigo, bishop of Padua, for whom in 1699 they requested the opening of the diocesan canon law process (ms. 443, fol. 23r), and in 1717 they sent three lengthy postulatory letters to Rome to pope Clement XI on the holy life, virtues, miracles, and intense pastoral, doctrinal, and charitable activity of this servant of God, of which they themselves had been direct witnesses (ms. 444, fols 99r-102v).

Tomb of Filippo Fabri

6. Regarding the personal bibliographical production of the theologians of the Collegium, up to the seventeenth century at least, we note a certain poverty and scarcity of results: of their many commentaries on individual books of the Bible, sermon collections rich in theological content, and questions on the books of the Lombard's *Sentences*, very little has been published and what has survived lies scattered and ignored in the manuscripts of various libraries. Nevertheless, as far as the fourteenth century is concerned, it would be unjust not to recall the figure and the work of the Augustinian Bonaventura Badoer, co-founder of the theological Collegium, author of ascetical and mystical works, and a close friend of Petrarca's, whose commemorative oration he delivered at his funeral in Arquà, as well as the presence of Pietro Filargo at the convent of Saint Anthony, compromised in his theological commentaries by a certain fideistic Ockhamism, who was to be illegitimately elected pope in Pisa in 1409 under the name of Alexander V.

In the fifteenth century standing out is the Augustinian Paolo Nicoletti of Udine, not only as a celebrated philosopher in the arts, but also as a theologian and proud polemicist against Jews and heretics. Among the Franciscans we have already mentioned Francesco Della Rovere, Maurizio Hibernicus, and Antonio Trombetta, while a separate word is due to the doctorate in theology and the first period of University teaching in Padua of the Dominican Tommaso de Vio, the great cardinal Gaetano who was to become the most famous theologian of the Thomist school. In the sixteenth century we find no great works of synthesis, but rather works on particular topics dictated by the rise of heresies to be confuted. Besides Cornelio Musso, mentioned above, who ironized and rejected the scholastic method of theology in vogue in the schools, given to interminable dis-

Portraits of Jacques-Hyacinth Serry and Giuseppe Maria Puiati

putes over otiose logical questions, proposing a return along Erasmian lines to the Bible and the Fathers with a new philological and critical intelligence, we find a hearty defence of the perennial validity of traditional Thomist theology by the teacher *in via Thomae*, Girolamo Vielmi, who later took part as a bishop in the Council of Trent, against the 'fatuous' innovations of the empty purist followers of Erasmus.

Among the more learned theologians of the seventeenth century we find, right at the beginning, the figure of the Conventual Franciscan Filippo Fabri, Scotist teacher in the arts, who besides an intense participation in the activities of the Collegium, published a complete cycle of *Disputationes theologicae*, tackling the most vital problems of the dogma and the sacraments of the Christian faith, as well as a strenuous confutation of the various forms of atheism put forward in the European philosophy of the time. The Dalmatian Matteo Ferchio, who produced a varied series of works ranging from theology to astronomy and literature, succeeded him to the same chair for many years (up until 1665). Strangely, the two most famous Scotists of the period, Bartolomeo Mastri and Bonaventura Belluto, regent masters at the convent of Saint Anthony from 1638 to 1641, do not appear as members of our Collegium of theologians. The cultural climate of libertinism, atomist materialism, Epicureanism, and scepticism drove the Dominican Serafino Piccinardi to a direct attack in the name of Aristotelo-Thomist thought (1671), while the French successor to the chair of theology, Nicolas Arnou, was to publish a profound commentary on the first part of Aquinas' *Summa Theologiae*.

The most outstanding figure of eighteenth-century Padua was another French theologian, Jacques-Hyacinth Serry, teacher on the Thomist chair from 1697 to 1738, committed to the defence of Thomas' doctrine of grace against the Molinist conception, always in the front line in the controversies over papal infallibility with a vein of moderate Gallicism, an adversary of the so-called Chinese rites, and prolific writer on the most varied fields of history, liturgy, and letters; one of his imposing works of lessons on dogmatic theology was published posthumously in Venice in 1742. They revolved around him in polemical opposition the Franciscan theologians *in via Scoti*, in particular Giuseppe Platina, with his anti-Gallican *Praelectiones theologicae* (1736). The Scotist metaphysician Bonaventura Luchi was one of the first in Italy to confute Spinoza's thought with his *Sintagma adversus spinozismi systema* (1738); in 1744 he moved to the chair of Holy Scripture, and together with his confrère Francesco Maria Leoni who taught Scotist Theology and Ecclesiastical History, in their lessons and the inaugural lectures to their courses, tackled the Biblical rationalism which destroyed the historicity and the divine inspiration of the sacred texts, and the Enlightenment Deism of the Anglo-French cultural élite.

From 1758 to '91, even after the two traditional chairs had been merged into one, we find as a teacher of Theology the Dominican Antonino Valsecchi, an excellent apologist for the Christian faith and the

Catholic Church, as well as acclaimed preacher in many Italian cities; one of his more significant works is precisely the *Dei fondamenti della religione e dei fonti dell'empietà*, in three volumes (1765-77). He was succeeded up to 1806 by an Istrian confrère (from Parenzo), Giorgio Maria Albertini, and the Thomist tradition was to be continued even in the new academic structure in the Habsburg model (1813) with the appointment in 1815 of the ex-Dominican (in 1810 all the religious orders and congregations had been suppressed) Tommaso Tommasoni, who in the following year was to have as a student the nobleman from Rovereto, Antonio Rosmini, who graduated in 1822.

Besides the dogmatic theologians listed so far we should mention the rich series of professors of Holy Scripture ('Scripturists' in bureaucratic language), which from 1551 to 1798 was taught on holidays mainly by Dominicans and then by Benedictines of the Cassino congregation. Unfortunately, of their lessons, introductions, and interpretations of the individual books of the Bible almost nothing remains, since we have lost the manuscripts even of those famous teachers such as Girolamo Bendandi (1648-59), Leone Matina (1663-78), and so on. Only the restless figure of the Cassino monk Giuseppe Maria Puiati (1786-98) survives in the form of a varied bibliography on the most disparate themes, with some worthy attempts at innovation in traditional biblical exegesis; Puiati was removed from his teaching post on the return of the Austrians (1798), after the brief Jacobin interlude, because of his Jansenist sympathies, his polemical excesses against the Roman hierarchy, and his bitter criticisms of the new popular devotion.

We can point to some good attempts at a critical approach to the history of the Church, related above all to dogmatic theology, by the Franciscans Alessandro Burgos and Francesco Leoni, as well as Tommaso Antonio Contin. It would be unjust, finally, to forget some of the members of the Collegium of theologians, who, although private teachers in the convents or on the various chairs of the arts, became famous with other historical and erudite works, still today the precious sources of reliable information of direct testimony: we can think of several publications on the history and the major figures of the Padua Studium by the canon of Santa Maria in Vanzo, Giacomo Filippo Tomasini, the admired history *Della felicità di Padova* by the Augustinian Angelo Portenari, and the collection of Paduan inscriptions by the Dominican Giacomo Salomonio, the historical documentation on the history of the University by Iacopo Facciolati, and still others.

Scientific and Cultural History:
The Modern University

PIERO DEL NEGRO

Jurisprudence, Political Sciences, Statistical Sciences, Economics

Jurisprudence

In 1806, after the annexation of the Veneto region to the Kingdom of Italy, the decision by Napoleon to place the University of Padua "on an equal footing" with the other Universities of the Kingdom involved among other things the disappearance of the centuries-old 'university' of law students, as well as that of the two Colleges, the "sacro" and the "veneto", which had up until then been charged with the task of conferring degrees in one or both branches of law. On the institutional ruins of the old regime a law faculty was established in accordance with the University reform which had been introduced in 1803 in Pavia and Bologna, while the legal disciplines, as far as content was concerned and on the basis of a scientific framework grounded on the one in force at the Institut National of Paris, were placed in the class of moral and political sciences. The length of the course was initially kept to four years, and was reduced to three in 1808 when six subjects, more or less removed from the legal context (among them Elements of Geometry and Algebra, Experimental Physics, Latin and Italian Eloquence, and Greek Language and Literature) were taken off the curriculum and the contents and the titles of the remaining subjects underwent a radical revision.

The Napoleonic cyclone which hit the University of Padua largely spared a teaching body which had in any case been forced to carry out a profound renewal of the curriculum of its courses; but it left very little standing - if anything at all - of the didactic order which the Austrian regime had inherited from the Venetians. Canon law, a discipline which had remained a pillar of legal education even after the late eighteenth-century reforms, was totally removed from the curriculum. The chair of Civil Law, which had remained a hostage of the Roman law tradition after the failure of the attempt by the Venetian government to bring its contents up to date by including the study of Venetian and municipal law, was transformed into the chair of the Code Napoléon compared to Roman law.

The new codes promulgated in the Kingdom also became the point of reference for Penal Law and Proceedings, Public Economics (combined together with Commercial Law), and Civil Proceedings. As a rule the general and generic teaching subjects were substituted by specific subjects which reflected the particular needs of the State: Public and Peoples' Law, for example was transformed into Public Law of the Kingdom. Once the

Hall of Jurisprudence, Palazzo del Bo

archaeological Roman-canon approach had been abandoned, as well as a conception of law that in as far as it looked back at the past tended to revolve around itself, legal knowledge was placed at the service of the new configuration of the State and society born of the French revolution and the Napoleonic regime, and Law became a 'practical' and hence a 'useful' science.

Enlightenment Venice had established the foundations of those disciplines concerning Public Law. The Kingdom of Italy enlarged them beyond measure not only and not so much because it introduced among the teaching subjects Public Economics (in any case the key discipline of the "moral and political sciences" in a socio-economic context which was feeling the first repercussions of the industrial revolution), but because it forced all or almost all of the disciplines of the faculty to reflect the institutions of the regime. It was a process which was consolidated in 1809, when a School of Legal Practical Eloquence was opened in Milan for those law graduates who intended to embark on a career as a lawyer. In as far as it was a 'technical school', that is a post-graduate school of specialization aimed at providing a professional training - an institution typical of the practical nature conferred on study by Napoleonic policy - the Milan school testified both to the way the area of legal studies was made equal to the technical and scientific disciplines and the preparatory nature of the training imparted by the law faculty.

This approach to University law studies was substantially maintained after Austria regained control of Padua in 1813. The law faculty, whose course of studies was brought back to four years (the Milan school was suppressed at the same time), was re-baptized politico-legal. The adjective 'political' was obviously used by Habsburg absolutism as a synonym for 'administrative': moving in the same direction was the introduction of a chair of Political Science applied to Austrian political legislation, a "legislation" which was meant sooner or later to substitute that of Napoleon. The wind of the Restoration led to the revival of Canon Law and – although Vienna was aware of its "limited application", as is testified by a "Sovereign resolution" of 1816 – also that of Feudal Law. Reversing the steps taken by Napoleon, the 'specific' Public Law of the Kingdom gave way to the 'universalistic' Private and Public Natural Law, while the General Introduction to Political and Legal Studies and General European Statistics and those specific to the Austrian monarchy, which in practice absorbed Public Economics, were borrowed from the Universities of the empire.

Nevertheless, despite these and other measures, it can be affirmed that the Napoleonic order survived both in the teaching subjects and in the organizational structure throughout the second, and after the brief revolutionary interlude of 1848, the third period of Austrian rule. The double organization of the teaching body, for example, was confirmed: in so far as it was a "teaching body" it depended on a "studium" headed by a director endowed with wide disciplinary powers; as an "academic body" it saw itself as a faculty guided by a dean with prevalently bureaucratic competencies. The stability of the institutional and didactic framework should not lead us however to neglect the profound changes which took place in the course of these sixty years both among the teachers and the students.

In the case of the teachers we must note their transformation into teacher-researchers, a change which took place almost completely over the course of a couple of generations. In the Napoleonic age and the first years of the Restoration as a rule the teachers, both because they were continually obliged to bring themselves up to date with regard to the text books with the rapid succession of different regimes, and because they were often burdened with the weight and the honour of teaching a plurality of subjects, devoted themselves solely, or almost, to teaching (and in any case they preferred to carry out research in disciplinary fields other than law). In the second half of the century, on the other hand, we find more and more teacher-researchers, specialized and qualified to varying degrees. At the same time, the large number of clerics holding chairs in the late eighteenth and early nineteenth century virtually disappeared from the University stage.

Angelo Messedaglia

The gap which separates the teachers of the early nineteenth century from those who were promoted to the chair during the course of the last period of Austrian rule is evident if, for example, we compare the figures of the abbés Antonio Marsand (1765-1842), professor of Economics, Commercial Law, and Statistics, but famous as a bibliographer and the editor of Petrarch's *Canzoniere*, and Giacomo Giuliani (1772-1841), who held courses on Political Science, Economics and Statistics, Public Law, and Penal Law and Proceedings, with those of Angelo Messedaglia (1820-1901), the "founder of scientific statistics in Italy" (Angelo Ventura), and Antonio Pertile (1830-1895), the holder – in 1857 – of the first chair of the History of Italian Law established in Italy (a concession to the patriotism of the inhabitants of the Lombard-Venetian Kingdom, to be placed in the context of the liberally-leaning programme of Archduke Maximilian of Habsburg, the governor in charge at the time) and founder, together with Francesco Schupfer (1833-1925), of the prestigious Paduan historico-juridical school subsequently continued by Nino (Giovanni) Tamassia (1860-1931).

We see a gradual increase in the number of law students up until the end of the 1820s when there was a boom in the number of enrolments, which in the early 1840s rose over the 800 mark, that is to say seven times the number registered in 1816. It was an increase so much the more amazing in that, as the worried Austrian authorities stressed, it was not justified by a parallel expansion in the job market. Indeed it is known that the legislation of the Lombard-Venetian Kingdom not only prevented lawyers from intervening in criminal trials, but it also limited their number (as well as that of the notaries), while job opportunities in the public sector, which in any case offered very little satisfaction at the lower levels, were certainly on the increase, but not to such an extent as to be able to absorb the exces-

Luigi Luzzatti
Emilio Morpurgo

sive number of graduates who came out of Padua. It is not by chance, therefore, that in 1848 we also see an explosion of the profound dissatisfaction of the legal class, which held itself to be greatly penalized by the Habsburg regime; in the Veneto region the revolution saw a large number of lawyers take to the scene (Daniele Manin first of all), as well as notaries, graduates - many of whom were underemployed or unemployed – and law students.

In the period after 1866, the period after the annexation of the Veneto region to Italy, that is, the problem arose yet again of fitting the University of Padua into an already consolidated University context, that defined by the Casati law and by successive regulations. Even if the aim of 'recognizing as equal' did not have to be reached until 1873 on the basis of a law approved by parliament the previous year, the change in regime immediately influenced the composition of the teaching body (two of the eight full professors were purged for having Austrian sympathies, and four 'junior' professors of reliable patriotic faith were appointed, among whom Schupfer and Luigi Luzzati), and the didactic palimpsest of the faculty (Constitutional Law was introduced, while National Economics became Political Economics). Jurisprudence – as the Paduan faculty was called after its 'official recognition of equality' - fitted into the new State framework with great authority, enjoying the interest of that cultural capital which it had accumulated above all in the final years of Austrian rule and which reflected in part the influence of Germanic culture and in part a liberal thinking adapted to the particular characteristics of the Veneto region.

The University and, within the University, the faculty of Jurisprudence was the "true political soul of the Veneto Right" (and, in the final decades of the nineteenth century, of a moderatism prepared to come to terms with the Left). The 'leading quartet' was made up of Messedaglia, in all respects, political and cultural, a "key figure" (Ventura) and his pupils and friends, Luzzatti (1841-1927), whose chair of Constitutional Law became, as he himself wrote, "a centre of political life", Emilio Morpurgo (1836-1885), who succeeded his master to the chair of Statistics and was rector of the University in 1880-82, and Giampaolo Tolomei (1814-1893), a jurist in all respects (he taught from five chairs; that which he held the longest was Criminal Law and Proceedings), who was rector in 1869-70 and from 1873 to 1879, and director (dean, that is) of the faculty from 1866 to 1873 and from 1881 to 1893.

Luzzati and Morpurgo were, during the years of the Right, influential general secretaries of the Ministry of Agriculture, Industry, and Commerce, and they promoted a generation of economist-bureaucrats destined to play a leading role in the life of Liberal Italy. In the late nineteenth and early twentieth centuries, Luzzatti, who in 1895 left the University of Padua for that of Rome, as Messedaglia had done twenty years earlier, was also Treasury minister and minister of Agriculture, Industry, and Commerce on more than one occasion. From the scientific point of view, the combination of Messedaglia, Luzzatti, and Morpurgo

Faculty of Jurisprudence,
Marsilio da Padua room

Giulio Alessio

worked successfully to counter the laissez-faire school of economics which its adversaries baptized as the "Lombard-Venetian school" or the "socialism of the chair", a school which in effect in no way renounced laissez-faire principles, but which was also convinced of the necessity of State intervention in the economy and in social legislation in defence of general interests and the interests of the weaker classes. In particular, in the 1860s, Luzzatti and Morpurgo were among the first admirers of the cooperative movement and of popular credit, and around 1880, in the context of the Jacini agrarian inquiry, Morpurgo published a weighty report on the Veneto region, in which he criticised the dramatic conditions of its peasant farmers.

The tight link between the Padua faculty of Jurisprudence, politics, and, even before politics, the State, did not weaken, as is demonstrated by Luzzatti's long career once the age of the Right was over. Indeed, it can be stated that every politico-ideological season which Italy lived through after Unification, with the exception, perhaps, of the Republican period (but we must not forget, for example, the criminalist Giuseppe Bettiol (1907-1982), an important exponent of the Christian Democracy Party), had to have a point of reference of greater or lesser standing from among the teachers of the faculty. Here we must remember, at least, among the teachers of the late nineteenth and early twentieth centuries, Carlo Francesco Ferraris (1850-1924), teacher of Statistics and then Administrative Law, rector of the University of Padua from 1891 to 1896 and minister in the Giolitti period, theorist of the science of administration, "the boldest and most coherent supporter of State intervention that Italian public life saw in the late nineteenth and early twentieth centuries" (Silvio Lanaro); Giulio Alessio (1853-1940), who from 1878 to 1928 taught first Political Economics and then Financial Law and Financial Science, a parliamentary member for the Radical Party and a minister in the Nitti and Giolitti governments, the greatest exponent of Padua's 'popular' season (from 1900 to 1912 the city was governed by a coalition of Radicals, Republicans, and Socialists), and the author of a great work, *Lo stato italiano*; and Achille Loria (1857-1943), professor of Political Economics from 1891 to 1903 and accredited exponent of a Marxism read in the light of positivist sociologism. In the course of the twenty-year Fascist period it was up to Alfredo Rocco (1875-1935), professor of Commercial Law from 1910 to 1925 and theorist of a nationalism based on an organicistic and totalitarian concept of the State, to play a fundamental role in the organization of the regime and also to favour, in the specific context of Padua, the fascistization of the faculty by means of pupils and colleagues who shared his political ideas.

Such a list might have us believe that the faculty of Jurisprudence kept solely to the aim assigned to it by a regulation of 1875, that is to say, "the study and the progress of the legal and social sciences, with particular attention to the needs and the constitution of the Italian State". In effect the profile of legal studies was, in Padua as elsewhere, mostly orientated, as a regulation of 1876 was meant to stress, towards the preparation "for the practice of the professions", above all those of the lawyer (from 1935 to 1982, except during the war, a School of legal specialization functioned, an heir of the Course for judiciary magistrates held in the first two decades of the twentieth century), the procurator, and the notary (from 1879 to 1918 a three-year course conferred the appropriate diploma), that is to say that it catered more for the "needs" of civil society than for those of the State. As is shown by the substantial continuity in its teaching (if the Fascist period imposed a conception of law totally different from that in force in the liberal and republican periods, it nevertheless largely maintained the tried and tested palimpsest which considered and considers Civil Law, Roman Law, the History of Italian Law, Criminal Law, and Administrative Law as particularly important subjects) and its loyalty to a monolithic training (it is not by chance that during the very recent University reform a single degree course was passed in the context of the faculty, that in Legal Science, and a second, Economy Law together with the faculty of Political Sciences), Jurisprudence distinguished itself in its respect for tradition.

From there derived the tendency to channel the impulses coming from the State and from society towards a change in the organization of studies into faculties and then into 'derived' faculties, from Political Sciences to Statistical Sciences, and, to a certain extent, to Economics. Again, from this we arrive at a historical curve in the student population which, though it basically followed the general rhythms and the trends of the University as a whole, distinguished itself from them in its relative loss of speed once, with the increase in demand for higher education and the multiplication of professional opportunities, the number of faculties grew and their profiles diversified. After having been the first of the faculties in its number of enrolments for much of the liberal period (if we exclude the last twenty years of the nineteenth century, when it was overtaken by Medicine), Jurisprudence has subsequently seen its quota reduced by around a quarter (in the years before the First World War) to a sixth (between the Wars), and then to a tenth (in the second half of the twentieth century) of the total number of students.

Political Sciences

From 1875 the regulations of the faculty of Jurisprudence included the possibility of introducing special courses in Political Sciences and therefore of its transformation into a Juridico-political faculty. But only in December 1924 was a School of Political and Social Sciences opened in Padua, in the context of the Gentile reform of the previous year. It was the first, together with those of Rome and Pavia, to be established within a State University in an ambiguous relationship of continuity, but above all of opposition, with the analogous initiatives of a private origin in the form

Donato Donati

of the Cesare Alfieri di Sostegno Higher Institute of Social Sciences (1875) and the faculty of Social Sciences of the Catholic University of the Sacred Heart (1922). It was probably this latter episode which prompted Corrado Gini (1884-1965), teacher of Statistics at Padua and a convinced fascist, to propose the establishment of a School of Social Sciences to the faculty council of Jurisprudence in 1923. But the person who was involved more than any other in the foundation of the school, becoming its first director in 1924 and then, after its transformation in 1933 into a Faculty of Political Sciences, the first dean, was the constitutional lawyer Donato Donati (1880-1946). Donati again was, to the same extent as Alfredo Rocco and the other teachers in support of the scheme, a resolute supporter of the new Fascist regime.

In the version of the statute put forward to the Ministry in May 1924 by the academic Senate, the school was defined as School of Social Sciences and was to have as its aim the "preparation for the civil service, free social activities, and political functions". But Rome preferred the title Political and Social Sciences and specified that the school should "provide the scientific preparation for the administrative, diplomatic, and consular careers, and for journalism", thus placing the stress on the Fascist State's need to form a high-level bureaucracy with a professional training no longer limited to the formalism of the jurists, but mindful of internal and international political 'contents'(even though the world abroad was taken into consideration almost only as a projection of the power of the Italian State), which were to be put into action taking into account the perspectives opened up by Mussolini, from corporativism to imperialism. The 'Roman' line was to prevail over the original 'Paduan' one: born with two distinct degree courses in Political Sciences and Social Sciences, by the mid 1930s the faculty was left with only one course, with the shortened title of Political Sciences.

In Padua, as elsewhere, the school came into existence as a branch of Jurisprudence, with which it physically cohabited in the Palazzo del Bo up until 1967, and from which it long borrowed most of its teaching subjects and teachers. Specific to the school and then to the faculty was its stress on geography, history (above all of international relations), statistics, and languages; as far as the legal disciplines were concerned, those regarding public law were obviously privileged. The quota of students with respect to the totality of those enrolled at Padua rose from the school's foundation to the second world war from 2 to 4%: a modest increase which can be explained above all by the difficulty in guaranteeing, despite the intentions of the regime, professional opportunities for its graduates.

In 1938 Donati was expelled from the University for being a Jew. In the seven years which immediately followed, four deans succeeded one another in presiding over the faculty, itself an indication of the critical situation. The second world war put paid, together with the regime, to the dream of a fascist faculty: indeed the origin and the militant configuration of Political Sciences led the government to close the faculty from 1945 to

1948, and only one of its degree courses survived in the faculty of Jurisprudence. From 1948 to 1968 the deans of the Faculty of Political Sciences were, for ten years each, the teachers of the History of International Treatises and Relations Anton Maria Bettanini (1884-1964) and Ettore Anchieri (1896-1988), who ensured that the faculty became less characterized by its dependence on that of Jurisprudence and favoured the expansion of the teaching body around four institutes (historical, political, economic, and juridical sciences). Despite this, in a period when the history of diplomacy prevailed, Political Sciences continued to attract a modest quota of the total number of students enrolled at the University of Padua, between 2 and 3%. An important phenomenon of the post-war period was the early feminization of the student body.

From 1968 Political Sciences changed decisively. The almost contemporary reform of the organization of the faculty, around five themes (politico-administrative, politico-economic, politico-international, politico-social, and historico-political) and the liberalization of University access, as well as, indeed above all, in the background, the profound social and economic transformation of the Veneto region towards the development of the tertiary sector, favoured a tumultuous growth in the student population (by over 5% at the end of the 1970s, to over 13% a decade later, and around 10% by the end of the twentieth century). But it was a process not lacking in strong tensions and contradictions, in particular in the second half of the 1970s, when the attempt was made by a group of teachers and a part of the student body to restore to the faculty that political role which it had originally had, but this time in a subversive key. The very recent University reform has brought to light, by means of new degree courses, some of them inter-faculty, the new disciplinary assets which have matured over the course of the last third of a century, and which stress the international and at the same time regional vocations of the faculty.

Statistical, Demographic, and Actuarial Sciences

One of the fundamental stages in the development of Statistical Sciences in Padua coincided, after the success of Messedaglia and his school, with the teaching in Padua of Gini (1913-1925). Gini was "the most eminent figure in Italian statistics of all time" (Bernardo Colombo), founder of prestigious journals such as *Metron* and, after his transfer to Rome, the first director of the Central Institute of Statistics and promoter of the first and, up until the establishment of its Paduan sister, the only Italian faculty of Statistical Science. In 1913 the laboratory, then institute, of Statistics, previously joined together with that of Geography, began its autonomous life; in 1924 moreover, Gini promised a two-year post-graduate School of specialization in Statistics. Gini's successor, Gaetano Pietra (1879-1961), who from 1938 to 1943 was to be the dean first of Political Sciences and then of Jurisprudence, created a School of statistics in 1927,

Corrado Gini

which conferred a diploma after its two-year course. Under the guidance of Albino Uggé (1899-1971), professor of Statistics in the faculty of Political Sciences, the school prospered to such an extent that the number of first year students enrolled was greater than that for Jurisprudence.

In 1965 the faculty council of Jurisprudence, having taken note of a success which placed the Padua School of statistics at the top of the national league, and appealing also to a politico-economic context which favoured national planning, approved the plan of establishing a degree course in Statistical Sciences in the faculty of Jurisprudence. Only in 1968, once a congruous number of chairs had been ensured for the discipline, was it possible to inaugurate the new faculty of Statistical, Demographical, and Actuarial Science under the guidance of a technical committee presided over by the well-known civil lawyer, Luigi Carraro. It was initially thought that the degree course should be in Statistical and Demographical Sciences, that is, that it should repeat the title of one of the courses of the Roman faculty, but the idea came to prevail of an original characterization, of a course, that is, in Statistical and Economic Sciences, which had "as its aim to provide a scientific culture and a professional training to graduates who are ever more useful and in demand for the purposes of the application of modern methods of business management and planning".

In 1970-71, when the degree course was fully functioning, the number of students topped six hundred. At the beginning of that same academic year the first dean of the faculty was elected, Bernardo Colombo, the person who more than any other had been involved in the implementation of the new initiative. Economic planning, which had been invoked when the faculty was established in the 1960s, taking up Gini's State interventionist approach in a highly different light, very soon disappeared from the scientifico-institutional horizon. As is testified by the degree courses approved during the recent reform, in which Statistics is linked to computer technology, economics and finance, business management, and social organizations, the faculty presents a highly complex cultural offering, attentive to the needs of the economy and civil society.

Economics

Economic Science has had prestigious exponents in Padua ever since the nineteenth century, as we hinted when dealing with the vicissitudes of the faculty of Jurisprudence. In the early twentieth century the most important figure was that of Marco Fanno (1878-1965), professor in Padua from 1920 to 1958 (excluding the years of anti-Jewish persecution, 1938-45) of Financial Science and Political Economics (from 1934 General and Corporative Economics): it was by no chance that the department, which holds most of the teachers of the discipline, was named after Fanno. The University of Padua established a faculty of Economics and Commerce at its Verona site actually from the years 1959-60, and formally from 1963, but the creation of an independent University in Verona was to remove such an achievement from the Paduan orbit. It was only in 1993 that a faculty of Economics was established in Padua – and activated two years later – initially with one degree course with a limited number of student places available, in Economics and Commerce, which in the context of the recent reform has been complemented by another course in Business Economics.

In its 'constituent' phase, under the guidance of the well-known constitutional lawyer Livio Paladin, the faculty elected as its first dean Francesco Favotto, professor of Business Economics. The cultural policy of Economics is based on five "strategic guide lines": a limited number of student places, organizational quality, a systematic linkage with the world of production by means of training workshops and the establishment of an Advisory Board made up of entrepreneurs, company managers, professionals, and experts, with the task of contributing critically to the teaching offered by the faculty, its high degree of internationalization, and the expansion of internet technology. The initial results have been extremely promising, as is shown by the high percentage of students who have taken part in workshops or followed courses in other European Universities, and of those who graduate within their fifth year of studies.

Marco Fanno

GIUSEPPE ONGARO

Medicine, Pharmacy, Veterinary Medicine

The radical upheavals which followed the fall of the Venetian Republic had a great impact on the life and the organization of the Studium and hence also on the teaching and the study of medicine. During the brief French occupation of 1797-98 and the first period of Austrian rule (1798-1805) the fundamental structure of the University was not modified. A ballet began, however, involving the professors most overtly partisan towards one regime or another, who were from time to time suspended, dismissed or taken on again as the occupiers changed. This is the case of Carburi, Simone Stratico (1733-1824), who taught Mathematics, Nautical Theory, and Experimental Physics, Pietro Sografi (1756-1815), who succeeded Calza to the chair of Obstetrics, and above all Gallini, who held the chair of Theoretical Medicine and was removed from teaching by the Austrians because he was suspected of Jacobinism. After the advent of the Napoleonic Kingdom of Italy the exile of 'revolutionary' professors ended temporarily in December 1805, when Gallini, Carburi, and Sografi re-obtained the teaching positions they had been deprived of by Austria. In 1806 Gallini was entrusted with the chair of Physiology and Comparative Anatomy, but on the return of the Austrians at the end of 1813, he, who also carried out the function of rector, was forced to abandon his post and withdraw to Venice, even though he later re-obtained the University teaching position which he kept until 1833.

The definitive loss of Padua University's institutional autonomy and its Venetian cultural tradition came with the annexation of the Veneto region to the Napoleonic Kingdom of Italy. The French, who reached Padua in December 1805, showed a decisive will to reform right from the beginning, a will which aimed to adapt the Studium too to the Napoleonic cultural model. Once the traditional division of the University into a 'university' of arts and one of law students had been abolished, three faculties arose, a physico-mathematical, a medical, and a legal one. The medical faculty included the teaching of Medical Clinics, *Materia Medica*, Surgical Institutions, Practical Medicine and Analysis of Clinical Observations, Pathology, Surgical Clinics, Botany, Human Anatomy, Pharmaceutical Chemistry, Obstetrics, Legal Medicine, Physiology and Comparative Anatomy, General Chemistry, and Natural History.

The return of the Austrians towards the end of 1813 initiated the long second period of Austrian rule, which lasted until 1866. By 1816 Vienna had completely reorganized the two Universities of the Lombard-Venetian

The anatomical theatre before the modifications it suffered in the Nineteenth Century. Lithography by Prosperini, based on a drawing by A. Dalola, from Pietro Tosoni, Della anatomia degli antichi e della scuola anatomica padovana *(Padua 1844)*

Kingdom, rendering them definitively equivalent to the other analogous institutes present in the various domains of the empire. In the medical-surgical-pharmaceutical faculty the traditional curricula for physicians and surgeons, which were articulated over five years, the first three of which were common for both branches of study, were supplemented by the introduction of a two-year course for pharmacists and a three-year course for the so-called "civil-provincial surgeons with a licence" destined, following the Austrian example, to practice in rural or mountain districts with a simple licence in surgery. The physicians and the surgeons followed lessons in Animal Physics, Natural History, Introduction to the Study of Medicine and Surgery, Physiology and Comparative Anatomy, Botany, General and Pharmaceutical Chemistry, General and Special Pathology, Surgical Institutions, and *Materia Medica*. The aspiring physicians then took courses in Special Therapy of Acute Illnesses, Human Anatomy, Special Therapy of Chronic Illnesses, Medical Clinics, Obstetric Art and Illnesses of the Puerpera and the New-born, Veterinary Medicine, Medical History and Literature, Surgical Clinics as spectators, Legal Medicine, and Medical Police. The curriculum for surgeons was very similar, with greater stress given to practical exercises. Those graduates in medicine who intended to take a degree in surgery too, and vice versa, had to frequent a further year. For the pharmacists, the curriculum included lessons in Natural History, Experimental Physics, Botany, General and Pharmaceutical Chemistry, Hygiene, Therapeutics, and *Materia Medica*. A two-year course was destined for the veterinary surgeons, with subjects such as Animal Physics and Comparative Anatomy, Rural Economics and the Principles of Botany, Veterinary Medicine relative to Pathology, Hygiene and *Materia Medica*, and Veterinary medicine relative to Internal and External Practice. Finally, the course for provincial licensed surgeons included the following disciplines: Animal Physics and Comparative Anatomy, Botany, Experimental Physics, Introduction to the Study of Medicine and Surgery, Human Anatomy, Physiology, Hygiene, Therapeutics and *Materia Medica*, Veterinary Medicine, Obstetrics, Legal Medicine, and Medical Police. The new University organization, which followed a more modern and specialist approach, was not accompanied however by an astute policy of recruitment of teachers, which prized loyalty to the government rather than merit. For a subject of the empire the obligatory University of reference was Vienna, and hence completing one's studies in the capital was a fundamental condition for those who aspired to obtaining a teaching position. The deliberate will to Austrianize the Veneto region thus led to a cultural monopoly, which – with all due respect to Austrian medicine of the period – was felt by the most lively spirits as a suffocating imposition which tried to render Padua submissive to its occupiers even on a cultural level. What is more, the Austrian government imposed several teachers of non-Italian origin and in general of modest ability, such as Martin Steer, a Hungarian of the Vienna school who in 1827 was entrusted with the chair of *Materia Medica* which he was forced to abandon after the 1848 uprisings. Other Hungarians were

Anton Rosas (1791-1855) who in 1819 was the first to hold Oculistic Clinics under the new organization, and who left to return to Vienna in 1821, however, leaving in Padua a series of wax preparations of ocular affections, and Wilhelm Lippich (1799-1845) who succeeded Valeriano Luigi Brera (1772-1840) to the chair of Medical Clinics from 1834 to 1841, and then he too moved to Vienna. Maximilian Vintschgau (1832-1902), professor of Physiology in Padua from 1858 to 1860, who then moved to Prague and finally to Innsbruck, was an Austrian. Rudolph Lamprecht (1781-1860), on the other hand, a native of Zagreb but who had studied in Vienna, was called in 1819 to the chair of Obstetrics and remained there until 1857, unlike other foreign teachers fully integrated into the Padua University environment, to such an extent that his assistant lecturer Luigi Pastorello (1811-1863), who succeeded him in 1858, was also his son-in-law. Lamprecht was the author of a valuable *Manuale di ostetricia teorica e pratica* (1837-40).

It is therefore understandable that in the first decades of the nineteenth century medical and physiological research in Padua was not able to develop independently according to the programme outlined by Gallini, which was in line with the most advanced and promising aspects of European science. Research and experimentation was reduced to a minimum, nor were any significant initiatives undertaken for the logistic improvement necessitated by the new institutional order. Thus, from 1842 to 1847, for example, at the request of the anatomy teacher, radical modifications were made to the anatomical theatre, which up until then had remained substantially unchanged since 1594, in particular the reduction of daylight and the establishment of an anatomical laboratory. Even though the teaching and research requirements which led to this radical step were quite understandable, it is impossible not to agree with Giampaolo Vlacovich (1825-1899) when in 1887 he wrote that "it would have been preferable [...] to transfer the school to another place, maintaining the theatre as it was": and indeed in 1873 the medical faculty was moved from the Palazzo del Bo to the ex-convent of San Mattia near the eighteenth-century "New Hospital", thus interrupting, around 1872, the activity of the anatomical theatre as such. The professor of anatomy who had dared to tamper with the anatomical theatre was Francesco Cortese (1802-1883), whose life and work were turned upside down by the eventful vicissitudes of 1848. He was more of a surgeon than an anatomist, so much so that he took over the clinical teaching of surgery from July 1844, to March 1845, after the illness and the death of Bartolomeo Signoroni (1796-1844). Up until 1825 Cortese had been the assistant lecturer to Cesare Ruggieri (1768-1828) on the chair of clinical surgery, and then he had specialized at the Specialist Institute of Surgery in Vienna. Once he returned to Italy at the end of 1828, Cortese was immediately appointed provincial surgeon in Venice, a post that he held for ten years, up until 1838, that is, when he was appointed professor of Anatomy at Padua after the death of Floriano Caldani (1772-1836). Greatly interested in the doctrine of Franz Joseph

Floriano Caldani. Portrait by Antonio Bernati (Padua, Palazzo del Bo, hall of the Faculty of Medicine and Surgery)

Francesco Cortese. Padua, Palazzo del Bo, hall of the Faculty of Medicine and Surgery.

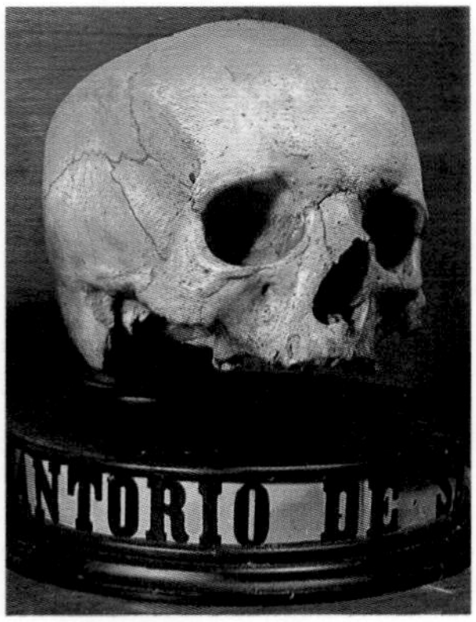

The cranium of Santorio. Padua, Palazzo del Bo, hall of the Faculty of Medicine and Surgery

Gall (1758-1828), called *phrenology* or *cranioscopy*, Cortese "collected with wise care, aided by fortune", seven crania "of esteemed scholars of science, who were almost all professors in our University" (Vlacovich), establishing the rudiments of an anthropological museum in the anatomical laboratory. The crania of Santorio Santorio, Salvatore dal Negro (1768-1839), Antonio Meneghelli (1765-1844), Floriano Caldani, Stefano Gallini, Pier Luigi Mabil (1752-1836), and Bartolomeo Signoroni – all collected by Cortese – were added to by his successors after his departure from Padua with those of Giacomo Andrea Giacomini and Carlo Conti (1802-1849). In 1873, after the transfer of the Anatomical Institute to the ex-convent of San Mattia, the nine crania also remained at the Palazzo del Bo and they are now on display in the hall of the faculty of Medicine and Surgery. Once the Austrians had been chased out of Padua on 24th March, 1848, Cortese took an active part in the provisional government and after three months, on the return of the Austrians, he fled to Venice with all his family. His wife, Anna Castelli, was the daughter of the lawyer Iacopo, who in 1848-49 was an authoritative member of Daniele Manin's provisional government. He managed an eventful flight from Venice and asked to be admitted to the Medical Corps of the Lombard militia: after the battle of Custoza, he followed the Piedmontese army. In 1850 he was recognised as a Sardinian subject and he subsequently moved definitively to the Piedmontese army Medical Corps, finally attaining the post of head of the Medical Corps of the Italian Army. His most well known work is the *Guida teorico-pratica del medico militare in campagna* (1862-63). After 1866, while he was still alive, Cortese's portrait was added to the series of portraits of Paduan professors of anatomy which decorate the walls of the anatomical laboratory: the portraits remained in the Palazzo del Bo after the Anatomical Institute was transferred to the ex-convent of San Mattia in 1873, and they are now preserved in the hall of the faculty of Medicine and Surgery, together with other portraits of illustrious physicians. According to a recent belief, which seems to date back to 1941, the most important nucleus of the collection is made up of the portraits, which Morgagni had painted for his study. In reality, there is no document to prove that Morgagni's collection was transferred to the University in one piece, although we cannot exclude that some portraits belonging to Morgagni were later added individually. The portraits of Giacomo Pighi and Michelangelo Molinetti were donated to the anatomical laboratory by one of Cortese's pupils, Pietro Tosoni (1817-1847).

Signoroni had also spent three years at the Specialist Institute of Surgery in Vienna. He arrived in Padua in 1830, from Pavia, where he had been professor of Surgical Clinics since 1824, actually under inquiry because of the contested outcome of some of his operations. A follower of the interventionist criteria of the Vienna school, his production concerns above all operational technique and some surgical instruments, which he invented or improved. In 1845 the temporary vacancy on the chairs of Surgical Institutions and Surgical Clinics was entrusted to the twenty-seven year old

Angelo Minich (1817-1893), who held the post until October 1847, when Carlo Cotta (1809-1866), a pupil of Luigi Porta and head surgeon at the hospital of Lodi, was appointed to both surgical chairs. Involved in the provisional government of Padua during the 1848 rebellion, Cotta was dismissed on the return of the Austrians. The same fate struck Francesco Marzolo (1818-1880), who was removed from the chair of Surgical Institutions, which he was able to return to definitively only twenty years later.

Francesco Fanzago (1764-1836), who had acquired fame with his studies on pellagra and the inoculation of the smallpox vaccine (1801) and who in 1801 succeeded Comparetti to the chair of Practical Medicine, was entrusted with the teaching of Pathology and Legal Medicine in 1806. In 1817 Dalla Decima took over his teaching on the chair of Pathology, while he continued to teach Legal Medicine and Medical Police up until 1827; in 1831 he was succeeded by Giuseppe Gianelli (1799-1872), author of a valuable *Trattato di medicina pubblica* (1836), who remained in the chair until 1837.

Francesco Fanzago

As we have seen with regard to Cortese, during the Austrian domination scientific and academic activity was interwoven with the political allegiance of the teachers who were often conditioned by it. In the third and fourth decade of the nineteenth century, Padua experienced a late revival of Giovanni Rasori's (1766-1837) vitalist doctrine of the "contrastimulus" in its final elaboration by Giacomo Tommasini (1768-1846). The fortunes of the anti-Hippocratic Rasori had collapsed with the fall of the Napoleonic Kingdom of Italy and – leaving aside any judgement of merit – the Austrians looked suspiciously on the doctrines of an author who was considered a Jacobin and a revolutionary. In this context, any adherence to Rasori's doctrines acted therefore as a veritable banner which also signified a show of dissent. This is the case of Giacomo Andrea Giacomini (1796-1849) – from 1824 professor of Theoretical Medicine for the surgeons, in 1826 taking on the temporary vacancy at Pathology and *Materia Medica* for the physicians, and then from 1831 to 1834 filling the vacancy at Medical Clinics for the surgeons – who after his degree had also spent his three good years in Vienna at the Specialist Institute of Surgery. A passionate vitalist, follower of Rasori and Tommasini and author of a *Trattato filosofico-sperimentale dei soccorsi terapeutici*, Giacomini was involved in violent controversies with Bufalini, denying that chemistry served a purpose in understanding vital phenomena. He found faithful collaborators and followers in Ferdinando Coletti (1819-1881) and Giambattista Mugna (1799-1866), who, although they tried their utmost to keep the vitalistic and Giacominian flag flying, were nevertheless forced to fall back on neovitalist positions in the second half of the nineteenth century. Mugna above all made a very intense effort to bring himself up to date, which finally led him to adhere to the "mechanical vitalism" of Rudolph Virchow (1821-1902), whose *Cellularpathologie* (1858) he published the first Italian translation of in 1863. Thus we arrive at the epic uprisings of 1848, after which the University remained closed until 1850.

On 12th July, 1866, Italian troops entered Padua. As was customary,

The portraits of Luigi Sabbatani and Egidio Meneghetti

there followed a purge of many teachers appointed by the Austrian government. Ferdinando Coletti, on the other hand, who had been one of the protagonists of the student revolt of February 8th, 1848, immediately obtained the chair of *Materia Medica*, which he held until his death in 1881. Still tenaciously linked to the vitalistic doctrines of his master Giacomini, he was inevitably excluded from the tumultuous succession of discoveries and new theories which during that period, in Europe and also elsewhere in Italy, were laying the bases of modern pharmacology. Nevertheless, his organizational activity was important as it contributed decisively to the transfer of pre-clinical teaching subjects from the hospital to the new school of Medicine established in the old convent of San Mattia where, in 1872, an independent laboratory of *materia medica* was established for the first time in Padua. Coletti was succeeded by Vincenzo Chirone (1847-1908), a strong advocate of the experimental method in pharmacology, who remained there until 1896. The title of the chair was changed from *Materia Medica* to Pharmacology with the arrival in Padua of Luigi Sabbatani (1863-1928), already well-known abroad for his pioneering research into the biological functions of calcium and the action of heavy metals, a convinced proponent of pharmacology as an independent science. In Padua, among other things, Sabbatani developed and completed his memorable research into the physiology and the pharmacology of calcium. During the First World War he was an organizer and a teacher of the "Battlefield University" which between December 1916 and October 1917 conferred degrees in medicine and surgery in Padua to 534 students from all war zones and territories. He can be credited with the Institute of Pharmacology in via Loredan, which became operative in 1919. After his death, which happened unexpectedly in 1928, the chair of Pharmacology was briefly entrusted to Italo Simon (1878-?), but in 1933 it was appointed to Egidio Meneghetti (1892-1961), a pupil of Sabbatani and the author of important research, above all into the action mechanism of drugs used in chemotherapy. In 1935 Meneghetti published a treatise on pharmacology which was profoundly innovative in its originality of approach and the modernity of its didactic contents, continually updated up until a ninth edition in 1958. A master of life and freedom, as well as of science, he was the recognized leader of the Resistance movement of the Veneto region; he was also rector from 1945 to 1947.

Once Italy had been unified, the regulations of the University of Padua were rendered uniform with those of the other Universities of the Kingdom. The medical-surgical-pharmacological faculty, which in 1842 had assumed the title of studium, reverted back to that of faculty in 1873, presided over by a dean. Briefly to run through the other principal chairs after annexation to the Kingdom of Italy, on that of Anatomy we find the already-quoted Vlacovich, from Lissa (Vis), who had been appointed to it at the age of only 27 and who held the chair honourably until 1898; in 1900 the glorious Paduan anatomical tradition continued with Dante Bertelli (1858-1946), who devoted himself mainly to research into the anatomy and the embryology of the diaphragm and the respiratory system of vertebrates.

The newly-established chair of Pathological Anatomy was entrusted from 1855 to 1888 to Lodovico Brunetti (1813-1899), educated in Austria, whose name is linked to the method of tissue tanning (1866); he was also the author of research into the cremation and the embalming of corpses. Respectful of Morgagni's glory, it has been said of him that he did not hesitate in any case in getting rid of the anatomical preparations of his predecessors, Morgagni included. In 1889 he was succeeded by Augusto Bonome (1857-1922), who remained in the chair until his death.

Roberto De Visiani (1800-1878), of Sebenico (Sibenik), appointed professor of Botany in 1837, was the author of a *Flora Dalmatica* (1842-52) and also a scholar of literary studies, the editor of a new manuscript of Brunetto Latini's *Tesoro*. He was succeeded by Pier Andrea Saccardo (1845-1920), whose fame is linked to his *Sylloge fungorum omnium hucusque cognitorum*, in 25 volumes (1882-1931, the last volumes in collaboration with G.B. Traverso and A. Trotter), which present systematically, according to a criterion based on spores, the Latin diagnoses of all the known species of fungi (then around 70,000). A scholar of the history of botany, he also assembled a rich collection of portraits of botanists.

The chair of Physiology was entrusted in 1867 to Felice Lussana (1820-1897), whose studies concern above all the physiology of the sensory centres and the cerebellum, the motor localizations, the entero-hepatic circuit, and the semi-circular canals and the cord of the tympanum. He was succeeded in 1890 by Aristide Stefani (1846-1925), who remained in the chair until 1920, the author of esteemed research into the physiology of the circulation and the nervous system.

The chair of Medical Clinics saw a series of highly prestigious figures, the first of which was Vincenzo Pinali (1802-1875), who held the chair from 1865 to 1875, known for his studies on, among other things, cholera, pneumonia, and the therapy of illnesses of the stomach; his name is linked to the library of the faculty of Medicine, established following the donation of his books and a large bequest to be used for the acquisition of medical works. Luigi Concato (1825-1880) stayed in Padua for only two years, then moving on to Turin: he made notable contributions to semeiotics and his name is remembered in Concato's syndrome, or *specific polysierositis*. Finally, Achille De Giovanni (1838-1916), who held the chair from 1878, is known above all for having advocated the need to direct medical study towards the identification of the various morphologico-functional characteristics. From 1876 onwards he worked to outline the methodological basis of this approach, and was the first to make use of the data of medical anthropometry. His morphological combinations are particular groupings of individuals, subdivided on the basis of the measurement of external somatic traits (trunk and limbs), and therefore of their constitution. According to this classification, individuals can be divided into three large groups: one represented by subjects with long limbs and small cross measurements (*first combination*); another characterized by

The portraits of Vincenzo Pinali and Achille De Giovanni

Edoardo Bassini and Pietro Spica

short limbs and a stocky body (*third combination*); and an intermediate group between the other two made up of individuals with a correct proportion between their various parts (*second combination*). These morphological combinations correspond respectively to the subdivision of individuals, carried out by Giacinto Viola (1870-1943), into longitypes, brachitypes, and normotypes.

For more than thirty years the Venetian Tito Vanzetti (1809-1888) held the chair of Surgical Clinics. Educated in Vienna, Vanzetti went first to Russia where he became the family doctor of General Naryškin; there he carried out an ovariotomy for the first time, and was appointed professor of Oculistics at the University of Char'kov. In 1853 he was given the chair of Surgical Clinics in Padua; among his merits is to have used, perhaps for first time, a rubber tourniquet as a means of obtaining haemostasis, and to have introduced (1846) a rigid dressing made of bandages soaked in glue in the treatment of fractures, the first step towards the plaster cast. The chair of Surgical Institutions was entrusted in 1882 to Edoardo Bassini (1844-1924), the hero of Villa Glori, who moved to Surgical Clinics in 1888, where he remained until 1921. Bassini became famous throughout the world for having revolutionized the treatment of the inguinal hernia with the invention of the operational method which bears his name and which was universally adopted, based on the anatomical and functional restoration of the inguinal canal after the tying and excision of the ruptured sac.

As regards the medico-surgical specializations, let us remember Pietro Gradenigo (1831-1904), who held the chair of Oculistic Clinics from 1873 to 1904, known for having been the first to describe the tuberculosis of the iris and for having invented some apparatus of his specialist field, among which the *ialopsifero*, a type of contact lens with a tube, designed to restore a part of lost vision to an eye with total leucoma. Achille Breda (1850-1934) was the founder of the modern Paduan school of Dermosyphilopathy, which he taught for all of 47 years, from 1878 to 1925 The name *Breda's disease* is also used to designate the buba, a variety of cutaneous leishmaniasis which he studied on those who returned from emigration to South America. From 1925 to 1942 Dermosyphilopathy was entrusted to Mario Truffi (1872-1964).

The pharmaceutical subjects remained in the faculty of Medicine up until 1874, the year in which the autonomous School of Pharmacy was established. The chair of Pharmaceutical and Toxicological Chemistry was entrusted in 1879 to Pietro Spica (1854-1929), only twenty-five years old, who was a pupil of Stanislao Cannizzaro (1826-1910) and Emanuele Paternò (1847-1936). Thanks to his initiative, in the academic year of 1882-83, the chair had its own laboratory in a specially constructed building opposite the General Hospital, which was enlarged in 1890 and 1909. In this institute for a good half a century Spica carried on his tireless activity as a teacher, researcher, writer of treatises, and organizer, setting the course for pharmaceutical science in Padua up until the present day. In

Two views of the Agripolis centre at Legnaro

1909 the teaching of Pharmaceutical Technics was established, which then spread to other Universities. The school initially granted the diploma of master in Pharmacy, later substituted by that of Pharmacist; in 1931 a degree in Pharmacy was established for the first time in Italy. In 1933 the School of Pharmacy became the Faculty of Pharmacy. Spica was succeeded in 1932 by Efisio Mameli (1875-1957), under whom the new institute of Pharmaceutical and Toxicological Chemistry (1937) came into being.

After the death of Orus, in 1797 Antonio Rinaldini of Brescia (1753-1838) was appointed professor of Veterinary Medicine; he had been Orus' pupil and assistant lecturer, also collaborating on the posthumous publication of his *Trattato medico pratico di alcune malattie interne degli animali domestici* (1793). Rinaldini held the post until 1804 and he was succeeded in 1817 by Girolamo Molin (1778-1851), who ceased teaching in 1838. After this, the importance of the school of Veterinary Medicine gradually diminished until it closed in 1873. More than a century was to pass before the faculty of Veterinary Medicine was established in the University of Padua, which began its activity in the academic year of 1992-93, finding a home two years later at Legnaro in the centre named Agripolis.

LIVIVS, PATAVINVS

GREGORIO PIAIA

Letters and Philosophy, Educational Science, Psychology

LETTERS AND PHILOSOPHY

After the radical transformation of the Padua Studium during the brief Napoleonic period, with the return of the Austrians to the Veneto region, the humanistic disciplines found themselves placed in the faculty of philosophy and mathematics. Under the Austrian regulations the 'philosophical' course (lasting three years, reduced in 1824-25 to two years) was to be preparatory for access both to the 'mathematical' course, and to the other three Padua faculties (the politico-legal, medical, and theological). In 1842, the year in which the faculties were named 'studia', the course in philosophy and that in mathematics came to constitute two independent studia. With the academic reform of 1852, grammar-school studies went from six to eight years; as from the same date philosophical studies no longer constituted a preparatory course, but they were kept in any case to allow future grammar-school teachers to complete their studies and those enrolled in other subjects to widen their cultural preparation. In the Restoration period, the professors of the philosophical and literary disciplines were generally of modest level, and their publications were less consistent than those of their late eighteenth-century predecessors. In this regard, it is significant that two of Padua University's most illustrious students, Antonio Rosmini and Niccolò Tommaseo, recall with admiration and affection the philosophical conversations they had with Cesare Baldinotti († 1821), a follower of moderate empiricism, who in 1808 had concluded his dignified academic career teaching Analysis of Ideas at Padua (as the traditional subject of Logic had been re-baptized under the French and later Napoleonic regulations).

In the dullness of the Restoration, it would be unreasonable to expect the teachers to have been open to the novelty of Romanticism, which indeed was accused by some professors of corrupting youth, as well as good writing style. The teaching of history was also affected by moral preoccupations, to such an extent that in the years 1817-1824 the text book used was Bossuet's famous *Discours sur l'histoire universelle* (1681), which with its providentialism inspired by Augustinian theology served to combat the persistent legacy of Enlightenment historiography. In this context any interaction between academic teaching, under rigid government control, and the intellectual environment linked to the literary journals of the Veneto region seems highly unlikely, even though the editors and collaborators of these journals had mostly completed their studies at the University

Arturo Martini, Tito Livio, *entrance hall of the Liviano*

Giacomo Zanella, Giuseppe De Leva and Roberto Ardigò

of Padua: this was true of the Venetian Luigi Carrer, the founder of the *Gondoliere* (1833), a law graduate who between 1827 and 1830 had had a short-lived academic experience as a "coadiutore" or assistant lecturer to the chair of philosophy, and who was one of the exponents of the Romantic movement of the Veneto region. And Legal Studies in Padua – it should be noted – saw some of the most representative nineteenth-century men of letters, from the already-quoted Tommaseo to the poets Arnaldo Fusinato, Giovanni Prati, and Aleardo Aleardi, and the novelists Ippolito Nievo and Antonio Fogazzaro. In the field of philosophy the text book which long dominated – as it did in other Italian Universities – was by father Francesco Soave, who offered a mitigated version of Condillac's sensism. Soave's work, which came out in Milan in the years 1791-92, was officially used in Padua from 1817 until 1837, when neo-professor Baldassarre Poli was allowed to use in his lessons his *Elementi di filosofia teoretica e morale*, which was very close to the eclecticism of Victor Cousin. Poli, who taught at the University of Padua until 1852, was also responsible for the effective launch of the teaching of the History of Philosophy, which had been established back in 1822.

With the annexation of the Veneto region to Italy came new men and new ideas, and this is also true for what had become the faculty of Philosophy and Letters. The faculty immediately called on the abbé Giacomo Zanella of Vicenza (1820-1888), who taught Italian Literature there for ten years, ending in 1876; besides his lively poetic sensitivity, Zanella brought a strong civil and patriotic commitment to his teaching, united to a belief in the difficult reconcilement between Christian faith and modern science. Nevertheless, we already find tangible signs of cultural renewal in the 1850s, with the beginning of the University teaching of the Latinist and Italianist Pietro Canal (1853), the modern historian Giuseppe De Leva (1855), the future author of vast research in five volumes into the emperor Charles V, and the palaeographer Andrea Gloria (1856), meritorious scholar of the official documents of medieval Padua and initiator of a school of palaeography and diplomatic which was to be made famous by Vittorio Lazzarini (1866-1957) and later by Paolo Sambin. In the subsequent decades the canons of philology and erudition were to make an impact on the literary disciplines, making Padua a true bastion of the "historical school". Italian studies saw the presence of Guido Mazzoni for seven years (then at the beginnings of his academic career), and then that of Francesco Flamini and Vittorio Rossi, who collaborated on the *Storia letteraria d'Italia* edited by Vallardi, writing the volumes on the Cinquecento and the Quattrocento respectively. At the same time a specific tradition of studies in philology and Romance literature was coming into being, whose founders were Ugo Angelo Canello (1848-1883), who died prematurely, and Vincenzo Crescini (1857-1932). We also see the establishment of the demanding chair of Sanskrit and Comparative History of Classical Languages held by the polyglot Emilio Teza (1831-1912), a friend of Carducci's.

The strong presence of the "historical school" was accompanied, thanks to the teaching of Roberto Ardigò (1828-1920), by the assertion of a decidedly positivistic philosophical tendency which acted as a foil to the long-lasting teaching of Francesco Bonatelli of Brescia (1830-1911), teacher in Padua of theoretical philosophy from 1867 and an exponent of Christian spiritualism, open however to the themes of neo-Kantism. Ardigò was appointed professor of the History of Philosophy at the beginning of 1881 and he was also employed for several years as a teacher of German Literature and Pedagogy; dean of the faculty in 1895-96, he retired in 1909. He wrote and published his most systematic works in Padua, becoming the acknowledged 'pontiff' of Italian Positivism and also exercising a notable influence in the field of psychology, sociology, and jurisprudence. The positivistic approach, in a more problematic form however, was carried forward in Padua by one of Ardigò's pupils, Giovanni Marchesini (1868-1931).

The 1920s marked a notable turning point in the history of the faculty of Letters and Philosophy (thus named with the Gentile reform). It took on a more "modern" face thanks to the appointment of teachers like the archaeologist Carlo Anti (1889-1961), who directed important campaigns of archaeological excavation before becoming dean of the faculty and then rector, and then the Latinist Concetto Marchesi (1878-1957) and the Hellenist Manara Valgimigli (1876-1965, who succeeded Augusto Rostagni in 1926), who were both open to the latest tendencies in aesthetic criticism and the history of civilization without renouncing their philological skill. To these we must add the historian Roberto Cessi (1885-1969), the poet and French scholar Diego Valeri (1887-1976), the Ancient Historian Aldo Ferrabino (1892-1972), the geographer Arrigo Lorenzi (1874-1948), whose legacy was continued by Giuseppe Morandini, and finally the Art Historian Giuseppe Fiocco (1884-1971), who initiated a school of scholars of the art of the Veneto region, from Rodolfo Pallucchini to Sergio Bettini and Camillo Semenzato.

New areas of research were established, moreover, such as Slavic studies (with Giovanni Maver, Ettore Lo Gatto, teacher in Padua from 1929 to '36, and Arturo Cronia), Glottology, Linguistics and Dialectology (with Benvenuto Terracini and Giacomo Devoto - who spent extremely fruitful years in Padua, from 1930 to 1935, before returning to Florence – and then with the long teaching of Carlo Tagliavini [1903-1982]), and Medieval Latin Philology, which took its first steps thanks to two young scholars, Ezio Franceschini (1906-1983) and Lorenzo Minio-Paluello (1907-1986), who subsequently ended up at the Catholic University of Milan and at Oxford respectively. It was to his pupil Franceschini that Marchesi gave the task in the 1930s of collaborating on the edition of the *Aristoteles latinus*, thus placing Padua on the international circuit and establishing a highly innovative link between philological and philosophical studies, which in 1956 was to lead to the establishment - on the initiative of the Greek scholar Carlo Diano – of the Centre for the History of the Aristotelian Tradition in the Veneto Region. Towards the end of the Thirties this multiplication of studies was accompanied by the construction of the Liviano, the faculty's new seat,

Concetto Marchesi, Manara Valgimigli and Diego Valeri

Gianfranco Folena

symbolically inspired by the meeting of the classical and the modern age.

For the role played by figures such as Anti, Marchesi, and Franceschini in the dramatic events which ended with the Liberation of Italy on 25th April, 1945, the reader must turn to the first part of this volume. It is interesting however to remember that within the University of Padua the faculty of Letters and Philosophy was the most averse to Fascism: many were the adherents to the manifesto of anti-Fascist intellectuals written by Benedetto Croce in 1925, while in July 1932 only three out of a total of 13 full professors and 'junior' professors were members of the National Fascist Party. But it must also be remembered that the political power enjoyed by Carlo Anti and his colleague Emilio Bodrero, professor of the History of Philosophy and a Senator (who in 1940 moved to Rome to the chair of the History and Doctrine of Fascism) did not have a negative influence on the appointment of teachers opposed to or estranged from the dominant regime, as long as they possessed the necessary scientific requirements.

Besides many of the teachers mentioned above, the post-war period was distinguished by the philosophical teaching of Luigi Stefanini (1891-1956), who from his initially idealistic positions reached a view centred on the unicity and the priority value of the "person". Stefanini's personalism was taken up again and developed in Padua by the Pedagogy scholar Giuseppe Flores d'Arcais and, from the point of view of philosophical historiography, by Giovanni Santinello. 'Classical' - that is to say, Aristotelo-Thomist - metaphysics, on the other hand, was the source of inspiration for Umberto Antonio Padovani (1894-1968) and Marino Gentile (1906-1991), as well as, although with a different stress, Carlo Giacon (1900-1984), active member of that Gallarate Centre for Philosophical Studies which produced among other things the monumental *Enciclopedia filosofica*. The field of literary studies too registered a notable increase in the Fifties, due above all to Carlo Diano (1902-1974), mentioned above, an acute interpreter of the relationship between literature and philosophy in the Greek world, and later to the Italianist Vittore Branca, known internationally for his studies on Boccaccio, and Gianfranco Folena (1920-1991), founder of the Philological and Linguistic Circle and promoter of multiple research in the field of the history of the Italian language and Romance Philology.

The advent of mass University education (from 211 students enrolled in the academic year of 1896-97 we move to 788 in the year 1937-38, 1265 in the year 1949-50, to reach a figure of 4206 in the academic year of 1975-76 and 6285 in the year 1998-99) dissolved the familiar-elitist atmosphere which still characterised the faculty in the immediate post-war period, and which today survives only in restricted seminars for PhD students. This evolution was marked by the student protests of 1968 and the troubled events of Seventies, when several teachers of the faculty became the object of terrorist attacks. At the same time, however, the changed cultural climate and the notable increase in the number of permanent professors (157 in the academic year 1999-2000) has favoured the introduction of a greater ideological and methodological pluralism, which has led to a reduction in some of the attitudes of rigidity and lack of openness typical of the traditional academic 'schools'. In the 1970s the faculty also expanded physically with the acquisition of the eighteenth-century Palazzo Maldura and its surroundings, while the need to enlarge the teaching prospectus on offer and to give the courses a more vocational character led to the creation of new degree courses besides the two traditional ones in Letters and Philosophy: the course in Foreign Languages and Literature was born in the academic year of 1963-64, that in Communication Science in 1996-97 (in collaboration with the faculty of Political Sciences), and that in History in 1998-99. Finally, a further and a richer range of courses will be created with the application of the University reform beginning with the academic year 2001-2002, to meet the challenges which modernization and globalization have posed to that "useless" but necessary thing, the humanistic disciplines.

EDUCATIONAL SCIENCE

The faculty of Educational Science, which began work in the academic year of 1994-95, is the final stage of a long course of development, which embraces almost two centuries. Indeed we must go back to 1817, when the teaching of the General Science of Education was introduced into the imperial royal University of Padua, in conformity with the Austrian regulations. This subject, considered compulsory in the reinstated faculty of theology and as the "free chair of philosophy" in the faculty of philosophy and mathematics, was first entrusted to the priest Angelo Ridolfi, who held the chair of German language and literature. In effect, pedagogy was almost always considered as a second post and from 1856 onwards it was regularly linked to a chair of philosophy; the combination of philosophy and pedagogy was maintained after the annexation of the Veneto region to Italy and it was further reinforced with the Gentile reform (1923).

In the second half of the nineteenth century, Italian Universities were obliged to take on the burden of an increased demand for school education on two fronts: training future secondary-school teachers and educating the governing personnel (primary-school headmasters and inspectors). An initial attempt to cater for this was made with the establishment in all Universities, from 1874 onwards, of a teacher-training college in Letters and Philosophy, which qualified students to teach the humanities, but whose pedagogical and didactic content was modest. Secondly came the establishment in 1906, in every faculty of Philosophy and Letters, of a (two-year) training course for those who had completed the 'Scuole Normali', that is to say those schools which prepared the future primary-school teachers. This course was suppressed in 1923 in the context of the Gentile reform by the decree which re-organized the two higher Institutes of Female Teacher Training (established in 1878 in Florence and Rome) and transformed them into faculties of teacher training. There were negative reactions to the suppression: in Padua the course's governing council,

Giovanni Marchesini

which since 1908 had been presided over by the philosopher and pedagogue Giovanni Marchesini, sent an official letter to the mayor, inviting him to promote the establishment of a teacher training College in agreement with the other major cities of the Veneto region. The proposal came to nothing, so much so that in the lengthy and detailed written report which, on 7th September 1943, accompanied the transfer of office from the "outgoing rector" Carlo Anti to the "incoming rector" Concetto Marchesi, the faculty of Teacher Training figured at the top of a list of new faculties whose establishment was greatly desired. The report also stated the wish that after the acquisition of the sixteenth-century Loggia del Capitanio (then occupied by government offices) and the necessary restoration, it could house the new faculty of Teacher Training. This is what happened, albeit twenty years later (1964)...

Finally established in the academic year of 1950-51, the University institute of Teacher Training (subsequently transformed into a regular faculty of Teacher Training), tackled the double educational demand mentioned above through its degree courses in Literary Subjects and Pedagogy, and its three-year diploma in Scholastic Supervision for primary-school headmasters, which were later complemented by a degree course in Psychology. The new faculty provided access to higher education for many of those who had finished the Teacher Training secondary schools from the whole north-east of Italy, and it carried out an essential function in the Sixties above all, when there was a huge new demand for new teachers after the establishment of the Middle School. But the Faculty of Teacher Training did not merely act as a duplicate of the Faculty of Letters and Philosophy, as was the case elsewhere. Thanks to the theoretical and organizational ability of Giuseppe Flores d'Arcais (who was dean of the faculty from 1955 to 1967 and long-term director of the institute of Pedagogy, now the department of Educational Science), it became a centre of Italian pedagogical research, open to new fields of study with the foundation of the institute of the History of Theatre and Drama, initially directed by Giovanni Calendoli (1912-1996). With the gradual disappearance of the reasons underlying the establishment of the faculty of Teacher Training, the need to respond more specifically to the educational challenges which today are no longer exclusively scholastic, has lead to the transformation of Teacher Training into the new faculty of Educational Science.

PSYCHOLOGY

The University of Padua has played a primary role in the development of psychology in Italy. Already present in the positivistic tradition embodied by Ardigò, psychological studies were radically renewed after the First World War when Vittorio Benussi of Trieste (1878-1927), teacher at the Austrian University of Graz, was appointed professor of Psychology at the Padua faculty of Philosophy and Letters for exceptional merit. This new chair was an addition to the only other three chairs, which had existed up to then in Italian Universities (at Rome, Naples, and Turin). These had been established by the Ministry of Education after the participants at the Fifth International Conference on Psychology, held in Rome in 1905, had expressed their disappointment at the unimpressive presence of this discipline in the Italian University. Thus a laboratory of psychology was founded in some rooms of the old building in piazza Capitaniato which was later to give way to the Liviano: it was a small structure with an extremely modest budget, supplemented by the patronage of count Novello Papafava dei Carraresi, a friend of Benussi and a scholar of psychology as well as philosophy. This was the "heroic age" of Paduan psychology, in which Benussi himself saw to the construction of some of the instruments for the newly founded laboratory, around which, nevertheless, there formed a little school open to the various research tendencies which characterized Central European psychology. With respect to the latter, Italian culture appeared decidedly dated, due in part to the aversion which neo-Idealism – which had become the official philosophy of the Fascist regime – showed for scientific psychology.

On the death of Benussi (1927), the teaching of psychology was entrusted to the young Cesare Musatti (1897-1989), then a teacher at the "Tito Livio" High School. In 1940 the notorious racial laws meant that Musatti was forced to leave Padua; he later became the foremost exponent of psychoanalysis in Italy. His post as lecturer and director of the institute of Psychology was taken up in 1943 by one of his pupils, Fabio Metelli of Trieste (1907-1987). In 1951, after having passed the selection process for promotion to the chair, Metelli was called first to Catania, then to Trieste, and in 1953 to the young faculty of Teacher Training at Padua. The training school in Psychology, which was set in motion by Metelli in 1962, contributed significantly to the spread of interest in the study of psychology. This role of cultural and scientific promotion was officially recognized at a national level in 1971 with the establishment in the faculty of Teacher Training of one of the first two degree courses in Psychology (the other one was opened in Rome). Thus for several years Padua became the point of reference for a vast and composite student population from many regions of Italy, which brought with it notable organizational problems and, towards the end of the 1970s, even problems of public order, given the strong presence of the *Autonomia proletaria* movement. The transfer of teaching and of two departments (that of General Psychology, heir to the old institute of Psychology, and that of the Psychology of Development and Socialization, guided by Guido Petter) to the new buildings in the Piovego area of Padua resolved these long-standing logistical problems. At the same time, the removal of the degree course in Psychology from the faculty of Teacher Training and its transformation into an autonomous faculty (1991) signalled the full maturity on an institutional level of a process which had begun back in the period after the First World War.

Vittorio Benussi, Cesare Musatti and Fabio Metelli

UGO BALDINI

Mathematical, Physical, Natural, and Agricultural Sciences

Introduction

At the end of the eighteenth century the scientific teaching at the University of Padua took place within the *universitas* of artists which had two functions: it led to academic qualifications in philosophy and medicine and, with some subjects, it provided a preparatory training for the courses in theology and law, which was not compulsory for those who had already studied them. Given that those who followed lessons in mathematics and philosophy often had not done so before, and that they were preparatory above all for the study of medicine, the curricula were not very advanced; the teaching of natural history, chemistry, nautical science, and special areas of mathematics introduced before 1797 did not aim to train engineer-architects, pharmacists, or surgeons (whose studies remained outside the University and had a slim theoretical basis), but only to provide those who followed the courses in philosophy and medicine with some grounding in these sectors too. Historically there was no direct connection between the University and research. Naturally, the division was partial, as is proved by the contributions made by lecturers in anatomy from the Middle Ages, but research was limited to a minority, usually private, and external to the Studium: it was of little help for a career, its results rarely made it into the lessons (even those of Galileo), and often the academic body denied that it was the University's job to produce knowledge, besides transmitting it. If the Degli Angeli and Montanari, then the Guglielmini, Vallisneri, Morgagni, and yet again the Poleni, Pontedera, and Caldani gave research an academic dignity and drove the University to improve its structures and its functions, then up until the late eighteenth century the pillars of the old order still stood.

Even the distinction between physical, mathematical, and natural sciences, and medical sciences (or human geography, or other subjects) was different from today. Natural disciplines such as botany, mineralogy, comparative anatomy, and chemistry, were included among the medical disciplines, or part of one of them. For this reason, strictly speaking the Padua faculty of sciences was born at the turn of the nineteenth century and coincided with a decisive modification of the disciplines and curricula everywhere; in Padua, however, this coincidence was highlighted by profound political change (the fall of the Serenissima and its transfer under other States), not necessary to the reforms which also took place in other more static Italian States, but which linked such reforms to foreign norms (Napoleonic and Habsburg). Moreover the reforms were carried out by an academic body which was mainly local but, despite the

View of the Specola, the Eighteenth Century astronomical Observatory

irredentism of the majority, one often linked to foreign scientific centres even after the Unification of Italy. In general, it is simplistic to look at the foreign control of Padua University in a political way, considering the French phase (1805-1813) as progressive, and the Austrian one (1813-1866) as conservative and static in its teaching and research.

From the End of the Eighteenth Century to 1866

The French occupation (1797-98) brought an epoch-making novelty: the transition from Latin to Italian as the language of the lessons. The first period of Habsburg government (1798-1805) opened with a decree that maintained the old order and reinstated Latin, but it also brought some modern initiatives: professional training for medical graduates, rigour in the examinations and the conferring of degrees (a old sore point), and the granting of chairs by a selection procedure (this never became a rule in Padua). Initially, however, war and political vicissitudes prevented its implementation, and the flight or the dismissal of teachers who had collaborated with the French meant recourse to supply teachers.

A new University began to take shape when, once the Veneto region had been annexed (December, 1805), the Napoleonic Kingdom of Italy extended its own scientific and disciplinary order to Padua. Between 1806 and 1807 the University was rendered uniform with those of Pavia and Bologna; the *universitates* were replaced by a disciplinary division into three 'classes' (mathematical and physical sciences, moral and political sciences, and letters) and a didactic division into three faculties (physico-mathematical, medical, and legal), governed by deans. The new lay attitude led the theology course to be moved to the Seminary; the mathematical, medical, and physical disciplines (the name which replaced "philosophy") went to the physico-mathematical faculty, ethics to the moral sciences, and analysis of ideas (heir of logic and metaphysics), Latin (which remained compulsory, even though teaching went back to Italian), and Greek went to letters. As far as the didactic order was concerned, the physical and mathematical subjects moved to the physico-mathematical faculty, while the naturalistic ones, devoid of any professional role, remained in the medical faculty. The transfer of the arts course to the physico-mathematical faculty was not only one of name or one concerning the contents of certain courses, because it transformed a philosophical course into a scientific one (in the late nineteenth century a philosophy course was to come back to life in a humanist context, despite positivism). Moreover, the reforms of 1806-07 brought vocational training to the University, previously entrusted to special schools or to the system of apprenticeship. The faculty of medicine conferred an academic qualification in pharmacy and a degree in surgery besides that in medicine; the physico-mathematical faculty conferred a degree in engineering-architecture and a diploma in land-surveying. To avoid an overlap between the secondary teaching subjects and preparatory teaching for the University, those who had already frequented the secondary subjects were exempted from taking

PHYSICO-MATHEMATICAL FACULTY	MEDICAL FACULTY
General Physics	Human Anatomy
Experimental Physics	Physiology and Comparative Anatomy
Introduction to *Sublime Calculus* (Calculus) and Geodesy	Practical Medicine
Sublime Calculus (Calculus)	Surgical Institutions
Applied Mathematics	*Materia Medica*
Civil and Military Architecture	Botany
Astronomy	Natural History
Agricultural Science (Rural Economics)	General Chemistry
	Pharmaceutical Chemistry
	Pathology
	Obstetrics
	Legal Medicine
	Medical Clinics
	Surgical Clinics

them; the preparatory subjects were reduced, but the new educational tasks required other subjects, which were part of the situation outlined above.

Like the Austrian one, the new order insisted on checks on progress and behaviour. Greater political stability introduced a continuity into the teaching subjects; the integration of the Veneto region into a State with other high-level academic centres meant that teachers came to Padua who had been educated elsewhere, preventing localism and traditionalism (two examples are Giovanni Santini, who was trained as an astronomer at Brera and the Venetian Antonio Collalto who completed his mathematical studies in Pavia and Paris). While most of the teachers had received their education in the Veneto region, with the exception of those from Emilia who came from the Bologna school, now education became Lombard-Venetian. This was true of the subsequent Habsburg period (when candidates for selection were accepted from Lombard-Venetian Kingdom or the Empire), influencing the composition and the scientific orientation of the teaching body. Nevertheless, urgencies, consideration for well-known local figures or those already active in the University, and political factors led to departures from the official selection procedure: valid teachers, such as the mathematicians Santini, Collalto, Pietro Cossali, and Francesco Maria Franceschinis, were called on directly.

The "stabilimenti" (the *Specola*; the library; the laboratories of Geodesy, Natural History, Physics, Comparative Anatomy; the Botanical and Agrarian Gardens) were improved or created. Santini began to provide up-to-date instruments for the Observatory; Stefano Andrea Renier, teacher of Natural History, enlarged Vallisneri's museum, dividing up the antique part and reorganizing the exhibits into new classes. The renewal of the curricula and the growth of the infrastructures did not only produce more specific competencies: in every structure besides the teacher there was at least one assistant lecturer and some technicians (operators of instruments and machines, gardeners), sometimes highly qualified. Thus collections, gardens, and laboratories became places for the development of programmes and advanced education and meet-

Roberto De Visiani

ing-places for scholars of a field, and (after 1850) conduits for the transition of the traditional "letture" (mere didactic pigeonholes) to the University institutes.

Naturally the teachers also had external relations. The University library (which received publications from the Universities and academies of the empire) grew, as did the circulation of Italian and foreign scientific journals and the bilateral links between scientific and agrarian academies from the Veneto and those from other areas of Italy, which also involved many teachers at Padua. Some were absorbed into the Italian Society of Sciences (the 'Accademia dei XL', founded in Verona in 1782 by Anton Mario Lorgna and, after an interlude, brought back to Verona by Antonio Cagnoli) and the Italian National Institute (1802, from 1810 Institute of Sciences, Letters, and Arts, with three of its five sections in the Veneto region). Some of them spent periods in Paris and Vienna and from 1839 they were constant participants in the Conferences of Italian scientists. Nevertheless, in the French period, as in the previous one, the teaching changed less than the regulations. Elderly teachers held back renewal: Marco Carburi, professor of Chemistry since before 1759, opposed the use of Lavoisier's nomenclature, making his assistant lecturer Girolamo Melandri Contessi, who had been trained in Pavia and was a convinced Lavoisierite, promise not to change criterion after he succeeded him (but Melandri disobeyed him). There were also contradictions in Botany. Giuseppe Antonio Bonato, who taught it from 1794 to 1835, followed Linnaeus in his courses and in the reorganization and enlargement of the Botanical Garden. By donating his books to the Garden he founded a specialist library, and once he had obtained a post for an assistant lecturer, trained researchers free from the need to practice medicine: one of them was Roberto De Visiani, who succeeded him in 1836. Nevertheless Bonato did not undertake large-scale collections and published little. A transitional figure was Angelo Dalla Decima, teacher of *Materia Medica* from 1786, who also dealt with natural history, which was not taught from 1777 to 1806. Acquainted with the work of the eighteenth-century Paduan school in physiology, nosology, medical physics, botany, and geology, he was not however original and was overtaken by progress made in the disciplines. Similar things can be said for Pietro Arduino and his son, Luigi, holders (1765-1805 and 1806-1829) of the first Italian chair of Agricultural Science, which moved in 1806 to the physico-mathematical faculty because it was useful for engineers and land-surveyors. Pietro (to whom Linnaeus dedicated a genus and a species), wrote notable studies on nutritional plants, but in other respects remained tied to the mid eighteenth-century naturalism of the Veneto region; Luigi wrote on the cultivation of exotic plants and on derivatives of colonial vegetables, also in relation to the problems of the continental blockade. Geology and mineralogy had a supporter from outside the University in Niccolò da Rio, who equipped a chemistry laboratory and collections, undertook important research in the Euganean hills, and held courses (against Carburi, he taught Lavoisier's chemistry). With his relations outside the University he aided the acceptance of recent geology and his *Giornale dell'italiana letteratura* (1802-1828) was the most qualified periodical in Padua, even for the sciences, along with the *Saggi* of the local Academy. In the Habsburg years – without ever having taught at the University – he directed the physico-mathematical studium.

In part there was a greater development in the teaching of physics by Salvatore Dal Negro and Giuseppe Avanzini. The former taught Experimental Physics from 1803 and Physics (experimental and general) from 1817. He worked on electricity and electromagnetism (he conversed with Volta), above all on their applications, designing instruments and apparatus which figure in the early history of electric motors (such as an "electromagnetic ram"). Avanzini, teacher of Analyses (1797-1801, 1817-29) and General Physics (1806-1809, 1813-1817), together with Stratico, Renier, and Collalto, one of the "Jacobin" science teachers, was one of the major pure and applied hydraulic engineers of the period, and increased the mathematical part of general physics. Like Dal Negro, however, he paid little attention to theoretical topics in optics, thermodynamics, and the structure of matter: the Padua school participated little in the most progressive debates on physics, and subsequently also contributed to the theoretical debate (that on fundamental forces, for example) above all with its mathematicians, while the most well-known contributions from the Veneto region came from non academics. Renier, who taught natural history from 1806 to 1830, besides modernizing the collections, adopted new systems of classification; like his friend Giuseppe Olivi, but with inferior results, he devoted himself above all to marine biology.

Stefano Andrea Renier

In astronomy, Vincenzo Chiminello, who succeeded Giuseppe Toaldo in 1797, was not an innovator. Nevertheless, his assistant lecturer Santini (from 1806), who had received an outstanding training from Barnaba Oriani (he was also a supply teacher for Analyses on more than one occasion), made progress by beginning to acquire adequate instruments; from 1813, when he succeeded Chiminello, he changed the contents. Among the mathematicians, who changed in 1806, Collalto, Cossali, and Franceschinis, mentioned above, who were all from the Veneto region but trained elsewhere, raised the level of the courses but were not top-level scientists (until after 1830 Padua was a mathematical centre inferior to Pavia and Pisa; Cossali was known for his works on astronomy or aerostatic flight and, above all, for *Origine, trasporto in Italia, primi progressi in essa dell'algebra*, the principal Italian work on the history of mathematics up until the late nineteenth century).

Thus, if in the biological and naturalistic disciplines the Veneto tradition, enriched by its relationship with Italian and foreign research, made valid contributions to teaching at least up until the Habsburg years, in the physical and mathematical disciplines – although its protagonists were mainly from the Veneto region – the direct relationship with other schools, above all that of Pavia, was more decisive. Moreover, the scientific life of the University in the first fifteen years of the century could no longer be separated from that of the academies, artistic circles like that of Da Rio, high schools, or religious schools (including the Padua Seminary), which at times had teachers of University level. Giuseppe Zamboni, teacher of physics at the Verona diocesan college, built original mechanisms of international renown in electrology. The chemist and physicist Giovanni Battista Polcastro, a pupil of Da Rio, designed a quadrant aerometer and a pneumatical linchpin and repeated the experiments carried out by Volta; Daniele Francesconi repeated Poleni's experiments on the fall of weights; in Biology, Giuseppe Olivi dealt with the University on substantially equal terms. Some of them later taught at the University or (like Zamboni) trained future teachers.

Austria re-occupied Padua in late 1813, but it acted on the University from 1815 onwards, more on the ideology underlying the Napoleonic reform than on technical lines. The organization into classes (now studia) and faculties remained, as did the distinction between preparatory subjects, which could be studied in the secondary schools, and the specialist subjects. The *Statuto disciplinare per gli studj Filosofici nella Imperial Regia Università di Padova* (1825) distinguished between subjects which were "compulsory" (for admission to the specialist courses), "free" (for those who wished to deepen their knowledge), and "special" (the specialist courses). Theology became a faculty so as to sanction the position of religion at the summit of knowledge and its harmony with positive learning. The previous faculties remained; the scientific ones maintained their basic approach. According to the regulations, the physico-mathematical faculty was to confer the qualification (later degree) in engineering and the diploma in land surveying; nevertheless it still conferred degrees in mathematics and physics. The medical faculty added the degree in chemistry (born between 1835 and 1838) and three licences, for "country" surgeons, midwives, and veterinary surgeons, to its degrees in medicine and surgery and its qualification in pharmacy.

In the physico-mathematical faculty it was compulsory for the degree to take theoretical philosophy, which revived the gnosiological and metaphysical dimension, and Latin returned in part. If the ideology of the model was conservative, the scope of the teaching subjects and the scientific curricula was enlarged; the separation between naturalistic and medical disciplines continued, and a division came into being between the 'philosophical' (mostly in the two-year preparatory course) and the mathematical disciplines, which in part foreshadowed the birth of the autonomous School of Engineering. This was not due to the specific merits of the Habsburg administration, but the result of scientific development which, with variants, also took place in other Italian Universities; nevertheless in Padua it was unhindered, and like Pavia - even though the two Universities were minor and peripheral within the empire - for fifty years the teaching of science as a whole was not inferior to that at other Italian Universities. This is shown by the list of disciplines (the legal and religious preparatory subjects are excluded):

Astronomy;
General Physics;
Particular Physics (in 1817 the two Physics were united, and remained so until 1873);
Elements of Algebra and Geometry (later Elementary Pure Mathematics; this ceased in 1841);
Introduction to *Sublime Calculus* (Calculus) (this ceased in 1842);
Sublime Calculus (Calculus);
Applied Mathematics and Geodesy (in 1836 divided into Applied Mathematics and Geodesy and Hydrodynamics);
Agricultural Science (from 1829 Universal Natural History and Rural Economics);
Civil and Military Architecture (from 1842 divided into Civil, Hydraulic, and Road Architecture, and Drawing);
Figurative Drawing;

Descriptive Geometry (from 1842);
Geometrical and Mechanical Drawing (from 1842);
Geography (from 1855);
General and Technological Chemistry (up until 1852 borrowed from the faculty of Medicine, then transferred to the physico-mathematical faculty;
Medical Chemistry remained at Medicine);
Special Natural History (transferred from Medicine in 1860);
Botany (also transferred from Medicine in 1860).

Giusto Bellavitis

The changes which took place between 1836 and 1842 came from a re-thinking of the relationship between the applied and the theoretical component. From 1843 the course prospectus distinguished between 'philosophical' and mathematical disciplines; from 1846, without modifying the whole, it qualified them as distinct faculties. The teaching subjects introduced between 1852 and 1860 responded to new scientific and technical needs, like some of the free courses activated between 1856 and 1866 (on mechanical and chemical technology, machine design and construction, probability theory, and techniques of calculus for engineering). All this shows a general move towards specialization, but also a difficulty. The distinction between philosophy and mathematics did not anticipate that between a course of physical, mathematical, and natural studies and one of engineering and architecture, but one between formal (pure or applied) disciplines and other disciplines which focused on phenomena and classes of natural objects (physical and biological, organic and inorganic). It probably would have been corrected, as it was later in other Habsburg Universities; but at Pavia and Padua, due to the events of 1859 and 1866, the correction did not come from Vienna but from Italy: in this, therefore, the political and the scientific turning point coincided.

By 1830, when the teachers trained in the eighteenth century had disappeared, the increase in the number of chairs, new posts for assistant lecturers, a degree of political stability and availability of funds, the choice of teachers via formal selection procedure, and support for those completing higher studies elevated the teaching standard and allowed research at a European level. Santini provided the Observatory with instruments by the best foreign manufacturers and he made others with qualified mechanics. He taught from 1813 to after 1870, obtaining European recognition in the calculation of the orbits of planetoids and comets for his star catalogues containing the highly accurate measurements of positions. The mathematical tone of his work also came through in his *Elementi di Astronomia* and his *Teorica degli stromenti ottici* (which compensated in part for the relative lack of interest in optics shown by the Paduan physicists of the period) and in the pupils who helped him in his observations and calculations (Carlo Conti, Virgilio Trettenero, Iacopo Michez, Ernesto Nestore Legnazzi) and who taught other mathematical disciplines, geodesy, and physics, thus contributing with him to the training of new teachers of mathematics: Serafino Raffaele Minich, prince analyst at Padua from 1834 to 1874; and Domenico Turazza, who between 1841 and 1891 held the principal teaching posts of applied mathematics, guided the transformation of the engineering course into an autonomous school, and developed the Veneto tradition of hydrodynamics (he was perhaps the greatest authority in the field in Italy).

After the early nineteenth century, which had been marked by a non academic great, Pietro Paleocapa, Turazza signalled the beginning of a different phase with Gustavo Bucchia, a pupil of Franceschinis and Santini, the holder of the chair of Civil Architecture (later Construction Science) from 1844, and around the time of Unification the major figure in Italian engineering. Giusto Bellavitis, too, who had benefited from the teaching of Santini, via Conti, and was teacher of Descriptive Geometry, Analytical Geometry, and Algebra (1845-1880), was with Minich the principal mathematician at Padua in that period (his calculation of equipollences was a milestone of geometric calculus before Hamilton, Peano, and Burali Forti). Minich and Bellavitis also dealt with hydraulics (the latter was involved in a controversy with Turazza over efflux theory).

In Physics the ambivalence described above continued. After Dal Negro, who up until 1839 did not form a real school, the teachers changed frequently (six in ten years, mostly supply teachers). One good pupil, Luigi Magrini, left Padua in 1840 after having dealt with electrology (in 1837 he put forward a telegraphic apparatus); only later did he work in acoustics. Neither do we reach a turning point with Giuseppe Belli, perhaps the greatest physicist at Padua before 1866 and an experimenter open to theoretical topics. He arrived in 1840 and returned to Pavia in 1843; his *Catalogo delle macchine esistenti nel Gabinetto fisico dell'I.R. Università di Padua* shows a notable increase in the number of instruments, thanks also to mechanics of the University. There seems to have been a period of more stability in 1849 with Francesco Zantedeschi, a pupil of Zamboni and a controversial but prepared researcher who also took an interest in the instruments and pursued research in electrology and optics, but had to leave his teaching post because of blindness (1857). The essay *Dell'origine e progresso* on the Padua school of physics (1851), where he lists the most notable contributions of his predecessors, confirms their almost purely experimental nature and a certain limitation in theme. He was succeeded by Trettenero (1859-63), who was waiting to succeed Santini and died young, and Bellavitis, who only held a four-year contract as a supply teacher, however (1863-1867). Between 1830 and 1850 in the faculty only an astronomer and mathematician like Conti seriously dealt with thermodynamics, then central to physical theory; when, after 1866, a teacher was sought who could begin work on a long-term basis, Francesco Rossetti was chosen. Rossetti had studied in Padua, but had pursued higher studies in Vienna, Paris, and Germany for a long period. Chemistry had a more stable teaching, but not more advanced. Melandri (who was judged by his pupil Bartolomeo Bizio to be simply a teacher) was succeeded by Francesco Ragazzini (1833-1858), who worked almost only on thermal waters, and by Francesco Filippuzzi (1858-1886). The latter, who had studied in University schools of chemistry in Austria, Germany, and France, and who had a modern preparation and good scientific relations, renewed the laboratory and reformed the courses, but once he received the teaching post, virtually ceased his research and publications.

In the two chairs, therefore, the organizational structure and equipment grew more than the scientific activity. But if mathematics was by now reserved for specialized professionals, elsewhere relatively simple apparatus still allowed advanced research. Each of the University chairs, which had not yet become institutes, were headed by only two or three specialists, while the scientific debate still centred on local academies and institutes, whose *Acts* mostly published their research (unlike Pavia, the University of Padua did not have any scientific journals of its own). In this context, after Zamboni, we find researchers of a certain level like Ambrogio Fusinieri and Bizio, in a field which stretched from the structure of matter to physical chemistry and biological chemistry. The former, who organized a true scientific centre in the Vicenza area, published the *Annali delle scienze del Regno Lombardo-Veneto* (1830-49), a qualified scientific periodical which often published the work of teachers at Padua. Fusinieri was the originator of the "Italian physical doctrine", a dynamist concept of matter born of phenomena observed in very thin liquid layers but extended to many others (from catalysis to optical phenomena). Short-lived but not without support (Bizio carried out some of the first microbiological observations and was the first to observe a metal, copper, in a living being), it raised great debate, not only in Italy: Bertelli and Zantedeschi gave it cautious attention; Bellavitis opposed it, but this confirms that in this fundamental area the University had a critical function but not the ability to put forward new ideas (at the conferences of Italian scientists held in Padua and Venice in 1842 and 1847 the non-academic researchers of the Veneto region were as active as the University teachers).

Tomaso Antonio Catullo and Antonio Keller

In the natural sciences, on the other hand, the University was central. Tomaso Antonio Catullo, teacher of Natural History (1831-1851), with interests in geo-mineralogy and palaeontology, in his *Zoologia fossile delle province venete* (1827), systematized the use of characteristic fossils for the relative dating of strata. His successor Raffaele Molin (1851-1866), who graduated and completed his studies in Vienna, cultivated Comparative Anatomy, but in restricted contexts and without innovation. The situation for Botany was more linear with De Visiani (from 1836 to 1877), who favoured its institutional evolution (in 1860 the chair moved from the medical to the physico-mathematical faculty). Hostile to evolutionism, but a good organizer and scientist (he was an authority on the flora of the Balkans and the Middle East and on fossil plants), he enriched the Botanical Garden and added to the equipment, had a vast network of relationships, and taught pupils of the level of Pietro Andrea Saccardo. The other chair of natural science, Agricultural Science, also played a socio-economic role, spreading the use of means and techniques. From 1819 to 1854 it was held by Luigi Configliachi, who had been trained in Pavia and was known for having founded an institute for the blind in Padua (1838); a good naturalist and botanist, he limited himself almost solely to teaching, however, and hardly published any contribution to research. Antonio Keller, who succeeded him from 1854 to 1900, had studied medicine and natural science in Vienna and Padua (he was De Visiani's assistant lecturer and a competent mineralogist and geologist). A herald of the discipline in academies and public bodies, he was a consultant in the schemes for reclaiming land for agriculture in the Veneto region in the late nineteenth century. Through him agricultural science brought together natural study and technico-economic themes, which later led it to move to the School of Engineering. Keller aimed at turning it into a distinct degree course, but this was not to take place until between 1946 and 1951, with the birth of the relative faculty.

3. *From 1866 to the Second World War*

Immediately after unification with Italy, there were significant innovations. In 1867 the engineering course conformed with the Casati law (1859) which was in force in the Kingdom, dividing Theoretical Geodesy (later united to Astronomy) from Practical Geodesy, changing Geography to Physical Geography, and making certain free subjects part of the compulsory curriculum. From 1868 Rational Mechanics became a subject in its own right; in 1869 Natural History was divided into Mineralogy-Geology and Zoology-Comparative Anatomy, with the consequent division of the collections; in 1870 came two-year licence courses for teachers of physics and mathematics and natural sciences. But the final organizational structure came with the law (May 1872) which rendered Padua University uniform with all the other Italian Universities. From 1873 the faculty, called Mathematical, Physical, and Natural Sciences, conferred four degrees (in mathematical, physico-mathematical, and physico-chemical sciences, and natural history); *Sublime Mathematics* (Mathematics) became Differential and Integral Calculus, Physics was divided into Experimental Physics and Mathematical Physics, Analytical Geometry separated from Descriptive Geometry, and General Chemistry became Organic and Inorganic Chemistry. The course in Graphic Statics began, held by Antonio Favaro, future historian of Galileo and of the University, as did other courses in Human Anatomy and Histology and Physiology, distinct from those for the medical students. Two regulations (1875-1876) transformed the course for engineers and architects into a technical School for Engineers, equal to those in Turin, Rome, Naples, and Palermo (and later Bologna) and inferior only to the Higher Technical Institute of Milan. The school, whose director was made equal to a faculty dean, was autonomous even before it became a faculty (1936); its creation freed engineers from their previous need for a preparation in extra-scientific subjects, and allowed the faculty, free of immediate applied aims, to increase its range of theoretical subjects:

1877-79: courses in Projective Geometry, Higher Analysis, Complementary Algebra and Anthropology (free course) established;
1882: course in Higher Mechanics established; separation between Geology and Mineralogy and their relative collections;
1884: the beginning of the course in Higher Geometry;
1885: the teaching of Theoretical Geodesy and Astronomy separated;
1891: the separation of Crystallography from Mineralogy;
1900: the beginning of the course in Electrochemistry.

Equipment and infrastructures grew, with mathematical laboratories and laboratories for subjects which later moved to the School of Engineering (Industrial Mechanics, Architecture, Hydraulics, Agricultural Science). At the end of the century there were laboratories for Mineralogy, Geology, Zoology, Physics, Technical Drawing, and Descriptive Geometry; there was a chemistry laboratory (enlarged in 1864), the Observatory, and the Botanical Garden. Between 1897 and 1907 laboratories were added for Anthropology, Bacteriology, Physical Geography, and Geodesy. From these structures, as we have said, were born the University institutes of sciences. The astronomical Observatory, at a distance from the University site, with its own staff, had been an institute in practice since the eighteenth century (in 1873 it formally became the University Observatory, thus accentuating its didactic role). The institutes came into being from 1873 onwards (Chemistry; 1874 Physics; 1886 Botany, Zoology, and Astronomy; 1903 Anthropology; 1904 Physical Geography; and 1907-08 Geology, Geodesy, and Mineralogy); the mathematical institutes came later, except in the School of Engineering. All the institutes formed their own libraries, often through donations made by teachers: at the end of the nineteenth century some of the larger ones were already educational resources for the students.

After the Unification of Italy, teachers and graduates of the faculty and the School of Engineering contributed to the building of the railways and roads, and the work of reclaiming areas of land from the sea for agriculture, which were set in motion by the new State, not only in the Veneto region; they also frequently held public office and – although civil engineering was considered most important academically – contributed to industrialization. But the faculty also became a respected centre on a scientific level. The prevalence of those from Veneto, Friuli, and Dalmatia, who had been trained at Padua or in the Habsburg domains, diminished, and Pavia was no longer the principal origin of external teachers. Completing one's studies abroad, however, still took place mostly in Austria and, above all, Germany: an effect of previous relations, but above all of the scientific primacy of these places in the late nineteenth century. All of this is clear in mathematics, which soon became the highest level area in the Faculty. Among the mathematicians only Legnazzi and Favaro were pupils of Santini, Minich, Bellavitis, or Turazza: they were teachers of great merit and, in the case of Favaro, eminent scholars in other subjects, but not original scientists. The years 1878 to 1885 saw the arrival of Francesco Flores D'Arcais, Giovanni Garbieri, Ernesto Padova, Gregorio Ricci Curbastro, Giuseppe Veronese, and Paolo Gazzaniga, pupils of masters such as Ulisse Dini, Enrico Betti, Luigi Cremona, and Felice Casorati. Ricci, Veronese, and Gazzaniga had completed their studies in Germany with mathematicians such as Klein, Weierstrass, and Kronecker. All were innovative in methods and topics, further increasing the range of teaching subjects; Veronese in Algebraic Geometry and Ricci in Differential Geometry (he introduced "absolute differential calculus", then "tensorial calculus") made the faculty a centre of research of international status: in 1915 Einstein used absolute differential calculus, formulated by Ricci and his pupil Tullio Levi Civita in *Méthodes de Calcul différentiel absolu* (1901), as a tool of general relativity. The qualitative peak involved Mathematical Physics, which Ricci had taken over in 1880; from 1882 Turazza's more applied teaching of Rational Mechanics was united with Higher Mechanics, entrusted to Padova, who worked on theoretical topics, some of them at the forefront of research. The horizons were further broadened when he also took over

Gregorio Ricci Curbastro and Giuseppe Veronese

Ruggero Panebianco

Turazza's teaching (1891), and then after his untimely death in 1896, when the two subjects were given to Levi Civita.

After Santini, the astronomers were natives of the Veneto region, but the change was considerable all the same. Santini was succeeded by his youngest pupil, Giuseppe Lorenzoni, from 1872 to 1914. The Observatory remained active in the fields of positional astronomy and astronomical calculation, due in part to the acquisition of a 19 cm Merz refractor; between 1898 and 1900 it took part in the international programme of studies on Eros (the first of the asteroids near the Earth to be observed): 180 observations by Antonio Maria Antoniazzi, pupil and then successor to Lorenzoni, were selected by an international committee. Above all, however, Lorenzoni grasped the turning point brought about by astrophysics and spectroscopy. The Observatory produced the spectroscopic instruments used by the Italian expedition to Bengal for the passage of Venus across the disc of the sun (December 1874) and sent specialists there guided by Antonio Abetti, a pupil of Santini and Lorenzoni. Their observations were the only spectroscopic ones among the international observations of the event; Lorenzoni subsequently designed specific apparatus and trained other pupils of repute, with whom the school of Padua spread itself to chairs throughout Italy.

There was continuity and innovation in Physics, too, with Francesco Rossetti (from 1866 to 1885), who had studied with Liebig, Bunsen, Helmholtz, Kirchhoff, and Regnault, and who established courses and curricula, created the institute of Physics (1874), bought instruments, updated methods, and trained future teachers in the School for Engineers or in other Universities. He worked on electricity, electromagnetism, and wave theory, and was one of the pioneers of telephony; nevertheless, although the chair was both experimental and theoretical, he paid more attention to the former aspect (partly due to the establishment of the teaching of mathematical physics in 1873). Augusto Righi, who arrived in 1885, might have been able to broaden the horizons, as he designed new instruments and began important research; but in 1889 he moved to Bologna, and his most notable successor too, Angelo Battelli, only stayed for two years (1891-93). Teaching only became continuous with Giuseppe Vicentini (1894-1931), an experimenter (he worked on seismic waves), who carried out a continual process of updating and paid attention to teaching, but was not at the centre of the essential processes of those decades. From 1896 the chair was again called Experimental Physics, almost anticipating the beginning of a theoretical subject, which did not take place, however: in the early twentieth century the most progressive work on physical topics was carried out by mathematicians and mathematical physicists.

From 1887 Giacomo Ciamician, who had studied in Austria and Germany and with Cannizzaro, could have renewed the school of chemistry; but after two years, he too moved on. The chemistry school only asserted itself with Raffaello Nasini (from 1891 to 1906), who had completed his studies with Cannizzaro and in Berlin, and who because of his interests in physical chemistry and the recent developments in atomic theory was also important for physics. In the natural and biological disciplines, after the division between

Giovanni Canestrini

Geology and Biology and that of Geology from Mineralogy, the situation was not uniform. Giovanni Omboni taught Geology from 1869 to 1904; Omboni had studied in Pavia, completed his studies in Paris, and was an assiduous researcher, but according to his pupil Giorgio Dal Piaz, was foreign to the theoretical debates of the time because of his excessive methodological scruple. The first teacher of Mineralogy, Ruggero Panebianco, a pupil of Cannizzaro, was at the centre of studies on systematic mineralogy and the optical behaviour of crystals; he founded the *Rivista di mineralogia e cristallografia italiana*, which he directed until 1918. His and Omoboni's teaching, that of eminent Geographers such as Giuseppe Dalla Vedova (1867-1873), and Giovanni Marinelli (1878-1892), and, later, the establishment of the teaching of Terrestrial Physics (1906) were at the origin of the high level of earth sciences at Padua in the early twentieth century. In the biological field, as we have already said, Natural History was replaced by Zoology and Comparative Anatomy, Physiology, Human Anatomy and Histology, and Anthropology. In Botany, from 1877 to 1915, Saccardo substituted the centrality of the Botanical Garden with herbals and the laboratory, and he subordinated the florae – which he nevertheless studied in exemplary fashion for the Veneto region – to a gigantic project in mycology, which discovered genera and species and created a systematic framework of such breadth as to make him a specialist of world-wide renown. Master of several researchers, he also wrote works on the history of botany, in part still relevant today. Equally involved, but scientifically less original was Giovanni Canestrini, teacher of Zoology, and Comparative Anatomy and Physiology (1869-1899) and Anthropology (1878-1880), who had studied in Vienna. He wrote on ichthyology, arachnology, anthropology, and bacteriology (then new), but he was known as a supporter of evolutionism and, with Panebianco, a prestigious exponent of the lay-positivist front among the teachers of the sciences, who at that period had the support of Roberto Ardigò from the philosophy course. Filippo Lussana was also close to positivism (he was a friend of Mantegazza); he had studied in Pavia, and was teacher of Physiology from 1867 to 1887, and a neurophysiologist who also worked on the entero-hepatic circuit and on pellagra. In 1873 his chair moved from the faculty of Medicine to that of the Sciences together with the chair of Anatomy and Histology held by Giampaolo Vlacovich, who had studied in Vienna like Canestrini, a teacher who was not original but significant because during his tenure the Paduan tradition of anatomy was enriched by recent developments in histology and cytology, opening itself up to a new season.

In 1902 a regulation for the science faculties distinguished between fundamental subjects (21) and complementary ones, maintained four four-year degree courses (mathematics, physics, chemistry, and natural sciences), and created two-year licence courses for teaching purposes (physical and mathematical sciences, chemistry, and natural sciences; in 1922 two became degrees, later abolished). Between 1903 and 1909 there were new teaching subjects: Mathematics for chemists, Physical Chemistry, Meteorology, History of Mathematics (entrusted to Favaro, but discontinued after a few years), Higher Mathematics, and Palaeontology. Three degree courses came into being in 1936

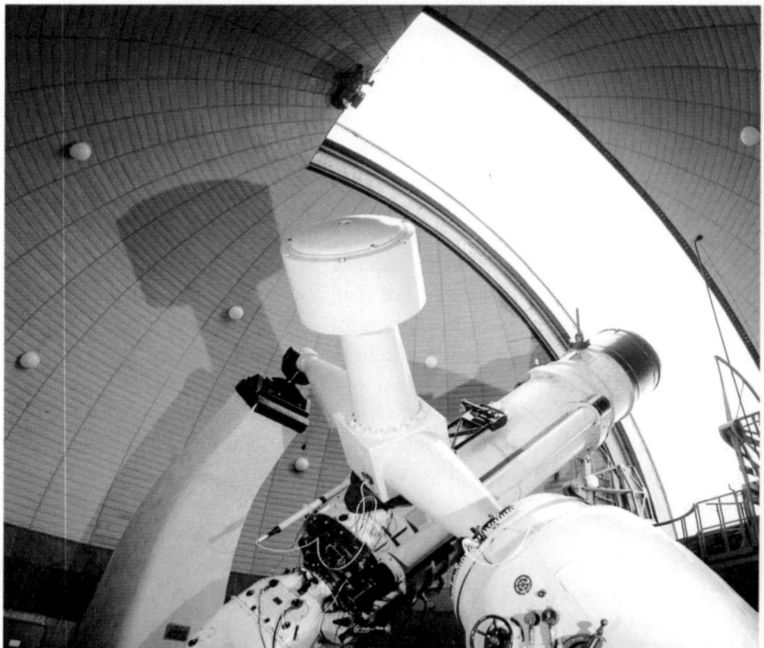

The Asiago astrophysical Observatory and the Galileo Galilei telescope

(Industrial Chemistry), 1939 (Biological Sciences), and 1941 (Geological Sciences, the first in Italy), and in 1940 and 1942 the hydrobiological station at Chioggia and the astrophysical Observatory at Asiago were added to the University. All this must be considered in relation to the facts of political and University geography which modified the University's old catchment area, reducing the flow of students from Istria, Dalmatia, Eastern Lombardy and the Trento region and influencing the teachers' choice of career. Among the mathematicians, however, Veronese and Levi Civita taught up to 1916, Flores d'Arcais to 1924, and Ricci to 1925; from 1901 they were joined by Giovanni Alfredo Bordiga and above all, from 1905 to 1921, by Francesco Severi. Thus towards 1920 the school remained excellent (Corrado Gini, who had carried out important studies into the calculation of probability, taught in another faculty from 1913 to 1925). The mathematicians between the two wars were in part pupils of their predecessors (Annibale Comessatti, Giuseppe Vitali, Angelo Tonolo, and Ugo Morin), and in part from other schools (Ugo Amaldi, Ernesto Laura, Giuseppe Scorza Dragoni, Renato Caccioppoli, and, for one year, Bruno De Finetti). In this phase, a period of settling-down with respect to the previous one, but not devoid of important contributions, the Mathematical Seminary (1926) and the relative *Rendiconti* (1930), still today the organ of common work, came into being.

In astronomy Antonio Maria Antoniazzi (1912-1925) and Giovanni Silva (1926-1952) pursued the new line, up to the construction of the Asiago Observatory; the school, which reached a high level, took part in international programmes. In physics, the theoretical progress which had been made firstly caused courses of general physics to be set up (1924-1931) then courses of higher and theoretical physics (from 1922 and 1933); from 1933 to 1938 relativity, quantum theory, and nuclear physics were represented by Bruno Rossi, followed by Antonio Rostagni, and Nicolò Dallaporta. After the war Padua was to become one of the three sections of the National Institute of Nuclear Physics and was to build an electrostatic accelerator at Legnaro (1959). In chemistry, after Nasini we must remember above all Arturo Miolati (1918-1937) and Giovanni Semerano (1932-1960); in earth sciences Giorgio Dal Piaz, teacher of Geology from 1905 to 1942 and guide of the *Carta geologica delle tre Venezie* (1921-62), the mineralogist Angelo Bianchi (from 1923 to 1962), and Luigi De Marchi, teacher of Physical Geography (1903-1932), glaciologist, and scholar of population dynamics. In the biological field, besides Saccardo's successors, Augusto Béguinot (1915-21) and Giuseppe Gola (1921-48), important figures were Davide Carazzi (Zoology, 1905-1917), a scholar of invertebrate anatomy, Paolo Enriques (Cytology and Comparative Physiology, 1921-1932), who studied Mendel's laws in simple organisms, Umberto D'Ancona (1937-1964), known for his statistical research into the fish population of the Adriatic carried out with the help of his father-in-law, the mathematician Vito Volterra.

After the war some of the above teachers guided the University towards a new process of modernization of its structures, teaching, and research. But the threads that stretch from this new phase to the present are not yet ready for the history books.

Giorgio Dal Piaz and Giuseppe Gola

ATTILIO ADAMI

Engineering

Although the word 'engineer' dates back to the Middle Ages, the professional figure, as we conceive of it today, came about after the industrial revolution, and therefore can only date back to around two centuries ago.

And in effect in Padua, the school of Civil Architecture was only established within the philosophical faculty in 1806 and, as we will see, freed itself much later, in 1876.

In short, the Faculty of Engineering did not belong to the original historical nucleus of 'faculties' which contributed to the birth of the University. It is much younger; nevertheless, its history is complex and full of change.

At its birth, the school prepared three professional figures: the Civil Architect, destined for the planning of buildings; the Land-Surveyor, for the operations of geodesy and land estimates; and that of the Civil Engineer who could carry out the activities of the former two, as well as all the operations concerning the science of water.

It is interesting to note that several years after its foundation there was an attempt to transform the school of Civil Architecture into an independent Polytechnic Institute: a sovereign resolution dated September 1818 declared this intention and asked the governors of the philosophical faculty, to which the school belonged, for opinions and clarifications on the subject. Although the initiative was viewed favourably by the academic authorities of the period, there is no trace in the University archives of the planned Institute, even though it was often quoted in the following years as if it already existed, and in 1825 a new curriculum was issued for the school by the governors of the physico-mathematical faculty, which made no reference whatsoever to its autonomy.

In 1839 the school was re-baptized with the name Institute for the Education of Land-surveyors, Engineers, and Architects, but as far as the organization of the studies and its dependence on the mathematical studium was concerned, in substance nothing changed, up until the end of Austrian rule.

With the Unification of Italy things changed thanks to the interest shown by several academics, among whom the figure of Domenico Turazza stands out, professor of Rational Mechanics (but better known as a hydraulic engineer), who enjoyed great prestige among his colleagues, so much so that he subsequently became rector of the University in 1870-71.

On 13th October, 1867, the Institute for Engineers was transformed into

Details of the new buildings of the Faculty of Engineering situated beyond the Piovego canal

The façade of Palazzo Cavalli, the old customs building, which was the first seat of the Faculty of Engineering in 1895

a technical school and the curriculum was profoundly changed, since the course was to last for five years (up until then it had been four), divided into two periods: an initial three years of theoretical studies and a further two years of practical study, with a total of twenty-four subjects.

On Turazza's initiative, in the academic year 1870-71 a new curriculum was introduced, which limited the period of theoretical studies to two years and increased that of practical studies to three.

Finally, in 1876, a royal decree, dated 8th October, recognised the independence of the technical schools for Engineers, with the task of "providing scientific and technical instruction necessary to confer the diploma in engineering and that in architecture". After this the Padua school created its own internal regulations, approved in 1877.

A ruling council made up of three members, who elected its own director, the first of whom was Domenico Turazza, headed the school. The school was made equivalent to a University faculty and the director fulfilled the functions of a dean.

In its first year of life the academic body was made up of three full professors, five 'junior' professors, and six temporary lecturers, to give a total of fourteen people.

As far as the student population was concerned, we can arrive at a relatively indicative figure: in the year 1880 thirty people were awarded a diploma.

Among the teachers of the first period the name of Enrico Bernardi stands out. Bernardi was 'junior' professor of Agricultural, Hydraulic, and Thermal Machines from 1878, and was responsible for the design and construction of the first Italian vehicle driven by an internal-combustion engine, in 1893.

The school did not initially have a single seat and almost all the teaching took place in the Palazzo del Bo. From 1895, the school had its own building in Palazzo Cavalli, the old customs building, which today houses the teachers of Geology. The building was extremely dignified and pretty vast, with its total surface area of 3750 square metres obtained after substantial renovation.

Regarding 1895 again, we can note that the number of those obtaining a diploma that year was 50, showing a consistent increase in the student population.

The school was structured in scientific laboratories annexed to individual chairs; there were eighteen laboratories, as was later recorded in the *Annuario* for the academic year 1922-23, which provided a list of them, with the dates of their foundation.

In 1905 the Veneto, Trentino, and Friuli region was hit by terrible flooding, after which the national government decided, with a law dated 5th May 1907, to re-establish the Magistracy of the Waters (an institution which dated back to the Serenissima) which was to be responsible for all initiatives regarding the safety of the water courses from the river Mincio to the eastern border.

This law also affected the engineering school, since article 12 ordered the reorganization of the teaching subjects of the hydraulic disciplines which already existed in the technical school of the royal University of Padua, as well as the establishment of other subjects on the same disciplines and their applications. Consequently, in the following year, on 21st June 1908, new regulations were issued for the school, which modernized its structure and, above all, its curriculum.

As far as the structure was concerned, the new regulations created a council of professors, made up of all the full and 'junior' professors and the lecturers; the council of professors appointed a ruling council made up of six members, four of whom were from the school and two from the physico-mathematical faculty. The ruling council put forward the name of the director who was appointed by the rector and who held the post for four years.

But the principal change concerned the curriculum, which was to consist of a first group of twenty-two compulsory subjects for everyone, after which the student could choose between a "general group" of another five subjects and a "group of hydraulic disciplines" of four subjects. The diploma in Civil Engineering was the same for everyone, but there was a special certificate in the hydraulic disciplines for those who had taken the second group of subjects. This is the first "specialization" of engineering studies.

In 1915 a new set of regulations came into force, which is important as it specified for the first time the awarding of the diploma of the degree in engineering.

As far as the curriculum was concerned, the special certificate in hydraulic disciplines remained, and a new special certificate joined it in electric disciplines. The exams, which had to be passed for the attainment of the degree diploma in Architecture, were also specified.

The building at the *Porte Contarine* soon became insufficient for the staff and the teaching, which increased progressively, and a new arrangement had to be thought out.

Domenico Turazza and Enrico Bernardi

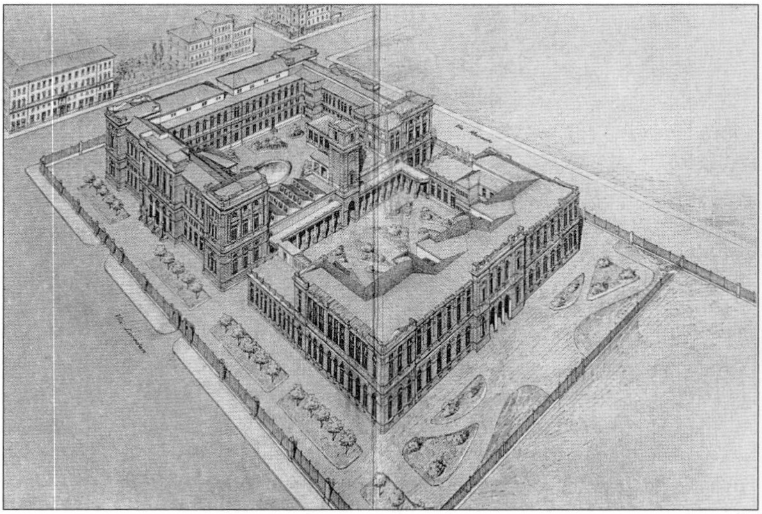

Axonometric view of the via Marzolo complex, seat of the Faculty in the 1930s

The via Marzolo complex, seen from via Loredan

In 1901 the director of the school, Ferdinando Lori, who later became rector, charged Daniele Donghi, professor of Technical Architecture, to draw up a plan for a new seat to be built on a site situated between via Marzolo and via Loredan, which had already been bought by the University. The plan underwent various modifications, and building consequently took several years: work began in 1912 and was completed only in 1929, when the entire school had been transferred to the new building.

Donghi's building was architecturally eclectic with notable points of merit; it must be observed, however, that the building now finds itself in extremely limited conditions with respect to those foreseen by its designer, due to the numerous additions it suffered almost as soon as it had been built. Because of all the subsequent modifications, Donghi's building went from an initial usable surface area of ten thousand to the present-day seventeen thousand square metres.

During the Great War sixty-two students of the school lost their lives on the battle fields, as commemorated by a memorial at the via Marzolo entrance which bears their names.

After the war, in 1919, the "Fondazione Sarpi" was established, set up by his father in memory of Antonio Sarpi, a pupil of the school who died in battle; the "Fondazione" began the custom of assigning a gold medal to the best graduate in engineering each year, a custom which still exists.

In the academic year 1923-24 an important change took place, by virtue of the royal decree of 30th September 1923: the Padua Royal School of Engineering was transformed into an autonomous institute of higher education and therefore became independent of the University. According to the statute, which the school created for itself, its studies led to the attainment of a degree in civil engineering or one in industrial engineering. At this point the University of Padua lost its ability to grant the title of architect.

The laboratories were substitute by institutes, much fewer in number: the *Annuario* of 1924-25 lists nine, plus the Botanical Garden and the Central Library, formed in 1920 by gathering together the collections of the various laboratories, which was rendered equivalent to an institute.

Three institutes soon became dominant with respect to the others:

- The institute of Machines, which enjoyed the prestige which derived from the figure of Enrico Bernardi, and which was favourably influenced by the process of mechanization which involved all sectors of production;
- the institute of Hydraulics, which had an extremely long tradition, dating back to the names of Poleni, Guglielmini, and the more recent one of Turazza, which was influenced by two important processes in progress: the reclaiming of land for agriculture and the use of water pipelines above all for the production of hydro-electric power;
- the institute of Electrotechnology, much younger and therefore without a tradition on which to base itself, but which benefited from the fallout from the great development of electrification in all fields.

In 1925 there were one hundred and forty-two graduates, out of a total of three hundred and thirty-eight students enrolled on the three-year course.

During its period of autonomy the school kept separate yearbooks from those of the University and published its *Annali della Regia Scuola d'Ingegneria di Padova* in the form of an independent journal.

But the school's autonomy ceased with the royal decree of 27th October 1935, with which the royal higher institute of Engineering was joined to the University of Padua as a faculty, and the following year another decree abrogated the school's statute and approved a new statute of the University of Padua, in which the faculty of Engineering appears.

The number of graduates in 1935 appears as 80, with two hundred students enrolled on the three-year course, showing a clear reduction in the student population in the previous years.

1936 was characterised by further building expansion of the faculty: a new building was put up next to Donghi's to house the institute of Technical Physics.

In 1938 a new royal decree came into force, which rigidly fixed the fundamental teaching subjects to be followed for the various Universities. It must be noted that the birth of new degree courses did not stop, since the curriculum for the degree in engineering included a civil section (with subsections in Construction, Hydraulics, and Transport), an industrial section (with subsections in Chemistry, Electrotechnology, and Mechanics), and the new section of Chemical Engineering.

In the war and the Resistance from 1940 to 1945 the faculty lost forty-two students, who were granted a degree *honoris causa*; one student and two assistant lecturers died as partisans were awarded a gold medal.

In 1945 the number of students had increased to 105 and those enrolled for the entire five-year course were now nearly a thousand.

After the war academic activity started up again with little change: to be noted is the importance which the institute of Electrotechnology was gradually gaining, in part thanks to the work of its director and true leader, Giovanni Someda, who was also dean of the faculty in the immediate post-war period, and was to remain so subsequently for a long period.

As far as the organization of studies was concerned, the greatest change came about in 1960, when a decree by the President of the Republic came into force, which was added to the statute approved in Padua in 1962. Under the new order the three degree courses became five: Civil Engineering (sections in Construction, Hydraulics, and Transport), Mechanical Engineering, Electrotechnical Engineering, Electronic Engineering, and finally Chemical Engineering.

By 1955 the number of graduates had risen to 241, indicating a notable increase with respect to the immediate post-war period, even though the student population had remained practically constant, around a thousand.

In 1965 there were 240 graduates, the same, that is, as the number ten years earlier, but the number of students enrolled had risen to around two thousand six hundred.

Towards the end of the 1960s we must note the liberalization of access to University, which provoked a sudden rise in the number of enrolments, causing serious teaching problems: the number of graduates in 1975 had risen to 510, more than double the number ten years earlier, and the number of students enrolled was in excess of 5600.

To cope with the new situation the fundamental courses most followed were duplicated, but the faculty faced a shortage of teachers and classrooms, causing serious problems for the student body.

This problem apart, the University dealt with the situation by building new infrastructures which had fortunately already been planned, and were therefore completed in a relatively short time.

The building constructed in the 1930s in via Marzolo as an extensionof the Faculty

Between 1964 and 1966 the new institute of Electrotechnology was built in via Gradenigo. The institute, as we have said, was going through a period of great development as a consequence of the development of electronics.

Between 1967 and 1971, the new Palazzo dei Paolotti was built to house the teachers of mathematics, with some very large classrooms which responded in some way to the great pressure of students on the two-year course.

The student protests of 1968 and the following years affected the faculty of Engineering only marginally and the extremist fringe of students always represented a tiny minority which did not create the same problems as it did in other faculties. In short, the period of protest did not cause any serious problems and has not left traces of any kind.

Due to the continual increase in staff, new building work had to be carried out: in 1974 the new seat of the so-called "Mechanical Department" began operating in via Venezia, which housed the institute of Machines, that of Applied Mechanics, and the newly-created institute of Business Organization.

In this way the faculty reached its hundredth birthday in 1976: it had started off with fourteen teachers, and twenty-nine subjects in a single degree course, and now it found itself with 237 teachers, 207 subjects (without counting the duplication of existing courses), and five degree courses.

The following years saw an even more intense development, with growth in all respects; various pieces of legislation, although relatively uncoordinated, allowed (and at times imposed) a profound renewal of the structures and the organization of studies. We are referring above all to law 382 of 1980 and the Decree by the President of the Republic dated 20th May, 1989.

The Balbino Del Nunzio bridge which crosses the Piovego canal

The first transformation to be mentioned is the structural one, which imposed the transformation of the institutes into departments, with a considerable degree of autonomy.

The process of departmentalization of the faculty was not easy and took more than fifteen years; we must recognise however that it involved situations that had been consolidated for decades, changing an equilibrium that was at times delicate.

In short, the faculty is today divided into twelve departments which entirely belong to it, plus two (that of Physics and that of Pure and Applied Mathematics) which only partially belong to it; if we compare this with the situation before 1980, we can see that the total number has not changed greatly: at that time the faculty was divided into twelve institutes, plus the usual situation of "cohabitation" of Physics.

We must remember, however, that the number of teachers has risen considerably in the meantime, so that the average number for a department today is over twenty-eight people, against an average for the old institutes of around nineteen people. Moreover, the present subdivision is more in line with the cultural needs of research and the teachers who carry it out.

But the greatest change concerns the organization of studies and the teaching in general, which in time have undergone the following modifications:

- In 1989 a new degree course in Computer Engineering was established;
- in 1990 a new degree course in Management Engineering was established, in Vicenza, making use of a building in the centre belonging to the Provincial Government, on free loan to the University;
- in the same year the "historical" course in Civil Engineering was divided into the new sections of Construction, Geotechnics, Hydraulics, Structures, and Transport, and the other "historical" course in Electrotechnical Engineering was reformed and took on the name of Electric Engineering;
- in 1991, given the continual increase in the number of student enrolments, a limited number of places was introduced;
- in 1992 the degree course in Construction Engineering detached itself from Civil Engineering to become an independent course;
- in the same year the first three-year diploma courses began: that in Mechanical Engineering and that in Electronic Engineering, both at Vicenza, as did the diploma in Computer and Automatic Engineering, which uses distance learning and has three local centres situated at Ceregnano (near Rovigo), Lancenigo (near Treviso), and Feltre.
- in 1994 the degree course in Engineering for the Environment and the National Territory and the diploma course in Biomedical Engineering began;
- in 1995 the degree course in Material Engineering began, as did the diploma in Chemical Engineering.

In conclusion, at the end of 2000, the teaching of the faculty was divided into eleven degrees and five diplomas, to give a total of 516 subjects which, counting the duplications of existing courses, correspond to almost 700 courses of teaching.

In the academic year 1999-2000 the number of students enrolled topped the 10,000 mark, with more than 1,600 first-year students.

But this is not enough: a new profound reform of studies will come into force imminently, which will allow a degree to be awarded after three years of study, to be followed by a specialist degree after a further two years. This imposes further change on a configuration, which had only just been reached, with unpredictable developments.

Finally, we must remember the contribution, which the faculty has made to the governing of the University, through the professors who have held the post of rector.

The first was Domenico Turazza, in the period 1870-1871, then Ferdinando Lori, in the period 1913-1919, then Emanuele Soler in the period 1927-29; after the war came Guido Ferro in the period 1949-1968 (the longest in the history of the University), then Luciano Merigliano in the period 1972-1984, to arrive at Giovanni Marchesini, who has been rector since 1996 and whose mandate runs out in 2002. Since the establishment of the faculty, a teacher of engineering has held the post of rector for a good forty-five years.

Bibliography

Political and Institutional History
The Medieval Period

Acta graduum academicorum Gymnasii Patavini ab anno 1406 ad annum 1450, cum aliis antiquioribus in appendice additis, eds C. Zonta–I. Brotto (Padua 1970)[2]

Acta graduum academicorum Gymnasii Patavini ab anno 1451 ad annum 1460, ed. M. P. Ghezzo (Padua 1990)

Acta graduum academicorum Gymnasii Patavini ab anno 1461 ad annum 1479, ed. G. Pengo (Padua 1992)

Acta graduum academicorum Gymnasii Patavini ab anno 1471 ad annum 1500, ed. E. Martellozzo Forin (Rome-Padua 2001)

G. Arnaldi, "Le origini dello Studio di Padova dalla migrazione universitaria del 1222 alla fine del periodo ezzeliniano", *La Cultura*, 15, 1977, p. 388-431

Id., "Il primo secolo dello Studio di Padova", in *Storia della cultura veneta*, II, *Il Trecento*, (Vicenza 1976), p. 3-18

M. Bellomo, "Giuristi cremonesi e scuole padovane. Ricerche su Nicola da Cremona", in *Studi in onore di Ugo Gualazzini*, I, (Milan 1981), p. 81-112

A. Belloni, *Professori giuristi a Padova nel secolo XV. Profili bio-bibliografici e cattedre*, (Frankfurt am Main 1986)

S. Bortolami, "Da Bologna a Padova, da Padova a Vercelli: ripensando alle migrazioni universitarie", in *L'Università di Vercelli nel medioevo. Atti del secondo Congresso storico vercellese (Vercelli, 22-25 ottobre 1992)* (Vercelli 1994), p. 35-75

Id., "Studenti e città nel primo secolo dello Studio padovano", in *Studenti, Università, città nella storia padovana. Atti del convegno, Padova 6-8 febbraio 1998*, eds F. Piovan - L. Sitran Rea (Trieste 2001), p. 3-27

G. Brotto - G. Zonta, *La facoltà teologica dell'Università di Padova (secoli XIV e XV)* (Padua 1922)

G. Cencetti, *Lo Studio di Bologna. Aspetti momenti e problemi (1935-1970)*, eds G.F. Orlandelli, R. Ferrara, A. Vasina (Bologna 1989)

H. Denifle, "Die Statuten der Juristen-Universität Padua vom Jahre 1331", *Archiv für Literatur- und Kirchengeschichte des Mittelalters*, 6, 1892 [= Graz 1956], p. 309-562

P. Denley, "The Collegiate Movement in Italian Universities in the Late Middle Ages", *History of Universities*, 10, 1991, p. 29-91

G. De Sandre Gasparini, "Dottori, Università, comune a Padova nel Quattrocento", *Quaderni per la storia dell'Università di Padova*, 1, 1968, p. 15-47

F. Dupuigrenet-Desroussilles, "L'Università di Padova dal 1405 al Concilio di Trento", in *Storia della cultura veneta*, 3/ii, *Dal primo Quattrocento al Concilio di Trento* (Vicenza 1980), p. 607-646

D. Gallo, "Lauree inedite in diritto civile e canonico presso lo Studio di Padova (1419-1422, 1423, 1424, 1428)", *Quaderni per la storia dell'Università di Padova*, 20, 1987, p. 1-50

Id., "Statuti inediti del Collegio padovano dei dottori d'arti e medicina: una redazione quattrocentesca", *Quaderni per la storia dell'Università di Padova*, 22-23, 1989-1990, p. 59-92

Id., *Università e signoria a Padova dal XIV al XV secolo* (Trieste 1998)

A. Gloria, "Antichi statuti del Collegio padovano dei dottori giuristi", *Atti dell'Istituto veneto di scienze, lettere ed arti*, s. VI, 7, 1988-89, p. 355-402

Id., *Monumenti della Università di Padova (1222-1318)* (Venice-Padua 1884) (anast. repr. Bologna 1972)

Id., *Monumenti della Università di Padova (1318-1405)* (Padua 1888) (anast. repr. Bologna 1972)

V. Lazzarini, "Crisi nello Studio di Padova a mezzo il Quattrocento", *Atti dell' Istituto veneto di scienze, lettere ed arti*, 109, 1950-51, part II, p. 201-211.

P. Marangon, *Ad cognitionem scientiae festinare. Gli studi nell'Università e nei conventi di Padova nei secoli XIII e XIV*, ed. T. Pesenti (Trieste 1997)

E. Martellozzo Forin, "Conti palatini e lauree conferite per privilegio. L'esempio padovano del sec. xv", *Annali di storia delle Università italiane*, 3, 1999, p. 79-119

F. Martino, "Un dottore di decreti arcivescovo di Messina. La laurea padovana (1281) di Guidotto d'Abbiate", *Rivista internazionale di diritto comune*, 4,1993, p. 97-120

G. G. Merlo, "Gli inizi dell'ordine dei Predicatori. Spunti per una riconsiderazione", *Rivista di storia e letteratura religiosa*, 31, 1995, p. 415-441

T. Pesenti, *Professori e promotori di medicina nello Studio di Padova dal 1405 al 1509. Repertorio bio-bibliografico* (Trieste-Padua 1984)

Id. "Università, giudici e notai a Padova nei primi anni del dominio ezzeliniano (1237-1241)", *Quaderni per la storia dell'Università di Padova*, 12, 1979, p. 1-61

A. Poppi, "Chiesa e Università", in *Diocesi di Padova*, ed. Pierantonio Gios (Venice-Padua 1996), p. 543-574

A. Rigon, "'Si ad scolas iverit'. Il canonico di Padova Tommaso Morosini, primo patriarca latino d'Oriente, in un inedito documento del 1196", *Quaderni per la storia dell'Università di Padova*, 33, 2000, p. 1-8

Id., "S. Urbano di Padova "procuratoria" del monastero di Praglia", in *L'Abbazia di Santa Maria di Praglia*, eds C. Carpanese - F. Trolese (Milan 1985), p. 56-62

E. Rigoni, "Il tribunale degli scolari dell'Università di Padova nel medioevo", *Atti e memorie dell'Accademia di scienze lettere ed arti in Padova*, n.s., 59, 1942-43, p. 19-34

N. G. Siraisi, *Arts and Sciences at Padua. The "Studium" of Padua before 1350* (Toronto 1973)

G. Zordan, *L'ordinamento giuridico veneziano* (Padua 1980)

Id., *Dall'università dei Giuristi alla Facoltà di Giurisprudenza nello Studio patavino* (Padua 1999)[2]

The Early Modern Period

Among the primary sources to be noted are the *Acta graduum academicorum Gymnasii Patavini ab anno 1501 ad annum 1550*, ed. E. Martellozzo Forin (Padua 1969-1971 and 1989); *Acta graduum academicorum Gymnasii Patavini ab anno 1551 ad annum 1565*, eds E. Dalla Francesca Helmann and E. Veronese Ceseracciu (Padua 1987); *Acta graduum academicorum Gymnasii Patavini ab anno 1601 ad annum 1605*, ed. F. Zen Benetti (Padua 2001); *Acta nationis Germanicae artistarum (1616-1636)*, ed. L. Rossetti (Padua 1967); *Acta nationis Germanicae artistarum (1637-1662)*, eds L. Rossetti – A. Gamba (Padua 1995); *Acta nationis Germanicae artistarum (1663-1694)*, eds L. Rossetti – A. Gamba (Padua 1999); *Acta nationis Germanicae iuristarum (1650- 1709)*, ed. G. Mantovani (Padua 1983); *Atti della nazione germanica artista nello Studio di Padova (1553-1615)*, ed. A. Favaro, I-II (Venice 1911-1912); *Atti della nazione germanica dei legisti nello Studio di Padova (1545-1609)*, ed. di B. Brugi (Venice 1912); *Matricula nationis Germanicae artistarum in Gymnasio Patavino (1553-1721)*, ed. L. Rossetti (Padua 1986).

Among the secondary works, some of which also enrich the documentary part, are:

P. Bianchi, "Università e riforme : la "Relazione dell'Università di Padova" di Francesco Filippo Picono (1712)", *Quaderni per la storia dell'Università di Padova*, 31, 1998, p. 165-203

H. F. Brown, "Inglesi e Scozzesi all'Università di Padova dall'anno 1618 sino al 1765", in *Monografie storiche sullo Studio di Padova. Contributo del r. Istituto Veneto di scienze, lettere ed arti alla celebrazione del VII centenario dell'Università* (Venice 1922), p. 137-213

B. Brugi, "Una descrizione dello Studio di Padova in un ms. del secolo XVI del Museo Britannico", *Nuovo archivio veneto*, n.s., 14, 1907, part. I, p. 72-88

Id., "Un parere di Scipione Maffei intorno allo Studio di Padova sui principi del Settecento, edizione del testo originale con introduzione e note", *Atti del R. Istituto Veneto di scienze, lettere ed arti*, 69, 1909-10, p. 575-591

S. De Bernardin, "I Riformatori dello Studio: indirizzi di politica culturale nell'Università di Padova", in *Storia della cultura veneta*, eds G. Arnaldi – M. Pastore Stocchi, 4/1, *Il Seicento* (Vicenza 1983), p. 61-91

P. Del Negro, "Appunti sul patriziato veneziano, la cultura e la politica della ricerca scientifica nel secondo Settecento", in G.P. Bozzolato – P. Del Negro – C. Ghetti, *La specola dell'Università di Padova* (Brugine 1986), p. 247-294

Id., "Bernardo Nani, Lorenzo Morosini e la riforma universitaria del 1761", *Quaderni per la storia dell'Università di Padova*, 19, 1986, p. 87-141

Id., "I 'Pensieri di Simone Stratico sull'Università di Padova' (1760)", *Quaderni per la storia dell'Università di Padova*, 17, 1984, p. 191-229

Id., "L'Università", in *Storia della cultura veneta. Dalla Controriforma alla fine della Repubblica*, eds G. Arnaldi - M. Pastore Stocchi, *Il Settecento*, 5/I (Vicenza 1985), p. 47-76

F. Dupuigrenet Desroussilles, "L'Università di Padova dal 1405 al Concilio di Trento", in *Storia della cultura veneta. Dal primo Quattrocento al Concilio di Trento*, eds G. Arnaldi - M. Pastore Stocchi, 3/II (Vicenza 1980), p. 607-647

A. Favaro, "Di alcune minacciate secessioni di scolari dello Studio di Padova durante il secolo decimosesto ed in particolare di quella dell'anno 1583", *Nuovo archivio veneto*, n.s., 40, 1920, p. 148-168

Id., "Informazione storica sullo Studio di Padova circa l'anno 1580", *Nuovo archivio veneto*, n.s., 30, 1915, part I, p. 247-271

Id., "Padova e il suo Studio nel MDCXLV, dal diario di viaggio di John Evelyn", *Atti e memorie della R. Accademia di scienze, lettere ed arti in Padova*, n.s., 30, 1914, p. 79-90

Id., "I Riformatori dello Studio di Padova in visita magistrale all'Università nell'aprile 1771", *Atti e memorie della R. Accademia di scienze, lettere ed arti in Padova*, n.s., 34, 1917-18, p. 46-60

R. Gallo, "Due informazioni sullo Studio di Padova della metà del Cinquecento", *Archivio veneto*, s. V, 72, 1963, p. 17-100

M. C. Ghetti, "Struttura e organizzazione dell'Università di Padova dalla metà del '700 al 1797", *Quaderni per la storia dell'Università di Padova*, 16, 1983, p. 71-102

G. Gullino, "Una riforma settecentesca della Serenissima : il collegio di S. Marco", *Studi veneziani*, 13, 1971, p. 515-586

F. L. Maschietto, *Elena Lucrezia Cornaro Piscopia (1646-1684), prima donna laureata nel mondo* (Padua 1978)

T. Pesenti Marangon, *La Biblioteca Universitaria di Padova dalla sua istituzione alla fine della Repubblica veneta (1629-1797)* (Padua 1979)

Relazioni dei Rettori veneti in Terraferma. IV Podestaria e Capitanato di Padova, [ed. A. Tagliaferri] (Milan 1975)

L. Rossetti, "I collegi per i dottorati 'auctoritate Veneta'", in *Viridarium floridum. Studi di storia veneta offerti dagli allievi a Paolo Sambin*, eds M. C. Billanovich – G. Cracco – A. Rigon (Padua 1984), p.

365-386

M. SAIBANTE – C. VIVARINI – G. VOGHERA, "Gli studenti dell'Università di Padova dalla fine del '500 ai nostri giorni", *Metron. Rivista internazionale di statistica*, 4, 1924-25, p. 163-223

M. SANGALLI, *Cultura, politica e religione nella Repubblica di Venezia tra Cinque e Seicento. Gesuiti e somaschi a Venezia* (Venice 1999)

F. WEIGLE, "Die deutschen Doktorpromotionen in Philosophie und Medizin an der Universität Padua von 1616-1663", *Quellen und Forschungen aus italienischen Archiven und Bibliotheken*, 45, 1965, p. 325-384

F. ZEN BENETTI, "Una proposta di riforma seicentesca: il 'Discorso di Ingolfo de Conti circa il regolare i scolari dello Studio di Padova'", in *Studenti, Università, città nella storia padovana. Atti del convegno di studio, Padova 6-8 febbraio 1998*, eds F. PIOVAN – L. SITRAN REA (Trieste 2001), p. 441-455

I. ZARAMELLA, "Laureati e licenziati dallo Studio di Padova dal 1719 al 1747 e provenienze degli studenti: dati statistici", *Quaderni per la storia dell'Università di Padova*, 20, 1987, p. 133-137

From 1797 to 1866

Annali della libertà padovana ossia raccolta completa di tutte le carte pubblicate in Padova dal giorno della sua libertà disposta per ordine de' tempi (Padua 1797), 6 vols

M. BERENGO, "Il numero chiuso all'Università di Padova. Un dibattito della Restaurazione", *Quaderni per la storia dell'Università di Padova*, 14 (1981), p. 41-53

G. BERTI, "Università e studenti a Padova durante la terza dominazione austriaca", in *Studenti, Università, città nella storia padovana. Atti del convegno, Padova 6-8 febbraio 1998*, eds F. PIOVAN - L. SITRAN REA (Trieste 2001), p. 521-536

G. GENNARI, *Notizie giornaliere di quanto avvenne specialmente in Padova dall'anno 1739 all'anno 1800*, II. Introduction, notes, ed apparatus by L. OLIVATO (Cittadella 1984)

M. C. GHETTI, "L'assetto statutario e didattico dell'Università di Padova dopo la riforma asburgica", *Quaderni per la storia dell'Università di Padova*, 32, 1999, p. 87-101

ID., "Struttura e organizzazione dell'Università di Padova dalla metà del '700 al 1797", *Quaderni per la storia dell'Università di Padova*, 16, 1983, p. 71-102

ID., "Struttura e organizzazione dell'Università di Padova dal 1798 al 1817", *Quaderni per la storia dell'Università di Padova*, 17, 1984, p. 135-182

ID., *L'Università, in Padova 1814-1866. Istituzioni, protagonisti e vicende di una città*, eds P. DEL NEGRO - N. AGOSTINETTI (Padua 1991), p. 65-79

A. GLORIA, *Cronaca di Padova dal 10 dicembre 1849 al 2 giugno 1867*. Introduction and notes by G. TOFFANIN JR. (Trieste 1977)

D. LAVEN, "Disordini studenteschi all'Università di Padova, 1815-1848", in *Studenti, Università, città*, cit., p. 491-504

ID., "Liberals or Libertines? Staff, Students, and Government Policy at the University of Padua, 1814-1835", *History of Universities*, 11, 1992, p. 123-164

ID., "Town, Gown and Garrison in Early Nineteenth-Century Padua, 1815-1835", *Quaderni per la storia dell'Università di Padova*, 28, 1995, p. 135-155

C. LEONI, *Cronaca segreta de' miei tempi*, with preface and notes by G. TOFFANIN JR. (Cittadella 1976)

L. OTTOLENGHI, *Gli avvenimenti dell'8 febbraio 1848 in Padova* (Padua 1898)

Professori di materie scientifiche all'Università di Padova nell'Ottocento, eds S. CASELLATO - L. PIGATTO (Trieste 1996)

Raccolta di carte pubbliche dal felice ingresso dell'armi austriache in Padova (Padua 1798)

Y. TOFFANIN, *Il dominio austriaco in Padova dal 20 gennaio 1798 al 16 gennaio 1801* (Verona-Padua 1901)

A. VENTURA, "L'8 febbraio nella storia dell'Università di Padova", in *Studenti, Università, città*, cit., p. 707-720.

From 1866 to 2000

Acta Universitatis Patavinæ - Septima sæcularia celebrantis (Padua 1925)

Annuari dell'Università degli studi di Padova per gli anni accademici dal 1866-67 (Padua 1866 ff.)

ANONIMUS, *L'Università di Padova durante l'occupazione tedesca* (Padua 1946)[2]

F. BERNARDINELLO, *Universitari padovani fra le due guerre*, dissertation for the degree in Contemporary History, supervisor P. DEL NEGRO (1999-2000)

N. BRIAMONTE, *La vita e il pensiero di Eugenio Curiel* (Milan 1979)

L. CANFORA, *La sentenza. Concetto Marchesi e Giovanni Gentile* (Palermo 1985)

Carlo Anti, Giornate di studio nel centenario della nascita (Trieste 1992)

P. DEL NEGRO, "I militari veneti morti nella grande guerra: dal mito alla storia", in *Archivio Veneto*, serie V, vol. 151, 1998, p. 207-231

A. FAVARO, *I professori della R. Università di Padova nel MCMXII* (Bologna 1922)

C. F. FERRARIS, *Cinque anni di rettorato nella R. Università di Padova 1891-'92 al 1895-'96. Ricordi in occasione del settimo centenario 1922* (Rome 1922)

E. FRANCESCHINI, *Concetto Marchesi. Linee per l'interpretazione di un uomo inquieto* (Padua 1978)

A. GAMBASIN, *'Theses' in sacra teologia nell'Università di Padova dal 1815 al 1873* (Trieste 1984)

M. Isnenghi, "Per una storia delle tesi di laurea. Tracce e campioni a Padova tra Ottocento e Novecento", in *Cento anni di Università. L'istruzione superiore dall'Unità ai nostri giorni*, eds F. De Vivo - G. Genovesi (Naples 1986), p. 99-122

A. Lazzaretto Zanolo, *La Fuci veneta nel ventennio fascista, Per una storia della sociabilità cattolica* (Vicenza 1998)

G. Lenci, "L'Università "Castrense" a Padova nella Grande Guerra", *Padova e il suo territorio*, 10, n. 58, 1995, p. 39-42.

C. Leoni, *Cronaca segreta dei miei tempi 1845-1874*, ed. G. Toffanin jr., (Cittadella 1976)

Libro del sacrificio e de la gloria MCMXV - MCMXVIII (Padua without year [1923])

A. Magro, "La parificazione dell'Università di Padova dopo l'Unità e la sua facoltà di Giurisprudenza (1866-1880)", *Annali di storia delle Università italiane*, 3, 1999, p. 143-169

L. Merigliano, *Eventi e risultati più significativi del mio Rettorato (1972-1984)* (Treviso 2000)

M. Minesso, *Tecnici e modernizzazione nel Veneto. La scuola dell'Università di Padova e la professione dell'ingegnere (1806-1915)* (Trieste 1992)

G. Muraro, *Scritti accademici 1993-1996* (Padua 1996)

Padova nel 1943. Dalla crisi del regime fascista alla Resistenza, eds G. Lenci - G. Segato (Padua 1996)

Il palazzo del Bo. Storia, architettura e restauri della facciata, ed. C. Semenzato (Venice 1989)

M. Quaranta, "L'impegno civile e politico di Giovanni Canestrini a Padova", in *Giovanni Canestrini Zoologist and Darwinist*, eds A. Minelli - S. Casellato (Venice 2001), p. 95-126

Storia d'Italia. Le regioni dall'Unità a oggi. Il Veneto, ed. S. Lanaro (Turin 1984)

Studenti, Università, città nella storia padovana, Atti del convegno Padova, 6-8 febbraio 1998, eds F. Piovan - L. Sitran Rea (Trieste 2001)

L'Università dalle leggi razziali alla Resistenza, Giornata dell'Università italiana nel 50° anniversario della Liberazione (Padova, 29 maggio 1995), ed. A. Ventura (Padua 1996)

L'Università di Padova. Notizie raccolte da A. Favaro *e* R. Cessi (Padua 1946)

L'Università di Padova per la Resistenza (Padua 1964)

A. Ventura, *Padova* (Rome-Bari 1989)

Id., "L'Università di Padova nella Resistenza", *Quaderni per la storia dell'Università di Padova*, 28, 1995, p. 157-172.

L. Zancan, *Egidio Meneghetti e la Resistenza nel Veneto* (Vicenza 1965)

Scientific and Cultural History: The Medieval and the Early Modern University

Jurisprudence

G. Arnaldi, "Le origini dello Studio di Padova. Dalla migrazione universitaria del 1222 alla fine del periodo ezzeliniano", *La cultura*, 15, 1977, p. 388-431

A. Battisti, *La cattedra di Diritto pubblico ecclesiastico eretta nell'Università di Padova nel 1768* (Rome 1952) (but 1957)

A. Belloni, *Professori giuristi a Padova nel secolo XV. Profili bio-bibliografici e cattedre* (Frankfurt am Main 1986)

E. Besta, *Riccardo Malombra professore nello Studio di Padova, consultore di stato a Venezia* (Venice 1894)

B. Brugi, "L'Università dei giuristi in Padova nel Cinquecento. Saggio di storia della giurisprudenza e delle Università italiane", *Archivio Veneto-Tridentino*, 1, 1922, p. 1-92

H. Coing, "Das juristische Vorlesungsprogramm der Universität Padua im XVII. und XVIII. Jahrhundert", in *Studi in onore di Edoardo Volterra*, IV (Milan 1971), p. 179-195

C. Dolcini, "Bologna e le nuove Università", in *L'Università di Vercelli nel Medioevo, Atti del secondo congresso storico vercellese (Vercelli, 23-25 ottobre 1992)* (Vercelli 1994), p. 23-33

D. Girgensohn, "Francesco Zabarella da Padova. Dottrina e attività politica di un professore di diritto durante il grande scisma d'Occidente", *Quaderni per la storia dell'Università di Padova*, 26-27, 1993-94, p. 1-48

E. Martellozzo Forin, "Annibale Buzzacarini e il cod. D 62 della Biblioteca capitolare di Padova. Un elenco di dottori giuristi della scuola padovana nel sec. XVI", *Quaderni per la storia dell'Università di Padova*, 1, 1968, p. 121-131

F. Martino, "Un dottore di decreti arcivescovo di Messina. La laurea padovana (1281) di Guidotto d'Abbiate", *Rivista internazionale di diritto comune*, 4, 1993, p. 97-120

Id., *Dottrine di giuristi e realtà cittadine nell'Italia del Trecento. Ranieri Arsendi a Pisa e a Padova* (Catania 1984)

G. Pace, *Riccardo da Saliceto. Un giurista bolognese del Trecento* (Rome 1995)

M. Roberti, "Diritto romano e cultura giuridica in Padova sulla fine del secolo XII", *Nuovo Archivio Veneto*, n.s., 4, 1902, p. 162-201

Id., "Il collegio padovano dei dottori giuristi. I suoi consulti del secolo XVI. Le sue tendenze", *Rivista italiana per le scienze giuridiche*, 35, 1903, p. 171-249

G. Zordan, "Il dottorato padovano di Carlo Goldoni tra fonti documentarie ed autorappresentazione", *Quaderni per la storia dell'Università di Padova*, 30, 1997,

p. 19-56

ID., *Dall'Università dei giuristi alla Facoltà di giurisprudenza nello Studio patavino* (Padua 1999)2

ID., "L'insegnamento del diritto naturale nell'Ateneo patavino e i suoi titolari", *Rivista di Storia del diritto italiano* 72, 1999, p. 5-76.

Medicine

Atti del convegno celebrativo di Johann Georg Wirsung nel quarto centenario della nascita (Padova, 6-7 dicembre 1990) (Padua 1992)

L. BELLONI, "Il primo ventennio della microscopia (Galilei 1610-Harvey 1628). Dalla microscopia alla anatomia microscopica dell'insetto", *Clio medica*, 4, 1969, p. 179-190

ID., "De la théorie atomistico-mécaniste à l'anatomie subtile (de Borelli à Malpighi) et de l'anatomie subtile à l'anatomie pathologique (de Malpighi à Morgagni)", *Clio medica*, 6, 1971, p. 99-107

ID., "L'opera di Giambattista Morgagni dalla strutturazione meccanica dell'organismo vivente all'anatomia patologica", *Morgagni*, 4, 1971, p. 71-80

B. BERTOLASO, "Ricerche d'archivio su alcuni aspetti dell'insegnamento medico presso l'Università di Padova nel Cinque e Seicento", *Acta Medicae Historiae Patavina*, 6, 1959-60, p. 17-37

ID., "Una cattedra veterinaria per medici nell'Ateneo patavino ed un teatro anatomico, ignorato o poco conosciuto del collegio veterinario", *Rivista di storia della medicina*, 4, 1960, p. 241-256

ID., "Sulla cattedra "Ad thermas Aponenses" (1768-1806) nello Studio padovano", *La clinica termale*, 13, 2, 1960, p. 72-77

ID., "La cattedra "De pulsibus et urinis" (1601-1748) nello Studio padovano", *Castalia*, 16, 1960, p. 109-115

ID., "Camillo Bonioli (1729-1791) maestro di chirurgia nell'Ateneo padovano", *Castalia*, 18, 1962, p. 73-77

C. F. COGROSSI, *Nuova idea del male contagioso de' buoi*, A facsimile edition, with an introduction by L. BELLONI, and English translation by D. M. SCHULLIAN (Milan 1953)

De sedibus, et causis. Morgagni nel Centenario, eds V. CAPPELLETTI - F. DI TROCCHIO (Rome 1986)

Epistolario di Felice Fontana, I, *Carteggio con Leopoldo Marc'Antonio Caldani, 1758-1794*, eds R.G. MAZZOLINI - G. ONGARO (Trent 1980)

G. FABRICI D'ACQUAPENDENTE, *The embryological treatises. The formation of the egg and of the chick. The formed fetus*, A facsimile edition, with an introduction, a translation, and a commentary by H. B. ADELMANN (Ithaca 1942)

A. FRANZ, "Vincenzo Malacarne (1744-1816) e il primo trattato italiano di traumatologia", *Castalia*, 10, 1954, p. 31-34

Leopoldo Marc'Antonio Caldani - Lazzaro Spallanzani: carteggio (1768- 1798), ed. G. ONGARO (Milan 1982)

P. MASAT LUCCHETTA, *Antonio Vallisneri medico naturalista. Scienza e filosofia nel Settecento* (Venice 1984)

Il metodo sperimentale in biologia da Vallisneri ad oggi (Padua 1962)

E. MORPURGO, "Lo Studio di Padova, le epidemie ed i contagi durante il governo della Repubblica Veneta", in *Memorie e documenti per la storia della Università di Padova*, I (Padua 1922), p. 107-240

G. ONGARO, "Contributi alla biografia di Prospero Alpini", *Acta Medicae Historiae Patavina*, 8-9, 1961-62/1962-63, p. 79-168

ID., "Spunti di anatomia e di fisiopatologia del sistema neuro-vegetativo negli "Occursus medici de vaga aegritudine infirmitatis nervorum" di Andrea Comparetti (1745-1801)", *Pagine di Storia della Medicina*, 11, 1, 1967, p. 35-55

ID., "Les apports de Vincenzo Malacarne (1744-1816) à la tératologie", in *Verhandlungen des XX. Internationalen Kongresses für Geschichte der Medizin (Berlin, 22.-27. August 1966)* (Hildesheim 1968), p. 186-194

ID., "La prima descrizione della borsa di Fabrici, organo linfoide centrale degli Uccelli", in *Episteme*, 4, 1970, p. 317-325

ID., "La scoperta della circolazione polmonare e la diffusione della Christianismi Restitutio di Michele Serveto nel XVI secolo in Italia e nel Veneto", *Episteme*, 5, 1971, p. 3-44

ID., "La medicina nello Studio di Padova e nel Veneto", in *Storia della cultura veneta. Dal primo Quattrocento al Concilio di Trento*, III/3 (Vicenza 1981), p. 75-134

ID., "Atomismo e aristotelismo nel pensiero medico-biologico di Fortunio Liceti", in *Scienza e cultura, Numero speciale in occasione del 350° anniversario della pubblicazione del "Dialogo sopra i massimi sistemi del mondo" di Galileo Galilei (1633) e del III Centenario della nascita di Giovanni Battista Morgagni (1682)* (Padua 1983), p. 129-140

ID., "La iatromatematica nello Studio di Padova e nel Veneto", in I *Riccati e la cultura della Marca nel Settecento europeo, Atti del Convegno internazionale di studio (Castelfranco Veneto, 5-6 aprile 1990)*, eds G. PIAIA - M.L. SOPPELSA (Florence 1992), p. 221-245

ID., "Morgagni uditore a Padova nel 1707", *Quaderni per la storia dell'Università di Padova*, 25, 1992, p. 323-358

ID., "L'insegnamento dell'anatomia nello Studio di Padova all'inizio del Settecento nella testimonianza di Giambattista Morgagni", *Atti e Memorie dell'Accademia Patavina di Scienze, Lettere ed Arti*, 105/II, 1992-93, p. 5-37

ID., "Storia della medicina dalla fine del Quattrocento alla fine del Settecento", in *Storia delle scienze. Natura e vita dall'antichità all'Illuminismo* (Turin 1993), p. 254-349

ID., "L'insegnamento clinico di Giovan Battista Da Monte (1489- 1551): una revisione critica", *Physis*, n.s., 31, 1994, p. 357-369

ID., R. G. MAZZOLINI, "Morgagni sconosciuto: le lezioni di anatomia e il diario medico-scientifico nel fondo morgagnano della Biblioteca Palatina di Parma", *Atti e Memorie dell'Accademia Patavina di Scienze, Lettere ed Arti*, 95/III, 1982-83, p. 19-32

W. PAGEL, *William Harvey's biological ideas. Selected aspects and historical background* (Basel-New York 1967)

ID., *New light on William Harvey* (Basel 1976)

F. PELLEGRINI, *La clinica medica padovana attraverso i secoli* (Verona 1939)

T. PESENTI, *Professori e promotori di medicina nello Studio di Padova dal 1405 al 1509. Repertorio bio-bibliografico* (Trieste-Padua 1984)

L. PREMUDA, *Personaggi e vicende dell'ostetricia e della ginecologia nello Studio di Padova* (Padua 1958)

S. SANTORIO, *De statica medicina*. Introduction, critical edition of the text, and translation by G. ONGARO (Florence 2001)

N. G. SIRAISI, *Arts and sciences at Padua. The 'Studium' of Padua before 1350* (Toronto 1973)

ID., *Avicenna in Renaissance Italy. The 'Canon' and Medical Teaching in Italian Universities after 1500* (Princeton 1987)

G. STERZI, *Giulio Casseri anatomico e chirurgo (c. 1552-1616)* (Venice 1909)

R. L. SUTTON, *Sixteenth century physician and his methods. Mercurialis on diseases of the skin, the first book on the subject (1572)* (Kansas City 1986)

M. TABANELLI, *Un chirurgo italiano del 1200: Bruno da Longoburgo* (Florence 1970)

G. TANFANI, "Pietro d'Abano nella evoluzione del pensiero scientifico medioevale", *Bollettino dell'Istituto Storico Italiano dell'Arte Sanitaria*, 12, 1932, p. 65-91 and 200-222

ID., "Jacopo Dondi, medico padovano del Trecento ed il suo metodo di estrazione del sale dalle acque termali", *Rivista di storia delle scienze mediche e naturali*, 26, 1935, p. 8-23

ID., "Giovanni Dondi medico e amico del Petrarca", *Atti e Memorie dell'Accademia di Storia dell'Arte Sanitaria*, 36, 1937, p. 26-33

ID., "La scuola medica padovana medioevale", *Atti e Memorie dell'Accademia di Storia dell'Arte Sanitaria*, 37, 1938, p. 71-79

ID., "Antonio, Uguccione, ed Enrigetto da Rio medici padovani 'doctores parisienses'", *Rivista di storia delle scienze mediche e naturali*, 30, 1939, p. 49-55

A. VEGGETTI, B. COZZI, *La Scuola di Medicina veterinaria dell'Università di Padova* (Trieste-Padua 1996)

G. WHITTERIDGE, *William Harvey and the circulation of the blood* (London 1971)

Philosophy

Aristotelismo padovano e filosofia aristotelica, Atti del XII Congresso internazionale di filosofia (Venezia 1958), 9 (Florence 1960)

Aristotelismo veneto e scienza moderna, ed. L. OLIVIERI (Padua 1983), 2 vols

L'averroismo in Italia. Atti del Convegno intern. (Roma, 18-20 aprile 1977) (Rome 1979)

Copernico a Padova. Atti della Giornata Copernicana [...], (Padua 1995)

Cesare Cremonini. Aspetti del suo pensiero e scritti, eds E. RIONDATO - A. POPPI (Padua 2000)

M.R. DAVI, *Bernardino Tomitano filosofo, medico e letterato (1517-1576)* (Trieste 1995)

A. DE PACE, *Le matematiche e il mondo. Ricerche su un dibattito in Italia nella seconda metà del Cinquecento* (Milan 1993)

G. FEDERICI VESCOVINI, *Astrologia e scienza. La crisi dell'aristotelismo sul cadere del Trecento e Biagio Pelacani da Parma* (Florence 1979)

A. FAVARO, *Galileo Galilei a Padova. Ricerche e scoperte, insegnamento, scolari* (Padua 1968) (anast. repr.)

ID., *Galileo Galilei e lo Studio di Padova* (Padua 1966) (anast. repr.), 2 vols

Galileo a Padova, 1592-1610. Celebrazioni del IV centenario promosse dall'Università degli studi di Padova (Trieste 1995), 5 vols

E. GARIN, *Storia della filosofia italiana* (Turin 1978)[3]

G.C. GIACOBBE, *Alle radici della rivoluzione scientifica rinascimentale. Le opere di Pietro Catena sui rapporti fra matematica e logica* (Pisa 1981)

Giuseppe Toaldo e il suo tempo, ed. L. PIGATTO (Cittadella 2000)

Istituzioni culturali, scienza, insegnamento nel Veneto dall'età delle riforme alla Restaurazione (1761-1818) ed. L. SITRAN REA (Trieste 2000)

P.O. KRISTELLER, *La tradizione aristotelica nel Rinascimento* (Padua 1962)

P. MARANGON, *Alle origini dell'aristotelismo padovano (sec. XII-XIII)* (Padua 1977)

ID., *"Ad cognitionem scientiae festinare". Gli studi nell'Università e nei conventi di Padova nei secoli XIII e XIV*, ed. T. PESENTI (Trieste 1997)

F.L. MASCHIETTO, *Elena Lucrezia Cornaro Piscopia (1646-1684), prima donna laureata nel mondo* (Padua 1978)

B. NARDI, *Saggi sull'aristotelismo padovano dal secolo XIV al XVI* (Florence 1958)

L. OLIVIERI, *Certezza e gerarchia del sapere. Crisi del-*

l'idea di scientificità nell'aristotelismo del secolo XVI (Padua 1983)

E. PASCHETTO, *Pietro d'Abano medico e filosofo* (Florence 1984)

G. PIAIA, *Marsilio e dintorni. Contributi alla storia delle idee* (Padua 1999)

A. POPPI, *L'etica del Rinascimento tra Platone e Aristotele* (Naples 1997)

ID., *Cremonini, Galilei e gli inquisitori del Santo a Padova* (Padua 1993)

ID., *Introduzione all'aristotelismo padovano* (Padua 1991)[2]

ID., *La dottrina della scienza in Giacomo Zabarella* (Padua 1972)

ID., *Saggi sul pensiero inedito di Pietro Pomponazzi* (Padua 1970)

ID., *Studi su Pietro Pomponazzi* (Florence 1965)

Rapporti tra le Università di Padova e Bologna. Ricerche di filosofia, medicina e scienza, ed. L. ROSSETTI (Trieste 1988)

G.A. SALANDIN - M. PANCINO, *Il "teatro" di filosofia sperimentale di Giovanni Poleni* (Trieste 1987)

G. SANTINELLO, *Tradizione e dissenso nella filosofia veneta fra Rinascimento e modernità* (Padua 1991)

CH. B. SCHMITT, *Filosofia e scienza nel Rinascimento*, ed. A. CLERICUZIO (Milan 2001)

Scienza e filosofia all'Università di Padova nel Quattrocento, ed. A. POPPI (Trieste 1983)

M.L. SOPPELSA, *Genesi del metodo galileiano e tramonto dell'aristotelismo nella Scuola di Padova* (Padua 1974)

ID., *Leibniz e Newton in Italia. Il dibattito padovano (1687-1750)* (Trieste 1989)

A. SOTTILI, *Studenti tedeschi e umanesimo italiano nell'Università di Padova durante il Quattrocento*, I (Padua 1971)

Storia della cultura veneta, eds G. ARNALDI - M. PASTORE STOCCHI, I-V (Vicenza 1976-1986)

Theology

The primary source for the history of the Padua 'faculty' of theology is constituted by the 40 manuscript volumes and 5 files of its ancient archive, containing the "acts" and the reports of the Collegium of theologians; besides the sections or chapters which recount the vicissitudes of the 'faculty' in the oldest general histories of the University, to be consulted in particular is I. FACCIOLATI, *Fasti Gymnasii Patavini* (Patavii 1757), and the inexhaustible mine of personal historical data contained in the various volumes of the *Acta graduum academicorum Gymnasii Patavini* published up to now by the 'Centro per la storia dell'Università di Padova'.

As far as secondary literature is concerned, the only specialized monagraph available, which goes up to 1509, is the praiseworthy and well-documented work by G. BROTTO - G. ZONTA, *La facoltà teologica dell'Università di Padova, I, (secoli XIV e XV)* (Padua 1922); for the following centuries one must turn to publications on periods, aspects, and figures of the various religious orders. Among these some of the most important are:

L. GARGAN, *Lo studio teologico e la biblioteca dei domenicani a Padova nel Tre e Quattrocento* (Padua 1971)

C. GASPAROTTO, *S. Maria del Carmine di Padova* (Padua 1955)

F. L. MASCHIETTO, *Benedettini professori all'Università di Padova. (Secc. XV-XVIII). Profili biografici* (Cesena-Padua 1989)

A. POPPI, *Ricerche sulla teologia e la scienza nella Scuola padovana del Cinque e Seicento* (Soveria Mannelli 2001), chs. I-VI and appendix 3

ID., "La teologia nell'Università e nelle Scuole", in *Storia della cultura veneta dal primo Quattrocento al Concilio di Trento*, 3/III, eds G. ARNALDI - M. PASTORE STOCCHI (Vicenza 1981), pp. 1-33

Storia e cultura al Santo di Padova fra il XIII e il XX secolo, ed. A. POPPI (Vicenza 1976)

The vicissitudes of the new theology faculty, from 1815 to its suppression by the Italian government in 1873, are recounted by A. GAMBASIN, *"Theses" in sacra teologia nell'Università di Padova dal 1815 al 1873* (Trieste 1984), pp. 1-58.

Scientific and Cultural History: The Modern University

Jurisprudence, Political Sciences, Statistical Sciences, Economics

A. AMORTH, *Commemorazione di Donato Donati* (Modena 1968)

B. COLOMBO, *Storia della nascita della facoltà di Statistica di Padova nella documentazione ufficiale*, typescript kindly made available by its author whom we warmly thank

D. DALL'ORA, *La facoltà di Giurisprudenza di Padova e i suoi docenti in epoca fascista (1919-1938)*, dissertation for the degree in Contemporary History, supervisor A. VENTURA (1998-99)

A. FAVARO – R. CESSI, *L'Università di Padova* (Padua 1946)

N. FEDERICI, "L'opera di Corrado Gini nell'ambito delle scienze sociali", in *Studi in onore di Corrado Gini*, II (Rome 1960), p. 3-33

M. C. GHETTI, "Struttura e organizzazione dell'Università di Padova dal 1798 al 1817", *Quaderni per la storia dell'Università di Padova*, 17, 1984, p. 135-182

S. Lanaro, *Nazione e lavoro. Saggio sulla cultura borghese in Italia, 1870-1925* (Padua 1979)

A. Magro, "La parificazione dell'Università di Padova dopo l'Unità (1866) e la sua facoltà di Giurisprudenza (1866-1880)", *Annali di storia delle Università italiane*, 3, 1999, p. 143-169

M. Manfredini Gasparetto, *Marco Fanno. L'uomo e l'economista* (Padua 1992)

F. Schiavetto, *La facoltà di Scienze Politiche di Padova: 1924-1990*. A short typescript historico-institutional outline kindly made available by its author, whom we warmly thank

P. Ungari, *Alfredo Rocco e l'ideologia giuridica del fascismo* (Brescia 1963)

A. Ventura, *Padova* (Bari 1989)

G. Zordan, *Dall'Università dei Giuristi alla Facoltà di Giurisprudenza nello Studio patavino* (Padua 1999)[2]

Medicine, Pharmacy, Veterinary Medicine

T. Berti, "1848-1948: un secolo di storia della farmacologia padovana, scuola di scienza e di libertà", *Atti e Memorie dell'Accademia Patavina di scienze lettere ed arti*, 109/II, 1996-97, p. 115-134

B. Bertolaso, "Ricerche d'archivio su alcuni aspetti dell'insegnamento medico presso l'Università di Padova nel Sette ed Ottocento", *Acta Medicae Historiae Patavina*, 5, 1958-59, p. 1-30

Id., "Francesco Luigi Fanzago (1764-1836) patologo e medico legale nell'Ateneo padovano", *Rivista di storia della medicina*, 5, 1961, p. 225-243

L. Bizzotto - G. Rialdi, "L'attività didattica e scientifica del fisiologo Maximilian Vintschgau (1832-1902) all'Università di Padova", *Acta Medicae Historiae Patavina*, 22, 1975-76, p. 9-20

S. Casellato - L. Pigatto, *Professori di materie scientifiche all'Università di Padova nell'Ottocento* (Trieste-Padua 1996)

G. de Laurentiis - L. Premuda, "Rodolfo Lamprecht (1781-1860) professore di ostetricia teorica e pratica all'Università di Padova", *Acta Medicae Historiae Patavina*, 23, 1976-77, p. 23-43

G. Federspil, "Giacomo Andrea Giacomini e l'evoluzione del pensiero medico nel primo Ottocento", *Atti e memorie dell'Accademia Patavina di scienze lettere ed arti*, 108/II, 1995-96, p. 167-174

M. C. Ghetti, "Struttura e organizzazione dell'Università di Padova dal 1798 al 1817", *Quaderni per la storia dell'Università di Padova*, 17, 1984, p. 135-182

G. Lenci, "L'Università "Castrense" a Padova nella Grande Guerra", *Padova e il suo territorio*, 10, 58, 1995, p. 39-42

E. Mameli, "L'insegnamento della chimica all'Università di Padova", *La chimica*, 24, 1948, p. 319-322

I Musei, le Collezioni scientifiche e le sezioni antiche delle Biblioteche, ed. C. Gregolin (Padua 1996)

M. Nicolini, "Pietro Spica Marcatajo", in *La chimica e le tecnologie chimiche nel Veneto dell'Ottocento. Atti del settimo seminario di Storia delle scienze e delle tecniche nell'Ottocento veneto, Venezia, 9-10 ottobre 1998*, ed. A. Bassani (Venice 2001), p. 285-294

G. Ongaro, "Interessi reumatologici in alcune dissertazioni di laurea padovane della prima metà dell'Ottocento", in *Atti della Rassegna mono-tematica di Storia della Reumatologia (Sanremo, 14-15 dicembre 1963)* (Sanremo 1964), p. 311-330

Id., "Medicina e chimica a Padova nella prima metà dell'Ottocento", in *La chimica e le tecnologie chimiche*, cit., p. 245-273

Id. - A. Gamba, "Pietro Tosoni (1817-1847), storico della scuola anatomica padovana", *Atti e Memorie dell'Accademia Patavina di Scienze, Lettere ed Arti*, 108/II, 1995-96, p. 23-43

E. Pastore, "Origine, vicende ed attualità della Scuola di veterinaria padovana", in *L'agricoltura veneta dalla tradizione alla sperimentazione attraverso le scuole e le istituzioni agrarie padovane*, ed. P.G. Zanetti (Padua 1996), p. 247-286

L. Premuda, "Ottocento padovano. Personalità ed interessi di Luigi Gianelli (1799-1872) professore ordinario di medicina legale e polizia medica", *Castalia*, 15, 1959, p. 7-9

Id., "Gli orientamenti scientifici e le strutture didattiche nell'Ottocento medico padovano", in *Atti del XXIII Congresso Nazionale di Storia della Medicina (Modena, 22-24 settembre 1967)* (Rome 1967), p. 557-581

Id., "L'asse Vienna-Padova nella medicina dell'Ottocento e i suoi riflessi sul piano didattico e scientifico", *Atti e Memorie dell'Accademia Patavina di scienze lettere ed arti*, 92/II, 1979-80, p. 129-143

Letters, Philosophy, Educational Science, Psychology

"Antonio Rosmini studente a Padova (1816-1822)", *Quaderni per la storia dell'Università di Padova*, 32 (1999), pp. 77-132

A. Arslan - F. Volpi, *Letteratura e filosofia nel Veneto che cambia*, intro. by E. Berti (Padua 1989), pp. 83-157

Atti del Convegno su Luigi Stefanini nel XXX anniversario della morte (Treviso 1987)

Carlo Anti. Giornate di studio nel centenario della nascita (Verona, Padova, Venezia, 6-8 marzo 1990) (Trieste 1992)

Cento anni di filologia romanza a Padova. Catalogo della mostra storico-bibliografica (Padua 1982)

F. De Vivo, *L'insegnamento della pedagogia nell'Università di Padova durante il XIX secolo* (Trieste 1983)

Id., "Il Corso di perfezionamento per i licenziati dalle Scuole normali presso l'Università di Padova (1906-1923)", *Quaderni per la storia dell'Università di Padova*, 32, 1999, pp. 177-191

C. Dionisotti, "Appunti sulla scuola padovana", in *Medioevo e Rinascimento, con altri studi in onore di Lino Lazzarini*, II (Padua 1979), pp. 327-348

E. Franceschini, *Concetto Marchesi. Linee per una interpretazione di un uomo inquieto* (Padua 1978)

Ezio Franceschini (1906-1983). Scritti, documenti, commemorazioni, testimonianze, ed. C. Leonardi (Bologna 1986)

Giornate di studio in ricordo di Fabio Metelli (Padova, 10-11 giugno 1987) (Padua 1987)

M. Isnenghi, "I luoghi della cultura", in *Storia d'Italia. Le regioni dall'Unità ad oggi. Il Veneto*, ed. S. Lanaro (Turin 1984), pp. 263-317

L. Lazzarini, "Un mio ricordo della Facoltà di Filosofia e Lettere a Padova dalla fine dell'Ottocento al primo trentennio del Novecento", *Quaderni per la storia dell'Università di Padova*, 25, 1992, pp. 549-565 (with bibliography)

A.M. Moschetti, *Cercatori dell'Assoluto maestri nell'Ateneo padovano* (Rimini 1981)

C. Musatti, "Il mio mondo giovanile nell'antica Padova", *Belfagor*, 41, 1986, pp. 81-94

"Roberto Ardigò: 'Una vita interamente dedicata alla scienza, alla scuola'", *Quaderni per la storia dell'Università di Padova*, 34, 2001

Storia della cultura veneta, 6, *Dall'età napoleonica alla prima guerra mondiale,* eds G. Arnaldi - M. Pastore Stocchi (Vicenza 1986)

Mathematical, Physical, Natural and Agricultural Sciences

G. Bozzolato - P. Del Negro - C. Ghetti, *La Specola dell'Università di Padova* (Brugine 1986)

La chimica e le tecnologie chimiche nel Veneto dell'Ottocento: atti del settimo seminario .... (Venice 2001)

A. Favaro, *I professori della R. Università di Padova nel MCMXXII* (Bologna 1922)

Id., *Saggio di bibliografia dello Studio di Padova* (Venice 1922)

Id. - R. Cessi, *L'Università di Padova* (Padua 1946)

M.C. Ghetti, "Struttura e organizzazione dell'Università di Padova dal 1798 al 1817", *Quaderni per la storia dell'Università di Padova*, 17, 1984, p. 135-182

Id., "L'assetto statutario e didattico dell'Università di Padova dopo la riforma asburgica", *Quaderni per la storia dell'Università di Padova*, 32, 1999, p. 87-10

Istituzioni culturali, scienza, insegnamento nel Veneto dall'età delle riforme alla Restaurazione (1761-1818). Atti del convegno di studi, Padova 28-29 maggio 1998, ed. L. Sitran Rea (Trieste 2000)

M. Minesso, *Tecnici e modernizzazione nel Veneto. La scuola dell'Università di Padova e la professione dell'ingegnere (1806-1915)* (Trieste 1992)

G. Piccoli - L. Sitran Rea, *Il Dipartimento di Geologia, Paleontologia e Geofisica dell'Università di Padova e le sue origini* (Padua 1988)

Professori di materie scientifiche all'Università di Padova nell'Ottocento, ed. S. Casellato - L. Pigatto (Trieste 1996)

Le scienze biologiche nel Veneto dell'Ottocento: atti del sesto seminario ... (Venice 1998)

Le scienze della terra nel Veneto dell'Ottocento: atti del quinto seminario ... (Venice 1998)

Scienze e tecniche agrarie nel Veneto dell'Ottocento: atti del secondo seminario di storia delle scienze e delle tecniche nell'Ottocento veneto (Venice 1992)

Le scienze matematiche nel Veneto dell'Ottocento: atti del terzo seminario ... (Venice 1994)

L. Sitran Rea - G. Piccoli, *La Facoltà di scienze fisiche, matematiche e naturali dell'Università di Padova. Origini e sviluppo* (Padua 1991)

M. L. Soppelsa, "Scienze e storia della scienza", in *Storia della cultura veneta*, 6, *Dall'età napoleonica alla prima guerra mondiale*, eds G. Arnaldi - M. Pastore Stocchi (Vicenza 1986), p. 493-551

Engineering

The information presented was mostly obtained from the book edited by the Faculty of Engineering, printed in Dolo in 1978, and entitled *I cento anni della Scuola per gli Ingegneri dell'Università di Padova, 1876-1976.* This book also includes an anastatic copy of the work by Antonio Favaro entitled *Notizie sulla Scuola d'Applicazione per gli Ingegneri Annessa alla R. Università di Padova*, printed in 1875 by the Tipography "Alla Minerva". See also M. Minesso, *Tecnici e modernizzazione nel Veneto. La Scuola dell'Università di Padova e la professione dell'ingegnere (1806-1915)* (Trieste 1992). For the more recent period, the information has been taken from the University *Annuari* and the *Bollettini* of the Engineering Faculty

FIRST PRINTED IN 2003
FOR SIGNUMPADOVA EDITRICE
BY THE OFFSET INVICTA PADOVA
LIMENA (PADUA)